FOUR THOUSAND
LIVES LOST

FOUR THOUSAND LIVES LOST

THE INQUIRIES OF
LORD MERSEY
INTO THE SINKING OF
the *TITANIC,*
the *EMPRESS
OF IRELAND,*
the *FALABA*
and the
LUSITANIA

A L A S T A I R   W A L K E R

The
History
Press

Back cover image: 'Remember the little lost children of the *Lusitania*', published in the *New York Herald*, 7 May 1918, artist W. A. Rogers (1854–1931). LOC

First published 2012

The History Press
The Mill, Brimscombe Port
Stroud, Gloucestershire, GL5 2QG
www.thehistorypress.co.uk

British Library Cataloguing in Publication Data.
A catalogue record for this book is available from the British Library.

ISBN 978 0 7524 6571 5
Typesetting and origination by The History Press
Printed in the EU for The History Press

CONTENTS

ACKNOWLEDGEMENTS

My interest in maritime matters began at the age of seven with the entry for Horatio Nelson in my parents' 1923 edition of the *Harmsworth Encyclopedia*, was nurtured by Arthur Ransome's wonderful Swallows and Amazons stories and came of age in yacht races in Belfast Lough. The fascination for the nautical never waned. An interest in *Titanic* was natural as my mother had seen the ship as a child of nine and a near neighbour of the family in the Woodvale area of Belfast had been lost. An uncle was a survivor of the torpedoing of the *Athenia* on the first day of the Second World War, so the topics covered here have a personal resonance.

I would particularly like to thank the Canadian National Archives for making me aware that the proceedings of the inquiry into the loss of the *Empress of Ireland* were available on the internet. I also express my appreciation for the work of the Titanic Inquiry Project in making the proceedings of both the *Titanic* and *Luisitania* inquires likewise accessible, and the Law Library of Yale University for the digitisation of the proceedings of the *Falaba* inquiry.

I am deeply indebted to two friends who agreed to read the draft of this book. Una Reilly and Stephen Cameron both provided very helpful and constructive comments. Thanks to Shaun Barrington and the staff at The History Press with whom it has been a pleasure to work.

Finally, go thanks go to my wife Barbara for the patience, understanding and forbearance without which a writing project such as this would never be started, let alone finished.

INTRODUCTION

The *Titanic* slowly disappeared into the chasm of the deep Atlantic, the *Empress of Ireland* rolled over in the shallows of the St Lawrence, the *Falaba* was dispatched into the waters off the south west of England and the *Lusitania* crashed bow first into the seabed off the south coast of Ireland. The man who links these four terrible tragedies, that cost close to 4000 lives, is Lord Mersey, who, as Commissioner of Wrecks, presided over a series of inquiries into the sinkings between 1912 and 1915. In the process of the inquiries he came to many significant conclusions, some of which, in retrospect, have turned out to be common sense, some have become controversial and some have been shown to be quite simply wrong. Many of those conclusions were judgements about the behaviour of eight men who were in charge of ships involved directly (or indirectly in one case) in the incidents. The purpose of this book is to look at those judgements, at the man who made them, the methods used to arrive at them and the captains whose lives or reputations were affected by them. Our concern will not principally be with the aspects of the tragedies linked to the actions of those in boardrooms, ministries and shipbuilders but rather with those who were held accountable for their actions at sea as the events took place.

Only four of the eight captains appeared before Mersey and, of these, two captained ships that had been lost. Two of the eight died with their ships and two were German submariners. The intention is to give a brief picture of their lives as well as an indication of their personalities and then to look at the way in which they were dealt with during the inquiries and to consider whether the outcomes affected their careers, in the cases of those who survived, or their reputations, in the cases of the two who did not. They are disparate in background and character. Three were quite well known to the public before the disasters took place. Of two we still know comparatively little. Most were reluctant actors in public events (the submariners of course not taking part in the inquiries) but there were also a couple of self-publicists.

It is important to place the incidents themselves and the people concerned firmly into historical context. It is all too easy to level criticisms based upon knowledge and understanding that has accrued over the century since then. We should therefore consider the maritime context of the early twentieth century, including commercial and technical factors, political and military developments and the activities of the press. To help in doing so we will consider some of the other accidents and tragedies that took place at sea during the same period so that we can better pick up patterns.

A great deal of research has already been undertaken into the sinkings of *Titanic* and *Lusitania* and there are many publications. Regarding the former, some might use the term 'overkill'. I have therefore approached that tragedy with some trepidation, but it would make little sense to look at the quartet of Mersey's inquiries without spending some time on the first and the longest. Less has been written about the *Empress of Ireland*, but the main events have been documented.

The story of the *Falaba*, however, has been entirely overshadowed by that of the *Lusitania,* which followed so closely after it and which resulted in the deaths of many more people. Nonetheless, the sinking of the *Falaba* raised significant issues and it contrasts with that of the *Lusitania* in interesting ways. Given the number of sources already in the public domain, a selection of which is listed in the Bibliography, this book is not intended to provide a full narrative of the incidents into which Mersey inquired and only sufficient background has been included to elucidate the issues being discussed.

In some of the material produced about these sinkings, particularly amongst the proliferation of books and films on *Titanic*, a mythology has developed that bears little relation to the actual events. Indeed, Mersey may have contributed, wittingly or otherwise, to the generation of some of the myths. What follows may help to puncture one or two of these; but the intention is to take an overview, to look for links and patterns and, perhaps by so doing, to gain some insight into the nature of disaster-related inquiries and their impact on the decision makers involved.

There are two themes that recur throughout. One, as just indicated, concerns the nature of the inquiry process and how it was influenced by the backgrounds and personalities of those who took part in it. The second is the extent to which events and reactions to them were influenced by the rapid technological change that was taking place at the time. There may be echoes of those themes that resonate down to the present day. Some of the major government-sponsored inquiries of recent times have demonstrated more than a few of the characteristics of those discussed here. We too live in a period of technological change, one even more rapid than that of the early twentieth century. To what extent do some of today's disasters arise from a mis-match between the pace of technological change and the speed with which people adapt their thinking and their practices to new circumstances?

In reviewing the judgements that were made about the eight captains, it will prove helpful to set them against two 'courts of opinion'. Firstly, how were those judgements received by other seafarers? Peer judgements by those who had to face the possibility themselves of being involved in this type of event are particularly valuable. There is also the court of public opinion. It may not be as well informed as the seafaring group and it may be considerably more variable, but it is important, particularly so far as reputation is concerned. The difficulty now, of course, is ascertaining, at this remove, what were the opinions of contemporary seafarers or of the general public on the conclusions reached by Lord Mersey. There are, however, some indications from the actions taken by shipping companies and others after the inquiries as to what those opinions were. The views which Mersey expressed, particularly in relation to *Titanic,* continue to influence writers today. Even in recent publications it is possible to see those opinions repeated uncritically, including some that have since been shown to be entirely in error. Perhaps one of the lessons we shall learn is the ease with which anything produced under judicial imprimatur acquires for some people the supposed infallibility of pronouncements 'ex cathedra'.

Altogether the loss of the four ships cost almost 4000 lives. Few people have chaired more than one inquiry into a maritime disaster. Mersey was unique in chairing four encompassing such a tragic number of deaths in a period of just three years and three months. Yet, to some he remains little more than a laughing stock, to others a symbol of judicial mediocrity, while a third group see him as a pawn of shipping bosses and government. Over the years he has received little appreciation for undertaking what must have been a series of daunting tasks and, while he is unlikely ever to be showered with accolades, we may just be able to qualify his infamy with a little more understanding.

1

A MARITIME WORLD IN TRANSITION

Shortly before he left England for the last time, in the late summer of 1805, Nelson attended a meeting at the Admiralty to discuss some new technological developments being promoted by Robert Fulton, an American inventor. Fulton had lived in England for some time, before moving to France and trying to persuade the French government that his ideas for a submersible boat were practicable. Having failed to do so, he was now back in Britain and trying to interest the British government in the same idea as well as his suggestions for an early form of 'torpedo', the term then being used to describe a transportable mine. Being a man of broad interests he was also raising the possibility of the navy making use of steam propulsion. There is no record as to how Nelson responded to such technological advances, although being conservative by nature he was probably not impressed. However, while Fulton made little progress with his submersible boat, in October 1805, the same month as Trafalgar, he demonstrated the potential of his torpedo when the resulting explosion sank a 200-ton brig. Just two years later, back in America, Fulton provided the first real evidence, with the *Clermont,* that steam propulsion was commercially viable.

Over the period of the next century one thinks of developments in maritime technology proceeding in a steady manner, decade by decade, culminating in the great liners, Dreadnoughts and submarines of the early years of the twentieth century. In fact, 50 years after his death Nelson would not have found the ships of the navy or of commerce so very different from those that he had known. Given the continued dominance of wood and sail, there would have been little to amaze him. Most of the really rapid changes took place in the period right at the end of that century and the beginning of the next.

Isambard Kingdom Brunel decided in 1852 to build a ship that was several times larger than any that had gone before. It was an idea ahead of its time, because, although it was then technically possible to create a hull of the requisite size, other elements of the technology necessary effectively to power and to control such a large ship were not in place. Some consider The *Great Eastern* to have been the biggest white elephant of all time, although it did achieve considerable success, not as the passenger ship it had been designed to be, but as a very effective cable layer. The iron monster, mixing paddle wheels, propeller and sails, laid much of the infrastructure required for the embryonic communications revolution. It was not until 1899 that the White Star *Oceanic* exceeded it in length and two years later the *Celtic,* also White Star and also built by *Titanic's* builder, Harland and Wolff in Belfast, exceeded it in tonnage. Within a decade, however, there were ships that were twice as large.

The speed that steamships were built to travel at depended on the purpose for which they were intended. The liners hoping to carry mails were normally the fastest of their day. Speeds did not increase dramatically with improvements to steam engines in the 1870s to 1890s. Rather, the quantity of coal needed to produce those speeds dropped significantly. Fuel costs were reduced and a greater proportion of ships' internal space was given over to revenue-generating passengers or cargoes. That changed suddenly on a single day, 26 June 1897. At the great Naval Review held at Spithead to celebrate the 60th anniversary of Queen Victoria coming to the throne, a small steam-boat called *Turbinia* streaked through the lines of ships, clearly visible to the Prince of Wales watching from the Royal Yacht (his mother was indisposed) and from every ship in the fleet. In modern times it would have caused a tremendous security alert, possibly with dire consequences. In 1897 it certainly created a stir, but for a very different reason. *Turbinia* was travelling at over 30 knots, a speed that not one of the other ships present could have approached. She was the product of a Dr Charles Parsons, who was aboard her at the time, and she had been built to show off his newly developed steam turbine engine. Instead of cylinders with pistons, cranks and shafts, all in a blur of reciprocating movement, *Turbinia* was driven by steam jets hitting blades in a casing on the shaft that led directly to the propeller. It was much smoother, involved much less wasteful thrashing of machinery, was more compact and it was much, much faster.

It is an immense tribute to the ability of late Victorian and Edwardian society to take hold of a new idea and apply it rapidly that, just ten years after the Jubilee Naval Review, a battleship, the *Dreadnought,* the biggest ever built to that time, was powered by the new engines. In the same year, the first of a new class of turbine-driven liner, *Lusitania,* emerged to take the Blue Riband speed record for crossing the Atlantic. The twentieth century has sometimes been called the century of the internal combustion engine because it is considered to be the most influential technical development of the period and also, perhaps, the most visible. The century could, with equal validity, be called 'the turbine century'. Not only did the turbine revolutionise propulsion at sea, it became the basis for all electricity generation, whether from coal, from nuclear power, from gas or from wind and water. Add to that the turbo-jet, turbo-prop and turbo-fan and we have the turbine to thank for modern flight as well.

For many ships not requiring high speeds the new propulsion system was not particularly advantageous and normal reciprocating engines continued to be built for several decades. A very few ships, of which *Titanic* was one, had a hybrid system of large, advanced reciprocating engines and a turbine as well. One effect was that the difference in speed between the fastest liners and the slowest cargo ships increased greatly. Plodding tramps continued to move at around 8 to 10 knots while some passenger ships raced past at 25 knots.

The first application of electricity in ships came in 1882. Cunard's *Servia* used it for lighting in passenger spaces. Over the next few years, however, applications relating to the operation of the ship gradually took effect. At around the same time, hydraulic control systems became available and the combination of electrical and hydraulic power made it feasible to manage the complexity of larger, faster ships in ways that had not been possible previously.

By the end of the century, all ships of any size were built of riveted steel plates. In a process of gradual development, rather than through any spectacular leap forward, the design of hulls gradually evolved to include watertight divisions both across the ship from side to side and also along the length of the ship. These divisions, or bulkheads, required doors through which crew members or passengers could pass. When, for any reason, it was necessary for the bulkheads to be watertight the doors needed to be quickly closed. At first this was done manually, then electro-mechanical methods were developed that allowed the doors to be closed by operating a single control on the bridge.

So, within a decade the means of propulsion, the size, speed and complexity of ships had all taken an enormous leap forward. However, there were two further inventions that were also to have a fundamental influence on the whole maritime world of the early twentieth century and were of major importance in the incidents with which we are concerned. These were the fruition of Robert Fulton's belief in the feasibility of submersible boats and the invention of wireless telegraphy.

The submarine was not the product of a single inventor. Going back to Fulton and beyond, many ideas for submersible boats had been produced and a few had made it off the drawing board. The American Civil War saw the first successful use of the submarine as a weapon of war, if an operation can be called successful that results in the loss of the submarine and its crew. Those early attempts at submarines were, like the contemporaneous *Great Eastern,* ahead of their time – navigating submerged was an aspiration that required further technical development before it could become established practice. Submarines could only become effective with a propulsion system, other than manpower, that could be made to work under water. They also needed much more sophisticated control systems to maintain the delicate balance of neutral buoyancy and trim which they required to operate submerged.

It was the electric motor and battery storage that provided the underwater motive power and it was electro-mechanical and hydraulic systems that facilitated sustainable trim with neutral buoyancy. Strictly speaking, the internal combustion engine was not necessary for submarine development. Britain built the K-Class steam turbine-powered submarines during the First World War, although they proved to be a failure that was costly in both material and human terms. Large-scale use of steam turbine propulsion in submarines had to wait for the emergence of nuclear reactors. The internal combustion engine, with its ability to stop and start readily and its absence of bulky boilers, made design of the early submarines so much easier; the coming of the marine diesel engine around 1910 made them safer, albeit never safe.

Marconi was not the only person who contributed to the early beginnings of wireless, but he was by far the dominant one and it is his name above all others that has come to be associated with it. His experiments, particularly the trans-Atlantic transmission in 1904, demonstrated the possibilities of radio as a communication tool and not just as a scientific curiosity. There had been earlier experiments at sea. In 1891, Captain Henry Jackson RN (later First Sea Lord) sent wireless Morse signals over a distance of a few hundred yards. In 1899 wireless technology was first used in naval manoeuvres. As with the turbine, the rapidity with which the new invention was applied was startling. The first occasion when radio enabled major loss of life to be averted in a maritime disaster was as early as 1909 during the sinking of the White Star *Republic*. Despite that success, the initial employment of radio at sea in the merchant service was primarily as a convenience for rich passengers and only marginally as a contribution to the operation of the ship. The terms of employment of the radio operators by The Marconi Company (not the ship owners) and their job descriptions left no doubt as to their commercial priorities. As with the submarine, it was how the invention was used that became controversial rather than the invention itself.

In the next two chapters we will be examining in some detail the nature of the risks that seafarers faced in the early 1900s, in peacetime and in wartime and both wireless and the submarine will feature strongly. Obviously the submarine only appears in the wartime scenarios, but wireless had major roles in both contexts. In one case it should have mitigated risk, but in the other it may well have exacerbated it.

One aspect of ship technology did not change over the two decades before the outbreak of the First World War, although it did so shortly thereafter. Coal continued to provide the energy source for steamships. That meant large bunkers had to be included in the ship's structure in such a way as to allow the coal to be loaded easily. The stability of the ship had to be managed during a voyage while bunkers were gradually depleted. There had to be arrangements for the movement of the coal to the stokeholds even under severe weather conditions and, finally, there needed to be large numbers of stokers to maintain the fires. For large, fast steamships of the period, the logistics of these processes were daunting and there were considerable dangers from bunker coal catching fire, or from explosion of the air and coal dust mixture remaining once the bunker was nearly empty.

The 'black gang' on an Atlantic liner moved hundreds of tons of coal every single day into the boilers. Smaller amounts, but still in the hundreds of tons, of ashes also had to be removed and dumped overboard. Although steam power was used in a large number of different contexts – on trains, in factories and mines and many others – there was something unique about the coal-fired stokeholds in ships, largely because they were subject to the vagaries of the sea and to changing temperature and weather patterns as ships moved through different climate zones. While the heat of the boiler fires might be quite welcome in the North Atlantic in winter, it was utterly intolerable in the Red Sea in summer. Keeping fires lit and steam pressure up in a severe gale required prodigious efforts by stokers and engineers. As can be imagined, the accident rate was appalling. It is a world which, apart from a few preserved ships, has now disappeared. Little remains by way of a record of the life of the men involved because few were communicators or even thought that their story might be of interest in the future.

Perhaps the most striking feature about the maritime scene of the early twentieth century was its variety. As well as the spread of steamers from large, fast passenger ships to small, slow cargo ones, there were still large numbers of sailing ships, both sea-going square riggers and coastal schooners and ketches. Add to them vast fleets of fishing vessels, both sail and steam and one is left with a vision of crowded seas in many parts of the world. The number of sailing ships, particularly ocean-going square riggers, was in steep decline although they continued to be built in small numbers right up to the outbreak of the First World War. The *Passat,* now preserved in Travemunde in Germany, was one of two sister ships launched in 1911. By the end of the First World War numbers of active ocean going sailing ships had dropped dramatically. Indeed, it has recently been calculated that with the building of replicas and of new sail training ships, there are more square riggers on the ocean now than at any time since 1919.

There were particular niches of the maritime world in which sail continued to flourish long after it had disappeared from the major trading routes. For example, the Grand Banks schooners from Canada and from Portugal continued to fish for cod on the Grand Banks almost as long as the cod held out. Sealers continued to hunt on the ice from small purpose-designed schooners well beyond the Second World War. Indeed, the last example of working sail in UK waters, the Falmouth Oyster fishery, continues to this day because the use of engines over the oyster beds is forbidden in order to reduce the risk of pollution.

We have seen that the early decades of the twentieth century were a period of intense change. It is interesting to reflect on the equally rapid changes in the latter part of that same century. When we look back to the events of 1912-1915 we do so from the perspective of a very different maritime world. Since 1980, there has been an enormous increase in the size of the largest ships, in propulsion systems and in the complexity of the electronics used for navigation and safety. Passenger liners have now largely disappeared except for ferries on short sea routes, but they have been replaced by large numbers of cruise ships. The biggest of those cruise ships are now the equivalent, in gross tonnage terms, of more than four *Titanics*. Taking into account the increase in the global population, there are probably now more passengers at sea around the world at any given time than was ever previously the case.

Perhaps the biggest change in recent decades has been in cargo handling methods. We still require bulk cargoes to be carried and the specialist ships that do this job are now much larger and more versatile but, in operating principle, they are much the same as they have been since oil stopped being transported in barrels. The real change has been in containerisation and the rapidly increasing numbers of containers being carried on a single ship. Where, early in the twentieth century, most non-bulk cargoes were carried loose in the holds of cargo ships, packed as well as possible to prevent them from being damaged, they are now almost all carried in standard containers on ships designed for that purpose alone. Very large container ships travel on ocean routes between massive container ports. Much smaller short-sea container ships then move goods between the container ports and ports around the coasts.

How does the maritime world of today contrast with that of a century ago? There is no longer such an enormous variety of ships. Standardisation of container ships, of the design of engines-aft bulk carriers and of smaller, but similarly standardised coasters means that there is a rather boring similarity to most modern ships. Cruise ships look like (and are like) floating hotels. They may be designed with some thought to an attractive appearance; but everyone seems to be using the same computer program to do so. The fleets of small fishing craft have disappeared in favour of large, super-efficient trawlers, each of which is capable of hoovering up complete shoals of fish.

On a flight across the Irish Sea it is now quite possible to go from one side to the other on a clear day and see hardly any ships at all. Had it been possible to fly across a hundred years ago, there would have been dozens. There are, of course, seas that remain as busy as ever because they contain main routes. The English Channel is the best known area where congestion, with its greatly increased risk of collision, is a continual concern. Out in the oceans, however, the great container ships, tankers and other bulk carriers travel along narrow sea corridors like juggernauts along motorways. Although the total amount of cargo carried has multiplied greatly over the last hundred years, the jump in the quantity carried by each ship and the speed with which they can be turned around, means that the total number of ships at sea has greatly decreased. The oceans are much emptier places.

Cruise ships, unlike the former passenger liners, frequent areas well away from those narrow corridors. They travel amongst the Caribbean islands, along the coast of Alaska, into Norwegian fjords and around the continent of Antarctica. For extremely large, deep ships they spend a lot of time in narrow, shallow waters, some of which are not as reliably charted as the main shipping routes. Many cruise in remote areas where there are few other ships. Some recent accidents, happily without large numbers of casualties, have demonstrated the element of risk that this type of cruising can sometimes involve.

The purpose of examining the changing maritime world from 1880 to 1910 is to help us to judge the events of the subsequent five years properly within their historical context. It helps us to understand better the minds of the principal actors, either those at sea or those in the inquiry rooms. The men who, in 1910, were at the apex of their profession, captaining large passenger or cargo liners, had spent their formative years in quite a different world. The ships in which they learned their craft were smaller, slower, usually wind- rather than steam-powered and relied only on lights and flags for communication. If they thought about wars at all (and they had little reason to do so) it was of fleets of battleships or of gun-firing surface raiders. It was probably even more difficult for those involved in the inquiries who were not seamen. The world of the big liners provided many stories for the newspapers and a lot of publicity centred on their size and speed. Some of the lawyers and others may have had first-hand experience of crossing the Atlantic on one of the modern leviathans, but even that would have provided them with little understanding of what was involved in guiding one at speed across a crowded ocean. None would have been aboard a submarine; indeed most would never have seen one. Even amongst the seamen, understanding of the dynamics of submarine operation and of their capabilities in terms of offensive action would have been quite limited.

Wireless did not become part of the daily experience of the population until broadcasting began in the 1920s. Until then it was rather a mysterious, almost slightly miraculous, technology confined to a relatively small range of applications. The size, power requirements and fragility of wireless equipment limited its use even in most military contexts. It was never a major factor in the great battles of the Western Front and did not appear in aircraft at all until much later. Most long-range communication continued to use telegraph technology based on the cables of the type that the *Great Eastern* pioneered, as is still the case to a certain extent today. Neither the seamen nor the lawyers at the inquiries would have had much understanding about how the new invention worked or what its capabilities and limitations were. As we shall see, however, one of the captains had become famous prior to the disaster in which he was involved by exploiting wireless in a new way.

A few years ago the author asked a group of educational technologists how they considered education had changed as a result of the immense increase in the availability of computers. Their answer was a unanimous one; the pace of change of technology was much faster than changes in the practice of the teachers using it. This is an issue that will interest us as we consider the events of 1912-15. To what extent were the disasters themselves the consequence of men not sufficiently adapting their habits at sea to the dramatic technological changes? To what extent also were the outcomes of the inquiries influenced by a failure to understand the new conditions under which seamen were operating? Finally, how much of our thinking about all of those events is a product of our own quite different perspective?

2

PEACETIME RISKS

Fear of flying is a well-known phenomenon and there are consultant psychiatrists who specialise in dealing with it. This is despite the fact that, statistically, travel by modern jet passenger aircraft is amongst the safest means of moving about the planet. In the 1950s, when jets were first being used for long distance flight, that was not the case. It seemed that rarely a month went by without a news announcer solemnly intoning the fate of yet another flight that had come down as a result of bad weather or mechanical problems. A lot of people died before the issue of metal fatigue on the early Comets was diagnosed. However, even the hazards of flying in early jet aircraft were small compared to ocean travel in the first days of steamships.

Our interest is in passenger ships in the North Atlantic in particular and, in order to arrive at an informed view about the actions of the captains and the pronouncements on them by the judge, we need to have some sense of the types of risk they faced at sea. In this chapter we will consider risks faced in peacetime before August 1914 and in the next the additional ones that war amongst the major powers rather obviously brought. Risk management is now a powerful tool that assists in the running of businesses and other organisations. Audit Committees review and update registers which detail the risks that an organisation faces, estimate the severity of those risks and set out measures which, it is hoped, will mitigate them. In a sense what we are now about to do is create retrospectively a sort of risk register for a liner at sea in the second decade of the twentieth century, such as the captain might have produced on the basis of his own knowledge and experience had he been asked.

Identifying risks is not the difficult part of the exercise, nor is listing the mitigating measures that either were or were not then in force. The contentious element in the process is measuring the relative severity of the risks. In modern management practice there is now a fairly standard approach to this.

Severity is quantified as the product of two estimations, the first of which is the likelihood of the risk materialising. The second is the level of damage created if it does. The risks that are easy to categorise in this way and to plan for are those at either extreme. An event that is highly likely to happen and is potentially very damaging requires urgent and extensive mitigating measures. It is probable that such risks are well understood and good preventative precautions are already in place. One which is unlikely and of little potential impact can largely be ignored. Even risks which are quite likely to materialise but which are of minimal potential impact do not cause too much concern so long as there are reliable procedures in place to deal with them.

The risks that most often give rise to sleepless nights are the ones that, although highly unlikely to happen, could have disastrous consequences. Their very improbability adds to the difficulty of establishing appropriate means of preventing them. If they are improbable, relatively few people in the past are likely to have experienced them. The underlying causes that give rise to such events may, for the same reason, be less well understood, so the effectiveness of any mitigating measures may be difficult to judge. The failure of some of the world's most prestigious financial institutions to prevent their own collapse in 2008 as a consequence of the effects of new types of highly complex but poorly secured loans is a classic example.

Audit Committees regularly update risk registers because the severity of risks changes over time and new ones are always emerging. That brings us back to the issue that we identified in the last chapter. How good were our captains at updating their personal estimates of the risks they were facing in the light of changing circumstances principally resulting from rapid developments in technology? For that matter, how well did the judge understand the relevant patterns of risk, even with the help of the nautical assessors who were provided to sit with him and assist him to do so? In the court of public opinion, guided by newspaper reports, it could only be expected that appreciation of what was involved in directing a voyage of a large, fast passenger liner was extremely limited.

In the era of wooden sailing ships casualty rates were extremely high. Indeed, it is surprising how many people were prepared to jeopardise their lives on long and perilous ocean voyages. Even well crewed and well found ships frequently came to grief. In 1707 Sir Cloudesley Shovell and his entire crew on HMS *Association*, as well as the crews of *Eagle, Romney* and *Firebrand* were lost when the squadron of which he was admiral ran foul of the Scillies in bad weather. Almost 2000 men died as the result of an inability to calculate longitude correctly. In 1811 an escorted convoy of merchantmen left the Baltic very late in the season and was caught in atrocious weather in the North Sea. Many ships were overwhelmed and, again, at least 2000 men and women perished.

The early liners were really wooden sailing vessels to which engines had been added. The engines were of limited power and did little to increase the ships' capacity to withstand hazards. Replacing the wooden hulls with iron allowed for larger ships to be built but had little impact on safety. The catalogue of disasters in the 1850s illustrates just how vulnerable these ships were; 1854 was an awful year. In March the Inman Line *City of Glasgow* left Liverpool for Philadephia with 480 on board but did not arrive. The sailing ship *Baldaur* reported sighting a ship of similar appearance to the *City of Glasgow* which seemed to be in some difficulty but was unable to get to her to help. In the days before wireless, hope lasted longer. For weeks people clung to the possibility that the ship had become disabled but had remained afloat. Eventually hope faded and nothing more was ever discovered as to her fate. She is likely to have foundered in heavy weather, but at that time of year there could have been icebergs in the area through which she was travelling and collision with one of them cannot be ruled out.

In September of that year the same line's *City of Philadelphia* grounded on Cape Race. All 600 on board were ferried ashore safely in the ship's boats, but the ship was lost. That same month the Collins Line *Arctic,* a large, fairly new and prestigious wooden paddle steamer, collided in fog in the area of the Grand Banks with the smaller iron-hulled French steam schooner *Vesta*. The badly mangled schooner managed to stay afloat but the damage to the *Arctic* proved fatal. So did the lack of discipline amongst some members of the crew who commandeered the boats and left the passengers, including many women and children, to fend for themselves. Only 21 of the 281 passengers survived, all of them male, while around 40 per cent of the crew were saved. Altogether around 350 perished and this remains the worst disaster to happen to an American flagged liner. The appalling stories brought back by the survivors created a wave of dramatic headlines in the press. Unlike the *City of Glasgow,* which simply faded out of public consciousness with little notice, the *Arctic* became notorious.

One aspect of that disaster which resonates with a later one was the fact that the number of lifeboats carried by the *Arctic* was nowhere near sufficient for the number of passengers that she carried, despite having the number that was required by law. Just as in the case of *Titanic* nearly 70 years later, the law had failed to keep up with an increase in the size of ships and the number of passengers carried. Also significant in terms of the level of media attention was the social standing of the passengers. Like the *Titanic,* the *Arctic* carried a number of wealthy citizens from both sides of the Atlantic while the *City of Glasgow* was transporting mostly poor immigrants.

The Collins Line suffered a further tragedy less than two years later. In January 1856 the *Arctic's* sister ship, *Pacific,* departed from Liverpool with 186 on board and was never seen or heard from again, at least not for almost a century and a half. When she failed to arrive the process of waiting and speculation began. There had previously been incidents when ships had gone missing for long periods but had eventually emerged having been damaged or in some way incapacitated. Although her normal passage time was ten or eleven days, it was three months before all hope was officially given up. Reports from other ships in the Atlantic at that time talked about a severe winter, with ice coming farther south than usual and there was speculation that this might have been the cause of her loss. It is difficult to know the extent to which that media speculation was shared by the community of seafarers who were better able to judge the risk. Only in 1991 was the question answered as to where the *Pacific* sank when her wreck was positively identified in the Irish Sea about 60 miles from Liverpool. It seems that some catastrophe occurred shortly after she left port that must have caused her to sink very quickly. Not only did no one on board survive, nothing identifiable from the ship reached the shore a mere twelve miles away. The riddle remains; we are none the wiser as to the cause of her loss except, of course, that we can remove ice from the list of possibilities. It is a tribute to the power of myth that still, in 2011, on the Ice Data website (http://www.icedata.ca/Pages/ShipCollisions/ShipCol_OnlineSearch. php), the ship is listed as having sunk following collision with an iceberg, the evidence quoted being a message in a bottle supposedly washed up in the Hebrides. The same website states that the *City of Boston*, which disappeared in January 1870 between Halifax and Liverpool, 'is assumed to have hit a berg.' There is, in fact, no evidence to that effect and many at the time considered it more likely that she was overwhelmed in an exceptionally severe storm reported by a number of other ships.

By the 1870s liners were steel-built with more efficient compound engines driving propellers rather than paddle wheels. They were therefore less dependent on their auxiliary sails, although they still carried them. Better control and reduced dependence on the wind helped to improve safety somewhat. A lee shore, with the wind forcing a sailing ship ever closer, does not present the same danger to a well powered steamship. Nonetheless, the changes in the structure and propulsion of ships also created some additional risk. As ships became bigger they carried more people so that a single accident put more lives in jeopardy. Greater speeds, without compensating improvements in navigation aids, meant some types of accidents were more likely to happen and not less. Two awful losses in just over a year illustrate the point.

In April 1873 the White Star Liner *Atlantic* crashed into rocks close to Halifax in atrocious weather. At least 550 died including all of the women. Only one child was saved. The ship had been turned towards Halifax because of fears aboard that she had insufficient coal left after days of fighting into heavy gales to reach New York. Her captain had left the bridge for a rest but was not awakened at the time he instructed. Either the speed of the ship was greater than estimated as a result of an easing in the weather, or the course plotted was incorrect, or both. Like *Arctic* before her and *Titanic* after, the agonies of the passengers were protracted and the stories of survivors heart-rending. An inquiry in Canada found that the captain had been negligent in not ensuring that greater care was taken in approaching a dangerous coast in bad weather. His certificate was suspended for two years, effectively ending his career. The owners, however, were also censured and were found negligent in sending the ship to sea with insufficient fuel. They raised such a clamour that a further inquiry was held in London and only after a very protracted process did they get the result that they wanted. Certainly on paper it seemed as if there ought to have been sufficient coal, so perhaps their exoneration was justified, but the fact that they were able to pursue the matter at such great length and to such good effect illustrated the extent to which, at that time, the Board of Trade, which was responsible for such matters, was open to lobbying by business interests. It is much more unlikely that the ship's captain, had he disputed the outcome of the first inquiry in Canada, could have achieved any such resolution.

As we have noted, the largest ship afloat in the 1870s was the *Great Eastern*. For a short time the second largest – although only one fifth of her tonnage – was the French Line *Ville du Havre*. Initially designed as a paddle wheeler she had been re-engined with screw propulsion as well as being lengthened and was fast, luxurious and well received on her return to service in 1873. Her nemesis was the sailing ship *Loch Earn* with which she collided in mid-Atlantic in the absence of fog in the early hours of 21 November 1874. Neither ship seems to have been aware of the other until the very last minute. There were heavy seas and it was overcast so, although visibility was good, the darkness meant that only the lights each ship was burning could have acted as warning. Either those lights or the look-outs on both ships were ineffective. *Ville du Havre* received a massive hole in her side allowing the sea access to the wide open spaces of her engine room; she sank in minutes. The loss of life amounted to 226 passengers and crew. It was over a week before news reached shore that the *Ville du Havre* had sunk and, despite all of the anguished analysis of survivors' reports, little emerged by way of explanation as to the reason for the collision. The disaster did illustrate the vulnerability of steel ships to collisions of this nature. As the number of bulkheads and watertight compartments gradually increased in the years following, the level of risk declined. Even so, ten years later, the Cunarder *Oregon,* then the fastest ship on the

Atlantic, was rammed off New York by a sailing ship and likewise sank as a consequence. In her case there was ample time to get the passengers off and assistance on hand to get them to shore, so no lives were lost. However, as the *Empress of Ireland* was to show in 1914, the potential consequences of such a collision remained extremely severe.

To the people involved in the peacetime accidents of 1912–1914, the losses that we have been considering would have seemed a long time ago, although well within the living memory of a significant number of them. Events of the 1890s and 1900s would have had a more significant impact on their understanding of the nature of the risks that they faced at sea. Unfortunately, there was no shortage of examples for them to consider. Some of those examples would not have provided help in determining the severity of risks because they were so unusual that their repetition was highly unlikely. They were extreme examples of the 'improbable but drastic' type of risk that we noted previously. On 17 March 1891, in Gibraltar harbour, the steamer *Utopia* was caught by wind and current as she came into the anchorage and was driven onto the ram of the anchored British battleship HMS *Anson*. The ram proved its effectiveness as a weapon by piercing the side of the *Utopia,* causing her to take on water so rapidly that she sank almost immediately with the loss of 571 lives. An even more bizarre accident, but fortunately one without loss of life, occurred on 22 September 1907 at Spezia in the Gulf of Genoa at the launch of what was then the largest liner built in Italy, the *Principessa Jolanda*. Some of the launching cradle remained stuck on the side of the ship as she went down the ways, causing her to take a list to port. As the openings in the side of the ship had not yet had their doors fitted at this stage, water flooded in and the list gradually became greater and greater until she capsized and sank in the harbour, a total loss witnessed by thousands of spectators.

Of much more relevance to the understanding of more general dangers at sea were the losses of the *Islander, Norge, Republic* and *Waratah*. The *Islander* accident was not in the Atlantic and did not involve a large liner, but it did involve ice. She foundered off Alaska after collision with an iceberg with the loss of 90 lives. Most collisions between ships and icebergs naturally involved ships that customarily went into ice prevalent areas because of the nature of the work that they did. Whalers, sealers, Grand Banks fishermen were all at significant risk from ice, although the great majority of collisions only involved damage rather than loss of the ship. Nonetheless, significant numbers of ships were lost and crew members killed. *Islander* was unusual in that passengers were lost, but the ship was engaged in travelling on a coastal route that took it through waters well known to have large numbers of bergs.

The risk from ice in the North Atlantic has already been noted. There was media speculation that the *City of Glasgow* and the *Pacific* had been lost through collision with ice and the latter possibility had not been discounted in 1912. The *Lady of the Lake,* a brig sailing from Belfast to Quebec in 1833, was caught in an icefield that eventually pierced her hull and caused to her sink. Reports of the numbers lost vary from 70 to 215. However, when it comes to collisions between Atlantic passenger liners and icebergs, there were, in fact, only two confirmed instances prior to the *Titanic* and neither resulted in any deaths. In January 1856 the Cunard liner *Persia* set out on her maiden voyage. She was at the time the largest and most luxurious ship afloat, although mechanically a little behind the times. Five days out she collided with an iceberg at 11 knots. Although quite badly damaged the ship survived and all aboard arrived safely, although very late, in New York. It may be that the knowledge of what had happened to the *Persia* encouraged speculation about ice being involved in the disappearance of the *Pacific* which set out on her fatal voyage on the 23rd of the same month. It was only weeks after the *Persia* arrived bruised and battered in New York that an explanation was being sought for the non-arrival of the *Pacific*.

The second liner to collide with an iceberg was the *Arizona* in 1879. The collision took place in the dark on a calm, clear night with good visibility. Again, the *Arizona* ran into the berg head on at almost full speed, again about 11 knots. The result was similar to the case of the *Persia*, a badly crumpled bow with the ship kept afloat by her watertight compartments. She limped to the closest port, St John's Newfoundland, and had to go back to the Clyde for repairs from there. There were some injuries amongst the crew but no fatalities. The excuse from the lookouts was that they thought the berg was low-lying cloud right up until the moment the bow crunched into it.

The danger of ice was, therefore, acknowledged by all, especially in combination with fog, but the overall risk assessment placed it much lower than many other hazards. In clear visibility, whether in daylight or at night, icebergs are easily seen. At night the phosphorescence from waves breaking on the base makes them readily visible from a considerable distance away as does the glint of moonlight or even starlight on the crystals formed on the surface. What probably was not recognised until after the *Titanic* disaster was that there was a particular set of circumstances where these conditions were not in force and an iceberg might not be seen until it was much closer. After some time drifting south into warmer water, the part of an iceberg under the water begins to melt. Eventually the berg becomes top heavy and rolls over. At that stage the part now out of the water is smooth, dark and free of crystals. On the very rare occasions in the North Atlantic when the sea is so calm as to be free of swell there is no phosphorescence at the base. Those were the circumstances that may have conspired together on the night of 14 April 1912 to create the most studied disaster in history.

It was early in the morning of the 28 June 1904 when the Danish immigrant ship *Norge* steamed at full speed into Hasselwood Rock just beside Rockall. Most passengers were in their bunks. The ship sank in only 20 minutes and, of the 800 or so on board, only 168 got away in the lifeboats, some of whom were not picked up for 8 days. It was the worst loss of life on the Atlantic up to that time and remains the worst sea disaster that Denmark has experienced. It resulted from a navigational error; clearly those on the bridge thought that they were many miles away from what is a well marked hazard on every chart. Although the sinking of the *Norge* has now largely been forgotten, it would have been very much in the minds of those responsible for navigating ships across the Atlantic for many years afterwards.

Navigational error leading to stranding was clearly therefore a major risk, but not one that featured in the peacetime accidents with which we are concerned, except that one of them took place in confined waters in fog and the risk of stranding may have influenced decisions about movements. The possibility of stranding did, however, feature in one of the wartime incidents, the sinking of the *Lusitania,* but we will have to consider that in the context of the additional risks that war created. Navigational error can lead to dangers other than possible collision with land and these include a risk that only emerged with the advent of wireless. If a ship is in distress and wishes to summon assistance with wireless, it is necessary to let others know accurately where the ship is. Prior to wireless a ship could only communicate with other ships that could see it. Sending out a wrong position by wireless could well jeopardise any rescue. That was a risk that materialised in the case of *Titanic.* It could have been significant in the case of the *Republic,* the first ever ship to summon assistance by wireless, as we shall see.

The area off the coast of America east of New York is notorious for persistent and dense fogs. During the night of 22/23 January 1909 the White Star liner *Republic* was slowly feeling her way through one of those fogs close to the Nantucket Light Vessel when she was struck amidships by the smaller Italian emigrant liner *Florida.* Although *Florida* was travelling slowly as well, this was another of those accidents, of which we have already noted several, where the smaller ramming vessel suffers serious bow damage but survives while the larger vessel struck in the side is fatally incapacitated. The difference in this case was that one of the two ships, *Republic,* was fitted with the new wireless technology manned by a single operator employed by the Marconi Company. Jack Binns took the brave decision to send out the world's first wireless distress call when he saw the damage to the ship without even wait-ing for instructions from the bridge. He followed that up with accurate details of the ship's position which were re-broadcast by much more powerful shore-based wireless stations. Nonetheless, it was over twelve hours before the first major rescue ship found *Republic* in the fog, also a White Star ship, the much larger *Baltic*. Had the position sent out by the *Republic* not been correct, it is extremely unlikely that the *Baltic* would have found her before she sank. By the time the *Baltic* did arrive the passengers had been transferred from the *Republic* to the *Florida,* who stood by despite the damage she had received, a process that required many hours. Eventually the passengers from both ships were rowed across to the *Baltic* and members of the *Republic's* crew were also rescued, the last two, Captain Sealby and Second Officer Williams, as the ship sank beneath them.

The stories of the protracted and dramatic rescue of almost all of those on the two ships became major world wide news. The collision itself killed three passengers on *Republic* and three crewmen on *Florida* but other than that everyone survived. One effect was to make a hero of Binns and raise the profile of wireless as a means of effecting rescue when a ship is in distress. Thereafter it became accepted without question that all ocean-going ships should be fitted with wireless capability. Nonetheless it is worth noting that, had the watertight bulkheads of the *Republic* not held out long enough to permit transfer of passengers and crew and had the ship been totally depend-ent on rescue by ships summoned through the distress calls, the story might have been quite different. At least the ship carried sufficient lifeboats for all on board and, in the absence of a rescue ship standing by, everyone might still have been evacuated. One of the notable features of the accident and the sub-sequent rescue was the quality of the leadership provided by Captain Sealby whose calm and powerful voice directed and reassured effectively throughout.

While the *Republic* was sinking off New York a brand new medium-sized liner was completing her maiden voyage from the UK to Australia. The *Waratah* was one of the last ships of her type to leave her builders without any wireless equipment. By the time she left on her return voyage to the UK in April 1909, possibly as a result of the publicity surrounding the loss of the *Republic*, the decision had already been taken to have it fitted on arrival back in the UK. That never happened because, having called at Durban and departed for Capetown on 27 July 1909, the *Waratah* disappeared. The loss of the ship has never been fully explained, partly because, despite extensive searches, the wreck has never been found. The most likely cause is an extremely large wave in the atrocious weather conditions that she headed into on leaving Durban. While stories emerged after her loss doubting her stability, these were never substantiated. It is the case that the area she passed through does experience combinations of wind and currents that, from time to time, give rise to freakishly large waves. However, the seabed along the course she would have taken has been meticulously searched for her wreck and it has not been located. A number of wrecks provisionally thought to be hers have been shown to be similar sized ships sunk by submarines during the Second World War; the mystery may never be solved.

What is of interest to us is not, however, the cause of her sinking but the reaction to the loss, given the fact that the ship did not have wireless. We have already noted that when the *City of Glasgow* and *Pacific* failed to arrive at their destinations, hope lasted for some time that they were still afloat. The same was true of the *Waratah*. For example, had the bad weather she experienced caused the loss of her propeller, the ship would have drifted disabled, but otherwise intact, with electrical and hydraulic power to operate her other life support systems on board and with sufficient food and water to last for a considerable time. Her drift would have taken her down into the roaring forties and gradually south towards Antarctica. Hence, several Royal Navy ships and a pair of chartered merchant ships mounted searches for the *Waratah* for a period of more than six months but nothing was ever found. Eventually all hope disappeared. Had the ship been fitted with wireless, how would that have affected what happened?

It is quite possible, likely even, that the *Waratah* was indeed suddenly overwhelmed and capsized by a freak wave. In such circumstances it is unlikely that a distress call could have been transmitted. In September 1980, the large bulk carrier *Derbyshire* sank during Typhoon Orchid in the Sea of Japan as a result, we now know, of structural failure. Her sinking was also so sudden that there was no time for a distress call and a search ensued that lasted a week before she was declared lost.

In her case it was the absence of radio messages that raised concerns about her safety. Had *Waratah* had wireless then the likelihood of her drifting for a prolonged period without contact would have been greatly reduced and the search would probably have been called off sooner. If the sinking was actually for a different reason and took place over a longer period of time, then of course the possibility exists that distress calls might have alerted other shipping in time to rescue some or all of those on board. The ability to make contact over long distances well beyond the horizon was, only a few years after it came about, beginning to alter the way people thought about risks at sea and how they were dealt with.

Without attempting any formal arithmetic in order to calculate estimates of the severity of the different risks, we can see that, in addition to the hazards of damage to a ship from bad weather, liner captains on North Atlantic routes were probably most concerned with avoiding other ships and avoiding running aground, particularly in fog, but that collision with icebergs was not particularly high on their list of worries, other than when visibility was restricted in certain parts of the ocean at certain times of year. The rapid increase in the size and speed of liners had not been matched by any significant improvement in their ability to see hazards or to determine their exact position. The human eye at high points on the ship remained the sole means of spotting any dangers. While the latest binoculars provided greater magnification than was available early in the nineteenth century this was of little benefit at night or in fog. In both situations binoculars tended to reduce the effectiveness of lookouts and not improve it. Navigation relied, as it had for a hundred years and more, on a combination of dead reckoning checked against sun or star positions calculated with a sextant. On a steam ship travelling on a course not subject to the vagaries of the wind, dead reckoning was generally more accurate than on sailing ships, except that, at higher speeds, any error became rapidly magnified over time. Captains of large liners racing across the Atlantic in poor weather, when the opportunity to take sights was limited, could find themselves with more uncertainty about their actual position at a given time than a sailing ship captain in Nelson's era.

Greater speed also reduced the available time in which to take avoiding action. It is a modern cliché, often used by politicians as an excuse for not having achieved what they promised, that it takes an awfully long time to turn around a supertanker. While modern supertankers may be many times the size of the Atlantic steamships, the principle does apply. The new large, fast generation of ships that emerged in the 1900s required greater distances in which to turn and much more time to stop than the slower, smaller predecessors to which their officers had previously been accustomed. Yet, as we have seen, the ability to spot potentially serious hazards had not changed.

These then were the major risks that liner captains had to consider as they traversed the Atlantic up to August 1914. Then the world went to war and an entirely new risk register had to be created.

THE WARTIME RISKS

Prize money paid for captured merchant ships and their cargo was one of the great recruitment motivators for the Royal Navy in the Napoleonic Wars at the beginning of the nineteenth century. Warships and their semi-official privateering colleagues of all navies saw the pursuit and capture of enemy merchant ships as a major part of their role. With the dominance of the Royal Navy and the navies of other European powers that followed those wars the need for the privateering element diminished and, eventually, the award of prize money was discontinued. One of the purposes of the Declaration of Paris at the end of the Crimean War was to regularise the position by international agreement. The result was the emergence over a period of time of a set of rules governing the behaviour of belligerent navies towards merchant ships, known as the Cruiser Rules. These were far from new, going back in much the same form to the time of Henry VIII. The Hague Conventions of 1899 and 1907 provided the last refinement of international codes of behaviour by belligerents prior to the First World War but did not materially alter the Cruiser Rules.

The Rules envisaged a scenario in which a warship of one nation encountered at sea a merchant ship belonging to a nation with which it was formally at war. There were separate agreements around the treatment of neutral ships which, while they proved highly controversial, do not directly affect the incidents with which we are concerned. Like all legalistic determinations, much hangs upon understanding what the terms mean and before looking at the rules themselves it is important at least to be clear as to when, so far as the rules are concerned, a merchant ship is a merchant ship. Obviously a ship mounting its own armament cannot claim to be solely a merchant ship. If a ship has been built so as to be easily converted into an armed cruiser, (as some liners were) that cast some doubt on its merchant status. Also of significance is the nature of the cargo the ship is carrying. If the ship is carrying cargo that is directly aimed at furthering the war effort of the country to which it belongs, then it is no longer a merchant ship under the rules. Such cargo is referred to as 'contraband'. The difficulty with that proviso is that the 'cruiser' may have no means of knowing what cargo the ship is carrying until its crew can board the ship and search it.

Thus the procedure envisaged by the Cruiser Rules was that the cruiser would order the merchant ship to stop, an order which the Rules required it to obey, so that the cruiser could send across crew members to carry out a search; if contraband cargo were found then the ship could be impounded. Ideally, the ship should then be directed into a port of the nation to which the cruiser belongs, or an ally. Should that prove impossible the Rules allowed the cruiser to sink the merchant ship on condition that the safety of the crew was ensured. 'Safety' here implied that the cruiser would take the merchant ship's crew on board itself or would put them into lifeboats, provided that they were close to shore and the crew could land easily. If, on approach, the cruiser could see that the ship was armed it was entitled to open fire without warning and without giving the crew time to leave the ship.

The rules were fine as far as they went, except that the scenario upon which they were based proved to be the exception rather than the rule when war broke out. That is not to say that they were ignored entirely. R K Lockner entitled his book about Captain Karl von Muller and his ship, the German Light Cruiser *Emden,* 'The Last Gentleman of War'. During the *Emden*'s cruise in the Pacific in the autumn of 1914 a number of merchant ships were sunk, but always the Cruiser Rules were meticulously obeyed and the safety of the crews was assured.

Defining contraband cargo as anything intended to further the war effort was an immediate source of controversy. Both sides eventually attempted to impose total blockades on the basis that even foodstuffs which sustained the population enabled that population to keep the war going. On that definition all merchant ships were deemed to be carrying contraband and therefore could be legitimately seized or sunk. Nonetheless, under the Rules the ship must first be stopped and the safety of the crew attended to. Unfortunately the Cruiser Rules were designed to deal with a surface warship as the cruiser and a merchant ship unable to send distress signals by wireless when approached. A submerged warship and a wireless-equipped merchant ship distorted the picture. It would be hard to blame the Tudor diplomats who penned the rules initially for a lack of foresight, but perhaps an opportunity was missed to update the rules in line with new technological developments when the refinements to the Hague Convention were agreed in 1907.

It is surprising, but also enlightening, to note how poorly the impact on warfare of both submarines and wireless were foreseen before the event. The occasional Jeremiah predicted the end of the battleship era as a result of the threat of submarine attack but, in fact, no Dreadnought type battleship on either side was lost to submarine action throughout the war. It was aircraft, not submarines, which eventually made battleships extinct. Likewise, the potential of German submarines to create complete mayhem with the seaborne trade of what was then the premier maritime nation was almost entirely unforeseen. Furthermore, the capability of wireless to provide intelligence and orders to widely spread warships at sea was also underestimated.

Submarines posed a major challenge to the Cruiser Rules because they combined enormous offensive potential with great defensive vulnerability, especially on the surface. They were capable of targeting a very large high explosive load, unseen and from great distances. But on the surface, damage that, to a surface ship, would be regarded as minor, could prove fatal to a submarine. It was quite unrealistic to expect a submarine to stay for a prolonged period on the surface in hostile waters while a party went across to a merchant ship to search the cargo and then facilitate the evacuation of the crew. It was also unrealistic to expect the merchant ship to sit quietly and not to use its wireless while this was going on.

What emerged as the war progressed was complete confusion characterised by partial adherence to the Rules by both sides, when to do so carried little risk, but total disobedience when judged expedient – and that was most of the time. What turned out to be almost as significant as actual behaviour in the war at sea was the propaganda campaign that each side mounted to exploit the supposed breaching of the rules by the other. Indeed, the two aspects interacted in that some of the activity at sea was engaged in for the purpose of generating a propagandist rather than a military success. The level of hypocrisy was quite extraordinary. The two incidents that we are interested in occurred quite early in the war at a time when both sides were still feeling their way with the new technology, uncertain as to what it could achieve, uncertain as to what they could legitimately use it for and, likewise, uncertain as to what they could get away with that was not legitimate.

The confusion as to how the war at sea with submarines would be fought was evident very quickly. A number of warships were sunk in August and September 1914, but the first merchant ship to be attacked was the *Glitra* on 20 October. The captain of U-17, Feldkirchner, kept his ship on the surface, requested the *Glitra* to stop, sent a party over to inspect the cargo, ordered the crew off on the lifeboats and then sank the ship. Just six days later, in the Dover Strait, the *Admiral Gentaume* was torpedoed without warning by Rudolph

Schneider in U-24, although she did not sink and was towed into port. By the end of 1914 just 10 merchant ships had been sunk by German submarines.

It must be remembered that the Allies were also making use of their submarines. Britain had declared a long range blockade of Germany and her submarines were involved in the North Sea and Baltic in enforcing it. In the North Sea the submarines were acting as scouts gathering intelligence as to the likely movements of the main German warships and they did not therefore pursue a very active role in stopping and sinking ships. In the Baltic they had a rapid impact on the carriage of iron ore from Sweden to Germany, sinking a large number of ore carriers in a short period. When the Gallipoli campaign began in April 1915, submarines were sent through the Dardanelles to the Sea of Marmara and the Bosphorus in order to disrupt Turkish supplies to their troops. It was a campaign that demanded much of the submarine crews in navigating very confined waters in a hostile environment and in operating completely isolated over long periods. Their bravery was recognised by the award of three Victoria Crosses. One of the commanders so honoured was Lieutenant Commander E.C. Boyle of E-14 for a patrol that lasted from 27 April to 18 May 1915. On 3 May, just four days prior to the sinking of the *Lusitania*, Boyle torpedoed the Turkish troop carrier *Gul Djemal*. This was a ship of 5000 tons which had begun life in Harland and Wolff's shipyard in Belfast as the White Star Line *Germanic* in 1875. There are several versions of what happened as a consequence of the torpedoing. In one, the ship sinks with the loss of almost all of the 6000 troops on board. In another, the ship is only slightly damaged and proceeds to port for repair with no human loss whatsoever. An 'intermediate' version has the *Guj Djemal* sinks in very shallow water so that her superstructure remains above water, but a large number of the 4000 troops on board drown. What is certain is that the ship was repaired and returned to service and performed various roles until scrapped in 1950. It is also the case that in 1922 surviving members of the crew of E14 shared £30 000 in 'bounty money' (at £5 per head of the supposed 6000 troops on the *Gul Djemal*) awarded by a British court, the largest such payment received by any group of individuals as a result of actions in the First World War. The court ruled that the rifles that the troops were carrying constituted 'ship's armament' and so the ship could be classified legally as a warship.

The commander of E14 knew that the *Gul Djemal* was in the service of the Turkish government as a troopship and, therefore, opened fire without warning as he was entitled to do. Towards the end of his patrol he also torpedoed a coal-carrying ship as it berthed in the harbour of Constantinople, also without warning, on the basis that coal was vital to the Turkish war effort. Altogether, during the Gallipoli campaign, British submarines sank 2 large warships, 1 destroyer, 5 gunboats, 11 transports, 44 steamships and 148 sailing boats. Although the actions of British submarines were never strategically as important as those of the U-boats and did not raise the same issues concerning the fate of neutral citizens or non-combatants, it would be wrong to suggest that the manner of their employment was radically different. That was not apparent from the statements of either government.

On 18 February 1915 the German government announced that, from that point on, in the area around the British Isles, its submarines would conduct 'unrestricted warfare'. That meant that the Cruiser Rules were being abandoned because all ships irrespective of cargo or of nationality were declared liable to be sunk without warning. Although the Germans withdrew the announcement in September that year as a result of pressure from neutral nations, particularly America, (only to re-instate it two years later) it was in effect during the period in which we are interested, through the spring of 1915. The U-boats immediately began to put the new policy into practice and numbers of ships sunk without warning increased. However, some U-boat commanders, where it was judged safe to do so, tried to follow the Cruiser Rules at least so far as giving the crew of the merchant ship a chance to get clear before the torpedo was fired. This most frequently occurred when small ships were attacked such as coastal steamers or sailing ships. Quite often the value of the target was judged to be so low as not to justify the expenditure of a torpedo. In such cases the submarine surfaced and used its gun to sink the merchant ship, often waiting long enough for the crew to get away in the boats before opening fire.

It is hard to pin down precisely why, in some cases, there was a genuine attempt to minimise losses amongst merchant ship crews and, in other cases, no attempt at all. It does seem to be the case that different U-boat captains exhibited different patterns of behaviour. Whether this was because they happened to operate in different patrol areas, some with high populations of British warships and others with fewer, or because some targets provided more opportunity for humanitarian gestures it is difficult to tell. A third possible explanation is that the different patterns of behaviour simply reflected the personalities of the captains involved and we will consider this further at a later stage.

The British Government attempted to hold the Germans to account in relation to the abandonment of the Cruiser Rules and some of the pressure from neutral nations demonstrated a measure of success in doing so. However, from the beginning of the war the British Admiralty had, in effect, abandoned the Rules as well, albeit in a different way. The advice given to the captains of merchant ships was that if they spotted a U-boat, they should ignore any instructions from it and either turn their stern towards it and run or else turn towards the submarine and attempt to ram it. They should also use their wireless to call for assistance, giving as much information about the submarine as possible. Turning stern on to the U-boat minimised the target size for the U-boat's gun or torpedo tubes and, obviously, going to full speed increased the chance of escape. Although we will later encounter one ship that did make an attempt to ram a submarine, the most common practice, certainly where passengers were involved, was to turn and run. However, the Cruiser Rules indicated that, if instructed to do so, the merchant ship should stop and permit a boarding party. The merchant ship was also not supposed to try to summon assistance.

The Admiralty encouraged captains to fly the flags of neutral nations instead of the Red Ensign so as to discourage U-boats. This was a legitimate 'ruse of war' sanctioned under the 1907 Hague Convention and was not itself a breach of the rules because, clearly, a search party could see through the ruse immediately. However, if a ship flying a neutral flag, which is told to stop by a U-boat, turns away at speed and calls for help on its wireless, it is difficult to see what option the captain of the submarine has other than to force the ship to stop by opening fire.

The advice given by the Admiralty was designed to try to reduce the success rate of U-boats and, if possible, to find them and attack them. Getting merchant ships to use their wirelesses increased the chance of warships being alerted in time to get to the scene before the U-boat had left. The priority of the Admiralty was to win the war. While they would not deliberately have put lives unnecessarily at risk, the saving of lives per se was not their first consideration.

The other advice that the Admiralty gave to captains was less contentious as it principally concerned the navigation of merchant ships in such a way as to avoid attack. Captains were advised to zig-zag irregularly in order to make it difficult for U-boats to target them with torpedoes. It was also suggested that merchant ships should not stay too close to coastlines and, in particular, they should avoid headlands. Headlands tended to be 'turning points' that also gave good opportunities for bearings to be taken that confirmed a ship's position. U-boat captains recognised this and tried to exploit the natural inclination of merchant ship captains to employ them in this way. Thus there was a tension between the advice offered by the Admiralty and what was regarded as normal, safe peacetime practice. Ships that perpetually zig-zagged had more difficulty in determining their dead reckoning position. If opportunities for taking sights with sextants had been limited for some time by weather conditions, then there was a greater need for sighting land in good time and good visibility. Running on towards land without knowing a ship's exact position of course raises the risk of stranding. As we have already observed, high speeds tended to magnify errors in dead reckoning positions. One degree of inac-curacy in a course steered at 10 knots over 12 hours produces half of the error that the same inaccuracy generates at 20 knots.

The British Admiralty also made adherence to the Cruiser Rules almost impossible through its use of Q-ships. These were small merchant ships, trawl-ers or sailing ships which were secretly converted into warships with hidden guns. They acted as decoys luring U-boats as close as possible before opening fire. They did have some success, although probably not commensurate with the effort and cost involved in terms of resources invested and manpower lost. They are not relevant to the episodes with which we are concerned as the first Q-ship success was not until 24 July 1915. It is worth noting, however, in the context of some of the attitudes being struck by the British Government in relation to the sinking of *Falaba* and *Lusitania,* that Q-ships had been con-ceived, had been taken up and converted and were operational by the time the second of those sinkings had occurred and before either inquiry had opened.

One criticism frequently levelled against the Admiralty is that it failed to put a convoy system in place at the very beginning of the war. After all, it is sometimes argued, convoys were successfully employed throughout the Napoleonic wars a century previously. Surely it was obvious that they were needed in 1914. In fact it would have been wrong simply to have extrapolated directly from actions fought by slow wooden sailing ships firing short range cannons to attacks on steamships by submerged, torpedo-firing submarines. Twentieth-century surface warships were also a world away from the sloops, brigs and frigates that used to prey on merchant ships in the early 1800s, being capable of accurate plunging fire from rifled guns fired at a distance of several miles. In the end the Admiralty became convinced that convoys would be beneficial and introduced them in 1917. Arguably they should have come to that conclusion a little sooner, but given the nature of the threat in early 1915 and the poor understanding there was about how effective the new technology would be and how best to counter it, the decision not to instigate a convoy system at that stage is at least defensible.

Perhaps the single word that captures the situation in the first half of 1915, therefore, is confusion. There was confusion amongst the politicians about the rules of war, confusion amongst the admirals and shipping companies as to how to interpret them and confusion amongst captains at sea, on either side, as to how best to balance out the risks of the new warfare while at the same time dealing with the peacetime risks that had not gone away when war was declared. And confusion persisted for a long time after 1915. The Cruiser Rules were included in the provisions of the 1930 Naval Treaty of London. Germany was not a signatory but added the relevant parts into German law.

Nonetheless, on 3 September 1939, the day Britain declared war on Germany again, a torpedo sank the Donaldson Line steamship *Athenia* off the north coast of Ireland with the loss of 117 lives. Oberleutnant Fitz-Julius Lemp, whose U-30 fired the torpedo, claimed afterwards that he had mistaken the ship for a troopship or armed merchant cruiser. Towards the end of that year, however, in the South Atlantic, Captain Langsdorf of the pocket battleship *Graf Spee* did make some attempt to avoid loss of life amongst the crews of merchant ships that he sank by taking them on board and transferring them to supply ships. He was almost the last person to do so. After that, war at sea became completely no holds barred.

THE NATURE OF INQUIRIES

Although by the beginning of the twentieth century, the UK was no longer the largest manufacturing nation in the world, having already been overtaken by Germany and soon to be relegated to third place by the USA, she was still the largest trading nation, handling a much greater proportion of the world's trade than any other. It is not surprising, therefore, that the post of President of the Board of Trade was an extremely important one, deemed to be of cabinet rank. Indeed, that remained the case until well into the second half of the century. It was one of the responsibilities of the holder of that office to decide when a public inquiry into a matter affecting trade was required and to determine its terms of reference.

There was never any doubt that the loss of the *Titanic* would be the subject of an inquiry, but it was not automatic. The President of the Board of Trade, Sydney Buxton in this case, had the right to consider the nature of any accident involving a British flagged ship and decide whether or not an inquiry was warranted. The Merchant Shipping Acts, 1894-1906 provided the relevant legislation. The most important appointment in an inquiry into the loss of a ship was the man (and in those days it was of course always a man) who would act as the rather oddly named Commissioner of Wrecks. This person was required to chair the inquiry and to write the report. It was normal for the Commissioner to have a legal background because the proceedings of the inquiry were quasi-judicial and, in the case of a judge being appointed, that was a matter for the Lord Chancellor. That meant that evidence was given as in court and witnesses could be cross-examined. It is important, however, to stress that an inquiry was not a court case in that there was no accused, no plaintiff, no jury and no 'verdict'. In the Royal Navy when an event occurred that caused damage to or loss of a ship, the captain of that ship was automatically charged, at least, with hazarding the vessel, if not with gross negligence. The Court Martial that followed was a trial in the usual sense with an accused, prosecutor, defence, verdict and, if appropriate, sentence. Sentence could include not only ignominious dismissal from the service but also a prison term.

Board of Trade inquiries, because there was no verdict as such, could not impose sentences. However, they could find that the accident into which the inquiry was being held had been the result of negligence on the part of one or more people involved. Acting on that finding, the Board of Trade could, for example, suspend or remove a certificate of competence from a captain or other officer of a ship. Even if no such steps were taken, a finding of fault against a seaman could adversely affect that person's career for many years afterwards. Not only seamen, however, could be considered to have been the cause of accidents, or the loss of life that resulted. Ship owners and ship builders, for example, were very sensitive to the findings of inquiries as a negative comment about them in a report could harm their reputation and future business. It would also greatly increase the likelihood of them being found liable for damages. For these reasons an inquiry had much of the feel of a trial about it; after all the consequences of the report might well be seen in other courts subsequently and the proceedings of the inquiry had to be such as to stand up to scrutiny in those courts.

One protection in case of future scrutiny of the proceedings of an inquiry was permission given to persons who were at all likely to be the subject of criticism in a report to be represented by counsel. At the discretion of the Commissioner of Wrecks, the counsel was permitted to cross-examine those witnesses whose testimony had a bearing on the behaviour of their client. In one of the inquiries in which we are interested, the issue of permitting representation became controversial and has remained so since.

One of Mersey's four inquiries was not a British Board of Inquiry but was created on a similar model by the government of the new Dominion of Canada. In fact it required an amendment to the existing legislation in order to establish an inquiry because no provision for one had previously been made. There were some differences in its constitution and that of the British ones, particularly in that it took the form of a tribunal with Lord Mersey acting as President and two Canadians sitting as Commissioners. It differed further in that the Canadian Ministry of Justice had a role in deciding which witnesses would be called to give evidence, a degree of government influence regarded as controversial at the time.

There was very little variation in the terms of reference given to inquiries into the loss of ships whether in peace or war. The terms of reference normally consisted of a long series of questions that the inquiry was asked to answer. The questions were specific to the incident being investigated, but taken together their overall effect was to require the inquiry to establish the cause or causes and to decide what should be done to prevent a repetition. There was a great deal of difference, however, between how a peacetime loss could be investigated and a wartime one. All of those surviving a peacetime sinking who had any hand in the event could be asked to provide testimony and have that testimony challenged. In wartime the enemy could not be made subject to questioning. An inquiry into a peacetime accident could make recommendations about the construction or navigation of ships, or their manning that would reduce the likelihood of a similar accident happening again. A Board of Trade inquiry, however, was not the place for the formulation of wartime strategy. The Admiralty was under no obligation to pay any heed to the suggestions of a Commissioner of Wrecks appointed by the Board of Trade. The first priority of the Admiralty was victory; the safe passage of ships came second.

The value of holding inquiries into wartime losses might therefore be questioned. If the Commissioner was limited in how he was able to investigate the event and not considered to be of any weight in determining future actions, there would appear to be little point in the inquiry taking place. As the number of merchant ship losses mounted during the First World War, the holding of inquiries became less frequent. The principal criterion for justifying an inquiry was loss of civilian lives and the great majority of sinkings did not meet that criterion. For those with responsibility for conducting the propaganda war, inquiries were significant events, either for good or bad and there was clearly a desire on their part to have some say in whether or not an inquiry was held and, if one were held, to influence the outcome. The extent to which that desire was or was not translated into action in the cases of the *Falaba* and the *Lusitania* is a highly controversial question to which we shall return in some detail.

The Commissioner of Wrecks was required to look into the actions of professional seamen and to make judgements as to whether or not those actions were correct. Coming from a legal background he was unlikely to have sufficient nautical expertise. For that reason, sitting with him, were Assessors whose job was to provide expertise in matters to do with the construction, equipping, manning and navigation of ships. The Assessors were not appointed by the Board of Trade but by the Home Secretary. So, although the inquiry (referred to in recognition of its quasi-judicial status as a Court of Inquiry) was regarded as a Board of Trade animal (and it was to the Board that it addressed its report) its personnel were appointed by other authorities, albeit within the same government. The number of assessors and their backgrounds were dictated by the circumstances of the sinking. In both of the wartime inquiries naval personnel were heavily involved, not always the case in inquiries into peacetime accidents.

Undoubtedly the assessors involved in the inquiries were all competent people with a good understanding of the issues faced by seamen and the nature of the decisions that they were required to make. It was not always the case, however, that they were able to convey their understanding fully to the Commissioner of Wrecks. In any situation involving expertise garnered from years of practical experience, communicating that expertise to a non-expert who has not had the benefit of that experience is difficult and it is not a negative reflection on either the Commissioner or his assessors to suggest that this did not always happen successfully. The origins of nautical terminology are often abstruse and their usage does not always appear logical. The terms 'larboard' and 'starboard' have little obvious meaning and the replacement for the former, 'port', no more so. That lack of any clear connection between the term and its meaning was compounded at the time of the inquiries by the archaic usage of giving helm, or tiller orders to steer a ship rather than wheel orders. A tiller is pushed to starboard if it is desired to make the ship turn to port. A ship's wheel, however, is turned anti-clockwise (i.e. the top of the wheel goes to port) in order to achieve the same effect. Yet, even on large ships using wheels operating hydraulically powered steering engines, orders on the bridge were still given as if the helmsman were operating a tiller. That was a matter of some significance in the *Titanic* inquiry but was eventually resolved, although not, it seems, to the satisfaction of many subsequent commentators right up to the present day.

One example of terminologically induced confusion that was not successfully resolved was the difference between a 'heading' and a 'bearing'. A heading is the compass direction in which a ship is pointing. A bearing is the compass direction from that ship to some other object, for example a headland or another ship. If two ships in sight of each other are stationary, either may swing clockwise or anti-clockwise with the wind or current and so its heading will alter. However, as long as neither ship actually changes position, the bearing of the one from the other will not change.

That seems really quite simple and had all of the evidence and discussion at the inquiries been based on compass directions confusion might (just might) have been avoided. Consider our two stationary ships again. If a witness is asked, for example,

'Where did you see the other ship?'
Answer: 'On the starboard beam.'
'Was it still there an hour later?'

'No, it was on the port quarter.'

'So it had moved then?'

'No it had not.'

Result, confusion. If the ship the witness was observing from had merely swung and changed its heading then the witness would have to look over a different part of it in order to see the other ship. When the conversation referred to a night time situation in which ships were observed only by their lights then the confusion could deepen when red lights changed into green lights and white lights altered their relative positions. Having got caught in this minefield, when a witness then reported that the bearing of a ship he was observing had altered over time, implying that it had changed its position, the significance was not always appreciated. The situation became so bad on occasion that witnesses themselves became confused and used terminology incorrectly.

Once an inquiry had been properly constituted under the legislation, its Commissioner appointed by the Lord Chancellor and its Assessors by the Home Secretary (or, in Canada, their equivalents), it was required to complete its business as speedily as possible and independently of any vested interest. Speed was not a problem with our judge who was never accused of being dilatory, but the matter of independence was an issue at the time of the inquiries and remains so.

Whatever we may think about someone's behaviour in the past from our own perspective, it is also important to judge them against the behaviour that their peers would have expected of them. Conflict of interest for example is much more clearly defined, and disregarding it more explicitly proscribed, now than was the case in Edwardian times; but it was still recognised as a potential source of bias. There was a famous exchange in the House of Commons when the *Titanic* inquiry was announced. Sir Edward Carson challenged Prime Minister Asquith for an assurance that the Board of Trade itself would not seek to influence the inquiry such that it would avoid criticism of itself. The irony of that exchange will become apparent when we consider the role that Sir Edward himself played in the inquiry into the loss of the *Lusitania*. The Canadian Deputy Minister of Justice was also challenged by the then Leader of the Opposition as to how he could select from a long list a much shorter list of witnesses to be called in the inquiry into the loss of the *Empress of Ireland* without compromising the inquiry's independence.

The potential for the inquiries to be biased as a result of influence from one quarter or another was not just a matter of formal representation or procedures. Despite the nineteenth century Reform Acts, power in the UK remained concentrated in the hands of a relatively small number of people, the great majority of them living within an hour's travel of the centre of London.

Not only was political power concentrated in this way, so was the ownership and management of the large industries. Although commercial interests in shipping were sometimes located at other major ports, there was normally a London HQ. Even Lord Pirrie, an Ulsterman chairing the then biggest shipbuilder in the world, operating in Belfast and Glasgow, had a house in London in addition to his splendid residence on the outskirts of Belfast. It was at a dinner party in that house in 1907 that the first discussions took place with White Star's Ismay on the shape of the new *Olympic* class liners of which *Titanic* was the second.

The ease with which interested parties could communicate with each other in the course of social gatherings or casual meetings was such (especially since the invention of the telephone, by then ubiquitous amongst the political and commercial elites) that knowing who was subject to influence and from whom was very difficult. It might almost be said that the concentration of power and influence amongst relatively small numbers of people all in close proximity meant that maintaining even the appearance of independence was almost impossible. Those who wanted to could point to potential sources of bias through X knowing Y, or having been in the same meeting as Z, or being married to a sister of P, or being seen having lunch with Q (also a cousin, perhaps) or any one of a hundred other forms of interaction amongst the coterie of males who ran the country and its industries. That is why it has been so easy to assert that the independence of some or all the four inquiries we are dealing with was subverted either by political or commercial vested interest. There was never going to be any shortage of circumstantial evidence. That is also why it is difficult to prove the case either way, although in at least one instance there now remains little doubt.

Having discussed the generalities of potential bias there is one specific issue that needs to be highlighted at this point and that is the difference between the independence of an inquiry in peacetime and wartime. In theory, of course, there is no difference. Once appointed and asked its questions, it is up to an inquiry to answer those questions as completely and as objectively as the evidence permits whether it is inquiring into a peacetime accident or an act of war. Only the most idealistic, however, would expect practice to match theory. It is inevitable that, irrespective of any undue influence that may be brought to bear, the personnel involved in an inquiry will be biased towards their own country's interests to some degree. There will be a tendency to make the most of any faults determined to lie with the other side and to minimise any on their own side. However, and this is a major caveat, there is a line to be drawn, on the one hand, between exhibiting in wartime some degree of bias in apportioning blame and, on the other hand, deliberately reporting something known to be untrue as a means of supporting the propaganda war. We will be looking to see whether that line may have been crossed.

There are four inquiries within the scope of this book, but there were also two other inquiries concerning two of the same incidents. In the case of *Titanic* there was an American inquiry and, in the case of the *Empress of Ireland,* one conducted in Canada under the auspices of the Norwegian Government. Both were quite unlike their British and Canadian equivalents. Senator William Alden Smith chaired the American Inquiry into the loss of *Titanic* that opened in the Waldorf Hotel in New York only days after the disaster. Senator Smith was a member of the Senate Committee on Commerce and when the proposal was put to the Committee that it should investigate the disaster, he was nominated as the Chairman of a Sub-Committee charged with doing so. Senators, of course are quite entitled to inquire into any matter they choose. However, in order to do so effectively they need the power to compel witnesses to attend. The legal basis for the right to subpoena witnesses, including witnesses not of US nationality, in this case came from the US Attorney General. He based his opinion on the ship's destination being New York, the landing of the survivors at New York and the American nationality of many of those on board. So, like the British inquiry, the US inquiry operated within a legal framework, but it was overtly political in nature.

The executive and legislative branches of government in the United States are separated in a way that is not the case in the United Kingdom. None of the Senators involved in the inquiry had personal responsibility for any actions of the American government in relation to shipping. In that sense, therefore, it was at least as free from conflict of interest as the British inquiry. Not that the American government would have had any particular reason to feel itself in the firing line, despite the owners of the White Star Line being an American company and the ship itself having been built to meet American quality standards rather than those of Lloyds of London. Each ship was certified when built as having met certain building standards. The most famous is the Lloyd's 100A1 classification. *Titanic* was never certified as being 100A1 because she was not assessed using that system, but using an equivalent American one. Some people have implied that not being awarded the prestigious 100A1 label meant that somehow the *Titanic* was inferior in quality. In fact, there is no reason to believe that the quality standards applied to her and her sisters were any less rigorous than would have been the case had Lloyds been the assessing authority.

The benefit of holding an inquiry very rapidly after the event was that witnesses generally were on hand in New York and could be told to remain there. It also meant that memories were fresh and the minds of those inquiring were less contaminated by the tidal waves of speculation that were already beginning to sweep both sides of the Atlantic. The drawback of course was that the proceedings were rushed and those involved had little time to prepare background documentation. Furthermore, although the Senate inquiry was independent of the American government, it was less clear that it was free of commercial interests.

International Mercantile Marine (IMM) was the American parent company of the White Star Line and it was a company that was part of the vast interests of J P Morgan. Senator Smith was a known critic of J P Morgan and he had had interests himself in railroads and Great Lakes shipping that competed with parts of the Morgan empire. There was a suspicion that Smith's intense interest in the *Titanic* disaster was motivated by a hope that the outcome of an inquiry would leave IMM exposed to claims for damages by survivors and the relatives of those who had perished. In fact, the disaster did prove a contributory factor in the demise of IMM just three years later, although the Senate inquiry itself did not materially affect that process. The inquiry was something of a one-man show with Smith leading from the front and peppering every witness with a multitude of questions. However, there did seem a genuine attempt in his interrogations to get at the truth, rather than to accumulate evidence against any particular party. For our purpose it is perhaps most important to note that for all their differences in constitution, timing and manner of investigation, the two inquiries came to quite similar conclusions.

That is far from the case when the outcomes of the Canadian and Norwegian inquiries into the loss of the *Empress of Ireland* are compared. The two sets of conclusions were diametrically opposed. It has already been noted that Canada was a very young nation in 1912 and required some additional legislation before an inquiry could be instituted. Norway was also a young country having only attained independence from Sweden nine years prior to the disaster. Because the ship that struck the *Empress of Ireland* was the Norwegian collier *Storstad,* the Norwegian government decided to hold an inquiry. It was held two days after the Canadian inquiry completed its hearings but before the findings were known. A Norwegian diplomat from Washington, W Maithe Johannesen, was chairman with two Norwegian captains acting as assessors. The inquiry, held at the Norwegian Consulate in Montreal, lasted just one day and the only witnesses heard were from the *Storstad*. Not surprisingly it found that all fault lay with the officers of the *Empress of Ireland*. The flawed process of the Norwegian inquiry must largely destroy its credibility, irrespective of the findings. Given the appalling scale of the loss of life involved in the sinking of the *Empress of Ireland*, it is rather a pity that there was not a second inquiry with reputable methodology, the conclusions of which could have been compared with that chaired by Lord Mersey.

There was one feature that all of the inquiries into these sinkings had in common. Each in their own way illustrated how poor the human ability to observe events and to record those observations accurately can be. Many of those giving evidence were recalling incidents that happened when they were under enormous stress and such conditions are bound to affect how we see and remember the things going on around us. Nevertheless, there were many instances of witnesses reporting on matters that happened when they were not under stress and many of the same weaknesses are apparent. In passing judgement on Mersey himself and the assessors who sat with him, it is important to remember the amount of doubt that witnesses expressed about their own memories of what they had seen and heard and also the extent to which different witnesses gave mutually conflicting evidence; indeed, some witnesses gave evidence which was not internally consistent. Whatever conclusions the inquiries came to they were inevitably going to be at variance with a proportion of the evidence. One of Mersey's principal roles was to try to determine which of the witnesses provided the most reliable evidence. As a judge that should have been second nature to him. His direction to juries must frequently have involved drawing their attention to the apparent reliability or otherwise of the different witnesses in a case. But as well as being a reputable and successful man of the law, Mersey was also a man of his time, a time when people were frequently judged by their background and their position in life as much as by their actions. One of the issues that we will be exploring is the extent to which his judgement about witnesses was subject to that type of influence.

The opening page of each of the four inquiry reports records the formalities of the constitution of the court of inquiry and the manner in which it went about its business. Following that there is a statement of the overall finding of the inquiry as to the reason for the sinking of the ship. Underneath that statement is Mersey's signature, followed by the words: 'We concur in the above Report'. Then appear the signatures of each of the Assessors. The Assessors were there primarily to provide the expertise that the inquiry required to assess the issues brought before it. They were not, however, just advisers. In theory, at least, they had the right to express a dissenting view on any of those issues. That did not happen in any of the four inquiries. All of the Assessors involved were content to go along with the conclusions reached and to sign their names to that effect. Some of the more extreme critics of those conclusions treat them as if they were attributable entirely to the personality, susceptibility to influence, prejudice or, indeed, ignorance of one man. However much Mersey may have been the dominant figure as the Commissioner of Wrecks, we must not ignore the role of the expert Assessors, many of them leaders in their professions.

5

THE COMMISSIONER OF WRECKS

When John Charles Bigham, Viscount Mersey, celebrated his 89th birthday on 3 August 1929, he probably looked back over his life with some considerable satisfaction. He had been a very successful lawyer, had risen to an elevated position in the judiciary, had been made Baronet and then raised to a Viscount. His saddest memory would have been of the death of his wife some four years previously after a marriage lasting 54 years. His two sons were each successful in their own spheres, the younger being Assistant Commissioner of the Metropolitan Police in charge of the CID. The elder, shortly to succeed to his title, had given him four grandchildren, and had also acted as Secretary to the *Titanic* inquiry. His satisfaction might have been moderated a little had he been able to read the obituary that *The Times* had prepared and which was to appear just a month later. He would have been quite appalled had he had any inkling that, half a century after that, people referred to as '*Titanic* buffs' would come to regard him almost as a figure of fun, or even as an icon of everything that was wrong with early twentieth-century British society.

The fact that his obituary in *The Times* ran to 2500 words was in itself an indication that he had achieved some standing in society; only a few sentences referred to his role as Commissioner of Wrecks. Given the social rigidities that existed during his lifetime and the journey he had travelled that was a considerable achievement. He came from 'trade' as they said, father John Bigham being a Liverpool merchant. He was educated in Liverpool and at the University of London, the latter after a short period in his father's business. In 1870 he was called to the bar at the Middle Temple and joined the Northern circuit, rapidly gaining a considerable reputation as someone who could grasp the essentials of a case quickly and expound them with confidence. He was not a particularly attractive speaker, but a deliberate and measured delivery gave him a gravitas appropriate to his calling. He quickly built up a successful practice and, in 1883, became a Queen's Counsel. By then he was specialising in commercial cases, although by no means exclusively, and he was becoming well known in London as well as on the Northern circuit. For someone ambitious to move up the professional and social ladders, politics provided a way of gaining attention and it was probably for this reason, more than from any desire to make a significant political impact, that he sought election as a member of parliament.

It was almost inevitable coming from a 'trade' background that he would choose the Liberal Party. He made his first unsuccessful attempt to become Liberal MP for the East Toxteth Division of Liverpool in 1885, one year before the Liberal Party split. Gladstone's Home Rule Bill for Ireland was the cause of the split and the dissidents formed the Liberal Unionist Party to indicate their opposition to self-government for Ireland because they felt that it would threaten the union of the United Kingdom. They were a disparate group with a conservative wing quite content to be allied closely with the Tories and a much more radical wing strongly influenced and eventually led by Joseph Chamberlain. Mersey stood for his second election in the Exchange Division of Liverpool in 1892 as a Liberal Unionist and there is little in his character or record to suggest that he was aligned with the radical element of the party. It took a third attempt in 1895, also in the Exchange Division, before he succeeded. He made little political impact in his two brief years in the House of Commons or in the House of Lords after 1910, when he was created Baron Mersey.

It was his ability as a barrister rather than any visibility as a politician that brought him success in the legal field. He had an excellent reputation as an able and hard-working advocate and when he was appointed as a Judge in the Queen's Bench Division in 1897 (and received the knighthood that went with it) it was generally considered a well merited promotion. He continued to specialise in commercial cases, including many involving bankruptcy, but also tried criminal cases. His record as a judge was generally sound and, unlike some others, he did not experience regular overturning of his judgements on appeal. Indeed, in some of the more difficult points of law with which he had to deal, his opinions were eventually upheld by the Law Lords. Not that he was untouched by criticism. On one occasion he was heavily castigated for a lenient sentence on a mother who had mistreated her child. As the mother in question was socially very well connected, the suspicion was that Sir Charles was operating a more lenient standard for the well-to-do than he would for the poor. His defence was that the worst of the accusations against the defendant had not in fact been proved.

The Edwardian era was one in which there was great public fascination with the dramas being played out in courtrooms up and down the land.

Court reports in newspapers were very extensive and lawyers along with others involved in the criminal justice system competed with the names in lights on theatres for celebrity status. Bigham never would have been into that celebrity league but one of his cases became quite notorious and his behaviour during the case is of relvant to what came later. Whitaker Wright was a self-made financier whose financial empire collapsed in suspicious circumstances that resulted in his prosecution for fraud. It was a high-profile case as the demise of Wright's company had caused a minor panic on the stock market and there can be little doubt that there was indeed fraud at the root of it. One of those caught up (although never suspected of fraud) was the man Wright had persuaded to act as Chairman of his company, the Marquess of Dufferin and Ava, ex-Viceroy of India and perhaps the most prominent of all the British Imperial diplomats. When news of the bankruptcy reached him, shortly after he had learned of the death of his son in the Boer War, the Marquess retired to his estate in Co Down and died a short time later in 1902.

It seems that Bigham was chosen for the case because he was regarded as one of the most astute corporate law experts at that time. The person prosecuting was Rufus Isaacs KC who was later, as Attorney General, to represent the Board of Trade at the *Titanic* inquiry. Even Bigham's *Times* obituarist was to comment that the manner with which he dealt with Wright was strange in that he showed open hostility to the defendant from the start of the trial. Bigham had clearly decided on the man's guilt irrespective of anything that was to come out at the trial and the defence lawyer complained that at one stage Bigham had made fun of Wright causing the jury to laugh at him. Wright was, as expected, found guilty and sentenced to seven years penal servitude. He left the courtroom and, in the room he was taken into, swallowed a cyanide capsule and died immediately. One might wonder what would have been the outcome had there been an appeal against sentence on the grounds of the judge's hostile attitude to the defendant throughout the trial.

Such behaviour was rather typical of the man. He was credited with a quick mind, but one that was quick not just to assimilate facts but to come to conclusions; having arrived at a conclusion he was not one for easily changing his opinion. He had a brusque manner in court and did not suffer either fools or solicitors gladly. Witnesses frequently got the sharp end of his tongue, but for all the tetchiness he was not thought to be knowingly unkind. In old age he was well regarded as a patron of the arts, particularly drama and a good companion who liked a bit of gossip, a pastime that became more difficult as deafness encroached in his late seventies.

Promotion came in 1909 to the post of President of the Probate, Divorce and Admiralty Division. His commercial work having included a number of cases involving the shipping industry, he was quite content with the Admiralty part of it and financial affairs in Probate caused him no concern. The matrimonial disputes that came before him, however, he disliked intensely and he resigned after only one year. Immediately he was elevated to the peerage, to the lowest rank as Baron Mersey. In the Lords, as already mentioned, he was not politically significant, but he did remain very active in appeals and in the Judiciary Committee.

When the *Titanic* disaster occurred and a Commissioner was required to lead the investigation, Lord Mersey was an obvious choice. Although approaching 72, he was fit, keen to work and a continuing participant in the legal system, albeit not in a full-time capacity. His previous experience in the commercial context, including shipping, was regarded as an advantage and his well known ability to assimilate a lot of information quickly meant that he could be expected to get to grips with this new context. Many people, however, now believe that his was actually a poor appointment, given the output of his work as a Commissioner. Obviously, succeeding Lord Chancellors and the Canadian authorities thought otherwise as he was re-appointed on three occasions, including undertaking a role that was recognised as being of some significance in the political and diplomatic dimensions of the First World War.

It is not a hypothetical question to ask if there were available to the Lord Chancellor other judges who, on the basis of their experience and records, were better qualified to investigate the *Titanic* disaster and who were available to take the role. Perusal of the judicial lists of the time may well identify some likely candidates. It is hypothetical to ask if it is likely that another judge, as well or better qualified as Mersey, would have accepted the role and would have done a different or better job. Certainly, Mersey's critics have not been forthcoming in suggesting the names of judges who might have been chosen by the Lord Chancellor and who might have been likely to have succeeded where they believe Mersey failed.

In a sense those questions go to the core of the issues that we are examining. For some commentators it is clear that they believe that any inquiry established at the request of and under the management of the Board of Trade would have displayed the same characteristics as that led by Mersey. Others, however, point to the personality of the judge himself and his foibles as being the source of the problems. One senses that, in their view, had a more enlightened, more effective and less intransigent judge been appointed Commissioner then all would have been well. As in most complex situations with many interacting variables, the answer is unlikely to lie entirely with one view or the other.

We have touched on the question of vested interests and the possible influence that they may have had on the outcomes of the four inquiries that Mersey led and it is now time to consider what the principal interests were and, in general terms, the nature of any influence they may have had. Obviously, we will consider later the possible impact of vested interests in relation to specific issues as they concerned each of the captains. Broadly the interests that are normally suspected of influencing the process or outcomes of the inquiries can be divided into three groups: the Board of Trade itself; commercial interests; and other government interests, particularly the Admiralty in relation to the *Falaba* and *Lusitania*. We also have to be aware that these separate interests sometimes complemented each other and acted in concert, but sometimes competed and tried to obstruct each other.

The Board of Trade was the sponsoring government department for the three British inquiries, making all of the arrangements and meeting the quite considerable costs involved. The role of the Board in relation to maritime matters was as the regulator for the shipping industry, administering the legal framework within which British flagged ships carried out their business. That included such matters as the load lines that all ships were required to display on their sides and which governed the amount of cargo they could carry. The Board was also responsible for proposing any relevant new legislation to Parliament or the updating of existing legislation. It was in the interests of the Board that British ship owners continued to prosper and that Britain continued to dominate the world's maritime trade. When the *Titanic* inquiry was established, for example, the Board would have had two main concerns. It would have wished to avoid too much criticism of the fact that the legislation governing lifeboats was so appallingly out of date, its only defence being that the issue having been raised in Parliament two years previously, the wheels of government machinery were slowly grinding into motion just as the *Titanic* hit the iceberg. It would also have been concerned to avoid criticism of the White Star Line being too barbed in that it was an important element in the lucrative British transatlantic travel industry. However, the civil servants were conscious that White Star was American-owned and they might have been even more concerned to protect Cunard, had it been the company involved.

We noted in Chapter 2 how, in 1875, following the loss of the *Atlantic*, also a White Star ship (although at that time the company was British owned) lobbying by the owners had succeeded in persuading the Board of Trade to set up a second inquiry, which eventually exonerated them from negligence. It is often the case that agencies responsible for regulating industries in which large and powerful companies operate find it difficult to maintain not just the necessary separation of regulator from operator but also the appearance of independence. It is very difficult to get past the circumstantial level of evidence in order to determine the extent of a regulator's susceptibility to unreasonable influence by one or more of the companies it is responsible for regulating. Some commentators on the inquiries chaired by Lord Mersey have simply made the assumption that where there was motive there was influence. Obviously it was in the interest of the ship owners to ensure that they received as little criticism as possible but that of itself does not prove that, either by lobbying the Board of Trade or by getting directly to Mersey or his Assessors, they were able to achieve an outcome to the inquiry more favourable for them than might otherwise have been the case. Even if the findings of one inquiry seem to favour a ship owner more than scrutiny of the evidence at a later date might support, that is not of itself conclusive evidence that the inquiry was 'fixed'. At the same time a pattern of such discrepancies across a number of inquiries might suggest that not all was above board.

The type of criticism that ship owners wished to avoid concerned the safety of the ship's equipment, the competence of its navigation and the behaviour of the crew both before and during the incident. The latter two of those focused attention on the captain who was responsible for the navigation and who also carried ultimate responsibility while at sea for ensuring that the crew knew and understood their duties and carried them out effectively. The other principal commercial interest was the ship builders who wished to avoid any responsibility for loss of life being found to result from defective design or construction. That is not an aspect that is of particular concern in this book although it has been a matter of intense debate in the plethora of books and documentaries that have appeared since the wreck of *Titanic* was found in 1985. It has never been a significant factor in consideration of the loss of the other three ships, despite the speed with which two of them sank.

A state of war brings to the fore entirely different issues. The jingoistic attitude that prevailed in the warring countries in 1914 and 1915, before the awful slaughter on the Western Front and elsewhere took its toll of morale, infected every aspect of society. It would be quite unrealistic to expect those taking part in the courts of inquiry to be immune. But added to the patriotic desire to support the war interest of their own country was the potential for government actively to attempt to subvert the process in order to obtain quite specific outcomes, irrespective of whether or not those outcomes corresponded with the facts as the government knew them to be. In discussing Mersey's treatment of the four captains involved in the sinkings of the *Falaba* and the *Lusitania,* we will be trying to separate those different types of influence.

How cynical ought we to be in considering the extent to which Mersey was effectively doing the bidding of the various vested interests? Was he simply a pawn of the Board of Trade (or, in Canada, the Ministry of Justice), given a set of questions above the table and passed the expected answers below it? Was Baron Mersey in the pockets of the boardroom barons who ruled the shipping companies? Was he in effect an Admiralty agent in 1915 working to further the anti-German propaganda campaign? The United Kingdom has always prided itself on the probity of its public services. The civil service has had a reputation for professionally and impartially serving governments of every political persuasion. Unlike the USA, senior public servants are not replaced when an administration changes. Neither has the UK been associated during the nineteenth and twentieth centuries with levels of financial corruption which appear to have been endemic in some other countries. We have already noted, however, the ease with which communication was possible amongst the various players and the difficulty of ever knowing the nature of the communications that took place outside official channels. Also, the UK was not immune from scandals linking commercial and political interests. One person, whose name has already appeared, was at the centre of perhaps the most significant such scandal of the era leading up to the First World War and was also a key player in the *Titanic* inquiry.

Rufus Isaacs, who had prosecuted Whitaker Wright before the then Sir Charles Bigham, had prospered and progressed by 1912 to become Sir Rufus Isaacs, Attorney General. In May and June 1912 he appeared in the *Titanic* inquiry on behalf of the Board of Trade, an indication in itself of the seriousness with which the Board regarded the proceedings. Just a matter of weeks later the so-called Marconi scandal broke in which a number of ministers in the Liberal government, including Isaacs and Lloyd George, the Chancellor, were accused of insider dealing in Marconi shares based on a tip from Isaacs brother who was then Managing Director of the company in the UK. A parliamentary select committee eventually investigated the matter and, voting along party lines, exonerated the ministers, but in the view of many at the time and since, innocence was far from fully established. It is worth reflecting, in terms of Rufus Isaac's role in the *Titanic* inquiry, that the wireless operators on the ships concerned at that time were Marconi employees and their roles were under close scrutiny. Indeed Guglielmo Marconi himself was present on the first day of the American inquiry and gave evidence on two different occasions, one of them in relation to the sale of his employee's stories to American newspapers.

It would seem, therefore, that we do need to bring at least a healthy scepticism to the matter of influence on the inquiries, acknowledging that most of the major players on the government, legal and commercial sides regarded themselves as part of the same establishment club, with a strong sense of their mutual loyalty to that club, and that norms of behaviour were somewhat different to those which we attempt to enforce today. To what extent ought we to apply that scepticism to Mersey in person? One must assume that his loyalty to the establishment club was at least as strong as that of most of his contemporaries in similar positions. It is sometimes said that there are none so aware of their social standing as those who have recently improved it. Mersey had, through his own efforts, moved from a background in trade to the House of Lords and a well respected position in the judiciary. He is likely to have felt that he was a recently joined member of the club and wanted to consolidate that sense of belonging. He showed little appetite for any rebellious actions that would have labelled him a member of the awkward squad. Stepping out of line is often a sign of someone whose membership credentials are so well established that a little bit of rebelliousness will not jeopardise them.

That instinct to conform to establishment attitudes and not to rock the boat would almost certainly have infected to some degree any of the people that the Lord Chancellor could have appointed Commissioner of Wrecks. Mersey, however, had spent a lot of his career dealing with cases involving commercial interests. As we have mentioned that may have been seen by the Lord Chancellor as an advantage in that it gave him valuable insights relevant to what he was being asked to do. However, many people since have pointed to this experience as the origin of close links with people who had an interest in influencing the outcomes of the inquiries. He regularly attended the Annual Dinner of the Chamber of Shipping and on one occasion, proposing a toast to 'The Shipping Interest', he said: 'Those connected with the industry had to see that nothing was done by legislation or in other ways which would decrease the carrying power of this great country.'

Our scepticism should therefore extend to some degree to Mersey as someone who may have been susceptible to influence by vested interests, although it must be remembered that throughout his life he was never subject to any suspicion of impropriety in any matter, professional or otherwise. With the exception of the wartime pressure from the Admiralty, it is doubtful if he himself considered that he had deviated in the slightest from following his own lines of investigation and forming his own opinions based on the evidence that emerged, opinions which, in every instance, were endorsed by the expert Assessors who sat with him.

6

THE EIGHT CAPTAINS

The captains were Smith of *Titanic*, Lord of *Californian*, Kendall of *Empress of Ireland,* Andersen of *Storstad*, Davies of *Falaba*, von Forstner of U-28, Turner of *Lusitania* and Schwieger of U-20. The most famous of these was Kendall. That fame had nothing to do with the loss of his ship, however. Rather it related to his prior involvement in the celebrated Crippen murder case. Smith became infamous after his death, more so a century later than in the years immediately following the sinking, when to many he was a hero. Lord, for some, became the archetypal scapegoat, for others a disgrace to the British Merchant Navy. Turner achieved a certain notoriety resulting from the loss of the *Lusitania* but became a recluse. Of Andersen and Davies relatively little is known but records of U-boat operations were well maintained and we know something of both of the German captains. Von Forstner became a minor celebrity in the 1930s amongst those who take an interest in the existence or otherwise of mythical sea-serpents. Schwieger might have been treated as a war criminal at the end of the war, had he lived to see it. The only thing linking these eight men is that one man was called upon to pass judgements on their actions.

Edward John Smith did not come from a seafaring family. His father was employed in the potteries in Stoke-on-Trent and also ran a shop for a while. Born in 1850, he was educated at the local school to the age of 13 and then signed on at 18 as an apprentice on the sailing ship *Senator Weber* leaving Liverpool, owned by Gibson and Co. He seems to have taken to the life readily and progressed steadily up the promotion ladder. By 1880 he had moved to steam and joined White Star, the line with which he stayed for the rest of his life. He was Chief Officer of the *Cufic* for a while and then, in 1887, aged 37, he was appointed captain of the *Celtic*. He moved rapidly from ship to ship, acquiring newer and bigger ships as his reputation as a safe pair of hands was established. By the early 1900s he was the premier captain of White Star and he was given command of each of the new, large ships as they were built. He captained *Olympic* on her maiden voyage and then moved across at the age of 62 to take over the new *Titanic* as she emerged from her builders in Belfast.

Smith, referred to familiarly as 'EJ', was known as the 'millionaires' captain' because he had an excellent reputation amongst the wealthy first class passengers as a calm, reassuring, competent sea captain. He held the rank of Honorary Commander in the Royal Naval Reserve and, in consequence, the ships he commanded were entitled to fly the prestigious blue ensign in place of the 'red duster'. He was imposing in appearance with neatly trimmed white beard and immaculate uniform and he was clubbable, well able to hold his own in the dinner table conversations. It seemed that the wealthy, often aristocratic passengers who had the privilege of dining with him almost regarded him as 'one of us'. By association, the captains of the great liners became elevated onto a social stratum to which other sea captains could never aspire. One of the qualities that the major lines expected of their senior captains was that they should be able to acquit themselves well in the social dimension of their work, a dimension almost entirely limited to the first class passengers. Smith met that requirement in full and clearly must also have satisfied his managers on his competence as a seaman in order for them to trust him with their latest and most valuable ships.

In the seamanship department Smith appears to have had a strange combination of good and bad fortune up to the point where he took over *Titanic*. He had the good fortune to avoid any seriously threatening mishaps at sea and the bad fortune to experience a significant number of smaller ones. In a press interview, reported in 1907 in the *New York Times*, on the occasion of the maiden voyage of the *Adriatic*, Smith was reported as saying:

> When anyone asks me how I can best describe my experiences of nearly forty years at sea I merely say uneventful. Of course there have been winter gales and storms and fog and the like, but in all my experience I have never been in an accident of any sort worth speaking about. I have seen but one vessel in distress in all my years at sea, a brig , the crew of which was taken off in a small boat in charge of my third officer. I never saw a wreck and have never been wrecked, nor was I ever in any predicament that threatened to end in disaster of any sort.

On the face of it this seems a quite remarkable statement for someone who had spent the last three decades of the nineteenth century at sea, given the statistics of losses at sea and the catalogue of disasters on the Atlantic that we considered in Chapter 2. Journalists, of course are very good at putting words into people's mouths that are a little different to the way that they came out. It is also the case that the interview that Smith gave would have been part of the corporate public relations campaign that White Star mounted to encourage passengers onto their new ship and Smith would have been wanting to play up the message that only good things happen to people who go to sea. Perhaps what appeared in print was the result of a combination of those two influences. Factually, it appears at least to be correct in that Smith had never been on a ship that was wrecked or sunk and had never been rescued from an immediately life-threatening situation. To use the term 'uneventful', however, was perhaps a little rich.

In 1889 and in 1890 ships under his command had run aground but had been refloated and he had experienced fires on board in 1901 and 1906. His record of significant but non-fatal incidents continued after he gave the interview when the *Adriatic* itself grounded in the Ambrose Channel in November 1909, but the most serious was in September 1911 when the *Olympic* collided with a cruiser, HMS *Hawke*. This was not *Olympic's* first accident, having had a collision with a tug when berthing at New York just after entering service. The two collisions, it seems, were both the consequence of the difficulties that were being experienced manoeuvring these new, enormous ships in confined areas, particularly as their movements created much greater levels of suction than had previously been experienced. It was taking time for practitioners to adapt to the advances in technology and it would be unfair to single out Smith in this regard.

If Smith's career had indeed been as free of major incidents as he suggested in his interview, not having involved participation even as a third party in major life threatening situations, how well prepared was he for the situation that he faced on the night of 14/15 April 1912? The reassuring captain needs to be able to convince those under his care of his ability to avoid the worst happening but also needs to be able to deal with the worst if it should come about. In Chapter 2 we discussed the use of risk management techniques in business as a way of identifying major risks and ensuring that they do not materialise. Despite the best efforts of the best management teams, however, those risks sometimes do become reality and the wise businessman has prepared 'business recovery plans' to deal with the consequences and either get the business back into a good position, or, if that is not feasible, arrange for it to be wound up in as orderly a manner as possible. Each of the four captains of the ships that were sunk at some stage realised that they were in the position of having to manage the loss of their ship with the smallest loss of life possible. Smith was in a different position to the other three because he had by far the greatest amount of time to accomplish this objective. One of the issues that we will be looking at will be the manner in which he went about it.

The question of whether or not Smith planned to retire at the end of *Titanic's* maiden round trip is of no consequence. Many believe that to have been his intention but others point to newspaper reports suggesting that he was planning to stay long enough to captain the third of the *Olympic* class ships (at that time possibly intended to carry the name *Gigantic* but subsequently it was decided to call her *Britannic*) by which time he would have reached the normal retirement age of 65. The fact was that he was approaching the end of a distinguished career. Like many in that position there may have been an element of coasting. The new big liners carried a large complement of well qualified officers, many of whom already held Master's or even Extra Master's certificates. One could see how someone in Smith's position might well become increasingly reliant on his immediate subordinates for the routine running and navigation of the ship. Indeed, that is probably how things should have been, up to a point. The increasing complexity of the electrical and hydraulic control systems on ships, the new wireless protocols that were to be observed and other recent developments all presented challenges that someone at Smith's stage in his career might well have found daunting. He may have largely relied on others to get to grips with these new-fangled gadgets while he got on with the more public face of captaining. While this might be a little speculative it does not seem at odds with what we know of his actions.

Captain William 'Will' Turner of *Lusitania* was in many respects in a similar position to that of Smith. He was Commodore of one of the other great Atlantic shipping lines and, in 1915, was coming towards the end of a highly successful career at sea. In almost every other respect, however, he was a very different character. Where Smith considered his time at sea to have been uneventful, Turner might have described his as having been punctuated by a seemingly never-ending series of dramatic episodes. Where Smith was the affable friend of the rich and famous, Turner was taciturn to the point of rudeness and disappointed his company as the public face of command in which Smith so excelled. It says something of the complexities of human relationships that the passengers whom Turner treated with such disdain clamoured to sail with him on the grounds, presumably, that if he was no good making small talk he must be an amazing seaman to hold down his job.

Turner was born in Liverpool in 1856 and did come from a seafaring background. His father Charles Turner was a sailing ship captain who took his young son to sea with him at the tender age of 7, signed onto the ship's register as 'cabin boy'. The ship was the barque *Grasmere*, and it was carrying 114 emigrants to New Zealand leaving Greenock on 14 December 1863. Slow progress because of contrary winds meant that she was off the Irish coast on the evening of 17 December, just south of the Copeland Islands. The *Grasmere* ran onto rocks off Ballyferis on the Ards Peninsula. All on board were rescued by the coastguards and were taken to Belfast but the ship was a total loss. At the subsequent Board of Trade inquiry Captain Charles Turner was censured for negligence in navigating his ship and his certificate was suspended for six months. So the Turners, father and son, lost ships for different reasons off the Irish coast and were both subject to scrutiny by Board of Trade inquiries.

Will Turner sailed with his father again as an apprentice on the *Queen of Nations,* again without much luck. The ship was badly battered by gales in the South Atlantic and had to jettison much of the cargo in order to stay afloat. She managed to make the Falklands and spent three months there under repair. He then sailed in a succession of sailing ships and having moved out of his apprenticeship was serving as second mate on *Thunderbolt* when he was washed overboard in heavy weather. Luckily the first mate reacted very quickly and threw him a lifebuoy on a line. He clung for over an hour before he was hauled back onboard. After that it was Will's turn to rescue others. In 1878 he left sailing ships with some regret to join the world of steam where the route to advancement now lay. Sailing as Fourth Officer on Cunard's *Cherbourg* on one occasion, the ship collided with a small barque *Alice Davies* in fog leaving Liverpool. The sailing ship sank but sufficiently slowly for a rescue party from the *Cherbourg* to rescue all but four seamen and the pilot. Will distinguished himself by saving a man and a boy from the rigging of the sinking ship. In February 1885 he distinguished himself again by jumping into the Alexandra Dock in Liverpool to rescue a young boy who had fallen in, a rescue for which he received the Silver medal of the Liverpool Shipwreck and Humane Society.

Turner returned briefly to sail in order to get experience of command, as Cunard only appointed captains with previous experience in the role, and on his return moved swiftly up the ranks. By 1897 he was Chief Officer of the *Catalonia*. On one voyage the ship came across a French schooner, *Vagne* , in a dismasted and sinking condition. Turner took charge of the rescue, which succeeded in saving all of the crew. For this he received an Illuminated Address to add to his Silver Medal. It was in 1903 that he was given his first command, the cargo carrying *Aleppo,* but he was quickly transferred onto larger passenger ships and in a remarkably short time was made captain of the *Lusitania,* the fleet's flagship, in 1908, on the recommendation of her retiring captain. In 1910 he was moved to her sister ship the *Mauretania* as Commodore of the Cunard Line and he also had the third of the trio, the *Aquitania,* for a while. It was on the *Mauretania* that he skilfully effected the rescue from a lifeboat of the captain and some of the crew of the *West Point,* a cargo ship that had sunk after a fire. For this he received another Illustrated Address from the Liverpool Shipwreck and Humane Society.

Following the loss of the *Lusitania* in 1915, Turner spent some time ashore recovering and was then appointed to a cargo ship, the *Ultonia*. Although a great come down from his previous role, Turner was glad of the opportunity to get back to sea and pleased also, no doubt, that Cunard had continued to support him. Towards the end of 1916 he was moved to the *Ivernia,* a troopship working in the Mediterranean. It was a short-lived appointment, as he was torpedoed for the second time, but once again he survived. That was the end of his sea-going career and he was awarded the OBE in 1918, formally retiring from Cunard in 1919. His retirement was overshadowed by the tragedy he had been part of and he became almost a recluse until he died in 1933.

Will Turner was therefore the tough old salt, gruff, strict disciplinarian and man of action. Smith was the urbane, elegantly presented senior sea officer. For all the contrast, however, they had much in common. Both became Commodores of their respective world class shipping lines, both received Transport Medals for their work on troopships taking men to the Boer War, both were Honorary Commanders in the Reserve and both were highly respected by their peers and by their paying customers. They had each begun their lives at sea in small sailing ships, little changed for hundreds of years, and ended them on liners attracting descriptions such as 'leviathans' and 'greyhounds of the seas', relying on sophisticated new technologies that had not even been conceived when they were young men.

The murder of Mrs Belle Crippen in February 1910 was an event that rivalled the horrors of Jack the Ripper in terms of worldwide press coverage. The Crippens were both Americans living in London and the story combined sex with ghoulish dissection, a transatlantic chase and the best forensic detection work available. That was a powerful mix, but what gave the story its unique twist was the fact that it involved the first use of wireless telegraphy to bring a major fugitive to justice. Once suspicion had been raised about the nature of Belle's disappearance some time after the event, Chief Inspector Walter Dew of Scotland Yard had Crippen's house searched and Crippen was interviewed but to no effect, despite the fact that his lover, Ethel Le Neve, was living with him at the house and using much of the missing wife's jewellery. Crippen, not realising that the detective had left empty handed, panicked and the couple fled to France and then on to Canada. Their flight triggered further investigations and parts of a corpse, subsequently identified as that of Mrs Crippen, were found buried in the basement. Crippen was such an incompetent criminal that, having left a trail littered with evidence, it was almost inevitable that the fugitives would be found. They were discovered on the SS *Montrose* en route to Canada by the ship's captain, Henry George Kendall, who recognised Crippen from a photograph issued by Scotland Yard despite his having removed his moustache. He also realised that Crippen's travelling companion was not the boy she was dressed as but his lover. A wireless message was sent which reached shore and Chief Inspector Dew was alerted. He took passage in the faster White Star liner *Laurentic* and arrived in Quebec a couple of days ahead of the *Montrose*. Dew arranged to be taken out to the *Montrose* as she came up the St Lawrence close to a place called Father Point. He was welcomed aboard by Captain Kendall and shortly afterwards Crippen and Le Neve were arrested, Crippen ostensibly relieved that it was all over.

Kendall's fame as the man who caught Crippen would be hard to overstate. The case had been on the front pages of newspapers all over the world for weeks and his photograph now accompanied the dramatic story of the arrest. It is a measure of how the Crippen case created celebrities and how short was the impact of the loss of the *Empress of Ireland* that, in November 1965 when Kendall died at the age of 91, the obituaries in newspapers recalled in detail the saga of the Crippen arrest and failed even to mention the deaths of more than 1000 people on the *Empress of Ireland*. A recent biography of Kendall by his great grandson, the motor racing journalist Joe Saward, is entitled *The Man Who Caught Crippen*.

Kendall's early life could have filled several issues of Boys' Own magazine. Although not from a seafaring background he went to sea at the age of 15 in steam on the North American run. Taken by the romance of sail he then spent some time as an apprentice on a barque from which he deserted as a consequence of a violent incident involving two other members of the crew. There followed a year on a small island off the north coast of Australia before an horrendous 197-day journey home in a small, leaky, poorly provisioned sailing ship carrying bird manure fertiliser. Despite all of that Kendall continued his career at sea, taking his certificates and progressing onto the promotion ladder on steamships, beginning as Fourth Officer of the *Lake Superior*. The Canadian connection was to stay with him for the remainder of his time at sea as he served with Canadian Pacific up to the outbreak of the First World War and his wartime service was on an Allan Line ship taken up as an Armed Merchant Cruiser.

Kendall was just 40 in May 1914 and in some ways he was a cross between younger versions of Smith and Turner. He was quite a tough character who had been physically and mentally tested in fairly extreme situations, but he was also an excellent conversationalist who enjoyed mixing with passengers and telling stories of his own adventures. Much later in life he was to write an autobiography called appropriately enough *Adventure on the High Seas*, although one hesitates to apply the term 'adventure' to something as unremittingly horrible as the sinking of the *Empress*.

Shortly after the disaster war broke out and he found himself in Antwerp as German troops advanced through Belgium. Along with the British Consul he organised the escape of two Canadian Pacific ships then in the port, one being his old *Montrose* and the other the disabled *Montreal*. He took command of the *Montrose* and towed the other ship, along with 600 refugees, back to England. Kendall was called up as a reservist with a commission in the RNR and spent the war as second in command of the Armed Merchant Ship *Calgarian* until it was torpedoed and sunk by U-19 near Rathlin Island off the north coast of Ireland in March 1918. A total of 49 men died but he got away and was picked up. There followed a period as a Convoy Commodore and that was the end of his seagoing career; after the war he was shore-based in jobs connected to the shipping industry.

Smith, Turner and Kendall were the three captains of large liners, each of whose losses resulted in over 1000 deaths, all in a period of just three years. In his treatment by the press, Smith was either a hero or a villain, depending on the newspaper; Kendall remained largely untouched by the disaster, being exonerated by the inquiry and remaining the Crippen celebrity; Turner felt the criticism he received both in the inquiry and in the press very deeply and never recovered. However, the man who received the worst criticism of all, both through the work of Mersey and in press reports was a captain who suffered no loss or damage to his ship. Captain Stanley Lord of the *Californian* protested that he had been badly treated by the *Titanic* inquiries for a year or two after the event but then settled into a highly successful second phase of his career and put the matter behind him. However, when he was an old man, the controversy blew up again with the publication of the book *A Night to Remember* and the release of the film based on it, from which spun out the entire *Titanic* industry. The story told in *A Night to Remember* relies almost entirely on the findings of the British inquiry as its factual basis. Compared to later film productions this one was a straightforward telling of the story, without fictional sub-plots, and in many respects was well done. The producer, Bill McQuitty, was inspired to make it because as a child he had watched *Titanic* being launched and then sailing out of Belfast along the County Down coast. Unfortunately, the film not only repeated the story of the *Californian's* close proximity to *Titanic* and its supposed failure to save lives, it also embellished the story by implying that Stanley Lord slept through the night of the disaster having had a couple of drinks. Lord, like Henry Kendall, was entirely teetotal at sea.

As a result of the hurt that this caused him Lord began again to try to clear his name, swearing out a lengthy affidavit in 1959 and asking the Board of Trade to re-open the matter. They refused to do this on the basis that no new evidence had become available. This was correct procedurally but missed the point that it was the interpretation of the evidence available in 1912 that was being questioned. Lord died before anything further could be done but others, including his son, carried on the campaign. When the wreck of the *Titanic* was found, some distance from where Mersey had believed her to be, the Board of Trade did eventually relent and a further inquiry was held into the particular circumstances relating to the *Californian*. The outcome was partial exoneration of Lord, but there was a significant caveat to which we will return.

Stanley Lord had achieved command at the early age of 29 and was only 35 at the time of the *Titanic* disaster. His record with the Donaldson Line, which owned the *Californian,* was exemplary and the company's management wanted to retain him even after the criticism of the inquiries emerged. It was the Board of Directors who asked for his resignation on PR grounds. They felt that his continued association with the company would not be good for business. He was recruited by the Lawther Latta Line and given a command a short time later and he remained with them until, at the early age of 50, he retired, partially on grounds of poor eyesight but also because he was in a financial position to do so. He received a glowing testimonial from his employers, describing him as one of the finest commanders ever to have served them. The only question mark against his competence as a captain in his entire career was his actions, or lack of them, on one particular night.

Those are the facts about the man's career, but what sort of person was he? This question is perhaps more important in his case than in those of the other merchant ship captains because much of the controversy that swirled around Stanley Lord was not just to do with his ability as a seaman, but with his integrity, his leadership style and his bravery. Those most ill-disposed towards him have portrayed him as an inveterate liar, an intimidating martinet and a coward. One recent writer even used the term 'sociopath'. On the other hand, to those who feel that he was gravely maligned by the inquiries, Lord was as upstanding and brave as the honest British seaman ever could be. It is now very difficult to discern the real Stanley Lord through the fog of war between the obsessive pro and anti factions. Those who met him in his later years, including some of his detractors, found a courteous, affable and even humorous old man quite different to the sour and bullying captain they might have expected. It would seem that either he had had a personality transplant sometime in middle age or else the view that his critics had formed of him was based on unreliable half truth and innuendo. As often is the case, however, the alternatives are probably not as wholly incompatible as they might seem.

Quite a number of people present quite different sides of their personality in a position of authority at work and relaxing at home. It is not unusual to be invited to a social occasion at your boss's house and to meet there an entirely different person to the ogre you have learned to know and loathe in the office. As a young captain of a hard working freighter on the North Atlantic, Stanley Lord would have been keenly aware of the need to impose strict discipline in a harsh environment populated by some quite tough characters who would have taken any informality as a sign of weakness. In that respect he would have been little different to the great majority of his peers and much the sort of person that junior officers would have been used to dealing with. Even if it were to be shown that the criticisms of his behaviour on the night of 14/15 April 1912 were justified, there seems no need to indulge in excessive character assassination for which there is little if any evidence from other periods in his life.

The unfortunate Fred Davies who died when his ship the *Falaba* was sunk has left little with which to build up a portrait. He served the Elder Dempster Line, sometimes described as an artery of the Empire, and his ship was one of the class of medium-sized passenger/cargo ships that carried people and materials back and forth to the colonies in West Africa. He had been with the company for 20 years, giving excellent service and was described as a quiet and unassuming man, well respected by his peers. Unlike others of our group of eight commanders, his actions at the time his ship was lost were not seriously questioned at the inquiry and there has been little said since that would call into doubt his competence or the courage with which he faced what turned out for him to be his demise. There is some confusion about the manner of his death. It appears that he was rescued alive from the sea as the ship took its final plunge but passed away shortly thereafter. One newspaper report said that he had struck his head on the gunwale of a boat as he jumped from the ship and it was this that killed him. In another report, however, the Quartermaster of the ship claims to have pulled him out of the water using a boathook but makes no mention of a head injury.

The ship that collided with the *Empress of Ireland* is usually described as a 'collier'. While accurate, that description may be a little misleading because the term collier has come to be associated in many people's minds with the image of a small coaster taking coal into little ports around the country. The *Storstad* might more properly now be described by the more modern term 'bulk carrier', as she was a sizeable ship for her time at 6000 tons and was used to transport a variety of bulk cargoes. It just so happens that the cargo she was carrying, fully loaded, at the time of the collision was coal, almost 9000 tons of it. Being built for northern, ice-ridden waters she had a strengthened bow making her just about the worst possible ship to ram a passenger liner. Her captain was Thomas Andersen and, like Davies, we only have a limited idea as to what he was like. He has been described as brusque, a typical tramp ship captain, again (like Davies) quiet and unassuming. We know that he and his wife were close. She frequently sailed with him and was on board at the time of the collision. Indeed, she played a significant role in helping rescued survivors and issued her own statement about the accident on arrival in port.

In none of the other cases have we introduced any of the other ship's officers, although some will feature later. However, the particular circumstances of the collision involving the *Storstad* require that we do mention the Chief Officer, Alfred Toftnes, a tall 33-year-old, recently promoted and holding his own master's certificate. The reason for bringing him onstage at this time is that it was his actions rather than Andersen's that were subject to the most intense scrutiny in the inquiry, as he was officer of the watch when the accident occurred and Andersen was not on the bridge until just before the ships collided. This meant that, when the stories coming from the two ships to explain the tragedy differed, the two people going head to head were the rather famous captain of a prestigious liner and the mate of a Norwegian tramp. Toftnes seems to have been quite a strong character who stuck firmly to his story. Both he and his captain continued on their careers afterwards with no apparent ill effects from the inquiry outcomes. The *Storstad*, with Captain Andersen still in charge, was torpedoed and sunk off the Irish coast in March 1917, all of the crew surviving.

It will hardly surprise the reader that two captains who did not come well out of Mersey's deliberations were von Forstner of U-28 and Schwieger of U-20. It is doubtful if either of them could possibly have conducted themselves in such a fashion as to please our learned Judge in the circumstances then pertaining. As the 'von' implies, Forstner was of aristocratic lineage, his full name being Georg-Günther Freiherr von Forstner and he had taken command of the submarine the previous year when it had been completed. The *Falaba* was by no means either the first or the last ship that he had attacked. The previous day he had sunk two ships, one called *Aguila*, killing several people by gunfire when she refused to stop. He retained command of the submarine until July 1916 and U-28 had several subsequent commanders before being lost in September 1917 when the munitions ship it was attacking exploded and took its attacker down with it. Von Forstner was appointed to a training role and survived the war.

In 1917 von Forstner published a journal that included a lot of material about how submarines worked and how U-boats went about their business. The journal was translated into English and published in Boston in November that year. It makes fascinating reading, remembering of course that it was obviously produced as a piece of German propaganda, probably to counter the growing antipathy in America to the war being fought by German submarines. Von Forstner refers in the journal to a number of the actions in which he had been involved as the captain of U-28, actions in which he claims to have made every attempt to abide by the Cruiser Rules. He describes in some detail the capture of two ships carrying food cargoes, which he escorted into German-held Belgian ports and also the sinking of another ship, the *Vosges,* like the *Aguila*, sunk the day before the *Falaba*. We will return to that incident later when considering the verdict that Lord Mersey arrived at in relation to his actions during the attack on the *Falaba*. We will also consider a report that appeared in the *New York Times* carrying a story by the doctor on the White Star *Iberian,* which was sunk by U-28 on 30 July 1915.

In his journal von Forstner makes no mention of the *Falaba,* nor does he record any strange sightings when the *Iberian* sank. However, twenty years later he wrote an article claiming that as the *Iberian* went down there was an enormous explosion, probably caused by the cold water hitting her boilers, an explosion that was confirmed in the report by the ship's doctor shortly after the event. As the mass of debris rose into the air von Forstner said that he and several other members of the submarine's crew saw a vast sea serpent rising up with it. Unfortunately at this stage none of the other members of U-28's crew whom he named were alive to corroborate the sighting, but his story became very well known amongst that strange group of people who continue to be fascinated about the possible existence of as yet undiscovered sea monsters. Needless to say there is no reference to the sea serpent in the report in the *New York Times.* Von Forstner died in 1940 just as the second round of U-boat warfare was getting under way.

One thing which von Forstner and Walther Schwieger of U-20 had in common was concern for the welfare of their crews. Schwieger in particular was known to avoid running unnecessary risks while always being prepared to press home an attack. Originally from Berlin, he was tall and fair haired. His thirtieth birthday came just a month before the sinking of the *Lusitania*. It seems that he and von Forstner differed, however in their mode of operation. While von Forstner clearly made some attempt to stick to international conventions, Schwieger seems largely to have ignored them. It appears, if differences between these two captains are typical, that there was no coherently imposed strategy by the German naval command as to the manner in which their submarines operated, at least in the early stages of the war. The lack of a consistent policy may have reflected tension between an aggressive naval hierarchy and a slightly less hawkish civil administration.

Walther Schwieger, like von Forstner, was a career naval officer having joined as a cadet in 1903, moving to submarines in 1911. His first command was U-14 and he took over the more modern diesel powered U-20 just four months after the war began. His concern for his crew was reflected in their respect for him. Conditions aboard submarines remained pretty grim until the large modern nuclear boats emerged after the Second World War. In the early boats that we are concerned with here they really were horrible with appalling sleeping conditions, limited washing facilities and obnoxious sanitary arrangements. In a boat that had been submerged for some time it was common for the atmosphere to become so thick and barely breathable that men would vomit when exposed to fresh air. Schwieger tried to make life as bearable for the men under his command as possible, although in the exposed seas off the west of Ireland or in the heavily patrolled waters around the English Channel he would have had little scope to offer relief. After U-20 was lost by stranding, Schwieger took command of U-88. He continued as a successful and well respected captain (in Germany) until September 1917 when, shortly after leaving harbour, U-88 hit a mine and all aboard were lost.

Now that we have been introduced to the eight men and seen a little of their stories, we need to consider briefly what was expected of a captain. Against what criteria should these men have been judged? Once away from land a captain is a sort of dictator because the law allows for no superior authority aboard a ship. Even the Chairman of the shipping line does not outrank a captain when at sea. Because he is the person who must always have the final say, the captain can, at least in theory, be held responsible for everything that happens while a ship is at sea, irrespective of whether or not he is directly involved. He can delegate authority but not responsibility. The practice of holding the man at the top accountable for everything that happens in an organisation has become increasingly the norm over the last thirty years or so. Chief Executive Officers of big companies justify their extremely large salaries with the mantra 'the buck stops here'. Ministers are called to account for the actions of quite junior civil servants in a way that would not have been thought reasonable a century ago. One of the issues we will want to consider is the extent to which our captains should or should not have been blamed for the shortcomings of members of their crews.

Once a ship docked, the merchant ship captain's role changed. He reverted to being an employee of the shipping company who had to fit into the management structure in his appropriate place. That meant reporting to the Superintendent, the manager responsible for the running of the fleet of ships, and also being amenable to the requirements of the senior management of the line and the Board of Directors. For some captains this transition from dictator to employee and back to dictator as the ship moved from port to port was not an easy one, particularly when management decisions limited the resources that were available to them when going to sea. If the calibre of the crew that the captain was permitted to recruit was poor, to what extent could he then be blamed for their failings? If the equipment on the ship was below standard, how could he be blamed for the consequences of its inadequacies?

There was also the matter of the policies that management laid down to which the captain was expected to adhere. These might indicate routes to be followed, speeds to be maintained, expected turn-around times etc. No captain could afford to ignore these, but they did have the right to put the safety of the ship first; indeed they were required to do so by law. If a conflict arose between what the company expected and what reasonable caution required then the captain should always choose the latter. No captain could excuse the loss of his ship on the basis that he was required to follow company policy.

The two submarine captains, however, were in a different position. In the Board of Trade inquiries into the loss of the *Falaba* and the *Lusitania* von Forstner and Schwieger were not being judged on their competency as captains. They were being judged solely as the agents of a foreign power with which Britain was at war. So far as we can tell they were both excellent seamen who were also good at the difficult job of commanding a highly complex type of ship with a very high level of risk in its operation. The question that was asked of them in the inquiries was whether or not the manner in which they employed this innovative technology in warfare was acceptable.

In the next section we will look at the stories of each of the incidents that became the subject of the inquiries and at the issues that these presented so far as the actions of the captains were concerned. After that we will review the judgments that Mersey arrived at on the actions of the eight captains and consider whether or not they stand up to scrutiny against the evidence with which he was presented. We will also want to see how they rate in those instances where evidence has come to light that Mersey did not have.

7

IMPROBABLE THINGS DO HAPPEN

Quite simply, the sinking of the *Titanic* should not have happened because the odds against such an event occurring were startlingly high. Some people have said the opposite; that the disaster was an inevitable consequence of the hubris and arrogance which, they claim, characterised Edwardian society to an exceptional extent. Perhaps there is a philosophical point that the author is missing here, but surely it is rare for societal attitudes to be connected in quite such a mechanical manner to specific events. We are dealing after all with the twentieth century and not the Bronze Age world of the Old Testament.

Given the manner in which some aspects of technology had progressed so rapidly since around 1880 (size, speed, complexity of ships, communication) while others had largely stood still (navigation, ability to see ahead), it was likely that some incident would occur that would draw attention to the developing discrepancy between what it was possible to do and what it was safe to do. However, it was not probable that the incident would take the form that it did. What were the chances that the incident would involve the largest ship in the world at the time; that it would happen on that ship's first voyage; that it would take the form of a collision with an iceberg rather than with land or another ship; that the collision with the berg would be precisely such as to open sufficient of the ship to the sea to make its sinking inevitable; that it would happen when legal requirements for lifeboats were out of synchrony with the size of the largest ships; that, despite the use of wireless, no other ship would come to its aid before it sank? Multiply those chances together and the odds against the entire event happening in the way it did are very, very large.

That improbability is one of the factors that has caused the *Titanic* disaster to exercise its peculiar fascination for so many people over such a prolonged period. Few readers will therefore lack familiarity with the basic story but it is repeated here as a necessary framework to what follows, partly also to separate the historical facts from some of the subsequently manufactured accretions. This is the 'stripped out' version including only what is, to the best of the author's knowledge, generally agreed to be beyond reasonable doubt; as is the description of the sinking of the *Empress of Ireland* which follows it. Perhaps we need to clarify the issue of reasonable doubt by stating unequivocally that the ship which sank in the early hours of 15 April 1912 was the *Titanic* and not her sister ship, *Olympic*. The preposterous notion that the two might have been switched is well beyond 'reasonable'; that would have required tens of thousands of shipyard workers to be complicit in a vast and successful conspiracy of silence. Nobody who knew Belfast shipyard workers would suggest that such a thing was remotely possible, to point up just one of the more absurd aspects of the hypothesis.

The *Titanic* was launched from the Harland and Wolff shipyard on 31 May 1911. Her fitting out was completed in time for trials to be held on the morning of 2 April 1912 and she left Belfast that same evening for Southampton. It is worth pointing out the brevity of the sea trials and the short time between them and the commencement of the maiden voyage. While many of the crew had had experience on similar ships (including a significant number on *Olympic*) there was very little opportunity to weld the crew into an effectively functioning team and, for the considerable number for whom this was their first experience of a large passenger liner, little chance to familiarise themselves with their new role and surroundings.

The ship departed Southampton at 1215 on 10 April on her maiden voyage and travelled to Cherbourg, arriving that same evening. Here a small number of passengers left the ship, having booked only that leg of the journey and a rather larger number joined. They embarked on the ship by means of two steam tenders, *Nomadic* and *Traffic*, each a small scale passenger ship in her own right. Unlike *Titanic,* the *Nomadic* was to have a long career, one which still continues. Having spent many years as a stationary quayside restaurant on the Seine in Paris, she has now been taken back to Belfast where she is being restored as a public exhibit. Not only is *Nomadic* an interesting part of the *Titanic* story, she is now the only example to be seen in the city of the enormous output of Harland and Wolff and other Belfast shipbuilders over a century and a half.

Titanic also stopped to drop off and take on some passengers at Cobh (or Queenstown as it was then known) in County Cork, transfer being effected by the tenders *Ireland* and *America*. Amongst the passengers leaving the ship was a trainee priest by the name of Brown, who was a keen amateur photographer. His photographs and those of a friend called McLean who was with him, in particular one taken from the tender looking up at Captain Smith peering over the side of his bridge, have become world famous. *Titanic* left Cobh at 1330 on 11 April and headed out into the Atlantic for the first and last time. On Sunday 14 April she began to receive ice warnings from some ships that were ahead of her. Some of the ice was reported to the north of her track but at least two messages mentioned ice that straddled her route. Both low lying field ice and large bergs were mentioned. Not all of the messages reached Captain Smith; one from the *Mesaba* was not passed to the bridge and one from the *Californian* a short time before the collision was excluded by the *Titanic's* wireless operators. The speed of the ship was not altered in response to the ice warnings.

The night of the 14/15 April 1912 was one of the calmest that anyone with experience of the North Atlantic could remember. There was no moon, just starlight, and it was clear with good visibility. The look-outs in the crow's nest saw the iceberg first at around 2340 and called the bridge by telephone. Officer of the watch, First Officer Murdoch, ordered the helm put to starboard in order to turn the ship's head to port. He also ordered the engines to go full astern, although this was by no means immediate in a ship with steam reciprocating machinery. As her head swung to port, the starboard side slid along the edge of the iceberg, opening six of her compartments to the sea. There is some doubt about how far the ship travelled before stopping and in what direction she was pointing when she did so. It took about twenty minutes to ascertain the nature of the damage, from which it was clear to the captain that she would sink. Orders were given to prepare the lifeboats and hoist them out ready to be filled.

Titanic's wireless operators had been very busy that evening sending personal messages on behalf of passengers. Now they were asked to send urgent calls for assistance. Anyone responding to such a call had to be told where the ship was and Fourth Officer Boxhall calculated the ship's position by dead reckoning and this position was broadcast. He made an error in his calculation and we now know, from the position in which the wreck was found in 1985, that he placed the ship between 10 and 13 miles almost due west of where she was. Preparations to load the lifeboats went ahead slowly and with some difficulty because for a time the noise created when the engineers released the high pressure steam from the boilers was such as to make any conversation on the boat deck almost impossible. Around 0030 the first sighting of another ship was reported and about 10 to 15 minutes later the first lifeboat was launched. It contained only 28 people instead of its full complement of 65. Captain Smith was reported to have advised those in the lifeboats to row to the ship whose lights had been seen and return for more people.

Around the time that the first lifeboat was leaving, the firing of rockets from the bridge began as a further attempt to attract assistance, in recognition that, in 1912, many ships were not equipped with wireless or did not operate it on a 24-hour basis. For the same reason attempts were made to contact the ship whose lights had been seen by morse code using one of the ship's large signal lamps. No response was seen. The evacuation continued with lifeboats leaving the ship at intervals, most of them containing fewer people than they were built to take. The last rocket was fired at around 0140 and the last lifeboat cleared the ship just after 0200. A final distress message was sent by the wireless operators a few minutes later and the ship sank at approximately 0220.

The wreck of the ship lies in two pieces on the sea floor at a depth of around 13000 feet. Arguments have raged over the years as to when the ship came apart. Some say that the split happened while the ship was still on the surface and was seen by a number of witnesses; others that it occurred just under the surface as the forward part submerged, and there is some witness evidence for this point of view as well. Given that the scope of this book is limited to the actions of the captains involved, the matter is not one that need concern us. What is of interest is the response that the distress calls elicited from nearby ships. There were a number of responses but none gave those on board *Titanic* assurance that a rescue ship would arrive before it was too late. Their best hope lay with the *Carpathia,* but only if *Titanic* stayed afloat for an unlikely four hours. Having made her best possible speed, *Carpathia* found the lifeboats at around 0400 and began to rescue the pitifully small number still alive. The number saved was 705, the number lost was 1522.

Some distance to the north and slightly west of where the *Titanic* collided with the iceberg the *Californian* lay stopped. Having encountered substantial field ice, Stanley Lord decided to wait until daylight before pushing on through it on his way to Boston. He put the engines on standby and the single wireless operator closed his set down for the night shortly after broadcasting the ice message that was excluded by the operators on *Titanic*. Normal watches were maintained by bridge officers and lookouts during the night. A short time after the ship had stopped another ship was seen approaching and it stopped with its masthead and navigation lights visible. An hour or so later a rocket was seen from the bridge of the *Californian* that appeared to come from this ship. The sighting was reported to Stanley Lord, who had retired to the chartroom for a rest after having been on duty for the entire day. He suggested that an attempt should be made to contact the ship by morse lamp. This was done without response and subsequently a number of further rockets were seen, again interpreted by those observing as coming from the nearby ship. Finally, the lights of the ship were observed to change in a way that the officer of the watch, Second Officer Stone, believed indicated that the ship was steaming off to the south west. Captain Lord was informed of these developments both by voicepipe and by a visit from the junior watch officer, Apprentice Gibson, to the chartroom. Arguments have continued ever since as to how much Lord did or did not understand of these messages in his sleep befuddled state. No instruction was given to investigate the matter of the rockets other than by attempting to signal to the ship from which they were thought to be emanating. The wireless operator was not roused to see if there was anything being broadcast that would shed any light on the reason for the rockets being fired. The fact that they had been seen only came to light when some members of the crew, in particular a donkeyman named Gill, spoke to reporters on the ship's arrival in Boston.

It was at 0600 that *Californian* received a wireless message to say that the *Titanic* had sunk. She got underway immediately and pushed through the ice field towards the position that had been given in the distress calls. On arrival there she found another ship stopped but no sign of wreckage or survivors. Discovering that the *Carpathia* was completing the rescue of survivors some distance to the south east, Lord again traversed the ice field to get to that position and arrived at approximately 0830. The *Californian* assisted the *Carpathia* until nothing more could be achieved and then resumed her passage to Boston. This is a very brief outline summary of events that took place in the space of two and a half hours that morning, the details of which have proved highly contentious. Witness evidence on movements and sightings by the different ships is confusing and contradictory to the point that no resolution is now possible, despite the many kilograms of paper and litres of ink that have been consumed fruitlessly in the attempt.

Of the 1522 people who died on *Titanic*, 832 were passengers. That was 8 fewer than the number of passengers who died when the *Empress of Ireland* sank just two years later in May 1914. Where the gradual foundering of the *Titanic* on a crisp clear April night was a protracted drama full of pathos, the sinking of the *Empress* was a brief, ugly convulsion shrouded in fog. If the sinking of the *Titanic* was highly improbable, that of the *Empress* was merely unlikely. As we saw in Chapter 2, collisions between ships in fog were a major risk, both in terms of the likelihood of them occurring and the seriousness of the consequences when they did. Even the coming of radar and GPS based navigation has not eliminated the risk. Ships still regularly collide in fog, particularly in crowded waterways. Mostly the ships affected are cargo ships and, unless there are serious environmental after effects such as oil spills, the accidents attract little publicity. But some have involved passenger ships. Amongst the most famous since the loss of the *Empress* have been the sinking of the *Egypt* in 1922, leading to one of the most exciting gold salvaging episodes ever, and the collision in 1956 off the eastern coast of the of the USA between the Italian liner *Andrea Doria* and the Swedish cargo vessel *Stockholm*. Forty six people died in the collision and the liner sank the following day.

What was unlikely about the accident that occurred in the St Lawrence in May 1914 was the fact that of all the possible combinations of ships and collision geometries, few would have been such as to lead to the enormous loss of life which occurred. A heavily loaded bulk carrier, with ice strengthened bow, striking a large passenger ship almost at right angles, in the area of the big open space of the engine room was a scenario for a major tragedy and so it proved.

When the *Empress* left Quebec in the late afternoon of the 28 May 1914 she was carrying 1057 passengers and 420 crew. Amongst her passengers, as well as a small number of people who were then well known in the theatre or business, there was also a large party, totalling 171, from the Salvation Army. This was the Canadian contingent on their way to a major International Conference being held by the Army in London. Included in the group was the full membership of the Territorial Staff Band from Toronto. The first part of the journey out into the Atlantic required the services of a pilot and, shortly after 1.00am on the 29th, he was dropped off at the usual disembarkation point for pilots at Father Point. As mentioned in the last chapter, it was at Father Point that Inspector Dew from Scotland Yard was taken out to the *Montrose* in order to arrest Crippen. The greatest triumph in Henry Kendall's life and the most harrowing tragedy were enacted in exactly the same place.

Just 10–15 minutes after moving off out into the seaway, which is approximately 30 miles wide at this point, the lights of another steamer were seen a few miles away, coming in the opposite direction. This was the *Storstad* and the officers on her bridge also saw the lights of the *Empress* at about the same time. A short while later each ship lost sight of the other as a bank of fog rolled across and what happened over the following ten minutes became obscured not only for that period of time but has remained so ever since because two entirely different versions emerged from the two ships. Probably all that we can be sure of is that, just before the fog reduced visibility, the *Empress* turned to starboard to come onto her course out to sea. Worried about the proximity of the other ship, Kendall, at some point, ordered the *Empress* to be stopped by putting the engines astern, although the timing of that order taking effect is in doubt. Also at some point, although again the timing is not certain, the *Storstad* stopped her engines and her helm was put over which may, or may not have had the effect of turning her to starboard. Suddenly those on the *Empress* saw the *Storstad* heading directly for the starboard side of the ship, already too close to prevent a collision. It was only a minute or two earlier that the Chief Officer of the *Storstad,* Alfred Toftnes, had called Captain

Andersen to the bridge. As the bow of the *Storstad* plunged into the side of the *Empress,* Kendall gave the order to close watertight doors. In many cases there was neither time nor access to enable the order to be carried out.

Briefly the two ships were locked together. Kendall called across to Andersen to ask him to put his engines full ahead in order to keep the ships together so that the collier would act as a plug in the wounded liner's side and limit the inflow of water. Andersen claimed afterwards that he did so. Kendall maintained that he did not because the two ships separated, the bow of the *Storstad* being heavily twisted in the process. Into the cavernous hole that was opened in the hull of the *Empress* the water surged with terrible force. Immediately she began to keel over to starboard. Although efforts were made to get lifeboats away, those on the port side were soon useless and within a few minutes more those on the starboard side were being forced under water on their davits. As one reporter described it, with a graphic but unpleasant simile, the ship rolled over 'like a hog in a ditch'. Just 15 minutes after the collision, the *Empress* disappeared leaving a mass of wreckage and people floating and struggling in the bitterly cold water.

Two tenders from Father Point and a tug did most of the rescue work, assisted by the crew of the *Storstad,* but only 465 people were pulled from the St Lawrence alive. Of these, just 217 were passengers; only 4 out of 158 children aboard survived. On the other hand almost 60 per cent of the crew were saved. The relatively large proportion of crew members compared to passengers surviving resulted from the circumstances of the accident. It took place when almost all of the passengers were in bed while a significant proportion of the crew were on duty. As the ship had only started her voyage a matter of hours before, the passengers had not had a chance to familiarise themselves with the ship while members of the crew knew their way around. This was critical because the electricity failed within a minute or two of the collision and the ship was in total darkness. The events in the passenger accommodation during the sinking must have been horrendous beyond description. Captain Kendall was amongst those rescued. He ended up aboard the *Storstad* and confronted Andersen with 'You sank my ship, Sir'. Both Captain Andersen and his wife worked tirelessly to try to bring some comfort, including dry clothes, to the distressed survivors brought onto their ship by the lifeboats the crew had lowered.

So, two very different accidents to Atlantic passenger liners had claimed the lives of 2534 men, women and children. One eventually became the symbol of all man-made disasters; the other was largely forgotten as the world went to war a few weeks after Lord Mersey completed his report and the newspapers began to carry stories of carnage on an even greater scale.

MEN OF STEEL

Earlier we discussed the international agreements that governed the use of raiders attacking merchant ships in wartime, informally known as the Cruiser Rules. Given their genesis at a time when knights still took part in jousts, it is hardly surprising that they have a whiff of an earlier age of chivalry about them. Events were to prove that they were entirely inadequate to deal with the type of warfare that commenced in August 1914. Initially it seemed as if the principal impact of the new submarine technology would be in devastating the ranks of surface warships, much as naval commentators had predicted. The first ship ever to succumb to a torpedo fired by a submarine was HMS *Pathfinder*, a light cruiser attacked by U-21 on 5 September in the Firth of Forth with the loss of around 250 men. The explosion of the torpedo set off one in the forward magazine that resulted in her sinking almost instantly.

Just over a fortnight later came an incident that not only demonstrated very clearly the power of the new underwater raiders but seriously embarrassed the British Admiralty. Early on a calm, autumn morning in the North Sea, Otto Weddingen in the primitive U-9, outmoded even by 1914 standards, torpedoed and sank the three old armoured cruisers *Aboukir, Hogue* and *Cressy* one after the other. The statement issued by the Admiralty sets out very clearly the nature of what happened and their attempt to cover their embarrassment.

The sinking of the *Aboukir* was of course an ordinary hazard of patrolling duty. The *Hogue* and *Cressy*, however, were sunk because they proceeded to the assistance of their consort and remained with engines stopped endeavouring to save life, thus presenting an easy and certain target to further submarine attacks. The natural promptings of humanity have in this case led to heavy losses which would have been avoided by a strict adherence to military considerations. Modern naval war is presenting us with so many new and strange situations that an error of judgement of this character is pardonable, but it has been necessary to point out, for the future guidance of his Majesty's ships, that the conditions which prevail when one of a squadron is injured in a minefield or is exposed to submarine attack, are analogous to those which occur in an action, and that the rule of leaving disabled ships to their own resources is applicable, so far, at any rate, as large vessels are concerned. No act of humanity, whether to friend or foe, should lead to a neglect of the proper precautions and dispositions of war, and no measures can be taken to save life which prejudice the military situation. Small craft of all kinds should, however, be directed by wireless to close on the damaged ship with all speed.

The loss of nearly 60 officers and 1400 men would not have been grudged if it had been brought about by gunfire in an open action, but it is peculiarly distressing under the conditions which prevailed. The absence of any of the ardour and excitement of an engagement did not, however, prevent the display of discipline, cheerful courage, and ready self-sacrifice among all ranks and ratings exposed to the ordeal.

The sense of the naval leadership struggling to come to terms with new technological developments that were turning their nicely ordered world upside down is evident in the statement, as is the view that what was happening was somehow a sneaky, underhand form of warfare. To say that the loss of so many men would 'not have been grudged if it had been brought about by gunfire in an open action' and to refer to the 'absence of any of the ardour and excitement of an engagement' displays an attitude to warfare into which submarines simply do not fit. The statement that no act of humanity or measures to save life should 'prejudice the military situation' is one with which the German authorities would have concurred in directing the use of their U-boats against merchant ships.

The mirror image of the Admiralty's attitude can be found in a book *Raiders of the Deep* written by an American, Lowell Thomas, published in 1928 and containing accounts of the exploits of U-boats provided to him in interviews after the war by their ex-crews. The book, like the Admiralty statement, exhibits a gung-ho, isn't war a jolly jape sort of attitude, but this time from the perspective of the men of steel who fought in these new-fangled and dreadfully dangerous contraptions beneath the waves. As Thomas puts it:

In setting down this account of the submarine war, straight from the lips of the U-boat commanders, I have disregarded all controversial ground, or at any rate have attempted to. The right and wrong of undersea war is not discussed here. The tales I have to pass on are tales of sheer adventure. Stranger than fiction? Aye! And tales, I believe, such as no other chronicler will have a chance to set down in our time. At any rate, we all hope the world has learned its lesson, and may there be peace among men for generations to come.

Setting aside the horrible irony of the latter part of the quote, the first part illustrates how the submarine itself had the potential to become the vehicle for tales of derring do and many accounts of the actions of British submariners in Gallipoli and the Baltic and elsewhere also appeared after the war ended.

Relatively few of the submariners' exploits, however, involved attacks on warships. The initial flurry of cruiser sinkings flattered to deceive and U-boats were relatively ineffective weapons against battle fleets during either world war. Just two days before the sinking of the *Falaba*, Otto Weddingen died in U-29 when attempting to attack the British battle fleet; his boat was rammed by HMS *Dreadnought*.

Gradually the focus of U-boat actions in late 1914 and early 1915 turned to attacks on merchant ships. The pace of such attacks increased significantly in February 1915 when the German government issued a statement to say that, from the 18th of that month in a designated area around the British Isles, all enemy ships would be sunk on sight. The statement went even further by indicating that the difficulty in determining the nationality of ships from some distance in a submarine was such that neutral ships could not expect to be spared in the designated area. The number of ships that were torpedoed without warning increased significantly but, at the same time, there were also examples of other ships being stopped and their crews getting away before the submarine opened fire. Although this German announcement of what was described by others as 'unrestricted submarine warfare' was rescinded later in 1915 as a result of pressure from neutral nations, principally the USA, it was in place at the time of the two sinkings in which we are interested.

The *Falaba* was a nine-year-old Elder Dempster liner used on the run from Liverpool out to West Africa. On her last voyage she left Liverpool on the evening of 27 March 1915 carrying 147 passengers and a crew of 95 and heading for Sierra Leone as her first stop. All but seven of the passengers were men, mostly colonial administrators and businessmen along with some soldiers joining or re-joining their regiments. One passenger who was to feature in the aftermath of the drama was a 31-year-old mining engineer from Massachusetts called Leon Chester Thrasher (spelled Thresher in many British publications, possibly because that was the spelling given in the published proceedings of the inquiry). In addition to the passengers she carried a general cargo and amongst it, her manifest recorded, were 13 tons of cartridges and gunpowder 'for government use'.

Chief Officer Walter Baxter was the officer of the watch the following morning when, about 1140, the conning tower of a submarine was spotted several miles away. Captain Davies joined him immediately on the bridge and ordered the ship's head to be turned directly away from the submarine and the engines to be brought up to full speed from the 13-knot cruising speed, actions that were in line with the instructions from the Admiralty. The submarine, now fully on the surface and showing a German flag, chased the fleeing *Falaba,* hoisting code flags calling on her to stop. The flag hoist was changed to one saying 'stop or I will fire' and some witnesses said that a flare was sent up to emphasise the threat. There followed a discussion on the bridge of *Falaba* as to the correct course of action. The officers were aware that the Admiralty wished them to try to save the ship by fleeing if possible, but the submarine had almost caught them up. Davies decided that to continue to attempt to flee would place the passengers in too much danger and he stopped the ship. He instructed the wireless officer to send a message reporting that the ship had been stopped by a hostile submarine and that he expected to be sunk. Two messages were sent in plain language, the latter requesting the assistance of a warship. The wireless station at Land's End confirmed that the message had been passed through to naval command.

Kapitanleutnant von Forstner in U-28 called across by megaphone to the *Falaba* and ordered Davies to abandon the ship as he intended to sink her. He may also have ordered all wireless transmissions to cease but this is not certain. Davies immediately ordered the evacuation of all of the passengers and crew. Some of the lifeboats had already been swung out the previous evening as a precaution and were ready for immediate use, but others were still on their chocks. Given the brief interval promised by von Forstner there was obviously a degree of haste that spilled over into near panic as the evacuation proceeded. It did not go well. The lowering of several lifeboats was mishandled or obstructed by jammed ropes that caused them to crash into the sea with their passengers. A couple of other lifeboats were not watertight by the time they were lowered and filled with water. The crewing of some boats was largely left in the hands of passengers and organisation was poor. Just as the final boat was being lowered towards the stern, U-28's torpedo hit amidships. The resulting explosion caused the last lifeboat to fall into the sea and the ship to sink very rapidly. The torpedo may have caused munitions in the ship's hold to explode although there is no clear evidence of this. Davies and Baxter were both picked up from the sea but Davies died shortly afterwards, possibly from a head wound. There was no evidence given at the inquiry as to how

Davies died. U-28 circled briefly and then submerged. The survivors were picked up by a couple of steam drifters and taken to Milford Haven. A total of 104 people died in the sinking, one of them being Leon C Thrasher.

A number of survivors told their stories to newspaper reporters and these were circulated to newspapers around the world. They had a number of features in common. One was complaint about the lack of organisation in the lifeboats and also the condition of the boats themselves and their equipment. But the one that had a big impact on headlines was a report from a number of sources that while the evacuation of the *Falaba* was taking place, the German sailors had lined the casing of the submarine and laughed and jeered at people struggling in the water. Survivors also claimed that von Forstner had fired his torpedo only five minutes after giving his warning, far too short a period to enable a proper evacuation of the ship. Such stories had enormous propaganda value, of course, and there was no attempt to prevent them appearing.

Once von Forstner had returned home the Germans felt obliged to respond and issued a statement giving their version of the event. In their version, U-28 actually allowed the British ship a total of 23 minutes before firing the torpedo as the evacuation had not been nearly completed after the 10 minutes which the Germans claimed had been given. The statement also denied absolutely that there had been any jeering or laughing by the submarine crew while this was going on. The torpedo had been fired, it was said, only because a warship had been seen approaching and it was considered too dangerous to wait any longer.

Leon Thrasher was the first American citizen to have died as a result of the actions of a German submarine. There was a bizarre postscript to his death. The body was not one of those recovered at the time of the sinking. Instead, it was washed up on the south coast of Ireland along with others from the *Lusitania*. Before its identity had been confirmed, Cunard had paid for the funeral as part of the mass burial of the *Lusitania* dead. It was reported that they tried subsequently to recover their costs.

It was the habit of the German authorities (and indeed the British ones) to use sympathetic Americans to seed supportive stories into the American popular press and this seems to have happened in this case. A cotton broker, J J Ryan, who had visited Germany on business, apparently met a gentleman called 'Commander Schmidt' who claimed to have been the captain of U-28. In fact it seems likely that Schmidt was von Forstner's second in command. Schmidt claimed that the German sailors had actually been crying when watching the distress of the passengers in the water and expressed regret at having to sink the ship. According to the report that appeared in the *Evening Press* in New York he went on:

I warned the captain of the *Falaba* to dismantle his wireless apparatus and gave him ten minutes in which to do it, and also to get out his passengers.

Instead of acting upon my demand, he continued to send out messages to torpedo boats that were less that twenty miles away to come to his assistance as quickly as possible.

At the end of ten minutes I gave him a second warning about dismantling the wireless apparatus and waited twenty minutes.

Then I torpedoed the ship, as the torpedo-boats were getting close up, and I knew they would go to the rescue of the passengers and crew.

The only ships which are known to have been within sight of the submarine at that time were the little steam drifters that were later to pick up the survivors. It is inconceivable that these could have been mistaken for torpedo-boats by the German look-outs, but it must be remembered that the incident took place in well populated waters with frequent Royal Navy patrols and that the *Falaba* had put out a wireless message requesting armed assistance. It is understandable that von Forstner was very nervous sitting for any length of time on the surface in those conditions, and even a smudge of smoke on the horizon may well have been interpreted as a hostile warship.

Walther Schwieger avoided this problem by remaining submerged when he sank the *Lusitania*. The two incidents were quite different in almost every other respect as well, not least in the scale of the human cost. The story of the *Lusitania* has become so overlaid by conspiracy theories that it is difficult to burrow underneath them to the fairly simple events that took place off the coast of Ireland on the morning of Friday 7 May 1915, six weeks after the destruction of the *Falaba*. Those readers who wish to believe that First Lord of the Admiralty, Winston Churchill, deliberately set the *Lusitania* up to be sunk, as bait to lure America into the war, need not feel threatened by the following. We can be sure that, whatever Churchill was up to in the spring of 1915 (and it would seem likely that his main preoccupation was in the Eastern Mediterranean), he did not take Will Turner and Walther Schwieger into his confidence. Their concerns were not with geopolitical strategy but with carrying out their duties. Had the actions of either of those captains been even slightly different that morning, none of Churchill's Machiavellian plans, if such there were, would have materialised.

Lusitania left New York just after midday on Saturday 1 May carrying 1257 passengers and 702 crew. Despite the appearance of adverts in the American East Coast press that morning warning passengers on ships leaving for Europe about the policy of the German government announced the previous February, the atmosphere on board was not particularly tense. Everyone knew that there was little chance of running into a surface attack in mid-Atlantic and that the submarine threat only became significant once the Irish coast was approached. At that time submarines had not ventured out into mid-Atlantic. As we have already noted, the Admiralty had issued advice to captains of merchant ships as to how the likelihood of a successful attack could be minimised. Advice was also provided as to how they should act in the event of being attacked by a submarine. This was updated at regular intervals and there was some confusion at the inquiry as to which specific communications Turner had seen. Because submarine warfare was so new and because the Germans were varying their tactics as they experimented with the new weapon, the initial advice issued by the Admiralty was sometimes contradicted by later updates. In the very early stages in 1914, captains were told to keep close to land as submarines would not operate in sight of the shore. That advice was quickly countermanded and ships were then advised to avoid coming close to shore, headlands in particular. Part of the difficulty that captains experienced was the sheer volume of material that was issued. Turner later described it as sufficient to paper the walls of his cabin.

Although what the Admiralty issued was formally regarded as advice, there were sanctions available to ensure that it would be obeyed. As normal marine insurance did not cover acts of war, the government had set up arrangements to indemnify owners who lost vessels to enemy action. Claims under those arrangements were made dependent on the ship that was lost having followed the Admiralty advice. The company whose captain recklessly ignored that advice could not expect to receive the same level of compensation.

By the end of April 1915 the advice that had been issued told masters that, in areas with a significant threat of submarine attack, they should not steer a straight course but should zigzag; they should stay well clear of headlands and stay out from land in mid-channel; they should keep speed up to the safe maximum, especially in the vicinity of ports; they should time their arrival at the port that they were sailing towards so that they did not need to linger outside it for tidal or other reasons. The advice, perhaps deliberately, was quite vague. While it was issued in confidential form, much of it was repeated in wireless messages that the Admiralty suspected were being decoded by the Germans.

The British were also decoding a substantial amount of the German wireless traffic and were able to tell in which area submarines were operating and, in many cases, identify the submarines concerned. As well as issuing generalised advice the Admiralty also issued specific warnings to ships in particular areas that there were U-boats operating. Such information was also available, of course, as a result of the attacks that were taking place. Although no convoy system was in operation arrangements were occasionally made to provide naval escorts for particularly valuable ships passing through areas where sub-marines were known to be active. On a previous voyage in March a destroyer escort had been provided for *Lusitania* as she approached the south coast of Ireland but had failed to meet up with her. It was the view of the Admiralty, with limited justification, that the best protection for a ship was speed as no ship travelling at high speed had yet been torpedoed.

In the 24 hours prior to the sinking, the *Lusitania* had received warnings of submarine activity off the south coast of Ireland and Will Turner was in no doubt that he was steaming into an area of heightened risk, just as Smith was in no doubt on *Titanic* that he was travelling towards ice. One warn-ing which proved to be of particular significance in later investigations was received shortly after 1100 on 7 May, reporting submarine activity about 20 miles south of Conninbeg lighthouse, at that time about 120 miles ahead of the ship. Early in the morning of 7 May there was fog and Turner reduced the speed of his ship to 15 knots until it cleared when he went back up to 18 knots. At the time the ship was running with one of her boiler rooms closed down because the company had seen a reduction in coal consumption as their only method of retaining profitability on the route. This limited her top speed to 21 knots instead of the pre-war 25 knots, but Turner deliberately kept her to 18 knots that morning because he wished to time his arrival at the Liverpool Bar such that the ship would not have to hang about but would be able to go straight in to port as the Admiralty advised. Also early that morning, Turner had the ship's lifeboats swung out and provisioned ready for filling and launching quickly if required. A further precaution entering the danger zone was an order that all portholes be closed so that, if the ship was damaged, it would not take on additional water through openings. It was an oral instruc-tion only that was not followed up to ensure compliance. Finally, to limit the movement of any water in the ship, the watertight doors were closed except for those that had to stay open for operational purposes such as the ones used by trimmers going back and forward with coal for the boilers.

Turner was concerned that navigation by dead reckoning was not suffi-ciently precise in these circumstances, particularly as the fog might return at any time, so he decided that he needed to get a good position fix by taking bearings on recognisable features on land. He altered course to port, therefore, to get closer to the Old Head of Kinsale. He had been keeping around 25 miles from land but this new course brought him in to about 12 miles. Even then, he was much farther out than would have been normal peacetime prac-tice where, in clear weather, the ship would have passed the headland at only one to two miles distance. Having come into where the fix could be taken, the ship was then turned to starboard back onto its original course. In doing so, Turner was not heading out to the 'mid-channel' area that the Admiralty had advised him to stay in but was running roughly parallel to the coast. It is doubtful whether the term 'mid-channel' had any meaning when the nearest land other than the coast of Ireland was over 100 miles away. Indeed, the Admiralty may only have meant the advice to apply in narrow waterways such as the English Channel or the North Channel between Ireland and Scotland where 12 miles out would have been mid-channel in both cases.

Walther Schwieger was also approaching the end of his voyage having left Germany on 30 April. Despite urgings to use the shortest route by his superior prior to setting out, he had cautiously brought U-20 down the west coast of Ireland rather than through the narrow and dangerous North Channel. The early part of his patrol had been unproductive and by 5 May he and his crew were becoming frustrated, their only attempted attack having failed as a result of a malfunctioning torpedo. That evening he sank the small schooner *Earl of Latham* by gunfire, her crew getting away in a boat but having a ten-mile row to the shore. The following morning matters improved from his point of view though not for the crews of the two Harrison Line ships he sank. U-20 attacked the *Candidate* on the morning of 6 May, initially by gunfire. The ship tried to flee but shell hits caused it to stop and the crew got away in boats in something of a panic as Schwieger lined up the torpedo shot that was the coup de grace.

Before encountering the second of the Harrison Line ships, the *Centurion*, Schwieger narrowly missed an opportunity to fire at the 16,000 ton White Star Liner, *Arabic*. Had she passed a little closer to U-20 and had visibility not been limited by fog, it is clear from Schwieger's war diary that he would have made an attempt to sink her with a torpedo. The *Centurion* came into view shortly afterwards in a favourable position and he sank her using two torpedoes, the crew succeeding in leaving in the lifeboats. This was by no means the first ship that Schwieger had torpedoed without warning. In January of that year he had sunk three merchant ships close to Le Havre without any warning and the following month had missed the hospital ship *Asturia* with a torpedo, claiming afterwards that he thought that she was a troop transport despite the white paint and red crosses. Schwieger's reputation, both leading up to the sinking of the *Lusitania* and after it, was that he was one of the more ruthless of the U-boat commanders, one who made the most aggressive interpretation possible of his orders while, at the same time, exercising considerable caution in their execution.

The sinking of the two Harrison Line ships on 6 May resulted in the warning that *Lusitania* received just after 1100 on 7 May to the effect that there were submarines active in the area twenty miles south of the Conninbeg

Lightship. The warning was vague and did not inform Turner that two ships had been sunk, nor that these attacks had taken place the previous day. The fog up to about 1100 that morning caused Schwieger to stay submerged to avoid being run down and when he came up to periscope depth he saw the cruiser *Juno* heading back into Queenstown. Travelling fast and zigzagging, the *Juno* gave him no opportunity to take a shot at her. It was at 1340, U-20 now on the surface, that the smoke, masts and funnels of the *Lusitania* were first spotted. Schwieger took his boat back under and looked to see if a shot would be possible. At first it seemed not, as the liner's course would not have brought her close enough to the submarine, which could only move slowly underwater. Then, as Schwieger watched through the periscope, he saw the liner's head swing to starboard as Turner brought her back parallel with the coast. Now coming broadside on at 700 metres the *Lusitania* presented a very hittable target despite her speed of 18 knots. Schwieger sent a torpedo off from one of his bow tubes and he and his crew waited in silence for the 35 seconds it took for it to reach its target. It is worth noting that the torpedo was fired not from the landward side of the liner but the seaward side and U-20 had actually come closer to the land in order to get into position to fire it.

On *Lusitania* the bubble track of the torpedo was spotted both on the bridge and by some of the passengers on the deck, but not with time for any evasive action to be effective. It struck the starboard side just abaft the bridge with an explosion that flung wreckage and water to a height well above the funnel tops. This was closely followed by a second explosion, the cause of which has remained contentious ever since. It was not caused by a second torpedo, nor by the explosion of munitions, either included on the cargo manifest or not. We know that it was not a second torpedo partly because Schwieger sent a wireless message back to HQ later that day informing them that he had sunk the *Lusitania* with a single torpedo. At that stage, before any second explosion had been mentioned, he had no reason to falsify his account. Also, all of the torpedoes aboard U-20 can be accounted for on her patrol. The signal sent by Schwieger was intercepted and decoded by the British Admiralty, who therefore knew that only one torpedo had been fired.

The second explosion was not the result of the torpedo setting off the munitions listed on the ship's manifest as these consisted of shell parts and small arms ammunition, neither of which would explode. If there were another secret cargo of explosives, as has sometimes been alleged, it would not have been stored close to the place where the torpedo struck. Furthermore, if such a 'contraband' cargo had exploded, it would have caused damage to the ship which Dr Robert Ballard did not find when he scrutinised the hull in 1993. The most likely explanation for the second explosion was the fracture of one of the large steam pipes taking steam from the boilers to the engines. Another possibility is that the torpedo set off a mixture of coal dust and air in the now nearly empty coal bunkers. The effect of the torpedo combined with the second explosion on the ship was immediate and dramatic. Electric power failed within a few minutes, the engines lost power and she developed a significant list to starboard. The loss of engine power frustrated Turner in two ways. His first thought after the ship was hit was to try to beach her. The absence of a response from the engine room quickly made him abandon this idea so that his next and only remaining option was to evacuate the ship. She needed to be stopped first and there was no power to put the screws astern and bring her to a halt. Witnesses were agreed that the *Lusitania* was still moving forward as her bows touched the bottom in the final stages of sinking eighteen minutes later.

The scenes that ensued, once the realisation caught hold amongst passengers and crew that the ship was sinking rapidly, were amongst the most distressing ever reported from a maritime disaster. The slow foundering of the *Titanic* evoked panic in some, but many remained calm and events happened relatively slowly and in a comparatively controlled manner. The speed of the *Empress*'s sinking, the darkness and the fact that so few passengers even made it to the deck shortened the horror and limited the extent to which surviving witnesses could report what had happened. On the *Lusitania*, in the middle of a calm sunlit May day, the frantic and often unsuccessful attempts to get lifeboats away amid crowds of terrified passengers, many separated from their loved ones, created an awful experience for all involved. The list made it nearly impossible to get the lifeboats down the port side and a number of people were killed and injured when boats swung in against the ship or fell to the sea. On the starboard side the boats hung out from the side of the ship and it was difficult to get them loaded. In one case the forward movement of the ship caused one lifeboat to land directly on top of another that had just been released.

As the ship gradually fell over on her starboard side and disappeared those lifeboats that had been successfully launched, many nowhere nearly filled, were left surrounded by a large amount of wreckage and a vast number of people struggling in the water. Most people going into the water had lifebelts, although some had not. There was an ample supply on the ship but some people had been unable to access them in time. In many cases they had been incorrectly fitted and caused injury or death when the wearers jumped from the ship. Many of the lifeboats made every possible effort to pull people who were still alive out of the water; some did not do so out of fear of being swamped. Rescue was not immediate. There were a few small fishing boats in the vicinity which got there as quickly as they could and started to take people on board. They could only take limited numbers and the boats that had left Queenstown on hearing of the sinking did not begin to arrive for over an hour. People were still being pulled from the water more than three hours after the liner had sunk.

Of the 1257 passengers on board, 785 were lost as well as 413 of the 702 in the crew. Undoubtedly the sheer magnitude of the disaster would have caused major headlines around the world, even while the terrible events of the Western Front were getting into their stride. However, it was the deaths of the 128 Americans amongst the passengers that gave the sinking an entirely different dimension. It is not within our scope here to consider the political implications of those deaths, but we will analyse the extent to which that outcome was the product of the particular personalities and actions of the captains of the submarine and the liner in a later chapter.

These then were the events that took place between April 1912 and May 1915 into which Lord Mersey and his teams of assessors were asked to inquire. What were the issues that the inquiries examined as they affected the captains – and the issues that they might have inquired into but chose not to?

9

ISSUES

There are two ways we can approach the identification of the issues that faced the Mersey inquiries as they concerned the eight captains. One is simply to take the sets of questions each inquiry was given as its brief and select those that raised matters relevant to their actions. The second is to consider from first principles what the job of a captain entails and see where those responsibilities sit in relation to the events. The latter would seem to be the more profitable if we wish to pick up on matters that might have been looked at in the inquiries but which did not in the event surface to any significant extent. In the following chapters the answers that Mersey produced to the questions that he was asked can be set against the issues which seem, from this perspective, to be the ones that matter so far as our eight captains are concerned.

Any captain was only as good as the resources he had at his disposal. So what was he expected to do with those resources? The captain was expected to bring his ship safely from port to port in good time and to arrive with the ship, passengers and cargo intact. He was expected to do this without any cost to the company beyond what had been budgeted for and he was required to avoid any bad publicity reflecting on the company. He was required to ensure that the treatment of passengers was such that they would wish to travel with the company on future occasions and to deal with cargo agents in a way that encouraged them to continue to trust their cargo to his company. Should any problems arise he was expected to use his expertise to overcome them so as to minimise their impact. That meant doing what was required to complete the voyage as close to time and budget as he could manage. If the problem were such as to prevent completion of the voyage he should try to keep the costs of any salvage or insurance claims to the minimum. If the problem threatened the survival of the ship, or of any of those on it, he was expected to do all in his power to save the ship and preserve the lives of those on board. Should he come across another ship experiencing a problem, he was required to offer assistance, especially if life was endangered, but without, in the process, running unnecessary risks to his own ship or incurring unnecessary expenditure. In short, the captain was a company man always subject to the crucial proviso that no expectation that the company laid on him could justify the taking of unreasonable risks with the safety of passengers or crew. Some commentaries on incidents at sea treat the captain of a ship as if he were a free agent able to set his own agenda and treat company requirements as of little import. Shipping companies were in business to make money and the ship captain, tasked with pursuing the company's interests, was no different to any of their other employees, except in one respect.

The role of the ship master differed from that of other company employees as a result of the Merchant Shipping Act. The Act gave him particular responsibilities that were laid on him personally because of the post that he held; they did not accrue to the company for which he worked. He was required to maintain discipline aboard, both amongst passengers and crew and was empowered to take such action as was needed in order to do so. This might include restraining a crew member who refused to obey orders and detaining him if necessary to prevent violence. If a crime was committed on board he was entitled to arrest a suspect and hold that person in detention until they could be handed over to port authorities. When death occurred on board he was permitted to order burial at sea, especially where retaining the corpse on the ship might present a health hazard. In these types of matters the captain was effectively the agent of the state of registry of the ship rather than of the company. He needed to be able to ensure that one role did not conflict with the other, although, in general, the Act itself had been designed so as to support captains in their work and not make life more difficult for them.

Moving away from the purely contractual and legal aspects of the job, the one quality that was most expected of a captain was that of leadership. He may have the guidelines of company policy as to how the crew were to be managed and he may have the sanctions of law to back him up, but he needed the ability at the personal level to guide, to motivate and to inspire confidence. Each of the six merchant captains we are focusing on was selected by his company as someone whom they believed to have that quality. Smith and Turner were more than that; they were Commodores, in effect the role model for other captains in the fleet. Kendall and Lord had shown leadership qualities early in their careers and were young for their roles.

There is a difference, of course, between the role of the merchant ship captain and that of the man who leads a warship. Where, for the captain of a liner or cargo ship, the safety of the ship and those on board is his single most important consideration, for the captain of a warship it is the achievement of his war objectives. He may be expected to sacrifice the safety of the ship and all on board if necessary in the pursuit of those objectives. Military discipline gives him even greater powers to enforce his decisions on his crew than the terms of the Merchant Shipping Act. Herman Wouk's novel *The Caine Mutiny* and the film made of it with Humphrey Bogart explore the limits of a warship captain's power in the US Navy, when a captain shows signs of serious mental instability. The message that emerges is that only in the most extreme circumstances can the power of a captain be successfully challenged. The responsibility that goes with such unlimited power is the obligation to demonstrate leadership at a very high level and under life threatening conditions.

When a warship is operating as one unit amongst others in a fleet under the control of a senior officer, that officer will take the big decisions that govern how the fleet acts. For the captain of the lone-wolf submarine on patrol, there is no such relief; all of the decisions must be his and his alone. Submariners then, and still today, tend to be young men. When navies began the submarine arms of the services in the first years of the twentieth century, those who volunteered for officer roles tended to be young, ambitious and action orientated, rather like the first pilots who became the dare-devil air aces over the Western Front. The actions of the air fighters, however, were not under the same ethical scrutiny as those of the submariners, although that was not true of their colleagues who dropped bombs away from the war zones. But fighter pilots flew on brief sorties either alone or with just an observer. A submarine captain had to lead thirty to forty men on an isolated patrol lasting for a couple of weeks and, as we have already noted, not only was their work dangerous, their living conditions were appalling. There can be few roles that have tested the ability of one man to lead others to such a degree. The two young men who led out U-20 and U-28 passed that leadership test, by all reports, but that is not the only criterion against which they must be judged.

Bringing a ship safely from port to port meant setting the correct courses and speeds and this could only be achieved if the position of the ship were known to an acceptable degree of accuracy. Deciding what was the appropriate course and speed, even in the largest ship, usually remained in the hands of the captain and was rarely delegated to a more junior officer, even one with an Extra Master's Certificate. An officer of the watch could change either course or speed if required, especially if safety were involved, but would usually be under orders to notify the captain immediately. Navigational decisions were important in each of the sinkings with which we are concerned, speed in particular. Was the *Titanic* travelling too fast as she headed towards the ice that had been reported? Did the reversal of the *Empress's* engines to take speed off her make the risk of collision greater rather than less? Did the speeding up of the *Falaba* when the submarine was spotted excuse a more belligerent approach by the submarine? Was the 18 knots at which the *Lusitania* was travelling critical to the success of the attack?

The direction in which each of the ships was going was also crucial. The *Titanic* deviated slightly from the normal track, running just a couple of miles farther south. However that did not take her clear of the area in which the ice had been reported. Should Smith have taken the ship a greater distance south in order to avoid the area altogether? Having dropped off the pilot and moved out into the St. Lawrence, Kendall turned his ship to starboard onto her course out into the Atlantic. Was that change of course executed properly, or did the ship yaw about and confuse those on the bridge of the *Storstad* just as the fog closed in? Did the *Falaba's* turn away from the submarine, like her increase in speed, aggravate the situation? Was the *Lusitania's* steady course about 12 miles or so from land, without the zigzagging that the Admiralty had recommended, a fatal mistake?

Each of these questions is really asking the same thing. Did the captain in question prioritise correctly the risks with which he was presented and take the right actions? We know now, of course, that, in each case, one or more of those risks did materialise, with dreadful consequences, so we must identify the issues which relate to the way the captains tried to limit those consequences. Some of the actions that were needed to reduce the danger to life actually had to be taken well before the incidents occurred. How well equipped and prepared was each ship to face the emergency that developed? How much of that preparation was the responsibility of the company rather than of the captain? It would not make sense to hold Smith to account for the fact that the *Titanic* lacked sufficient lifeboats. We have already observed that the brief interlude between leaving the builders and starting her maiden voyage left little time to work up the *Titanic's* crew into coherent teams in the different departments. However, did Smith do all that might reasonably be expected to prepare the ship and the crew in the time available to deal with an emergency? The same question might also be asked of Kendall, Davies and Turner. Kendall had only been in charge of the *Empress* for a month but Davies and Turner had both had charge of their ships, or their sisters, for some time and the ships were in mid-life. On the other hand, both of them suffered from the difficulties of recruiting and retaining good quality, experienced seamen during wartime.

Preparing passengers to deal with an emergency was part of the captain's remit. Although the captain had the power to give passengers orders so as to preserve good order and could instruct them to undertake lifeboat drill, for example, it is clear that many captains found some conflict between the need to deal with safety matters and the desire to give passengers the sort of pleasant experience that would tempt them back on a future occasion. Too much emphasis on preparing for nasty things to happen might not be good for business. Associated with that was the reluctance of passengers to engage with safety issues. This was evident even on the *Falaba* and *Lusitania* when the threat of German attack was quite explicit. One passenger claimed to have been quite relaxed when he saw a German submarine only 100 yards from the *Falaba;* he thought that the Germans just wished to come aboard to inspect the papers. All of us have a remarkable capacity to deal with threats by ignoring them in the hope that they will go away.

Good preparation might be important, but the crucial factors when disaster has struck are organisation and discipline. The captains of each of the four ships that sank faced the same problem, albeit in very different circumstances. They each needed to ensure that the evacuation of their ship was carried out in such a way that as many people as possible were safely into lifeboats that were equipped and manned. That objective could only be achieved if the crew knew what they had to do, were in a position to do it and did not panic. Furthermore, the passengers needed clear instructions as to what they should do, with order maintained. The situation on *Titanic* differed from that on the other three ships because of the relatively long period of time between the collision and the ship sinking. It is possible as a result to ask more meaning-ful questions of Smith as to how well the 2 hours 40 minutes were used on *Titanic* compared to the 14 minutes on the *Empress* or the 18 minutes on the *Lusitania.* On *Falaba* the amount of time is shrouded in controversy, but that incident differed from the others in that, for most of the time that the evacu-ation was taking place, the ship was undamaged, it was daylight and there was no list or other factor complicating the process. Could any of the captains have done things differently, in a way that would have resulted in the death toll being lower?

It is not just the actions of each of captains, but their manner, their compo-sure and their assertiveness that might well have made a difference. In Chapter 2 we saw how the calm, clear voice of Captain Sealby when the *Republic* was sinking provided real leadership and was so reassuring to his passengers. Was there any indication of that kind of leadership being displayed by Smith, Kendall, Davies or Turner? Was that even a matter on which an inquiry such as the ones Mersey chaired could have commented upon? Would a judge in his seventies, his life spent in the court room, appreciate the impact that such qualities might have in the midst of the drama of a sinking ship?

While the general expectations on Stanley Lord and Thomas Andersen as captains of merchant ships were the same as for the other four, their roles in the incidents that we are examining were different so the issues concerning their actions are also different. Lord was unique amongst the eight captains in that neither he nor his ship was present when the incident took place. Exactly how far away the *Californian* was from the sinking *Titanic* is unlikely ever to be known with certainty, but we do know that rockets were seen from her bridge at around the time when they were being sent up by Fourth Officer Boxhall on *Titanic*. For Stanley Lord that was the start of something that was to have almost as great an impact on his life as on many of those who succeeded in the struggle to stay alive that was taking place just over the horizon. Leaving aside for the moment the question as to whether or not the rockets that Second Officer Stone and Apprentice Gibson saw on *Californian* were actually those fired by Boxhall, the issue for Mersey was whether they should have been treated as distress signals irrespective of which ship they had emerged from. If they should have been treated as distress signals, then why did Lord not take action? Was it a failure of communication or of will? If of communication then was Lord at fault in the way he led his officers such that communication was ineffective? If of will, does that raise an issue about Lord's duty to come to the assistance of another ship in difficulty? There would then be implications as to Lord's character.

Once the *Californian* had received the news of the sinking of *Titanic* Lord then moved his ship. Did he do everything possible to get to the scene as quickly as possible and did he do as much as he could have done once there? Given that the *Carpathia* had already brought all of the survivors from the lifeboats aboard, it may be that there was no further reason for the *Californian* to remain. There is one further issue that concerns Stanley Lord's actions and how they were dealt with by Mersey. It has often been alleged that Lord attempted to cover up the facts of what had taken place on his ship prior to the inquiry and gave evidence that was, at the very least, less than the full truth. While the opinions of many witnesses at the four inquiries have been challenged and the memories of others doubted, Lord is the only one who has subsequently been accused of deliberately attempting to mislead Mersey on matters of fact.

Chief Officer Toftnes called Thomas Andersen to the bridge of *Storstad* a bare minute or so before his ship rammed the side of the *Empress of Ireland*. Andersen had given instructions that he was to be called in the event of fog. Should Toftnes therefore have called him when the fog came down rather than when an emergency was developing? Was Andersen at fault for not ensuring that his instructions were sufficiently clear and for failing to impress on his officers the need for them to be obeyed to the letter? We touched on the question earlier as to the extent to which a captain should be held accountable for the failures of his subordinates and this is a case in point. There are echoes here of the sinking of the *Atlantic* in 1873 described in chapter 2. Her captain also was not called as he had he instructed but was subsequently found guilty of negligent handling of his ship.

Once the *Storstad*'s bows had disappeared into the side of the *Empress* Andersen's first consideration was for the safety of his own ship and crew. He did not immediately know the extent of the damage that *Storstad* had received and thought that she might sink. Once satisfied that she was not in immediate danger, did he do enough to minimise the impact of the collision on the *Empress?* Kendall maintained that Andersen should have put his engines full ahead in order to keep his ship embedded in the hole that it had created, thus reducing the flow of water into the *Empress*. Was that the right thing to do and, if so, did Andersen make the attempt with sufficient determination?

Once the ships had split apart, Andersen was again pre-occupied with ensuring that he could rely on the *Storstad* staying afloat. Had she been in real danger, fully loaded as she was, of slipping under, there would have been little point in bringing people from the *Empress* on board just to undergo a second evacuation. He satisfied himself that she was safe and then went back to use his own boats to bring survivors on board from the rapidly sinking *Empress*. One of them was Kendall who was clearly upset and confrontational towards Andersen, whom he blamed for the collision. This was the only face-to-face meeting between any of the captains. The overarching question for the sixth merchant ship captain was simply whether or not he did all in his power to save life.

Mersey had no interest in the competence of von Forstner or Schwieger either as seamen or as captains of their ships. He was concerned with one issue only and that was whether or not they had behaved in an acceptable manner in wartime. This issue could be sub-divided. Were the ships they attacked legitimate targets? Were the methods they used in their attacks justifiable under the international conventions then in force? The first question can actually be dealt with now because it did not surface in the inquiries either as a question asked of Mersey in his brief nor in the outcomes. It was simply assumed that *Falaba* and *Lusitania* were legitimate targets. We mentioned in Chapter 3 that the propaganda war on both sides during the First World War, as it related to the use of submarines, was carried out with shameless hypocrisy. Hypocrisy is only effective, however, if you have at least some semblance of cover for your own sins. For Britain to claim that either of these ships was not a proper target would have lacked any credibility given the activities of her own submarines in promoting the blockade against Germany and in attacking Turkish shipping in the Dardanelles.

The second question, as to the methods the two U-boat captains had used, was a valid one. Britain had not sunk without warning a large passenger liner carrying civilians and so, in the case of the *Lusitania*, could take the high moral ground. In the case of the *Falaba* the issue was more about the detail of the attack, because a warning had been given, and in most respects the sinking was not that different from the types of attacks being carried out by British submarines. The timing of Mersey's appointment is germane here. He was appointed for the second time as Wreck Commissioner on Monday 3 May 1915 when the *Lusitania* was in mid-Atlantic on her final voyage. On the Tuesday the Board of Trade announced that it required an inquiry to be conducted into the loss of the *Falaba*. Mersey was in the process of preparing for the opening of that inquiry when, late on the Friday, news came through of the sinking of the *Lusitania*. The *Falaba* inquiry held its hearings on 20, 21, 27 and 28 May. It is difficult to know how much the appalling stories of the suffering that those on the *Lusitania* had experienced, which were on every page of every newspaper throughout the run-up to the *Falaba* hearings, influenced Mersey in his approach to the earlier sinking. How much his view of the behaviour of von Forstner was influenced by what he now knew of the actions of Schwieger?

E. J. SMITH

The British inquiry into the loss of the *Titanic* lasted from 2 May 1912 to 3 July with sittings on 37 days during that period at two different venues. The report was read by Mersey at a final session on 30 July. By any standards it was a long and detailed inquiry at which a total of 97 witnesses gave evidence. The cast list was impressive, with the Attorney General Sir Rufus Isaacs appearing for the Board of Trade and Butler Aspinall KC for the government. We have already mentioned the Marconi connections of the former and the fact that his client, the Board of Trade, was the sponsoring department of government for the inquiry. Butler Aspinall was to be almost as much of a fixture in these inquiries as Mersey himself, appearing for Canadian Pacific in the *Empress* inquiry, for Elder Dempster in the *Falaba* inquiry and for Cunard in the *Lusitania* one.

We touched on the possible impact on the *Falaba* inquiry of the timing of the sinking of *Lusitania*. In the case of the *Titanic* we need to be aware of the timing of the American Senate hearings as they preceded the British inquiry and attracted considerable publicity on both sides of the Atlantic. The Senate Sub-Committee began to hear witnesses on Friday 19 April, just four days after the tragedy and completed its sessions on Saturday 25 May. Its final report was issued just three days later on 28 May. There was, therefore, quite a long period of overlap as both inquiries heard testimony. Because almost all of the witnesses were in America at the start of the process, the pattern was almost always that those who testified at both appeared first in front of the Senators. Not all who appeared at one testified at the other; the American inquiry had much more evidence from passengers, for example, than Mersey heard. It is impossible to gauge the extent to which the evidence given at the sessions in New York exerted an influence on any of those taking part in the ones in London. It may be that Mersey himself or the lawyers representing the different

1 Viscount Mersey.

2 (Below left) Captain Stanley Lord of the *Californian*.

3 (Below) Captain E.J. Smith of the *Titanic*.

4 The *Titanic* at Queenstown.

5 A depiction of the sinking of the *Titanic* in the *London Illustrated News*.

6 The *Californian* photographed from the *Carpathia* on 15 April 1912. (Courtesy of The National Archives at New York City)

7 Captain A.H. Rostron and under officers of the *Carpathia*, 29 May 1912. (Library of Congress)

8 (Top) The *Empress of Ireland*.

9 (Above) The *Storstad* with her damaged bow.

10 Captain Henry Kendall of the *Empress of Ireland*.

11 Captain Thomas
Andersen of the *Storstad*.
(Courtesy of the artist,
John Andert)

12 Victims of the sinking of the *Empress of Ireland*. (Library of Congress)

13 (Top) Captain Kendall giving evidence to the *Empress* inquiry.

14 The *Falaba*.

15 (Below left) Kapitanleutnant Walther Schwieger of U-20.

16 (Below) Captain Will Turner of the *Lusitania*.

17 The *Lusitania* passing the Old Head of Kinsale. (Courtesy of the Peabody Essex Museum)

18 An artist's depiction of the moment the second torpedo hit the *Lusitania*. (Library of Congress)

19 The body of a victim of the sinking of the *Lusitania* is unloaded from the *New York*. (Library of Congress)

20 An anniversary parade to mourn the sinking of the *Lusitania* marches towards Marble Arch bearing a model of the stricken vessel.

interests were prompted by what they knew of the proceedings in America to ask some additional questions. Bruce Ismay, of White Star, amongst others, was questioned by the Attorney General on differences between his answer to a question in New York and his answer to the same question in London. In one case he had quoted Chief Engineer Bell as saying that he 'thought' the pumps would cope with the inflow of water while in the other he had used the word 'hoped'. Rufus Isaacs thought that the difference might have been significant; Ismay blamed it on his unreliable memory. When we come to consider how the *Californian* incident was dealt with, however, the overlap might be thought to have impinged on more than quibbles about words.

The American and British press not only reported the proceedings of the two inquiries, they also commented on their very different styles and approaches. To the American press the Senate hearings were purposeful, direct and effective, with nobody given any favour. Their description of the British inquiry, however, from the very beginning, was of a carefully staged white-wash in which the people really to blame were being given an easy ride. Senator Smith was perceived as a persistent terrier, chasing down the culprits who had caused the deaths of 1500 people. Mersey, on the other hand, was regarded as a rather curmudgeonly old duffer, more concerned with maintaining proper protocol than finding any real answers. There were also echoes of that type of thinking in some the British press as well, including the *Spectator*, but most British newspapers regarded the American hearings as a bizarre form of theatre, lacking in the dignity that such a solemn undertaking warranted. There was confidence that the more measured judicial approach of the British inquiry would produce a better considered outcome. The antipathy towards the American inquiry was heightened by the openly anti-British tone of much of what was emerging in New York. No-one was in any doubt that, so far as the Senators were concerned, all responsibility for the disaster resided firmly on the eastern side of the Atlantic.

Senator Smith launched his report with a barnstorming speech blaming, in the most extravagant language, Captain Smith for speeding into an iceberg, the Board of Trade for not requiring sufficient lifeboats to be carried and Captain Lord for not bothering to save those who died. Any other fault lay entirely with White Star. The British press mostly responded with an anti-American rant which, if it did not include the word hillbilly, it was certainly implied. Perhaps not surprisingly, over the years, respect has grown for what that the Senate Sub-Committee achieved. People have seen through the bluster to a process that, although rushed, was a genuine seeking after truth. Senator Smith may have shown some lack of nautical understanding, but he was direct and focused and he did not display any softness towards big business or government agencies. To recognise the value of the work of the inquiry in New York, however, is not to endorse its findings uncritically.

The written report of the Senate Sub-Committee (as against the Chairman's speech launching it) implied criticism of the speed at which *Titanic* was travelling when the accident happened but did not make criticism of Smith explicit and did not include any specific recommendations about the speed of ships in the vicinity of ice. Mersey went into this in rather greater detail and included amongst his witnesses other captains with experience of this route in the North Atlantic. They were asked to describe their normal practice when close to ice. The following is an extract from the evidence of Captain Edwin G Cannons of the Atlantic Transport Company.

The Attorney General: There is only one further question I want to put to you. When you do sight an iceberg do you reduce your speed or do you keep your speed?
– I keep my speed.
What is the speed of the vessel?
– Sixteen knots.
You keep your speed – that, of course, is, I suppose, in the day or it might be at night?
– Both day and night.
The question I put to you, and you have answered, is when you have sighted an iceberg?
–Yes.
Then you have time, I suppose, from what you said, to get clear of the iceberg going at the speed at which your vessel then is?
– I have never had any difficulty to clear when I have met ice ahead.
Does that mean that you see the ice some distance ahead?
–Yes.
How far as a rule?
– Well, I have seen it over three miles and at less distances.
Are you speaking of the day or night?
– At night.
Do you mean you would see it further in the daytime?
–Yes, decidedly, in clear weather.
At night you have seen it at three miles and sometimes less?
–Yes.
And supposing that your look-out is properly kept and that the night is clear is there any difficulty in your sighting an iceberg at sufficient distance to enable you to steer clear of it?

– None whatever.

And supposing you received reports of icebergs in a latitude and longitude which you would expect to be crossing during the night would you take any precaution as regards speed?

– I should maintain my speed and keep an exceptionally sharp look-out until such time as I either had the ice-blink or some sight of ice ahead or in the track of the vessel.

This evidence was broadly consistent with those of the other captains although there were differences in terms of the numbers and positions of lookouts. Cannons was also asked about the visibility of ice in different sea states, most particularly when there was a calm sea with no swell, something very rarely seen in the North Atlantic. In his view this would make no difference – ice would still be visible from a distance that would permit easy avoidance even at night. He did admit never to having seen 'black' ice, that is a berg that had recently overturned. It is also worth emphasising that 'maintain speed' for Cannons meant keeping to 16 knots, not the 22 knots at which *Titanic* was travelling.

Second Officer Lightoller, the senior surviving *Titanic* officer, had the watch prior to Murdoch's on the evening of 14 April, which ended at 2200. At about 2100 Smith joined him on the bridge and they had a conversation about the ship, the weather and the ice warnings. In light of Cannon's evidence it is worth recalling what Lightoller remembered of that conversation. On the subject of the weather they agreed that the night was so clear that no additional precautions were necessary but that if any problem should arise (if it became hazy, for example) Smith was to be called immediately. Lightoller was also asked if he spoke to Smith about the sea being so calm:

The Solicitor-General: Had not you better tell us as accurately as you can what passed between him and you when he came on the bridge at five minutes to nine?

– I will.

If you please.

– At five minutes to nine, when the Commander came on the bridge (I will give it to you as near as I remember) he remarked that it was cold, and as far as I remember I said, 'Yes, it is very cold, Sir. In fact,' I said, 'it is only one degree above freezing. I have sent word down to the carpenter and rung up the engine room and told them that it is freezing or will be during the night.' We then commenced to speak about the wind. He said, 'There is not much wind.' I said, 'No, it is a flat calm as a matter of fact.' He repeated it;

he said, 'A flat calm.' I said, 'Yes, quite flat, there is no wind.' I said something about it was rather a pity the breeze had not kept up whilst we were going through the ice region. Of course, my reason was obvious; he knew I meant the water ripples breaking on the base of the berg.

You said it was a pity there was not a breeze?

– Yes, I said, 'It is a pity there is not a breeze,' and we went on to discuss the weather. He was then getting his eyesight, you know, and he said, 'Yes, it seems quite clear,' and I said, 'Yes, it is perfectly clear.' It was a beautiful night, there was not a cloud in the sky. The sea was apparently smooth, and there was no wind, but at that time you could see the stars rising and setting with absolute distinctness. And also…

Then you both realised at the time, did you, that since it was a flat calm it would be more difficult to see the ice?

– As far as the base of the berg was concerned, yes, it would be more difficult; naturally you would not see the water breaking on it if there were no wind; and so you would not have that to look for.

Also included in the conversation was a reference to 'blue' ice. Ice that has no frost crystals on it because it has recently been immersed in water is sometimes referred to as blue and sometimes as black ice. Cannons, of course, had testified that he had never encountered this phenomenon although he had spent many years on the North Atlantic.

Lightoller: We then discussed the indications of ice. I remember saying, 'In any case there will be a certain amount of reflected lights from the bergs.' He said, 'Oh, yes, there will be a certain amount of reflected light.' I said, or he said; blue was said between us – that even though the blue side of the berg was towards us, probably the outline, the white outline would give us sufficient warning, that we should be able to see it at a good distance, and, as far as we could see, we should be able to see it. Of course it was just with regard to that possibility of the blue side being towards us, and that if it did happen to be turned with the purely blue side towards us, there would still be the white outline.

So just two and a half hours before the collision with the berg, Smith discussed with one of his senior officers the peculiar effects of the exceptional calmness of the sea that night on the visibility of icebergs and the possibility that 'blue' ice might be more difficult to see. Lightoller confirmed, however, that the only specific mention of speed in the conversation was Smith saying that were the visibility conditions to change it would be necessary to slow the ship. We do not know whether or not the iceberg that the ship struck was one that had recently inverted and was showing blue ice. The chances of that being the case are low, but we do know from the timings given at the inquiry that it was only seen at less than a thousand yards distant. The expectations of other captains giving evidence was that, even at night under the conditions existing on 14 April, a berg should have been seen at well over a mile, possibly two and, therefore, should have been easily avoidable. There were lookouts both in the crow's nest and the bridge and they had been warned to be especially vigilant. It seems unlikely that the reason for the late sighting of the berg was negligence on their part.

Captain Rostron of *Carpathia* provided another insight into this question when he was asked about bringing his own ship past icebergs on the way to rescue the survivors. He reported seeing about six bergs on the journey. All of them, except the last, were spotted at a distance of one to two miles. The last was seen less than half a mile away and he had to make an emergency swerve to avoid it. He was questioned as to why he had seen this berg so late when he had had ample warning of the earlier ones. This is the relevant passage from his evidence.

The Commissioner: You cannot account to me for your seeing some of these bergs a couple of miles away, but not seeing this particular one till it was about a quarter of a mile away?
– No.
You cannot account for it?
– No.
It happened to yourself?
– I cannot account for it at all.
It did happen to yourself?
–Yes, it did happen.
The Attorney-General: That would seem to indicate a considerable risk in going through the ice region, does it not?
–Yes.
The Commissioner: Is that a common experience, that when you are amongst icebergs you will detect one two or three miles away and another not till it is within a quarter of a mile? Is that within your experience?
– No, I do not think it is common experience. I think it is rather uncommon, as a matter of fact.
The Attorney-General: Rather uncommon?
– I think so.
I want to understand this a little more if we can. If I correctly followed you, you said you only saw this one at about a quarter of a mile distance from

you by the streak of a star upon it?

– No, the first one I saw was about one and a half to two miles away; that was the one we saw at about a quarter to three with the streak of the star. That was the first one we picked up; it was a large one.

That one we understand, but this last one that you saw about 4 o'clock when you were getting ready to pick up the boat on the port side, was there anything at all special about the colour of that iceberg?

– No, but I suppose it must have been because of the shadow or something of that kind that we could not make it out before. I cannot account for it.

Rostron clearly believed, as he made clear in answers to subsequent questions, that the failure of the men on *Carpathia* to spot that particular berg was because of some characteristic of its shape that prevented starlight being reflected. Sides that fell precipitously or which had a concave shape, he felt might have made the berg less visible than others. It should be stressed that the berg he saw so late was quite a low one and therefore not the one with which *Titanic* had collided earlier. Rostron had clearly found the experience quite disturbing as it was so abnormal. In his evidence to the British inquiry, Second Officer Lightoller was quite sure that the berg with which *Titanic* collided was one that had recently capsized and did not, therefore, reflect starlight in the usual way. He described that factor, combined with the complete absence of swell and the fact that there was no moon as a combination of circumstances that would only arise once in a hundred years.

Mersey's conclusions on the basis of this evidence were possibly amongst the most sensible of the opinions he arrived at in all four inquiries. This is what he said in his report.

Why, then, did the Master persevere in his course and maintain his speed? The answer is to be found in the evidence. It was shown that for many years past, indeed, for a quarter of a century or more, the practice of liners using this track when in the vicinity of ice at night had been in clear weather to keep the course, to maintain the speed and to trust to a sharp look-out to enable them to avoid the danger. This practice, it was said, had been justified by experience, no casualties having resulted from it. I accept the evidence as to the practice and as to the immunity from casualties which is said to have accompanied it. But the event has proved the practice to be bad. Its root is probably to be found in competition and in the desire of the public for quick passages rather than in the judgment of navigators. But unfortunately experience appeared to justify it. In these circumstances I am not able to blame *Captain Smith*. He had not the experience which his own misfortune has afforded to those whom he has left behind, and he was doing only that which other skilled men would have done in the same position. It was suggested at the bar that he was yielding to influences which ought not to have affected him; that the presence of Mr. Ismay on board and the knowledge which he perhaps had of a conversation between Mr. Ismay and the Chief Engineer at Queenstown about the speed of the ship and the consumption of coal probably induced him to neglect precautions which he would otherwise have taken. But I do not believe this. The evidence shows that he was not trying to make any record passage or indeed any exceptionally quick passage. He was not trying to please anybody, but was exercising his own discretion in the way he thought best. He made a mistake, a very grievous mistake, but one in which, in face of the practice and of past experience, negligence cannot be said to have had any part; and in the absence of negligence it is, in my opinion, impossible to fix Captain Smith with blame. It is, however, to be hoped that the last has been heard of the practice and that for the future it will be abandoned for what we now know to be more prudent and wiser measures. What was a mistake in the case of the *Titanic* would without doubt be negligence in any similar case in the future.

When we considered peacetime risks in Chapter 2 and discussed the different types of risk, we identified collision with icebergs as one of those with very serious potential consequences but very low probability of occurrence. That type of risk we thought presents problems because there would be insufficient experience to establish just what type of avoidance measure would be needed. That, in effect, is what Mersey acknowledged and so he decided that Smith had not been negligent. There was one aspect, however, that he omitted to mention. He spoke of how it was usual practice to maintain normal speed in the vicinity of ice. He did not draw attention to the fact that, over the previous decade or so, 'normal' speed for the large liners on the North Atlantic route had gradually risen from around 16 knots to 22 or even 25 knots. *Titanic* was not the fastest, but she was amongst that group of very fast liners. Had Smith slowed *Titanic* to what had recently been 'normal' speed of 16 knots he not only would have missed that particular berg (it would have drifted south of his track by the time he reached it), he would also have been judged by his officers to have been unnecessarily cautious. Captain Rostron of the *Carpathia* was praised by Mersey for taking the risk of keeping his speed up to his maximum of 16 knots as he approached the ice field in the race to save the *Titanic* survivors. The words 'full speed' or 'keeping up speed' did not refer to an absolute value.

Mersey not only exonerated Smith as to *Titanic*'s speed, he also exonerated the management of White Star. There was never anything but the flimsiest hearsay evidence to suggest that the Chairman of White Star, Bruce Ismay, had pressurised Smith into maintaining a higher speed than he otherwise would have done. It makes perfect sense that Smith, as Mersey suggested, was simply sticking to normal practice by maintaining speed despite the ice warnings. His colleagues in other similar ships were doing exactly the same thing in identical circumstances. He had no need of a Chairman whispering in his ear to persuade him to do so. And, as we noted earlier, the captain is the supreme authority on a ship whether the Chairman of the Line is there or not. Smith was the archetypal company captain in some respects, but in matters of seamanship he appears to have been his own man.

It took about 20 minutes to half an hour after the collision to establish how seriously *Titanic* was damaged. There is relatively little information about what was happening on the bridge during that time because hardly anyone present survived. We know that various people, including the carpenter and the Chief Engineer, were reporting back the extent of the damage and it seems that shortly after midnight Smith knew that the ship would inevitably sink and that her time afloat was limited to about two hours. We will not detail the events of those two hours –many other people have already done so – but focus on the one man who had the ultimate responsibility of ensuring that the maximum number possible of those on board stayed alive.

The order to begin readying the lifeboats was given at 0005 and the first distress call, with Boxhall's incorrect position, was sent at 0015. Taking this latter point first, it is only since Dr Robert Ballard discovered the wreck of *Titanic* in 1985 that we have had conclusive evidence of the mistake that Boxhall made. During both the American and British inquiries there was evidence given that cast some doubt on the the accuracy of his calculation but, in both cases, it was accepted as gospel. Mersey, in particular, seemed reluctant to entertain any doubt about a position computed by a White Star officer holding an Extra Master's Certificate. That being the case, he was in no position to ponder as to whether Smith had been sufficiently careful in using a quick calculation by one officer as the sole basis for the position given on the distress calls. The history of the ship's navigation that evening was that, at about 1930, Lightoller took some stellar sights with his sextant. He gave the results to Boxhall who worked out the position and noted it in the chart room. At about 2200 the captain asked about the position and Boxhall gave him the piece of paper on which he had written the 1930 calculation. Smith himself then marked it on the chart. It was that position that Boxhall used later at about 0010 to calculate the position sent out by the Senior Telegraphist in the first CQD message. Boxhall testified that, having worked it out, he showed it to the captain and then took it to the wireless room himself. The surviving Junior Telegraphist, Bride, however, testified that Phillips was given it by Captain Smith. Where exactly in the chain of events from the taking of the stellar observations by Lightoller to the transmission by Phillips the mistake occurred is unknown and forever will remain so. In retrospect it might have been prudent for someone to have checked Boxhall's figures, but in the event the error probably did not materially alter the outcome.

Smith's final task, on what he must have realised was likely to be the last night of his life, was to manage the evacuation of the sinking ship in the knowledge that there was lifeboat accommodation for fewer than half of those on board. No one from what might be described as the senior management team on the ship survived and we are therefore very reliant on the evidence of the officers Lightoller, Pitman, Boxhall and Lowe, who did. While many other crew members were involved in getting people off the ship and in seeking help, it is the evidence of these men that provides the most valuable insight into how the process was organised. The inquiry transcripts contain such a wide range of evidence, much of it contradictory, from so many different people that, like the Bible, one can always find supporting quotes for almost any proposition. It seems reasonable, therefore, in considering the role of Captain Smith during the last two hours of his life and the life of his ship, to focus principally on the evidence of his senior surviving officers, evidence that shows what they were thinking, seeing and doing during that time.

Second Officer Lightholler began his posting to *Titanic* as First Officer, but a last minute change of crew, the insertion of Wilde as Chief Officer, had moved him down to Second. He had held an Extra Master's Certificate since 1902 and had been with White Star for over twelve years. He had had an adventurous youth experiencing shipwrecks, fires, gold mining, riding North American trains as a hobo and working as a cowboy before settling down as a career merchant navy officer. It was a pattern that repeated itself throughout his life. During an eventful period as an RN officer in the First World War he was awarded a DSC and Bar. More peaceful times between the wars were spent mostly ashore running guesthouses and farming chickens. In May 1940, at the age of 66, he was asked to hand his motor yacht over to the navy for use at Dunkirk. He refused and took the boat across himself with his son and one of his son's friends. They brought more than 120 troops back to Ramsgate under continuous threat from German aircraft. Lightoller spent the remainder of the war helping with the navy's small boats. He died in 1952.

Charles Lightoller is frequently described as the hero of the *Titanic*. He certainly seems to have been one of the most clear headed and purposeful crew members that night and it was his part that the male lead, Kenneth Moore, played in the film *A Night to Remember*. He impressed as a witness in both inquiries giving relatively straightforward and consistent answers over long periods in the witness box. He was called on three separate occasions by Mersey. He has been accused of being somewhat defensive of his senior officers and his employers, whether out of loyalty or conviction it is difficult to be sure. It may be that he felt that it was not his place to be critical of them; it may also be that those questioning him did not make sufficient attempts to elucidate that criticism. While it is worth bearing that concern in mind, it does not devalue the detailed recall of events that he provided. Lightoller and his wife were clearly deeply affected by the tragedy and both were present at all 37 sessions of the British inquiry

We have already seen something of his testimony about the conversation he had with the captain prior to the collision. He had gone off watch and retired to bed when the collision happened. He went on deck to see what had happened, could see nothing unusual, spoke to Third Officer Pitman who knew no more than he did, saw that there appeared to be no alarm on the bridge and returned to his cabin. He was lying down for between 20 and 30 minutes, he reckoned, when he was awoken by Boxhall. At this point Smith gave the orders to uncover the lifeboats, swing them out and prepare to load them with women and children. Lightoller detailed the available crew members to begin undoing the covers on the lifeboats on both sides, using hand signals to do so because of the deafening noise from the escaping steam. Then, at Wilde's request, he took charge of the boats on the portside (even numbered) beginning with number 4. When boat 4 had been prepared he had it lowered to A-Deck in order to fill it with passengers from there. When he discovered that the closed windows of the promenade on A-Deck prevented that being done he ordered that the passengers be told to come back up to the boat deck, left boat 4 and got boat 6 ready to load from the boat deck. He was quizzed about the time taken up to that point, partly in order to establish how soon he noticed that the ship was down by the head. This is the relevant extract from his evidence.

The Commissioner: At what point of these events did you notice that the ship had begun to be down by the head or to have a list?
– It was when I was at No. 6 boat, My Lord.
As I understand, that would be about half-an-hour after you had come on deck?
– I think it is longer than that.
Well, let us say three quarters of an hour?
–Yes, perhaps three quarters of an hour.
You had been half-an-hour in your bunk before you came on deck at all?

– I said approximately half-an-hour.

So this would be an hour or an hour and a quarter after the collision. And was it then for the first time you noticed the vessel had a list?

– At whatever time that was, My Lord. However, it works out it was about when I was at boat No. 6.

The Solicitor-General: What you had been doing in the interval was, you had been getting No. 4 unstripped; you had been getting her swung out, her falls cleared and let down as far as the A deck, and there you had ascertained that it was not possible to open the windows and get the people through?

– Not immediately, and therefore rather than delay I did not go on with it.

The questions in this part of the evidence were designed to try to establish the timetable of events on board the ship and not to cast doubt on the way that the process was managed. It did not seem to strike anyone during Lightoller's evidence that the time taken to perform the various operations he described was longer than it might have been. Nor was any criticism implied regarding the way Lightoller went about them. One wonders what the reaction from Mersey might have been had the *Titanic* been the fourth of his quartet of inquiries rather than the first. The crews of *Empress, Falaba* and *Lusitania* each had 20 minutes or less to evacuate their ships. None of them fully succeeded, but each managed to launch some of the lifeboats and, in the case of the *Falaba* an attempt was made to lower all of them. At the *Empress of Ireland* inquiry the report of a Board of Trade inspection conducted on the liner in Liverpool was submitted in evidence and it included a report on an exercise in getting out the lifeboats. The following is an extract:

As soon as the muster was over the bugle was sounded and all hands repaired to the boat deck when the order 'out all boats' was given. All the boats under davits, sixteen in number, were at once swung out. Two sailors were in each and they shipped the thole-pins, passed the ends of the painters out and shipped the rudders, the rest of the boats' crews setting up the guys and clearing away the falls. From the time the order was given to the time the boats were ready for lowering about four minutes had elapsed.

Those on *Lusitania* and some of those on the *Falaba* had been uncovered and swung out before the emergency arose, but, even so, the timetable followed on *Titanic* seems remarkably slow. Lightoller was asked about this at the American inquiry and his response was that 'there was no urgency'. Later in his evidence he was asked at the British inquiry about the time taken to lower the boats and this was his response:

Mr. Lewis: I want to know the general methods adopted by the company as far as this Witness knows. (To the witness.) With regard to particular life-boats, I understood you to say in your evidence that it took about an hour and a half to two hours to prepare and lower the boats upon which you were engaged, is that so?

The Commissioner: Yes, he has said it, and I know it, you know.

Mr. Lewis: Do you consider that under the circumstances of the case, when the ship was sinking rapidly, that that was a reasonable time to take?

−Yes.

What is the object of a boat list and boat drill?

− It is rather obvious; it is to teach the men to know their stations.

In the event of danger is not the object to be prepared to lower the boats simultaneously?

− Not necessarily.

If, for instance, the accident was even worse, if it is possible to conceive, and you had knowledge that the ship was to sink in an hour, obviously it would be desirable to get the boats down speedily, would it not?

−Yes.

Is not the object of having boat stations in order that you may station men at the different boats to lower them at once if necessary?

− No.

What is the object of having firemen and stewards on the boat list?

− To know their stations.

Is it not a fact that you ran a risk by proceeding from boat to boat to lower those boats of having several boats left?

− They were not left.

Is it not the fact that you did have boats left, collapsible boats or rafts that you could not get off in time?

− No.

The Commissioner: Now what is the real object of your questions. They are not helping me at all. Is your real object that you think more men belonging to your Union ought to be employed? These questions do not assist me one bit.

Finally, on this topic, Lightoller was asked:

You considered that everything was done that was reasonable with regard to the launching of the boats?

−Yes.

These questions were asked by one of the lawyers representing the Seamen's Union and Mersey here is seen at his peremptory worst, dismissing them as self serving when he should have been considering the issue seriously.

We need to take stock here of the picture that Lightoller has painted and then consider how Mersey dealt with that picture in his report. As Second Officer Lightoller apparently had no designated emergency role but did as he was detailed to do on the night by the Chief Officer. He assigned men to work on the boats irrespective of their actual stations, if indeed they knew them. He did not know which deck lifeboats were filled from, sending number 4 down to the Promenade deck and only then finding that it could not be loaded from there and recalling the passengers. There was another major factor that became clear from some of the evidence given by the Second Officer. He thought that lifeboats should only have a small number of passengers in them when they were lowered and should receive the remainder of their quota once they were in the water because they would not be strong enough to carry the weight of a full load going down on the falls. He told how he had despatched the Boatswain to open the forward gangway doors low down on the ship in order for passengers to go down ladders into the boats after they had been launched. He never saw the man again and did not know whether or not the doors had been opened. If they had been the large additional openings low down would almost certainly have shortened the life of the ship. No passengers were ever instructed (so far as we know) to go down below to the gangway doors to embark on the lifeboats.

Lightoller also insisted that it was correct to lower the boats sequentially rather than simultaneously and this clearly was the order that he and Murdoch on the starboard side had been given. We really need to remind ourselves that this was a highly competent seaman with over twenty years experience at sea but one who clearly had little training in emergency procedures on this ship or any other. The idea that passengers might climb down ladders from the gangway doors into the floating lifeboats is quite bizarre even on a night as calm as 14/15 April 1912.

The idea that it might not be safe to lower a lifeboat with its full complement of 65 people was not just Lightoller's. Fifth Officer Lowe testified that the same approach was being adopted for a while on the starboard side under Murdoch's supervision until eventually the later lifeboats were filled. He also thought that there was a plan to add more people into the boats through the gangway doors and had heard that someone had been sent down to open them. He knew nothing of any passengers being directed to leave the ship by that means. Third Officer Pitman was sent away in a boat by Murdoch quite early in the evacuation as the officer to take charge of the lifeboats so he had relatively little to offer about events on the ship. He was told by Murdoch to keep close to the ship and to stay within reach of the aft gangways although he said that he was not told why. When asked he expressed the view that the filling of lifeboats by ladders from the gangways was not a practical proposition.

So what was Smith's role in this process? The only mention of the captain was a reference by Lightoller to having heard Smith call out to the boats through a megaphone. This is what he recalled.

> *The Solicitor-General:* After these boats had been launched and left the side of the ship, did you hear any orders or call given to any of them?
> —Yes.
> By whom?
> — By the Commander.
> Through the megaphone?
> —Yes.
> Did that happen more than once?
> — More than once, yes.
> What was the order?
> —To come back.
> Was he hailing any particular boats?
> — No. I heard the Commander two or three times hail through the megaphone to bring the boats alongside, and I presumed he was alluding to the gangway doors, giving orders to the boats to go to the gangway doors.
> *The Commissioner:* When was this?
> — During the time I was launching the boats on the port side, I could not give you any definite time.
> *The Solicitor-General:* You heard the orders given and you heard the orders repeated; could you gather at the time whether they were being obeyed or not?
> — No.
> You did not know one way or the other?
> — I did not know anything at all about it.

Lightoller indicated that the last interaction that he himself had with Smith was when he was at the early stages of getting the port side boats organised. He wanted confirmation that he was to begin loading and lowering them.

> *The Solicitor-General:* What was the order?
> — After I had swung out No. 4 boat I asked the Chief Officer should we put the women and children in, and he said 'No.' I left the men to go ahead

with their work and found the Commander, or I met him and I asked him should we put the women and children in, and the Commander said 'Yes, put the women and children in and lower away.' That was the last order I received on the ship.

So far as can be estimated, this conversation took place between 0030 and 0045. The last order that the Second Officer received from any of his seniors was at least an hour and a half before the ship sank.

After Boxhall had helped to estimate the extent of the damage he went to help on the boat deck. He appeared to be 'floating', helping out as he was needed. At some stage after the order to get the boats prepared he spoke to Smith and asked him if the situation was serious. Smith told him that he had been advised that the ship would only stay afloat for an hour or an hour and a half. Boxhall assumed that this advice had come from the ship's designer, Thomas Andrews. He went back onto the bridge and began firing off the distress rockets, having cleared that with the captain. He, Smith and others on the bridge watched the lights of a ship which he judged to approach to within about 5 miles and then to turn and head away. He was asked to try to contact her by Morse lamp which he did without detecting any reply. Boxhall was certain that the ship was within signalling range and the captain appeared to be of the same opinion. Those were the only interactions that he reported with Smith and he did not include in his evidence any other steps taken by the captain.

The other person who reported significant interaction with Smith during this time was Junior Telegraphist Harold Bride, Phillips having been lost. In his testimony he mentioned that Smith had come to the wireless room to give the order to send the distress calls and give the position. Bride had taken responses to the calls for help to Smith on a few occasions and he reported that on one of those the captain had been on the boat deck supervising the lowering of boats on the starboard side, that is the side for which First Officer Murdoch was responsible. At a late stage the captain came back to the wireless room to tell the two operators to leave and save themselves. That was the last time Bride saw him.

What then did Mersey make of this evidence as to the organisation of the evacuation? Too much and too little would appear to be the answer. In his comments he deplored the fact that so many boats went away with less than their full complement, in some cases by a very large margin. The following is an extract from the report of the inquiry.

Many people thought that the risk in the ship was less than the risk in the boats. This explanation is supported by the evidence of Captain Rostron, of the *Carpathia*. He says that after those who were saved got on board his ship, he was told by some of them that when the boats first left the *Titanic* the people 'really would not be put in the boats; they did not want to go in.' There was a large body of evidence from the *Titanic* to the same effect, and I have no doubt that many people, particularly women, refused to leave the deck for the boats. At one time the Master appears to have had the intention of putting the people into the boats from the gangway doors in the side of the ship. This was possibly with a view to allay the fears of the passengers, for from these doors the water could be reached by means of ladders, and the lowering of some of the earlier boats when only partly filled may be accounted for in this way. There is no doubt that the Master did order some of the partly filled boats to row to a position under one of the doors with the object of taking in passengers at that point. It appears, however, that these doors were never opened. Another explanation is that some women refused to leave their husbands. It is said further that the officers engaged in putting the people into the boats feared that the boats might buckle if they were filled; but this proved to be an unfounded apprehension, for one or more boats were completely filled and then successfully lowered to the water.

Mersey jumped to the conclusion that Smith had been responsible for the idea that passengers should join lifeboats already in the water from the gangways and that he had ordered lifeboats to come back to the gangways for that purpose. The only evidence for that was Lightoller's supposition as to the reason for Smith calling lifeboats back towards the ship. In this, Mersey was making too much from too little.

The inquiry evidence presented two different explanations for lifeboats leaving half full or even less. One was the reluctance of passengers to get into the boats. The other was the extraordinary belief amongst at least some of the officers (which may or may not have been shared by Smith) that it was unsafe to lower lifeboats with a full load of passengers. Which of these reasons was the more significant? If the officers loading the boats were of this view, how hard did they try to persuade passengers to get into the boats on the boatdeck? Mersey was clearly perplexed that so many lifeboats went away with fewer on board than should have been the case and he suggested that perhaps they should have been held longer before lowering, or that men should have taken the place of women reluctant to leave husbands, or that the gangway doors should have been used to fill the boats. If this is criticism it is mild indeed and not directed at anyone in particular. So far as the conduct of the officers was concerned he said that: 'The officers did their work very well without any thought for themselves.' He added that: 'The discipline among passengers and crew during the lowering of the boats was good, but the organisation should have been better, and if it had been it is possible that more lives would have been saved.'

Coming from someone with a reputation for rushing to judgment, this is a considered, cautious understatement. So were the recommendations that he made based on these conclusions, which were as follows:

Manning the Boats and Boat Drills

13. That in cases where the deck hands are not sufficient to man the boats enough other members of the crew should be men trained in boat work to make up the deficiency. These men should be required to pass a test in boat work.

14. That in view of the necessity of having on board men trained in boat work, steps should be taken to encourage the training of boys for the Merchant Service.

15. That the operation of Section 115 and Section 134 (a) of the Merchant Shipping Act, 1894, should be examined, with a view to amending the same so as to secure greater continuity of service than hitherto.

16. That the men who are to man the boats should have more frequent drills than hitherto. That in all ships a boat drill, a fire drill and a watertight door drill should be held as soon as possible after leaving the original port of departure and at convenient intervals of not less than once a week during the voyage. Such drills to be recorded in the official log.

17. That the Board of Trade should be satisfied in each case before the ship leaves port that a scheme has been devised and communicated to each officer of the ship for securing an efficient working of the boats.

The last recommendation is the only one with any bearing on the training of officers in how to deal with emergencies. The remainder deal with the role of the 'men'. In 1912 any reference to 'men' automatically excluded the officers. It was not the 'men' who failed the passengers on *Titanic;* it was the lack of understanding of the officers of the nature of the emergency that they were dealing with and their lack of skill in the processes involved in evacuating their ship. How much of that inadequacy on the part of the officers should have been laid at the door of the ship owners and how much was the responsibility of Smith?

When we come to the ship owners, we are obliged to consider industry norms as we did with speed. What was normal industry practice and to what extent was White Star following those norms? If Smith could be exonerated for maintaining speed despite the ice warnings because that was normal industry practice, then White Star likewise could claim that their officer training in matters of safety was no worse than anyone else's. It seems quite likely that White Star was not an exception in this area.

Mersey tacitly acknowledged that ship owners and ship builders have to be coerced into dealing with matters of safety as they see their self-interest as being better served by skimping where they can get away with it. His final recommendation, however, went some way to taking the matter more seriously. Under the heading 'General' he recommended that an International Conference be called to agree a common line of conduct in a number of areas affecting safety at sea. The conference was called in 1913 and was chaired by Lord Mersey himself. It was the first of a series of such conferences that continue to the present day and which have had a considerable influence on the construction of ships, the provision of safety equipment and the training of crews. Perhaps we should temper our concern at his understated response to the inadequacies of the evacuation of the *Titanic* with some acknowledgement that he initiated a process that, over time, has led to a substantial improvement in maritime safety.

There is one matter, however, that we have not yet explored so far as Smith is concerned and that is the quality of his personal leadership. While one can understand a reluctance to speak ill of the dead, it does seem wrong that the lack of leadership during the sinking of *Titanic* was not the subject of comment in the report. Smith knew by midnight that his ship would sink in around two hours or so and yet it was a further 45 minutes before the first lifeboat left on one side of the ship and almost an hour before the first one left on the other side. Clearly there was no sense of urgency, as Lightoller admitted at the American inquiry. Why not? There were only two ways in which the number of deaths could have been substantially reduced given the shortage of lifeboats. One was to transfer people to a rescue ship and the second was to create more floats or rafts to support people and keep them out of the water. Smith was well aware of exactly what had happened when the *Republic* sank five years previously. He knew how long it took to transfer passengers and crew by lifeboat to another ship. While wireless messages had not given any promise of a ship arriving before *Titanic* sank, there was always a possibility of a ship appearing, given the number still without any wireless or with only part-time operation. To facilitate a rapid transfer the first requirement was for *Titanic's* lifeboats to be off the ship, full and roped together. That way they could be emptied and sent back as quickly as possible to re-load. Smith had men available, massive amounts of wood and substantial quantities of tools to work with. It would never have been possible to construct rafts to hold all who needed them, but many more might have been saved nonetheless.

The picture that emerged from the evidence at the inquiry was of the crew all working as best they knew how, but without any clear strategy from above. It could be that this absence of strategy was a result of Smith's own lack of experience of emergencies – his 'uneventful' career – or that Smith's one central strategy was to avoid panic. Trying to speed up the launching of the boats and coerce into them reluctant passengers, while at the same time breaking up furniture and panelling to make rafts might have induced a state of disorder amongst passengers or crew that would have been difficult to deal with. Perhaps Mersey should have reflected on how captains ought to lead in this type of situation in such a way that the risk of panic can be managed and set against the potential gains of urgent action. It seems doubtful that the right answer was the laissez faire policy that Smith adopted and that resulted in 1500 people losing their lives.

STANLEY LORD

The controversies surrounding Stanley Lord are such that it would be better, in this instance, to start with the conclusions that Mersey reached and work back, rather than trace the evidence through to the report. Mersey dedicated a complete chapter in the report to '*The Circumstances in Connection with the S.S. Californian*' although the original set of questions forming the inquiry brief had not included one about the actions of other ships. On 22 May, the thirteenth day of the inquiry, Sir Rufus Isaacs proposed and Lord Mersey agreed that the Board of Trade should be asked to add an additional question to the brief and question 24(b) was adopted: 'What vessels had the opportunity of rendering assistance to the *Titanic* and, if any, how was it that assistance did not reach the *Titanic* before the SS *Carpathia*?'

Although the question was added six days before the report of the American inquiry was published, it came after Stanley Lord and other members of his crew had given evidence to Mersey as well as in New York and after it had become clear that the Senators were in no doubt as to his culpability in failing to come to the assistance of those on the sinking ship. The phraseology of the question clearly reflected the concerns that had developed in the press as the blame game gained momentum. It is hardly surprising that the answer of the Mersey inquiry to the question that it had asked of itself was brusque and to the point:

> The *Californian*. She could have reached the *Titanic* if she had made the attempt when she saw the first rocket. She made no attempt.

There followed a recommendation to the effect that:

> The attention of Masters of vessels should be drawn by the Board of Trade to the effect that under the Maritime Conventions Act, 1911, it is a misdemeanour not to go to the relief of a vessel in distress when possible to do so.

If the conclusion in the report avoids any specific criticism of Lord in person, the recommendation could scarcely be more pointed. Mersey explained in the discursive chapter on the *Californian* exactly how the evidence led him to his findings. Irrespective of one's views as to what actually happened that night one can admire the judicial style of Mersey's summary of the evidence.

> There are contradictions and inconsistencies in the story as told by the different witnesses. But the truth of the matter is plain. The *Titanic* collided with the berg 11.40. The vessel seen by the *Californian* stopped at this time. The rockets sent up from the *Titanic* were distress signals. The *Californian* saw distress signals. The number sent up by the *Titanic* was about eight. The *Californian* saw eight. The time over which the rockets from the *Titanic* were sent up was from about 12.45 to 1.45 o'clock. It was about this time that the *Californian* saw the rockets. At 2.40 Mr. Stone called to the Master that the ship from which he'd seen the rockets had disappeared.
>
> At 2.20 a.m. the *Titanic* had foundered. It was suggested that the rockets seen by the *Californian* were from some other ship, not the *Titanic*. But no other ship to fit this theory has ever been heard of.
>
> These circumstances convince me that the ship seen by the *Californian* was the *Titanic*, and if so, according to Captain Lord, the two vessels were about five miles apart at the time of the disaster. The evidence from the *Titanic* corroborates this estimate, but I am advised that the distance was probably greater, though not more than eight to ten miles. The ice by which the *Californian* was surrounded was loose ice extending for a distance of not more than two or three miles in the direction of the *Titanic*.' The night was clear and the sea was smooth. When she first saw the rockets the *Californian* could have pushed through the ice to the open water without any serious risk and so have come to the assistance of the *Titanic*. Had she done so she might have saved many if not all of the lives that were lost.

Eloquent it might have been, but Mersey's summary was a triumph of conviction over objectivity. No jury, having heard a summary such as that, could have returned any verdict other than 'guilty as charged'; except of course that Lord had not been charged. We saw earlier how the rules for inquiries permitted anyone who was liable to be subject to criticism in an inquiry to be represented by an attorney. Even after the formulation of the extra question, Mersey refused Stanley Lord the right to be represented. Furthermore, despite the reference to a 'misdemeanour' and despite also some subsequent clamour in the press, Lord never was charged with any offence nor was action taken against him to remove or suspend his certificate. Perhaps the most inaccurate sentence (of many) in Mersey's summary was the assertion that the truth of the matter was plain. A century later it is still not possible to make that assertion with the confidence that Mersey displayed.

Following years of controversy, much of it conducted in a spirit of animated hostility, the government decided in 1990 to ask the recently formed Marine Accident Investigations Branch to carry out a reappraisal of the evidence. In March 1992 MAIB produced a report that was distilled from a strange mixture of opposing opinions. The initial work was done by an Inspector who came to the conclusion that a substantial southerly current had brought the *Californian* much closer to *Titanic* than the position in which she had stopped. Thus he believed that the two ships had seen each other and so he broadly concurred with Mersey's findings. The MAIB Chief Inspector was unhappy with his conclusions and asked his Deputy to review the evidence again. He came to the view that the two ships were much farther apart and that it was most unlikely that either could have seen the other. The Chief Inspector endorsed his Deputy's views and, in March 1992, submitted a report to that effect. The report was accepted by the government and now replaces Mersey's original findings as the 'official' position. It is the only example of any of Mersey's conclusions being officially overturned.

The MAIB report, notwithstanding the internal disagreements that preceded it, is quite a contrast to most of the other literature on the subject. When one has perused the sometimes dense and turgid polemics that characterise much of what has been written, the MAIB report appears brief, logical and clear. There is no need to repeat here what the MAIB investigators did twenty years ago. There is no new evidence; the position of the wreck is the main piece of evidence that has emerged since Mersey completed his work and that was known to the MAIB. We shall therefore use the 1992 findings as the basis for evaluating the earlier inquiry and then reflect on what that tells us about Stanley Lord and how he was treated in 1912.

The MAIB report concluded that *Californian* was between 17 and 20 miles North by North West of the *Titanic* as she was sinking. This means that, in normal circumstances, the ships would not have seen each other's lights. The Chief Inspector acknowledged that a phenomenon known as 'super-refraction' might have made it possible for one ship to have seen something of the other even at that distance, but he did not consider this likely and advanced a number of reasons for ruling it out. These included the impossibility at that distance of distinguishing coloured navigation lights even with super-refraction. Witnesses on both *Titanic* and *Californian* testified to seeing the navigation lights of the ship that they were observing. This question of the distance at which navigation lights are visible in clear conditions was also raised at the inquiry into the loss of the *Empress*. The Chief Officer of the *Storstad* was asked how far the ship's sidelights were visible and he replied about four or five miles. The MAIB report, therefore, endorses the view that the ship seen by the *Californian* was a third ship, identity never likely now to be known. The ship seen from *Titanic*, as reported by a number of witnesses, including Boxhall, was either that third ship or some other unidentified vessel.

On the matter of the relative position of the two ships, the MAIB report therefore agrees with Lord's view, to which he stuck for the rest of his life, that the ship seen by *Californian* was not the *Titanic*. However, Lord also maintained, again consistently, that the rockets that his officers had observed, and which appeared to come from that ship, were not the rockets that Boxhall fired from the bridge of *Titanic*. Here, the 1992 report agrees with Mersey. No-one, in all of the time since the disaster, has found any evidence of any ship sending up rockets that night other than *Titanic* and, much later, the *Carpathia* as she raced towards the lifeboats. One of the justifications that Lord gave for believing that the rockets could not have come from *Titanic* was the fact that the direction in which they were observed from *Californian* was different to that of the *Titanic's* radioed position. Mersey perhaps ought to have taken that fact rather more seriously than he did, but he was convinced of Lord's guilt and had discounted almost all navigational evidence from *Californian* as a result. He was also more than a little confused as to the distinctions between bearings, headings and directions. The position of the wreck, discovered by Ballard in 1985, both helps to confirm Lord's navigational evidence while, at the same time, removing the substance of his argument. We now know that the direction in which the rockets were seen from *Californian* was the direction in which *Titanic* lay stopped at the time. It now seems clear that the white rockets that were seen by Second Officer Stone and Apprentice Gibson were indeed the distress rockets fired from the sinking *Titanic*.

Two questions now remain. Firstly, why were the rockets not properly recognised as distress signals and appropriate action taken? The second is something of a 'what if' question that historians generally dislike. If Lord had acted in response to the rockets, could the *Californian*, as Mersey maintained, have substantially reduced the death toll? In beginning to answer the first question, we should note that Lord himself did not see any rockets. Just before the first rocket was seen he had retired to the chartroom for a rest having been continuously on the bridge since early in the day. The only people who gave evidence as to the rockets that were seen were Stone and Gibson.

The regulations about the use of rockets as distress signals at sea at the time, give a simple description: "Rockets or shells throwing stars of any colour or description, fired one at a time at short intervals.' Mersey himself read this out to the inquiry after a vast amount of time had been spent questioning witnesses as to the interpretation they placed on the rockets observed having been white. The various lawyers had pressed Gibson, Lord and Stone (in that order) as to what they believed at the time the rockets had signified, largely on the assumption that informal company signals would have been coloured while white signals meant distress. The important words in the regulations were the last ones, 'one at a time at short intervals'. 'Short' has been interpreted by some as meaning intervals of a minute or less but the regulations themselves did not specify this. It seems that the ones fired by *Titanic* were at fairly irregular intervals but rather longer than a minute.

Without going into the details of the long and confused interrogations of the three *Californian* officers, all of which have been analysed *ad nauseam*, the following sequence seems reasonably certain, although timings are approximate.

- Just before he went to sleep in the chartroom, at about 0040, Lord spoke to Stone by voice tube. Stone assured him that the steamer that had come up and stopped close to them was still there, that he had tried to contact her by morse lamp and that no reply had been received.

- At 0115 Stone called Lord on the voice tube to report that the ship had fired five rockets and was now steaming away to the South West although Lord's memory of this conversation is that only one rocket was mentioned. Lord questioned Stone about the colour of the rockets and was told that they were white. He then instructed Stone to watch the other ship, continue trying to morse, and to send Gibson down to report to him when he had any news.

- Gibson went down to the chartroom to report to Lord just after 0200. He told him that the ship had fired a total of 8 rockets and was now disappearing in the South West. Lord asked him about the colour of the rockets and asked Gibson the time. Gibson then left and went back to the bridge. Lord said that his only memory was of Gibson opening and closing the door some time between 0115 and 0430.

- At 0245 Stone again called Lord by voice pipe to report that the steamer had now disappeared to the South West and again mentioned that the rockets were white. Lord claimed to have no memory of that conversation whatsoever.

When pressed as to their interpretation of the meaning of the rockets both Gibson and Stone denied that they had ever believed them to have been distress signals. The idea that they might have been calls for assistance only occurred to them the following day when they knew about the sinking of *Titanic.* However, they had no other rational explanation for what they saw. They spoke of company signals but admitted they had never before seen company signals of this nature. Stone also admitted that they met the description that he had been taught to look for in distress signals, except for two features. They were much lower in the sky than he would have expected of distress signals fired from a ship he estimated to be only about 5 miles away. Secondly, the ship they were apparently being fired from was moving while firing them, her bearing gradually changing, he claimed, from around South East to South West. This second observation is a rather puzzling one to which we will return later. Stone and Gibson both testified to a discussion between them on the bridge about the rockets during which they agreed that whoever was sending them up must have some good reason for doing so. They also reported observing that the lights of the ship that they were watching behaved oddly as she was steaming away. Here the inquiry descended into farce at times, a frustrating exercise in semantics in which the questioners tried desperately to get the witnesses to use a form of words that could be interpreted in line with what someone might have seen if what they had been observing was the *Titanic* sinking.

Notwithstanding the points about the apparent lowness of the rockets, the moving ship and the oddness of the lights, the MAIB report concluded that Second Officer Stone should have interpreted the rockets as being in all likelihood distress signals. That being so, he should have been more forceful in bringing them to the attention of his captain. In particular, when Gibson returned from the chartroom to say that the captain had not indicated that any further action should be taken, Stone should have left the bridge to inform him in person exactly what had been observed. It was a serious matter for the officer of the watch to leave the bridge, even when the ship was stationary; but, in the view of the Chief Inspector of MAIB, the circumstances warranted that course of action. There may be two reasons why Stone did not do so. One, of course, is that it genuinely did not occur to him that what he had seen was a call for assistance. That indeed is what he testified in the inquiry; his inability to provide a convincing alternative, however, at least leaves him open to doubts as to his competence.

The second possible reason is that he was scared of Lord's reaction if he had appeared in front of him in the chartroom. Lord was asked about what Stone should have done if he had believed the rockets were distress signals. This is the relevant section of the proceedings.

Mr. Dunlop: You were surprised about the *Titanic*. Did you question your Second Officer as to why you had not been called?
– I did.
What was his explanation to you?
– He said that he had sent down and called me; he had sent Gibson down, and Gibson had told him I was awake and I had said, 'All right, let me know if anything is wanted.' I was surprised at him not getting me out, considering rockets had been fired. He said if they had been distress rockets he would most certainly have come down and called me himself, but he was not a little bit worried about it at all.
If they had been distress rockets he would have called you?
– He would have come down and insisted upon my getting up.
And was it his view that they were not distress rockets?
– That was apparently his view.

Lord therefore testified to his expectation that Stone would have come to him in person had he felt the need to do so. Some commentators have stated that in doing so Lord was, at best, disingenuous. He appears to have been something of a martinet and must have been aware at least of the possibility that his second officer might have been very wary of waking him in that way, if it turned out that there was insufficient reason to do so. At the same time, if we take Stone's testimony at face value, we cannot then set Lord's aside without some evidence.

The background and personality of the captain have been brought into this discussion, but not that of the other two actors who, together with him, determined how the *Californian* reacted. Second Officer Stone was described by Lord in testimony as being reliable, but was also described elsewhere as being somewhat unimaginative. Although he did not suffer any consequences because of his association with the sinking of *Titanic*, in his subsequent career he was not a high flyer. Stone continued to serve for some time with the Leyland Line rising to become Chief Officer and he served as a Sub-Lieutenant in the RNR in WW1. He worked on Harrison Line ships after the war until he suffered some form of breakdown in 1938 after which he worked in Liverpool docks as a supervisor.

Apprentice Gibson, who appears to have been viewed as a bright young lad in the context of the inquiry, progressed even less well in his career at sea. He only passed his exams for his Masters' Certificate 28 years later, in 1940, and rose no higher than third officer, spending time as an AB, a Bosun and a Quarter Master as well as an officer. He was described by one captain as a 'positive menace on the bridge'. These post-*Titanic* histories of the two junior officers do not lead us, directly or indirectly, to any specific conclusions about what happened that night. They are presented only for the purpose of completeness.

In accepting the MAIB's conclusions, we are therefore suggesting that Stone (and Gibson, but the responsibility lay with Stone) should have recognised the rockets as distress signals and should have ensured that Lord was aware of that. Before considering the second of our questions, however, we do need to make some reference to the 'moving ship' issue. If the rockets that Stone saw were being fired from the (stationary) *Titanic*, how could he have observed the compass bearing of their point of origin changing during the time that they were fired? There appear to be only two answers. Either he was entirely mistaken and had failed to take bearings on the compass but had noted the change visually, a change that had actually resulted from the *Californian* swinging round while stopped. That seems by far the more likely explanation despite Gibson's assertion in evidence that he understood Stone to have taken bearings. Gibson himself did not claim that the ship sending up the rockets had been moving while doing so, but did not argue with Stone's evidence. During the period when four of the first five of the rockets were sent up, Gibson was not on the bridge. The other possibility, at least in theory, is that the *Californian* and *Titanic* were each being moved by significant (but different) currents. While that eventuality cannot be ruled out, the scale of the movement that Stone reported seems beyond the capacity for currents alone to cause within the timescale of his observations.

Our second question is an important one because of Mersey's wholly unsubstantiated assertion that, had the *Californian* responded to the rockets, she could have rescued some, or even all, of those on *Titanic*. The MAIB report is clear on this matter also. Even had Lord been awakened and action taken at the point when Stone should have realised that the series of rockets represented a call for help, the *Californian* could not have reached the scene of the sinking in time to prevent the loss of any lives. There was of course the confusion over the *Titanic's* position. If Lord had woken Evans, his Marconi operator, and received the CQD signal with the wrong position where would he have headed? In the direction of the ship which was still in sight and which Stone had reported as firing rockets, or in the direction of the position given by *Titanic*? The MAIB report suggests that Lord would have recognised the significance of the discrepancy and sent a wireless message to *Titanic* querying the position being broadcast. Presumably then either Phillips or Bride would have gone from the wireless room along the boat deck to the bridge and told Smith (or Boxhall?) that the position was being queried by a ship that reported seeing the rockets. The position might then have been checked, the error discovered and a correct position broadcast. Lord would then have known where to head. There is a considerable element of speculation in that chain of events and a rather large number of possible breakdown points. However, even if Lord had set off in the right direction at a safe pace through the ice field surrounding the *Californian,* it is most unlikely that he could have been at the disaster site before *Titanic* had sunk. As the survival time of those not in the boats was very short the *Californian* might only have succeeded in gaining the kudos that, in the event, went to the *Carpathia* as the ship that found the lifeboats.

In Chapter 9 we posed the question as to whether the failure of the *Californian* to take action in response to the rockets was a failure of communication or of will. On balance the MAIB report comes down on the side of communication, preferring to believe Lord when he said that he was not properly awake when Stone and Gibson spoke to him and did not appreciate the significance of what he was being told. Undoubtedly Lord was very tired when he went for a rest. He had been on duty for over 15 hours and had experienced an ice field for the first time in his career. That having been said, one of the characteristics of the sailor that is often spoken of is the ability to take short periods of sleep and awaken from them immediately if called. It is also worth remembering that the voicepipe that Stone used twice to speak to Lord was not in the room beside him where he was resting but was in the neighbouring room. Lord therefore had to walk from one room to the other to take the call. The nature of what he was told, however, was not such as to give rise to concern instantly, as Stone was at pains to stress that the ship he was watching was moving away and at no time did he use the word 'distress' or even hint that he thought someone was in trouble. The tone of the messages was reassuring rather than rousing and it is certainly quite possible that, in his sleepy state, that is exactly how Lord interpreted them. There is no need to paint Lord as a paragon of ship-mastery (as his more fervent supporters do) in order to accept that the failure to take action was not a failure of will on his part. The description of him as a sociopath, coming from the anti-Lord camp, surely falls into the category of what the MAIB report itself describes as 'scurrilous'.

In the last chapter we decided that Mersey was fair in his treatment of Smith on the speed issue but was not as critical as he should have been of his lack of effectiveness during the period between the collision and the ship foundering. We can draw mixed conclusions here also. Mersey was mistaken in supposing that the two ships were in sight of each other but he was right in believing that the *Titanic's* rockets were seen. The confusion that was apparent in the minds of the officers of the *Californian* over what sort and colour of rockets constituted a distress signal should have been the subject of more direct comment and, indeed, should have led to a recommendation about the better standardisation of practice. The claim that the *Californian* could have rescued many of those in danger on the *Titanic* showed little understanding, amongst other things, of the logistics of transferring a very large number of people between ships at sea in the dark, especially when one of those ships is sinking rapidly by the head. The barbed recommendation about masters being reminded of their obligation to go to the relief of a ship in distress was, at the very least, unwarranted by the evidence.

HENRY KENDALL AND THOMAS ANDERSEN

The inquiry into the loss of the *Empress of Ireland* was quite different to any of the other three inquiries over which Mersey presided. The reason for the difference was not the fact that it took place in Quebec, three thousand miles from London, or that it took place under Canadian rather than British jurisdiction. It was different because of the adversarial legal battle it foreshadowed. Within minutes of the *Empress* sinking, when Kendall was fished out of the water and brought aboard the *Storstad*, accusations of blame began as he confronted Thomas Andersen. By the time the inquiry commenced reciprocal law suits had already been filed and the inquiry itself became the cockpit within which claim and counter-claim were made. It was understood by all concerned that whatever emerged from the inquiry would, in all probability, determine the outcomes of the lawsuits and, in fact, that is exactly what happened.

Thus the *Empress* inquiry resembled a criminal trial more than an investigation into a horrible tragedy. It was a trial with two competing defendants. If one was found guilty the other must be innocent and vice versa – or so it was played out. The lawyer representing the Canadian Pacific Railway acted as defence lawyer for his client and, in effect, also as prosecutor of the Dominion Coal Company who had chartered the *Storstad*. The lawyer for the Dominion Coal Company played the opposing two roles. Caught somewhere in the middle, rather uncomfortably, were the lawyers representing, amongst others, the Canadian government and the Union of Seamen. We must not forget also that the inquiry was not a 'one man show', with Mersey as the only judicial presence. This inquiry was a tribunal. Mersey sat, as President, with Sir Adolphe Basile Routhier, a retired Chief Justice of the Superior Court of Quebec and the Honourable Ezekiel McLeod, Chief Justice and Judge in Admiralty for New Brunswick. The Canadian Government was represented by Edward L Newcombe who, as well as being a lawyer, was the Deputy Minister of Justice.

The role played by Newcombe was a slightly controversial one. Before the inquiry began he arranged for the existing Canadian Commissioner of Wrecks, a Captain Lindsay, to take preliminary statements from all potential witnesses and to advise as to which ones should be called to testify. This was a process which greatly helped the inquiry to focus on those who had the most information about the tragedy, but it did open the Ministry to accusations of self-interest. In the event these accusations do not seem to have been of any substance and there were witnesses called who had not been included in the list drawn up by Lindsay and Newcombe. The process exposed Newcombe to some sharp exchanges with Mersey, who was less than happy with a few of the outcomes. One does wonder if Mersey would have spoken with quite the same asperity to a Home Office minister in London, had one appeared in front of him in a similar role.

Butler Aspinall KC, whom we met previously representing the Board of Trade in the *Titanic* inquiry, was the lawyer for the CPR. An establishment figure with experience in maritime matters, he also had a killer instinct for exposing what he considered to be weaknesses in the opposition case. For the most part he and Mersey communicated in a relatively relaxed manner; appropriate deference was always shown to the bench and apologies for over-stepping the mark were suitably profuse. When Aspinall argued the toss with Mersey, he always took care to point out at the start that his lordship would win anyway. Aspinall was persistent in following issues through. Witnesses cross-examined by him were worn down through multiple probes, rather than being demolished by a masterstroke. While he clearly did have an under-standing of nautical terminology and his knowledge of ship construction was quite impressive, there were occasions when he failed to appreciate the sig-nificance, or the implications, of the testimony from the sailors involved.

We have already noted the comments of the British press about the different styles of the American and British *Titanic* inquiries. Those differences owed something to the fact that the American one was composed of a committee of politicians while the British one was judicial in character. But the differ-ences reflected as well a less formal and rather more theatrical approach that characterised American courtroom procedures. The lawyer for the Dominion Coal Company, representing the *Storstad* interest, brought something of that approach to the *Empress* inquiry. Charles Sherman Haight was a well known New York lawyer specialising in Admiralty cases who had a reputation for daunting courtroom performances. He had a relationship with Mersey that was much less relaxed; the two came from quite different backgrounds and legal traditions so it would only be expected that there might be some fire-works. It is probably to the credit of both that the fireworks did not burn the house down and Haight certainly had all the latitude he desired to present his case in his own way. In the event, his client might have been better served had he been somewhat more restrained.

Our two captains were both present throughout the inquiry sitting in close proximity. We do not know what words, if any, were exchanged between them during the nine days of testimony and the two days of summing up. They listened to the testimony of 60 witnesses in addition to each other's. Kendall was recalled to the stand twice, but Andersen only testified once. At the start of the inquiry Kendall was obviously suffering from his ordeal and walked hesitantly using a stick, despite which he refused a seat when giving evidence. Kendall knew that he had more to lose than Andersen. He had been on the bridge of the *Empress* throughout the entire incident and was personally responsible for every order given on the bridge. Andersen had been resting below as the two ships approached and was only called a minute or so before the actual collision. While he might have to answer for the fact that he was not on the bridge when the fog came down, he could not be so directly criticised for the orders given by his officers.

Because the inquiry had the appearance of a criminal trial but not the reality, the lawyers involved were not restricted by the protocols that would normally prevent collusion between prosecuting and defence counsel. There was clearly frequent contact between Aspinall and Haight during the inquiry and there appears to have been agreement between them at least as to the ground that they would fight over. They agreed that the navigational evidence from both ships was so imprecise as regards timings, positions and speeds as to be nearly worthless. The story told by those on the *Empress* was wholly incompatible with that coming from the crew of the *Storstad*. For this reason the two lawyers agreed that no collision would have taken place unless one of the two ships had altered her course while in the fog, despite firm denials from all involved. Therefore, one crew was lying to the court. Their only disagreement was about which crew had conspired to commit perjury. When, in their summings up, both Haight and Aspinall had described their respective positions, Mersey challenged Aspinall as to whether there might be another possibility.

Lord Mersey: If your story is right it follows logically that the witnesses for the *Storstad* are either telling deliberate lies – and I don't think you can escape from saying it – if on the other hand Mr. Haight's story is right it follows as he says that the witnesses from the *Empress* must be deliberately putting forward a story which they know is untrue. That seems to me to be the position involved by the pretensions of the two sides. What I am asking is this, is it according to your view possible that there may be a middle course involving both sides in blame?

Mr Aspinall: As your Lordship says of course it is possible, but what I submit is the manner in which your Lordships will approach the consideration of this case will be, your Lordships will consider the evidence, and I submit that in a court of law that the court is slow, and properly slow to arrive at a conclusion which neither party to the dispute invites the court to come to, and to which conclusion neither party has addressed its evidence.

Lord Mersey: Of course you must remember that this is not a suit.

Mr Aspinall: I admit that.

Lord Mersey: This is an inquiry.

Mr Aspinall: That is clear, but nevertheless I submit I am entitled to put forward this contention, that where you find two ship-owners represented, if I may say so, by counsel who know their business, if in accord with this view that it is one to blame, and not both, and when it is remembered that the evidence on both sides has been massed so to speak to arrive at that conclusion, that whether it be a tribunal which is inquiring, or whether it is a tribunal which is determining liability, that that tribunal would be slow to say that they propose under these circumstances to arrive at a middle course.

Judge McLeod: What this commission wishes to do is not to try the case between the *Empress* and the *Storstad* but to satisfy ourselves and, if we can, satisfy the public, just how this accident happened, and if coming to that conclusion we have to find that both are to blame we are entitled to do it.

This is really quite an extraordinary passage. Aspinall is speaking not only on his own behalf but also that of his opponent and his rather weasel attempt to pin the tribunal down to an interpretation of its role with which both lawyers would be happy was very sensibly rejected by McLeod.

Newcombe was the one who summarised the evidence as he saw it from a perspective not governed by a financial imperative to find any particular party at fault. He suggested that the middle way which Mersey had identified was the correct answer. He argued that there had been mistakes on both ships, mistakes which he considered might amount to negligence, but that it was not necessary to assume anyone was lying in order to envisage how a collision was possible. His belief was that the *Empress* had inadvertently stopped across the path of the *Storstad* but that the *Storstad* had not reacted sufficiently to the signals from the *Empress* telling her that she was stopping. It was a brave attempt, but he was not able to square enough of the evidence with this explanation to make it wholly convincing to the tribunal and, in the end, Aspinall won the day so far as the report was concerned. It is worth noting, however, that there is no suggestion in the inquiry report that the crew of the *Storstad* deliberately conspired to mislead the court and no witnesses were ever charged with perjury.

Reading the transcript of this inquiry and thinking back to the *Titanic* one, it seems as if some of the informality that Haight brought to the proceedings rubbed off on the judge. Mersey remained as gruff as ever, but here one can sense a hint of a smile behind some of his bearishness, as when he called to a witness: 'Speak up man, I'm old and deaf!'

Mersey made no secret of his dislike for one witness and it is unlikely that he was alone in that reaction as he does seem to have been quite an annoying character. He was a man called Galway and he was the Quartermaster on the *Empress* who had had the watch prior to the one in which the collision took place. Some of his testimony was flatly contradicted by the colleague who took over the wheel after him and also by the pilot who was on the bridge with him. One of the sources of Mersey's annoyance was Galway's habit of repeating each question he was asked before beginning to answer it. Perhaps he was just putting into effect in the courtroom the training that he had had on a ship's bridge. All quartermasters are drilled to repeat each order that they are given parrot fashion before executing the order and then report-ing it done. Mersey was not amused by that, but he was amused by a phrase which Galway used more than once in which he described a ship's steering mechanism as its 'principal asset'. When it turned out that Galway had given a lengthy newspaper interview without referring to the ship's steering, Mersey quipped: 'So the principal asset was left out.'

The words that the court reporter put on paper no doubt give a very accu-rate record of exactly what was said by witnesses, by counsel and by those on the bench. They only occasionally provide insights into what the atmosphere was like and how different witnesses reacted to the sometimes robust cross-examinations to which they were frequently subjected. One such insight came in a remarkable attack in the summing up by Haight on two of the witnesses from his own ship. (Incidentally, it is slightly odd to read how both Aspinall and Haight had acquired first person ownership of their respective ships. Each spoke of 'my ship' and 'our captain' etc.) Haight had a problem in that the engine room log from the *Storstad* did not entirely back up the story being given by the bridge personnel. Haight wanted to make sure that it was the bridge story that carried credibility. This is how he lashed into the ship's Chief Engineer and the engineer in charge in the engine room at the time of the collision.

Lord Mersey: Was the chief engineer there at that time?

Mr Haight: He was in his bed, my Lord, but as I saw him on the stand he might as well have stayed in his bed all the time.

Lord Mersey: Does that mean that you do not care about him, or what does it mean?

Mr Haight: It was an inadvertent expression of my contempt for the man who went to the lifeboats instead of going below to be on the scene of action with his assistant engineer; perhaps I should not have allowed myself …

Lord Mersey: Do you mean that he came up on the deck instead of going to his engine room?

Mr Haight: I do, my Lord. The engineer who was in charge of these engines stood before your Lordships a pitiable exhibition of absolute terror. Your Lordship may remember it; drops of cold perspiration formed on his forehead, ran down his face and dropped from his chin. He stood there for 15 minutes, the most pitiable exhibition of terror that I ever saw.

Mersey's response to this tirade was cryptic and, surprisingly for him, possibly even an attempt at tact: 'My eyesight is getting bad.'

There was another difference between this inquiry and the other three. A considerable number of the witnesses were not native English speakers. Captain Andersen, Chief Officer Toftnes and a few other crew members from *Storstad* were questioned in English but others required the assistance of a Norwegian interpreter.

There was one moment of light relief when a seaman from the ship failed to respond to the interpreter. Only then was it discovered that he was a Russian Finn. Luckily the interpreter was able to cobble together sufficient Finnish for his evidence to be heard. The pilots on the St Lawrence and some of the shore staff involved in the rescue were French Canadian but their English was sufficient for them to manage without an interpreter, although with a little difficulty in the cross-examination.

One witness, Third Officer Saxe of *Storstad,* posed problems when it was found that he was a German speaker who was struggling to cope with questions in English. Mersey himself came to the rescue by asking him questions in German to which he responded in kind, resulting in the following record of the proceedings;

Lord Mersey Let us go step by step. What does one long blast mean?

– (No answer).

Do you speak German?

– Jawohl, mein Herr.

(At this point Lord Mersey asked a few questions of the witness in the German language, and was answered in the same tongue).
Lord Mersey: The witness answers that one long blast means: I am going straight on my course.

The third day of the inquiry saw the worst of the blow-ups between Haight and Mersey. The context was Galway's evidence and the flare-up probably owed something to Mersey's resentment that Haight had foisted such an objectionable witness on him. Galway was a late addition to the list of witnesses because he had come forward about a supposed problem in the *Empress's* steering very late in the day, so late, in fact, that Haight had interviewed him in his hotel room just the night before. That was the cause of the row as Haight persisted in asking the witness to repeat what he had said the night before instead of giving his evidence directly to the court. After all, a witness could truthfully repeat in court lies that he had spoken the night before without committing perjury. This culminated in the following passage.

Mr Haight: You said on your cross-examination that you had heard about their wanting you to go home on the *Caligarian* today. When did you hear about that?
– I heard about it last night.
From whom?
– From the office lad,
Did you make any statement to me last night on this subject?
Lord Mersey: This is becoming a most curious examination. In all my life I have never heard any counsel ask a witness to repeat the statements that he made to him in private.
Mr Haight: I thought that having been cross-examined by the other side as to what he had said –
Lord Mersey: It is becoming to my mind, so utterly irregular that I really cannot interfere – you must finish it in your own way.
Mr Haight: I do not care to press the question.
Lord Mersey: If we were to pursue this to the end we should have you in the witness box and have you cross-examined and that, at all events, I am not going to allow.
Mr Haight: It would not be a matter that I would object to. If anybody wishes to cross-examine me I would be willing to submit to it.
Lord Mersey: Well then, you are a very odd man.

Both men having had time to reflect overnight, the fourth day began with apologies and statements of mutual respect. Haight said that: 'If I had had an opportunity to choose my words with a little more care I should have expressed myself quite differently.' Mersey responded:

> Mr. Haight, your conduct in this case hitherto, in my opinion, has been quite irreproachable. You have done your best, and in my opinion you have acted in the wisest way in the conduct of the cause which has been entrusted to you here. It may be – let me say it – that in my conduct of the inquiry yesterday I became a little heated because I did not like one of your witnesses, but do not attribute my observation to anything you said or did for whatever you said or did was done with proper care and in the best interests of the people you represent. I am glad you have given me an opportunity to say that.

We noted that during the course of the *Titanic* inquiry the Board of Trade had been asked to alter the terms of reference so as to include an additional question which then provided the basis for castigating the inaction of the *Californian*. The *Empress* tribunal agreed to a similar request to the Canadian Government, on this occasion to permit them to include a significant type of evidence omitted from the original set of questions. It related to the whistle signals that each of the ships had sounded while in the fog, signals that were of great importance in attempting to piece together the movements of the ships as they approached each other. Clearly, if a situation arose in which an inquiry felt, on the basis of testimony that it had heard, that the questions which it had been asked to follow up did not cover all of the relevant issues, it was entitled to draw this to the attention of the government and have the matter addressed. The change in the *Titanic* inquiry's terms of reference has been interpreted as part of a sinister conspiracy to attack Stanley Lord, but in procedural terms it was unexceptional.

In evaluating the findings of the tribunal one must be conscious that the inquiry had available the assistance of a team of expert assessors who brought to the tribunal's work knowledge of the conditions in the St Lawrence and an understanding of steamship handling that cannot now be replicated. With that caveat in mind it is now intended to approach the evaluation with a discussion of the issues as devoid of nautical terminology as possible.

We take up the story of the events of the early hours of 29 May 1914 given in Chapter 7 at the time that the *Empress* dropped her pilot about a mile off Father Point. She headed out from shore into the St Lawrence and between 15 and 20 minutes later the lookout reported the masthead lights of the

Storstad. Both of the surviving officers on the bridge at that time estimated the distance at about 6 miles. The night was then clear and it seems that the crew of *Storstad* spotted the masthead lights of the *Empress* at about the same time. They gave a similar estimate of the distance. Having made the necessary offing from the shore Kendall then turned the *Empress* through about 30° onto her course down the St Lawrence. Shortly afterwards he observed the *Storstad* carefully, measuring her compass bearing and noting that he could now be sure that the *Empress* would pass her right side to right side. First Officer Jones confirmed that he also believed this to be the position.

The evidence of the bridge personnel on the *Storstad* at this stage now diverges. They observed the *Empress* change course, but were convinced from their observations that the ships would pass left side to left side. As Aspinall kept emphasising in his summing up, despite the difference in their observations of each other, neither crew seems to have had any concern about the possible risk of collision at this stage. However, all then saw a fog bank rolling out from the shore and very soon the lights of each ship gradually became obscured from the other. One has to take all timings given from this point on as being quite unreliable because there are no reference points, up until the collision itself, to calibrate them. Human memories are very unreliable in estimating time, even in situations where the memory is not being reconstructed on the other side of a highly traumatic incident.

Henry Kendall decided, shortly after visibility had seriously deteriorated, to stop his ship. He did so as quickly as possible by putting the engines into reverse for around three minutes, although there is some doubt as to whether this was sufficient to bring it to a complete halt. In the witness box he explained his action as being one of caution, but he was not entirely convincing as to the reason why he considered such a dramatic act to be necessary in a situation where the ships were on courses that would allow them to pass each other in safety. Haight at the time and some later commentators have questioned the legitimacy of his action in terms of the regulations governing the avoidance of collisions at sea. Mersey ruled that it was acceptable in those terms and was not unseamanlike, although he did question its wisdom. The regulations advised captains to maintain existing courses and to proceed with caution in fog, but there was also a catch-all clause that allowed a captain to take whatever action was necessary in order to avoid a collision. What the regulations did require, however, was that any change in the situation of a ship in fog should be clearly signalled using the ship's whistle. Kendall did this, blowing three short blasts on two occasions to indicate that his engines were in reverse. There was little agreement amongst witnesses as to the whistle signals that were blown by the two ships when in the fog, except so far as these two sets of three short blasts were concerned. Everybody agreed that the *Empress* had made these signals, although the timing varied depending on the witness.

Alfred Toftnes, Chief Officer of *Storstad,* was in charge of the bridge when the *Empress's* signals were heard. Despite orders to call the captain in the event of fog he had not yet done so. Thomas Andersen was generally supportive of his Chief Officer in the witness box but he did agree with Aspinall that it had been a mistake on Toftnes' part not to call him to the bridge sooner. One has the impression, in reading Toftnes' evidence, that, although he seemed to become flustered under cross-examination and even a little nonplussed at times (which may have been the language problem), he was quite a strong, outgoing character who may have resented the implication that he was not capable of dealing with any situation that arose. Andersen was in the witness box for a shorter time; his answers were generally brief and to the point. Reading the text at this remove can give only a tentative impression of the man but he seems to have been a rather more introvert character than his Chief Officer and one wonders who might have been the more dominant personality on the ship.

Toftnes' reaction to the indication from the *Empress* that she was stopping was to stop his own engines; he did not reverse them so the ship carried on, gradually losing speed. At this stage the *Empress's* crew all maintained that they could hear the *Storstad's* whistle blowing to their right, as expected. Likewise, the *Storstad's* crew testified that they could hear the *Empress's* whistle coming from their left as they expected. It is not necessary to suppose that any of the witnesses were lying to explain this anomaly. Determining the direction from which sound is coming in fog is dreadfully difficult and there is ample evidence that we tend to assume that it is coming from the direction that we expect.

At some stage, before the ships saw each other just prior to the collision, the order was given by Toftnes to turn the ship's wheel. In the witness box he said that he was worried that the current coming downstream in the St Lawrence would push the ship's head to the left and decrease the distance between her and the *Empress* so he wanted to counteract this effect. This was not the initial explanation for the manoeuvre that was given in the inquiry. In his opening remarks Haight argued on behalf of the *Storstad* that the order to turn the wheel had been with the intention not of keeping the ship steady on her course against the influence of the current, but of turning her to the right to keep farther away from the *Empress.* Either Haight had been incorrectly briefed or the story changed in the course of the inquiry. This was a point picked up by Mersey that appears to have had some influence with the tribunal.

Irrespective of the motive for the order, all of the crew on the bridge testified that the ship had slowed so much that turning the wheel had no effect;

the *Storstad* had lost steerage way. What happened next is one of the most puzzling aspects of the whole tragedy. Seeing that the ship had lost steering way and was not responding to the rudder, Third Officer Jacob Saxe, who was on watch with Toftnes, pushed the helmsman away from the wheel and swung it hard over. He said that he did so because she was not responding and he was worried that the current might catch her and swing her round. Under cross-examination he agreed that he had not been given any order to put the wheel hard over, nor had he any indication from the compass that the current was having any such effect. It seems rather like someone reacting in something of a panic when, up to that time, there had been no indication of any danger according to the evidence that he and the others had given. In order to give the ship steering way, Toftnes then ordered the engines to 'slow ahead' and at last called the captain to the bridge.

Thomas Andersen was in his day cabin when the call came. His wife was accompanying him on the ship and told reporters afterwards that her husband had seemed worried, sensing something was wrong. Toftnes had not hinted as much, telling Andersen only that visibility had deteriorated and the light at Father Point, their destination to pick up the pilot, was no longer in sight. He did not mention the proximity of another vessel. Andersen had scarcely reached the bridge when the first indication of real danger appeared as the *Empress's* masthead light was seen above the fog quickly followed by her other lights and silhouette on the port bow of the *Storstad*. Andersen testified that he just had time to confirm that the *Storstad* was still pointing in the direction of her original course before ordering the engines full astern, knowing even then that a collision could not be avoided.

Whatever way the fog was lying or moving, it seems that the *Storstad* saw the *Empress* first, as those on her bridge estimated the distance between them at that point at about 200 metres. On *Empress* they thought that when the *Storstad* was first seen she was only 30 metres away, although this estimate seems remarkably low. This was not the only point of disagreement; those on *Storstad* thought that the *Empress*, far from being stopped, was moving through the water quite quickly, those on the *Empress* that the *Storstad* was close to her full speed of 10 knots. Again, it is not necessary to assume anyone was lying in order to arrive at such conflicting evidence. Witnesses were reporting momentary impressions of events in the dark in swirling fog and it is highly likely that those impressions were extremely unreliable. One must be a little suspicious at the degree of uniformity of the evidence within each ship, for there were opportunities for witnesses to chat amongst themselves and, if not to collude in falsehood, at least to reinforce in discussion a dominant impression that each then become convinced was his own. We know now more than was understood in the early part of the twentieth century about group dynamics and how suggestible we all are in arriving at agreed outcomes and convincing ourselves that these were our own beliefs from the beginning.

Whatever the speed of either ship, just a few seconds later the two collided. The bow of the *Storstad* travelled around 5 metres into the hull of the *Empress* almost in the middle of her right side and with dire consequences. It is important to reflect on how the tribunal judged the events up to this point. As we have seen, both Aspinall and Haight argued that only a change of course by one ship in the fog could have caused the collision. No evidence came from the *Empress* of any movement of the wheel or any indication of her changing the way that she was pointing, even after she came to a halt, assuming that she did so. Haight could offer no explanation as to why she might have altered course deliberately. He chose instead to produce evidence of problems with the *Empress's* steering gear that might have led to an involuntary change of course to which no-one on the ship was admitting. This was one of the areas in which he probably over-reached himself as he did not restrict his argument to one explanation of this steering problem but rather argued the case for three different explanations. Two years after being in service the *Empress* had had her rudder enlarged and a similar operation had been carried out on her sister ship the *Empress of Britain*. Haight argued, quite correctly, that this indicated a need to improve the steering qualities of the ships. Aspinall responded by saying that the rudder alterations had had the desired effect and that no further problem with the steering had been noted since. Haight then turned to the hydraulically operated telemotor steering system as a source of problems. One difficulty with presenting his evidence was the complete lack of understanding amongst the lawyers, the bench, or even some of the witnesses, as to how such a system worked. All get full marks for persistence; the transcript of this evidence runs to many pages and it is not easy reading. Haight tried to show that leaking fluid from a system, which, he claimed, with little evidence, might have been poorly maintained, could cause the ship to yaw about and not keep to a straight course. His called as witnesses representatives of the crew and the pilot of another Norwegian collier, the *Alden*, that the *Empress* had passed on the way down the St Lawrence that night. They maintained that the *Empress* had been swinging about erratically on her course but their evidence was contradicted by the pilot on board the *Empress*.

The now notorious Galway was called to give evidence that the *Empress's* steering gear was also prone to jamming. Galway said that when he had been on watch prior to midnight the steering had jammed briefly once and that when he went off watch he had warned both his successor at the wheel and the pilot. Both men flatly denied any such warning. If Haight appeared to be clutching at multiple straws in presenting his evidence on the steering, he tried in his summing up to hold tight to just one of them and magnify its significance. He presented a scenario in which, at the point just prior to the fog obscuring vision when the *Empress* had changed course, the steering had jammed, causing her to swing much too far to the right. Wrenching the wheel over eventually corrected the jam only to send the ship careering off to the left, right across the bows of the approaching *Storstad*. He went so far at this point as to suggest that Kendall was in a state of complete panic and had lost control of himself as well as his ship. These theatricals might have been the right approach for a New York jury but clearly did not have the desired effect on an elderly English judge and his learned Canadian colleagues. Kendall had come across as the sort who stayed calm in a crisis. We know from his earlier history (Chapter 6) that he had dealt with a number of dangerous situations in his life and the court's impression of him does not seem inconsistent with that history.

Aspinall argued his case in a more prosaic fashion, concentrating on a rather simpler argument that, despite protestations to the contrary from Andersen and the other members of the *Storstad* crew, the turning of the *Storstad's* wheel did alter her heading and that she was carrying sufficient forward motion, particularly once her engines resumed at slow ahead, to take her into the side of the *Empress*. This was the story that the tribunal accepted, although it still leaves some big questions unanswered. Perhaps the biggest was the fact that those on the *Storstad* were so emphatic that what they saw convinced them that the *Empress* would pass left side to left side and not, as those on the *Empress* maintained, right side to right side. At night, of course, observations depend on interpreting the lights that are seen. In this case Toftnes and Saxe both were adamant that, after the *Empress* made her change of course to head down river, they could see her red, left side, navigation light. Kendall and Jones were equally adamant that they were showing the *Storstad* their green, right side, light. Haight argued that 'his' crew were right; Aspinall tried to take the issue out of the equation by maintaining that, either way, the ships would have passed safely had not one of them changed course in the fog. What might the explanation be, given that it would seem that this might just be the crucial mistake that resulted in the tragedy? One explanation of course was Haight's supposed problem with the steering gear that caused the ship to weave. If, in making the change of course, the inadequacy of the rudder, or depletion of hydraulic fluid in the telemotor system, had caused the *Empress* to turn too far for a while showing her red light to the *Storstad*, the correction being obscured as the fog came down, then this would explain the discrepancy. However, Aspinall's defence of the steering gear on the *Empress* was quite robust and this explanation lacks credibility in the absence of better supporting evidence.

New helmsman on ships mostly make the error of oversteering. When ordered to alter course they swing the wheel over to start the turn, but fail to straighten up in time. The ship then swings past the desired course and a similar error of overcorrection leads to the sort of serpentine wake that gives officers of the watch nightmares. The author can testify to this, having been justly on the receiving end of abuse more than once from an officer of the watch on a sailing ship for exactly that offence. The quartermaster on the helm of the *Empress* was not a novice, but it is possible that he suffered a momentary lapse of concentration. It is a plausible explanation as an excess turn of only around 5° would have been sufficient to show the red light to the oncoming *Storstad* at least briefly. If that is indeed what happened and Toftnes and his colleagues had reason to believe that the ships would pass left side to left side, then making sure that the *Storstad* did not deviate at all towards her left made sense. Toftnes might have ordered the wheel turned, as Haight originally suggested, to increase the passing distance of the two ships although, if he did, he failed to indicate on his whistle that he was doing so. It seems a terrible thing to suggest that over a thousand people may have died as a result of a momentary lapse on the part of a helmsman, but it is a possibility that cannot entirely be ruled out.

Two aspects of events deserve particular attention at this stage. One is the decision by Kendall suddenly to throw his engines into reverse to stop the ship. The second is the suggestion of panic by Saxe on the bridge of *Storstad* before any real danger was apparent. The puzzling thing about Kendall's decision was not so much the fact that he made it but his reticence in explaining it in the witness box. Was there a reason other than his extreme caution that he did not want fully to share with the inquiry? Two possibilities present themselves. One is that he was aware of *Empress* having wavered on her turn and realised that this might have caused some confusion on the other ship. The other, probably more likely, is that he felt that the passing distance between the ships was safe enough in clear visibility but that there was not a sufficient margin of safety in foggy conditions. One can see why he might have been reluctant to share the former possibility with the court, but the second seems relatively innocuous. Perhaps he thought that it might not reflect too well on his seamanship in making his 30° turn when he did.

Saxe's behaviour in pushing the quartermaster away from the wheel and turning it to its maximum extent, without any order to do so, on the face of it seems even less explicable. Had he heard the *Empress's* whistle again and suddenly realised that it was not coming from the expected direction? Is it possible that he had even heard the sound of the other ship's machinery (her generators for example) which told him she was much closer than she should have been? Given the trauma that ensued soon afterwards, it is quite possible that he simply forgot the real reason for what he did and the story he gave the court of holding the ship against the current was the one that he then believed.

The issue that occupied more of the tribunal's time than any other was the speed with which the *Empress* sank immediately after the collision. There was lengthy evidence given concerning the ship's structure. When the ships came together, Kendall called through a megaphone to tell Andersen to keep his engines going ahead so as to hold the *Storstad* in the hole she had created, thereby reducing the inflow of water into the *Empress*. Andersen claimed that he had already given the order to go full ahead even before he heard Kendall shouting. No reply was heard on the *Empress*, possibly because Andersen had no megaphone, and within a few moments the ships separated as the *Storstad* twisted around and slid backwards down the right side of the *Empress*. Kendall maintained that the separation happened because Andersen had failed to respond. Andersen said that he had done his best but that the forward motion of the other ship had caused his to twist out of the hole. The argument between the lawyers on this point was protracted and probably pointless. It was important to Aspinall to establish that his ship was at rest when the collier had crashed into her. It was vital for Haight's case that the *Empress* was moving as it was her erratic movements that he blamed for the collision. Each lawyer produced an expert witness and each of the two experts proposed a different angle for the collision, Aspinall's that it had taken place almost at right angles, Haight's that the ships had been at an angle of only 40°. If Haight's expert was right about the angle (and he may well have been) then it actually would provide an explanation for the parting of the ships that did not require the *Empress* to be moving. If the collision took place at a narrower angle, the *Empress* would have absorbed the component of the *Storstad's* momentum that was driving her into the *Empress* but not the lateral component along the side of the *Empress*. With the *Storstad's* bows being stopped, her stern would then have swung on down the *Empress's* side until the two separated. The damage to the *Storstad's* bow was consistent with that scenario. Haight seems to have sensed that his own expert's evidence as to the angle of the collision was actually working against his desire to prove the *Empress* to be at fault, because in his summing up he referenced his argument to Aspinall's assumption of a collision angle of about 80°, at which angle there would be little lateral momentum to effect a separation; only movement on the part of the *Empress* could explain it.

After the separation, with fog still obscuring the scene, Andersen first ensured that his own ship was seaworthy and then brought her around in a circle to a position as close as he felt he could safely go to the sinking *Empress*. He launched the ship's lifeboats as quickly as possible and sent them away to pick people up from the water whose shouts they could already hear. From that point on his crew (including his wife) worked tirelessly to rescue and care for as many as possible, the *Storstad's* boats making a number of trips to fill up with survivors and bringing them back to such care as those on the *Storstad* were capable of giving them. The few of the *Empress's* boats that got away from her before she sank also brought some survivors to the *Storstad,* others went to the rescue ships once they arrived on the scene.

Only half a dozen boats got away from the *Empress*. Because of the rapid and severe list that she developed the boats on the port side were useless. Some even fell down across the deck of the ship injuring and possibly killing some people. On the starboard side the boats that were released were mostly dropped almost empty into the sea with few on board other than their allocated crew. This was done deliberately because of the rapidly deteriorating situation on the ship; their crews were instructed to pick survivors up from the water. Most of those who survived were picked up in this way either by the *Empress's* boats or those which rowed across from the *Storstad*. Most of the boats made several trips, their crews becoming exhausted in the process. Numbers rescued decreased rapidly with each trip, but initially were of the order of 50 or so. Contrast that scene with the situation when the *Titanic* sank and people were likewise being thrown into the sea. Third Officer Pitman was in boat No 5 and after leaving *Titanic* the half-filled boat sat off about 100 yards distant. This what Pitman said about going back to pick up people struggling in the water:

As the *Titanic* sank and immediately after did you hear any screams?
– Immediately after she sank? Yes?
– Yes.
Were you able to go in the direction of the screams and render any assistance?
– I did not go.
But do you think you could have gone? I am not suggesting anything; I only want to get the facts from you. Do you think it would have been safe or reasonable to go?
– I do not.
What is your reason?
– Well, there was such a mass of people in the water we should have been swamped.
In your view you had a sufficient number of people on your boat. Is that so?
– No, but I had too many in the boat to go back to the wreck.

In Mersey's report on the loss of the *Titanic* he quite rightly expressed concern about the behaviour of those in the boats failing to pull people from the water, although his language was probably too measured to have the impact that it should have had. He was appropriately complementary about the work of the boats' crews in saving as many as possible from the wreck of the *Empress*.

Our last mention of Henry Kendall was when he was shouting across with the megaphone to the *Storstad*. Once the separation had occurred he considered the possibility of beaching, only to find himself in a similar position to Will Turner on *Lusitania* almost exactly a year later. The steam lines had been cut and there was no power for the engines. All that was left to do was to try to save as many lives as possible. He was, however, criticised at the inquiry on two counts. The first was that the order to close all watertight doors was not given until the collision had taken place. While this was not a breach of existing procedures, the view was expressed by Haight that a more prudent captain would have closed them when the fog appeared. This was the recommendation of the tribunal; in future all ships were advised to close watertight doors below bulkhead level in fog. It was suggested that they also be closed at night, along with all portholes below the same level. That was the second point of criticism of Kendall; the speed with which the ship sank was partly attributed to the fact that some of the portholes were open low down on the ship, something that was against the ship's own regulations. There was a suggestion that discipline was not sufficiently strict in enforcing that regulation, although the difficulty of doing so on a warm evening was recognised. Neither of these criticisms was included in the tribunal's report.

Captain Kendall, therefore, was almost given a clean sheet (bar slightly negative remarks about his changing course when he did and his caution in stopping his ship) and was exonerated from responsibility for the collision and for the loss of life that ensued. Neither did Andersen suffer any direct criticism, but his ship was found to have been at fault and there was an implication that he was not as fully in command as he should have been. Toftnes was found to have been negligent in turning the *Storstad's* wheel. Were these findings reasonable on the basis of the evidence presented? Like much of Mersey's work in this area there is an unjustifiable certainty about the way that the findings are expressed. It is as if no other explanation is now possible once he has arrived at his conclusions. However, expressed with more caution as a consequence of the conflicts in the evidence, what the tribunal concluded seems to be the most likely explanation for the disaster. It is necessary to set aside more evidence to arrive at any other explanation but Mersey and his colleagues too lightly dismissed the evidence of both Toftnes and Saxe regarding the sighting of the *Empress's* red sidelight. In the report they are simply described as mistaken, only because what they claimed does not fit in with the inquiry's preferred explanation. The tribunal should, at least, have allowed for the possibility that Toftnes and Saxe were correct in what they saw, even if it led to an erroneous assumption about the *Empress's* intention. Perhaps Newcombe was right at least in his suggestion that there was blame on both sides, a possibility that Aspinall and Haight had placed off limits in deciding how their personal jousting match was to be played.

Only one individual in all four disasters considered in this book was wise before the event, rather than after. It was reported that the ship's cat Emmy, who had never once missed a voyage, repeatedly tried to escape near the departure of the *Empress* on 28 May. The crew could not coax her aboard and the *Empress* departed without her. Apparently Emmy watched the ship sail away from Quebec City sitting on the roof of the shed at Pier 27, which would later temporarily house the dead pulled from the river after the *Empress* went down.

13

FREDERICK DAVIES AND WILL TURNER

The two inquiries into the wartime sinkings were both considerably shorter than those into the peacetime accidents. Those numbers do not provide a statistically significant sample, but even this very limited correlation may have had a reason. Much of the focus in the peacetime inquiries was on establishing the cause of the accidents and allocating blame. In the cases of the *Falaba* and *Lusitania* the causes of the sinkings were not in question and the allocation of the principal blame by a British inquiry under the circumstances could be taken for granted. However, there was still a question to be asked as to whether or not the actions of those on the two ships might have in some way contributed to their loss. Equally, it was necessary to ask if some additional actions might have been taken that would have improved the outcome.

The *Falaba* inquiry began on 20 May 1915 and had just four sittings. A total of 46 witnesses were heard. The four Assessors sitting with Mersey were the same four who were to sit with him through the *Lusitania* inquiry a few weeks later. It is the only inquiry in which neither of the two captains involved gave evidence. The inquiry took place at Caxton Hall in London and the report was published on 8 July, after the evidence of the *Lusitania* witnesses had been heard. The Solicitor-General, Sir Stanley Buckmaster, represented the Board of Trade for the first two days of the inquiry before being elevated to the post of Lord Chancellor, the role being continued in the other two sessions by the existing junior counsel. None of these inquiries would be complete without the presence of Butler Aspinall and, in this case, he represented the ship's owners, Elder Dempster, as well as the senior surviving member of the crew, Chief Officer Baxter and the company's Marine Superintendent, Fred Davies' brother-in-law Captain Thompson. The relatives of Captain Davies paid for their own barrister to be present on his behalf.

There was only one explicit reference to the *Lusitania* during the course of the inquiry. The witness who naively explained that he believed that the Germans only wanted to look at the ship's papers then incongruously pointed out that the *Lusitania* had been given no warning whatsoever. Mersey slapped him down by stating that he was not now 'trying the *Lusitania*'. It is apparent, however, in reading the transcript of the *Falaba* inquiry, that Mersey seems at times distracted. In the proceedings of all four inquiries there were examples of Mersey losing the thread of an argument by counsel or the examination of a witness, sometimes because of his deafness, sometimes because of his lack of nautical or technical knowledge, sometimes because what he was listening to did not actually make sense. In this inquiry there are a number of occasions when his interventions indicate that he has been missing quite significant stretches of input. It would hardly be surprising if the forthcoming *Lusitania* 'trial' were pressing on his mind.

Mersey and Buckmaster had an interesting exchange following the evidence given by one passenger who had asked to be allowed to give his evidence in his own words unprompted by questions. Mersey was unimpressed, but Buckmaster argued in support:

> *The Commissioner:* We had one gentleman here yesterday who asked to be allowed to tell his story in his own way. I said he might, and he did. He told us a very great deal of what we did not want to know and which was quite immaterial. Once you get a witness telling his story in his own way he will tell you the colour of his coat and how his hair had been brushed and all sorts of things.
>
> *The Solicitor-General:* I am as keenly alive to that as any one, but I can see something on the other side. These people have been in peril of their lives and they do not understand that matters which are of very real importance to them are matters which, for the purposes of this Inquiry, we do not want to know about.
>
> *The Commissioner:* You must as far as possible let them have their say.
>
> *The Solicitor-General:* I am obliged to your Lordship.
>
> The next witness, Mr. T. D. Woolley was sworn.
>
> *The Commissioner:* Now, Sir, will you tell us all you want to tell us?
>
> – I would rather have questions asked me.
>
> *The Commissioner:* I think you are quite right.

The *Lusitania* inquiry began on Tuesday 15 June 1915 in the Central Hall, Westminster. It lasted 5 days and there were just 36 witnesses. Part of the inquiry was heard in camera owing to the sensitive nature of the evidence. For obvious reasons, given the strategic political issues that the case raised, the cast of the *Lusitania* inquiry included some famous names. Leaving aside Mersey himself, who was quite well known as a result of the *Titanic* inquiry but probably not a name recognised in every household, there was the Attorney General, Sir Edward Carson representing the Board of Trade with the recently appointed Sir Frederick (F.E.) Smith, the Solicitor General. Smith was an extrovert, enormously self-confident and assured, with acknowledged courtroom charisma.

Carson's position as Attorney General was remarkable considering his recent political history. Less than a year before the *Lusitania* sinking he had been the political leader of what had threatened to become the most serious armed rebellion against the crown since Bonnie Prince Charlie in 1745. With large quantities of arms in the hands of the Ulster Loyalists and a threatened mutiny by sections of the British Army, Carson was set to create serious trouble for the government until the First World War intervened and the Irish problem was postponed for another day. His dramatic transition from rebel leader (even a 'loyal' one) to the senior law officer of the Crown was more reminiscent of events in the courts of the Tudor monarchs than in a twentieth century democracy. In Mersey's short parliamentary career, his party affiliation had been with the Liberal Unionists so we can assume that there was no frisson of political difference between him and the Attorney General.

Appearing for Cunard was the ubiquitous Butler Aspinall KC, by now regarded as a leading specialist in the field of maritime law. One of the questions it is fair to ask (although impossible to answer with any authority) is the extent to which a rapport had developed between Mersey and Butler Aspinall and the effect such an understanding might have had on the outcome. Aspinall had successfully represented the government interest in the *Titanic* inquiry in 1912 and Mersey had, in 1914, found that his defence of Henry Kendall's handling of the *Empress of Ireland* had been wholly convincing. As we shall see, his defence of the Elder Dempster interest in the case of the *Falaba* was likewise successful in persuading Mersey, in that case entirely in the face of the evidence. Aspinall had been given permission by Cunard to represent the interests of Will Turner in the *Lusitania* inquiry as well as the company interests. Was Mersey as swayed by the arguments that he heard from the same man yet again in defence of Turner?

The *Lusitania* inquiry might also have been relatively brief because the government wanted it so. Carson gave the distinct impression he was seeking brevity. In his opening statement he suggested that the 21 questions that made up Mersey's brief from the Board of Trade could effectively be reduced to just two. Did the navigation of the ship, in the light of Admiralty instructions, contribute to the disaster? Was everything done that could have been done to save life once the ship had been torpedoed? These are certainly the pertinent issues, particularly so far as Captain Turner is concerned; we are not addressing matters of strategic interest in relation to the war nor will we be adding to the debate on what level of conspiracy there may or may not have been in connection with the 'Lusitania incident'. We can therefore be content to accept Carson's narrowing of the focus, even if others see it as one element of an attempted cover-up.

Carson's two questions can also be used to assess the fundamentals of the Falaba inquiry. Was Davies' handling of his ship a contributory factor in its loss and was the evacuation of the ship as successful as it could have been in the circumstances? It makes sense to consider the first question for both Davies and Turner and then move on and do likewise for the second. In doing so the differences between the two incidents will be apparent and it will be of interest to consider whether or not Mersey's findings reflected those differences.

Prior to the sighting of the submarine, the Falaba was holding a steady course. Although in a known danger zone for submarines, Davies was not following Admiralty advice by zigzagging at irregular intervals because the advice had not yet been issued. Had von Forstner mounted an attack by torpedo without warning, as did Schwieger, the absence of zigzagging might have been important. However, as the Falaba was approached on the surface by U-28 in clear sight, it was immaterial. There is therefore no reference to zigzagging in the report. Once the submarine had been spotted, it was correctly assumed to be German and Davies did as his instructions told him to do. He turned away from the submarine and increased to maximum speed, sending a wireless message giving his position and the nature of the threat. The possibility of turning towards the submarine to ram it, the alternative Admiralty option, appears not to have been seriously considered, unsurprisingly given the fact that the ship was carrying passengers. Mersey made no comment about these actions in the report, simply referring to them in court as sound common sense. He also accepted without question the stopping of the ship once it was clear that escape was impossible.

Davies' attempt to run away from the submarine was fairly perfunctory. His call for full speed appears not to have had much effect as the ship was close to that anyway and he stopped when von Forstner threatened to open fire. To have continued was futile and would have put his passengers in immediate danger. Any shots would in all likelihood have caused casualties.

So far as the first question was concerned, Fred Davies was therefore entirely in the clear and it would be hard to dispute that finding. The one issue that might be raised was in relation to the wireless message. Sending the message was in accordance with Admiralty advice but was it really in the interests of the passengers on the *Falaba?* There was only one other ship in sight at the time. It was a small steam fishing drifter without either armament or means to summon help. Davies must have known that even if his wireless message succeeded in bringing a warship on the scene, his ship would have been long destroyed and the submarine departed. Knowing that the message had been sent, however, put pressure on those in the submarine to get the job done quickly and get as far from the scene as possible before help arrived. Visibility from the low height of a submarine conning tower is much more restricted than from the bridge of a substantial cargo liner. Von Forstner would have had little warning of the arrival of a destroyer. The Germans could have argued also that a wireless message aimed at bringing a warship to the scene put the *Falaba* outside the terms of the Cruiser Rules and made her eligible to be sunk without any further efforts to save those on board. However, it is vital to remember that this incident took place in the first few months of submarine warfare and of the first war in which wireless had been available on merchant ships. In the circumstances it is difficult to envisage Davies not sending that wireless message and impossible to guess how the result might have been altered, if at all, had he kept radio silence.

For Turner the issues that were raised about his handling of the *Lusitania* were much more complex and occupied a considerable amount of the inquiry's time. Questions had been asked in the press shortly after the sinking about the *Lusitania's* course and speed, questions that were the result of some briefing of journalists by the Admiralty. Churchill himself, First Lord of the Admiralty at the time, was party to serious criticism of Turner in private and even gave hints of it in Parliament. The First Sea Lord, Admiral 'Jacky' Fisher was apoplectic and virtually demanded Turner's head on a plate, describing him as traitorous. This disgraceful outburst probably revealed more about Fisher's own mental instability at the time than the culpability of Will Turner. There were however significant and more rationally argued criticisms of Turner from lower levels within the Admiralty, particularly from within Naval Intelligence. Some of the criticism was obviously motivated by self-defence. Was it not the job of the most powerful navy in the world to protect the country's ships, especially those carrying large numbers of vulnerable passengers? How had such a failure of protection occurred – was poor intelligence to blame? Turner has frequently been described as the scapegoat, with some justification given the nature of the briefing against him. Nonetheless, given the evidence at the inquiry, there were real questions to be asked about the wisdom of Turner's decisions on the morning of the sinking.

The inquiry had a considerable amount of information before it concerning the events of 7 May 1915. There was evidence about the general advice to mariners given by the Admiralty in relation to the submarine menace as well as specific warnings issued about the situation at that time in the area the ship was passing through. Aspinall maintained that there was a tension between the two; Turner, he claimed, by obeying the general instructions would have increased his risk in relation to the specific warnings. F.E. Smith, who led the attack on Turner by the Board of Trade, argued that he had not used the options available to him and might have avoided the submarine if he had done so.

There was a second source of tension, one that Turner relied on in his defence, (which we identified back in Chapter 3) and which concerned the balance between the normal peacetime risks to a ship and the additional ones resulting from war. The need to navigate the ship safely as it completed the crossing of the Atlantic and approached land meant that an accurate determination of position was required. Turner argued that, on the morning of the 7 May he had to approach close enough to the Old Head of Kinsale to complete what is called a 'four-point bearing'. He pointed out that he remained at least ten miles farther out from the headland than he would in peacetime. Smith countered by suggesting that it was quite possible for Turner to have used other methods of fixing his position that did not require such a close approach to land.

The specific criticisms of Turner were that he ignored Admiralty advice by approaching land near a headland, that he did not zigzag and that he failed fully to exploit the speed of the ship as a means of protection. Aspinall's arguments in rebutting the first two of these criticisms were linked as the following passage demonstrated:

> *Butler Aspinall* … Mr. Bestic [the Junior Third Officer], and those associated with him, were at the time in question doing what was perfectly legitimate, I submit, and perfectly proper, engaged in taking a 4-point bearing, and it was during that half an hour that the catastrophe happens. If they had been zigzagging, they could not have carried out the operation of taking the 4-point bearing.
> *The Commissioner:* Is that so?
> *Admiral Inglefield:* Yes. They must run steady on a direct course at a regular speed while the bearing is being taken.
> *The Commissioner:* So that the zigzagging would have defeated that object.
> *Mr. Butler Aspinall:* It would have defeated a legitimate operation in navigation.

Despite the apparent support given to Aspinall's argument by the Admiral, it was really quite specious on two counts. Firstly, it was not necessary, as the Solicitor-General pointed out, for Turner to have used that particular method of fixing his position. He could have achieved his objective without the necessity of keeping the ship on a steady course for an extended period. Turner was quite right in maintaining that he required assurance as to his position and it was normal practice in peacetime for him to approach the Old Head much closer. No doubt he then habitually used that headland to carry out a four-point fix. That procedure may well have been common to many of the Atlantic liner captains approaching the St George's Channel. Turner evidently felt that keeping an additional ten miles out to sea was sufficient to counter the submarine risk and then carried on as normal. On the previous wartime voyage in which he had been in command the ship had passed the Old Head at this same distance. As we have already seen with Captain Smith on *Titanic*, there was a powerful inclination to stick closely to standard practice irrespective of warnings received. In fact, had Turner taken the *Lusitania* a few miles farther out to sea, he might only have saved Schwieger the trouble of bringing U-20 closer inshore to get lined up for the shot.

Much was made at the inquiry and much has been made since of Turner's reaction to the warnings about submarine activity 20 miles south of Conninbeg lightship, warnings which resulted from Schwieger's activities the day before. Turner had not been told either that the reported activity was 24 hours previously or that it had resulted in the sinking of two ships. In one sense this is something of a red-herring because, although Turner had decided what he was going to do in response to the warnings, the attack by U-20 came before he took any action. There was still some 80 miles to go before he hit the supposed danger zone. It has been suggested that he came closer to the Old Head because he was intending to take an inshore course as he approached Conninbeg, to stay away from the supposed submarine lurking 20 miles out. However, as already noted, his distance off the Old Head was the same on this trip as it had been on the previous one when there had been no similar warnings. Furthermore, the 18-knot speed of the *Lusitania* had been set before the warning was received.

The second reason for Aspinall's argument being groundless was that Turner had not been zigzagging prior to taking the four-point fix and, it seemed, had no intention of doing so when it was completed. The fact that the ship was torpedoed during that procedure was entirely coincidental. The questioning of Turner in camera about his decision not to zigzag is one of the most crucial passages in the inquiry and so a lengthy extract (edited to omit some duplication) is given below to illustrate the nature of the questioning, Mersey's own part in the process and the character of Turner's responses. Carson, the Attorney General, has rightly been criticised for his overly forthright grilling of a man who was clearly very disturbed by what he had suffered and by the loss of so many of his close colleagues. At the same time, Haight's cross-examination of a similarly distressed Kendall had also been very direct and somewhat harassing. The general rule seems to have been to let the dead rest in peace but to lean heavily on the living.

The Attorney General: Now, tell me this. Did you zigzag the boat?
– No.
You were told to do that?
– I understood it was only when you saw a submarine that you should zigzag.
You had information that there were submarines about, and the instructions to you were to zigzag.
The Commissioner: And I think the reason is stated, too.
The Attorney General: Yes, my Lord. *(To the Witness):* You told me you read this: 'War experience has shown that fast steamers can considerably reduce the chance of a successful submarine attack by zigzagging – that is to say, altering course at short and irregular intervals, say ten minutes to half an hour. This course is invariably adopted by warships when cruising in an area known to be infested by submarines.' Did you zigzag?
– No
Why?
– Because I did not think it was necessary until I saw a submarine.
You were told zigzagging was a safeguard; you were told submarines were infesting the southern part of the Irish coast; you had plenty of time in hand, and you did not obey the orders?
– I did not.
You would have plenty of time. I understand zigzagging takes more time, but why did not you zigzag?
– Because I thought it was not necessary until I saw a submarine.
The Commissioner: But the whole point of that is that it is the submarine that is looking at you?
–Yes.
The Commissioner: And if you are zigzagging you confuse him and put him into difficulties?
The Attorney-General: How could you think that, because this is very clear: 'War experience has shown that fast steamers can considerably reduce the chance of a successful submarine attack by zigzagging' – nothing about when you see the submarine. You see, when you are torpedoed it is too late?
– Of course it is.
Do not you see now that you really disobeyed a very important instruction?
– (No answer.)

Turner later accepted that he had 'mis-read' the Admiralty advice. At a different point in the inquiry, Mersey himself picked up the logical flaw in Turner's evidence. As he was at this time finalising the report of the *Falaba* inquiry, it was perhaps natural that he would be the one to point out that Admiralty advice to ships when a submarine was spotted was not to zigzag but to turn away at maximum speed – exactly as the *Falaba* had done – or to turn towards the submarine to ram it. Turner came across as someone who had not properly assimilated the thinking behind the Admiralty advice. It is worth pointing out that in the case of the zigzagging instructions, he had had very little time to consider them before his ship was torpedoed. They had only been issued the day before the ship left Liverpool on the outward voyage and were not drawn specifically to his attention at that time. It has been suggested that Carson bullied him into agreeing that he had read a document that, in fact, he had never seen, but Turner confirmed in the much friendlier questioning by Aspinall that he had read it and never subsequently indicated otherwise. It seems fair to assume that he had actually read the Admiralty advice to zigzag but possibly had not given it the attention it deserved.

Although Mersey's was the only formal inquiry into the sinking of the *Lusitania* there were other court proceedings at a later date in America resulting from claims for damages against Cunard. UK witnesses were not asked to put themselves at risk by travelling across the Atlantic and depositions were taken, including cross-examinations, in London in mid-1917. Naturally Turner was one of the crucial witnesses and he was again questioned about his decisions that morning, including the fact that he had not been zigzagging. His responses differed to those of two years earlier in that he no longer claimed to have mis-read the instructions, interpreting them as only applying after a submarine had been spotted. Instead, he maintained that he thought them not to apply to a fast ship such as his, which is rather odd as the Admiralty wording specifically indicated that zigzagging was particularly effective in the case of faster ships. He also maintained that Admiralty advice was little more than helpful suggestions to masters which they were under no obligation to observe. Turner, probably with some degree of satisfaction, pointed out that he had been torpedoed a second time when the *Ivernia* had been sunk at the end of 1916 and he had been zigzagging at the time. There were other captains who gave evidence to the American court in support of Turner, indicating that few of their peers had paid any attention to the advice on zigzagging when it had been issued. Indeed some had described it as 'a joke'.

The zigzagging issue also connects through to the third element of the criticism levelled at Turner, that of the 'slow' speed at which the ship was travelling when it was hit. The ship, with its boiler capacity reduced deliberately by Cunard to save coal and so money, was capable of 21 knots but was only doing 18 knots when spotted by Schwieger. The Chairman of Cunard, Albert Booth, was first of all questioned about the reduction in boiler capacity and its effect on the ship's speed:

> *The Attorney General:* With that boiler power you have told us, and we have been told that they got an average maximum speed of about 21 knots?
> – That is right.
> Is that as fast or faster than most Atlantic-going steamers?
> – That is considerably faster than any Atlantic steamer which was running during last winter or is running now.

The inquiry seemed satisfied by Booth's point that 21 knots was faster than any other ship. Perhaps it should not have been. The level of safety depended on the absolute speed, not the speed relative to other ships. A ship travelling at 25 knots was safer than one travelling at 21 knots. There are echoes here of the 'maximum speed' issue as *Titanic* approached the ice. The real point was nothing to do with whether or not it was the fastest that the ship could go, it was the relationship of the absolute speed to the capacity of lookouts to spot things ahead that mattered. In the case of a submarine attack, the faster a target is moving the lower the chances of hitting it. Probability is all important here. Neither speed nor zigzagging offer any absolute defence against torpedoes. Each reduces the statistical probability of a strike somewhat and the combination of the two has even greater effect. Add an escort and the probability is reduced even further. Examples can still be found, nonetheless, of fast, zigzagging ships with escorts being torpedoed.

Booth was also questioned about Turner's decision not to use even the full speed he did have available and he defended his employee by arguing that, prior to the sinking of the *Lusitania,* no ship travelling at even 14 knots had been 'caught' by a submarine. Mersey immediately responded by (incorrectly) pointing out that the *Falaba* had been travelling at above that speed when caught by U-28. Booth had, however, provided an insight into thinking in Cunard, and probably other shipping lines as well. The primitive state of submarine technology and experience of it at work up to that point had created a sense, if not of invulnerability, at least of very limited risk. Despite the blustering of the German government in the adverts they had placed in the American press, the upper echelons of Cunard did not really believe that large, fast liners were seriously threatened by the new weapons. Hence Turner had given little more than perfunctory attention to Admiralty advice on the matter and had made only the minimum concession in his navigation to the supposed risk. One may wonder, in fact, how much he knew about the capabilities of submarines and how they operated. It is likely that a landlubber who has watched the film *Das Boot* has a better understanding of submarine operations than did Will Turner.

Turner's explanation of his decision to stick at 18 knots superficially seemed a good one because it did appear to be a response to one aspect of Admiralty advice. Captains had been told to try to arrive at their destination port at night and at a state of tide that allowed them to enter immediately. Turner had calculated that a steady 18 knots would bring him to the Mersey Bar just as the sun was about to rise and with water enough to allow him to cross it. F E Smith correctly pointed out that the time could just as well have been managed by zigzagging at greater speed. An erratic zigzag pattern at 21 knots would have taken much the same time to reach the Bar as 18 knots on a steady course. Aspinall defended Turner, rather lamely, by suggesting that zigzagging caused the ship to cover a slightly greater area and thus marginally increased the risk of being spotted by a submarine. As the extract given previously indicated, it is not the avoidance of being spotted that is the object of zigzagging.

In recording the events of 7 May in Chapter 8 we mentioned that, just before coming across the *Lusitania*, Schwieger had seen the cruiser HMS *Juno*. Although not a modern ship, sinking her would have made a fine ending to Schwieger's patrol. Despite being in range, Schwieger could not attack because the cruiser was travelling at speed and was zigzagging. This combination of speed and erratic changes of course had been recognised quickly as making an important contribution to defence against submarine attack and it remained so right through the Second World War. The two great Cunard liners of that period, the *Queen Mary* and the *Queen Elizabeth,* spent most of that war crossing the Atlantic, not in convoy, but travelling very fast and zigzagging, albeit with a heavy escort to reduce the probability of a successful attack even further. It was a successful ploy, the only loss of life coming from a collision between the *Queen Mary* and her escorting cruiser that may have resulted from confusion over the zigzag pattern. While recognising the benefit of hindsight, it does seem to be the case that, had Turner maintained the 21 knots his ship was capable of and steered an irregular zigzag pattern, it is less probable that Schwieger would have been able to mount a successful attack.

Given the criticisms of Turner that had been voiced even before the inquiry began, there was some surprise at the lack of criticism of him in the report. It was widely supposed (and still is by many) that Mersey himself was under pressure by the Admiralty to find Turner guilty of contributing to the loss of his ship. Admiral Inglefield was thought to be the assessor who was looking after the Admiralty's interest in the procedure, there being no counsel with that specific brief. In reading through the transcript, it does not seem that Inglefield showed any particular hostility to Turner and, as we have seen, he lent support to some of Aspinall's arguments in the captain's defence; but one cannot rule out pressure being exerted on Mersey through less official channels. The issue of the second torpedo does not concern us at this point, but the case is well made by Diana Preston in *Wilful Murder* that influence was brought to bear to persuade the inquiry that at least two torpedoes had been fired when in fact it was already known that there had only been one. There was also an incident in the inquiry when it was discovered that the Admiralty had prepared two versions of a communication sent to the *Lusitania*. The intention seemed to be to demonstrate that the instructions that Turner had received were less vague than in fact they had been. Mersey was extremely angry about the apparent deception and it may have made him more sceptical about the Admiralty position. There remains the possibility that Mersey, with agreement from the assessors, came to the conclusion without outside influence that Turner should not be blamed. A second possibility was that he resisted Admiralty pressure, possibly to demonstrate that, having been pushed around on the matter of the second torpedo, he was still his own man. A third possibility was that the government itself recognised that putting blame on Turner might detract from the anti-German propaganda value of the report, so that the influence on Mersey was in quite a different direction. Our focus must be to consider the merits of the outcome rather than to speculate without additional evidence about the murkiness of its origins.

The exoneration of Turner's handling of his ship on the morning of 7 May in the report is comprehensive – no blame was attached to him – but it was not unqualified. The section was obviously written with great care by a skilled wordsmith. It read:

> Captain Turner was fully advised as to the means which in the view of the Admiralty were best calculated to avert the perils he was likely to encounter, and in considering the question whether he is to blame for the catastrophe in which his voyage ended I have to bear this circumstance in mind. It is certain that in some respects Captain Turner did not follow the advice given to him. It may be (though I seriously doubt it) that had he done so his ship would have reached Liverpool in safety. But the question remains, was his conduct the conduct of a negligent or incompetent man. On this question I have sought the guidance of my assessors, who have rendered me invaluable assistance, and the conclusion at which I have arrived is that blame ought not to be imputed to the Captain. The advice given to him, although

meant for his most serious and careful consideration, was not intended to deprive him of the right to exercise his skilled judgment in the difficult questions that might arise from time to time in the navigation of his ship. His omission to follow the advice in all respects cannot fairly be attributed either to negligence or incompetence.

He exercised his judgment for the best. It was the judgment of a skilled and experienced man, and although others might have acted differently and perhaps more successfully, he ought not, in my opinion, to be blamed.

There are three points to note here. Firstly is the reference (unusual in Mersey's reports) to his having consulted with the assessors on a difficult judgment. Perhaps this was included deliberately in order explicitly to tie Admiral Inglefield into the exoneration of Turner. Second are the doubts expressed by Mersey that different decisions by Turner, more in line with Admiralty advice, might have saved the ship. He gives no reason for this view and there is nothing in the evidence given to the inquiry that would seem to justify it. Had Turner been travelling at any different speed on any different course in any different position around 2pm on that day the probability of a successful attack would have been altered. Like each of the other four ships whose sinking Mersey investigated, *Lusitania*'s fate depended on the coming together of a very particular set of circumstances on a specific occasion.

The third and most significant point to note is the last sentence, which implies that a different person might have made different, and more successful, decisions. Presumably such different decisions would have been more in line with Admiralty advice (they could hardly have been less so) and, if more successful, would, one assumes, have prevented the ship being lost – in contradiction of the opinion expressed in the first paragraph. If it was not negligence or incompetence that prevented Turner from making more successful decisions, what was it? Perhaps the answer lies in how Turner the man came to be viewed by Mersey during the course of the inquiry.

Butler Aspinall at times encouraged Turner to portray himself as the crusty old man of the sea, as in the following exchange:

Mr. Butler Aspinall: Is it your view that the modern ships, with their greasers and their stewards and their firemen, sometimes do not carry the old-fashioned sailor that you knew of in the days of your youth?
– That is the idea.
That is what you have in your mind?
– That is it.
You are an old-fashioned sailor man?

−That is right.

And you preferred the man of your youth?

−Yes, and I prefer him yet.

We will come back to the point concerning the seaman-like qualities of the crew later, but the passage also displays the brevity of Turner's answers, almost to the point of being curt. Reports at the time described him as ill at ease and clearly under stress from the dreadful experience of losing his ship and so many of the passengers for whose safety he was responsible. Mersey showed flashes of impatience with Turner on occasions in the earlier part of his evidence in particular, but then flashes of impatience from Mersey towards both witnesses and counsel were the norm rather than the exception. They do not appear to have carried any meaningful insight into Mersey's attitude to the person at whom they were aimed.

Towards the end of the inquiry there was a conversation between Mersey and Butler Aspinall about Turner as a witness, one that took place in camera in the absence of all of the witnesses. It was surprisingly frank and is worth quoting in full. It took place immediately prior to Aspinall beginning his defence of Turner's actions.

Mr. Butler Aspinall: At the outset of my remarks on behalf of the Captain what I want to emphasise, and I think it is a material matter, is this, that the Captain was undoubtedly a bad witness, although he may be a very excellent navigator.

The Commissioner: No, he was not a bad witness.

Mr. Butler Aspinall: Well, he was confused, my Lord.

The Commissioner: In my opinion at present he may have been a bad Master during that voyage, but I think he was telling the truth.

Mr. Butler Aspinall: Yes.

The Commissioner: And I think he is a truthful witness. I think he means to tell the truth.

Mr. Butler Aspinall: Yes.

The Commissioner: In that sense he did not make a bad witness.

Mr. Butler Aspinall: No.

The Commissioner: He made a bad witness for you.

Mr. Butler Aspinall: Well, what I was going to say about him was this, that it was very difficult to get a consecutive story from the man, but I was going to submit that he was an honest man.

The Commissioner: I think he is, and I do not think Sir Edward Carson or Sir Frederick Smith have suggested anything to the contrary.

The Solicitor-General: No, my Lord.

The Commissioner: The impression the man has made upon me is – I came here prepared to consider his evidence very carefully, but the impression he has made upon me is that he was quite straight and honest.

Mr. Butler Aspinall: Quite. He had gone through naturally the very greatest strain both physical and mental. He lost his ship; he lost his comrades, or many of them; there was very great loss of life, and he was in the water for a very long period of time.

It is interesting to see Mersey at this quite late stage (the penultimate session) saying that, in his opinion, Turner may have been a 'bad Master' during the voyage, but the main thrust of the passage is the recognition by all of the senior personnel taking part that Turner was honest and straight forward despite the brevity and lack of coherence of his answers. This is rather a different view to the hysterical picture painted by First Sea Lord Fisher of a captain traitorously presenting his ship to the enemy for destruction. The impression of Turner that comes across is akin to Jack Hawkin's portrayal of the Captain of the *Compass Rose* in the film of Nicholas Monsarrat's novel *The Cruel Sea* – taciturn, introverted, dogged and reliable, but not without charisma that inspired admiration and loyalty in others. A collection of photographs taken by him, many on board the *Lusitania*, were auctioned in the spring of 2011 and the catalogue described the 400 photographs as providing an intimate insight into the life of a captain who seemed fun-loving and happy.

The benefit of the doubt that Mersey gave to both Captains Smith and Turner in the handling of their ships may, in each case, have had a similar origin, despite the very different circumstances of the events they were associated with and the different characters of the men themselves. Butler Aspinall touched on it in his defence of Turner when he suggested to Mersey that 'He may have been a courageous sailor, but, after all, one has got to judge him by who he is and what experience he has had in the past.'

As we have seen, Mersey acquitted E J Smith of reckless speeding in the known proximity of ice because he was convinced, probably correctly, that other captains with similar experience to Smith would have done the same. There was evidence given in the *Titanic* inquiry to that effect. In the *Lusitania* inquiry there was, of course, no evidence given as to the practice of other master mariners so far as following Admiralty advice on the avoidance of submarines was concerned. In the sailing ship era there had been a resistance amongst merchant ship captains to being dictated to by their naval colleagues and convoy operations in the Second World War were often fraught with the same tension. Without hearing any evidence directly in court, Mersey may have been aware that Turner's non-compliance was very much in line with current practice amongst his peers on the larger, faster ships and he may, therefore, have been reluctant to single him out. The concern within the Admiralty at Mersey's failure to censure Turner probably arose not so much from a desire to punish that individual, but because they wanted their 'advice' to be regarded as instructions that were to be obeyed to the letter, except in the most unusual circumstances. Mersey appeared to endorse the notion that the captain's discretion was sacrosanct and should not be challenged. This is, perhaps, the critical issue so far as this inquiry is concerned. The Admiralty was collecting all of the data it could find about U-boat activity and was having considerable success in de-coding German signals. Using that intelligence it was providing the best advice it could in what were novel and difficult circumstances. That advice was the only source of expert help for merchant ship captains. While the requirements of safe navigation would always have to be taken into account, captains would have been well advised to stick as closely as possible to what the Admiralty believed to be the best way of avoiding attack. Our natural sympathy for Turner and understanding of Mersey's reluctance to censure him should not detract from the view that a strong exhortation in the report to captains to regard the Admiralty advice as instructions in all but name might well have been effective.

When Carson condensed the brief of the *Lusitania* into just two questions, his second one related to the steps taken to minimise the loss of life. Given the short time between the torpedo striking *Lusitania* and its sinking there was limited scope for a systematic evacuation. Mersey was satisfied that the lifeboats were in good order and that the collapsible boats designed to float free as the ship sank had been released to do so. One or two witnesses complained about lack of organisation, about lifeboats taking in water and about a degree of panic amongst the crew and some passengers. Mersey was not impressed by the complaints. Perhaps the fact that one of the complainants appeared to be motivated by the prospect of being paid to keep quiet prejudiced the Commissioner to some extent, but he was probably correct in suggesting that problems with lifeboats were a consequence of those on the port side crashing against the side of the listing ship as they were lowered. On the matter of panic, however, Mersey's wording left him open to an accusation of class bias. He suggested that any panic had only occurred when steerage passengers 'swarmed' onto the boat deck. It was an unfortunate choice of words. The class division in ships resulted in steerage passengers, who were aboard in larger numbers, having farther to go than passengers in the other classes to reach the lifeboats. When they began to get there, having climbed through a darkened, listing ship, they were suddenly faced with the appalling sight of the bow rapidly disappearing into the sea. It is not surprising that some became hysterical.

The loss of steam pressure from the boilers almost immediately after the *Lusitania* was hit prevented her engines being put into reverse in order to stop her. She carried on moving, gradually slowing down, right up until the time she sank. This created considerable difficulty in lowering the lifeboats as we noted in Chapter 8. Turner in his evidence mentioned that he had stopped the launching of lifeboats for some minutes in order to allow the ship to slow. As a consequence, some passengers reported that they had been ordered out of a lifeboat that they had already clambered into and this had obviously caused them distress. There was some confusion as to who told them to leave the lifeboat and how the instruction was explained to them. One witness said that the captain had shouted from the wing of the bridge to get out of the lifeboat as the ship was not going to sink. A second witness reporting the same incident said that it was Staff Captain Anderson who shouted to them. There may well have been some confusion as Anderson, who lost his life in the tragedy, carried the title of Captain and may have been better known to many than the passenger-shy Turner. Nonetheless, it is surprising that passengers were actually removed from lifeboats and even more surprising if they were assured that the ship would remain afloat at least until beached. It is an incident that has not been entirely explained but may indicate a communication glitch between captain and staff captain. Telling the passengers already in the lifeboats to get out because the ship was not going to sink may have been a white lie, to allow the ship time to slow.

Turner cast doubt on the competence of his own crew in manning the lifeboats. There are two sides to this. Like other captains he was very concerned about the number of good quality seamen who had been taken up by the navy as reservists and the difficulty in finding able replacements. At this stage of the war it was a major problem and, as we shall see in the next chapter, it was one of which the German submariners were well aware. However, in this criticism he was also exhibiting his old seadog nature, complaining that seamen in 1915 were not what they had been in his youth. He comes across as someone uncomfortable with the dramatic changes he has lived through and has found that for him they posed more threats than opportunities.

Turner's attitude to the passengers, from whom he made his living, was demonstrated when he claimed, without giving any specific instance, that their attempts to assist with the launching of the lifeboats had actually been a hindrance. While one or two other witnesses from the crew suggested that some of the efforts of passengers to help had been futile, there was not the same implication of interfering busybodies that emerged from Turner.

Surprisingly, Mersey reflected Turner's view, indeed seemed to amplify it in the inquiry report. It was an issue that had also surfaced in the *Falaba* inquiry; this from Henry Ashton, a steward on the ship giving evidence:

> You say the passengers meant to help, but were interfering with you?
> —Yes.
> At which boats?
> — At the two I was working at.
> You mean No. 2 and No. 4?
> —Yes.
> But they did not prevent your lowering No. 4?
> — No; but I mean most things would have been done much quicker and better and less lives lost if it had been left to members of the crew to do it.

One suspects that it may have been this evidence in the *Falaba* inquiry that influenced Mersey's comments in the *Lusitania* report as much as Turner's throwaway remark.

Fred Davies was not at that peak of the profession occupied by both Smith and Turner, but he was nonetheless on its higher reaches. He was not alive to give evidence on his own behalf, but his reputation did not suffer as a consequence. There is no hint of any criticism of him in Mersey's report. We have already observed that the two wartime inquiries were short by comparison with the peacetime ones but there was another significant difference. The inquiries into the *Titanic* and *Empress* disasters both finished with a set of recommendations intended to prevent similar disasters occurring or at least to ameliorate the consequences. Neither the *Lusitania* nor the *Falaba* reports contain any such recommendations. So, not only did Davies evade any criticism, there were no suggestions as to how things might be improved on future occasions. In the wartime context in 1915 it was almost certain that such occasions would arise with distressing frequency. The sinking of the *Falaba* was not a freak accident unlikely ever to happen again, as in the case of *Titanic*. Arguably the absence of recommendations in these two reports was one of Mersey's greatest failings. Not only did he not do what he should have done to support the Admiralty in their measures to help ships to avoid submarine attack, he missed entirely a crucial opportunity to highlight the failures in practice that led to so many casualties in the sinking of the *Falaba*.

In the evidence given to the *Falaba* inquiry Mersey was told that von Forstner's warning, shouted from the conning tower through a megaphone, had given Davies just five minutes to clear his ship. In fact only one witness, a passenger, claimed to have heard mention of five minutes in the hail from the submarine but admitted to being unsure of what he had heard. Another witness reported that, just before the torpedo hit, the captain remarked to him: 'They have only given us five minutes to clear the ship.' Other witnesses failed to decipher what had been shouted across the gap. The German side claimed that Davies had been given a ten-minute warning, but that 23 minutes actually elapsed before the torpedo was fired. In one sense the actual amount of time is immaterial. Davies knew that he had to evacuate the ship as quickly as it could be achieved. What followed was a shambles and although the last boat (a small one) was being launched when the torpedo struck, only two got away cleanly with the number of passengers they were expected to carry. Three were lost by accidents when being lowered, one broke up after launch and one was swamped. Why?

The inquiry report contains some answers to that question, but does so purely in the matter of fact manner that might be expected of an able journalist reporting events but making no comment or judgement. The difficulty of obtaining competent crew in wartime that we have already noted resulted in high turnover amongst crews from one voyage to the next. Over half of the crew that sailed on *Falaba* on her last voyage had not sailed on her previous one. Some of those may have been on the ship or her sister on another occasion but the majority were probably there for the first time. Some crew only arrived on board just before sailing time and this was the reason given for the fact that when she sailed crew members had not been allocated to lifeboats. The Purser was in the process of doing this when U-28 appeared.

It was the custom on Elder Dempster Line ships to conduct lifeboat drill on Saturdays or Sundays. The ship was attacked on Saturday morning and no drill had been attempted. Presumably, one would have been carried out sometime in those two days after the crew boat list had been completed. There were a series of vociferous complaints from the passengers who gave evidence about the equipment and the organisation on the ship. One, Cyril Bressey, summarised his five complaints and they mirrored the tone of the evidence given throughout the inquiry.

> The first thing is that there were no boat stations for the passengers – no list of boat stations and no passengers knew where they were to go to. Secondly, the submarine was apparently seen by a large number of passengers before any action was taken by the ship in altering the course to bring that boat directly astern. Thirdly, there were no instructions given to the passengers at the crisis, or to me anyhow. I say there were apparently no instructions given; in fact, I can say definitely that there were no instructions given me, as I heard none. Fourthly, the regulations also

provide for a crew, as far as I remember, from the ship's boats station list—it is somewhere about ten, with a competent officer in charge of each boat. The boat that I was dropped into the water in apparently had no officer. I heard none, because I had no directions given me there. The boat which ultimately picked me up was being steered and commanded by passengers, so that if there was a ship's officer on board he was not in charge and he gave no directions, he gave no orders. And the fifth is the apparently unsatisfactory condition of the boats.

The last complaint is one that was refuted with some degree of success by Aspinall and his team. Several of the passengers had described the timber in the boats as having been rotten. As some of the boats had been cast up on the Cornish coast they were examined and found to be sound. The boats on the *Falaba*'s sister ship were also examined on her next docking and were also found to be sound. While there may have been some doubts about the equipment in the boats and there was a possibility that one or two of the seams in the hulls had dried out and were leaking, the boats themselves do seem to have been generally fit for purpose.

Aspinall dealt with the complaints by passengers at length in his final statement. He began with a hand-wringing and patronising dismissal of the evidence from all of the passengers:

> A large number of them came forward, some seventeen or eighteen of them, in support of those charges, and I want those gentlemen to understand that in saying what I am going to say. I am speaking in no spirit of hostility to them. I am not attacking their veracity and I am not impugning their good faith. I have no doubt they perfectly honestly believed what they told the Court. They formed the impression at a time when their opportunities certainly for accurate observation were not good, but they undoubtedly have come to the conclusion that they have a grievance against the Elder Dempster Line, and against the sailors of the Elder Dempster Line who were managing the boats under the very trying circumstances of this lamentable tragedy.

Regarding organisation on the ship he was on particularly weak ground. This was his answer to the accusation about the lack of boat lists for crew members:

> Now with regard to the other points of attack, point No. 2 was that there were no boat lists for the crew or passengers. With regard to that, we have been told that the practice in this vessel, and I submit it is a reasonable

practice, is that the boat list is got out as soon as it can practically be got out. One cannot, of course, do impossibilities. I suppose perhaps it would be more desirable that one should have a boat list up as soon as ever the anchor is up and the vessel sails. But, in fact, that is impossible, if it could be done readily, of course, it would be done. The ship, no doubt, came out of dock at 6 o'clock in the morning, and did not sail until 6 p.m., 12 hours afterwards; but as Captain Thompson told us, it is very difficult to collect your men, and in this particular case four of the crew came on board as late as the passengers did, and that is, as common experience teaches one, what happens. Some of the sailors, unfortunately (not those of engine room staff as your Lordship elicited), came on board suffering from intoxication, and there always are out of a large crew unfortunately a certain number of men who do not act up to the higher standard of conduct, but when they get to sea they are not a whit worse as sailors. But we must deal with human nature as we find it, and I submit it is quite impossible under these circumstances for shipowners to do more than the Elder Dempster Line did in this case with regard to boat lists.

In a way it is rather sad to see a highly respected and intelligent lawyer being forced to come out with such claptrap in defence of his client. What on earth did the sobriety or lack of it amongst some members of the crew have to do with the purser putting a list of names and boats together unless the purser was himself amongst the intoxicated? This is perhaps the most transparent example across all four of the inquiries of a commercial interest pleading, and successfully pleading, innocence when the evidence so clearly pointed to guilt. At what point do crude financial considerations give way in the corporate mind to broader ethical concerns?

Aspinall's answer to the reports of the mishandling of the lowering of the boats that resulted in so many of the deaths was even less edifying. It consisted of a marriage of half-truth and innuendo in which he attempted to pass most of the blame onto the passengers concerned. The story of boat number 2 can serve to illustrate. This boat was one of the ones that had been lifted off its chocks and swung out ready for launching shortly after leaving Liverpool. When the emergency arose the first four people to go into the boat were four male passengers, including a father and son. Before any other people arrived the boat's stern suddenly fell and the ringbolt holding the bow broke. The boat fell heavily into the water still with the four men aboard and floated away, partially disintegrating in the process. It was held together with a rope that the passengers found and tied around what was left of the gunwale and it served to provide flotation for some of the other passengers who had been thrown into the water as a result of other boats being damaged. All four of the passengers who had climbed into the boat gave evidence. There was also evidence from one of the crew on the deck at the boat as the accident happened. He maintained that the ship's butcher had let go the fall at one end of the boat and the captain had told him to run out the other as quickly as possible. It had jammed and that was when the ringbolt had broken free. This was Aspinall's take on the story of boat 2, no doubt building on the evidence of the steward Ashton quoted earlier.

> That, my Lord, was the undoubted cause of this boat getting into trouble – the fact that the fall ran through the man's hand, and, possibly, the fact that the disaster was in some way contributed to by the efforts, and very zealous efforts, of these four passengers to get the boat into the water.

So, when von Forstner gave his warning, crew members did not know their duties and passengers did not know which boat to go to or what to do when they got there. Most of the casualties resulted from people being killed or injured in the accidents that occurred during the attempts to launch lifeboats or through being thrown into the sea when boats were upset. Mersey should have appreciated that a complete change in attitude to passenger safety was required if ships such as this were going to continue to sail with a major risk of submarine attack. The evidence he had heard had made it clear beyond any doubt that this ship had sailed into a submarine-infested zone totally unprepared to deal with the consequences of an attack. In all likelihood it was typical of many others. There should have been a clear recommendation that no ship should be permitted to sail unless all members of crew fully understood what was required of them in an emergency and all passengers had been well rehearsed in evacuation procedures. Habits that had become ingrained in peacetime, such as only holding lifeboat drill on a Saturday or Sunday, became quite absurd in wartime. Mersey might, yet again, have excused Davies personally as he was only following similar practice to others, but that did not detract from the need to ensure that obvious, life-threatening deficiencies in practice were addressed for the future. Instead Mersey, in his report, put all of the disorganisation of the crew and the catastrophes in the launching of the boats down to the haste engendered by von Forstner's inadequate warning.

The lack of recommendations in the two wartime reports may be associated with the desire to achieve maximum propaganda effect by heaping all responsibility for the loss of life onto the German submariners and their controllers. In the next chapter we will consider the nature of their culpability in relation to the terms in which Mersey chose to describe it.

GUNTHER VON FORSTNER AND WALTHER SCHWIEGER

When Mersey issued his report on the *Falaba* he summarised his findings as follows:

> The Court, having carefully enquired into the circumstances of the [sinking of the *Falaba*] finds … that the loss of the said ship and lives was due to damage caused to the said ship by a torpedo fired by a submarine of German nationality, whereby the ship sank. In the opinion of the Court the act was done not merely with the intention of sinking the ship but also with the intention of sacrificing life.

It is the final four words that we are concerned with, as all of the rest was already well established. While the first part of the statement is factual, those four words are an inference. Mersey did not question von Forstner and had no means of knowing what was in his mind during the attack. The inference seems to have been drawn from the brevity of the supposed five minute warning – Mersey was quite convinced that the torpedo had indeed been fired just five minutes after the ship was stopped. If von Forstner had no intention of killing people, why did he not allow adequate time for everyone to get clear? However, one might equally ask why he allowed any time at all. Had he fired immediately he could have sacrificed even more lives. Mersey presumably considered the five minutes a token behind which the Germans could hide their murderous intent.

In this case, we may be in a slightly better position to arrive at a judgement than was Mersey as we have access to more information about von Forstner and his pattern of behaviour as a submarine captain. Our view of Mersey's conclusions should not, however, be overly influenced by material of which he knew nothing. In Chapter 6 we referred to the journal that von Forstner published in 1917, following his transfer to a training role, and which included his descriptions of some of the actions in which he was involved. Before looking at what he says in his accounts of these actions, it is necessary to be absolutely clear that the journal must be regarded as a propaganda exercise. Those who lived through the Cold War will be attuned to a form of Soviet propaganda that was jargon laden. Words and phrases such as 'proletariat', 'workers' democracy' 'western imperialism' appeared so often as to become meaningless. Von Forstner's journal is not overt propaganda of that nature; parts of it seem almost to be extracts from training manuals, understandable considering his role at the time. He makes reference to British authorities in describing the nature of submarine warfare and uses the exploits of British boats in the Dardanelles as examples of what can be done. However, in his outline of submarine activity in the early part of the war, and in particular in his description of events in which he had been engaged, the journal is patriotic bluster, seeing the war as a glorious and often enjoyable exercise in the demonstration of German superiority over the hated enemy, 'our dear cousins across the Channel'. Needless to say the same sort of jingoistic material, replete with patronisingly contemptuous references to the 'Hun' was being produced in Britain; examples are not hard to find.

The journal was translated by Ana Crafts Codman and published in Boston in November 1917, America having entered the war that April. She added a foreword to the document which casts an interesting light on how the journal was regarded in the newly belligerent United States. This is her view of the Gunther von Forstner who emerges from the journal:

> Several chapters in this book are simple narratives of the commander's own adventures during the present naval warfare waged against commerce. His attempts at a lighter vein often provoke a smile at the quality of his wit, but he is not lacking in fine and manly virtues. He is a loyal comrade; a good officer concerned for the welfare of his crew. He is even kindly to his captives when he finds they are docile victims. He is also willing to credit his adversary with pluck and courage. He is never sparing of his own person, and shows admirable endurance under pressure of intense work and great responsibility. He is full of enthusiastic love for his profession, and in describing a storm at sea his rather monotonous style of writing suddenly rises to eloquence. But in his exalted devotion to the Almighty War Lord, and to the Fatherland, he openly reveals his fanatical joy in the nefarious work he has to perform.

In addition to personal recollections there are references to other aspects of the war in the journal, some surprisingly objective in tone. This is von

Forstner's take on the Battle of Jutland, which the German authorities at the time hailed as a great victory.

> If one should examine the course of this battle, which has been represented by lines graphically showing the paths of the British and German fleets, one could easily see how the British imposed their will upon the Germans in every turn that these lines make. It reminds one very much of the herding of sheep, for the German fleet was literally herded on May 31, 1916, from 5:36 in the afternoon until 9 o'clock that night. Admiral von Scheer, however, fought the only action which it was possible for him to fight. It was a losing action, and one which he knew, from a purely mathematical consideration, could not be successful.

There is also a brief passing reference to the *Lusitania* to the effect that 'destiny overtook her', surely one of the most euphemistic descriptions ever of such a terrible event. Our principal concern, however, is von Forstner's own actions during the spring and summer of 1915. There is a long description of his sinking of the *Leuwarden* in which great care is taken to ensure the safety of the crew and much made of their expressions of gratitude. The theme that runs through the journal is that captains who stopped their ships immediately and did precisely as ordered could thereby ensure the safety of their passengers and crew. Those who disobeyed, who attempted to escape or who tried to summon assistance could expect to suffer the consequences. Here is how he wrote of the sinking of the *Glitra* by another U-boat in October 1914.

> At the end of October, 1914, the first English steamer *Glitra* was sunk off the Norwegian coast. It carried a cargo of sewing machines, whisky, and steel from Leith. The captain was wise enough to stop at the first signal of the commander of the U-boat, and he thereby saved the lives of his crew, who escaped with their belongings after the steamer was peacefully sunk. If others later had likewise followed his example, innocent passengers and crew would not have been drowned; and after all, people are fond of their own lives; but these English captains were following the orders of their Government to save their ships through flight.

The problem that Britain was experiencing manning its merchant ships because of the massive expansion of the Navy was well known. Wages of merchant seamen had been increased in order to attract more and better people. In the journal, von Forstner claims that he had observed the effects of this problem and his observations were directly relevant to the sinking of the *Falaba*.

> I had made an interesting study of the manner in which the English crews
> of the present day were composed. Apart from the British officers there
> were but few experienced seamen on board. This was made evident by the
> awkward way the men usually handled the lifeboats. Even with the enor-
> mous increase of wages, sailors could not be found to risk their lives in the
> danger zone, and a lot of untrained fellows … revealed by their clumsy
> rowing that they had only recently been pressed into service.

To emphasise the point, he mentioned in his description of the sinking of the
Flamian the fact the crew took to the boats with a perfect discipline 'we
were little accustomed to witness'.

The action in which we are particularly interested is one that took place
on the day prior to the sinking of the *Falaba*. As well as sinking the *Aguila*
that day, U-28 met the *Vosges* in heavy weather in the entrance to the Bristol
Channel. In this case the captain refused to stop and even, according to von
Forstner, turned and attempted to ram the submarine. The submarine's gun
was used to damage the ship and set it on fire and a running 'battle' went on
for four hours. The *Vosges* was damaged enough to sink when U-28 had to
leave because of fear of warships arriving. Von Forstner then reported what
happened after he returned to Germany.

> We had been truly impressed by the captain's brave endurance, notwith-
> standing his lack of wisdom, and we knew that the men-of-war were
> coming to his rescue. We read in the papers, on our return to a German port,
> that the *Vosges* had sunk soon after we had departed, and what remained of
> the passengers and crew were picked up by the English ships. The captain
> was rewarded for his temerity by being raised to the rank of Reserve officer,
> and the crew were given sums of money; but all the other officers had per-
> ished, as well as several sailors and a few passengers, who had been forced to
> help the stokers in order to increase the speed of the flying steamer.

The 'brave but stupid' theme was a recurring one in descriptions of British
master mariners. What is really odd about this passage is the acknowledgement at the end of the large number of people who had been killed, numbers
that he had obtained from a German newspaper. In fact there was only one
fatal casualty, the Chief Engineer, and four wounded, one of them a woman.
The suggestion that passengers were killed who had been forced to assist the
stokers was surely nonsensical.

Von Forstner makes no specific reference to the events of the following day. He simply says that in the next few days they stopped and searched many neutral steamers and sank many English ones. With regard to these actions he says:

> The captains were occasionally stubborn and refused to obey our signals, so a few accidents occurred; in one case, for instance, a stray shot struck some passengers in a lifeboat, which collapsed; but as a rule passengers and crews were picked up by the many sailboats and fishing boats which circulate in the Irish Sea and in St. George's Channel, and it was we who generally summoned these fishermen to go to the rescue of their shipwrecked countrymen.

We are left to wonder if the 104 deaths of passengers and crew from the *Falaba* was one of the accidents of which he speaks. There is no mention in the journal either of the sinking of the *Iberian* on 31 July that year, the event which later gave rise to the story of the sea monster. It is worth looking at as there was a report provided to the *New York Times* by the doctor on the ship, Dr Patrick S Burns, who happened to be American. As such the story in the paper was rather less partial than those syndicated across from London, as many of them were. Given that the incident happened two months after the sinking of the *Lusitania*, when sentiment in America was largely hostile to the actions of German submarines, the tone is surprisingly neutral. There are a couple of inaccuracies and inconsistencies in the report, which may be the result of mistakes by typesetters. The submarine is wrongly numbered as U-58 and the lifeboat that Dr Burns used to leave the ship is number 3 on one occasion and number 8 on another. The *Iberian* refused to stop when ordered to do so and attempted to outrun the submarine. Captain Jago had succeeded in escaping from a submarine on a previous occasion but this time von Forstner's gunfire proved conclusive. One shot killed six members of the crew and wounded a number of others while another blew away the aerial, although not before a message asking for assistance had been sent. Eventually Jago realised that escape was impossible and stopped the ship. The crew, including the wounded, were successfully evacuated before the torpedo was fired. Shortly afterwards there was a tremendous explosion inside the ship, probably as the result of a boiler coming into contact with cold water. Dr Burns made no reference to the sea monster which, twenty years later, von Forstner claimed to have seen.

Interestingly, the lifeboats came alongside the submarine and von Forstner lectured Jago on the foolishness of his refusal to stop. He also asked if a wireless message had been sent and Jago denied sending one. That seems odd, as one would have expected the submarine wireless operator to have detected the transmission himself. Von Forstner left the lifeboats to their fate around 75 miles from the Irish coast. Arguably that was his first departure from the Cruiser Rules in the attack as they were too far from land to be sure of getting there safely. Luckily the survivors kept the boats close together and they were picked up later that night.

So how does this additional information about the man commanding U-28 help us to second guess Mersey's assertion that his actions during the sinking of the *Falaba* were governed by a desire to kill? The term 'collateral damage' came to prominence in the first Gulf War as Western military leaders explained the regrettable deaths of civilians as a result of their operations. It was a phrase that came to have a callous ring from overuse and application to circumstances where its validity was, at best, dubious. Perhaps it does have value in the context that we are examining. Von Forstner, on the evidence we have available, suffered no moral anguish over the deaths of non-combatants as a result of the actions in which he was involved. He regarded them either as the inevitable consequence of a modern conflict at sea, or the result of the refusal of British authorities to be compliant in their part of the 'bargain'. He was quite prepared to shell a ship that he knew had passengers aboard and he left a group of filled lifeboats in deteriorating weather 75 miles from land. There is not, however, any evidence that he sought to magnify the number of casualties beyond what he regarded as the inevitable 'collateral damage' of submarine operations.

Mersey appears to have recognised this, despite his accusation of murderous intent. One of the questions that his inquiry was asked to consider was whether or not the submarine captain had made any attempt to save the lives of people struggling in the sea. The response was that he had not made any attempt as to do so would have risked the safety of the submarine. Mersey understood the pressure that von Forstner was under keeping his submarine on the surface for an extended period after a wireless call for assistance had been broadcast. The inclusion in the report of the phrase 'intention to sacrifice life' was pure propaganda – but it resonated with many people. Von Forstner had become a bête-noir with many newspaper readers around the world because of the stories of some of the survivors that were published. The *Falaba*, being the first passenger liner to be torpedoed, had been extensively covered in papers across the world before it was entirely overshadowed by the *Lusitania*. As mentioned earlier, amongst the stories reported by survivors was one that the crew of U-28 had lined the deck of the submarine and laughed and jeered at people struggling in the water. Several of the witnesses to the inquiry referred to this but, suspiciously, almost all used the same phrase, 'laughing and jeering', unprompted.

One witness however, a passenger called Primrose, one of the four involved in the accident to boat number 2, had a different slant:

Did you notice the people on the submarine at all ?
– Yes, I saw them quite plainly.
Did you see them doing anything ?
– I did not see them jeering at anybody in the water at that time, but when the *Falaba* heeled over I could see one or two men clinging on to the rail at the high side of the vessel, and it was then I heard the Germans shouting and pointing excitedly to these men as they fell off.

In the report, Mersey was judiciously non-committal:

There was evidence before me of laughing and jeering on board the submarine while the men and women from the *Falaba* were struggling for their lives in the water; but I prefer to keep silence on this matter in the hope that the witness was mistaken.

In all likelihood the witnesses and the other survivors who gave the story to the press were mistaken. It is much more probable that some of the crew of the submarine were on deck (including those manning the gun) and were trying by shouting and with gestures to direct lifeboats to people that they could see in the water. What was the basis of an accusation of callous disregard for life may well have been the one attempt made at a humanitarian gesture.

As a final word on the time allowed for the evacuation of the *Falaba* it is worth noting that survivors' estimates in newspaper reports were varied but, in several instances, spoke of the torpedo being fired 'barely ten minutes' after the warning. Given the time taken to launch the boats, the five minutes assumed by Mersey seems much too short; on the other hand the 23 minutes claimed by the Germans seems rather long. Around ten minutes or a little more would be a reasonable guess and only a handful of people were on the ship when the torpedo struck. One passenger registering his anger at the bungled evacuation pointed out in his evidence that had the crew been well organised and the passengers well led, all of those on the ship could have been safely evacuated before the torpedo was fired. The sinking of the ship was down to von Forstner and U–28; responsibility for the loss of life, however lay with Elder, Dempster, their Marine Superintendent and his brother-in-law Fred Davies.

Before moving on to focus on von Forstner's colleague Walther Schwieger, we might just glance in passing at an example of what his translator described as the 'quality of [Gunther's] wit'. At one stage very early in the war, U–28 carried out an operation more akin to the privateering era than the First World War. A Dutch ship trading with the UK was captured in the Channel, a small prize crew of an officer and a seaman put on board and it was escorted as a prize, along with a second ship acquired similarly, to Zeebrugge. Von Forstner was initially concerned about the safety of the officer on the captive ship and wrote:

> So we proceeded towards the shores of Flanders; we, in the proud consciousness of a new achievement, and the Dutchman lamenting over the seizure of his valuable cargo. The passengers must have wondered what was in store for them. Many of the ladies were lightly clad, having been roused in fright from their morning slumbers, and their anxious eyes stared at us, while we merrily looked back at them.
>
> Our officer on board exchanged continual signals with us, and we were soon conscious, with a feeling of envy, as we gazed through our field glasses, that he was getting on very friendly terms with the fair sex on board our prize. We had feared at first that he might have some disagreeable experiences, but his first message spelled, 'There are a great many ladies on board,' and the second, 'We are having a delicious breakfast,' and the third, 'The captain speaks excellent German,' so after this we were quite reassured concerning him.

The women it turned out were members of a troupe going to perform in London. One suspects that the event did not seem quite so light-hearted from their perspective as it did for Gunther and his prize-captain officer.

Mersey's judgment on Wather Schwieger was, unsurprisingly, no less damning than that on von Forstner. The language used to describe the German captain was uncompromising in its condemnation. In answer to the question, 'What was the cause of the loss of life?' Mersey wrote:

> The answer is plain. The effective cause of the loss of life was the attack made against the ship by those on board the submarine. It was a murderous attack because made with a deliberate and wholly unjustifiable intention of killing the people on board.

On the face of it the accusation of intent to kill is much more readily justified than in the case of the *Falaba*. Schwieger gave no warning of the attack but launched a torpedo against a defenceless, unescorted passenger liner with dreadful consequences. For all the talk since of conspiracies, of Britain trailing the *Lusitania* like a bait across the Atlantic to tempt the Germans, of the German authorities secretly ordering Schwieger to lie in wait for the ship, few have attempted to justify the decision that Schwieger took that afternoon. The present author is not going to join their number. Schwieger's attack on the *Lusitania* was morally wrong, it should not have been made and there was nothing in the political or military context that justified it. That is not exactly the same as saying that he acted with the deliberate intention of killing the people on board.

Despite the evidence given to Mersey that the ship was hit by two torpedoes (and, indeed that there may have been a third that missed) we know that Schwieger only fired one. Later that day he fired another at a different ship, which missed. Why did he fire only one torpedo when he had the option to fire a second? He had used two torpedoes to sink the *Centurion* just the day before. Surely the *Lusitania,* the greatest 'prize' on the sea at the time, was worth two torpedoes if any ship was. German torpedoes early in the war were unreliable (something of which Schwieger himself had had recent experience) and sometimes failed to run true or to explode when they did hit a target. A second torpedo would have been an insurance against such a failure. What was Schwieger's real intention in firing just one torpedo? As well as keeping the formal ship's log, each U-boat captain was required to keep a war diary that was handed over to the German War Office on arrival back at base. Schwieger's war diary for that day cannot be relied upon to give any indication of his thinking, as there is clear evidence of it having been doctored, possibly even after his death.

What we can do is to look at the various possible outcomes and ask how they might have presented themselves to Schwieger in the circumstances of May 1915. His torpedo may have missed entirely and gone unseen by anyone on the *Lusitania.* It would probably have been too late at that stage to fire a second and the attack would have failed. Had the torpedo missed by a small margin and been seen by passengers and crew on the ship, that in itself would have been a propaganda coup for the Germans without the downside of a major loss of lives, particularly American lives. A similar outcome would have resulted if the ship had been hit but only damaged, stayed afloat and been taken in to Queenstown for safety. Any casualties would have been limited to those hurt by the explosion. A mortal blow which sank the ship, but which allowed sufficient time for a safe evacuation, might also have been a 'win-win' scenario for the Germans. The catastrophic destruction of the ship that actually occurred and the enormous number of deaths which resulted were what might be described as a 'win-lose' result for Germany. It was a win in the sense that the attack had succeeded, but a major loss in terms of the opprobrium that it generated and the consequent hostility towards Germany in the USA.

When Schwieger fired just one torpedo at the *Lusitania,* then travelling at 18 knots and about 700 metres distant, he almost certainly considered this last possibility to be the least likely outcome and not the one he was hoping for. In that sense, and in that very limited sense only, he probably did not intend to cause the loss of life on the scale that took place.

Already by that point in the war a number of large ships had been sunk even by a single torpedo, some with big numbers of casualties. None had been as large as the *Lusitania* and most had been warships which lacked the life saving equipment of merchant ships. Nonetheless, there was ample evidence for Schwieger to be fully aware that a torpedo explosion in a vulnerable place could create sufficient damage to cause any ship to sink quite quickly. He must also have known that the rapid evacuation of the numbers of people on the *Lusitania* would have been a very dangerous process risking substantial loss of life. He had no right to take that risk with those on the ship. Mersey's condemnation in that respect was not harsh.

In examining the actions of the two submarine captains we have drawn a distinction between them, based on their modus operandi in a number of attacks on merchant ships. Von Forstner clearly made some attempt to follow the spirit of the Cruiser Rules and give passengers and crew an opportunity to escape before sinking their ship. Schwieger, on the other hand, rarely did and he fired torpedoes at a number of ships without ever coming to the surface. It was a pattern that continued after the *Lusitania*. On 4 September 1915 at 8.30pm he torpedoed without warning the Allan Line liner *Hesperian* approximately 70 miles off the Irish coast and about 130 miles west of Queenstown. The ship sank comparatively slowly and most of those on board were able to get into lifeboats and were picked up. The death toll still came to 32. The German authorities, still suffering embarrassment as a result of the *Lusitania*, tried to pretend that the ship had hit a mine. Schwieger was reined in and told to stick strictly to instructions which by then forbade no-warning attacks on passenger liners.

There is an intriguing question that probably should not be asked, a 'what if' kind of speculation that historians reject as invalid because it is not possible to change just one variable in history while keeping all of the others the same. The question is this. Had U-28 been the submarine that was in the track of the *Lusitania* on 7 May and not U-20, what action would von Forstner have taken? Would he have surfaced and ordered the ship to stop, firing his gun when she refused? Given how close the situation was to the naval base at Queenstown, that would have been a rather risky thing to do. Had he done so, however, the propaganda victory for Germany of the flagship of the British merchant fleet being fired at by a surfaced submarine a few miles from one of their own naval bases would have been tremendous.

Mersey was correct on the basis of the limited evidence in front of him in questioning whether von Forstner gave those on the *Falaba* sufficient time to make good their escape but wrong to blame the deaths that ensued solely on that time limitation. He was also correct in his outright condemnation of Schwieger in torpedoing a crowded passenger liner without warning. His failure was in not distinguishing between the two actions by ascribing the same murderous intent to both captains.

EIGHT CAPTAINS AND A JUDGE: THE LINKS

As an aid to drawing the threads of the four inquiries together, it might help just to summarise their findings so far as the eight captains are concerned. Even though it was acknowledged that *Titanic's* speed contributed to the loss of the ship, her captain was judged blameless as he had been following well attested custom and practice. E.J. Smith was not held personally responsible either for the disorganised evacuation that followed the accident nor was attention drawn to a lack of dynamic leadership during the time it took for the ship to sink. Neither government nor the White Star Line came in for serious criticism either. The principal focus of blame for the loss of life was someone who was many miles away when the ship sank. Mersey's castigation of Stanley Lord, the man who did nothing, was at least partially set aside by the MAIB inquiry over seventy years later. There still remains a question mark about the lack of response aboard the *Californian* to the rockets that were seen by Second Officer Stone and Apprentice Gibson. The MAIB inquiry regarded this as most likely a failure of communication, for which Lord must accept some responsibility, rather than a lack of will.

The *Empress of Ireland* inquiry turned into a pseudo-trial as a result of collusion between lawyers of the opposing parties. Mersey and his two fellow Commissioners came down firmly in favour of Kendall and against Andersen. Despite the strange and not fully explained action of Kendall in stopping his ship with dramatic suddenness when the fog obscured the *Storstad*, he was entirely exonerated. The Commissioners dismissed the *Storstad's* legal team's several attempts to cast doubt on the steering gear of the *Empress* and concluded that First Officer Toftnes on the bridge of *Storstad*, having failed to call his captain as instructed, had caused the ship to veer to the right into the side of the *Empress*. The appalling speed with which the *Empress* turned over and sank left little opportunity for a systematic evacuation and everyone involved on that ship, the *Storstad* and the rescue boats was judged to have done all that was possible to save life.

Although still called inquiries and still sponsored by the Board of Trade, the two wartime inquiries were quite different to the peacetime ones in many respects. Fred Davies and Will Turner were both held not to have contributed to the loss of their ships even though the latter disregarded Admiralty advice and the former followed it. Likewise, the two German submarine captains were dealt with similarly, each being accused of acting with intent to kill, despite von Forstner making some effort to preserve life while Schwieger made none. The manner of the rapid sinking of the *Lusitania* with a heavy list, like the *Empress,* left everyone on board struggling for survival and Mersey found no fault with Turner's leadership. Most of the casualties on the *Falaba* resulted from the crew being unbriefed and passengers not being properly informed, but still there was no censure of Davies personally and no attention drawn to the obvious deficiencies in practice in merchant ships at that stage of the war.

A constant theme running through all four inquiries was that of distinguishing lines of responsibility. Where did the responsibility of the government, either as regulator of the shipping industry in peacetime or as Admiralty in wartime, end and that of the shipping companies begin? For how much of what happened to their ships were the companies accountable and for how much the captains? Did the 'buck always stop' with the captain when it came to the mistakes of his subordinates? None of those questions was answered in any systematic way by the outcomes of the four inquiries and it is arguable that the failure to do so undermined their value.

As well as attributing blame, the purpose of holding an inquiry was to identify things that could be done to prevent a recurrence. The *Titanic* report is by far the best in this respect with a total of 24 formal recommendations. This compares with only three so-called 'suggestions' in the *Empress* report. Part of the discrepancy can be attributed to the fact that in the tragedy on the St Lawrence there was little to be learned from the post-collision phase. The recommendations in the *Titanic* report covered matters concerning the watertight subdivision of ships, provision of lifeboats and rafts, the manning of boats and boat drills, sight tests for look-outs, policing the passengers and, not surprisingly, the moderation of speed in the vicinity of ice. Then there was the pointed recommendation, already noted in the context of the *Californian* incident, that masters should be reminded of their obligation to go to the assistance of ships in distress. Finally, Mersey recommended the calling of an international conference to examine the issues raised by the *Titanic* disaster, particularly as regards mitigating the risk to ships of ice. We cannot tell to what extent Mersey was the author of this suggestion. He may well have been prompted by one or more of his assessors or by civil servants in the Board of Trade, but, if it can be said that his role between 1912 and 1915 as a Commissioner of Wrecks had any lasting legacy, this is it. The recommendation proved its worth not because the conference which was called in 1913 as a consequence dramatically improved safety at sea, but because it acted as the forerunner of a further series of such conferences which arguably have indeed had that effect.

Although the First World War prevented the ratification of the outcomes of the 1913 conference which Mersey chaired, some of its recommendations, for example in instigating an Ice Patrol to warn of serious ice hazards in the North Atlantic, were acted upon. Further Safety of Life at Sea or SOLAS conferences were held in 1929, 1948, 1960 and 1974, each incrementally adding measures to improve safety. Article VIII of SOLAS 1974 enabled further amendments to be put in place under the auspices of the International Maritime Organisation, without the need for further large international gatherings – provided a large number of nations did not dissent – and that process continues. In 2010 a number of the older cruise liners had to be withdrawn because the cost of bringing them into line with the latest SOLAS regulations was uneconomic. A number of people who, understandably, get great pleasure from seeing old, well-designed, attractive looking ships with character still at work were upset by their demise. It is perhaps ironic that there have been accusations that SOLAS has now become part of an overbearing 'health and safety' regime.

The suggestions at the end of the *Empress* inquiry were at a relatively low level, dealing with the closing of portholes and watertight doors at night or in fog, the provision of rafts on deck that would float off should the ship sink and the avoidance of ships crossing on the St Lawrence by staging the pick-up and drop-off points for pilots. The middle one of those is worth noting because it had a relevance to the *Lusitania*. Mersey clearly became quite engaged with his role as Commissioner of Wrecks. He mentioned in the *Empress* inquiry how, on his journey across the Atlantic on the *Mauretania,* he had noted the sort of lifebelts provided and their storage. In reading the transcripts one can see how he follows through on points from one to the other. One follow-through occurred in the *Lusitania* inquiry concerning the additional lifeboats that had been fitted as a consequence of his recommendation in the *Titanic* report. The *Lusitania* could not easily be adapted to take additional lifeboats on davits and instead a number of collapsible boats were placed, mostly underneath the existing boats on their davits. These were designed to be released easily so that, in the manner mentioned in the *Titanic* report, they would float free of the ship. Quite some time was spent in the *Lusitania* inquiry questioning Turner and other members of the crew so that Mersey could be satisfied that the collapsible boats were released and did float off as intended. Towards the end of the inquiry there was an odd exchange between Mersey and Turner about the value of the additional boats. When Turner was asked by Mersey if he thought that it had been worthwhile increasing the number of lifeboats as a response to the *Titanic* disaster, Turner responded that he did not think so. It was not clear whether Turner considered that they did not make any material difference in the particular circumstances of the rapid sinking of the *Lusitania* or whether he was of the view that cluttering up a ship's decks with extra boats was in general a bad thing.

The two wartime inquiries contained nothing even by way of 'suggestions', let alone recommendations. One cannot be sure if this was because the Commissioner and his Assessors found nothing of value to suggest, or because they were directed not to. The questions asked by the Board of Trade in those two instances were primarily retrospective and did not require forward looking responses. It is just possible that in either case (but probably more likely in the *Lusitania* one) Mersey provided some thoughts to the Board of Trade that were not included in the published report in case they might be of material or propaganda value to the Germans. If no recommendations were in fact made, one has to ask what purpose was served by holding the inquiries. Each report concluded that, as the whole world knew, the ship had been sunk by a German submarine and, as the Allies were in no doubt, the Germans were thereby failing to obey the accepted rules of warfare. It is hard to conceive that any propaganda gain from the reports was worth the trouble and expense of creating them. There is no evidence that either inquiry had any impact whatsoever on subsequent events. Their main benefit perhaps is to us a century later in providing additional windows through which we can observe some aspects of the first ever phase of submarine warfare, albeit at times as through a glass darkly.

There seems much to have been gained and little to have been lost if Mersey had stressed in the *Falaba* report the need for all merchant ships to be fully prepared before leaving port for an immediate evacuation and had pointed out in the *Lusitania* report the value of adhering as far as was possible to Admiralty instructions (the only source of expert advice for mariners) for the avoidance of attacks by submarines. In relation to both issues the inquiries had clearly shown that practice in the merchant service in the early stages of the war had failed to adapt with sufficient urgency to the new threat posed by the advent of submarines. As became clear from von Forstner's journal, this was at least as well understood by the German submariners themselves. They had nothing to learn from such recommendations in the report of a British inquiry.

In Chapter 4 we looked at the nature of inquiries of this type and wondered about the extent to which they were subject to external influence from government or from commercial interests. As the focus of this book has been on the men at sea and not those in Whitehall or in corporate boardrooms, we can only say that ship's captains, as has been noted, are company men and severe criticism of them may reflect badly on the company that employs them. That is exactly what happened with Stanley Lord. It was the Directors and not the Marine Superintendent of the Leyland Line that demanded his resignation for PR reasons following the criticism he received in the reports of both the American and British inquiries. The permission given to Butler Aspinall to represent Kendall, Baxter and Turner's interests, even though the shipowners were his clients, also seems to have been aimed at preventing any criticism of the captain making the company look bad. At the same time, given the public criticism of Turner, in particular, that had been aired prior to the inquiry, the fact that Cunard adopted this approach was a vote of confidence in Turner and in his ability to answer the criticisms that had been made. It might also be interpreted as an indication that Turner's decisions had indeed been in line with the company's view of Admiralty advice at the time.

The Canadian government may have had some concerns that Mersey would have found fault with the navigation system in the St Lawrence for which they were responsible and that may be why the junior Minister of Justice acted as their counsel in the *Empress* inquiry. In the event they had nothing to worry about. The final suggestion in the report that the pick-up and set-down points for the pilots might be staged was offered purely as a constructive idea without any hint of criticism. The British government had much more at stake, particularly the Board of Trade in the case of the *Titanic* and the Admiralty in the case of the *Lusitania*. Mersey has frequently been criticised for his lack of forthright condemnation of the Board of Trade for its anachronistic regulations governing lifeboats. At the same time, changing those was a matter for Parliament; responsibility lay with politicians rather than civil servants. With changing governments and changing faces in ministries it is rarely possible to pin blame on any particular politician (one of the attractions of the profession). The President of the Board of Trade had already initiated moves to have the regulations changed when the disaster occurred, albeit the pace of change would have made the movement of tectonic plates seem fast.

White Star Line also avoided censure for only fitting the minimum number of lifeboats to *Titanic*. The defence that 'we were only sticking to the inadequate regulations' obviously served its purpose. There is a debate to be had on corporate ethics in a situation of regulatory laxity but this is not the place for it. Arguably, the real criticism of White Star Line should have centred on the woefully inadequate corporate training provision for its officers in dealing with emergencies on its ships. No panic by the steerage passengers or by the 'black gang' from the stokeholds can justify the utter waste of valuable time between the collision and the sinking. Similar comments could be made about the disordered attempts at evacuating the *Falaba* even if wartime shortages of expertise exacerbated the crew's inadequacies.

Was this absence of negative comment on government and commercial interests the result of Mersey being leaned on or did it represent the outcome to be expected from inquiries headed up by an 'establishment man' who, in his previous role, had been close to the shipping companies? The only instance where there is circumstantial evidence of one of these inquiries being pushed is in the case of the *Lusitania*. We can now be reasonably certain that it was known in the Admiralty that only one torpedo had been fired but they did everything in their power to engineer a finding by Mersey of at least two torpedoes as a way of deflecting speculation on the cause of the second explosion. Mersey obliged, although there is no indication that he himself had any knowledge contrary to the evidence he heard in the inquiry. Turner has been criticised for being complicit in this deception and yet the matter was put to him in the manner of 'When did you stop beating your wife?'

> *The Attorney General:* Did you notice any other concussion that would lead you to believe there was a second torpedo?
> – One immediately after the first.

Turner acquiesced in response to a leading question to confirm, as he had to, that he had heard a second explosion, but he did not explicitly indicate that he believed that there had been a second torpedo. It was in character with his pattern of clipped answers that he did not try to provide any further explanation of his views. He seemed later in life to have come to the view that there was only one.

Butler Aspinall's maxim, already quoted in relation to Turner, that a man should be judged 'by who he is and by what experience he has had' is probably also a fair basis for us to come to a view on Mersey. Even before he had opened the first of his inquiries there were those voicing expectations of a 'whitewash' and few at the end of it came forward to say that their prediction had been wrong. One of the themes running through the book has been the inability of people in a variety of contexts to adapt practice to rapid changes in technology or to new risks suddenly emerging. If it was accepted as a valid excuse for Smith, Turner and Davies that they had simply done things the way that they had always been done, it surely was also a valid excuse for Mersey himself. Would it have been realistic to expect a judge in his seventies, a member of the House of Lords and with all of the connections that implied at the centre of the British establishment, to bring to his work as Commissioner of Wrecks a radical viewpoint, heavily critical of the status quo and the oversight of it by government legislation and corporate policy?

The view that in circumstances requiring a major public inquiry, confidence in the process can be assured by appointing a well-known legal brain to oversee it, is one that has had a long history continuing right up to the present day, despite the cynical expectations that often result. The appointment of Lord Hutton in 2004 to inquire into the circumstances surrounding the death of Dr David Kelly in the wake of the Iraq invasion is a case in point. From the time when the decision was announced until the publication of his report there were continual predictions that his findings would fail to point the finger at the 'guilty' parties. Few of those making the predictions were disappointed by the result. That is not to cast doubt on Hutton's findings; there is no basis here for such a comment. It is simply a matter of the historical record that the appointment of a Law Lord to undertake such an inquiry did not create confidence in the process; quite the opposite.

Perhaps the most positive judgment we can make of Lord Mersey is that, within the limitations of who he was and the experience he had had, he did quite an efficient job in the conduct of the four inquiries. He was diligent in ensuring that most of the issues that were raised during the inquiries were properly followed through. With the exception of the refusal to allow Stanley Lord representation, he was generally quite good in giving each of the parties involved in the tragedies full opportunity to put their cases. When the issue of the *Empress's* steering was suddenly brought up after the inquiry was well underway he allowed considerable additional time to investigate it. His understanding of the maritime context within which he was working improved somewhat during the course of the four inquiries although it remained deficient and a source of misunderstanding and confusion to the end. As we have already hinted, the outcomes of the *Titanic* inquiry might just have been a little different had it been the fourth rather than the first of the series.

One of the unusual features of Lord Mersey's work as Commissioner of Wrecks was the number of very powerful men with whom he had to deal, both in government (Lord Chancellor, Home Secretary, Attorney-General, Solicitor-General, President of the Board of Trade) and in business (Chairmen of the two most prestigious shipping companies). Mersey did not appear to be daunted in having the likes of Isaacs, Carson and F E Smith appearing in front of him and there is nothing in the transcripts that speaks of subservience other than the rather overblown and at times apparently obsequious courtesies of legal protocol. The tasks that were given to him were challenging and he was subject to more intense public scrutiny than he had ever previously experienced. For all the inadequacies of the outcomes we must allow Mersey credit for applying his legal experience and considerable intellect in as effective a manner as could be expected of the man. Many people would be content to rest on such laurels, as circumscribed as they are.

The sinking of *Titanic* was a freak accident; the *Falaba* and *Lusitania* were both destroyed in a form of warfare that we hope will never return. The accident in the St Lawrence, however, was different in that it fitted a pattern, even if it was unusual in its scale. Yachtsmen have a graphic description of this type of collision. When racing yachts are tacking against the wind in close proximity, collisions frequently occur when a yacht with the wind on the port side fails to see and give way as it ought to one with the wind on the starboard side. Striking almost at right angles, the bow of one driving into the side of the other, the collision is called 'T-boning'. That is exactly what happened to the *Empress of Ireland;* she was T-boned by the *Storstad*. As we saw in Chapter 2, other passenger liners that were also sunk by T-boning prior to 1914 included *Arctic, Ville du Havre, Oregon, Utopia* and *Republic.* Just a month before the *Titanic* disaster, an elderly liner, *Oceana,* also a product of Harland and Wolff in Belfast, was setting out on what was intended to be her final trip to India. Just off Beachy Head she was T-boned by a German sailing barque and sank quickly, luckily with relatively small loss of life. There have been others since including *Andrea Doria* (in 1956). Modern technology ought to ensure that this type of accident should not happen, but the risk, however minuscule, is always there and it continues to have the potential for dreadful consequences. The effect of one of the new 200,000-ton super cruise liners with close to 5000 passengers and crew aboard being T-boned by a fully loaded modern bulk carrier could be truly awful. Should such a terrible event happen, to whom should a government turn to carry out the inevitable inquiry? The second *Titanic* inquiry in 1992, limited to the role of the *Californian,* was conducted without the benefit of legal minds or legal trappings by the Marine Accident Investigation Branch. This organisation professionally examines each maritime incident with a UK involvement, however minor, and produces excellent reports designed to provide the maximum learning benefit for all concerned. Following a major maritime disaster there might still be media pressure for a 'public' inquiry headed by someone with establishment status. Before acceding to any such pressure, a government might do well to reflect on the record of such inquiries in the context of specialised technical environments. It is the qualities of the findings that matter and not the standing of the inquirers. Mersey should not be blamed that, in the second decade of the last century, governments failed to make that distinction.

POSTSCRIPT

There is a harmless joy in finding random historical connections. Just a few miles from Ballyferis, where the future Captain Turner was shipwrecked as a child, is my home town of Bangor in North Down. The author of *Shipwrecks of the Ulster Coast*, from which came the information that it was Turner senior's ship that was lost, is Ian Wilson, past Director of the North Down Museum. The Museum is housed in Bangor Castle, previously the home of Lord and Lady Clanmorris. One of the naval heroes of the First World War, Commander Barry Bingham, was a son of the family and grew up in the house. He was awarded the VC for leading his destroyer flotilla against the German High Seas Fleet during the battle of Jutland in an attack reminiscent of the Charge of the Light Brigade. Bingham's ship, *Nestor,* was sunk and he and the other survivors of the crew were captured.

At the end of the war, to commemorate the award of the VC, a gun removed from a surrendered U-boat was given to the town and installed on a concrete plinth in front of the War Memorial, where it remains. The submarine was U-19, the boat that torpedoed the *Calgarian* with Henry Kendall aboard and had also previously delivered the ill-fated Roger Casement on his mission to Ireland. At that time the boat's captain was Raimund Weisbach. Before taking over U-19, Weisbach was Torpedo Officer on U-20. It was his hand that, on Schwieger's order, pulled the lever that released the torpedo …

BIBLIOGRAPHY

Primary Sources

The proceedings and reports of the inquiries into the loss of the *Titanic* and the *Lusitania* are both available online via the *Titanic* Inquiry Project at www.titanicinquiry.org.

The proceedings and report of the American Senate Inquiry into the loss of the *Titanic* are also available through the same website.

The report of the second *Titanic* inquiry on the role played by the *Californian*:
Marine Accident Investigation Branch of the Department of Transport, *RMS Titanic- Reappraisal of Evidence Relating to SS Californian* (HMSO: London, 1992)

The proceedings and report of the *Empress of Ireland* inquiry:
Canadian Government Sessional Paper No 21B, *Commission of Inquiry into the loss of the British Steamship Empress of Ireland through collision with the Norwegian Steamship* Storstad (1915).

The proceedings and report of the *Falaba* inquiry:
Proceedings before the Rt. Hon. Lord Mersey, Wreck Commissioner of the United Kingdom ... on a formal investigation ordered by the Board of trade into the loss of the Steamship *Falaba*, (1915).

Gunther von Forstner's journal:
von Forstner, G-G, *The Journal of Submarine Commander von Forstner,* Trans: Ana Crafts Codman, Gutenberg Project, E-book #30114 (2009)

Lord Mersey's obituary appeared in *The Times* newspaper on 4 September
  1929.
The report on the sinking of the *Iberian* appeared as 'Six of Iberian's Crew
  Slain With One Shell' in the *New York Times* newspaper on 31 July 1915.

Published Sources

Ballard, R.D., *Exploring the Lusitania* (Weidenfeld and Nicholson, London
  1992)
Ballard, R.D., *The Discovery of the Titanic* (Madison Publishing Inc., Toronto
  1987)
Bartlett, W.B., *Titanic, 9 Hours to Hell, The Survivors' Story,* (Amberley
  Publishing, Stroud, 2010)
Butler, D.A., *The Other Side of the Night* (Casemate, Newbury 2009)
Cameron, S., *Titanic Belfast's Own* (Colourpoint, Co. Down, 2011)
Eaton, J.P. and Haas, C.A., *Titanic Destination Disaster* (Haynes, Somerset 1987)
Eaton, J.P. and Haas, C.A., *Titanic Triumph and Tragedy* (Haynes, Somerset,
  1988)
Flayhart, W.H., *Perils of the Atlantic* (Norton, New York, 2003)
Fox, S., *The Ocean Railway* (HarperCollins, London, 2003)
Gordon, A., *The Rules of the Game* (John Murray, London, 1996)
Harris, J., *Lost at Sea* (Guild, London, 1990)
Harris, J., *Without Trace* (Guild, London, 1988)
Keegan, J., *The Price of Admiralty* (Arrow, London, 1990)
Lee, P., The *Titanic and the Indifferent Stranger* (self published, 2008)
Lochner, R.K., *The Last Gentleman of War* (Arrow, London, 1990)
Lynch, D. and Marschall, K., *Titanic An Illustrated History* (Hodder and
  Stoughton, London, 1992)
Molony, S., *Titanic and the Mystery Ship* (Tempus, Gloucestershire, 2006)
Preston, D., *Wilful Murder* (Doubleday, London, 2002)
Ramsay, D., *Lusitania: Saga and Myth* (Chatham, Rochester, 2001)
Reade, L. and de Groot, E.P., *The Ship that Stood Still* (Haynes, Somerset, 1993)
Saward, J., *The Man Who Caught Crippen* (Moienval, France, 2010)
Stringer, C., '*Falaba's* Sinking Begins March to War', *Voyage,* vol 53, pp.30-35
Thomas, L., *Raiders of the Deep* (Doubleday, Doran, New York, 1928)
Wilson, I., *Shipwrecks of the Ulster Coast* (Impact, Coleraine, 1997)
Zeni, D., *Forgotten Empress* (Avid, Merseyside, 2001)

INDEX

QuickBooks® Online

2023 Edition

by David H. Ringstrom, CPA

A Wiley Brand

QuickBooks® Online For Dummies®, 2023 Edition

Published by: **John Wiley & Sons, Inc.**, 111 River Street, Hoboken, NJ 07030-5774, www.wiley.com

Copyright © 2023 by John Wiley & Sons, Inc., Hoboken, New Jersey

Published simultaneously in Canada

For general information on our other products and services, please contact our Customer Care Department within the U.S. at 877-762-2974, outside the U.S. at 317-572-3993, or fax 317-572-4002. For technical support, please visit https://hub.wiley.com/community/support/dummies.

Wiley publishes in a variety of print and electronic formats and by print-on-demand. Some material included with standard print versions of this book may not be included in e-books or in print-on-demand. If this book refers to media such as a CD or DVD that is not included in the version you purchased, you may download this material at http://booksupport.wiley.com. For more information about Wiley products, visit www.wiley.com.

Library of Congress Control Number: 2022946641

ISBN 978-1-119-91000-8 (pbk); ISBN 978-1-119-91002-2 (ebk); ISBN 978-1-119-91001-5 (ebk)

SKY10036600_101122

Contents at a Glance

Table of Contents

Introduction

Welcome to QuickBooks Online! In this book, my goal is to help you get up and running quickly if you're new to QuickBooks, and then carry out tasks in QuickBooks in the most efficient way possible. Accounting programs such as QuickBooks Online are designed to take the pain out of accounting, and in some cases, they even make it easy. In other cases, they may infuriate you. I point out the good, the bad, and the ugly of QuickBooks Online, which is aimed at business users, and QuickBooks Online Accountant (QB Accountant), which is aimed at — you guessed it — accountants and bookkeepers. Both programs are web-based products that offer mobile versions, so your accounting records can be at your fingertips no matter which device you have at hand. Business owners can share access with their accountants, and accountants can gracefully support multiple clients who use QuickBooks Online.

Intuit, the maker of QuickBooks Online and QB Accountant, also offers QuickBooks Desktop, which is a version of the software that you must also subscribe to but then install locally on individual computers. I discuss migrating QuickBooks Desktop to QuickBooks Online in Chapter 3 and Appendix B. If you're in need of a QuickBooks Desktop reference, please get a copy of Stephen L. Nelson's *QuickBooks All-in-One For Dummies 2023* (John Wiley & Sons, Inc.).

About This Book

Everything that can be done in QuickBooks Online can be accomplished in QB Accountant as well. QB Accountant offers additional tools that are useful to accountants who manage multiple clients and/or multiple companies. As you'll see, QuickBooks Online requires a subscription fee for every set of books you want to maintain, whereas accountants get free access to QB Accountant for overseeing their clients' books.

QuickBooks Online and QuickBooks Online Accountant aren't for everyone. Before you commit to Intuit's web-based solution, you need to explore the available editions and examine the requirements for the products. In that regard, I've divided the book into five parts:

>> Part 1, "Getting Started with QuickBooks," helps you choose a subscription level, set up your company, and if needed, migrate your accounting records from QuickBooks Desktop.

- >> Part 2, "Managing Your Books," covers the nuts and bolts of using QuickBooks, such as adding customers, vendors, employees, and inventory items, plus all of the transactions related to each.

- >> Part 3, "Reporting and Analysis," shows you how to run reports within QuickBooks Online, and then how to crunch your numbers in Excel.

- >> Part 4, "Working in QuickBooks Online Accountant," helps accountants set up shop in QB Accountant and explore the software's accountant-specific features.

- >> Part 5, "The Part of Tens," covers ten features of the Chrome browser that help you optimize your use of QuickBooks.

REMEMBER

As I discuss in Chapter 1, QuickBooks Online offers different subscription levels. I used QuickBooks Online Advanced to write this book because it is the most feature-laden offering.

Before diving in, I have to get a few technical conventions out of the way:

- >> Text that you're meant to type as it appears in the book is **bold**. The exception is when you're working through a list of steps: Because each step is bold, the text to type is not bold.

- >> Web addresses and programming code appear in monofont. If you're reading a digital version of this book on a device connected to the Internet, note that you can tap or click a web address to visit that website, like this: www.dummies.com.

- >> You can use QuickBooks Online and QB Accountant in a web browser or a mobile app. Example web browsers include Microsoft Edge, Google Chrome, Mozilla Firefox, and Apple's Safari. QuickBooks and QB Accountant mobile apps are available for Android and iOS. QuickBooks Advanced subscribers and QB Accountant users also have a desktop app available.

- >> When I discuss a command to choose, I separate the elements of the sequence with a command arrow that looks like this: ⇨. For example, when you see Sales ⇨ Invoices, that command means that you should click Sales in the left bar and then click Invoices in the drop-down menu that appears.

- >> You may be surprised to learn that QuickBooks Online has more than one version of its Navigation bar that appears along the left-hand side. Your navigation is mostly likely set to the Business View, which consolidates commands into fewer top-level choices. In this book, I used the Accountant View, which provides more top-level choices. To change your view, click the gear-shaped Settings button at the top right-hand corner of the screen, and then toggle the view setting at the bottom right-hand corner of the menu that displays.

Note that you don't have to change to Accountant View to follow along in this book. When necessary, I list the Accountant View commands first, and then parenthetically list the Business View commands. For instance, a reference to the Invoices screen looks like this: Sales ⇨ Invoices (Sales & Expenses ⇨ Invoices).

If you have identified yourself as an owner or partner, your Business View may differ even more. If you have any problems finding a command that I reference, you can briefly switch to Accountant View to carry out your task and then toggle back to Business View if that's more your speed.

Foolish Assumptions

I had to assume some things about you to write this book, so here are the educated guesses I made:

>> You know that you need to manage a set of accounting records for one or more businesses, and you might even have some sort of setup in place already. I *did not* assume that you know how to do all those things on a computer.

>> You may want to analyze some of your accounting data outside QuickBooks, which is why I include a couple of chapters on using Microsoft Excel, some of which translate to Google Sheets as well.

>> You have a personal computer running Windows 10 or 11 (I wrote this book in Windows 10) or a Mac running macOS 10.11 or later.

>> You have a copy of Microsoft Excel on your computer, or you plan to use Google Sheets at https://sheets.google.com.

Icons Used in This Book

Throughout the book, I use icons to draw your attention to various concepts that I want to make sure that you don't skip over in the main part of the text. Sometimes, I share information to help you save time; in other cases, the goal is to keep your accounting records safe.

TIP

This icon points out time-saving tricks or quirks that you may encounter in QuickBooks.

REMEMBER

This icon points out tricky aspects of QuickBooks that you'll want to keep in mind.

WARNING

This product can burn your eyes. Oh, sorry, wrong type of warning. Don't worry, you're safe! Pay careful attention to warnings that you encounter so that you can avoid problems that could wreak havoc in your accounting records or more often simply cause you frustration.

TECHNICAL STUFF

At some points, I may include some geeky stuff about QuickBooks, your web browser, or your computer. You can safely skip over the technical stuff if that's not your cup of tea.

Beyond the Book

In addition to the book content, this product comes with a free, access-anywhere Cheat Sheet that lists keyboard shortcuts for QuickBooks Online (QBO) and Quick-Books Accountant and handy toolbar buttons in QBO as well as info on using the multicurrency feature, Desktop conversion tips, and entering payroll history. To get this Cheat Sheet, go to www.dummies.com and search for "QuickBooks Online For Dummies Cheat Sheet."

You can keep the learning going with the most up-to-date information and tutorials from School of Bookkeeping (https://schoolofbookkeeping.com/). The folks there (one of whom is the technical editor of this book) have broken down every version of QuickBooks Online, QuickBooks services (Payments and Payroll), and other tasks into bite-sized lessons that you can watch and get back to business. Use promo code QBO4DUMMIES to save 20 percent on any membership. If you're looking for video-based Excel training, please visit my site at http://www.professionalsexcel.com.

Where to Go from Here

Simply turn the page. Seriously. You can dive in anywhere you want and come back as often as you like. You don't have to read through this book cover to cover, as you would a John Sandford thriller, because each chapter stands alone and provides step-by-step instructions for common tasks. You should consider this book to be a reference that you can use when you need it.

That said, if you're getting started with QuickBooks Online or QuickBooks Online Accountant, you may want to read the chapters in Part 1 in order. Then feel free to explore any chapter you want, using the table of contents or the index to find topics that interest you.

1

Getting Started with QuickBooks Online

Chapter **1**

Welcome to QuickBooks Online

Welcome to QuickBooks Online! Why devote a whole book to this software? First of all, I'm going to assume that you're most likely not an accountant but are either the owner or the employee of a business that has chosen to keep their accounting records in QuickBooks Online. Or maybe you're an accountant and you want to understand the ins-and-outs of QuickBooks Online better. No matter where you fall on this continuum, my goal is to empower you to use QuickBooks Online more effectively. To do so you'll find that I sometimes broaden the discussion to include Microsoft Excel and Google Sheets, because no accounting software can meet every single need that you may have. Another complicating factor with QuickBooks Online that accountants in particular may notice is that the functionality available varies widely between the different subscription levels. Throughout the book I help you keep tabs on what you can, and cannot, accomplish within each level of QuickBooks.

In this chapter I explain some differences between QuickBooks Online and QuickBooks Desktop, and then I give you a sense of what your annual costs might look like if you choose to use QuickBooks. Pricing and features are directly related, and most businesses may find the Plus and Advanced subscriptions are best suited to their needs, but less expensive options are available for those who don't need quite as much functionality. I briefly touch on QuickBooks Online Accountant here, but rest assured, that version gets full-bore treatment in Chapters 16 to 18.

What Is QuickBooks Online?

QuickBooks Online is a cloud-based accounting software, as opposed to Quick-Books Desktop, which is a traditional accounting software installed locally, along-side your data, on your office computers. Conversely, with QuickBooks Online, both the software and data are housed securely in remote data centers and accessed securely over the Internet. Working in the cloud can increase your efficiency by offering you the opportunity to work anywhere, communicate easily with others, and collaborate in real time. Further, your data is backed up automatically, which can help you avoid disasters such as fire or flood, which can take out both your workspace and your accounting records. Traditionally, QuickBooks Desktop allowed you to choose when to pay for a software upgrade, but starting with QuickBooks 2022, the desktop version became subscription-based, just the same as QuickBooks Online.

REMEMBER

Some folks see the "anywhere, anytime" aspect of the cloud as a potential disad-vantage because it makes information too readily available — and therefore a target for hackers. Rest assured that Intuit stores your data on servers that use bank-level security that creates encrypted backups of your data automatically.

Perhaps you're currently using QuickBooks Desktop and wondering, "Should I switch to QuickBooks Online?" The answer, as you might expect, is that it depends. Because QuickBooks Desktop is no longer offered on a perpetual license basis, the cost distinction between the two has been somewhat removed. Chapter 3 describes the conversion process, and Appendix B offers a nuts-and-bolts analy-sis of what data you can move to QuickBooks Online from QuickBooks Desktop, and what you can't.

REMEMBER

QuickBooks Desktop enables you to create unlimited companies at no additional charge, while QuickBooks Online subscription fees are on a per-company basis.

On the other hand, using web-based software can be attractive simply because you always have immediate access to your accounting records from any device as long as you have an Internet connection. The QuickBooks Online mobile app allows you to track your mileage, and keeps your accounting records in the palm of your hand. Further, your accountant and/or bookkeeper has access from any-where as well. As you'll see, QuickBooks Online Accountant (QB Accountant) empowers accountants and bookkeepers to quickly toggle between their clients' accounting records and to keep up with deadlines and tasks, and provides a cen-tralized communication hub. Conversely, QuickBooks Desktop requires you to send an electronic Accountant's Copy to your accountant, and specify a dividing date before which you cannot make any changes until your accountant returns the Accountant's Copy to you. QuickBooks Desktop also requires you to install periodic software updates, which are a thing of the past with QuickBooks Online. Most modern computers should easily exceed the minimum requirements for Quick-Books Online, but you can get the nitty gritty computer specification details here: https://intuit.me/3yEaSJL.

WARNING

Because updates occur so frequently in QuickBooks, by the time this book is published, some features (and screens) may have changed. Make that *will* have changed.

TIP

My technical editor extraordinaire Dan DeLong has created a free QuickBooks Chooser chatbot that will help you choose the right version of QuickBooks Online based upon your specific business needs. Check it out at https://sob.drift.click/QBChooser.

SHOULD YOU MOVE TO THE CLOUD?

Before you decide to move your accounting records to the cloud, you should consider the needs of your business in the following areas:

- Invoicing, point of sale, electronic payment, and customer relations management
- Financial and tax reporting
- Budgeting
- Time tracking and payroll
- Inventory, job costing, and job scheduling
- Management of company expenses and vendor bills

Beyond the advantages described in this section, the needs of your business may dictate whether you can use QuickBooks Online. The platform won't work for you if your business has industry-specific needs or is midsize, for example. In addition, QuickBooks Online won't work for you if you need to do any of the following things:

- Track your balance sheet by class.
- Manage a robust inventory that supports making and selling finished goods.

In any of these cases, you'd probably be better off with Intuit's desktop-based QuickBooks Enterprise or perhaps QuickBooks Premier. Another consideration is the speed and quality of your Internet connection. You will be mightily frustrated if you can't get to your books simply because the Internet is out again.

Checking on QuickBooks Pricing

QuickBooks subscriptions can be canceled at any time, but the service is billed in monthly periods with no refunds or prorations. You can no longer create new transactions once your subscription expires, but you can view your accounting records and run reports for up to one year. As you see in the next three sections, you may find that using QuickBooks costs much more than the base subscription price that you pay. Further, pricing is per company, so if you maintain the books for two or more entities, you'll have to pay for two or more subscriptions. Add-ons such as payroll and specialized apps are generally priced on a per-company basis as well.

QuickBooks subscription pricing

As shown in Table 1-1, QuickBooks Online is available in six different versions and price points, but most likely you'll need to choose one of the three shaded options. QuickBooks Online Self-Employed and Simple Start are best suited to fledging businesses, while QuickBooks Online Accountant is a free portal that accountants and bookkeepers can use to support their clients. You can get more details and start a QuickBooks Online subscription at https://quickbooks.intuit.com/pricing/ or start using QuickBooks Online Accountant at https://quickbooks.intuit.com/accountants/products-solutions/accounting/online.

TABLE 1-1   QuickBooks Online Subscription Pricing per Company

Version	Monthly	Annually	Users
Self-Employed	$15	$180	1 billable user + 2 accountant users
Simple Start	$30	$360	1 billable user + 2 accountant users
Essentials	$55	$660	3 billable users + 2 accountant users
Plus	$85	$1,020	5 billable users + 2 accountant users
Advanced	$200	$2,400	Up to 25 billable users + 3 accountant users
Accountant	$0	$0	No limit

TIP

QuickBooks allows you to choose either a 50 percent discount for the first three months of your subscription, or a free 30-day trial. You may also be offered a discount during the 30-day trial. If so, take the deal immediately if you plan to move forward with QuickBooks, as it's unlikely that it will be offered again during your trial period. The 50 percent discount will save you more money, but the 30-day trial lets you test drive the software without making a financial commitment. You will have to cancel your subscription if you opt for the discount and decide QuickBooks isn't right for you, whereas the 30-day trial simply expires at the end.

PROADVISOR PREFERRED PRICING

Accounting professionals can arrange a 30 percent discount on QuickBooks Online (all versions except QuickBooks Self-Employed), QuickBooks Payroll, and QuickBooks Time. The 30 percent discount is ongoing for accountants who agree to be billed directly by Intuit. Accountants can pass all or part of the savings on to their clients if they wish. As discussed in Chapter 16, Intuit sends you a single consolidated bill for all the QuickBooks subscriptions you manage. Conversely, accountants also use the ProAdvisor Preferred Pricing program to arrange a 30 percent discount for 12 months for charges billed directly to their clients.

If your client initially sets up their own QuickBooks subscription, you can move it to your consolidated bill at the discounted wholesale rate. If your arrangement with your client doesn't work out, you can remove the client from your consolidated bill, which means that the client resumes paying for their own subscription.

Payroll and time track pricing

It's best to think of the amounts in Table 1-1 as the base cost for QuickBooks, as it's likely that you'll need to add additional functionality, such as payroll processing. As shown in Table 1-2, QuickBooks offers three different payroll options. I've calculated the associated costs for a hypothetical team of five employees to give you a frame of reference.

TABLE 1-2 **QuickBooks Payroll Subscription Pricing for Five Employees**

Version	Monthly	Annually
Core	$65 ($45/month + $5/employee x 5 employees)	$780
Premium	$115 ($75/month + $8/employee x 5 employees)	$1,380
Elite	$175 ($125/month + $10/employee x 5 employees)	$2,100

All QuickBooks Payroll plans include the following features:

>> Paying employees with printed checks or by direct deposit

>> Calculating tax payments automatically and paying them electronically

>> Processing federal and state quarterly and annual reports, and preparing W-2 and 1099 forms

>> Processing payroll for employees who work in your company's state or another state

>> Keeping payroll tax tables up to date without having to install updates (as you do with the QuickBooks Desktop product)

>> Using the QuickBooks Payroll mobile app to pay employees, view past paychecks, file tax forms electronically, and pay taxes electronically

The Core tier offers next-day direct deposit, while the Premium tier enables same-day direct deposit and adds time tracking. The Elite tier also adds project tracking, tax penalty protection, and a personal human resources advisor. You can get more details and start a payroll subscription at `https://quickbooks.intuit.com/payroll/pricing/` or you can choose Payroll from the left-hand menu within your QuickBooks company.

TIP

A QuickBooks company is a set of accounting records for a single business entity. Each QuickBooks company entails separate subscription fees, and you will need to establish a QuickBooks company for each company that you own or maintain accounting records for.

TIP

You can test-drive the QuickBooks payroll service at no charge for up to 30 days.

WARNING

When you establish QuickBooks Payroll, you must connect your bank account and provide your tax identification numbers. Make sure that you're ready to start processing payroll immediately before you embark on a QuickBooks Payroll subscription. If you'd like to try before you buy, use the online test drives I mention later in this chapter in the sections, "QuickBooks Online Plus" and "QuickBooks Online Advanced."

Table 1-3 shows the additional annual cost for the Premium plan for five employees, which provides time and attendance tracking. The Elite tier adds project tracking as well. It's worth running the numbers for the various offerings, because QuickBooks Core Payroll for five employees at $65 per month plus QuickBooks Premium Time at $60 per month is $125 per month versus paying $115 per month for QuickBooks Premium Payroll, which also offers time tracking.

TABLE 1-3 **QuickBooks Time Subscription Pricing for Five Employees**

Version	Monthly	Annually
Premium	$60 ($20/month + $8/employee x 5 employees)	$720
Elite	$90 ($40/month + $10/employee x 5 employees)	$1,080
ProAdvisor	Free for accounting professionals	$0

REMEMBER

You can add time tracking on an á la carte basis by adding QuickBooks Time (formerly known as TSheets). Think twice before doing so, as it typically makes more financial sense to use the time tracking bundled into the upgraded payroll service tiers. Further, you may encounter complications if you start out with QuickBooks Time and then try to switch to a QuickBooks Payroll tier that offers time tracking.

Other add-on pricing

QuickBooks Payments enables you to accept electronic payments from customers, and entails per-transaction fees instead of a monthly subscription. Table 1-4 shows the current rates as of this writing.

TABLE 1-4   **QuickBooks Payments per Transaction Fees**

Payment Type	Rate per Transaction
ACH Bank payments	1% up to a maximum of $10 per transaction (customer enters bank information online)
Swiped credit card	2.4% plus 25 cents (mobile reader available)
Invoiced credit card	2.9% plus 25 cents (customer enters credit card online)
Keyed credit card	3.4% plus 25 cents (you key the credit card information online)

TIP

QuickBooks Payments deposits money from qualifying credit or debit card transactions into your bank account the next business day. Your payments and deposit transactions are recorded into your books automatically, based upon the funding date.

Companies with e-commerce offerings might opt for QuickBooks Commerce, an add-on that allows you to position your inventory products on a variety of major shopping platforms for $100 per month or $1,200 per year. You can find out more or start a QuickBooks Commerce subscription at https://quickbooks.intuit.com/quickbooks-commerce. In Chapter 2, I discuss the QuickBooks App store, which offers dozens of free and paid apps that add even more functionality to QuickBooks.

Comparing QuickBooks Features

As you can see, the ongoing expenses for QuickBooks can add up fast. You can upgrade or downgrade your subscription at any time, although downgrading can entail disabling inventory and/or removing users. Use the search term **downgrade** at `https://quickbooks.intuit.com/learn-support/en-us` for more details. Let's take a look at the various tiers so that you can find the right fit for your needs.

I used a QuickBooks Online Advanced subscription as I wrote this book because it offers the whole enchilada with regard to QuickBooks functionality. Accordingly, there's a good chance that you'll see references throughout the book to features you don't have.

QuickBooks Online Self-Employed

This version of QuickBooks is aimed at freelancers and self-employed people who file Schedule C of IRS Form 1040 (`https://www.irs.gov/forms-pubs/about-schedule-c-form-1040`). Unlike the higher-level offerings, QuickBooks Self-Employed allows you to mix business with pleasure, meaning that you can track personal and business expenses, as well as mileage. It's best suited to someone with a side hustle who wants to keep track of their business and simplify income tax filing.

QuickBooks Simple Start

A QuickBooks Simple Start subscription is great for a new business with basic bookkeeping needs. With Simple Start, you can

>> Track your income and expenses

>> Download transactions from your bank and credit card accounts

>> Create an unlimited number of customers

>> Send estimates and invoices

>> Print checks and record transactions to track expenses

>> Track and pay sales taxes

>> Track mileage

>> Categorize expenses by taking pictures of receipts

>> Pay contractors and send 1099 forms

>> Import data from Microsoft Excel or QuickBooks Desktop

>> Integrate with available apps in the QuickBooks Online App Center

>> View and customize over 50 reports

Although the Simple Start version supports accounts-receivable functions, you can't set up invoices to bill customers on a recurring basis or track unpaid bills. If you're on the fence between Self-Employed and Simple Start, you'll have more options in the future with Simple Start.

QuickBooks Online Essentials

Established businesses that do not have inventory may be able to use QuickBooks Essentials, which includes all of the Simple Start functionality and also allows you to

>> Set up invoices to bill automatically on a recurring schedule

>> Use accounts-payable functions, including scheduling payment of vendor bills and free online bill payment

>> Create and post recurring transactions

>> Track time for unlimited users

>> Control the areas of QuickBooks that your users can access

>> View and customize up to 85 reports

REMEMBER

QB Accountant users can create Simple Start, Essentials, Plus, or Advanced subscriptions and then serve as the primary administrator (previously known as the master administrator), or transfer that role to their client at any time, as discussed in Chapter 17.

QuickBooks Online Plus

A Plus subscription goes beyond the Essentials level by adding the ability to

>> Create, send, and track purchase orders.

>> Track inventory using the first in, first out (FIFO) inventory valuation method. QuickBooks Online supports light inventory needs: If you sell finished goods, then QuickBooks Online should be able to meet your needs. But if you need to assemble finished goods to sell, QuickBooks Online won't meet your needs on its own. You can look for an add-on app to supplement your inventory needs; I talk about add-on apps in Chapter 2.

>> Categorize income and expenses by using class tracking.

>> Track sales and profitability by business location. You can assign only one location to a transaction, but you can assign multiple classes to a transaction.

- Give employees and subcontractors limited access to the QuickBooks company to enter time worked.

- Track billable hours by customer. QuickBooks Online supports light job-costing needs, but it doesn't allow you to cost labor automatically.

- Track projects.

- Create budgets to estimate future income and expenses. You can create multiple budgets per year, location, class, or customer.

- View and customize 124 reports, along with unlimited reports-only users.

TIP

You can test-drive the QuickBooks Online Plus sample company at `https://qbo.intuit.com/redir/testdrive`.

Usage limits for QuickBooks Simple Start, Essentials, and Plus

Simple Start, Essentials, and Plus subscriptions are subject to the limits shown in Table 1-5. Long-term users may be allowed higher limits but won't be able to add any element that exceeds the use limit without upgrading to a higher-level plan. As you'll see in the next section you can work without limits in QuickBooks with an Advanced subscription.

TABLE 1-5   **Usage Limits for Simple Start, Essentials, and Plus Subscriptions**

QuickBooks Element	Use Limit
Annual transactions	350,000
Chart of accounts	250
Classes and locations	40 combined; further, you cannot track your balance sheet by class.
Billed users	1 for Simple Start, 3 for Essentials, 5 for Plus
Unbilled users	2 Accountant users for most plans, 3 for Advanced; unlimited reports-only users in Plus and Advanced; Unlimited time tracking-only users in Essentials, Plus, and Advanced.

WARNING

QuickBooks Simple Start, Essentials, and Plus have hard limits on the chart of accounts and number of classes and locations. Once you max out, you have to deactivate accounts, classes, or locations to free up space, or else upgrade to an Advanced subscription.

QuickBooks Online Advanced

QuickBooks Online Advanced is the flagship subscription for users who have out-grown QuickBooks Online Plus, and allows you to

>> Have unlimited accounts, transactions, and classes.

>> Connect with a dedicated customer success manager to handle support questions. (Support calls go to the front of the line instead of waiting in a queue.) Customer success managers also provide information on online training and QuickBooks products; Advanced subscribers are entitled to five free on-demand training courses annually.

>> Establish custom permissions for your users.

>> Efficiently import hundreds of invoice transactions into QuickBooks by way of a comma-separated-values (CSV) file. You can create such a file in Microsoft Excel or Google Sheets.

>> Use Spreadsheet Sync to create customized reports in Microsoft Excel, as well as edit existing records, such as customers and vendors, in Excel, and then post the changes back to QuickBooks.

>> Create custom reports using the Custom Report Builder.

>> Edit or delete multiple invoices.

>> Batch-reclassify and batch-create transactions, including invoices, bills, checks, and expenses.

>> Enable workflows to trigger reminders for customers and team members.

>> Use up to 48 custom fields.

>> Visualize your data in the Performance Center with customizable chart widgets.

>> Employ premium app integration with services such as Bill.com, HubSpot, Salesforce, LeanLaw, and DocuSign. (Third-party subscription fees apply.)

>> Restore QuickBooks data to a particular date and time. You can also schedule automatic backups and reverse changes made to customers, vendors, and company settings.

>> Set up workflow automation to generate payment and invoicing reminders and assign tasks to team members.

TIP

You can test-drive the QuickBooks Online Advanced sample company at `https:// qbo.intuit.com/redir/testdrive_us_advanced`.

QuickBooks Online Accountant

QuickBooks Online Accountant (QB Accountant) is a free cloud-based portal that accounting professionals use to access clients' QuickBooks Online companies and communicate with clients. QB Accountant includes a free QuickBooks Online Plus subscription that accountants can use to keep track of their own businesses, but the standard subscription fees apply for each additional QuickBooks company that is created. I discuss QB Accountant in great detail in Chapters 16 to 18, and you can create your QB Accountant account at https://quickbooks.intuit.com/accountants/products-solutions/accounting/online.

Once you choose a subscription, the next step is to start building out your QuickBooks company, which you do in Chapter 2.

» **Understanding the dashboard**

» **Updating the chart of accounts**

» **Establishing company settings**

» **Finding out about the app options**

Chapter **2**

Creating a QuickBooks Online Company

Once you subscribe to QuickBooks Online, you're prompted to create your company. You can then start entering data from scratch, import your data from QuickBooks Desktop if applicable, or import lists such as customers and vendors, which I discuss in Chapter 4, along with importing inventory items in Chapter 5. You can also ask your accountant for assistance.

TIP

If you're in the market for an accountant or bookkeeper, visit the ProAdvisor marketplace at `https://quickbooks.intuit.com/find-an-accountant/` to seek expert advice from certified QuickBooks advisors. Or try the QuickBooks Live Bookkeeping service at `quickbooks.intuit.com/live`.

Signing Up for QuickBooks Online

I discuss the features available at each subscription level in Chapter 1. Follow these steps when you're ready to start your subscription or 30-day trial of QuickBooks Online:

1. **Visit** `quickbooks.intuit.com/pricing`.

    This page has the current pricing as well as any sale prices.

2. **Look for four boxes describing the Simple Start, Essentials, Plus, and Advanced subscriptions.**

   If you're looking for QuickBooks Self-Employed, scroll down past the boxes to the freelancer and independent contractor section.

   Typically, you can choose between a free 30-day trial and three months of reduced prices for Simple Start, Essentials, and Plus. The Advanced subscription doesn't offer a free trial, but you can access the test drive at `qbo.intuit.com/redir/testdrive_us_advanced`. For more information, see Chapter 1 and check out `quickbooks.intuit.com/accounting/advanced`.

3. **To sign up for a free trial, click the slider button above the QuickBooks versions shown in Figure 2-1 to activate the Free Trial for 30 Days option.**

   Be aware that the price you ultimately pay for QuickBooks depends on whether you choose the Buy Now option or the Free Trial for 30 Days option. If you opt to buy now, you'll pay less for your subscription because discounts don't apply to the free trials. Be aware that promotional pricing usually ends after three months. However, ask your accountant if they're able to extend a ProAdvisor Preferred Pricing discount to you, which I discuss in Chapter 1.

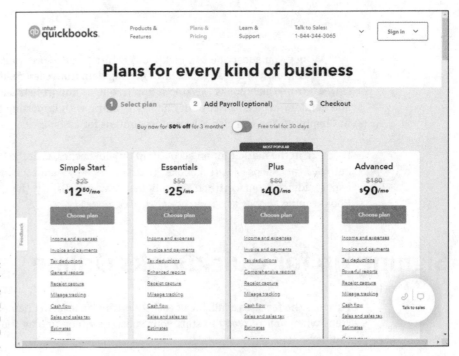

FIGURE 2-1: Use the slider button to toggle between a short-term discount and a free trial.

4. **Click Choose Plan for the subscription level that you're buying or trying.**

The optional Add Payroll page appears; this page allows you to add a free payroll service test drive to your QuickBooks trial if you want.

5. **Click Add to Plan or Continue without Payroll to move to the Checkout screen.**

You can always add payroll later, so don't feel that you need to make a heat-of-the-moment decision here. If you start your paid subscription, payroll will also be 50 percent off for three months; if you opt for the free trial, it will be free for 30 days instead.

6. **Review your choices and then click Checkout to establish your QuickBooks Online account.**

The amount(s) shown are what you'll be charged each month for your subscription once your free trial or promotional pricing ends.

7. **Fill in your email address, mobile number, and a password, as shown in Figure 2-2.**

FIGURE 2-2:
Fill in the information needed to start your subscription or the free trial.

Your password must be between 8 and 32 characters and consist of a mix of uppercase and lowercase letters, numbers, and one or more special characters (such as an exclamation point or pound sign). The email address and password will serve as your credentials for accessing QuickBooks. You can use your mobile number to recover your account if you mislay your credentials. If you already have an Intuit account, look for the tiny — and I mean tiny — Sign In link.

8. **Click the One More Step button.**

    If you're starting a subscription, you are prompted to enter your payment information. If you're starting a trial, you're offered one more chance to skip the free trial and buy the product at a discounted rate for three months. I clicked the Continue with Trial button.

Exploring Your New Company

When you've established your paid or trial subscription, the first screen of the setup wizard appears, as shown in Figure 2-3. Click Next after you complete each screen of the wizard, which asks you to enter your company name, industry, and type of business; your role in your company; any team members; and your goals for QuickBooks. Click Skip for Now to skip any questions that seem too personal, such as the one that asks you to link your bank and credit card accounts, and the one that asks you to list the apps that you use. You can indicate which activities you want to use QuickBooks for or skip that item as well.

TIP

You might be able to temporarily bypass the wizard by pressing the Escape key, but you will have to complete it eventually.

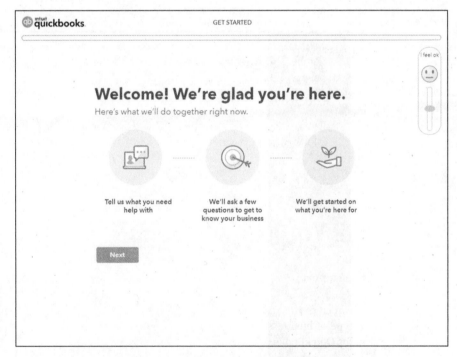

FIGURE 2-3:
A loquacious wizard walks you through the setup process.

TIP

The wizard asks whether you want to import your QuickBooks Desktop data, but you can defer that decision until later, which I discuss in Chapter 3. Once you complete or bypass the wizard, you see the opening screen, which has some combination of two or three of these tabs.

» **Get Things Done:** As shown in Figure 2-4, this page provides one-click access to common tasks in QuickBooks.

» **Business Overview:** If you bailed out of the startup wizard, clicking here launches it again. Once you have capitulated to the entire wizard, this space, as shown in Figure 2-5, serves as a financial dashboard for your company when your QuickBooks menus are set to Accountant View. Depending upon your subscription level, you may see a Cash Flow Forecast included in your Business Overview. Toggle the Privacy slider on whenever you want to hide this information. You can also carry out tasks such as connecting bank accounts and creating invoices from this page.

» **Tasks:** Advanced subscribers see this task-tracking option when the QuickBooks menus are set to Business View. The aforementioned Business Overview becomes a menu option on the left menu bar.

» **Workflows:** Advanced subscribers can establish reminder and approval workflows for accounting transactions.

FIGURE 2-4:
Get Things
Done page.

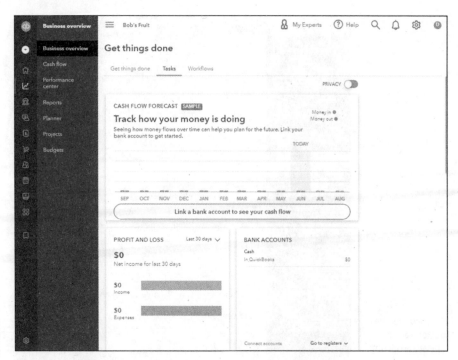

FIGURE 2-5:
The Business
Overview page.

Reviewing the QuickBooks interface

The left menu bar runs down the side of the QuickBooks interface, and leads off with the +New button shown in Figure 2-6. This is your starting point for creating most transactions in QuickBooks. If the list of options feels overwhelming, click Show Less in the bottom right-hand corner to collapse the list down to the basics: Invoice, Estimate, Expense, and Check. You can always click Show More at any time to get the full list of transactions back again. The full list of commands is grouped into four columns: Customers, Vendors, Employees, and Other. When you click any choice on the menu, the corresponding transaction window opens in QuickBooks. Any commands that have an arrow after them are not available in your subscription level. You're prompted to upgrade to a higher level if you choose any of these commands, but you can always click Stay On Plan and get back to work.

REMEMBER

Descriptions on the left menu bar sometimes vary, based on your version of QuickBooks and the preferences that you've set. For example, you may see Sales & Expenses or Invoicing instead of Sales, as shown in Figure 2-5. Once you make a selection, a highlighted entry in the navigation bar helps you identify the section of QuickBooks that you're using.

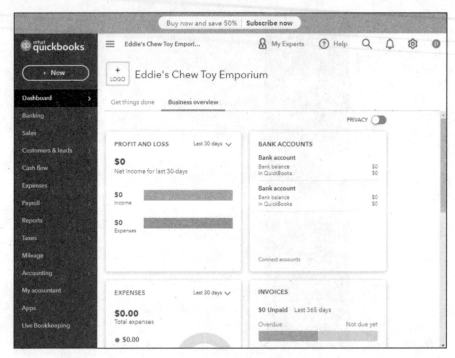

FIGURE 2-6:
Click the +New
button to create a
new transaction.

Other buttons that you should be aware of include the following.

REMEMBER

» **Three stripe button:** This appears to the right of the QuickBooks logo at the top left, and collapses the left menu bar so that you can have more screen space for reports and tasks. Click the three stripe button again to restore the left menu bar.

When you collapse the left menu bar, the +New button is represented by a plus (+) icon at the top of your QuickBooks screen.

» **My Experts:** This button initiates a chatbot that can enable you to get support from QuickBooks or enlist their paid Live Bookkeeping service.

» **Help:** This displays a task pane with two tabs.

   • **Assistant:** This is a bot that offers answers to common questions.

   • **Search:** This is a searchable menu of common topics that might be of interest to you, as shown in Figure 2-7.

» **Search:** This looks like a magnifying glass and appears to the right of the Help command. As shown in Figure 2-8, you are initially presented with search tips, but recent transactions appear here as you start working in your company. You can also click Advanced Search if you want to search based on multiple filters.

» **Notifications:** This feature keeps you informed of action items that need your attention.

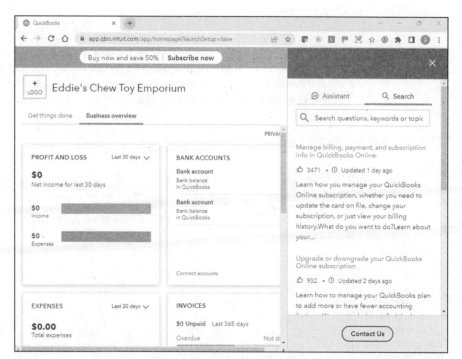

FIGURE 2-7:
The Search tab of
the Help pane.

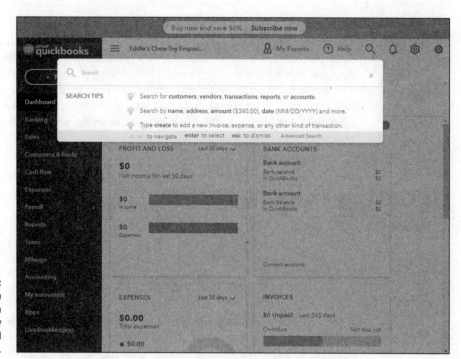

FIGURE 2-8:
Click the Search
button to search
for previously
entered
transactions.

» **Settings:** This looks like a gear and displays the menu shown in Figure 2-9. From here, you can review and change QuickBooks settings; view lists; work with features such as import and export, reconciliation, and budgeting tools; and view information about your QuickBooks account. Note that the Settings menu is divided into four columns that organize related commands.

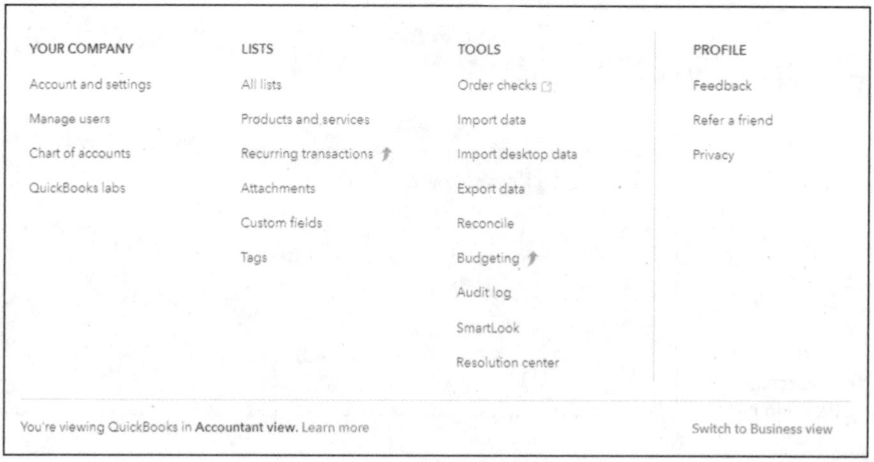

YOUR COMPANY	LISTS	TOOLS	PROFILE
Account and settings	All lists	Order checks	Feedback
Manage users	Products and services	Import data	Refer a friend
Chart of accounts	Recurring transactions	Import desktop data	Privacy
QuickBooks labs	Attachments	Export data	
	Custom fields	Reconcile	
	Tags	Budgeting	
		Audit log	
		SmartLook	
		Resolution center	

You're viewing QuickBooks in **Accountant view**. Learn more   Switch to Business view

FIGURE 2-9:
Use the Settings menu to work with settings, lists, tools, and your QuickBooks account.

REMEMBER

The bottom right-hand corner of the Settings menu contains a link that displays either Accountant View or Business View, which controls how the navigation bar displays in QuickBooks. Business View groups things into fewer categories, whereas Accountant View is more detailed. You can toggle between these modes to find what feels most comfortable for you. For the record, I used Accountant View for most of the images in this book, because as an accountant, I find that this view resonates with me more than the Business View.

Updating the Chart of Accounts

QuickBooks automatically sets up the chart of accounts it thinks you'll need when you create a new company. If you're not happy with this list, you can replace it with one you set up in Excel, in a CSV file, or in a Google Sheet, which I discuss in the later section, "Importing a Chart of Accounts."

You'll probably want to modify the chart of accounts that QuickBooks establishes for your company. To do so, choose Settings⇨Chart of Accounts or choose Accounting⇨Chart of Accounts. On the page that appears, click the See Your Chart of Accounts button to display a page similar to the one shown in Figure 2-10. This page lets you perform a variety of functions. You can print a list of your accounts, for example, if you click the Run Report button at the top of the page or the Print List button above the Action column. You also see a Currency column if you've enabled the Multicurrency feature, which I discuss in Appendix A.

Be mindful when adding accounts to QuickBooks, as you cannot delete accounts from the list. As you see in the later section, "Editing or inactivating accounts," your only option for unwanted accounts is to mark them as inactive. Inactive accounts reduce the number of accounts that you can create, which is limited to 250 for all plans other than Advanced.

FIGURE 2-10:
The Chart of Accounts page.

QuickBooks confusingly has three different screens for adding accounts, which are predicated on the aforementioned Accountant View or Business View, and your subscription level. The following steps show you how to add an account to your chart of accounts when your Settings menu indicates that you are using Business View in QuickBooks Simple Start, Essentials, or Plus:

1. **Click the New button on the Chart of Accounts page to open the New Account task pane, shown in Figure 2-11.**

2. **Make a selection from the Account Type list.**

   This list contains the major categories that typically appear on the balance sheet and profit-and-loss reports for a business.

3. **Make a selection from the Detail Type list.**

   Depending upon the Account Type you chose, you may only have one choice here, or you may have many.

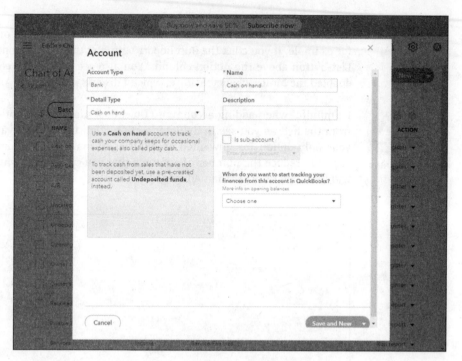

FIGURE 2-11:
The task pane
you use to create
an account in
Business View for
Simple Start,
Essentials, and
Plus subscribers.

4. **Fill in the Name field to assign a name to your account.**

   Only enter words in this field. Later in the chapter, I show you how to enable account numbers for your chart of accounts if you wish. Don't be fooled by the relatively small size of the field; you can enter up to 100 characters into it.

5. **Optional: Enter a description for your account.**

   Enter up to 100 characters providing additional documentation as to the purpose of the account.

6. **Optional: Click Is Sub-account if you want to have this account roll up into a higher-level account on your reports.**

   You must specify a parent account for each sub-account that you create.

7. **Choose an option from the When Do You Want to Start Tracking Your Finances from This Account in QuickBooks? list.**

   Always defer to your accountant or bookkeeper if you're unclear how to answer a question like this. Options include Beginning of the Year, Beginning of This Month, Today, and Other, which allows you to specify any date that you wish.

8. **Click Save and Close if you only need to create one account; otherwise, click the arrow and choose Save and New.**

REMEMBER

This is an example of a sticky preference in QuickBooks. When you alter the functionality of a button, the button retains that functionality going forward until you make another choice from that button's drop-down menu.

If you've enabled the Multicurrency feature, the task pane you use to create a bank account — or any type of asset or liability account except an A/R or A/P account — also contains a list box in which you select the currency for the account. QuickBooks automatically creates currency-related A/R and A/P accounts when you create transactions for foreign customers and vendors.

Here's how to add an account to your chart of accounts when your Settings menu indicates that you are using Accountant View:

1. **Click the New button on the Chart of Accounts page to open the New Account task pane, shown in Figure 2-12.**

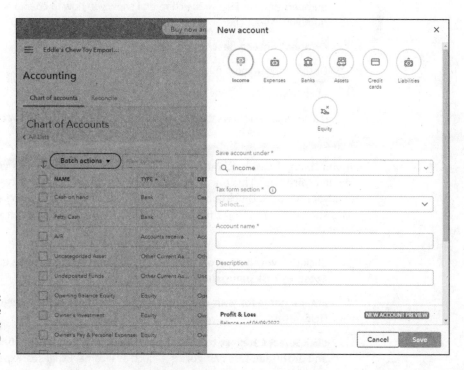

FIGURE 2-12:
The task pane you use to create an account in Accountant View.

2. **Optional: Choose a balance sheet category from the top of the screen.**

This is an abbreviated version of the Account Type list that appears in Business View. Your options are Income, Expenses, Assets, Credit Cards, Liabilities, or Equity.

3. **Make a selection from the Save Account Under list.**

   If you made a choice in Step 2, your options are filtered to that type; otherwise, you see the entire list.

   If you choose an account name from this list, rather than a balance sheet or profit-and-loss report category, then your new account is a sub-account of the parent account that you chose. However, you can turn off the sub-account status by editing the account, which I discuss in the next section.

4. **Specify a Tax Form Section.**

   Depending upon the choice you make in Step 3, this field may default to an appropriate value, or you may have to make a selection from the list.

5. **Enter an account name.**

   Enter up to 100 characters in this field. Only enter account names and not numbers here, as later in the chapter, I show you how to enable account numbers in your chart of accounts.

6. **Optional: Enter a description.**

   Describe the account further here if you wish.

7. **Click Save.**

   QuickBooks redisplays the Chart of Accounts page, and your new account appears in the list.

If you thought two methods of adding accounts in QuickBooks was wacky, how about a third one? This one materializes in Business View for Advanced subscribers. Not only does QuickBooks offer a third approach, but it also very confusingly uses the word *categories* instead of *accounts*. Are you having fun yet? Here's the lowdown:

1. **Click the New button on the Chart of Accounts page to open the New Category task pane, shown in Figure 2-13.**

2. **Enter a name for your new category (er, account) in the Category Name field.**

3. **Click Select Category to choose between highly generalized balance sheet and profit-and-loss categories** — such as Income, Expenses, Expensive Items, Loans & Money Owed, Owner Investments or Expenses, Bank & Credit Cards, or Other Accounts — **and then click Next.**

   You'll certainly be excused for casting an eye about to see if Rod Serling or Ashton Kutcher is nearby. The intent of this screen is to remove some of the accounting from your accounting, which in my experience has the opposite effect of making simple tasks more complicated than they should be.

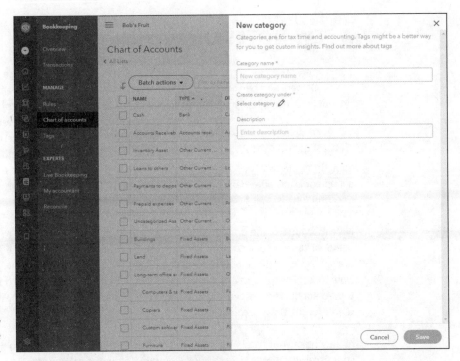

FIGURE 2-13:
The task pane
that Advanced
subscribers in
Business View
use to create
accounts.

4. **Choose a parent account that your new category will be placed under as a sub-account, and then click Select.**

5. **Optional: You can provide a description for your new category/account and then click Save.**

   If you find yourself in the New Category task pane and yearn for a good old-fashioned account screen, click Cancel. Choose Settings and then Switch to Accountant View, and then click the New button once again on your chart of accounts.

REMEMBER

Editing or inactivating accounts

Any editing or inactivating tasks must be initiated from the Chart of Accounts list, which you can display by choosing Settings ⇨ Chart of Accounts to display your Chart of Accounts list. The Action column gives you the following options.

>> **View Register:** This displays a register report detailing all of the transactions for a balance sheet account.

>> **Run Report:** This generates a QuickReport that shows activity for the past 90 days for accounts that appear on your profit-and-loss report. This option also appears on the View Register drop-down menu if you want a QuickReport.

A FEW NOTES ON PAYING OWNERS

Many small-business owners wonder about the accounts they should use to pay themselves. Owners and partners typically aren't considered to be employees and therefore are not paid through payroll. To pay an owner or partner, use the Chart of Accounts page to set up a Draw account (Owner's Draw, Partner's Draw, or whatever is appropriate; if you have multiple partners, set up Draw accounts for each partner) and use it to pay owners. The Draw account is an equity account. Similarly, owners and partners sometimes put their own money into the business. To account for these contributions, set up equity accounts (again, one for each owner or partner), called Owner's Contribution, Partner's Contribution, or whatever is appropriate.

Note that you use the Draw account not only to pay the owner, but also to account for personal items an owner might buy with the business's money. You record the withdrawals by using the appropriate bank account and the appropriate Draw account. Note that these transactions don't show up on your profit-and-loss report because they're not business expenses. To find out the total amount paid to an owner, run a report for the Draw account.

At the end of your fiscal year, you need to enter a journal entry, dated on the last day of your fiscal year, that moves the dollar amounts from the appropriate Draw or Contribution account to Retained Earnings — another equity account. If I've just lost you, talk to your accountant about how to handle closing the year.

>> **Edit:** Click the View Register or Run Report drop-down menu to access this command, as shown in Figure 2-14. Choose this command to display the task pane shown in Figure 2-11 if your Settings menu is set to Business View in Plus or below, Figure 2-12 if the Settings menu is set to Accountant View, or Figure 2-13 for Business View in QuickBooks Online Advanced.

REMEMBER

Certain accounts, such as Accounts Receivable, do not display an Edit button when you are working in Business View, but they do when you're working in Accountant View.

>> **Make Inactive:** As shown in Figure 2-14, this is the equivalent of deleting an account from the chart of accounts. In QuickBooks Plus and below, most accounts parenthetically state "won't reduce usage," which means that inactivating the account won't help you if you're concerned about hitting the 250-account limit. Some balance sheet accounts state "reduces usage," but those are very much the exception. Click the Settings button just above the Action column and choose Include Inactive to view your inactive accounts. You can deactivate two or more accounts at once by clicking the checkboxes along the left-hand side of the chart of accounts and then choosing Batch Actions ➪ Make Inactive. Advanced subscribers have no limit on the number of accounts in the chart of accounts.

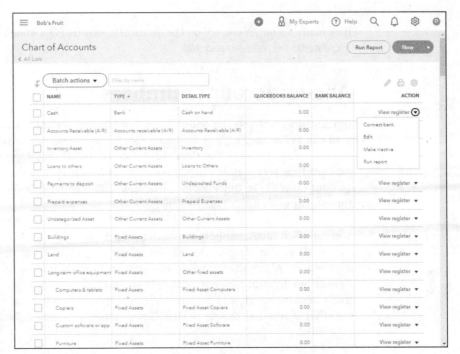

FIGURE 2-14:
A typical action
menu for the
Chart of Accounts
page.

>> **Make Active:** This option appears as a top-level option in the Action column
next to inactive accounts if you have chosen to display them on your Chart of
Accounts page.

>> **Connect Bank:** This option appears as a drop-down menu option when you
are working in Accountant View, and enables you to connect your bank
account on your chart of accounts to your physical bank account so that
transactions can be synced into QuickBooks.

TIP

Click the Batch Edit button, represented by a pencil icon above the Action column,
to be able to change any account name on your chart of accounts. If you have
enabled account numbers, which I discuss shortly, you can edit those here as well.
Click Save when you've finished your changes.

I'd like to point out a few other aspects of the Chart of Accounts page. First, a settings button appears just above the Action menu. This enables you to turn the
Type, Detail Type, QuickBooks Balance, and Bank Balance columns on or off on
the Chart of Accounts page. The menu also has an Include Inactive option that you
can enable to display inactive accounts. Finally, this menu allows you to control

how many accounts you see on the Chart of Accounts page at one time, in various increments between 50 and 300.

Adding account numbers

QuickBooks gives you the option to assign account numbers to each account on your chart of accounts. To do so, choose Settings ⇨ Account & Settings ⇨ Advanced. Click the pencil icon in the Chart of Accounts section and toggle on the Enable Account Numbers option. Click Show Account Numbers if you wish to display the account numbers in QuickBooks. Click Save and then click Done. You can change these settings as needed at any time.

You can click the Batch Edit command (which looks like a pencil icon above the Action column in Figure 2-14) to edit all account numbers at once, as shown in Figure 2-15. Alternatively, when you edit an individual account, you see a new field called Account Number or simply Number, depending upon whether you're using Accountant View or Business View, respectively. Click Save above or below the chart of accounts listing, or click Cancel above the Action column if you change your mind.

FIGURE 2-15: Batch Edit mode enables you to assign or change multiple account numbers at once.

QuickBooks sessions time-out after 60 minutes of inactivity, so save periodically as you enter account numbers in case you get pulled away unexpectedly. After you add account numbers, you can sort the chart of accounts in account-number order by clicking the Number heading of the Chart of Accounts page.

Importing a chart of accounts

When you create a new company, QuickBooks automatically sets up the chart of accounts it thinks you'll need, but you can replace it by importing one that you've set up in Microsoft Excel, as a CSV file, or as a Google Sheet spreadsheet. The import file can include sub-accounts and parent accounts.

Use the convention *Account: Sub-account* when establishing sub-accounts, with *Account* representing the parent account.

Click the New drop-down menu on the Chart of Accounts page to display the Import Accounts page, shown in Figure 2-16. Notice the links to download a sample CSV or Excel file or to preview a sample Google Sheet.

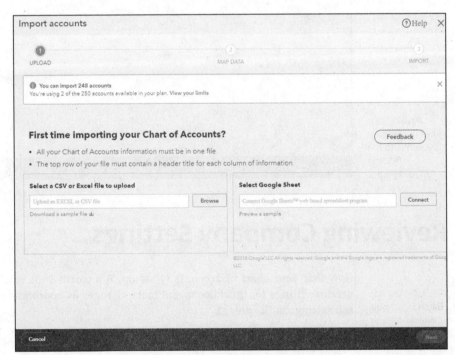

FIGURE 2-16:
The Import Accounts page.

After you set up your chart of accounts file, click the New drop-down menu again on the Chart of Accounts page and choose Import. Click Browse or Connect, as shown in Figure 2-16, to select your import file, and then click Next to display the Map Data page, shown in Figure 2-17. Map the headings in your import file to the fields in QuickBooks by making selections from the drop-down lists in the Your Field column. Click Next after you finish mapping the import file to display a preview of the accounts to be imported. Click Import if everything looks to be in order.

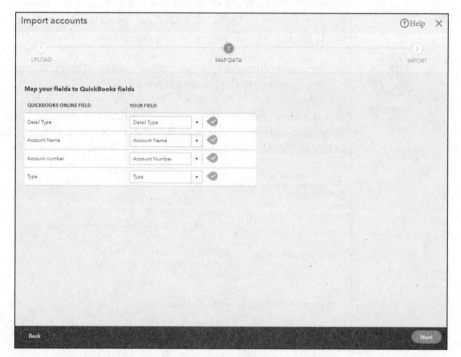

FIGURE 2-17:
Map the fields in your file to the fields in QuickBooks.

Reviewing Company Settings

Now that your chart of accounts is set up, it's worth your while to review the default settings for QuickBooks and make changes as appropriate. I discuss payroll settings in Chapter 12.

Company preferences

Choose Settings ⇨ Account and Settings to display the Company tab of the Account and Settings page shown in Figure 2-18. You can edit your company name, address, and contact information, as well as your marketing preferences for Intuit. Click anywhere in the group where the setting appears to make updates, and then hit the Save button before you move on to another group of settings. Click Done to close the Account and Settings page.

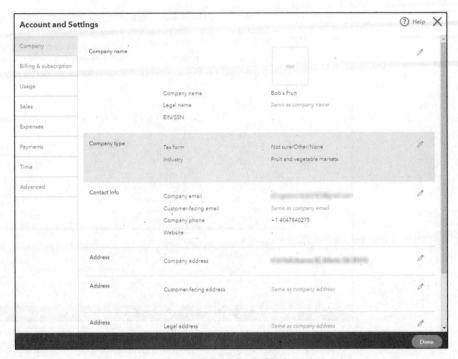

FIGURE 2-18: Company preferences.

Billing & Subscription preferences

If you've left the Account and Settings page, choose Settings ⇨ Account and Settings (or Your Account in QuickBooks Online Accountant) to review the current status of your subscription and to change your payment method.

REMEMBER

You don't see the Billing & Subscription pane if your QuickBooks company is being managed by an accountant who participates in the ProAdvisor Preferred Pricing program, which I discuss in Chapter 1.

The page shown in Figure 2-19 shows you the status of your QuickBooks, QB Payroll, and QuickBooks Payments subscriptions. You can convert your trial version of QuickBooks and of the QB Payroll product to a regular subscription, but doing so terminates the trial period that you opted into. You can also scroll down on this page to order checks and supplies. I discuss QuickBooks Payments in the later section, "Payments preferences." As of this writing, you can also reduce your QuickBooks subscription fees by roughly 10 percent by opting into annual billing instead of monthly billing.

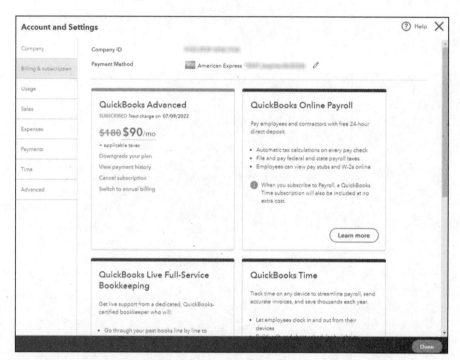

FIGURE 2-19:
Billing &
Subscription
preferences.

Usage statistics

Click Usage on the left side of the Account and Settings page to display the subscription-based usage limits that apply to your QuickBooks company. The User Count in Billable users section is a clickable link that displays the Manage Users page from which you can add, edit, or remove users.

Sales preferences

Sales preferences enable you to customize certain fields within your sales forms, including determining whether or not to show Product/Service and/or SKU fields, as shown in Figure 2-20. You can indicate if you want to add a default charge to overdue invoices, utilize progress invoicing, customize default email messages, and include an aging table at the bottom of account statements.

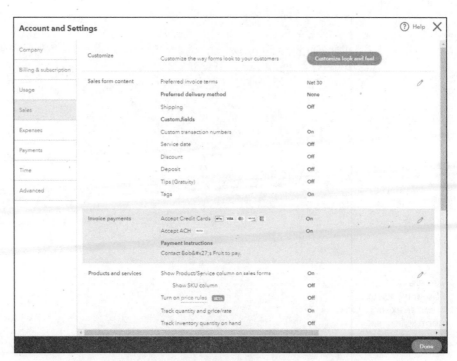

FIGURE 2-20:
Sales
preferences.

Customizing sales forms

Every QuickBooks subscription level offers a Customize Look and Feel button in the Customize section to display the Custom Form Styles page, as shown in Figure 2-21.

TIP

QuickBooks is rolling out a new "invoice and estimate experience" for customizing and using these forms. You can choose Old Layout to return to the classic experience, or if available, click Try the New Invoices to customize your forms in the new interface.

The Custom Form Styles page lists any form styles you have already created. By default, QuickBooks creates one Standard form style for you when you sign up; this style is used by default for invoices, estimates, and sales receipts.

You can an existing form — including the default forms — or you can create new customized forms for invoices, estimates, and sales receipts. To do so, click New Style in the top-right corner of the Custom Form Styles page, and choose (from the drop-down menu) the type of form you want to create. For this example, when I choose Invoice, the page shown in Figure 2-22 appears, which varies only slightly if you opt to edit a different form. If you opt to create a form style, the page displays a form name for the form you're creating.

FIGURE 2-21:
Use this page to edit an existing form style or set up a new form style.

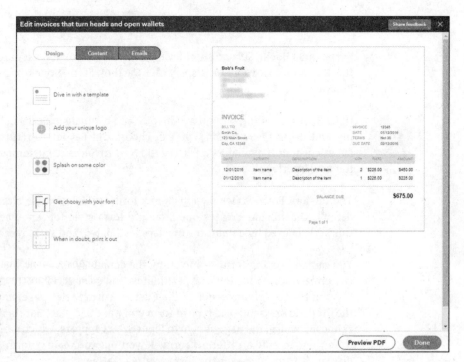

FIGURE 2-22:
The page you use to customize existing sales forms or create new forms.

You use the tabs in the top-left corner to establish form style settings.

» **Design:** This tab allows you to either click Dive In With a Template the first time that you edit a form, as shown in Figure 2-23, or click Change Up Template thereafter. You can choose between several styles for the form: Airy New, Airy Classic, Modern, Fresh, Bold, or Friendly. The preview shown in Figure 2-23 is the Airy New form style. You also use the Design tab to modify the appearance and placement of your logo, set the form's font, and apply different colors.

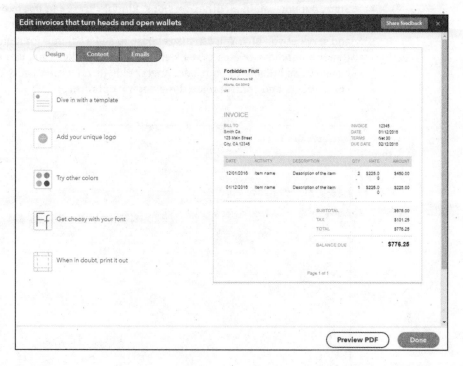

FIGURE 2-23:
Edit Invoices
page.

» **Content:** Click on any section of the form on this tab to turn fields and columns on or off, as well as edit labels and widths.

» **Emails:** This tab enables you to configure the outgoing emails that your invoices will be sent with. A preview of the email appears onscreen while you're making your changes.

» **Payments:** This tab — only present if you've enabled QuickBooks Payments — allows you to specify which means your customers can use to pay online, meaning, by bank transfers or credit card, or both. As noted in Chapter 1, fees can apply to both methods.

Click Preview PDF in the bottom-right corner of the screen to preview your invoice in PDF format, or click Done to save your changes. If you change your mind about editing the form, you can either press Escape or click the Close button at the top right-hand corner of the page. You're asked to confirm if you want to exit without saving, so you don't have to worry about accidentally losing your changes during an editing session.

Expenses preferences

You cannot configure the settings shown in Figure 2-24 in QuickBooks Simple Start, but you can in all other versions. Eligible users can opt to display a table of expense and purchase forms so that you can itemize and categorize the products and services you buy. You can also choose to add a column for identifying the customer a purchase relates to, as well as a column where you can mark items and expenses as billable to your customers. Plus or Advanced users can enable purchase orders and control related messaging options.

FIGURE 2-24:
Expenses preferences.

Payments preferences

Connect an existing QuickBooks Payments account here or click Learn More to initiate creating a new account. This service entails per-transaction fees that

I discuss in Chapter 1. The service enables you to accept credit cards or bank transfers from your customers and to email invoices that contain a Pay Now button for your customers. You may know this service as GoPayment or Merchant Services.

Time preferences

Your options here vary, based upon your subscription level, but at a minimum, you can set the first day of the work week and determine if a service field should appear on timesheets, and if time should be billable.

Advanced preferences

The Advanced section shown in Figure 2-25 contains preferences mostly related to nitty-gritty accounting settings that you'll probably want to hand off to your accountant. These include indicating the first month of your fiscal and tax years; specifying Cash or Accrual for your accounting method; optionally specifying a tax form; and, as mentioned earlier, determining if you want to use account numbers in your chart of accounts.

FIGURE 2-25: Advanced preferences.

CATEGORIES, CLASSES, AND LOCATIONS . . . OH, MY!

Don't confuse the Classes and Locations options you see in the Categories section of the Account and Settings page with the Product Category feature. The Product Category feature is separate from the features shown in the Account and Settings page.

If you are a Plus or Advanced subscriber you enable the Class and Location options in the Account and Settings page. This allows you to assign classes and locations to transactions to help you break down financial data beyond the account level. To create classes and locations, first enable them in the Account and Settings page; then choose Settings ➪ All Lists ➪ Classes to create new classes, and click Locations to create new locations.

Product categories, which don't need to be enabled, replace sub-items and are available to users of QuickBooks Plus and Advanced to help organize item information for reporting purposes; see Chapter 5 for details.

TIP

The Automation group of preferences enables you to control whether QuickBooks prefills forms with previously entered content, and whether credits are applied automatically. The Other Preferences section enables you to change the Sign Me Out If Inactive setting to as much as three hours.

Additional groups of preferences appear based upon your subscription level.

TIP

If you're about to contact Intuit for technical support, choose Settings ➪ Smart-Look to get a number that you can share with the support agent that will grant temporary permission to view your QuickBooks company (but nothing else on your computer). I can attest from decades of work as a software consultant that being able to see someone's screen turbocharges the support process.

QuickBooks Online Apps

Now is a good time to see the app options that are available to you now that you've reviewed your settings and configured your sales forms. This section felt a little tricky to write, because the word *app* has so many meanings these days. As you're about to see, there's a QuickBooks Online app for Windows, there are mobile apps for iOS and Android, and then there's an app store that features functionality that you can plug into your QuickBooks Online company. After I cover the various forms of apps, I discuss QuickBooks Labs, which is not an app but rather gives you an opportunity to beta-test new features that Intuit is contemplating.

QuickBooks Online Desktop app

Advanced subscribers can download and install the QuickBooks Online Desktop app for Windows, which, to be clear, is simply an interface for QuickBooks Online, and is no way related to QuickBooks Desktop, which is a separate accounting software. You can start the process by choosing Settings ⇨ Get the Desktop App. From there, you scroll down and click Download For Windows. Using the desktop app means you remain perpetually signed into QuickBooks Online, and you can create tabs that enable you to switch effortlessly between companies. The app also comes with an additional set of drop-down menus across the top that feel familiar to anyone accustomed to QuickBooks Desktop. Apart from that, you have exactly the same user interface and functionality as you do in your browser, as shown in Figure 2-26, but you don't have to worry about booting yourself out of QuickBooks by closing the wrong browser tab. You can choose File ⇨ Sign-Out if you don't want anyone to be able to access your books by simply launching the desktop app.

REMEMBER

You can only access QuickBooks Online Advanced companies with the desktop app, so you can't access Simple Start, Essentials, or Plus companies in this fashion.

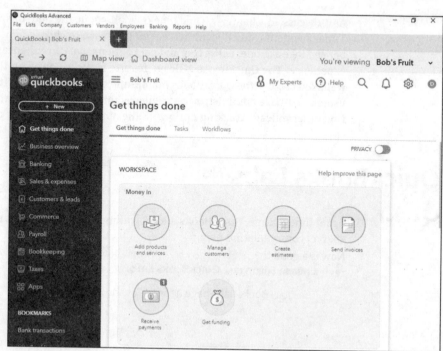

FIGURE 2-26:
QuickBooks
Online Desktop
app for Advanced
subscribers.

QuickBooks Online Mobile apps

Your QuickBooks subscription includes mobile apps for iOS/iPadOS and Android devices. These apps are optimized for touch interaction and on-the-go workflows such as customer management, invoicing, estimates, and signatures. You can also use the mobile apps to track the status of invoices, take payments, reconcile bank accounts, capture expenses, record mileage, and check reports. Pinch-and-zoom functionality works in both the apps and browsers on mobile devices.

WARNING

Mileage tracking in QuickBooks Online Mobile is only available to administrative users. To me, this is a whack-a-mole situation where you solve one problem — making it easy for employees to track mileage — and replace it with another: granting employees administrative access to your books.

You can get the mobile apps from the app store for your device or request a link at `https://quickbooks.intuit.com/accounting/mobile`. Alternatively, you can use your browser to log into your books at `https://qbo.intuit.com` without installing anything. Keep in mind that the mobile apps offer a subset of QuickBooks functionality, so you still need to use a web browser to carry out certain tasks, such as customizing templates.

QuickBooks App Store

As I discuss in Chapter 1, QuickBooks is all about the add-ons, such as Payroll, Time, Payments, and E-commerce. You may wish to choose Apps in the left menu bar and take a gander at the free and paid options that can enhance your QuickBooks experience. The QuickBooks Mileage feature is tucked away on the Apps menu as well. You can use the QuickBooks Mobile app to track mileage, with the caveat that users must have administrative privileges to your company. Fortunately, you can find other mileage tracking options in the app store, albeit on a paid basis.

QuickBooks Labs

From time to time, QuickBooks allows willing users to beta-test new features that they're contemplating using:

1. **Choose Settings ➪ QuickBooks Labs.**

   The QuickBooks Labs page appears, as shown in Figure 2-27.

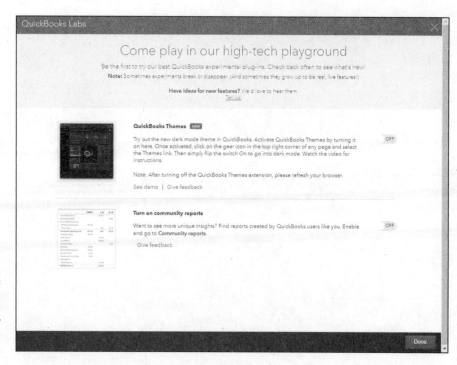

FIGURE 2-27:
Enable beta
features and
community
reports in
QuickBooks Labs.

2. Toggle the Off button for the features you want to try.

The Off button changes to an On button. You can always turn features off again if you don't like the effect or you simply change your mind.

TIP

Click Give Feedback on any feature to share your thoughts on any QuickBooks Labs feature. You can also click the Tell Us link to suggest new features that you'd like to see added to QuickBooks.

3. Click Done when you've enabled or disabled any features.

Your QuickBooks company reappears, with the features you selected enabled.

REMEMBER

You may need to refresh the browser page to see the new features you chose to make them available. Click your browser's Refresh button or press F5 on your keyboard.

Chapter **3**

Importing from QuickBooks Desktop and Sage 50

I f you're not presently using QuickBooks Desktop or Sage 50, you can safely skip this chapter. Otherwise, stick around while I walk you through converting your data from QuickBooks Desktop or Sage 50 to QuickBooks Online. You need to carry out these steps for each QuickBooks or Sage company that you wish to migrate. Keep in mind that each set of books that you've been keeping on your desktop, typically referred to as a company, will entail a separate QuickBooks Online subscription fee. Accounting software conversions always have some rough edges, so read on to see what to expect when moving your books from your desktop to the cloud.

Knowing the Ins and Outs of Converting Data

When you convert a QuickBooks Desktop company or Sage 50 company to QuickBooks Online, some data fully converts, some partially converts, and some doesn't convert at all. In addition, QuickBooks Online contains comparable alternatives for most, but not all, QuickBooks Desktop and Sage 50 features. Some of the more visible elements that don't convert includes the following:

>> **Reconciliation reports:** Save your Reconciliation reports in QuickBooks Desktop or Sage 50 as PDF files in case you need to access them later. In QuickBooks Online, continue reconciling where you left off. See Chapter 10 for details on reconciling accounts.

>> **Recurring credit card charges:** In QuickBooks Desktop Merchant Center, cancel each existing automatically recurring credit-card charge and re-create it in QuickBooks Online as a recurring sales receipt. All other recurring transactions convert and import. You'll need to cancel and reset up any charges that run through Sage Payment Services as well.

>> **Reports:** Find a similar report in QuickBooks Online and customize it to your preference. See Chapter 14, and check out the QuickBooks Online App Center or the app store at `https://quickbooks.intuit.com/app/apps/home` for a list of reporting apps that can help your business.

TIP

In Chapter 15, I discuss how QuickBooks Online Advanced subscribers can use the new Spreadsheet Sync feature to create custom reports in Microsoft Excel.

>> **Audit trail:** Your desktop audit trail won't transfer, but all changes going forward will be captured in the Audit Log within QuickBooks Online.

>> **Nonposting transactions or accounts:** Only estimates and purchase orders are converted from QuickBooks Desktop. Non-posting entries are not included in Sage 50 conversions.

WARNING

You must have a QuickBooks Online Plus or Advanced subscription to migrate your inventory items.

QuickBooks Desktop users should review the "QuickBooks Desktop Conversion Considerations" section in the QuickBooks Online for Dummies Cheat Sheet available at `www.dummies.com`. This supplemental guide describes the conversion limitations in detail so that you can avoid unpleasant surprises. I'd like to share a few additional caveats about importing into QuickBooks Online:

>> You can't import QuickBooks Desktop or Sage 50 data into any QuickBooks Online company that was created more than 60 days ago, except for accountant company files.

REMEMBER

When I say "accountant company files," I'm talking about importing a QuickBooks Desktop company file into the Your Books company available in QB Accountant. You have up to 1,060 days from the time that you create your account to import your data.

>> Importing QuickBooks Desktop data into an existing QuickBooks Online company overwrites any list and transaction data already stored in that company. Conversely, you must first delete your QuickBooks Online data before you can import from Sage 50, which means cancelling your current subscription and then starting a new company.

>> Importing your data into QuickBooks Online in no way limits your ongoing use of QuickBooks Desktop or Sage 50. Indeed, you may want to run parallel for a period, meaning that you temporarily enter transactions into both your desktop software and QuickBooks Online until you're sure that QuickBooks Online will meet your needs.

>> QuickBooks Online supports Intuit Online Payroll and QuickBooks Online Payroll to manage payroll. In some cases, your QuickBooks Desktop payroll data will update your year-to-date totals automatically. But if that data doesn't migrate, and you intend to use QuickBooks Online Payroll, you need to enter payroll totals as described in Chapter 12. The Sage 50 conversion process does not convert any payroll, so you'll have to migrate that information manually.

WARNING

Do not turn on or set up QuickBooks Online Payroll until *after* you convert your desktop data. If you've already turned on payroll in your QuickBooks Online company, see the nearby sidebar, "Payroll and desktop data conversion."

>> Make sure that all your sales tax filings are current before you export your QuickBooks Desktop data or Sage 50. You may need to make adjustment entries to sales tax filings in QuickBooks Online after you import the information.

>> You can only import an international QuickBooks Desktop company into its associated QuickBooks Online edition.

PAYROLL AND DESKTOP DATA CONVERSION

If you've already turned on payroll in your QuickBooks Online company, cancel your subscription or allow the free trial to lapse. Start a new subscription to create a new, empty QuickBooks Online company file, and only enable payroll after you've imported your data from QuickBooks Desktop into the new company. To cancel a subscription, choose Settings ⇨ Account and Settings ⇨ Billing & Subscription.

>> You can't import non-Intuit accounting software company files other than Sage 50. If you need to import company data from a non-Intuit product, you need to work with the Intuit customer service team.

>> You can't directly import accounting data stored in spreadsheet files. However, you can import this data via a third-party app called Transaction Pro, available at http://appcenter.intuit.com/transactionproimporter.

Using an online tool to migrate QuickBooks Desktop online

You can use an online tool to migrate your QuickBooks Desktop data to QuickBooks Online if your data meets the following requirements:

>> You're currently using QuickBooks Pro, Premier, or Enterprise or QuickBooks for Mac.

>> You have a company file (.QBW), portable file (*.QBM) or backup file (.QBB). QuickBooks for Mac users must convert their data to QuickBooks for Windows. The resulting backup file (.QBB) file can be converted to QuickBooks Online. For more details visit https://quickbooks.intuit.com and then choose Learn & Support ⇨ Support Topics and then use the search term **Convert Mac** and then click on the first link.

Here are the steps to convert your data from QuickBooks Desktop to QuickBooks Online:

1. **Access the online tool that matches your version of QuickBooks Desktop and then log in with your Intuit account, which you can create if needed:**

   - QuickBooks Pro/Premier/Mac: https://http-download.intuit.com/http.intuit/oii/html/quickbooksmigrationProPrem.html

   - QuickBooks Pro/Premier/Mac: https://http-download.intuit.com/http.intuit/oii/html/quickbooksmigrationEnt.html

You can access clickable versions of these links at https://quickbooks.intuit.com. Choose Learn & Support ⇨ Support Topics and then use the search term **Move Books Online** and then click on the first link.

2. **Click the File icon and then Temporary Files ⇨ Upload Files.**

3. **Browse to the .QBW, .QBM, or .QBB file that you wish to load.**

4. **Close the pop-up window once your file is uploaded and then click Refresh.**

From here your data will be automatically updated to the latest desktop version of QuickBooks, and then converted to the QuickBooks Online format. After the automatic update has occurred, you'll have the option to move your data now or to test drive a free trial of QuickBooks Online.

Using an online service to migrate Sage 50 to QuickBooks Online

Intuit has established a partnership with Data Switcher (www.dataswitcher.com), a company that specializes in accounting software conversions. Migrating your data is as simple as providing a back-up of your Sage 50 company and creating an Intuit account. The basic conversion, which covers two years of transactions, is free and completed within 72 hours. Nominal fees apply to additional conversion options.

Presently the following data cannot be converted from Sage 50 to QuickBooks Online:

- >> Payroll records
- >> Non-posting entries such as estimates, sales orders, and purchase orders
- >> Jobs, phases, and cost codes
- >> Memorized transactions
- >> Budgets
- >> Invoice templates and other templates
- >> Attachments

Conversions involves a four-step process:

1. Complete a series of pre-conversion steps.

Data Switcher will provide you with a pre-conversion checklist.

2. Share your data.

You'll provide a copy of your Sage 50 data to Data Switcher, as well as temporary access to your QuickBooks Online company.

3. Migrate your data to QuickBooks Online.

Data Switcher converts your data and imports into QuickBooks Online.

4. Review the data.

Data Switcher provides a Migration Report to help you confirm that everything moved over seamlessly.

To get started, visit `https://quickbooks.com/dataswitcher`, enter your email address in the Make Your Move section, and then click Let's Go.

TIP

Data Switcher offers a wide range of accounting software conversions as a paid service. This provides a pathway to convert from say FreshBooks or MYOB to QuickBooks Online. If you become disenchanted with QuickBooks Online, the service can migrate your accounting records to say Xero or NetSuite instead.

Double-Checking Your Data After Conversion

When conversion finishes, you need to double-check the data to make sure that it looks the way you expected. At this point, I suggest that you run and compare the following reports in both QuickBooks Desktop or Sage 50 and QuickBooks Online:

- Profit & Loss
- Balance Sheet
- Accounts Receivable and/or Open Invoices
- Accounts Payable and/or Unpaid Bills
- Sales Tax Liability (if applicable)
- Payroll Tax Liability (if applicable)

Run these reports using Accrual basis with the dates set to All. Due to differences between the platforms, cash-basis reports may not match, so make sure to do your comparisons on the accrual basis.

If the unthinkable happens and your data doesn't convert, you receive an email telling you that there was a problem. A report is attached for you to review so you can resolve the issues.

REMEMBER

You should plan to keep your QuickBooks Desktop data file around, if for no other reason than to refer to it for historical data as needed. Some people opt to run QuickBooks Desktop and QuickBooks Online simultaneously for a month or two to make sure that QuickBooks Online is performing as they expect. This process is referred to as running the accounting systems in parallel.

UNDOING AN IMPORT

You can purge all existing data if your Essentials, Plus, or Advanced subscription is 60 days old or less. Beyond this time frame, you must cancel your subscription and start a new company by resubscribing.

To undo an import, open your QuickBooks Online company and click Dashboard to display the home page. Enter `https://qbo.intuit.com/app/purgecompany` in your browser's address bar and then press Enter. A confirmation page reminds you that purging will delete everything in your QuickBooks Online company. The page also informs you of how many days you have left to perform the purge. If you want to proceed, type **yes** in the bottom-right corner and click OK to purge the data from your company; otherwise, click Cancel. You cannot halt or undo a purge once it begins.

QB Accountant users should not purge the Your Books company, as doing so may cause irreparable damage. Contact QuickBooks support if you need to purge the Your Books company.

2
Managing Your Books

IN THIS CHAPTER

» **Creating new records**

» **Managing records**

» **Deciding the settings for lists**

» **Getting up and running with importing customers and vendors**

» **Looking at Spreadsheet Sync**

Chapter **4**

Customer, Vendor, and Employee Lists

I n this chapter, I show you how to create customers, vendors, employees, and contractors. The mechanism is the same for each list, so I demonstrate by using the customer list, but most of the techniques you use are exactly the same for the other lists. Chapter 5 is where I discuss creating inventory and service items., while in Chapter 12, I show how Plus and Advanced subscribers can use the Projects feature to monitor certain customer-related transactions.

Adding New Records to a List

You create new customers, vendors, employees, and contractors in pretty much the same fashion. You start by choosing the appropriate section in the left menu bar and then choosing from your list.

» **Customers:** Sales ➪ Customers (Sales & Expenses ➪ Customers)

» **Vendors:** Expenses ➪ Vendors (Sales & Expenses ➪ Vendors)

» **Employees:** Payroll ➪ Employees

» **Contractors:** Payroll ➪ Contractors

Don't worry about having all of your ducks in a row with regard to completeness, as you can create each type of record by filling out only one or two required fields, and then circle back later to fill in any missing information.

>> **Customers:** Customer Display Name

>> **Vendors:** Vendor Display Name

>> **Employees:** First Name and Last Name

>> **Contractors:** Name and Email

REMEMBER

QuickBooks emails contractors and instructs them to set up their own account and complete a profile.

Creating a new record

Because the process for creating customers, vendors, and employee records is so similar, I won't bore you by walking through basically the same screens three times. Instead, I'll walk you through setting up a customer and then discuss differences for vendors and employees along the way. Customers have a couple of special characteristics that vendors and employees do not. For instance, you can create and assign customer types and create sub-customers. You cannot create a sub-vendor or sub-employee, but Advanced subscribers can create custom fields to store vendor or employee types.

REMEMBER

Essentials, Plus, and Advanced subscribers can enable the Multicurrency feature to set a foreign denomination for customers, vendors, and bank accounts. Check out the *QuickBooks Online For Dummies Cheat Sheet* for information on working with multiple currencies at www.dummies.com.

Follow these steps to create a customer:

1. **Choose Sales ⇨ Customers (Sales & Expenses ⇨ Customers) to display the Customers page.**

2. **Click Add Customer Manually if you're presented with that option; otherwise, click New Customer to display the task pane shown in Figure 4-1.**

   A bit of chicken-versus-egg arises in brand-new QuickBooks companies. In such instances, QuickBooks instead presents a page that gives you the option to import customers or add a customer manually instead of showing a blank customer list.

TIP

   I discuss how to import customers and other lists toward the end of this chapter.

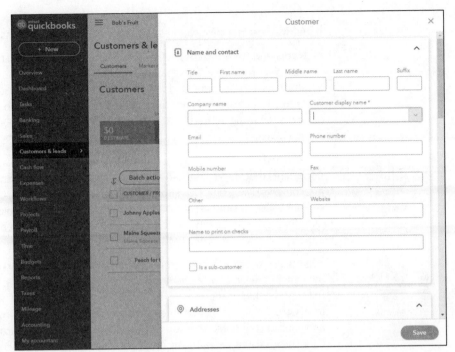

FIGURE 4-1:
Customer task
pane.

3. Complete the Customer Display Name.

This is the only required field in the Customer task pane.

4. Optional: Click Is a Sub-Customer.

More 'chicken versus egg' surfaces here, in that you must create a parent customer first, but after that, you can assign sub-customers as needed. Clicking Is a Sub-Customer causes a Parent Customer field to appear, which is a required field if the related checkbox is enabled. Once you choose a parent customer, a Bill Parent Customer checkbox appears. You can clear this checkbox if you want to bill the sub-customer directly instead of sending invoices and/or statements to the parent customer.

TIP

Sub-customer balances roll up into the parent customer balance. Transactions for sub-customers appear in both the sub-customer and parent customer registers. You can create up to four levels of sub-customers beneath a parent customer.

5. Optional: Complete the other aspects of the record.

The Customer task pane includes the following sections.

- **Name and Contact:** The name and contact information for your customer. The vendor task pane includes the name to print on checks.

- **Addresses:** The billing address and optional shipping address.

- **Notes and Attachments:** A free-form notes field allows you to add any sort of narrative, while a separate Attachments field gives you the ability to attach files to customer and vendor records. These may include copies of contracts, approvals, or any files that you wish, up to 20MB in size, in any of the following formats: PDF, JPEG, PNG, DOC, XLSX, CSV, TIFF, GIF, and XML.

REMEMBER

You can add attachments to customers, vendors, and their transactions. Any documents that you've attached appear in sequential order within the Attachments dialog box. QuickBooks notifies you of file types that are unacceptable, such as compressed ZIP files and Excel Binary workbooks (`.xlsb` files). To be clear, attachments can collectively exceed 20MB, but any single attachment cannot exceed 20MB in size.

WARNING

You can remove attachments from a record or transaction by clicking the X to the right of the filename in the Attachments field. However, doing so only unlinks the attachment from the record or transaction and does not remove it from QuickBooks. Any attachments that you add to become permanent additions to your books that you can attach to other records or transactions. Click Show Existing beneath any Attachments field to see all attachments, and choose Unlinked to view attachments that are not tied to a specific transaction or record.

- **Payments:** A section related to customers that allows you to specify the primary payment method, customer terms, and sales form delivery options, and to choose from up to six languages to use when sending invoices.

- **Additional Info:** The customer task pane allows you to specify a customer type, which I discuss in the next section, along with sales tax exemption details and opening balance details for the customer.

REMEMBER

QuickBooks often allows you to add new items on the fly to a drop-down list, such as new customers and vendors, but you can only choose from existing customer types on the Additional Info tab.

- **Custom Fields:** Advanced subscribers can create custom fields for customers, vendors, and transactions, as shown in Figure 4-2.

6. **Click the Save button to display the corresponding page or list for the record, as shown in Figure 4-3.**

There's a slight nuance here, in that you're returned to the customer page after you create a customer, but you're returned to the corresponding list when you add a vendor or employee. Click any vendor or employee to view their page. On the customer and vendor pages, you can click the Edit button to edit the record, or click New Transaction to initiate a transaction for that customer or vendor.

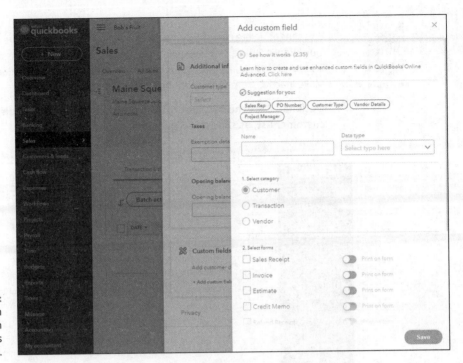

FIGURE 4-2:
The Add Custom
Field task pane in
QuickBooks
Online Advanced.

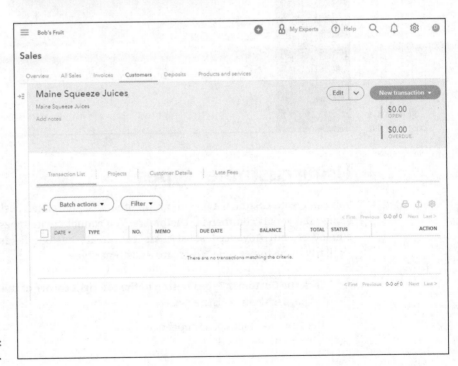

FIGURE 4-3:
Customer page.

REMEMBER

You cannot delete customers, vendors, employees, or contractors from QuickBooks Online, but you can mark them as inactive as long as their balance is zero. Choose Make Inactive from the Edit button drop-down menu, or click Make Inactive from the Action menu on the respective page.

7. **Optional: Click the Customers tab at the top of the page to display your customer list, as shown in Figure 4-4.**

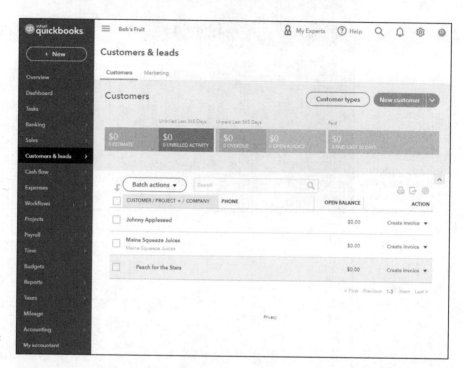

FIGURE 4-4:
Customer list.

Using customer types

You can create customer types to group otherwise-unrelated customers, such as residential versus commercial customers. You cannot create types for vendors or employees, but Advanced subscribers can create custom fields that function similarly to customer type. To create a customer type:

1. **Click the Customer Types button in the top-right corner of the Customers list page, shown in Figure 4-4.**

   The Customer Types page appears.

2. **Click New Customer Type.**

3. **Fill in the New Customer Type field in the dialog box that appears, and then click Save.**

4. **Add additional customer types as needed or click the Customers link at the top left of the screen to return to your customer list.**

You can now assign customer types to individual customers by editing their record, or assign customer types to multiple customers by using batch mode, which I discuss in the section, "Working with a batch of records," later in this chapter.

QuickBooks offers four reports that allow you to view transactions or customers by type.

>> **Sales by Customer Type:** No modification required.

>> **Sales by Customer Type Detail:** No modification required.

>> **Sales by Customer:** Click Customize, expand the Filter section, select Customer Type, and then choose one or more types.

>> **Customer Contact List:** Filter in the same fashion as the Sales by Customer report.

The first report doesn't require any modifications, but you need to group the Sales by Customer report by Customer Type. You also need to enable the Customer Type column on the Customer Contact List.

You can read more about running reports in Chapter 14.

Working with Records

Most lists enable you to sort, export, and perform group actions, particularly the customer, vendor, and employees lists. There's always an exception to the rule, though. For instance, you can only search or prepare Form 1099s from the contractors list. However, you can print a basic report for any list by clicking the Print List button, which appears in the margin, just above the Action column.

Searching lists

To search for a particular record, type some characters that match the person or company name in the Search box shown in Figure 4-4 that appears above the list, and then click the name when it appears on the list. As shown in Figure 4-5, a customer page appears that may have multiple tabs, such as Transaction List, Projects (if applicable), Customer Details, and Late Fees. Vendors have Transaction List and Vendor Details, while the employee list doesn't show tabs unless you subscribe to one of the QuickBooks payroll offerings.

REMEMBER

My transaction list in Figure 4-5 is blank because at this point, I haven't yet discussed how to create inventory items or transactions. I discuss inventory items and services in Chapter 5, invoices and payments in Chapter 6, estimates and purchase orders in Chapter 7, and paying bills and writing checks in Chapter 8.

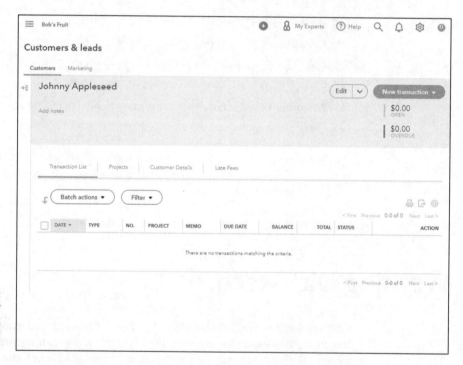

FIGURE 4-5:
An empty
transaction list
for a new
customer.

Click the Edit button on any customer or vendor tab to edit information about that record. Click the New Transaction button to add a transaction associated with that record. The Employee page doesn't have an Edit button; instead, you click Edit in the Action column.

Accessing attachments

You can add an attachments column to your customer or vendor list:

1. **Display the customer or vendor list.**

2. **Click Settings above the Action column.**

3. **Click the Attachments checkbox in the resulting menu, as shown in Figure 4-6.**

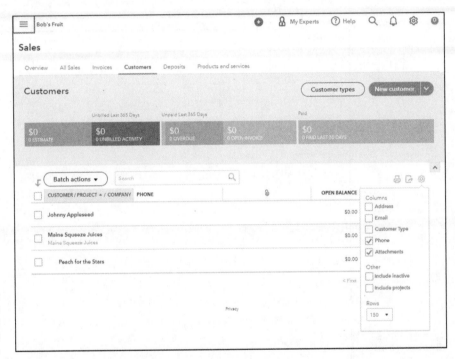

After you've enabled the feature, the Attachments column appears as part of the table grid. A paper clip in that column indicates that a record has an attachment. You see the number of attachments in the column for each transaction. Click the number to list the transaction's attachments, and then click any attachment to open it.

TIP

You can add an Attachments column to your transaction lists as well. Click any customer or vendor to display their page, and then carry out Steps 2 and 3.

Switching from record to record

When you finish working with one record, you can easily switch to another in that list by using the list's Split View pane.

 You can click the Split View icon shown in Figure 4-7, which looks like an arrow pointing to the right toward three stripes, to display a pane that shows the records stored in the list. The Split View icon only appears when you're displaying a page related to the record; the icon vanishes when you're viewing the customer or vendor list.

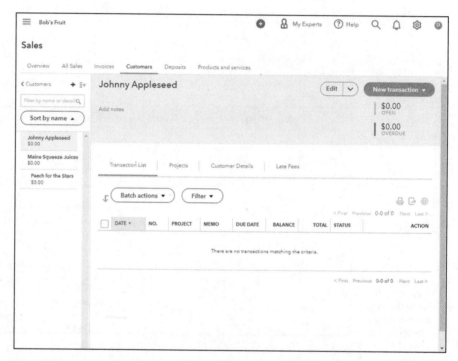

FIGURE 4-7:
Displaying a list's
Split View.

While working in the Split View pane, you can scroll down to find a record, or you can type a few letters of the person's or company's name in the Search box at the top of the list to find that record. You can use the Sort By drop-down list to sort the list by name or by open balance. Click a record to switch to that page.

To add a new record to the list, click the plus (+) symbol at the top of the list in the Split View pane to see the dialog box shown in Figure 4-7. To return to the Customers & Leads list page shown earlier in Figure 4-4, click Customers at the top of the Split View list, or click Sales (Sales & Expenses) on the left menu and then click Customers.

To close Split View, click the Close Split View button, which is an arrow pointing left toward three stripes.

Sorting a list on the Customers and Vendors page

You can sort the lists on the Customers and Vendors page by name or open balance. By default, the entries on these pages are sorted alphabetically by name in ascending order.

TIP

You can sort employees in alphabetical order and reverse alphabetical order, by pay method, or by status (active or inactive). The contractors list always appears in alphabetical order and can't be sorted. I talk more about employees and contractors in Chapter 12.

Follow these steps to sort the customer or vendor lists:

1. **Click Sales or Expenses (Sales & Expenses) on the left menu bar; then click Customers or Vendors to display the appropriate page.**

   I'm using the Customers list for this example.

2. **Click the heading for the column by which you want to sort.**

   If you click the Customer/Company column heading, the customers appear in descending alphabetical order. If you click the Open Balance column heading, the list appears in Open Balance order, from lowest to highest.

3. **Click the column again to sort it in reverse order and display balances from highest to lowest** (which, I'm sure, will be of much more interest to you because we all like to see the big numbers first).

Working with a batch of records

Certain lists allow you to carry out simultaneous actions for a group of records, such as sending emails, paying bills online, or making records inactive. You can also create and send customer statements and assign customer types in this fashion.

You must open the corresponding list before you can carry out a batch action, such as the Customers list. Click the checkboxes next to the records you want to include in your action, and click the Batch Actions button, shown in Figure 4-8. Select the action you want to take, and follow the onscreen prompts to complete the action.

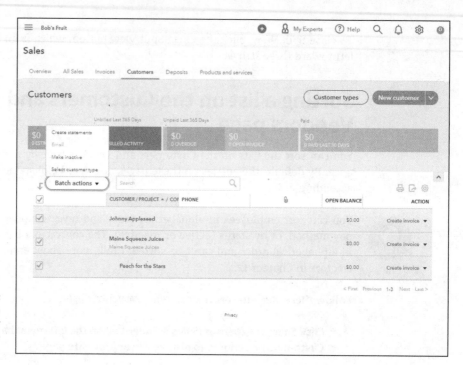

TIP

Advanced subscribers can also use the Spreadsheet Sync feature that I discuss at the end of this chapter to export lists, such as customers, vendors, employees, inventory, class. and locations in Excel; edit the records as needed, and then post the changes back to QuickBooks.

Changing Settings for Lists

You can control the appearance of certain lists by determining which columns are displayed and whether to include inactive records:

1. **Display a list, such as Customers, and then click the Settings button above the Action column, as shown in Figure 4-6.**

2. **Toggle checkboxes as needed to display or hide columns in the list and control how many records are shown per page.**

3. **Click the Settings button again to close the menu.**

REMEMBER

The elements you can show or hide depend on the list you're using. You can show or hide address information in Customers and Vendors lists, for example, but not in Employees and Contractors lists.

To adjust the width of any column, hover over the right edge of a column heading, and drag the double-headed arrow to the left or right, as shown in Figure 4-9. When you start to drag, the mouse pointer changes to a pointer, and a vertical bar appears to guide you in resizing the column. Release the mouse button when you're satisfied with the column width.

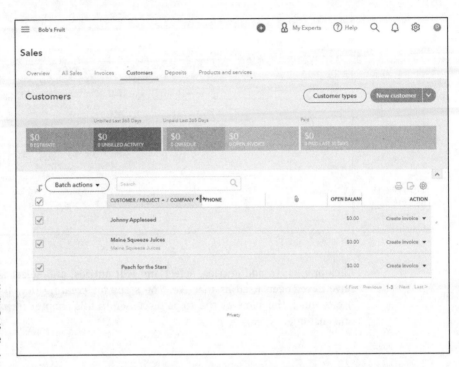

FIGURE 4-9:
Adjusting the width allotted to the customer's name on the customer list.

TIP QuickBooks remembers column width adjustments that you make in registers and on pages like Customers and Vendors, even after you sign out.

Accessing Other Lists

 QuickBooks lists range beyond just customers, vendors, employees, and items. Some examples include Payment Methods, Recurring Transactions, Attachments, and more. Choose Settings ⇨ All Lists to display the Lists page, as shown in Figure 4-10, to access these lists.

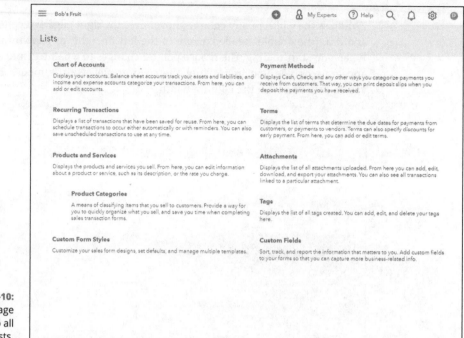

FIGURE 4-10: The Lists page links to all available lists.

Click any list to add entries, select and edit entries, and select any entries that have never been used as inactive. The steps for creating new list elements are pretty much the same as the steps discussed in this chapter for creating records and customer types.

Importing Customers and Vendors

If you have a QuickBooks Online Advanced subscription, skip this section and move on to the "Introducing Spreadsheet Sync" section later in this chapter. Otherwise read on to see how you can spend less time getting up and running with QuickBooks by importing your customers and vendors. If you're migrating from QuickBooks Desktop to QuickBooks Online, you can bring over all of your records, or choose to selectively import only some lists if you want to start with a clean slate. For instance, it's easy to import customers and vendors, as well as inventory items for products and services that you offer, which I discuss in Chapter 5.

REMEMBER

Importing lists isn't the same thing as importing a QuickBooks Desktop company. For details on importing a company, see Chapter 3.

Most accounting and contact management platforms allow you to export the customer and vendor information you've saved to a Microsoft Excel workbook or a comma-separated-values (.csv) file. Then you can use Excel or Google Sheets to access the exported data. Open the export file in the spreadsheet of your choice to review the information. If you happen to make any edits, be sure to save your file. You can import your list into QuickBooks.

TIP

The steps that follow assume that you've installed Excel on your computer. If you don't own a copy of Excel, you can use Google Sheets (https://sheets.google.com) and then choose File➪Import to open an Excel workbook in Sheets. QuickBooks allows you to import directly from Sheets, so you don't have to save the file back to your computer.

Downloading the sample file

You can download a sample file that illustrates what each import file should look like. In this case, I walk you through creating the sample file that will allow you to import customers:

1. **Choose Sales ➪ Customers (Sales & Expenses ➪ Customers).**

2. **Click Import Customers or choose Import Customers from the New Customer drop-down menu to display the Import Vendors page, shown in Figure 4-11.**

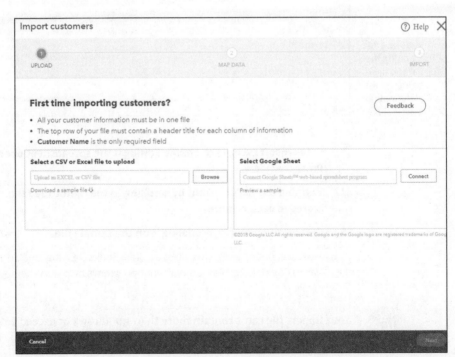

FIGURE 4-11:
The Upload page of the Import Customers wizard.

Import Customers and Import Vendors buttons appear on the Customers and Vendors pages until you've created your first customer or vendor. From that point on, you must click the corresponding New menu and choose the Import command.

3. **Click Download a Sample File if you're using Excel, or click Preview a Sample for Google Sheets.**

   The sample file appears in the downloads bar of most browsers. Otherwise, you can find it in your Downloads folder.

4. **If you're using Excel, open the sample file by clicking it on the downloads bar of your browser window or double-clicking the file in your Downloads folder.**

   The sample file opens in Excel, as shown in Figure 4-12.

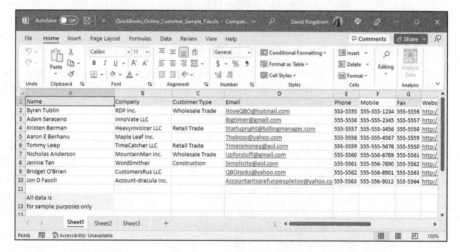

FIGURE 4-12:
A file showing the format you need to import list information successfully.

5. **In Microsoft Excel, click Enable Editing if the spreadsheet opens in Protected View.**

6. **Examine the file's content by scrolling to the right to see the information stored in each column.**

7. **Create your own file, modeling it on the sample file.**

   Most accounting programs, such as QuickBooks Desktop, enable you to export lists to CSV or Excel files. Consult your program's help documentation for details.

Your import file can't contain more than 1,000 rows or exceed 2MB. You can save your file as either an Excel workbook or a CSV file.

REMEMBER

THE SAMPLE IMPORT FILE'S LAYOUT

You can see that information in the sample file is in a table format, where each row in the spreadsheet contains all the information about a single customer or vendor (each row is referred to as a *record*), and each column contains the same type of information for all customers and vendors (each column is referred to as one *field* in a record). In Figure 4-19, all the information about Aaron E. Berhanu appears in Row 5, and all customer email addresses appear in Column D. You can safely delete all rows from the sample file except Row 1. The headings must remain in place for the import process to work properly.

TIP

Dates that you import must be in *yyyy-mm-dd* format. If you have a date entered in cell A1 of an Excel worksheet, you can use this formula to transform a date such as 2/15/2024 into 2024-02-15:

```
=TEXT(A1,"yyyy-mm-dd")
```

Copy the formula down the column, and then select all of the cells that contain the formula and choose Home ⇨ Copy, or press Ctrl+C (Cmd+C in Excel for Mac). Next, choose Home ⇨ Paste ⇨ Paste Values to convert the formulas to static values in the *yyyy-mm-dd* format.

REMEMBER

The Name column is the equivalent of the Customer Display Name field (as opposed to a contact name) and is the only required field in the import file. The Company column is the equivalent of the Company Name column, so you may wish to put the same information in both columns. You can import up to 16 fields of customer data into QuickBooks via this feature, but you have to manually enter in any elements. If this makes you do a face palm, check out the Transaction Pro app in the QuickBooks App store. Transaction enables you to import up to 38 fields, including detailed contact information, billing and shipping addresses, customer terms and payment information, and more. A free 7-day trial with limitations is available, or pricing starts at $10 per month.

Importing lists

Here's how to import a customer or vendor list:

1. **Make sure that your spreadsheet or CSV file is not open in Excel or Google Sheets.**

2. **Navigate to the corresponding list page, such as Customers.**

3. Click the Import Customers button or choose Import Customers from the New Customer drop-down list.

4. Click Browse for an Excel or CSV file or Connect for a Google Sheet, as shown in Figure 4-13.

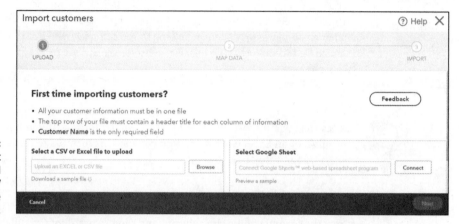

FIGURE 4-13:
You can import from an Excel workbook, CSV file, or a Google Sheet.

5. Navigate to the folder where you saved the file containing your list information.

6. Specify the file and click Open for an Excel or CSV file, or Select for a Google Sheet.

   The Import page displays the name of the file you selected.

7. Click Next to upload your file to a staging area.

8. Map the fields in your data file to the corresponding QuickBooks fields.

   Use the Your Field drop-down lists, shown in Figure 4-14, to match the columns in your file with the import files.

9. Click Next to display the final page of the wizard.

   As shown in Figure 4-15, a confirmation screen displays the records to be imported. You can widen the columns as needed.

10. Review the records to make sure that the information is correct.

    You can change the information in any field by clicking that field and typing. You can also deselect any rows that you've decided you don't want to import.

11. When you're satisfied that the information is correct, click the Import button shown in Figure 4-15.

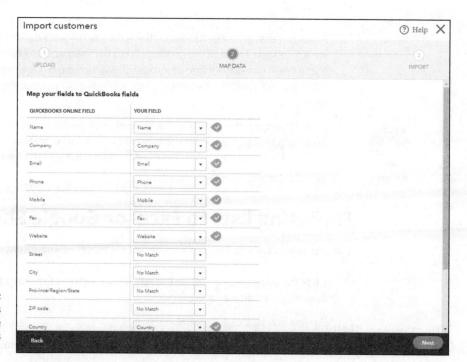

FIGURE 4-14:
Match the fields in your data file with QuickBooks fields.

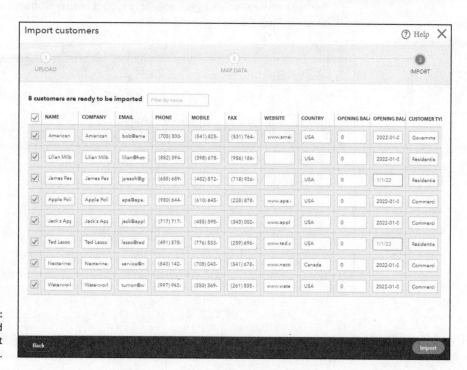

FIGURE 4-15:
Records uploaded from your import file.

A status message briefly flashes on the screen to tell you how many records were imported. I tried to trip up the process with two opening balance dates that were in *mm-dd-yyyy* format instead of *yyyy-mm-dd*, but the records were still imported. QuickBooks simply ignored the invalid input but imported the valid fields.

WARNING

If the Import button is disabled, some portion of the data can't be imported. Look for a field highlighted in red to identify information that can't be imported. If the problem isn't apparent, contact Intuit support for help, or set up the records manually.

Exporting lists to Excel or Google Sheets

You can export lists to Excel or Google Sheets by doing the following:

1. **Click the appropriate link on the left menu, such as Expenses (Sales & Expenses), to display a list.**

For this exercise, click Vendors.

2. **Click the Export to Excel button just above the Action column.**

Typically, an Excel spreadsheet appears in your browser's Downloads bar, as shown in Figure 4-16.

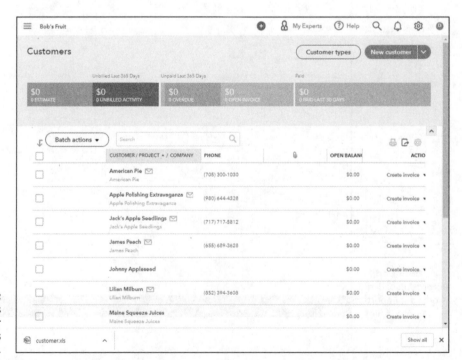

FIGURE 4-16:
Excel exports typically appear in your browser's downloads bar.

In Chapter 20, I discuss how to change a browser setting that enables you to choose where to save files that you export to Excel, as opposed to defaulting to your Downloads folder.

3. **Click the button at the bottom of the screen or look in your Downloads folder to open the file.**

4. **If you're using Microsoft Excel, you may have to click Enable Editing to exit Protected View.**

   I talk about how to disable Protected View and to streamline opening Excel files exported from QuickBooks in Chapter 15.

If you're using Google Sheets instead of Excel, choose File ⇨ Import. Follow the prompts to upload your workbook, after which you can work with the spreadsheet in the usual way.

Introducing Spreadsheet Sync

Advanced subscribers can utilize the Spreadsheet Sync feature in order to create a direct connection between QuickBooks and Microsoft Excel. Spreadsheet Sync enables you to create custom reports in Excel, as well as to export list records and transactions into Excel, make any changes you wish, and then post the updated records back to QuickBooks (see Chapter 15). Spreadsheet Sync enables you to pull the following data over to Excel, make changes, and then post the changed records back to QuickBooks:

» Vendors & Customers

» Inventory Items

» Classes & Departments

» Time Activities

» Purchase Orders

» Employees

» Estimates

You have to complete a one-time installation process on each computer with which you want to use Spreadsheet Sync.

Installing the Spreadsheet Sync add-in

The first step is to install the free Spreadsheet Sync add-in within Microsoft Excel:

1. **Choose Settings ⇨ Spreadsheet Sync.**

An instructions page appears, as shown in Figure 4-17.

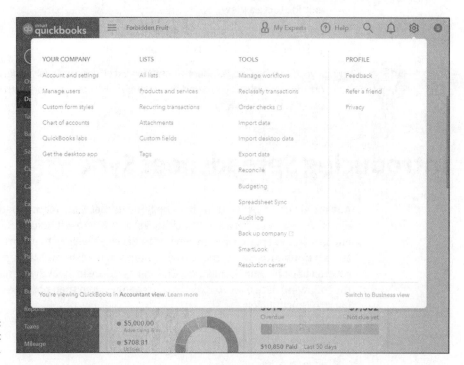

FIGURE 4-17:
Spreadsheet Sync
instructions.

REMEMBER

Spreadsheet Sync is only available in QuickBooks Online Advanced.

2. **Click Let's Go to begin the installation process, and then choose Open Excel if prompted.**

Your browser may ask you for permission to open Excel. Alternatively, a Spreadsheet Sync.xlsx workbook may appear in your Downloads folder; you can open it in Excel by way of the File ⇨ Open command.

WARNING

At this point, Excel for Mac users may encounter a warning that the file format and the extension of "Spreadsheet Sync.htm" do not match, and that the file could be corrupted or unstable. You can safely disregard this warning and click Yes to continue.

3. **Click Trust This Add-In, as shown in Figure 4-18.**

   Excel add-ins enhance the application with additional functionality. At this point, a new Spreadsheet Sync command appears on the Home tab of the ribbon interface in Excel.

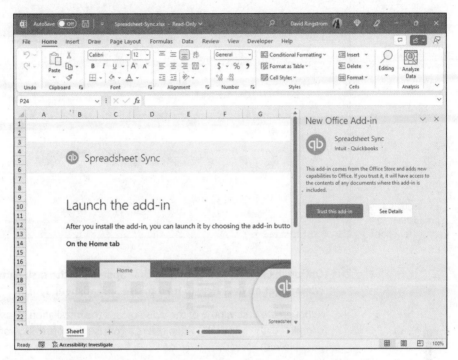

FIGURE 4-18:
Installing the
Spreadsheet Sync
add-in.

4. **Choose File ⇨ Close to close the Spreadsheet Sync workbook.**

   Spreadsheet Sync is now part of your Excel application.

5. **Choose File ⇨ New or press Ctrl+N (Cmd+N for Mac) to create a blank workbook.**

6. **Choose Home ⇨ Spreadsheet Sync to display the task pane shown in Figure 4-19.**

   All Spreadsheet Sync–related commands appear in this task pane.

7. **Click Sign-In and enter your email or user ID and password, in the same way you do when logging into QuickBooks Online.**

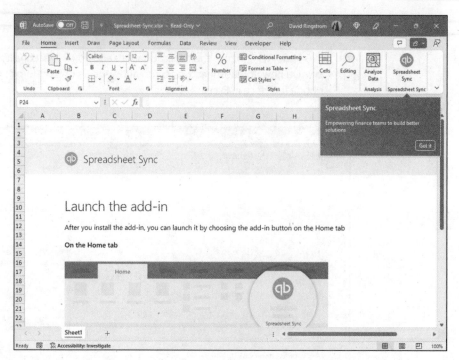

FIGURE 4-19:
Spreadsheet Sync
task pane.

8. **Optional: Click Play on the video that appears in the task pane if you want to get an overview of how to use Spreadsheet Sync.**

   Although the first minute of the video recaps the installation steps that you just completed, the rest of the video offers a concise demonstration of what's possible with Spreadsheet Sync.

You've now completed all of the one-time steps required to install Spreadsheet Sync.

Managing list records with Spreadsheet Sync

Spreadsheet Sync allows Excel to become an extension of QuickBooks, meaning you can retrieve data from QuickBooks, make changes in Excel, and then post the changes back to QuickBooks. This makes reviewing records, such as customers and vendors, far easier than by running reports or pulling up one record at a time. Even better, you can make corrections or fill in missing information in Excel, and then save your changes back to QuickBooks.

Here's how to edit or create customer and vendor records:

1. **Choose Home ⇨ Spreadsheet Sync in Excel, unless the Spreadsheet Sync task pane is already displayed.**

You must carry out the installation steps in the previous section on each computer with which you want to use Spreadsheet Sync.

2. **Choose Vendors & Customers or Employees from the Select Template list.**

A blank template appears in your spreadsheet, as shown in Figure 4-20, along with a separate Notes and Controls worksheet that documents certain restrictions and procedures to use with Spreadsheet Sync.

3. **Optional: Choose a company from the Company or Group section if you have more than one Advanced subscription.**

This field is not editable if you only have a single QuickBooks Online Advanced subscription.

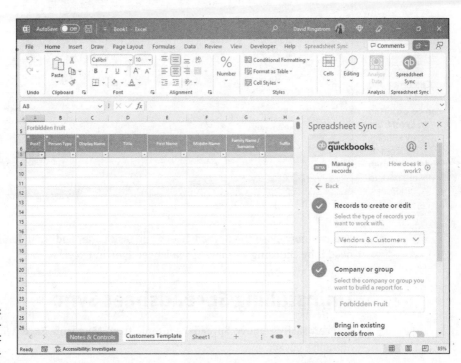

FIGURE 4-20:
Blank Spread-
sheet Sync
template.

4. **Optional: Toggle on the Bring in Existing Records from QuickBooks option. When the warning prompt informs you that any transactions or unposted changes on the template worksheet will be discarded, click OK.**

Whether you retrieve your records or not, you can use the template to post new customers and vendors to the list. Choose Yes in Column A for any rows where you edit an existing customer or vendor record, or enter **Yes** in the rows where you add new records. Enter **Customer** or **Vendor** in Column B for new records, and at a minimum, enter a display name in Column C.

5. **Click Post Data to QuickBooks at the bottom of the Spreadsheet Sync task pane, as shown in Figure 4-21.**

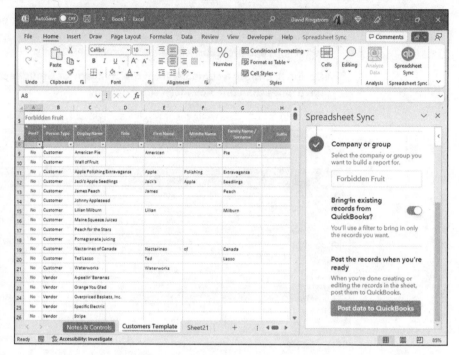

FIGURE 4-21: Customer and vendor records can be exported to Excel from QuickBooks, updated as needed, and then posted back to QuickBooks.

You can now close the Spreadsheet Sync task pane, and then display it when you need it by choosing Home ⇨ Spreadsheet Sync in Excel.

Uninstalling Spreadsheet Sync

You can easily remove Spreadsheet Sync from Microsoft Excel with just a couple of mouse clicks:

1. **Choose Insert ⇨ My Add-Ins in Microsoft Excel.**

   The Office Add-Ins dialog box appears.

2. **Hover your mouse over the Spreadsheet Sync add-in to display a three-dot menu, and then choose Remove.**

3. **Click Remove in the confirmation prompt.**

Spreadsheet Sync no longer appears on the Home tab of the Excel ribbon. You can install and uninstall Spreadsheet Sync as often as you wish.

IN THIS CHAPTER

» Setting up sales tax and automated sales tax

» Taking a look at the Economic Nexus feature

» Creating custom sales tax rates, and reporting and paying sales tax

» Distinguishing between inventory and non-inventory items

» Figuring out how to import and export products and services

» Editing and creating inventory records with Spreadsheet Sync

Chapter **5**

Managing Sales Tax, Services, and Inventory

H ello, dear reader, it's time to play "choose your adventure!" Jump ahead to the "Working with Products and Services" section if you aren't required to collect sales tax. Don't worry, I won't be offended. Otherwise, hang with me for a minute before you start adding the stuff you sell to QuickBooks. There's no question of which comes first, you really do want to set up sales tax before you start adding your goods and services to QuickBooks. Once you see how to add what you sell to QuickBooks, I cover some finer points, like categories, which function like sub-items, and the automation opportunities that pricing rules and bundles offer. I wind up this spirited discussion with the steps you can use to import and export products and services into or out of QuickBooks. The Spreadsheet Sync feature is a cherry on top that allows Advanced subscribers to maintain their product and services list in Excel.

REMEMBER

QuickBooks uses the term *categories* in two different contexts. In this chapter, you see how to use categories to organize items that you sell, while in Chapter 7 I show you how to use a Categories field to classify non-inventory related expenses. In short, you choose an account from your chart of accounts from the field named Category. If I had any say about it, I promise you that field would be named Account, and not Category. I have no say, but at least now you know!

Setting Up Sales Tax

Sales tax calculations are an automated affair if you're creating a new company in QuickBooks. Once you walk through a short wizard, QuickBooks calculates sales tax automatically on the fly based upon your customer's address. Conversely, existing QuickBooks companies, or those converted from QuickBooks Desktop, may still be using the old system, which required manually establishing sales tax rates, assigning the corresponding rates to each customer. Here, I show you how you can switch to the Automated Sales Tax feature if you're currently using the manual system. In addition, I discuss how the Economic Nexus feature can help you identify situations where you might not be collecting sales tax but are legally required to. Taxes come in all sorts of shapes and sizes, so I show how to create custom sales tax rates when needed, such as for tariffs or excise taxes. Government agencies will look to you for any taxes that you fail to collect, so I show you a hard way to review your sales tax settings if you're a Simple Start, Essentials, or Plus subscriber, and a hidden easy way if you are an Advanced subscriber. After that you discover how to report and pay sales taxes to the corresponding taxing authorities.

Understanding sales tax liability

Depending upon your volume of taxable transactions, you are required to remit sales tax to your taxing authority monthly, quarterly, or annually. When you enable the Sales Tax feature, you are asked to specify the method QuickBooks uses to calculate your sales tax liability for each period.

>> **Accrual:** QuickBooks considers sales tax due in the period that you create the invoice, regardless of whether your customer has paid the invoice or not. If you later write the invoice off, you get a credit for the sales taxes you previously paid.

>> **Cash:** QuickBooks considers sales tax due in the period that your customer pays the invoice. Tracking this liability is easiest if your customers pay their invoices in full. Partial payments, non-taxable items, and discounts or credits that you apply can make it harder to follow how sales tax has been calculated.

REMEMBER

You have to provide accurate mailing addresses for your company and your customers once you enable the Sales Tax feature. QuickBooks verifies the addresses in real time, and rejects illegitimate addresses. Your home state taxing authority is determined based upon your physical address, while sales taxes are computed automatically based upon your customers' addresses.

Enabling the Automated Sales Tax feature

You're prompted to set up sales tax the first time that you click the Taxes command in the left menu in a recently created QuickBooks company:

1. **Choose Taxes and then click the Get Started button.**

The wizard asks you to verify or enter your company's physical address, after which you click Next.

TIP

As is the case throughout QuickBooks, the State drop-down list is a little tricky. You can type the two-letter abbreviation for your state, but you then have to choose it from the list with your mouse. If I had my way, you'd be able to type in an abbreviation and press Enter.

2. **The next screen asks if you need to collect tax outside of your state.**

If you choose No, you can click Next to advance to the next screen. If you click Yes, you're prompted to specify the additional tax agencies. If you're not sure, check out the section, "Exploring the Economic Nexus feature," later in this chapter.

You cannot edit or delete tax agencies that you set up in your company.

WARNING

3. **Click Next once you've answered the Yes or No question to display an Automated Sales Tax Is All Set Up page.**

You can either click Create Invoice or close the page; however, spoiler alert, sales tax isn't completely set up at this point. You have one more screen at a minimum, plus you may need to mark certain customers as tax-exempt.

4. **Specify your filing frequency for each agency when the How Often Do You File Sales Tax window appears, and then click Save.**

   This step marks the true end of the sales tax wizard, so your next step is to indicate any tax-exempt customers.

QuickBooks assumes that all customers are subject to sales tax, so you need to edit any tax–exempt customers (such as government agencies, schools, and charities) by following these steps:

1. **Choose Sales ⇨ Customers (Sales & Expenses ⇨ Customers or Get Paid & Pay ⇨ Customers).**

2. **Select a tax-exempt customer and then click Edit.**

3. **Scroll down to the Additional Info section and click This Customer Is Tax Exempt, as shown in Figure 5-1.**

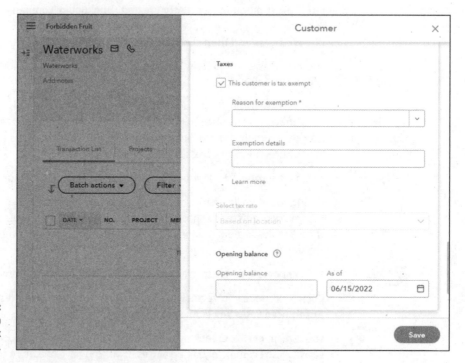

FIGURE 5-1: Marking a customer as tax exempt.

4. **Specify a choice from the Reason for Exemption, which is a required field.**

5. **Optional: Enter up to 16 characters in the Exemption Details field.**

   You can record a customer's exemption certificate ID in this field, or optionally upload a copy of the exemption certificate in the Notes and Attachments section.

Converting sales tax from QuickBooks Desktop

Setting up sales tax is a little different if you've imported your books from QuickBooks Desktop:

1. **Choose Taxes and then click the Get Started button.**

   This screen gives you the option to Do It Later, but let's seize the moment and click Get Started.

2. **Confirm your business address on the first screen of the wizard and then click Next.**

3. **A Bulk Matching screen asks you to link your tax rates from QuickBooks Desktop to the tax agencies recognized by QuickBooks Online.**

   Click the checkbox to the left of the Tax Rate Name column heading if all of your tax rates relate to a single tax agency. You can then make a choice from the Official Agency drop-down list, and then click Apply.

4. **Click Next to display a Review Your Rates page.**

   Click Change next to any tax rates that you wish to modify.

5. **Click Save to finalize your changes.**

6. **Click Continue when prompted.**

   A two-screen help wizard appears to give you background about the Sales Tax Center. You can click through this wizard or close it without reviewing it.

7. **Specify your filing frequency for each agency when the How Often Do You File Sales Tax window appears, and then click Save.**

   You can continue forward with your custom sales tax rates from QuickBooks Desktop, or you can enable automated sales tax.

Switching from manual to automated sales tax

You can easily switch to the Automated Sales Tax feature whether you've just converted from QuickBooks Desktop, or you've been continuing on with the traditional manual sales tax method as a long-term QuickBooks Online user:

1. **Choose Taxes and then click the Sales Tax Settings button to display the Edit Settings page.**

2. **Click Turn Off Sales Tax, and then click Yes when prompted to confirm.**

In effect, this puts all of your sales tax in a deep freeze, meaning the sales tax fields and settings vanish out of QuickBooks, but you're just a few clicks away from restoring them again.

I discuss the steps for enabling automated sales tax earlier in this chapter, in the section, "Enabling the Automated Sales Tax feature."

REMEMBER

You can control whether QuickBooks automatically calculates sales tax for your customers or uses a custom tax rate that you establish. Click once on any customer in your customer list and then click Edit. Scroll down to the Additional Info section and choose a custom tax rate from the Select Tax Rate field. Alternatively, choose Based On Location to instruct QuickBooks to automatically calculate sales tax instead.

Exploring the Economic Nexus Feature

As your business grows, you may draw in customers from other states and then start wondering, am I subject to sales or use tax in those states? The Economic Nexus feature removes all doubt by analyzing your sales for a time period of your choosing from January 2022 onward. You can run a report that informs you where you should be collecting and paying sales tax:

1. **Choose Taxes and then click Economic Nexus to display the Economic Nexus page.**

2. **Select a state from the drop-down list.**

3. **Specify a date range, such as Year to Date (YTD).**

4. **Click Run Report.**

This is where things get a little confusing, as you don't actually see a report appear on the screen. Instead, QuickBooks updates the row for the state that you chose, as shown in Figure 5-2. The Sales and Transaction Count columns report any activity for the period. The Threshold Met column reports Yes or No. Hover your mouse over that response to see a pop-up window that tells you the threshold for that state, and also provides a link to the taxing agencies' online documentation. The Agency Setup column informs you if you've already established that tax agency in your books. Finally, the Date Last Run column contains a timestamp for when you last ran the Economic Nexus tool for a given state.

5. **Optional: Repeat Steps 2 to 4 for each state that you do business in.**

Um, yes, this does mean that if you do business in all 50 states, then you have to run the report 50 times. Hopefully, QuickBooks will update this feature to automatically update all 50 states at once so that you don't have to.

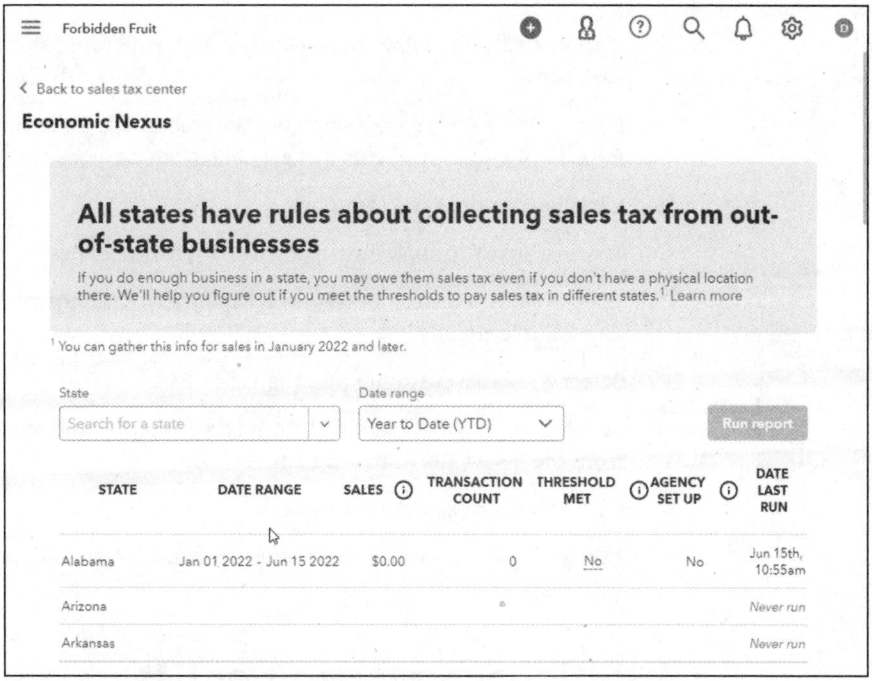
Forbidden Fruit
Back to sales tax center
Economic Nexus
All states have rules about collecting sales tax from out-of-state businesses
If you do enough business in a state, you may owe them sales tax even if you don't have a physical location there. We'll help you figure out if you meet the thresholds to pay sales tax in different states.1 Learn more
1 You can gather this info for sales in January 2022 and later.
State
Search for a state
Date range
Year to Date (YTD)
Run report
STATE
DATE RANGE
SALES
TRANSACTION COUNT
THRESHOLD MET
AGENCY SET UP
DATE LAST RUN
Alabama
Jan 01 2022 - Jun 15 2022
$0.00
0
No
No
Jun 15th, 10:55am
Arizona
Never run
Arkansas
Never run

FIGURE 5-2: The Economic Nexus tool for sales and use tax compliance.

Custom sales tax rates

You can establish custom tax rates if you have a tariff, excise tax, or other amount that you must collect on behalf of a governmental agency that QuickBooks does not automatically compute. Or you may be a free spirit that prefers to handle sales tax calculations on your own. Either way, just follow these steps:

1. **Choose Taxes and then click the Sales Tax Settings button to display the Edit Settings page.**

   This page enables you to add agencies.

2. **Optional: Click Add Agency if you wish to add a new tax agency.**

   A task pane prompts you to select an agency, specify your filing frequency, indicate your start date for collecting sales tax, and specify accrual or cash for your reporting method.

   TIP

   Your sales tax reporting method can be the same as the reporting basis for your books, or you can have it be different.

3. **Click Save to close the task pane.**

   Your new agency appears in the Tax Agencies list.

4. **Optional: Click Add Rate to display the Add a Custom Sales Tax Rate task pane.**

   Choose Single if you have a single tax rate paid to a single agency or Combined if you have multiple tax rates that get paid to one or more agencies.

5. **Click Save to close the task pane.**

   The next step is to apply the custom rate to your customers as needed.

6. **Choose Sales ⇨ Customers (Sales & Expenses ⇨ Customers or Get Paid & Pay ⇨ Customers).**

7. **Select a taxable customer and then click Edit.**

8. **Scroll down to the Additional Info section and choose the custom tax rate from the Select Tax Rate drop-down menu.**

9. **Click Save to close the task pane.**

   Repeat Steps 7 to 9 as needed to apply your custom tax rates to your customers.

Auditing your customer list

As I discuss in Chapter 4, you only need to fill in a single Customer Display Name field when creating a new customer. That means it's easy to set up a customer if you intend to circle back later and fill in their address. You may also wish to review the tax rates assigned to each customer. The Sales Tax Center offers a Taxable Customers Report button that purports to make the process easier but as you're about to see, quickly turns Kafkaesque.

TIP

At the end of this chapter, I describe how QuickBooks Online Advanced subscribers can use the Spreadsheet Sync feature to create an auditable sales tax listing.

Here are the steps to run a report that QuickBooks purports can be used to audit your sales tax settings by customer:

1. **Choose Taxes from the left-hand menu to display the Sales Tax Center.**

2. **Choose Taxable Customer Report from the Reports drop-down menu.**

   As shown in Figure 5-3, a modified version of the Custom Contact List report shows Customer Name, Billing Address, and Shipping Address, along with Taxable and Tax Rate columns. I don't know about you, but in my mind, a column labeled Taxable should display Yes if a customer is subject to sales tax, and No if they're not. I also would not expect to see a Tax Rate for customers that I've marked as Tax Exempt, like Waterworks. This means that the Taxable Customer Report is going to be of limited use for auditing the sales tax settings of your customers.

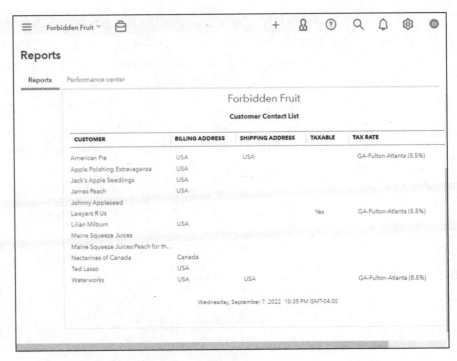

Forbidden Fruit

Customer Contact List

CUSTOMER	BILLING ADDRESS	SHIPPING ADDRESS	TAXABLE	TAX RATE
American Pie	USA	USA		GA-Fulton-Atlanta (8.5%)
Apple Polishing Extravaganza	USA			
Jack's Apple Seedlings	USA			
James Peach	USA			
Johnny Appleseed				
Lawyers R Us			Yes	GA-Fulton-Atlanta (8.5%)
Lilian Milburn	USA			
Maine Squeeze Juices				
Maine Squeeze Juices:Peach for th...				
Nectarines of Canada	Canada			
Ted Lasso	USA			
Waterworks	USA	USA		GA-Fulton-Atlanta (8.5%)

Wednesday, September 7, 2022 10:35 PM GMT-04:00

FIGURE 5-3:
The Taxable Customers Report is a modified version of the Customer Contact List.

TIP

A bit of cold comfort is that customer names on the report are clickable links that enable you to edit a customer's record, so that you can easily fill in any missing billing or shipping addresses or perform your audit by viewing customer records one at a time. In case you're wondering, the Spreadsheet Sync feature that Advanced subscribers can use to maintain customer records in Excel only includes a Tax Identifier/VAT Number column, but no other information related to sales taxes.

3. **Optional: Click the Export button and choose Export to Excel if you wish you view the report in Excel.**

   In Chapter 15, I discuss how to use the Filter feature, which can make it easy to view all customers that have the same tax rate, or to display customers where the billing or shipping addresses are blank.

Reporting and paying sales taxes

You or your accountant can manage and pay sales tax. Click Taxes on the left menu; then click Sales Tax to display Sales Tax Center, where you see all sales tax returns that are due and any that are overdue. To file and pay a particular return, click the View Return button on the right side of the page next to the return you want to file, to display a page similar to Figure 5-4.

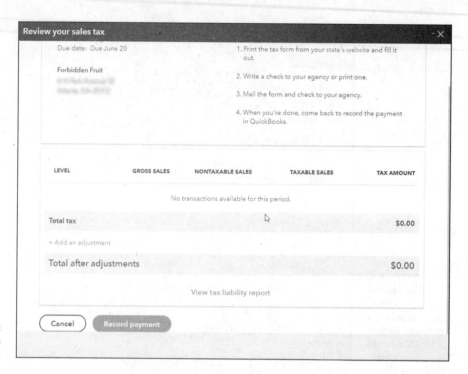

Review your sales tax

Due date: Due June 20

Forbidden Fruit

1. Print the tax form from your state's website and fill it out.

2. Write a check to your agency or print one.

3. Mail the form and check to your agency.

4. When you're done, come back to record the payment in QuickBooks.

LEVEL	GROSS SALES	NONTAXABLE SALES	TAXABLE SALES	TAX AMOUNT
		No transactions available for this period.		
Total tax				$0.00
+ Add an adjustment				
Total after adjustments				$0.00

View tax liability report

Cancel   Record payment

FIGURE 5-4:
Reviewing a sales tax return.

If you need to add a sales tax adjustment, click the Add an Adjustment link that appears below the Total Tax line. An Add an Adjustment task pane appears on the right side of the screen. Provide a reason for the adjustment and the adjustment date, along with an account and an amount for the adjustment. Click Add to post the adjustment, or click the X at the top right-hand corner to close the task pane.

When the Review Your Sales Taxes page appears (see Figure 5-5), click the Record Payment button to display the Record Payment page. You'll then need to file your sales tax return(s) with the corresponding governmental agencies.

QuickBooks calculates and displays the amount due to your sales tax agency, and you can confirm the amount or change it. Be aware that although you can change the amount due that QuickBooks supplies, if you do, you risk underpaying your sales tax liability. To see the details of the amount due on the Sales Tax Liability report, which breaks down the tax amount due, click the Report link in the first step listed on the page. (This downloads your full report.)

To complete the payment and sales tax filing, supply a payment date and a bank account from which you want to pay the liability; then click the Record Payment button, which I couldn't squeeze into Figure 5-5 but that I promise you see when you scroll down when you're looking at your own screen.

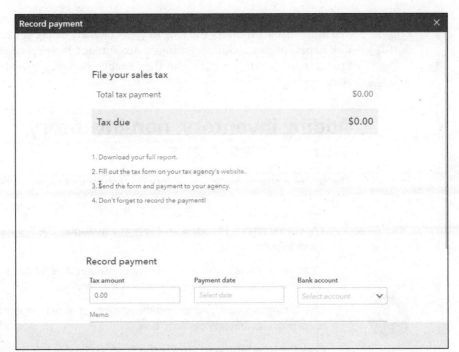

FIGURE 5-5:
Use this page to
record a sales tax
payment.

Working with Products and Services

Depending upon your subscription level, you can create up to three types of products and services.

>> **Inventory:** Plus and Advanced subscribers can use the FIFO (First In, First Out) accounting method to track inventory quantities on-hand for physical goods kept in stock.

>> **Non-inventory:** These include items that you don't physically own, such as drop-ship items, or consumable items that are of immaterial value, such as nuts and bolts, where it's not feasible to charge for each individual nut or bolt. Simple Start, Essentials, Plus, and Advanced subscribers can create non-inventory items.

>> **Services:** These items can streamline the invoicing process by giving you a way to standardize descriptions and pricing. Simple Start, Essentials, Plus, and Advanced subscribers can create service items.

WARNING

If you are based in the United States and currently using another accounting method, such as LILO (last in, last out) or Average Cost for valuing your inventory, then you must file Form 3115, Application for Change in Accounting Method (https://irs.gov/forms-pubs/about-form-3115) with the Internal Revenue Service.

REMEMBER

You must enable inventory tracking in your company before you can create inventory items. To do so, choose Settings ⇨ Account and Settings ⇨ Sales. Click on the Products and Services section and then enable the Track Inventory Quantity On Hand setting.

Adding inventory, non-inventory, and services items

The following steps walk you through creating inventory, non-inventory, and service items:

1. **Choose Settings ⇨ Products and Services to display the Products and Services page.**

   Alternatively, choose Sales ⇨ Products and Services (Sales & Expenses ⇨ Products and Services) or Get Paid & Pay ⇨ Products and Services.

   TIP

   Click Settings above the Action column and then choose Compact to squeeze more products and services onscreen.

2. **Click the New button to display the Product/Service Information task pane shown in Figure 5-6.**

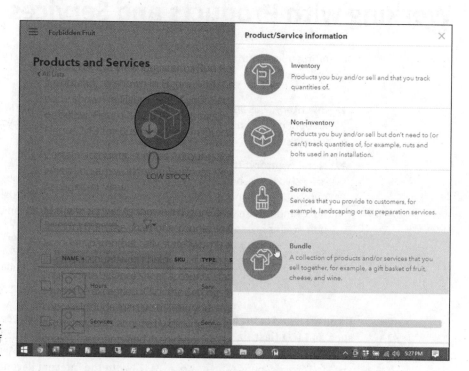

FIGURE 5-6: Select a type of item to create.

3. **Choose Inventory, Non-Inventory, or Service.**

   I discuss the fourth option, Bundles, in the section, "Working with bundles."

   For this example, I chose Inventory Item, which resulted in the Inventory task pane appearing, as shown in Figure 5-7. You set up Non-Inventory and Service items in exactly the same fashion; the only difference is that you have fewer fields to fill in.

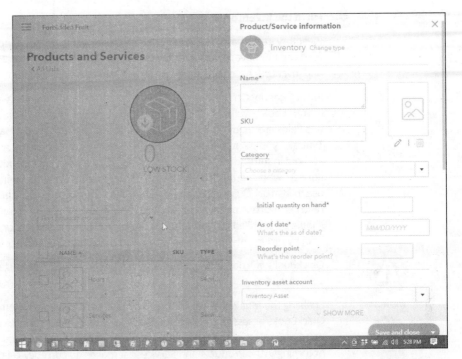

FIGURE 5-7:
Use this task pane to create an inventory item.

4. **Supply a name for the item and optionally enter a SKU.**

   SKU is short for *stock-keeping unit*, and is another way of referring to a part number or other identifier for your products and services.

5. **Optional: Upload a picture of the item by clicking the Upload button, which looks like a pencil, and navigating to the location where you store the picture.**

6. **Optional: Assign the item to a category or identify it as a sub-item.**

   Assigning items to categories enables you to group related items together. If you don't see the Category field on your task pane, then you see the option to make an item be a sub-item instead. When you enable the Subitem checkbox, you are then prompted to choose a parent item. You can tell if you have categories by clicking More on the Products and Services page. Companies with the Categories feature have a Manage Categories command on the drop-down menu along with a Run Report option. Companies that don't have the Category feature only have a Run Report option here.

7. **Optional: Assign a default class to the item if you've enabled the Class feature.**

   I discuss classes in more detail in Chapter 2.

8. **Fill in the Inventory Items fields.**

   Inventory Items have four additional fields that Non-Inventory and Service Items do not have: Initial Quantity On Hand, As Of Date, Reorder Point, and Inventory Asset Account.

   Initial Quantity On Hand is the starting inventory count that you want to record in your books, while As Of Date is the date on which the count was valid. These two fields are required, so enter zero for the Initial Quantity On Hand if needed. Typically, you want to use the first day of your fiscal year for the As Of Date, entered in mm/dd/yyyy format, or make a choice from the calendar that appears when you click in the field. Reorder Point is an optional field you can use to instruct QuickBooks to alert you when the quantity on hand for an item reaches or drops below a certain level. The Inventory Asset Account field should be prefilled for you, but you can create a new asset account if you wish by clicking the drop-down arrow and then choosing Add Account.

WARNING

   QuickBooks will not allow you to enter transactions prior to the start date of your company.

REMEMBER

   Enabling the Multicurrency feature has no effect on inventory item valuations; QuickBooks assesses and reports inventory item values in home currency units, regardless of the currency used by the vendor who sold you the items. Accordingly, the Products and Services list makes no currency-related distinctions. To learn more about this feature, check out the Cheat Sheet for *QuickBooks Online For Dummies*.

TAKING ADVANTAGE OF SKUs

You can control whether SKU information appears in the Products and Services list and on transaction forms from the Account and Settings task pane. Choose Settings ⇨ Account and Settings ⇨ Sales. In the Products and Services section, toggle the Show SKU option, click Save, and then click Done. If you like, you can add the SKU to any custom invoice forms, which I discuss in Chapter 2.

9. **Fill in the Description field for how the item should be described on sales forms.**

TIP

Clear the I Sell This Product/Service to My Customers checkbox if you want to create an item that is basically a note that you can add to your sales forms by choosing its item ID. I would classify such an item as Non-Inventory.

10. **Fill in the Sales Price/Rate field and specify an Income Account.**

The Income Account is prefilled, but you can choose or add a different account if you wish.

11. **Optional: Click Edit Sales Tax to verify or change the sales tax settings.**

QuickBooks asks you to specify the type of product or service so that sales tax can be calculated correctly. If your item is nontaxable, scroll down and choose Non-Taxable, and then click Done.

12. **As shown in Figure 5-8, click I Purchase This Product/Service from a Vendor if applicable to display a description to be used with purchase forms, cost, expense account, and preferred vendor.**

FIGURE 5-8:
Add purchasing information for the item.

The checkbox is preselected for Inventory Items, while you need to click it when applicable for Non-Inventory and Service items. All four of these fields are optional.

13. **Click Save and Close.**

The Products and Services list appears, displaying your new item.

At any point, you can click Edit in the Action column of the Products and Services page to edit an existing inventory item. The arrow in the Action column displays a menu with up to six choices, depending upon the item type.

>> **Make Inactive:** Choose this command to make an item inactive. To view items that you have marked inactive, click the funnel icon just above your list of products and services, change the Status to Inactive, and then click Apply. The Action contains a link that enables you to make an item active again.

WARNING

QuickBooks enables you to make items inactive even if the quantity on hand is not zero. The Quantity On Hand field is automatically adjusted to zero when you make such items inactive. Making an item active again does not restore any quantity on hand that was present when you marked the item inactive.

>> **Run Report:** Choose this command to run a Quick Report for the last 90 days of transactions for this item.

>> **Duplicate:** Choose this command to display the Product/Service Information task pane that you used earlier in the chapter to create a new item. In this case, some, but not all, fields are prefilled to ease the process of setting up similar items.

>> **Adjust Quantity:** Choose this command to adjust the quantity on hand of Inventory items, which I discuss in more detail in the section, "Creating inventory adjustment transactions."

>> **Adjust Starting Value:** Choose this command to adjust the starting value of Inventory items, which I discuss in more detail in the section, "Creating inventory adjustment transactions."

>> **Reorder:** As I discuss in more detail in the section, "Reordering inventory items," this command enables you to create a purchase order to reorder Inventory items.

TIP

Plus and Advanced subscribers have basic inventory tracking capabilities available. QuickBooks Desktop Premier or Enterprise versions offer more robust, advanced inventory capabilities, such as to support manufacturing.

You use the Products and Services list pretty much the same way you use the Customer and Vendor lists. For example, you can search for an item by its name, SKU, or sales description. You can identify the columns you can use to sort the list by sliding your mouse over the column heading; if the mouse pointer changes to a hand, you can click that column to sort the list using the information in that column.

Reordering inventory items

You can also use the Products and Services list to identify inventory items that are below their reorder level or out of stock. As shown in Figure 5-9, click Low Stock at the top of the list to show only items that have either a quantity below the reorder point you set, or an on-hand quantity of one. Click Out of Stock to view items that have an on-hand quantity of zero or a negative inventory quantity. Click the X that appears to the right of either graphic to display all items again.

There are two ways you can reorder low-stock or out-of-stock inventory items:

>> Click the arrow in its Action column and choose Reorder from the drop-down menu that appears.

>> Select the checkbox to the left of two or more item names that you are ordering from a single vendor and then choose Batch Actions ⇨ Reorder to add multiple items to a purchase order.

In either case, a purchase order reflecting the item(s) you choose appears. Complete the purchase order and then send it to your supplier. QuickBooks only allows you generate purchase orders for one vendor at a time, so you need to repeat these steps for each vendor that you want to order from.

REMEMBER

The Reorder option is only available in the Action column for Inventory items. You have to manually create purchase orders for Non-Inventory and Service items that you purchase from others.

Creating inventory adjustment transactions

On occasion, you may need to adjust inventory item quantities on hand or starting values, particularly after performing a physical inventory count. You can print the Physical Inventory Worksheet report by choosing Reports (Business Overview ⇨ Reports) and then typing the word **Physical** in the Search field. This worksheet makes it easy to record item quantities on hand as you count inventory. You can then compare the report to your accounting records and make adjustments as needed.

Adjusting inventory quantities

If your physical count results in a discrepancy from your accounting records, then you need to create an adjustment to reconcile your books with the reality in your warehouse. Follow these steps to create an inventory adjustment:

1. **Choose New ⇨ Inventory Qty Adjustment to display the Inventory Quantity Adjustment page, shown in Figure 5-10.**

Click Show More if you don't see the Inventory Adjustment command on the New menu. Alternatively, you can click the drop-down menu in the Action column for any item on your Products and Services page and then choose Adjust Quantity.

2. **Optional: Change the adjustment date and/or the inventory adjustment account.**

You can also change the reference number if you wish.

3. **Click the Product field in Row 1 and choose an inventory item from the drop-down menu.**

The description field is populated, along with the current quantity on hand. The New Qty field defaults to the current quantity on hand.

REMEMBER

If you've enabled class and location tracking, you can supply information for those fields as you complete the Inventory Quantity Adjustment window.

FIGURE 5-10:
You can adjust
one or more
inventory items
at a time.

4. **Update either the New Qty or Change in Qty field.**

   If the Qty on Hand field indicates that you should have 345 giant bows, but you only counted 330 bows in your warehouse, then you need to reduce the quantity on hand in QuickBooks by 15. You can do either of the following:

   - Enter **330** in the New Qty field.
   - Enter **–15** in the Change in Qty field.

5. **Repeat Steps 3 and 4 for each inventory item you need to adjust.**

   Click Add Lines if you wish to add more items.

   The Clear All Lines button next to Add Lines completely erases the Inventory Quantity Adjustment screen without asking you to confirm. To guard against accidentally clicking this button, you can click the Save button at the bottom of the screen to save your work in progress. Conversely, the Cancel and Clear buttons at the bottom of the screen provide a confirmation prompt.

WARNING

6. **In the Memo field, enter a description that explains why you made this adjustment.**

   Your accountant, or perhaps your future self, will thank you for your diligence in documenting why the adjustments were made.

7. Click the Save and Close button.

TIP

You can prefill the inventory adjustment screen by choosing one or more items from your Products and Services page, and then choosing Adjust Quantity from the Batch Actions menu.

Making an inventory quantity adjustment

You can review or amend inventory adjustment transactions by carrying out these steps:

1. Choose New ⇨ Inventory Qty Adjustment or use the Change Quantity command on the Action menu on the Products and Services page to display the Inventory Quantity Adjustment window.

2. Click the Recent Transactions button in the top-left corner of the window, to the left of the words "Inventory Quantity Adjustment."

Recent inventory adjustment transactions are shown in Figure 5-11.

FIGURE 5-11:
Recent inventory
adjustments.

3. **Choose an adjustment from the list, or click View More to display the Search page where you can provide additional criteria.**

4. **Once you have displayed a transaction, you can make edits as needed or delete the transaction.**

   You can remove a line from an adjustment by clicking its Delete button at the right edge of the row. You can delete the entire transaction by clicking the Delete button at the bottom of the screen.

5. **Click Save and Close in the bottom-right corner of the window.**

Adjusting an inventory item's starting value

Let's say that in spite of your best-laid plans, you made a mistake when you entered the starting value for an inventory item. You can edit the starting value for any inventory item that you created subsequent to November 2015.

WARNING

Changing an item's starting value can have wide-ranging effects, and a note to this effect appears when QuickBooks senses that you're trying to edit an inventory item's starting value. If you're not sure what you're doing, ask your accountant. Please. They won't mind.

To adjust an inventory item's starting value, follow these steps:

1. **Choose Settings ⇨ Products and Services.**

2. **Click the arrow in the Action column for the inventory item you want to adjust, and then choose Adjust Starting Value from the drop-down menu.**

   A warning appears, explaining that changing an inventory item's starting value may affect the initial value of your inventory.

3. **Assuming that you heeded the preceding warning and know what you're doing, click "Got It!"**

   The Inventory Starting Value window appears, as shown in Figure 5-12.

TIP

   If you've enabled class and location tracking, note that you can supply information for those fields along with other fields that affect the inventory item's starting value.

4. **Adjust the Initial Quantity On Hand, As Of Date, and Initial Cost as needed.**

   Although you could also change the Inventory Adjustment Account, I don't recommend doing so unless you want to *really* get under your accountant's skin.

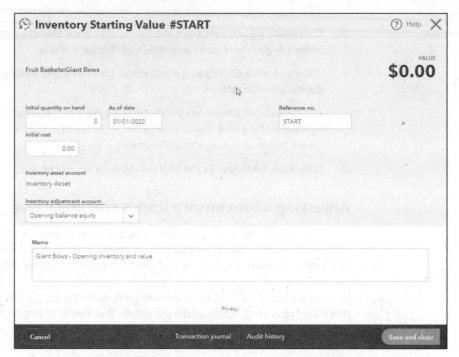

Inventory Starting Value #START · ? Help · X

Fruit Baskets:Giant Bows

VALUE
$0.00

Initial quantity on hand
5

As of date
01/01/2022

Reference no.
START

Initial cost
0.00

Inventory asset account
Inventory Asset

Inventory adjustment account
Opening balance equity ∨

Memo
Giant Bows - Opening inventory and value

Privacy

Cancel · Transaction journal · Audit history · Save and close

FIGURE 5-12:
Use this window to adjust an inventory item's starting values, but only if you're sure of why you're making the adjustment.

REMEMBER

You're in the wrong place if you want to change the inventory asset account. Choose the Edit command in the Action column of the Products and Services page for the item you wish to modify, and make the change in the Product/Service Information task pane.

5. **Click Save and Close.**

Establishing categories

Categories can help you organize what you sell and can group related items on your inventory and sales reports. Categories don't affect your accounting or your financial reports, and you can't assign categories to transactions — that's what classes and locations are for, which I discuss in Chapter 2. The Category field in the Product/Service Information task pane that you use to create an item enables you to create new categories on the fly, or you can use the Product Categories page:

1. **Click Settings ➪ All Lists to display the All Lists page.**

2. **Click Product Categories in the first column, just below Products and Services, to display the Product Categories page, as shown in Figure 5-13.**

3. **Click New Category to display the Category Information task pane.**

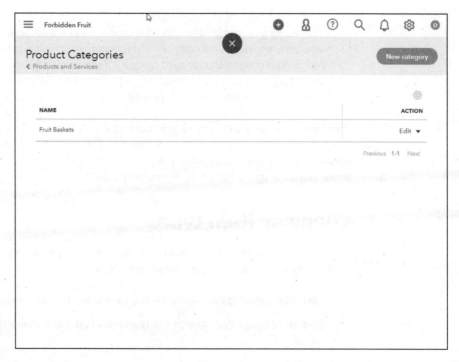

FIGURE 5-13:
The Product
Categories page.

4. **Enter a category name; then (optionally) choose Is a Sub-Category and then select a parent category.**

   REMEMBER

   You cannot use existing item names as a category name. For instance, if you have a product called Fruit Basket, you can't use the words *Fruit Basket* as a category name, but you could be clever and use the plural *Fruit Baskets*.

5. **Click Save to create your new category, or click the Close button at the top right to cancel this action.**

   TIP

   You can create subcategories up to four levels deep, such as Clothing ⇨ Shoes ⇨ Women's Shoes ⇨ Sneakers. You can't create a subcategory for Sneakers because it's four levels down, but you can create another subcategory for Women's Shoes, which is three levels down, called *Dress Shoes*.

6. **Optional: Choose two or more items from the Products and Services list, and then use the Assign Category drop-down menu to update the category of the selected items.**

   You can also click an individual item and then choose Edit on the next page to change the category for that single item.

7. **Click Edit from the Action column of the Product Categories page if you wish to modify or delete a category name.**

The resulting Category Information task pane includes a Remove button that you can use to delete the category. The Remove command also appears on the Action drop-down menu for each category. If you remove a subcategory, any items assigned move one level up. Any items assigned to a top-level category that you remove become uncategorized.

WARNING

Categories are an exception to the normal QuickBooks convention of keeping deleted items in an inactive state. When you remove a category, you physically remove it with no ability to undo your change other than to re-create the category again and associate it with your items as needed.

Changing item types

You can change a service or non-inventory item's type individually or in batch mode. Here's how to a change a single item's type:

1. **Click Edit in the Action column for the item in the Products and Services list.**

2. **Click the Change Type link at the top of the task pane above the item's name.**

   A task pane similar to Figure 5-7 appears. The only differences are that Bundle isn't an option and that the current item type contains a checkmark.

3. **Click the new item type to redisplay the Product/Service Information task pane with the new item type.**

4. **Make any other necessary changes.**

5. **Click Save and Close.**

Changing the type of a single item by using this method works well when you need to change just one or two items or when you're converting a Non-Inventory or Service item to an Inventory item.

TIP

You can change multiple Service items to Non-Inventory, or multiple Non-Inventory items to Service, by selecting similar products on the Products and Services list and then choosing the new type from the Batch Actions menu.

Simplifying your invoicing process

Invoicing your customers generally involves a lot of rote work. QuickBooks offers two features that can speed things up for you. First, *pricing rules* enable you to automatically discount or increase the price of items for some or all customers, either permanently or for a specified period. Second, *bundles* allow you to add a collection of two or more items to an invoice by selecting a single item.

Using pricing rules

QuickBooks Online doesn't record a price change as a discount but as an override of the sale price. This feature seems to be in perpetual beta testing, and apparently for good reason. When I tried to create a price rule for an individual customer, QuickBooks acted as if I hadn't created any customers yet. If you're willing to work around that constraint, here's how to enable the Price Rules feature:

1. **Choose Settings ➪ Account and Settings ➪ Sales.**

2. **Click in the Products and Services section and toggle on the Turn on Price Rules setting.**

3. **Click Save and then click Done to close the Account and Settings page.**

The Price Rules feature in QuickBooks Online is known as *price levels* in QuickBooks Desktop.

TIP

Intuit recommends that you keep the total number of price rules to 10,000 or less. Once you've enabled price rules, follow these steps to create one or more rules:

1. **Click Settings ➪ All Lists ➪ Price Rules.**

   The new Price Rules section appears below Products and Services on the All page.

2. **Click Create a Rule to display the Create a Price Rule page, shown in Figure 5-14.**

3. **Assign a name to your rule.**

4. **Choose All Customers, Select Individually, or if available, choose a Class from the Customer list.**

   If you choose Individually, checkboxes appear to the left of your customer names on the page so that you can select the applicable customers.

5. **Choose All Products and Services, All Services, All Inventory, All Non-Inventory, Select Individually, or if available, choose a category from the Products and Services list.**

6. **Choose Percentage, Fixed Amount, or Custom Price Per Item from the Price Adjustment Method list.**

   If you choose Custom Price per Item, your Products and Services list appears along with an Adjusted Price column that you can use to selectively override individual prices.

7. **If you chose Percentage or Fixed Amount, choose Increase by or Decrease from the Percentage or Fixed Amount lists, respectively, and then enter an amount in the adjacent field.**

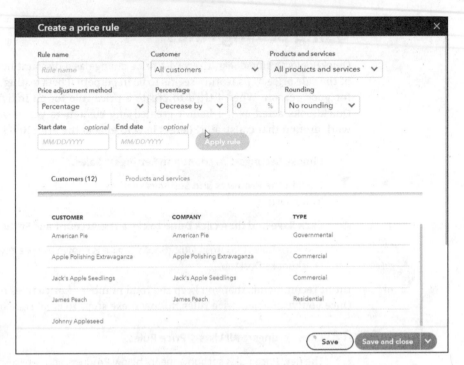

FIGURE 5-14:
The Create a
Price Rule page.

Create a price rule

Rule name | Customer | Products and services
Rule name | All customers | All products and services

Price adjustment method | Percentage | Rounding
Percentage | Decrease by | 0 % | No rounding

Start date *optional* | End date *optional*
MM/DD/YYYY | MM/DD/YYYY | Apply rule

Customers (12) | Products and services

CUSTOMER	COMPANY	TYPE
American Pie	American Pie	Governmental
Apple Polishing Extravaganza	Apple Polishing Extravaganza	Commercial
Jack's Apple Seedlings	Jack's Apple Seedlings	Commercial
James Peach	James Peach	Residential
Johnny Appleseed		

Save | Save and close

8. **Optional: If you chose Percentage or Fixed Amount, choose a rounding increment from the list.**

9. **Optional: Provide a Start Date and/or End Date for the price rule.**

10. **Click Save and Close, or choose Save and New if you wish to create another price rule.**

REMEMBER

You can't assign a price rule to a bundle, but you can assign price rules to individual items within a bundle.

Working with bundles

Essentials, Plus, or Advanced subscribers can group two or more items together into a bundle, meaning a collection of products and/or services that a customer buys from you in a single transaction. A company selling fruit baskets might create one or more bundles that comprise products at various price points so that they don't have to add the items to sales transactions one by one.

TIP

Bundles in QuickBooks Online are known as *group items* in QuickBooks Desktop.

Follow these steps to create a bundle:

1. **Choose Settings ⇨ Products and Services.**

2. **Click the New button to display the Product/Service task pane and then choose Bundle.**

   The Bundle task pane appears, as shown in Figure 5-15.

FIGURE 5-15:
The Bundle
task pane.

3. **Provide a name, an SKU if appropriate, and a description to appear on sales forms for the bundle.**

4. **Optional: Upload a picture of the item by clicking the Upload button, which looks like a pencil, and navigating to the location where you store the picture.**

5. **Optional: Click Display Bundle Components When Printing or Sending Transactions if you want to see the individual components listed on your transaction forms instead of a single line item that uses the description you entered in Step 4.**

REMEMBER

A bundle is *not* an assembly. QuickBooks Online does not create a bill of materials or track bundles as separate items with quantities or cost. The price for a bundle is the sum of the prices for the individual components, which can be modified with pricing rules, as I discuss in the previous section.

6. **Use the table at the bottom of the task pane to identify the products included in the bundle, and then add products or services and the associated quantities as needed.**

7. **Click Save and Close, or choose Save and New if you wish to create another price rule.**

Importing and Exporting Products and Services

If you have a QuickBooks Online Advanced subscription, skip this section and move on to the later section, "Managing products and services with Spreadsheet Sync," in this chapter. You can spend less time getting up and running with QuickBooks by importing your products and services. In Chapter 4, I discuss how to import customers and vendors, and I provide much more detail about the process. I only offer a quick sketch here because importing and exporting products and services is virtually identical to importing customers and vendors.

Most accounting platforms allow you to export inventory and service items to a Microsoft Excel workbook or a comma-separated-values (.csv) file. Then you can use Excel or Google Sheets to access the exported data. You then need to copy and paste your data into the sample file that QuickBooks Online offers.

Downloading the sample file

You can download a sample file that illustrates what each import file should look like. In this case, I walk you through creating the sample file that will allow you to import products and services:

1. **Choose Settings ⇨ Products and Services to display the Products and Services page.**

2. **Click Import Inventory or choose Import from the New drop-down menu to display the Import Products and Services page.**

3. **Click Download a Sample File if you're using Excel or Preview a Sample for Google Sheets.**

   The sample file appears in the downloads bar of most browsers. Otherwise, you can find it in your Downloads folder.

4. **If you're using Excel, open the sample file by clicking it on the downloads bar of your browser window or double-clicking the file in your Downloads folder.**

5. **In Microsoft Excel, click Enable Editing if the spreadsheet opens in Protected View.**

6. **Examine the file's contents by scrolling to the right to see the information stored in each column.**

7. **Create your own file, modeling it on the sample file.**

REMEMBER

Your import file can't contain more than 1,000 rows or exceed 2MB. You can save your file as either an Excel workbook or a CSV file.

TIP

Dates that you import must be in yyyy-mm-dd format. If you have a date entered in cell A1 of an Excel worksheet, you can use this formula to transform a date such as 2/15/2024 into 2024-02-15:

```
=TEXT(A1,"yyyy-mm-dd")
```

Copy the formula down the column, and then select all of the cells that contain the formula and choose Home ➪ Copy or press Ctrl+C (Cmd+C in Excel for Mac). Next, choose Home ➪ Paste ➪ Paste Values to convert the formulas to static values in the yyyy-mm-dd format.

REMEMBER

The Product/Service Name and Type are the only required fields in the import file.

THE SAMPLE IMPORT FILE'S LAYOUT

Information in the sample file is in a table format, where each row in the spreadsheet contains all the information about a single product or service. Make sure to specify Inventory, Non-inventory, or Service in the Type column. Unlike customers in particular, QuickBooks Online enables you to import every field related to creating an inventory item, except for any pictures that you want to associate with the items; that remains a manual effort.

Importing lists

Here's how to import your products and services list:

1. **Make sure that your spreadsheet or CSV file is not open in Excel or Google Sheets.**

2. **Choose Settings ⇨ Products and Services.**

3. **Click the Import Products and Services button or choose Import from the New drop-down list.**

4. **Click Browse for an Excel or CSV file or click Connect for a Google Sheet.**

5. **Navigate to the folder where you saved the file containing your list information.**

6. **Specify the file and click Open for an Excel or CSV file or click Select for a Google Sheet.**

7. **Click Next to upload your file to a staging area.**

8. **Map the fields in your data file to the corresponding QuickBooks fields.**

9. **Click Next to display the final page of the wizard.**

10. **Review the records to make sure that the information is correct.**

    You can change the information in any field by clicking that field and typing. You also can deselect any rows that you've decided you don't want to import.

11. **When you're satisfied that the information is correct, click the Import button.**

    A status message briefly flashes on the screen to tell you how many records were imported.

WARNING

If the Import button is disabled, some portion of the data can't be imported. Look for a field highlighted in red to identify information that can't be imported. If the problem isn't apparent, contact Intuit support for help, or set up the records manually.

Exporting lists to Excel or Google Sheets

You can export your product list to Excel or Google Sheets by doing the following:

1. **Click the Export to Excel button just above the Action column on the Products and Services page.**

2. **Click the button at the bottom of the screen or look in your Downloads folder to open the file.**

3. **If you're using Microsoft Excel, you may have to click Enable Editing to exit Protected View.**

TIP

If you're using Google Sheets instead of Excel, choose File ⇨ Import. Follow the prompts to upload your workbook, after which you can work with the spreadsheet in the usual way.

Managing Products and Services with Spreadsheet Sync

QuickBooks Online Advanced subscribers can edit or create product and service records with the Spreadsheet Sync feature, which turns Microsoft Excel spreadsheets into a direct extension of QuickBooks. At the end of Chapter 4, I explain how to install Spreadsheet Sync; here, I focus on how you can use Spreadsheet Sync to edit and/or create inventory items in Excel, which is but one of many uses for Spreadsheet Sync:

1. **Choose Home ⇨ Spreadsheet Sync in Excel to display the Spreadsheet Sync task pane.**

2. **Sign in if prompted otherwise click Get Started.**

   Spreadsheet Sync sessions expire if you close Excel, or after a certain amount of time elapses.

3. **Click Manage Records and then choose Inventory Items from the Select Template list.**

   A blank template appears in your spreadsheet, as shown in Figure 5-16.

4. **Optional: Choose a company from the Company or Group section if you have more than one Advanced subscription.**

   This field is not editable if you only have a single QuickBooks Online Advanced subscription.

5. **Optional: Toggle on the Bring in Existing Records from QuickBooks option. A warning prompt appears to inform you that any transactions or unposted changes on the template worksheet will be discarded; depending on the prompt, click OK or Clear Data.**

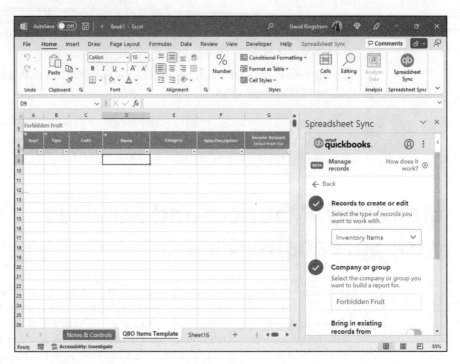

FIGURE 5-16: Blank Spreadsheet Sync template.

Whether you retrieve your records or not, you can use the template to add new inventory items to the list. Choose Yes in Column A for any rows where you edit an existing inventory record or enter **Yes** in the rows where you add new records. Enter **Stock**, **Non-Stock**, or **Service** in Column B for new records, and at a minimum, enter a name in Column C.

6. **Click Post Data to QuickBooks at the bottom of the Spreadsheet Sync task pane, as shown in Figure 5-17.**

You can now close the Spreadsheet Sync task pane, and then display it when needed by choosing Home ⇨ Spreadsheet Sync in Excel.

Now let's see how you can audit the sales tax settings for your customers:

1. **Choose Home ⇨ Spreadsheet Sync in Excel to display the Spreadsheet Sync task pane.**

2. **Sign in if prompted otherwise click Get Started.**

3. **Click Build a Report and then click My QuickBooks Data.**

4. **Click Select Data Source and then choose Data Tables.**

5. **Choose Contacts and then Customers.**

6. **Click Select Data to Get and then click Add to New Sheet.**

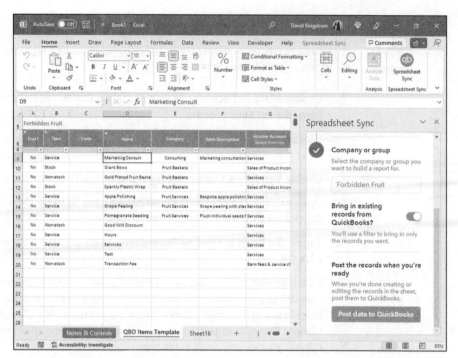

FIGURE 5-17:
Inventory records
retrieved from
QuickBooks.

A much more detailed listing of your customers appears. I'd like to draw your attention to a couple of specific columns:

>> Active – click the Filter button in cell I2 and choose clear the checkbox for FALSE to hide inactive customers.

>> Default Tax Code Ref. Value – A number appears in column O if you specified marked a customer as tax exempt.

>> Taxable – Unlike the pesky Customer Contact List report that I discussed earlier in this chapter, column P displays TRUE for customers marked as taxable and FALSE for customers you've marked as exempt.

>> Resale Num – Column AE lists the contents of the Exemption Details field within a customer's record.

>> Tax Exemption Reason ID – Column AF displays a number that corresponds with the selection you made from the Reason for Exemption field within the customer's record.

REMEMBER

This is a report, meaning a one-way export from QuickBooks, so you'll need to make any corrections manually in QuickBooks. You can edit customer records in Excel with Spreadsheet Sync:

1. **Choose Manage Records (instead of Build a Report) at the start of the Spreadsheet Sync process.**

    Click the Back button as needed to work your way to the screen where you can make this selection.

2. **Choose Vendors & Customers from the Select Template list.**

3. **Optional: Select a company if you have access to more than one QuickBooks Online Advanced subscription.**

4. **Toggle the Bring In Existing Records from QuickBooks on and then click OK.**

    An editable list of customers and vendors appears in Excel, from which you can choose **Yes** in column A to indicate that you want to post the changes back to QuickBooks in the same fashion as inventory items above. The catch is the Manage Records template does not include the five fields that I noted above, nor can you add any fields to the template.

5. **Optional: Click Post Data to QuickBooks at the bottom of the Spreadsheet Sync task pane if you make changes in Excel that you wish to post back to QuickBooks.**

Chapter **6**

Invoicing Customers and Receiving Payments

When you're using new software, it always helps to carry out actions a few times to get familiar with them. If you have any unpaid invoices for your customers, for example, recording them in QuickBooks now will help reinforce what you read here. You'll also want to record all bank deposits that you've made since the starting date that you've chosen for using QuickBooks.

Getting Oriented with Sales Transactions

TIP

The left menu bar in QuickBooks has two modes: Business View and Accountant View. Even if you're not an accountant, you'll find it easier to navigate QuickBooks if you choose Settings ⇨ Switch to Accountant View. You can't access the Sales Transactions page shown in Figure 6-1 if you're in Business View, for example, because QuickBooks hides the command. In Business View you can add bookmarks to the bottom of the menu. Also, the ability to reorganize the menu in Business View is in the works as of this writing.

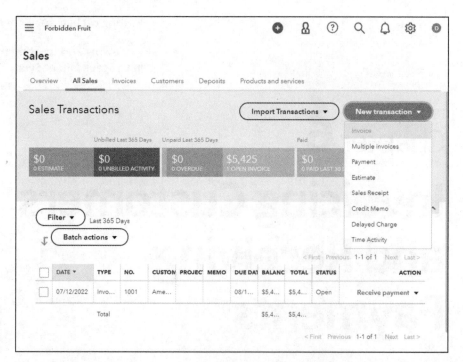

FIGURE 6-1:
The Sales Transactions page.

You can choose Sales ⇨ All Sales on the left menu bar in Accountant View to display the Sales Transactions page shown in Figure 6-1, and create almost every sales-related transaction. There's always an exception, so if you're looking to create a Refund Receipt, then click the New button and make a choice from the Customers column shown in Figure 6-2. Also, there's a temporary exception you should note: the New Transactions button does not appear until you've created at least one invoice, so if you're just getting started with QuickBooks, choose Create Invoice on the Invoices tab, or create a Sales Receipt from the menu shown in Figure 6-2.

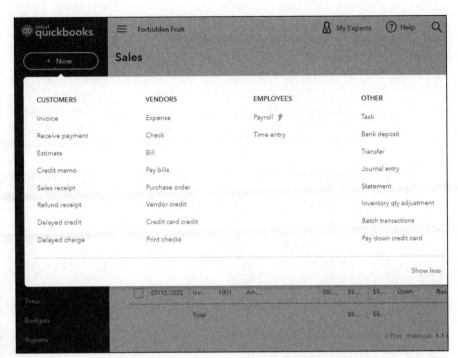

FIGURE 6-2:
Sales transactions
appear in the
Customers
column of the
New menu.

TIP

I discuss invoices, payments, credit memos, sales receipts, and refund receipts in this chapter. I dig into estimates, delayed credits, and delayed charges, among other topics, in Chapter 7.

Creating Invoices

Invoices are written requests for payment for any goods and/or services that you've provided to your customers. An effective invoice makes it clear what value was provided. If you try to save a minute up front by creating a summary invoice with little detail, it could cost you time and frustration later in the form of delayed payment until you provide more detail about what the invoice covers.

Follow these steps to create an invoice:

1. **Choose New ⇨ Invoice from the left menu bar.**

A new invoice window opens, as shown in Figure 6-3.

REMEMBER

If you're working with a project and need to associate the invoice with that particular project, you can choose Projects on the left menu bar, select the project, and then click Add to Project. I discuss estimates, purchase orders, and projects in Chapter 7.

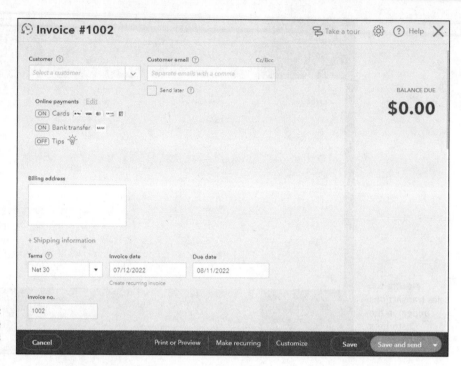

FIGURE 6-3:
A blank invoice window awaits your input.

Invoice #1002   Take a tour   ⚙   ⑦ Help   ✕

Customer ⑦
Select a customer   ⌄

Customer email ⑦   Cc/Bcc
Separate emails with a comma

☐ Send later ⑦

BALANCE DUE
$0.00

Online payments   _Edit_
(ON) Cards
(ON) Bank transfer
(OFF) Tips

Billing address

+ Shipping information

Terms ⑦   Invoice date   Due date
Net 30   ⌄   07/12/2022   08/11/2022
             Create recurring invoice

Invoice no.
1002

Cancel   Print or Preview   Make recurring   Customize   Save   Save and send ⌄

2. Choose a customer.

The customer's mailing address, payment terms, invoice date, and due date appear, along with the Send Later option.

TIP

Any pending estimates or billable time entries appear in a transaction pane on the right side of the screen. I talk about estimates in Chapter 7, and time entries in the section, "Creating Billable Time Entries," later in this chapter.

3. Optional: Enable or disable online payments.

As shown in Figure 6-3, QuickBooks assumes that you want to offer online credit card and ACH payments to your customers by way of their QuickBooks Payments service. I discuss the per-transaction fees for this service in Chapter 1. Click Edit to disable (or enable) these options for the current invoice only.

WARNING

If you leave the online payment links enabled, your customer will be able to submit a payment for your invoice even if you haven't completed your QuickBooks Payments profile. This can result in customer payments getting stuck in limbo. To permanently disable these links, click Edit and then click Go to Settings in the Edit Payment Methods dialog box. Click the pencil icon in the Invoice Payment section and then turn off both Accept Credit Cards and Accept ACH.

REMEMBER

On the other hand, if you do want to use QuickBooks Payments, choose Settings ➪ Account and Settings ➪ Payments and then click Confirm Your Info in the Payment Methods section to start the onboarding process. You may be able to secure a discount on the transaction fees by working with a QuickBooks ProAdvisor. My technical editor Dan DeLong offers a free course on maximizing QuickBooks Payments at https://www.schoolofbookkeeping.com/offers/wqYuirSe/

4. **Optionally, click the Send Later checkbox and then confirm the Invoice Date, Due Date, and Terms.**

   The Send Later checkbox appears beneath the customer email field and allows you to indicate that you want to email an invoice at a future date. Terms, Invoice Date, and Due Date appear further down the screen.

TIP

You can customize the outgoing email messages for your sales forms. To do so, activate your dashboard and choose Settings ➪ Account and Settings ➪ Sales. Edit the Messages section to create and then choose a sales form from the list. In addition to editing the actual message, you can provide email addresses to which you want to CC: or BCC: all sales documents. If you want to change the email address that the sales forms are sent from, choose Settings ➪ Account and Settings ➪ Company and then edit the Customer-Facing Email field in the Contact Info section.

5. **Enter products and/or services.**

   QuickBooks Online requires you to provide an item name in the Product/Service field for each row of your invoice. If you try skipping the Product/Service field, a generic item such as Services is entered for you.

   a. **Click the Product/Service column shown in Figure 6-4, and select an item for the invoice you're creating.**

      A list of matching items appears as you type a few characters in this field.

TIP

      If you type an item name that doesn't exist, you can click Add New at the top of the list to create the new item. See Chapter 5 if you're not clear on the process of adding items for products and services.

   b. **Optional: Edit the Description column for the selected item.**

   c. **Fill in the Qty and Rate columns to provide the quantity and price of the goods or services provided.** If you fill in these two columns, the Amount column calculates automatically. Or fill in Quantity and Amount, and the Rate column auto-populates.

   d. **Repeat Steps (a) to (c) as needed to add more items to the invoice, as shown in Figure 6-4.**

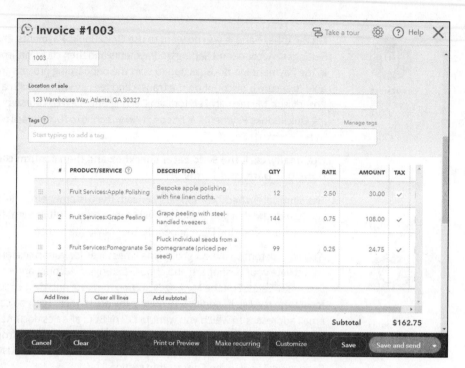

Invoice #1003

Take a tour · Help

1003

Location of sale

123 Warehouse Way, Atlanta, GA 30327

Tags ?

Manage tags

Start typing to add a tag

#	PRODUCT/SERVICE ?	DESCRIPTION	QTY	RATE	AMOUNT	TAX
1	Fruit Services:Apple Polishing	Bespoke apple polishing with fine linen cloths.	12	2.50	30.00	✓
2	Fruit Services:Grape Peeling	Grape peeling with steel-handled tweezers	144	0.75	108.00	✓
3	Fruit Services:Pomegranate Se	Pluck individual seeds from a pomegranate (priced per seed)	99	0.25	24.75	✓
4						

Add lines · Clear all lines · Add subtotal

Subtotal | $162.75

Cancel · Clear · Print or Preview · Make recurring · Customize · Save · Save and send

FIGURE 6-4:
Add as many line items as needed to your invoice.

TIP

Click the Add Subtotal button at the bottom of the screen if you want to subtotal two or more items on an invoice. QuickBooks allows you to subtotal a single item if you want, but doing that would be like wearing both a belt and suspenders. I discuss enabling automatic subtotals on your sales forms in the section, "Configuring Automatic Subtotals."

6. **Optional: Specify discount amount or percentage or override the location-based sales tax with a custom rate, as shown in Figure 6-5.**

The Discount field is hidden by default. To enable this field, click Settings in the top-right corner of the invoice screen, and click the Total Discount checkbox on the panel that appears.

The Sales Tax Rate option appears on invoices only if you enabled Sales Taxes by choosing Sales Tax ⇨ Set Up Sales Tax Rates. Chapter 5 has all the gory details.

TIP

If you enable both sales tax and discounts, you can use the switch that appears to the left of these fields to control whether discounts are pretax or after-tax. Position the discount above sales tax for pretax or below sales tax for an after-tax discount.

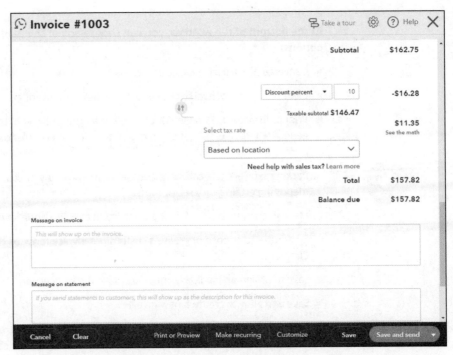

Invoice #1003   Take a tour   Help

	Subtotal	$162.75
Discount percent ▼ 10		-$16.28
	Taxable subtotal $146.47	
Select tax rate		$11.35
		See the math
Based on location ∨		
Need help with sales tax? Learn more		
	Total	$157.82
	Balance due	$157.82

Message on invoice

This will show up on the invoice.

Message on statement

If you send statements to customers, this will show up as the description for this invoice.

Cancel   Clear   Print or Preview   Make recurring   Customize   Save   Save and send ▼

FIGURE 6-5: Use the bottom of the Invoice window to handle sales tax, discount information, messages, and attachments.

The Deposit field is hidden by default as well. To enable this field, click Settings in the top-right corner of the invoice screen, and click the Deposit checkbox on the panel that appears. If you turn on the preference to display the Deposit field at the bottom of the invoice, you can use it to reduce the amount of the invoice by a deposit amount paid by the customer.

7. **Optional: Enter an invoice and/or statement message as shown in Figure 6-5.**

   The bottom portion of the invoice screen allows you to include messages for your customer by typing an invoice and/or statement message. A statement message is the description for an invoice when you send customer statements.

8. **Optional: Attach an electronic document to the invoice by clicking the Attachments field. You can then navigate to the document, or drag the document into the Attachments field.**

   Supporting documents must be no more than 20MB in size, and one of these file types: PDF, JPEG, PNG, DOC, XLSX, CSV, TIFF, GIF, or XML. This means you can include pictures of your work, Aunt Mabel's pie recipe, a shipping confirmation, or anything else you want to include.

9. **At the bottom of the window, you can choose any of the following options:**

- Cancel to discard the invoice and close the window

- Clear to erase the invoice but keep the invoice window open

- Print or Preview to choose Print Later, see a print preview of the invoice, generate a PDF version of the invoice from the Print or Preview screen, or print a packing slip

TIP

Packing slips are basically invoices that don't show any prices — kind of like menus in certain fancy restaurants.

- Make Recurring to schedule the transaction as a recurring invoice

- Customize to choose or create a customized invoice form, as described in Chapter 2

- Save to assign an invoice number and save the transaction

- Save and New to create a new invoice

- Save and Send to assign an invoice number, save the invoice, edit the default email message, preview the invoice, and then send a copy to the customer

TIP

The email time and date-stamp information appears in the header of invoices that you send. Invoice emails are mobile-friendly and include invoice details so that customers see everything at a glance.

- Save and Share Link to copy a unique URL for the invoice for inclusion in an email you want send outside of QuickBooks

TIP

Choose between Save and New, Save and Send, and Save and Share Link by clicking the arrow on the button. The option you choose becomes the default behavior for invoices until you make a different selection in the future.

ACCESSING RECENT TRANSACTIONS

Every transaction screen in QuickBooks has a Recent Transaction button that appears in the top left-hand corner, and looks like a clock with an arrow around it. Click this icon to access any recent transactions that you have created. Alternatively, click the Search button on the Dashboard page to view a list of recent transactions from across QuickBooks. You can also view recent transactions on the corresponding page for a customer, vendor, and so on.

Configuring Automatic Subtotals

You can use the Add Subtotal button on Sales Transaction forms to add a subtotal manually to any set of items on a form. Or you can take subtotals to the next level by enabling QuickBooks to subtotal your items automatically by customizing your forms.

Certain actions, such as customizing forms, can't be performed in the iOS and Android mobile apps, but you can customize your forms in a web browser and then use your customized forms in a mobile app. See https://intuit.me/3qs5MOH for details on what you can and can't do in mobile apps. Depending on your screen resolution, you may be able to use your web browser on your mobile device to carry out these actions.

You can add subtotals to invoices, estimates, and sales receipts. For instance, here are the steps to add subtotals to an invoice:

1. **Choose Settings ⇨ Custom Form Styles.**

    The Custom Form Styles page displays any form styles you've set up.

2. **Select a form to customize and then click Edit in the Action column.**

    The Customize Form Style page contains three buttons in the top-left corner: Design, Content, and Emails.

    I discuss customizing forms in detail in Chapter 2. If you don't already have a custom form to choose, click New and then select a form type, such as Invoice.

3. **Click Content, as shown in Figure 6-6.**

    The Content page appears, with all sections disabled.

4. **Click the Table section.**

    The Table section is where you see column titles such as Date, Product/Service, and Description. As shown in Figure 6-7, the section is available to edit.

5. **Scroll down the page, and click Show More Activity Options in the bottom-left corner.**

    Additional options for the Table section appear, as shown in Figure 6-7.

6. **Click the Group Activity By checkbox, and make a choice from the drop-down list.**

    You can group items by day, week, month, or type. For this example, choose type.

7. **Click Subtotal Groups.**

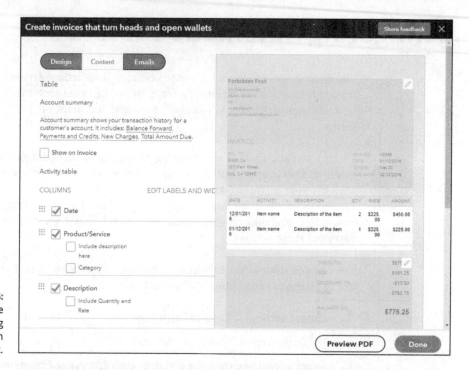

FIGURE 6-6:
The Content page after choosing the Table section to edit.

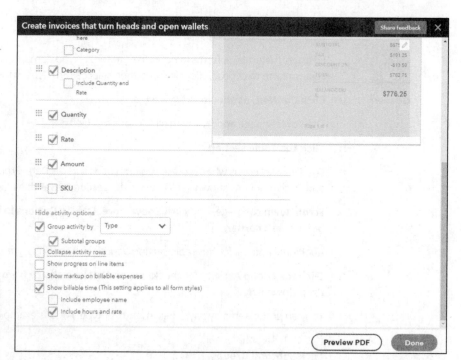

FIGURE 6-7:
Turning on the setting to enable grouping in the selected sales forms.

8. **Click Done in the bottom-right corner of the window to save the settings.**

Although you can click Preview PDF, there's not much point in this context as QuickBooks doesn't show you the subtotals in use until you actually create an invoice.

REMEMBER

You need to repeat the preceding steps to include subtotals for estimates and sales receipts if you want a consistent look and feel across all the forms you use.

Creating Billable Time Entries

Your employees may complete activities required to run your company (such as preparing customer invoices or entering accounting information), and they may also perform work related directly to your customers. In the latter case, you may want to track the time employees spend on client-related projects so you can bill your customers for your employees' time. This section focuses on the time-tracking tools that are native to QuickBooks Online.

To track time using tools available within QuickBooks Online, make sure that you turn on Time Tracking options. Choose Settings ➪ Account and Settings ➪ Time, as shown in Figure 6-8, and enable these two options:

>> Add Service Field to Timesheets

>> Allow Time to Be Billable

TIP

If your business has time-tracking needs that go beyond the basics, click See Plans, as shown in Figure 6-8, to check out QuickBooks Time (formerly known as TSheets). This is one of several timekeeping apps that fully integrate with QuickBooks Online to enable your employees to track time on their mobile devices. Any time entries that they record sync automatically with your books, with all the appropriate customer, job, and employee information.

Entering time activities

Let's say that you want to record two hours that an employee worked on a consulting project. Follow these steps to open the Add Time For window:

1. **Click the New button and then choose Time Entry in the Employees column.**

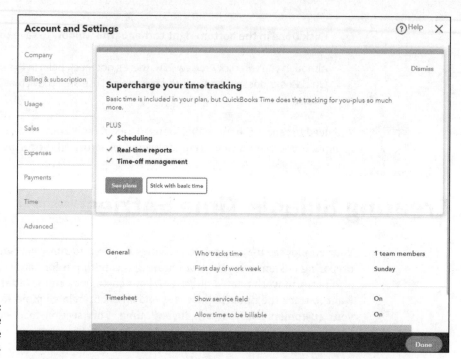

FIGURE 6-8:
Enabling the
built-in Time
Tracking options.

REMEMBER

If you're working with a project, you can choose Projects (Business Overview ⇨ Projects), select the project, and click Add to Project.

2. **Choose an employee from the Add Time panel.**

   The Add Time For panel appears, as shown in Figure 6-9.

3. **Choose the date when the work was performed.**

4. **Click Add Work Details.**

   The Add Work Details pane opens, as shown in Figure 6-10.

5. **Enter a time amount in the Duration field, such as 2 for two hours.**

   Alternatively, you can enter start and end times by toggling the Start/End Times option.

6. **Select the customer for which the work was performed.**

7. **Select the service that was performed.**

   You cannot add new services on the fly from the Add Work Details screen, so make sure to set any new services up before you try to create time entries.

REMEMBER

8. **Toggle the Billable (/hr) option if applicable.**

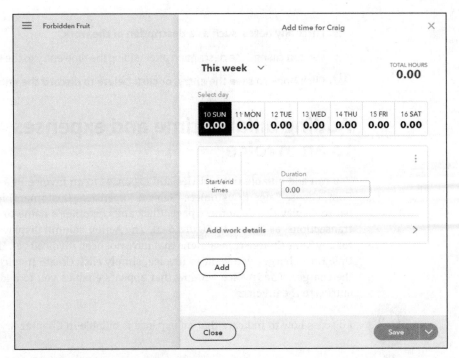

FIGURE 6-9:
The Add Time For panel enables you to enter time for one or more billable activities.

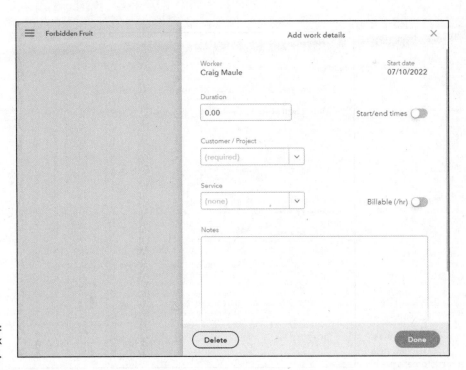

FIGURE 6-10:
The Add Work Details pane.

9. Enter any notes, such as a description of the work.

You can change the description after adding the time entry to the invoice.

10. Click Done to save the entry, or click Delete to discard the entry.

Adding billable time and expenses to an invoice

You can add billable time entries and expenses to an invoice in a couple of ways. First, choose Sales ⇨ Customers (Sales & Expenses ⇨ Customers) in the left menu bar to display the Customers page. Click any customer's name to display a list of transactions, as shown in Figure 6-11. The Action column displays Create Invoice for any Time Charge transactions that have not been invoiced yet. If you have multiple time charges you want to invoice, simply click Create Invoice for any one of the charges. The Invoice window that appears enables you to add the other time entries to the invoice.

TIP

I discuss how to indicate that an expense is billable in Chapter 8.

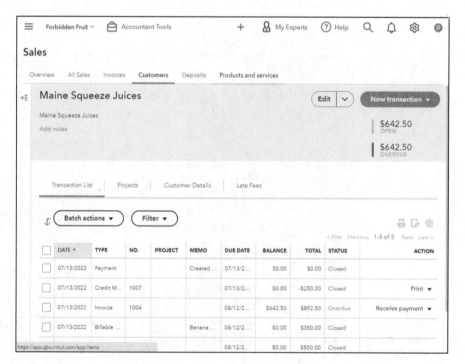

FIGURE 6-11:
Viewing a customer's page.

On the other hand, QuickBooks prompts you to add unbilled expenses to any invoice you create when you choose New ⇨ Invoice and select a customer. Any billable expense entries also appear in the pane on the right side of the screen, as shown in Figure 6-12.

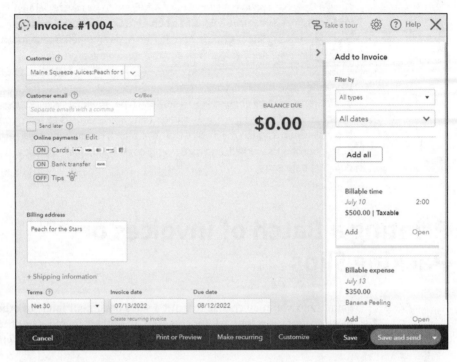

Use the Filter options to limit the billable time entries that appear. Then click the Add button in each billable time entry that you want to add to the invoice. Or, to add all the entries, click the Add All button at the top of the pane. Each billable time entry's information is added to the invoice as a line with the service, description, quantity, rate, and total amount filled in. By default, time entries appear individually in the invoice, but you can opt to group time entries by service type. You can edit any information as needed. Fill in the rest of the invoice as described in the section, "Creating Invoices," earlier in this chapter, to add other lines that don't pertain to time entries.

Don't forget that you can add a subtotal for time entries, or any group of line items on an invoice by clicking the Add Subtotal button, or see the "Configuring Automatic Subtotals" section to automatically group and subtotal time entries.

QUICKBOOKS ONLINE AND GOOGLE CALENDAR

If you record work that you perform in Google Calendar, you can use the Invoice with Google Calendar app in the QuickBooks App Store to pull event details into an invoice. This app is free if you have a Gmail account or a Google Workplace subscription (formerly known as G Suite). Choose Apps ⇨ Find Apps and then search for *Invoice with Google Calendar*. Click Get App Now and then follow the prompts.

When the app is installed, you can click the Google Calendar icon that appears on the invoice form. A panel enables you to set search parameters, such as choosing a Google Calendar, specifying a time frame, and entering any keywords to search on. You can choose events to add to the invoice from the search results, which will record the title, description, hours worked, and date from Google Calendar — a great way to eliminate duplicate data entry.

Printing a Batch of Invoices or Packing Slips

Sometimes you may choose to print a sales document later. In other cases, one or more customers might ask for copies of all of their invoices or other forms from a specific period of time. You can handle both of these situations with ease:

1. **Choose Sales ⇨ All Sales (Bookkeeping ⇨ Transactions ⇨ All Sales) from the left menu bar.**

   A listing of all sales transactions appears.

2. **Click the Filter button to choose one or transaction types, customers, as well as specify other criteria as needed.**

   You can display a list of all transaction types at once, or you can choose a single transaction type. However, you cannot choose, let's say, Invoices and Sales Receipts at the same time. Similarly, you can view a list for all customers, or a single customer. You cannot choose display transactions for two or more customers at once.

3. **Within the transaction list, click the checkbox adjacent to each transaction that you want to print or generate a packing slip for, or click the Select All checkbox at the top of the list.**

4. **Click the Batch Actions button and then choose Print for sales transactions, or choose Packing Slip for, wait for it, packing slips.**

REMEMBER

All choices on the Batch Actions menu are disabled until you select one or more transactions. Further, the Print Transactions command will remain disabled unless you choose a specific customer.

5. **A Print Preview window appears, as shown in Figure 6-13, from which you can print or download the sales forms.**

TIP

The download button is the downward-pointing arrow in the top right-hand corner. All documents that you selected are saved to a single PDF file.

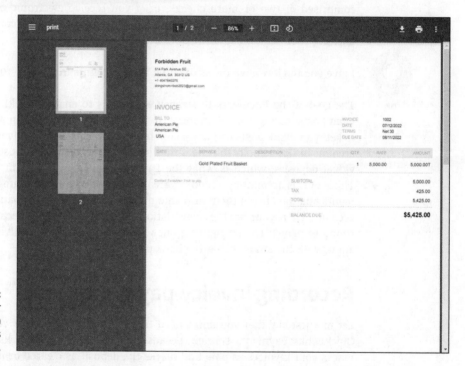

FIGURE 6-13:
Printing or downloading a batch of sales documents.

Recording Customer Payments

Alright, now it's time for the good stuff. It's one thing to send out an invoice, but it's another thing completely to record the payment on that invoice. Or perhaps you want to bypass creating an invoice and record a sales receipt instead. As you'll see, sales receipt transactions are a mash-up of an invoice and customer payment. Before you look at recording payments, let me first describe the Payments to Deposit account.

Understanding the Payments to Deposit account

Older QuickBooks companies may still have an Undeposited Funds account, which could feel like an oxymoron. You're going to deposit those funds pronto, of course! Thus, QuickBooks now refers to this as the Payments to Deposit account. If your bank deposits are always comprised of a single check or ACH payment that does not incur a processing fee, you can skip this section. But if you make bank deposits comprised of two or more checks, or if you receive electronic payments from which have been deducted, utilizing the Payments to Deposit account makes reconciling your bank account much easier.

TIP

I give you the lowdown on reconciling bank accounts in Chapter 10.

The goal of the Payments to Deposit account is to enable QuickBooks to mirror what posts to your bank statement. If you deposit five checks on a single deposit ticket, your bank posts one lump sum to your account. You ideally want your bank account in QuickBooks to reflect that lump sum as well, as opposed to five individual deposits, which is what the Payments to Deposit account accomplishes. Think of this account as a holding area where you can accumulate customer payments and then batch them into amounts that match what the bank posts to your account. Then your bank-reconciliation process sails along, because you're not trying to play Tetris by figuring out which combination of individual payments aligns with the amount that the bank posted.

Recording invoice payments

Let me first say that you don't need this section of the book if you opt into the QuickBooks Payments service, because in that case, QuickBooks automatically marks your invoices as paid and marks the deposit as cleared or matches it with your bank deposit. But let's say that a customer pays you by check, or perhaps sends you money through PayPal or Venmo. In such cases, there's a two-step process: 1) record the customer payments, and 2) record the bank deposit.

There are a few ways that you can initiate receiving an invoice payment:

>> Click Receive Payment in the Action column of the sales transaction list on the customer page shown in Figure 6-11.

>> Choose New Transaction ⇨ Payment on the Sales Transactions page and choose Payment.

>> Choose New ⇨ Receive Payment.

>> Select the project on the Projects page and click Add to Project.

REMEMBER

I discuss using projects in Chapter 7.

The first method in the preceding list displays the Receive Payment window, pre-filled with the information for the invoice you selected as well as a default payment amount. The second and third methods display an unfilled Receive Payment window. Any unpaid invoices appear in the Outstanding Transactions section once you select a customer, as shown in Figure 6-14.

	DESCRIPTION	DUE DATE	ORIGINAL AMOUNT	OPEN BALANCE	PAYMENT
☐	Invoice # 1001 (07/12/2022)	08/11/2022	5,425.00	5,425.00	
☐	Invoice # 1002 (07/12/2022)	08/11/2022	5,425.00	5,425.00	

< First   Previous   1-2 of 2   Next   Last >

Amount to Apply $0.00
Amount to Credit $0.00

Clear Payment

Memo

Note

Attachments   Maximum size: 20MB

Drag/Drop files here or click the icon

Cancel   Clear   Print   Save and close ▾

FIGURE 6-14: The Receive Payment window after selecting a customer with unpaid invoices.

And now — the moment you've been waiting for — instructions for how to post a customer payment:

1. Confirm the payment date.

Make sure that the payment date matches the date you're depositing the funds to make reconciling your bank account easier.

2. **Optional: Choose a payment method.**

Default methods include Cash, Check, and Credit Card, but you can add others as needed.

3. **Enter a reference number.**

This number is the check number if your customer paid by check. You can leave the reference field blank for cash for electronic deposits or repurpose it as a note field.

4. **Specify the account in which you want to deposit the payment.**

If you're posting a single check or payment for which no fees are deducted, you can choose your bank account from the drop-down list. If you're depositing two or more checks in your bank on the same day, or an electronic payment that incurs a processing fee, choose Payments to Deposit (Undeposited Funds).

5. **Select the invoice(s) being paid by clicking the checkbox for individual invoices, or the checkbox at the top of the column to select all invoices.**

If your customer makes a partial payment, you can adjust the Payment field as needed for each invoice.

REMEMBER

You cannot record payment-processing fees, such as those assessed by Stripe or PayPal, on the Receive Payment screen if your customer has paid you electronically. You can enter those fees on the Bank Deposit screen, which I discuss in the upcoming section, "Recording Bank Deposits."

6. **Click Save and Close or click Save and New.**

The Save button is a sticky preference, meaning you can click it and change the default behavior for future transactions.

Entering a sales receipt

Sometimes, you may get paid at the time you provide goods or render services. Rather than entering an invoice and then immediately receiving a payment against it, you can create a sales receipt instead. You can also print a packing list based on the sales receipt. This approach also works well when you receive payments that you didn't invoice in advance via an electronic payment platform such as Stripe or PayPal.

To create a sales receipt, choose New ⇨ Sales Receipt, or choose New Transaction ⇨ Sales Receipt on the Sales Transactions page. The sales receipt form closely resembles the invoice form, but in this case your saved transaction is recorded to your bank account or the Payments to Deposit account, instead of your Accounts Receivable account. Fill out the form in much the same way that you do an invoice: provide the payment-specific details, such as payment method and reference number, and select the account where the funds should go. See the section, "Understanding the Payments to Deposit account," earlier in this chapter for information on selecting an account from the Deposit To list.

TIP

You can add a row for electronic payment transaction fees, such as those assessed by Stripe or PayPal. In this case, you need to create a Service or Non-Inventory item labeled Payment Processing Fee or something along those lines. Choose the Payment Processing Fee item, and record a negative amount. QuickBooks displays a "This value is out of range" warning when you type the minus sign, but you can safely disregard the prompt. The net amount of the sales receipt should match the net deposit that posts to your bank account.

HANDLING OVERPAYMENTS

From time to time, a customer might pay you more than you're expecting. You can choose to give your customer credit for this overpayment or keep the excess as a gratuity. Either way, you must first instruct QuickBooks to apply credits automatically. Choose Settings ⇨ Account and Settings and then click Advanced on the left side of the Account and Settings task pane. In the Automation section, toggle on Automatically Apply Credits and then click Save. Going forward, QuickBooks will create credit transactions for overpayments automatically.

You receive payment as described earlier in this chapter, but include the overpayment when you fill in the Amount Received field. You can choose from three scenarios:

- **Apply the overpayment to an existing invoice.** Select the invoice(s) you want to apply the payment against in the Outstanding Transactions section of the Receive Payment window. Most likely, this option results in partial payment for at least one invoice and possibly payment in full for other invoices.

- **Apply the overpayment to a new invoice.** Choose an invoice to apply the overpayment to in the Outstanding Transactions section of the Receive Payment window. If the invoice is $100, but you received $120, show the amount paid as $120. QuickBooks creates a credit transaction for $20 when you click Save and Close. This credit is applied automatically to the next invoice you create for this customer.

- **Keep the overpayment as income.** Add a Gratuity income account to your chart of accounts and a Gratuity service item assigned to the Gratuity income account. Create a new invoice for the customer, using the Gratuity item and the overpayment amount. QuickBooks automatically marks the invoice paid because it uses the overpayment credit that it created from the overpaid invoice.

TIP

If you use QuickBooks Payments, you can enable a Tips (Gratuity) field on your invoices that gives your customers the option to express appreciation for a job well done. To enable this option, choose Settings ⇨ Account and Settings ⇨ Sales ⇨ Sales Form Content and then enable the Tips (Gratuity) option. You need to specify if the tips only go to you or are distributed to your team for income tax tracking purposes.

Recording Bank Deposits

It's important to remember to post your bank deposits in QuickBooks so that the money doesn't end up in purgatory within your Payments to Deposit (Undeposited Funds) account. This account should always have a zero balance after you've recorded any current bank deposits. Here's how to post a bank deposit:

1. **Record one or more customer payments as described in the section, "Recording Customer Payments," earlier in this chapter.**

    Make sure to apply the payment to your Payments to Deposit (Undeposited Funds) account.

2. **As shown in Figure 6-15, select the payment(s) you want to deposit.**

    Click the checkbox next to each payment that you're including in this deposit.

3. **Optional: Enter a payment processing fee or bank charge:**

    a. Choose a vendor name in the Received From field of the Add Funds to This Deposit section, such as Stripe or PayPal. If the name of the payment platform doesn't exist, type it the Received From field and then click Add New. Change the type to Vendor and then click Save.

    b. Choose an account, such as Bank Charges and Fees, or see Chapter 2 to add a new account to your chart of accounts, such as Payment Processing Fees.

    c. Enter a description, such as Payment Processing Fee.

    d. Optional: Choose the same payment method that you chose when applying the payment, as shown in the Payment Method column of the Select the Payments Included in This Deposit section.

    e. Enter a negative amount in the Amount field. QuickBooks displays a "This value is out of range" warning when you type the minus sign, which you can ignore. Simply enter the amount as usual, albeit with a minus sign in front.

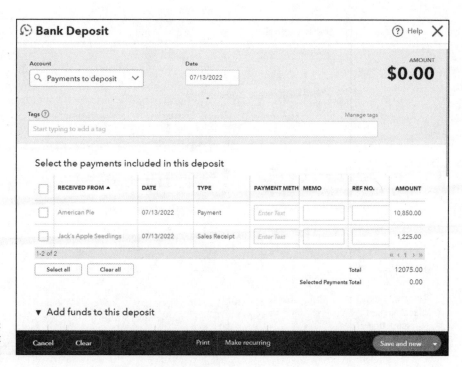

FIGURE 6-15:
A bank deposit
transaction.

WARNING

Make sure to enter a negative amount in the Add Funds to this Deposit section; otherwise, you overstate your deposit by *adding* the transaction fees to the deposit amount instead of *deducting* the fees.

4. **Confirm that the deposit total matches the net amount that posts to your bank account.**

Figure 6-16 shows that if I deposit $12,075 and post –$350.18 in the Add Funds to this Account section, the net deposit is $11,724.82. Conversely, if you're simply depositing paper checks that you take to your bank, you likely don't need to enter anything in the Add Funds to This Deposit section, so the Total should match the sum of the checks that you're about to deposit.

5. **Click Save and Close or click Save and New.**

Click the arrow on the Save button to toggle between those two settings. Your choice then becomes the default for future transactions.

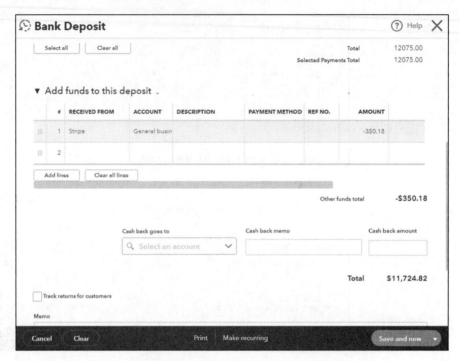

FIGURE 6-16:
Recording an electronic payment processing fee.

Keeping Tabs on Invoice Status and Receiving Payment

Choose Sales ⇨ Invoices (Sales & Expenses ⇨ Invoices) any time you want to get a bird's-eye view of your sales activity. Graphics show you at a glance the dollar amount of your unpaid and paid invoices. The unpaid invoices bar divides the total into Overdue and Not Due Yet. As shown in Figure 6-17, the bar for paid invoices breaks the total into Not Deposited and Deposited.

Click the Status column for any transaction to see the underlying details, including if your customer has viewed the invoice yet. Figure 6-18 shows the status of an invoice for which payment has not yet been deposited. If you look closely, you see the invoice was never sent, so of course it hasn't been paid yet. The status window also shows you any payment dates and amounts. Click the Status column for the transaction again to hide the details or click the Close button in the Status window.

A Status of Deposited means exactly what you think: You received a payment, and you deposited it. Partially paid invoices show an amount in the Balance column that differs from the total, helping you keep track of how much is still due, while overdue amounts appear in orange.

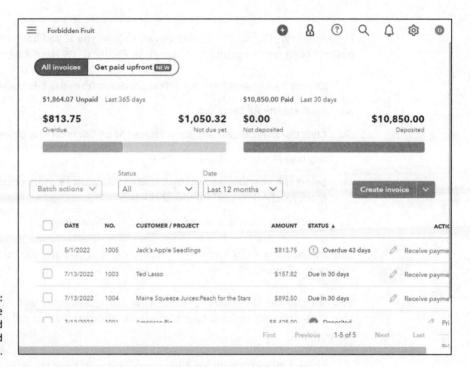

FIGURE 6-17:
Determining the amounts of paid and unpaid invoices.

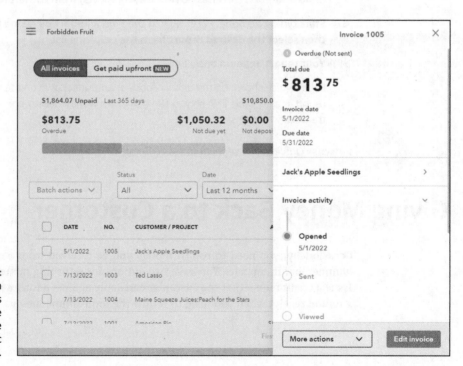

FIGURE 6-18:
Click anywhere in the Status column to see the details for the specific transaction.

Unfortunately, the status column doesn't show you if you have any invoices that haven't been sent or printed, as shown in Figure 6-17. Here's what to do instead:

1. **Choose Sales (Bookkeeping ⇨ Transactions) from the left menu bar.**

2. **Activate the All Sales tab.**

3. **Click the Filter menu and then choose Send Later for the Delivery Status.**

   Any unsent invoices appear onscreen.

4. **Select the checkboxes for any invoices you want to send, or click the Mark All checkbox at the top of the list.**

5. **Click Batch Actions and then choose Send Transactions.**

TIP

You can use these same steps to print invoices that you marked Print Later; simply change the Delivery Status to Print Later.

You can also use the Accounts Receivable Aging Summary and Accounts Receivable Detail reports to keep tabs on unpaid invoices. To run either report, follow these steps:

1. **Choose Reports (Business Overview ⇨ Reports) from the left menu bar.**

2. **Start typing** Accounts Receivable **in the Find a Report By Name field and then select the desired report from the resulting list.**

3. **Your report appears onscreen.**

   Each invoice shown on the detail report, or amount shown on the summary report, is a clickable link, so you can drill down within these reports to the transaction screens.

TIP

I discuss QuickBooks reports in more detail in Chapter 14.

Giving Money Back to a Customer

Occasionally, you need to return money you've received from a customer. It's a bummer, but it happens. You have two options for returning money to customers: Issue a credit memo that the customer can apply against a future invoice, or issue a refund receipt when you need to return the funds immediately.

Recording a credit memo

Credit memos allow you reduce the outstanding or future balance for your customer when warranted. You enter a Credit Memo transaction pretty much the same way that you enter an invoice. To display the Credit Memo window shown in Figure 6-19, you can choose New⇨Credit Memo, or on the Sales Transactions page, you can click the New Transaction button and choose Credit Memo.

REMEMBER

Enter credit memo amounts as a positive number. It can get confusing, because you're trying to offset an invoice, so you might think that the credit memo needs to reflect a negative amount, but you want both transactions to reflect positive amounts, and then you match them against each other.

Select the customer, fill in the products or services for which you're issuing a credit memo, or create a non-inventory item with a name such as Good Will Discount, fill in the bottom of the Credit Memo window with appropriate information, and save the transaction. This transaction window is like the Invoice transaction window; refer to the section, "Creating Invoices," earlier in this chapter for details.

You can enter a credit memo for a customer even if that customer currently has no outstanding invoices; when you enter the customer's next invoice, the credit memo is applied to the invoice automatically unless you've disabled that option. Conversely, credit memos are applied automatically to outstanding invoices. If you view the Sales Transactions list for that invoice, you notice that its status is partially paid, as shown in Figure 6-20.

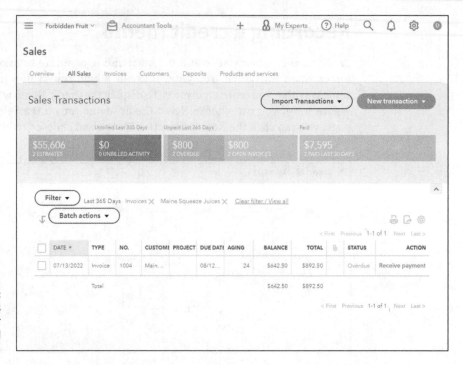

Sales

Overview   **All Sales**   Invoices   Customers   Deposits   Products and services

Sales Transactions

[Import Transactions ▾]   [New transaction ▾]

Unbilled Last 365 Days		Unpaid Last 365 Days		Paid
$55,606	$0	$800	$800	$7,595
2 ESTIMATES	0 UNBILLED ACTIVITY	2 OVERDUE	2 OPEN INVOICES	2 PAID LAST 30 DAYS

[Filter ▾]   Last 365 Days   Invoices ✕   Maine Squeeze Juices ✕   Clear filter / View all

[Batch actions ▾]

🖨 ☐ ⚙

‹ First   Previous   1-1 of 1   Next   Last ›

☐	DATE ▾	TYPE	NO.	CUSTOMI	PROJECT	DUE DATI	AGING	BALANCE	TOTAL	📎	STATUS	ACTION
☐	07/13/2022	Invoice	1004	Main...		08/12...	24	$642.50	$892.50		Overdue	Receive payment
	Total							$642.50	$892.50			

‹ First   Previous   1-1 of 1   Next   Last ›

FIGURE 6-20: Invoice 1004 has a credit memo for $250 applied against it.

TIP

By default, credit memos are applied automatically to outstanding or future invoices. If you want to change that behavior, choose Settings⇨ Account and Settings⇨ Advanced⇨ Automation, toggle off the Automatically Apply Credits option, click Save, and then click Close.

If you click the invoice to view it, you see a link just below the outstanding balance indicating that a payment was made (and the amount of the payment). And if you scroll to the bottom of the invoice, you see the credit amount on the Amount Received line at the bottom of the invoice, as shown in Figure 6-21.

Issuing a refund to a customer

Create a Refund Receipt transaction if you need to refund money to a customer instead of reducing an outstanding or future balance. In this example, you're going to issue a refund check to a customer, which deducts the amount of the refund from a bank account and reduces an income account. The customer didn't return any items.

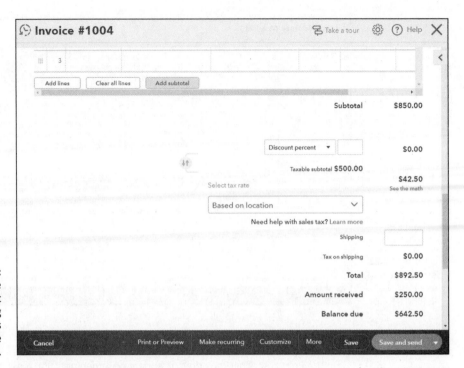

Subtotal	$850.00

Discount percent ▼ [   ] $0.00

Taxable subtotal $500.00

Select tax rate $42.50
See the math

Based on location ✓

Need help with sales tax? Learn more

Shipping [   ]

Tax on shipping $0.00

Total	$892.50
Amount received	$250.00
Balance due	$642.50

FIGURE 6-21: Credit memos are applied against outstanding invoices unless you decide otherwise.

TIP

To account for refunds, you issue when a customer doesn't return an item, first set up an account called something like Returns and Allowances. Assign this account to the Category Type of Income and a Detail Type of Discounts/Refunds Given. If you need the particulars, I discuss adding accounts to your chart of accounts in Chapter 2. Next, set up a service on the Products and Services list, and call it something like Customer Refunds or even Returns & Allowances. Do *not* select Is Taxable for the service. Assign the service to the Returns & Allowances account, and don't assign a default Price/Rate. I discuss creating services in Chapter 5.

Filling in the Refund Receipt window is similar to filling in the Sales Receipt window. If you need more details than I supply here, refer to the section, "Entering a sales receipt," earlier in this chapter. Follow these steps to display and fill in the Refund Receipt window, as shown in Figure 6-22:

1. **Choose New ⇨ Refund Receipt.**

2. **Select a customer to fill in related information.**

3. **Select a payment method and make a choice from the Refund From drop-down list.**

   If you select a bank account, the current balance and the next check number associated with the account appear.

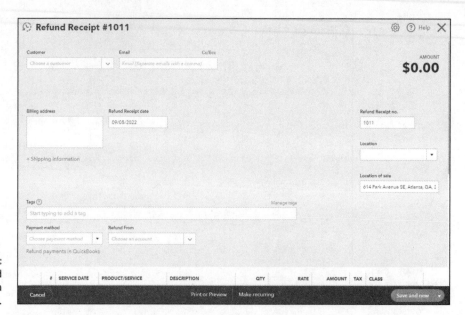

FIGURE 6-22:
Issuing a refund
check by way of a
Refund Receipt.

4. **Optional: Click the Print Later checkbox.**

   The Print Later checkbox doesn't appear onscreen until you make a choice from the Refund From drop-down list.

5. **If your customer is returning items, select the item that the customer is returning in exchange for the refund in the Product/Service column, and otherwise create or choose a non-inventory item with a name along the lines of Good Will Discount, as shown in Figure 6-22.**

   In this example, the customer isn't returning any items, so I selected the Refunds & Allowances item.

6. **Optional: Scroll down to the bottom of the window, and fill in the information (the same as the information at the bottom of an invoice).**

7. **Click either Print or Preview at the bottom of the screen and then choose Print Check if you want to print a check, or make a choice from the Save button.**

   The transaction is saved when you print the check, or you simply save the transaction if you want to print it later. The Save button allows you to choose between Save and New, Save and Send, or Save and Close. The Print or Preview button allows you simply print the check as well.

REMEMBER

If you are using QuickBooks Payments, you can only refund credit card charges processed through your payment account. You cannot refund ACH payments electronically. You have to kick it old school and print a paper check or facilitate an electronic transaction outside of QuickBooks.

Writing Off Bad Debt

An unfortunate reality is that at some point you may not get paid for products delivered or services rendered. It's a frustrating aspect of being a business owner or manager, but is part of the hard-fought knowledge that one accumulates over time. Some setup is required before you can write off an invoice, but once you accomplish those two one-time tasks, going forward writing off bad debt is as simple as creating a credit memo that you then apply as a payment against the defunct invoices.

Setting up a bad debt account and item

The first task is to add a Bad Debt account to your chart of accounts:

1. **Choose Settings ⇨ Chart of Accounts to display your chart of accounts.**

2. **Click New in the upper right-hand corner.**

3. **The following steps depend on whether you're using Business View or Accountant View, as two different screens appear.**

   - **Business View — Accounts on your chart of accounts are referred to as Categories in Business View.** I think this is a misguided attempt at trying to make accounting terms more understandable. Regardless, here we go:

   a. **Enter a name such as** Bad Debt **in the Category Name field.**

   b. **Click Select Category, choose Expenses, and then click Next.**

   c. **Choose Uncategorized Expenses and then click Select.**

   d. **Optional: Complete the Description field if you want.**

   e. **Click Save to create your new account.**

   - **Accountant View — The process is a little more traditional on this screen:**

   a. **Type** uncat **to filter the Save Account Number list and then choose Uncategorized Expense.**

   b. **Choose Bad Debts from the Tax Form Section list.**

   c. **Enter a name such as** Bad Debt **in the Account Name field.**

   d. **Optional: Complete the Description field if you want.**

   e. **Click Save to create your new account.**

The next one-time step is to create a Bad Debt item. Fortunately, the steps here are the same for both Business View and Accountant View:

1. **Choose Settings ⇨ Products and Services to display your item list.**

2. **Click New in the upper right-hand corner and then choose Non-Inventory.**

3. **Assign a name, such as** Bad Debt.

4. **Optional: Assign the Bad Debt item to a category.**

   I skipped over the SKU field in this context because a stock-keeping unit isn't typically assigned to an administrative item like Bad Debt.

5. **Optional: Enter a description such as $*#@_% (which stand in for curse words in comic strips), or be more reserved and enter** Bad Debt Write-Off.

6. **Choose Bad Debt from the Income Account list.**

REMEMBER

   Make sure that you've already added Bad Debt to your chart of accounts; otherwise, you won't be able to choose it here.

7. **Click Save and Close.**

Creating bad debt write-off transactions

Once you've created the Bad Debt account on your chart of accounts and created a Bad Debt non-inventory item, you're ready to grit your teeth and start writing off some uncollectible invoices.

1. **Choose New ⇨ Credit Memo.**

2. **Select your nemesis, er, I mean customer.**

3. **Choose Bad Debt in the first line of the Products/Services section.**

4. **Enter the amount that you're writing off in the Amount column.**

   In the particularly unfortunate event that you're writing off two or more invoices, the amount you enter here can be the sum of all invoices that you're writing off.

5. **Optional: Enter something along the lines of** Write Off Bad Debt **in the Message Displayed on Statement field.**

6. **Click Save and Close, or click Save and New if you have other non-paying customers to dispatch as well.**

7. **Choose New ⇨ Receive Payment.**

8. Choose your customer.

9. Select one or more invoices from the Outstanding Transactions section.

10. Select the credit memo you created from the Credits section.

11. Click Save and Close.

REMEMBER

A bit of cold comfort: if you file your taxes on the accrual basis, you'll most likely get a deduction for the bad debt. There's no deduction if you file your taxes using cash-basis because you don't count invoices as taxable income until you receive payment.

Reviewing and Creating Transactions with Spreadsheet Sync

QuickBooks Online Advanced subscribers can edit or create invoices, bills, and purchase and sales records with the Spreadsheet Sync feature, which makes Microsoft Excel spreadsheets become a direct extension of QuickBooks. At the end of Chapter 4, I explain how to install Spreadsheet Sync, so here I just focus on how you can use Spreadsheet Sync to edit and/or create customer transactions in Excel:

1. Choose Home ⇨ Spreadsheet Sync in Excel to display the Spreadsheet Sync task pane.

2. Sign in if prompted.

Spreadsheet Sync sessions expire if you close Excel or after a certain amount of time elapses.

3. Choose Manage Records if prompted.

4. Choose Invoices and Bills or Purchases & Sales Receipt from the Select Template list.

A filter dialog box appears, as shown in Figure 6-23.

5. Optional: Toggle on the Bring in Existing Records from QuickBooks option and then click OK or Clear Data, depending upon the warning prompt that appears to inform you that any transactions or unposted changes on the template worksheet will be discarded.

6. Optional: Make selections from the Txn Date field and Due Date field.

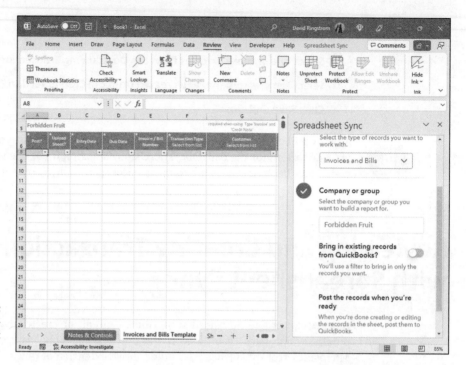

FIGURE 6-23:
Blank Spreadsheet Sync template.

7. **Optional: Select Invoice, Bill, Credit Note, or Supplier Credit Note from the transaction type list.**

   In this context, a Credit Note is another way of referring to Credit Memos that you issue to customers. Conversely, a Supplier Credit Note is referred to as a Vendor Credit within the QuickBooks interface.

8. **Click OK to retrieve your existing transactions from QuickBooks into Excel, as shown in Figure 6-24.**

9. **Optional: Click Post Data to QuickBooks at the bottom of the Spreadsheet Sync task pane, as shown in Figure 6-24, if you make any changes to the transactions, or add new transactions.**

   You must set Column A to Yes for any transactions that you want to post to QuickBooks.

You can now close the Spreadsheet Sync task pane, and then display it when needed by choosing Home ➪ Spreadsheet Sync in Excel.

WARNING

Be mindful when editing transactions because you can very easily solve one problem and create new ones, such as creating discrepancies between the payments posted against invoices or bills. Study the template carefully and read all notes and warnings.

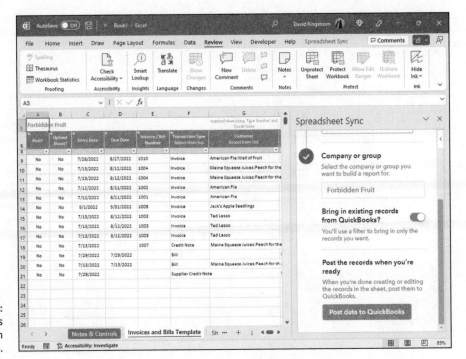

FIGURE 6-24:
Transactions retrieved from QuickBooks.

Chapter **7**

Paying Bills and Writing Checks

t's always more fun to record money coming in as you did in Chapter 6, versus going out as you'll do in this chapter. Alas, paying bills is part of life — unless you're a penguin and you eat with your one bill, but I digress. This chapter explores the transactions you use in QuickBooks to meet your financial obligations, which accountants often generalize as accounts payable, or A/P for short.

Looking at Expense and Bill Payment Methods

First, I want to make sure that you're aware of the various payment method options that you have for recording expenses and bill payments, as it isn't always readily apparent from the user interface.

>> **Printed check:** QuickBooks enables you to fill out a check form onscreen and then print the check immediately or batch it for later.

>> **Electronic transactions:** These include direct debits to your bank account, such as ACH (Automated Clearing House) transfers, wires, online bill payments, and debit card transactions.

>> **Credit card:** You can record expenses or bill payments that you make via credit card in a similar fashion to recording a check. Simply choose your credit card account from the payment account instead of a bank account.

I discuss other types of credit card–related transactions, such as Credit Card Credit and Pay Down Credit Card in Chapter 10.

TIP

Understanding the Transaction Types

Let's begin by looking at the various types of accounts payable transactions that you can enter, so that you make the proper choice.

>> **Expense:** This type of transaction is well suited to recording automatic drafts from your account for bank fees, utility payments, rent payments, and so on, as well as expenses that you pay for with a credit card.

>> **Check:** Check transactions are a virtual twin of Expense transactions, with the exception that you are assumed to be either recording a handwritten check or planning to print or write a check.

>> **Bill:** This type of transaction allows you to record the expense now and pay it later. You can track unpaid bills on the A/P Aging Summary and A/P Aging Detail reports.

>> **Pay Bills:** This type of transaction comes into play when it's time to pay one or more bills in part or in full. You can choose to print a check, or you can record an online payment that you've scheduled through your bank. Bills drop off the A/P Aging Summary and A/P Aging Detail reports once they are paid in full.

>> **Vendor Credit:** You could think of a vendor credit as a reverse bill, where a vendor is waiving all or part of a bill, or perhaps making a goodwill gesture against a future bill. Vendor credits can be applied against open bills in a similar fashion to making a payment.

As I discuss in Chapter 12, purchase orders are a way of tracking obligations for goods and/or services that you've requested from a vendor, and serves to document the price that you and the vendor have agreed to.

TIP

As of this writing, Advanced subscribers may be able to beta-test creating Expense Claims transactions, which enable employees to submit expense reports for reimbursement. This feature is available under Expenses ⇨ Expense Claims (Sales & Expenses ⇨ Expense Claims). Onscreen documentation shows you how to get started with this feature.

TIP

Now that you have the lay of the land, let's explore how to use each transaction type.

Entering an Expense

Expense transactions are for situations where the money has already been spent, or, as they say, "the horse has already left the barn." As you'll see, expense transactions are an alternative to entering a bill for expenses that you plan to pay later, and checks for expenses that you want to pay at this moment. You typically use expenses to record automatic withdrawals from your bank account, debit card transactions, handwritten checks, outgoing ACH transactions, and so on. Here's how to enter an expense:

1. **Click the + New button near the top of the left-hand menu bar and choose Expense from the Vendors column, or choose Expenses ⇨ Expenses (Sales & Expenses ⇨ Expenses), click New Transaction, and then choose Expense.**

   The Expense Transactions page appears, as shown in Figure 7-1.

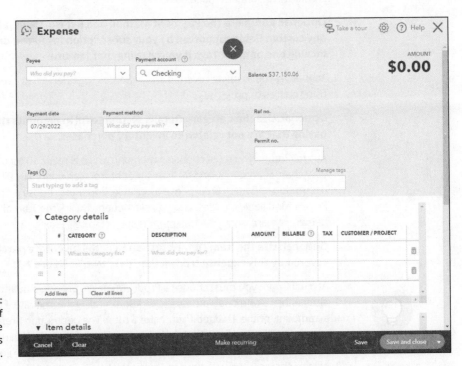

FIGURE 7-1:
The top half of the Expense Transactions page.

2. **Select the payee from which you incurred the expense or choose Add New from the drop-down list to add a new payee.**

   The vendor's mailing address information appears if you choose an existing vendor; otherwise, a Vendor task pane appears. Fill in at least the Vendor Display Name and then click Save to create a new payee.

3. **Choose a Payment Account.**

   This is typically a bank or credit card account.

TIP

   The Payment Method list in QuickBooks applies to both customers and vendors. Choose Gear icon ⇨ All Lists ⇨ Payment Methods to view your existing payment methods. Choose Make Inactive from the Action column if you want to disable a particular method.

4. **Confirm the Payment Date.**

   Using the actual date of the transaction will make reconciling your bank or credit card statement much easier.

5. **Optional: Complete the Payment Method and Ref No. fields, along with any custom fields supported by your subscription level. You can also include one or more Tags if you're using that feature.**

   Tags allow you to relate revenue and expenses together, as an alternative to using classes or projects.

6. **Optional: Use the Category Details section to fill in amounts that you're paying that are not related to inventory purchases.**

   At a minimum, you must choose a category, which is really an account from your chart of accounts, and fill in an amount. You can optionally fill in a description and mark an expense as billable. You must choose a Customer/Project for billable charges, and you can optionally click the Tax column if the reimbursement from your customer is subject to sales tax.

7. **Optional: Use the Item Details section to detail inventory purchases covered by this expense transaction, as shown in Figure 7-2.**

   At a minimum you must choose a Product/Service, provide a quantity, and enter either a rate or an amount (QuickBooks calculates the rate if you enter an amount, or the amount if you enter a rate). The description prefills when you choose the Product/Service. You can optionally mark the inventory purchases as billable. If you do, you must choose a Customer/Project for billable charges, and you can optionally click the Tax column if the reimbursement from your customer is subject to sales tax.

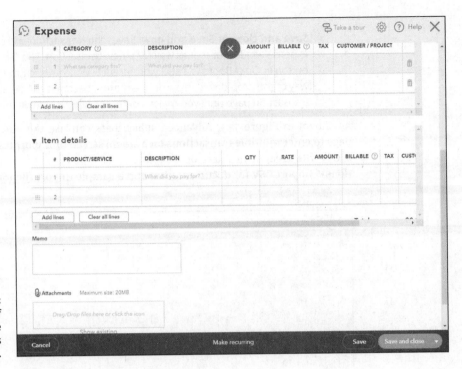

FIGURE 7-2:
The bottom half
of the Expense
Transactions
page.

8. **Optional: Provide a memo.**

   This can be any sort of notes that you want to enter related to the transaction.

9. **Optional: Add one or more attachments.**

   You can upload any of the following document types: CSV, DOC, GIF, JPEG, PDF, PNG, TIFF, XLSX, XML. Each file can be no more than 20MB in size.

10. **At the bottom of the page, you can choose any of the following commands.**

    - **Cancel:** Discards the transaction and closes the Expense window if you indicate yes, you would like to leave without saving.

    - **Clear:** Erases the Expense window but keeps it open if you indicate yes, you would like to clear without saving.

    - **Make Recurring:** Sets up a recurring expense on a schedule that you choose, such as a monthly insurance payment that is automatically debited from your bank account or charged to your credit card. See the section, "Managing recurring transactions," later in this chapter for details on recurring transactions.

    - **Save:** Saves the transaction but keeps the Expense window and the transaction on the screen.

- **Save and close or Save and new:** Saves the transaction and closes the Expense window or makes way for a new transaction. The "Save and . . ." button in QuickBooks is a sticky preference. Whichever choice you make by way of the drop-down arrow on the button, becomes the default for that transaction page until you make a different selection down the line.

As shown in Figure 7-3, Advanced subscribers can use the Batch Transactions page to enter multiple transactions on a single screen or import transactions from a CSV file created in Excel or Google Sheets. Choose + New ➪ Batch Transactions ➪ Import CSV for documentation and a sample import file format.

FIGURE 7-3:
The Batch
Transactions
page in
QuickBooks
Online Advanced.

TIP

The Batch Transactions page allows you to enter invoices, bank deposits, sales receipts, bills, expenses, and checks. You can also click Import CSV to import invoices. A secondary way of importing invoices involves choosing Settings ➪ Import Data ➪ Invoices. As of this writing that route is a dead-end if you're using Sales Tax — QuickBooks will inform you that they're working on the feature, which means Advanced subscribers that charge sales tax have a workaround for importing invoices that other subscribers don't.

Writing a Check

Check transactions enable you to print a physical check to cover an expense that hasn't been paid yet, such as when the window washer is tapping their toes by your desk. You also have the option to click Print Later to queue up one or more checks that you'll print later as a batch. To write a check, you can do either of the following:

>> Choose + New ⇨ Check from the Vendor column.

>> Choose Expenses ⇨ Expenses from the left menu bar, click New Transaction, and then choose Check.

In either case, the Check window appears, as shown in Figure 7-4.

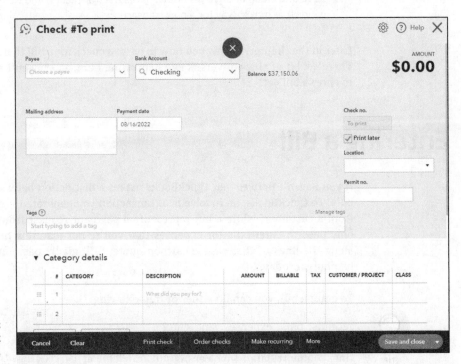

FIGURE 7-4:
The Check
window.

As for writing a check, hold onto your hat here: the screen is almost identical to the Expense page that I just covered. The only differences are spots to enter a check number and, as I mentioned, to choose to print the check later. Everything else works in the same fashion. However, you have some different command choices at the bottom of the screen.

>> **Cancel:** Discards the transaction and closes the Check window if you indicate yes, you would like to leave without saving.

>> **Print check:** Saves the transaction and displays a Print Preview window.

>> **Order checks:** Displays a QuickBooks Checks and Supplies page from which you can order various paper checks. Unfortunately, they only sell blank checks, so don't expect to see your name on the payee line.

>> **Make recurring:** Sets up a recurring check on a schedule that you choose, such as a monthly rent payment that you want to physically print a check for each month. See the section, "Managing recurring transactions," later in this chapter for details on recurring transactions.

>> **More:** The Void check command lurks on a submenu here, ostensibly so that you only purposefully void a check that you've written.

>> **Save and close or Save and new:** Saves the transaction and closes the Check window or makes way for a new transaction.

Later in the chapter, I show you how to write a check for a bill that you've entered. There's a bit of chicken versus egg happening here, as I haven't shown you how to enter a bill yet.

Entering a Bill

If you haven't noticed yet, QuickBooks makes a distinction between invoices and bills. To QuickBooks, an invoice is a transaction you generate to request payment from a customer, while a bill represents a payment request from a vendor. You only need to enter bills for expenses that you're not planning on paying today, along the lines of that classic cartoon quote, "I'll gladly pay you Tuesday for a hamburger today."

To enter a bill, you can do either of the following:

>> Choose + New ⇨ Bill from the Vendor column.

>> Choose Expenses ⇨ Expenses from the left menu bar, click New Transaction, and then choose Bill.

In either case, the Bill window appears, as shown in Figure 7-5.

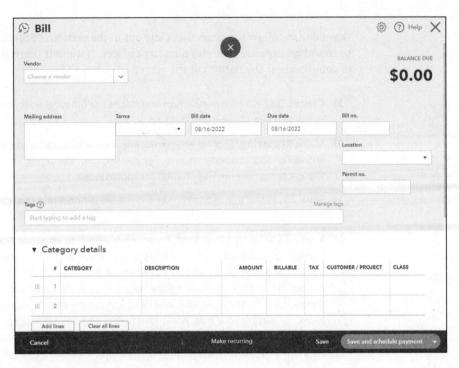

FIGURE 7-5:
The Bill window.

Alrighty, brace yourself for a bit of déjà vu, because the Bill window looks eerily like the Expense and Check window. Additional fields that you won't see on the other two windows include the following.

TIP

>> **Terms:** This is where you document the payment terms that you want to use for this bill, such as Due on Receipt, Net 15, Net 30, and so on. You can also choose Add New to create a new type of payment term.

The Terms list in QuickBooks applies to both customers and vendors. Choose Gear icon ⇨ All Lists ⇨ Terms to view your existing terms. Choose Make Inactive from the Action column if you want to disable a particular payment term.

>> **Bill Date:** This is the equivalent of the Payment Date field in the Expense and Check window. Enter the date that your vendor issued the bill here.

>> **Due Date:** The Due Date recalculates automatically based upon the choice that you make from the Terms field, but you can override the default date provided.

>> **Bill No.:** This is the equivalent of the Ref. No field in the Expense window and the Check No. field in the Checks window. You enter your vendor's invoice number in this space.

Beyond that, follow the steps that I laid out in the section, "Entering an Expense," to record an expense that you plan to pay later. Note that there is a different mix of commands at the bottom of the screen.

>> **Cancel:** Discards the transaction and closes the Bill window if you indicate yes, you would like to leave without saving.

>> **Make Recurring:** Sets up a recurring check on a schedule that you choose, such as annual property tax bills. See the section, "Managing Recurring Transactions," later in this chapter for more details.

>> **Save:** Saves the transaction but keeps the Bill window and the transaction on the screen.

>> **Save and Schedule Payment:** Saves the transaction and then sneakily displays QuickBooks Online Bill Pay service, which enables you to pay two bills by for free each month, plus $1.50 per check thereafter. A 2.9 percent fee applies to bills that you want to pay via credit card. Alternatively, you can choose Save and new, or Save and close if you have other avenues you prefer to use for paying your bills. Another way to schedule online bill payments is to choose Expenses ⇨ Vendors (Sales & Expenses ⇨ Vendors) and then click Schedule Payments in the Action column for any vendors that have unpaid bills.

REMEMBER

QuickBooks Online Bill Payment is not available to Simple Start subscribers.

Paying Bills

You typically won't have to revisit expenses or checks that you enter, because you're either recording a financial event that has already occurred, or you're settling up in the moment by printing a check. Conversely, bills always entail follow-up unless you schedule payment online, as I describe in the previous section.

QuickBooks offers two different ways that you can pay bills. The first is the Pay Bills command, which is designed for you to quickly decimate your bank balance by paying multiple bills. Or you can take the slow-bleed approach by using the Write Checks command to pay bills one vendor at a time.

Paying two or more bills at once

This then brings you to the Pay Bills transaction screen, which you can display in a couple of ways:

>> Choose + New ⇨ Pay Bills from the Vendor column.

>> Choose Expenses ⇨ Expenses from the left menu bar, click the arrow next to Print Checks, and then choose Pay Bills.

REMEMBER

The button to the left of the New Transaction button on the Expenses window remembers the last choice that you made. This menu enables you to Print Checks, Order Checks, and Pay Bills. Your most recent choice becomes the default state for this button until you make another choice.

Either action displays the Pay Bills window shown in Figure 7-6, which is designed to streamline the process of paying two or more bills at once. As you see in the next section, you can also choose to pay one bill at a time by writing a check.

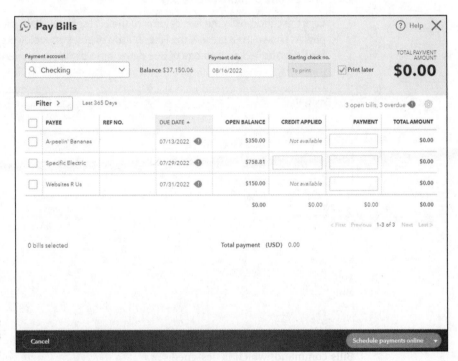

FIGURE 7-6:
The Pay Bills window.

Use the following steps to use the Pay Bills window:

1. **Choose a payment account.**

   An Add New command enables you to add a new payment account on the fly if necessary.

2. Select a payment date.

This date will apply to all bills that you choose as a part of this Pay Bills transaction.

3. Confirm the starting check number.

Typically, this automatically increments for you, but you can override the check number shown if needed.

4. Optional: Click Print Later if you want to print paper checks at a later time.

This field only applies when you plan to print checks from QuickBooks later on, so skip it if you use the QuickBooks Online Bill Pay service.

5. Choose one or more bills to pay.

Click the checkbox in the first column of the bill list for any bills that you wish to pay. As shown in Figure 7-7, the Filter button enables you to display open bills for a specific vendor or range of due dates, or to display only overdue bills.

FIGURE 7-7: Filtering options for paying bills.

6. **Optional: Adjust the payment amounts.**

   Although QuickBooks assumes that you want to bills in full, you can override the payment amounts for any bills to reflect a partial payment.

7. **Choose Schedule payments online, Save, Save and print, or Save and close.**

   Schedule payments online displays the QuickBooks Online Bill Pay service screen, which is free for payments made from your bank account or debit card, or incurs a 2.9 percent fee for any bills that you pay via credit card. Choose *Save* if you want to save the work that you've done but keep working in the Pay Bills window; choose *Save and print* if you're ready to print paper checks at this moment; or choose *Save and close* if you choose to print later and have finished your work on this screen.

The only other option you have in this window is to Cancel, which causes Quick-Books to ask if you want to leave without saving.

Writing a check to pay a bill

Earlier in this chapter, I discuss how to write a check for an expense that you want to pay on the spot. In that case, it would be double the work to enter a bill that you then immediately pay. However, from time to time you may realize that you need to write a one-off check to pay a bill that perhaps slipped your memory. Let's revisit the Write Checks screen to see what those steps look like:

1. **Display the Write Checks screen by choosing + New ⇨ Check or Expenses ⇨ Expenses from the left menu bar, click New Transaction, and then choose Check.**

2. **Select a payee from the list.**

   Any outstanding bills appear in the Add to Check task pane shown in Figure 7-8. You only see this task pane for vendors that have unpaid amounts due.

3. **Click Add All if you want to pay all open bills for the vendor, or click Add below specific bills.**

   The ground may feel like it has shifted on you, because the Write Check screen transmogrifies into a Bill Payment screen, as shown in Figure 7-9. The bill or bills that you've chosen to pay appear in an Outstanding Transactions section, in place of the typical Category Details and Item Details sections.

4. **Optional: Adjust payment amounts as needed or click Clear Payment if you change your mind about paying the bills.**

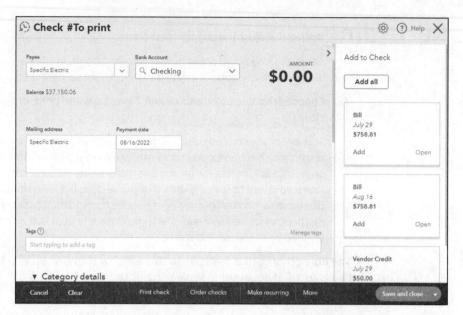

FIGURE 7-8:
Add to Check task
pane.

FIGURE 7-9:
A Bill Payment
window shape
shifts from the
Check window
you were just in.

Clear Payment returns you to the Check screen you were on, but without the
Add to Check task pane. You have to close and then reopen the Check window
at this point to get access to the Add to Check task pane again.

5. **Use any of the commands along the bottom in the same fashion as I
    describe in the previous section, "Writing a Check."**

Recording Vendor Credits and Refunds

You could consider a vendor credit to be a negative expense. Vendor credits may arise when you return goods that you've paid for, or perhaps when a service that was provided didn't meet your expectations and the vendor offers you a credit to be applied against future transactions. Or, you may have the good fortune of having a refund check in hand from your vendor. Either way, you begin the process by recording a vendor credit transaction.

Entering a vendor credit

Use these steps to record a vendor credit or vendor refund check:

1. **Choose + New ⇨ Vendor Credit.**

   The Vendor Credit window appears, as shown in Figure 7-10.

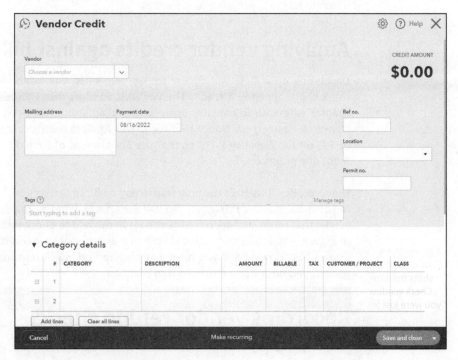

FIGURE 7-10:
The Vendor
Credit window.

2. **Select the vendor that issued the credit.**

3. **Enter the date of the credit.**

4. **Enter the credit amount or refund amount as a positive amount.**

   Don't fall down any rabbit holes here and overthink things. Yes, I know this is basically a negative expense, but the Vendor Credit memo knows that, and so you enter a positive amount here, as opposed to a negative amount.

5. **Optional: Select the account used on the original bill in the Category Details section if the credit relates to expenses that are not related to purchasing inventory.**

6. **Optional: Enter the inventory items that you returned in the Item Details section if appropriate.**

7. **Optional: Attach a digital copy of the credit in the Attachments section.**

8. **Choose Save and close or Save and new.**

If the vendor submitted a credit memo, you can apply the credit against an existing or future bill, as I discuss in the next section; or, if you have a refund check in hand, skip to the section, "Recording vendor refund checks and payments," immediately following the next section.

Applying vendor credits against bills

Depending upon how you choose to pay your bills, you might not even have to think about applying a credit. The Pay Bills window that I discuss earlier in this chapter automatically applies open credits against bills that you want to pay, as shown in Figure 7-11. Notice that the Credit Applied column contains an amount of $75.00 for Websites R Us, so that the bill amount of $150.00 results in a payment due of $75.00.

However, Pay Bills isn't the only way to pay a bill. In the section, "Writing a check to pay a bill," I show that you can use the Checks window to pay bills as well. If you go that route, any open credits appear in the Add to Check task pane, as shown in Figure 7-8. Either way, it's a simple process to apply a credit memo against an unpaid bill. However, if you have a vendor refund check burning a hole in your pocket, you have a few more steps to carry out.

Recording vendor refund checks and payments

If your vendor has done you a solid and gave you an actual check or electronic payment as opposed to a credit memo, make sure that you have entered a vendor credit memo (as described in the section, "Entering a vendor credit") first, and then carry out these steps:

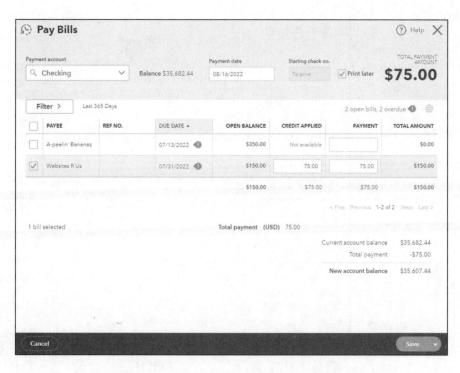

Pay Bills   (?) Help ✕

Payment account
🔍 Checking ⌄   Balance $35,682.44

Payment date
08/16/2022

Starting check no.
To print   ☑ Print later

TOTAL PAYMENT
AMOUNT
$75.00

Filter >   Last 365 Days   2 open bills, 2 overdue ❶ ⚙

	PAYEE	REF NO.	DUE DATE ▲	OPEN BALANCE	CREDIT APPLIED	PAYMENT	TOTAL AMOUNT
☐	A-peelin' Bananas		07/13/2022 ❶	$350.00	Not available		$0.00
☑	Websites R Us		07/31/2022 ❶	$150.00	75.00	75.00	$150.00
				$150.00	$75.00	$75.00	$150.00

< First Previous 1-2 of 2 Next Last >

1 bill selected   Total payment (USD) 75.00

Current account balance $35,682.44
Total payment   -$75.00
New account balance $35,607.44

Cancel   Save ⌄

FIGURE 7-11:
The Pay Bills window automatically applies applicable vendor credits.

1. **Choose + New ⇨ Bank Deposit from the Other column.**

   The Bank Deposit window appears, as shown in Figure 7-12.

2. **Choose the bank account that you will deposit the check into, or choose Payments to Deposit (Undeposited Funds) if you plan to take the check to the bank with one or more other checks.**

3. **Enter your vendor's name into the Received From column of the Add Funds to This Deposit section.**

4. **Choose Accounts Payable (A/P) from the Account column.**

   If you're thinking, "Wait, what?", remember that you posted the credit to the actual expense account when you entered the credit memo. Thus, you're now posting the check to your Accounts Payable account as a step toward zeroing out the vendor credit that you entered. I say a step toward because you still need to match the vendor credit and bank deposit together, so hang with me here.

5. **Optional: Fill in the Description, Payment Method, and Ref No. fields.**

   Don't worry, mum's the word if you choose to skip these fields.

6. **Enter the refund check amount into the Amount field.**

7. **Optional: Record any other amounts that you want to include on the same bank deposit.**

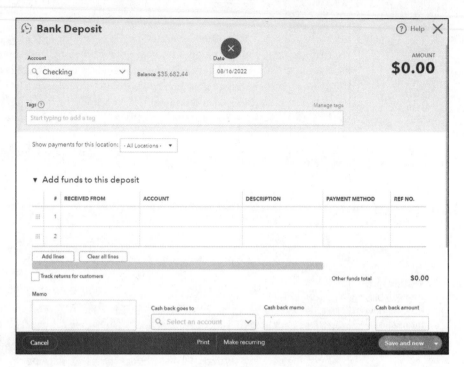

FIGURE 7-12:
The Bank Deposit window.

8. **Choose Save and close.**

9. **Choose + New ⇨ Pay Bills.**

   I know, I know, you're saying, "Wait, what?" again. You need to match the vendor credit and the bank deposit together, so that the credit is applied, and *then* you'll be free of this gauntlet.

10. **Select the bank deposit transaction that you saved in Step 8.**

    The vendor credit appears in the Credit Applied field and the Total Payment becomes zero.

11. **Choose Save and close.**

    Whew! You made it! Your vendor refund check or payment is applied and properly accounted for.

Managing Recurring Transactions

Have you ever had that dream where you keep doing the same task over and over again? For some of us, it's more of a real-life nightmare. Fortunately, recurring transactions can help eliminate some of the repetitive nature of your accounting transactions. Well, that is unless you have a Simple Start subscription, which doesn't offer this feature. In all other subscription levels, you can set any transaction up as recurring except for bill payments, customer payments, and time activities. Rest assured, you're in control here because you can decide whether a recurring transaction posts automatically to your books, serves as a tickler that a transaction needs to be posted, or just serves as a template that you can use to get a jump start on future transactions. Here are the types of recurring transactions that you can create.

>> **Scheduled:** These types of recurring transactions post automatically to your books based upon the schedule that you establish, and are ideal for transactions that have fixed amounts that rarely change, such as monthly rent payments. For instance, recurring bills scheduled for the first of the month will post to your books automatically without any intervention from you, and are even emailed automatically if you choose.

>> **Reminder:** This type of recurring transaction prompts you when the scheduled date comes around on the calendar. You can edit the transaction details before posting. This is well suited to transactions where the amount varies from month to month, such as a utility bill.

>> **Unscheduled:** This type of transaction hangs out in the background and does not remind you or post to your books but is available for use at any time in posting new transactions. Payroll journal entries or year-end closing transactions are ideal candidates for unscheduled recurring transactions.

With that background in mind, let's see how to create a recurring transaction. I think you'll find it easiest to click the Make Recurring button at the bottom of the screen the next time that you create a transaction that you'd like to recur, but I'll also show you how you can purposefully create recurring transactions.

Creating a recurring transaction on the fly

QuickBooks allows you to set most first-stage transactions as recurring, such as invoices, bills, sales receipts, expenses, and so on. Conversely, transactions such as Receive Payment and Bill Pay are second-stage transactions, as they offset first-stage transactions, and thus cannot be set to recur.

Follow these steps to make a recurring version of an existing transaction:

1. Click Save to preserve the transaction that you have on screen, particularly if you've just entered it.

2. Click Make Recurring at the bottom of the transaction screen to display the Recurring version of the transaction type you started with, such as Recurring Bill shown in Figure 7-13.

   You can only recur transactions that have a Make Recurring button at the bottom of the screen.

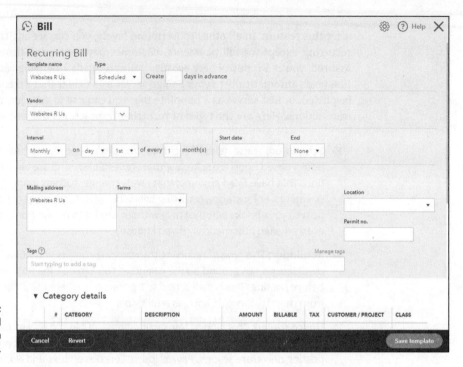

FIGURE 7-13:
The Recurring Bill
transaction
window.

3. **Optional: Change the template name.**

4. **Choose Scheduled, Reminder, or Unscheduled from the Type list.**

5. **Fill in the number of days in advance that a scheduled transaction should be created, or the number of days before the transaction date that you want to be reminded.**

WARNING

Be aware that QuickBooks sets the date on the scheduled transaction by using the scheduled date, not the date that you enter the transaction. But a recurring transaction charges a customer's credit card or ACH payment on the day you record the recurring transaction. So the charge gets processed on the day it's recorded, but the transaction date could be a future date.

6. **Ensure that the vendor (or customer) is correct.**

7. **Select the frequency for scheduled or reminder transactions, along with the time frame.**

   • **Daily:** Specify the number of days between when this transaction should post.

   • **Weekly:** Specify the number of weeks between when this transaction should post, and the day of the week that you want for it to post.

- **Monthly:** Specify the interval in months and the day of the month to pay the bill. For instance, you can schedule a transaction to post on a specific day each month or, say, on the last Tuesday of each month.

- **Yearly:** Specify the month and day for the transaction to post each year.

- **Start Date:** Indicate the first date when QuickBooks should post the transaction, along with an end date if appropriate. For instance, you might set an end date for a rent bill to coincide with the end of your lease.

8. **Confirm that the mailing address and terms are correct, scroll down the window to confirm that the detail section(s) of the transaction are correct, and add any memo information or attachments to the transaction.**

   Any lines in the Category Detail or Item Detail sections that have a value of $0 won't be saved.

9. **Click Save Template in the bottom-right corner of the window.**

Adding to the recurring transaction list

You can also add new transactions directly to the recurring transaction list by following these steps:

1. **Choose Settings ⇨ Recurring Transactions to display the Recurring Transactions list.**

2. **Click New to display the Select Transaction Type dialog box, choose a transaction type, and then click OK.**

   Available choices include the following: Bill, Non-Posting Charge, Check, Non-Posting Credit, Credit Card Credit, Credit Memo, Deposit, Estimate, Expense, Invoice, Journal Entry, Refund, Sales Receipt, Transfer, Vendor Credit, and Purchase Order.

3. **Complete the recurring transaction window in the same fashion as described in the preceding section, and then click Save.**

Making changes in recurring transactions

To work with existing recurring transactions, choose Settings ⇨ Recurring Transactions to display the Recurring Transactions list shown in Figure 7-14.

As shown in Figure 7-14, click Edit in the Action column to modify a recurring transaction. Any changes you make in recurring-transaction templates only affect future transactions. You will have to manually edit any existing transactions that have been posted to your books.

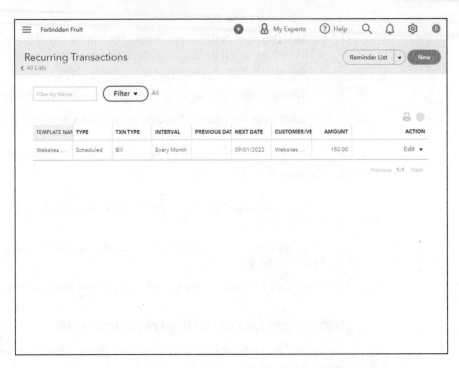

FIGURE 7-14:
The Recurring
Transactions list.

REMEMBER

QuickBooks automatically updates recurring transactions when you modify a customer or vendor record, such as recording a change of address.

The Action column also includes the following options.

>> **Use:** Enables you to record a Reminder or Unscheduled transaction to your books.

>> **Duplicate:** Creates additional recurring-transaction templates from existing recurring-transaction templates. You might use the template for your rent to create another template to pay monthly insurance, for example. You can also use this option to create backup copies of complex transactions, such as a detailed payroll journal entry.

>> **Delete:** Removes unwanted recurring-transaction templates.

REMEMBER

In many areas, deleting a record in QuickBooks translates to making a record inactive. Recurring transactions get deleted, and QuickBooks does not offer an undo capability, so think twice before deleting recurring transactions.

Finally, you can print a report of your existing recurring-transaction templates. Choose Reports on the left menu bar, type **recu** in the Search box (that's all you need to type to find the Recurring Template List report), and click on the report name to display the Recurring Template List report.

Reviewing and Creating Transactions with Spreadsheet Sync

Advanced subscribers of QuickBooks Online can edit or create invoices and bills as well as purchase and sales records with the Spreadsheet Sync feature, which makes Microsoft Excel spreadsheets become a direct extension of QuickBooks. At the end of Chapter 4, I explain how to install Spreadsheet Sync, as well as how to edit lists such as customers and vendors, so here I just focus on how you can use Spreadsheet Sync to edit and/or create vendor-related transactions in Excel.

1. **Open a blank Excel workbook, or an existing workbook that you want QuickBooks to insert a new worksheet into.**

2. **Choose Home ⇨ Spreadsheet Sync in Excel to display the Spreadsheet Sync task pane.**

3. **Sign in and/or click Get Started if prompted.**

   Spreadsheet Sync sessions expire if you close Excel or after a certain amount of time elapses.

4. **Choose Manage Records.**

   I discuss the Build a Report button in Chapter 15.

5. **Choose Invoices and Bills or Purchases & Sales Receipt from the Select Template list.**

   A new worksheet appears in your workbook, such as the Invoices and Bills Template shown in Figure 7-15, along with a Notes and Controls worksheet that offers additional instructions.

6. **Optional: Toggle on the Bring in Existing Records from QuickBooks option, and if prompted, click OK or Clear Data, depending upon the warning prompt that appears to inform you that any transactions or unposted changes on the template worksheet will be discarded.**

   A Filter dialog box appears.

7. **Optional: Make selections from the Txn Date field and Due Date fields for Invoices and Bills, or the Entry Date field for Purchases & Sales Receipts.**

8. **Optional: Select Invoice, Bill, Credit Note, or Supplier Credit Note from the Transaction Type list if you chose Invoices and Bills.**

   In this context, a Credit Note is another way of referring to Credit Memos that you issue to customers. Conversely, a Supplier Credit Note is referred to as a Vendor Credit within the QuickBooks interface. Similarly, Purchase transactions may have been recorded in QuickBooks as Expenses or as Checks.

9. Click OK to retrieve your existing transactions from QuickBooks into Excel.

Your existing QuickBooks transactions appear in the workbook, as shown in Figure 7-15.

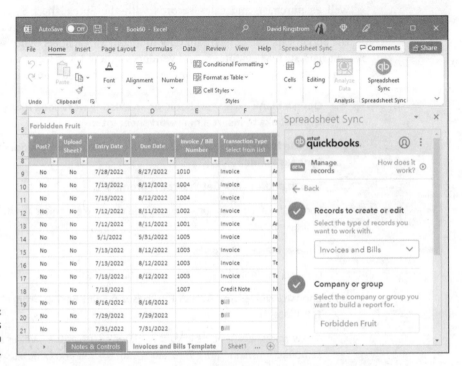

FIGURE 7-15:
Transactions
retrieved from
QuickBooks.

10. Optional: Click Post Data to QuickBooks at the bottom of the Spreadsheet Sync task pane, as shown in Figure 7-15, if you make any changes to the transactions or add new transactions.

You must set column A to Yes for any transactions that you want to post to QuickBooks.

You can now close the Spreadsheet Sync task pane; you can then display it when needed by choosing Home ⇨ Spreadsheet Sync in Excel.

WARNING

Be mindful when editing transactions because you can very easily solve one prob-lem and create new ones, such as creating discrepancies between the payments posted against invoices or bills. Study the template carefully and read all notes and warnings.

Chapter **8**

Paying Employees and Contractors

As an employer, you have a responsibility to pay both your employees and any contractors who work for you. In this chapter, I explore both responsibilities. Running payroll is more than just issuing paychecks to your employees. After you've prepared paychecks, you need to remit amounts withheld for deductions and benefits to the appropriate parties. QuickBooks Payroll handles the tax deposits and files payroll tax returns with the appropriate taxing authorities for you.

In the past, QuickBooks Online users could prepare payroll in one of two ways: using QuickBooks with Self Service Payroll or using QuickBooks with Full Service Payroll. Intuit has revised its offerings to blur the lines between these two methods. All QuickBooks Payroll plans now offer automated tax deposits and tax forms. Initially you could not opt out of the automatic filings and tax payments, but now you retain control over these tasks if you want. All three plans also offer Auto Payroll, which, if enabled, instructs QuickBooks to process payroll automatically as well. Among Auto Payroll, automated tax deposits, and automated payroll return findings, much of your payroll process can be set-and-forget.

REMEMBER

At the end of this chapter, I explore the ways that QuickBooks users typically pay — and report on paying — contractors, who are vendors who perform work for a company but don't qualify as employees.

TIP

If you're wondering about Intuit Online Payroll, all accounts have been migrated to QuickBooks Payroll, and that offering is no longer available. Intuit has been working to consolidate its payroll offerings down to three choices.

Getting Started with QuickBooks Payroll

When you prepare payroll, the process involves doing setup work so that you can calculate payroll checks accurately. You must also account for payroll taxes withheld from each employee's paycheck. The payroll service remits federal, state, and (in some cases) local payroll taxes to the appropriate tax authorities. You remit to the appropriate institutions any required deductions and contributions that affect each employee's paycheck.

This section examines the payroll setup process and details differences in the process for new employers and established employers.

TIP

I discuss how to add employees and contractors to QuickBooks in Chapter 4.

Turning on QuickBooks Payroll

This service uses a to-do list approach to walk you through the payroll setup process. You start by turning on payroll in QuickBooks Online. Then you complete tasks in the to-do list that walk you through setting up your company so that you can pay your employees.

REMEMBER

You can set up employees without a payroll subscription. After you establish your subscription, you can enter previous payroll data back to your subscription date.

Choose Payroll on the left menu bar to display the Employees page, and then click the Get Started button. On the first page, shown in Figure 8-1, choose the options that appeal to you, and clear the ones that don't, to have QuickBooks recommend a plan that best fits your needs. Alternatively, scroll down to compare the Core, Premium, and Elite payroll processing options. All three plans include automated tax deposits and payroll tax form filing. Click Try Now to start a free 30-day trial. Once you confirm your billing details, you're returned to the Welcome to Quick-Books Payroll page, on which you click Get Started.

FIGURE 8-1:
Choosing an option for payroll.

Follow these steps to embark on the process:

1. **When the Getting Started wizard asks you whether you've paid any employees in the current year, make a choice from No, I'm Not Sure, or Yes; then click Next.**

2. **On the next screen, select a date for your next payday and then click Next.**

3. **A series of address and contact information screens appear. Complete each one and then click Next.**

   The contact information you provided when you initially set up your company appears.

4. **Edit the contact information fields if necessary.**

   After you finish this part of the wizard, you're returned to a Setup Tasks list.

5. **Click Finish Up to begin adding your employees.**

   The Your Team page appears, as shown in Figure 8-2. In this case, the first employee is marked incomplete because they were added before QuickBooks Payroll was activated.

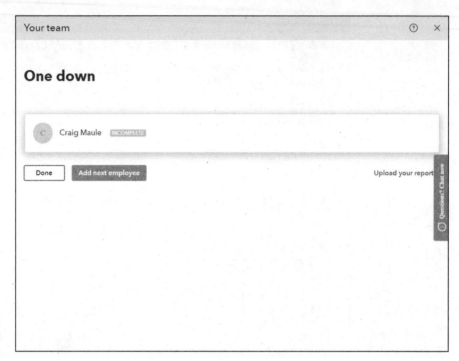

One down

C Craig Maule INCOMPLETE

[Done] [Add next employee]   Upload your report

FIGURE 8-2:
The Your Team
page.

6. **Choose an existing employee or click Add Next Employee.**

   The wizard displays a lengthy screen for you to complete.

7. **On the first part of the screen, shown in Figure 8-3, provide the employee's name, email address, and hire date.**

   Notice the option to allow the employee to enter their data directly in QuickBooks Workforce. You can deselect this option, but you may prefer to push the data entry work to your employees, which enables them to ensure that the information is entered correctly.

REMEMBER

   Form W-4 is the Internal Revenue Service form that employees complete to specify their withholding allowance. If you need to complete Form W-4 for any employee, visit www.irs.gov, and click the W-4 link in the Forms & Instructions or use this link: www.irs.gov/pub/irs-pdf/fw4.pdf.

   For this example, I'm going to assume that you want to provide the information yourself. Scroll down the page, and fill in the following information:

   ● Personal information, which includes the employee's address, Social Security number, birth date, gender, and phone number.

Add personal info ⑦ ✕

Tell us more about Craig

First name | M.I. | Last name
Craig | | Maule

Email

We'll email them an invite to QuickBooks Workforce. They can view their pay stubs, W-2s, and more. Learn about Workforce

Employee self-setup ⬤

Turn this on if you want this employee to enter their personal, tax, and banking info in Workforce.

Birth date
mm/dd/yyyy

Street address
🔍 Search by address

City | State | ZIP code

Cancel | Save

FIGURE 8-3:
Fill in the basic information about the employee, and decide whether the employee should add their own information.

- Tax withholding, which includes the employee's tax filing status (single, married, head of household, and so on) and withholding amount, as shown in Figure 8-4. State payroll tax information appears at the bottom of the screen and isn't shown in Figure 8-4. The requirements vary from state to state, but QuickBooks prompts you to supply information for the state in which your business operates.

TIP

To identify your state's payroll tax requirements, visit your state's website and search for payroll *taxes*. I live in Georgia, so I search the Georgia Department of Revenue's site.

- The method you want to use to pay the employee (such as paper check or direct deposit). If you choose direct deposit, specify the bank account information for the employee (account type, routing number, and account number).

TIP

For direct-deposit checks, you can choose to deposit the paycheck in its entirety in a single account, deposit the check into two accounts, or deposit a portion of the check directly and pay the balance as a paper check.

- Employment details, which include employee status, hire date, pay schedule, work location, job title, employee ID, and workers' comp class.

- Pay types (see Figure 8-5), which include the amount you pay the employee (hourly, salaried, or commission only), along with time-off pay policies and additional pay types.

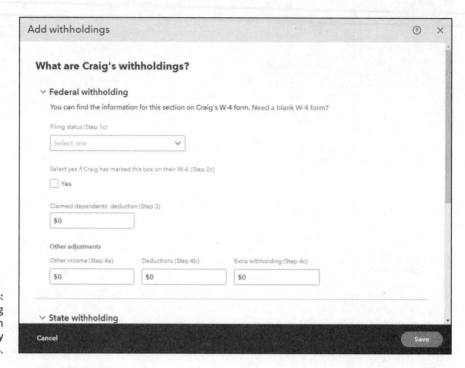

FIGURE 8-4:
Tax withholding information provided by federal Form W-4.

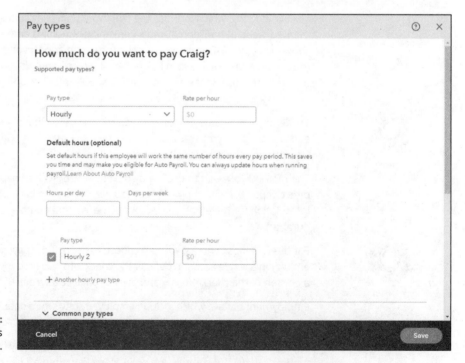

FIGURE 8-5:
The Pay Types window.

WARNING

Make sure to pay close attention when working in the How Much Do You Want to Pay section. For hourly employees, QuickBooks makes it easy and intuitive to enter regular time. Make sure to scroll down on this page and enable any other types of pay that the employee could accrue, such as overtime, holiday pay, bonuses, and so on. If you don't enable the fields here, you won't be able to enter the amounts when you process payroll.

- Deductions or contributions (add in whether the employee has any).

8. **When you finish supplying the employee's information, click Done.**

   The Your Team page appears again, listing active employees, as shown in Figure 8-2. On this page, you can edit employees, add employees, and start a payroll. At this point, you probably should add the rest of your employees.

Setting payroll preferences

In addition to adding employees, you should review payroll preferences and set up payroll taxes. You won't be able to process your payroll and payroll tax returns fully until you complete all the setup fields.

To review payroll preferences, choose Settings ⇨ Payroll Settings (Your Company column) to display the Payroll Settings page, shown in Figure 8-6.

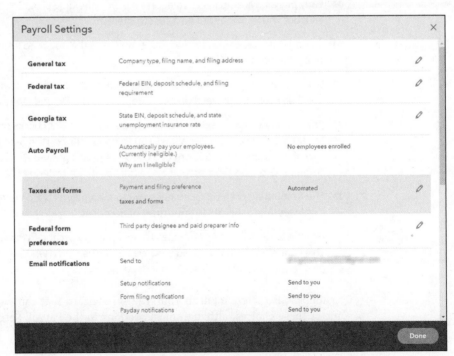

FIGURE 8-6: The Payroll Settings page.

The page contains a series of sections that you can use to review or establish various settings related to payroll. Understanding this page may make you feel less overwhelmed by what you see:

>> General Tax allows you to edit your company type, filing name, and filing address, as well as change your first payroll date if necessary.

>> Federal Tax allows you to indicate your Employer Identification Number (EIN), opt out of workers' comp offers from Intuit partners, and specify a filing requirement and deposit schedule.

>> Special federal programs such as the CARES Act may appear here if payroll tax deferrals or other relief is available.

>> A state tax section allows you to specify your state EIN, payroll tax deposit schedule, and state unemployment rates.

>> The Auto Payroll option indicates if you have any employees set up on automatic payroll.

>> The Federal Forms Preference enables you to designate third parties and paid preparers authorized to represent you before the Internal Revenue Service.

>> Email notifications allow you to opt in or out of payroll-related email notifications.

>> Early pay allows employees to access a payday lending program, at no cost to you, but you know there'll be a cost to them.

>> Shared Data allows you to give your employees the option to import their W-2 data into TurboTax.

>> Bank Accounts requires you to connect your bank account to remit deductions, pay your employees via direct deposit, and e-file and e-pay your taxes.

>> Printing allows you to specify whether you want to print checks on plain paper (assuming that your printer allows you to use a MICR cartridge to generate the row of numbers at the bottom of a check) or on preprinted QuickBooks-compatible checks. This section also offers a link for ordering checks.

>> The Accounting preference enables you to map payroll tax payments, expenses, and liabilities to your chart of accounts.

TIP

Be sure to set aside a few minutes to review every section in Payroll Settings. This review will help you avoid surprises and frustration when you make a tax payment or attempt to e-file near a deadline.

QuickBooks also offers a Fill In Your Tax Info wizard that can walk you through some of these choices, although most sections in the Payroll Settings screen are limited to a few fields at a time.

Setting up payroll taxes

Before you start using payroll, you should also review the to-do list on the Payroll Overview page, shown in Figure 8-7. If you've been completing steps as you've read through this chapter, your to-do list may look like Figure 8-7.

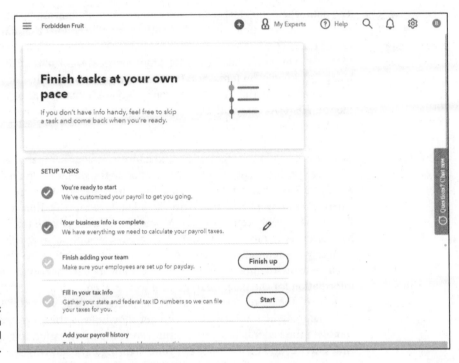

FIGURE 8-7:
The to-do list on the Payroll Overview page.

As shown in the figure, you can click Edit to edit any data that you've already entered, or you can click Start next to add a workers' comp policy. A wizard first asks you to choose between Yes, I'm Covered and No, I Don't Have It. If you choose No, QuickBooks offers to help you find a policy, or you can opt to do the work yourself. If you choose Yes, you're asked whether you want to connect your policy to QuickBooks. If you do, select the checkbox titled Help Me Add My Policy to QuickBooks and then click Next. If you skip the checkbox and click Next, you return to the to-do list.

At this point, you can use the Fill In Your Tax Info wizard to set up your payroll by clicking Start. The wizard first asks you to confirm your general business info, such as your company's legal name and address, and company type. Click Next to continue to the next screen.

The next step in the list relates to workers' compensation insurance. If workers' compensation insurance is required in your state, QuickBooks asks you whether you're already covered or whether you'd like a quote on a policy that integrates with QuickBooks Payroll. You can connect your workers' compensation policy or simply click Next.

TIP

The date when you start using QuickBooks Payroll determines the "as of" date of historical information you need to collect and determines that date to be the first day of the current quarter. Try to start using QuickBooks on January 1 of any year; that way, you don't need to enter any historical information. If you can't start using QuickBooks on January 1, try to start using it on the first day of an accounting period, either the first day of your company's fiscal year or the first day of a month. Historical payroll transactions can be summarized before that date but must be entered in detail after that date.

Next, you provide the legal name and address of your company, as well as federal and state tax information. After you complete the General screen, a single Federal and State Tax Details page appears if you indicated that you're a new employer. Existing employers see the more detailed Federal Tax Info screen, shown in Figure 8-8. Supply your federal EIN, and confirm the payroll tax form you use and how often you must remit payroll taxes. You should also specify whether your company is a federally recognized not-for-profit organization that isn't required to pay federal unemployment taxes. Also indicate whether you want to share your information for the purpose of getting workers' comp insurance offers. When you click Next, the State Tax Details form appears; provide your state tax ID number and unemployment information. I'm not showing you this page because when you complete the Federal Tax page, Intuit sends the information to the Internal Revenue Service, and I don't need any folks wearing dark suits and sunglasses knocking on my door because I submitted fake data. Click Done to complete this part of the to-do list.

TIP

Some of the figures in the remainder of this chapter are from the sample company in QuickBooks, because there's no way to process payroll without providing valid information, which makes it hard on an author writing about a mythical company.

WARNING

If you enter data in a field incorrectly, the wizard can appear to be broken or frozen. Scroll back up to look for any fields marked in red. You can't progress through the wizard until you clear up input errors such as indicating that you have an employee who works 40 hours a day or 8 days a week (instead of 8 hours a day and 5 days a week).

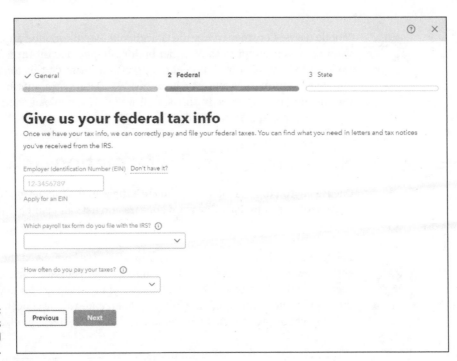

The final task in the Payroll Setup to-do list is to link your bank account. This step is required because as of this writing, QuickBooks automatically deposits your payroll taxes for you and files your payroll tax forms. This means you can't deposit your payroll taxes or file your payroll returns on your own, and hey, who really wants to, anyway? Ceding control does mean that you'll need to plan accordingly to ensure that your bank account has sufficient funds to cover both payroll and the tax deposits.

You can use the links on the Payroll Tax Center screen to change any of the settings you provided as you worked through the checklist.

Preparing Payroll

Processing payroll in QuickBooks Online involves a three-step process:

1. Record paycheck information.
2. Review paycheck information.
3. Generate paychecks.

TIP

Mobile users: Consider trying the QuickBooks Payroll mobile app, which you can use to pay your employees. You can optionally pay payroll taxes and file payroll tax forms electronically if you opt out of letting Intuit do this for you, and review employee information and paycheck history. Data syncs automatically between the mobile app and your Intuit payroll account. Download the free mobile app from the Apple App Store or from the Google Play Store.

Recording payroll information

Choose Payroll link ⇨ Employees and click the Run Payroll button to start processing payroll. The Run Payroll wizard appears and lists all your employees, as shown in Figure 8-9.

WARNING

The Run Payroll button doesn't appear until you've completed the tax setup step, entered your payroll history, and depending upon your automation choices, connected your bank account. Check the bottom of the setup list for any required tasks that you haven't completed. If you try to do an end-run by choosing + New ⇨ Payroll, you're simply returned unceremoniously back to the payroll setup list.

FIGURE 8-9:
Use this screen to enter payroll information for your employees.

TIP

Click the arrow next to Run Payroll to review a Bonus Only option for generating bonus checks. You can enter bonus amounts as net pay, meaning you specify how much you want the employee to receive, and QuickBooks works backwards to figure out the gross pay, or you can choose the As gross pay option and have QuickBooks calculate the net pay.

Verify the bank account from which you'll pay employees and double-check the pay period and pay date. By default, a checkmark appears to the left of each employee scheduled to be paid, but you can remove the check if appropriate. Enter the hours that any hourly employees worked during the pay period.

TIP

You can squeeze more employees onscreen by choosing Settings ⇨ Compact just above the top-right corner of the employee list.

Enabling employee time tracking

In QuickBooks Online Essentials or higher, you can set up time-tracking users who can log in with limited privileges that enable them to record time activity (and do nothing else). Alternatively, QuickBooks Payroll Premium and Elite offer the QuickBooks Time Tracker app (previously called TSheets), which allows workers to use a free mobile app to log their time. Your employees and contractors will be notified automatically when you provide their email addresses in the employee setup screens.

If you want to use the time tracking built into QuickBooks Online, you need to set up the affected employees as users:

1. **Choose Settings ⇨ Manage Users ⇨ Add User ⇨ Time Tracking Only.**

2. **Click Next, select an employee (or vendor), and then provide an email address.**

3. **Click Next and then Finish to send an invitation email.**

Your employees (or vendors) will create a QuickBooks Online account if necessary. Once they log in they'll be presented with a summary screen that shows hours for the current week and month. When your employees then click Add Time, they have three options:

>> Weekly: Enables employees to complete or add to a weekly time sheet.

>> Single Activity: Enables employees to record a single time-related activity.

>> Go To Report: Displays the Time Activities by Employee Detail report.

See Chapter 12 if you want to use the Project feature to track time and other transactions in QuickBooks Online Plus or Advanced subscription. In that case, you can create time sheets without using QuickBooks Payroll and view hours entered on time sheets by time-tracking employees. To do so, click the + New button on the left-menu bar, select Weekly Time Sheet, and then select an employee. Or, run the Time Activity by Employee report by clicking the Reports link on the left menu bar and searching for Time Activities by Employee Detail. You can customize the report to display any time frame that you want. I cover reports in more detail in Chapter 14.

Reviewing and generating payroll checks

When one of everyone's favorite days of the month, known as payday, has come around on the calendar, it's time to process payroll:

1. **Choose Payroll from the left menu bar.**

The Payroll Overview page appears.

2. **Click the Let's Go button beneath the large It's Time to Run Payroll banner.**

QuickBooks really doesn't want you to miss payday. Your employees don't either. The Run Payroll page appears to help you with this process.

3. **Enter regular pay hours and an optional memo.**

Your active employees appear in individual rows. If you need to override federal or state withholdings for a single paycheck, click Edit at the right-hand side of an employee's row.

REMEMBER

QuickBooks only shows you fields for pay types that you've enabled within each employee's record. Infrequent pay types, such as holiday pay or bonuses, can suddenly feel like a pop quiz when there's no place to enter the information. To enable additional pay types on the fly, click the employee's name on the Run Payroll page, and then scroll down to the How Much Do You Pay section. Within this page, you see checkboxes for enabling additional pay types.

4. **Click Preview Payroll.**

If you need more time, click the arrow on the Preview Payroll button and choose Save for Later to save your work in progress rather than abandoning a payroll run completely.

5. **Use the Review and Submit page shown in Figure 8-10 to make sure everything looks in order.**

Click Edit next to each employee's Net Pay amount if you need to edit their check, or click the Compare to Last icon to display a chart that compares this paycheck to the employee's previous check.

Run Payroll: Every month

Review and Submit

$5,044.63
TOTAL PAYROLL COST

$3,419.65
NET PAY

$913.85
EMPLOYEE

$711.13
EMPLOYER

1
Paper check for $3,419.65
Deliver these paychecks by 08/19/2022

Pay period: 07/18/2022 to 08/17/2022   **Pay date:** 08/19/2022

EMPLOYEE	PAY METHOD	TOTAL HOURS	TOTAL PAY	EMPLOYEE TAXES	NET PAY	COMPARE TO LAST
Maule, Craig	Paper check	173.34	$4,333.50	$913.85	$3,419.65 ✎	
TOTAL		173.34	$4,333.50	$913.85	$3,419.65	

Back   Preview payroll details   Submit payroll ▼

FIGURE 8-10:
Reviewing paychecks before generating them.

WARNING

If you use the Compare to Last Payroll page, make sure that you click the Close (X) button in the upper-right hand corner. If you're like me and press the Escape key to close windows on your computer, you'll not only close the Compare to Last Payroll page, but you'll cancel your payroll run as well.

6. **Optional: Click Preview Payroll Details, as shown in Figure 8-10.**

This command is a little tricky as it doesn't look clickable but is. A detailed report shows every aspect of your employee's compensation, withholdings and deductions, and any employer costs such as the employer portion of payroll taxes.

7. **Click Submit Payroll to finalize your payroll.**

If you have any issues that you need to resolve before submitting your payroll, you can click the arrow beside Submit Payroll and choose Save for Later.

8. **The Payroll Is Done page appears.**

Hold your horses, though; you might not be completely done yet. If you use direct deposit and don't need to print pay stubs, you can skip the next two steps. Otherwise, you still have some unfinished business to attend to.

9. **Optional: Click Auto-Fill to assign check numbers, or manually enter check numbers if you use handwritten checks.**

If you happen to catch a last-minute issue, you can click an employee's pay amount to display a screen from which you can edit their check. Payroll isn't over until it's over.

10. **Optional: Click Print Pay Stubs to preview paychecks and stubs and print them, as shown in Figure 8-11.**

This report appears in an additional browser tab.

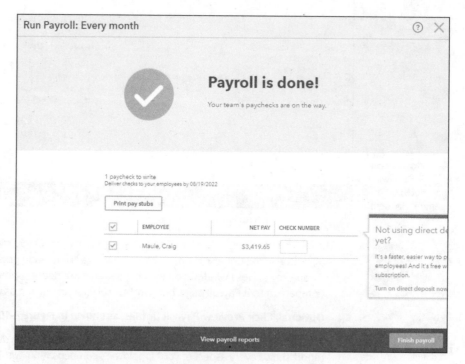

Run Payroll: Every month

Payroll is done!

Your team's paychecks are on the way.

1 paycheck to write
Deliver checks to your employees by 08/19/2022

Print pay stubs

	EMPLOYEE	NET PAY	CHECK NUMBER
☑	Maule, Craig	$3,419.65	

Not using direct d
yet?

It's a faster, easier way to p
employees! And it's free w
subscription.

Turn on direct deposit now

View payroll reports   Finish payroll

FIGURE 8-11:
When you don't direct-deposit paychecks, you see a page like this one.

11. **Optional: Click View Payroll Reports.**

The Your Payroll Reports Are Ready page allows you to pick the reports that you want to export to Excel. Each report is placed on a separate worksheet that you can open in Microsoft Excel or Google Sheets. Click OK to close this page.

When you open your payroll report workbook, you could encounter a warning prompt in Excel that informs you that the file format and extension don't match, and that the file could be corrupted or damaged. You can safely click Yes to open the report. The geeky details are that the programmers at Intuit are generating a workbook that has an .xls file, but the workbook itself is in the modern .xlsx format. In short, there's nothing to see here. Click Yes and move along.

12. **Click Finish Payroll.**

Take a deep breath. Now, my friend, you are truly done with payroll.

You can click Edit at the right edge of the line for any employee to see the details associated with the employee's paycheck. If necessary, you can change certain paycheck details, such as hours worked and federal/state tax amounts.

If you pay your employees by direct deposit, expect next-day deposits for Payroll Core, or same-day deposits for Premium or Elite for transactions initiated by 7 a.m. Pacific time.

Establishing or correcting payroll exemptions

Although it's unlikely you'll need to, you can establish payroll tax exemptions when necessary by following these steps:

1. **Choose Payroll ⇨ Employees and select the name of the employee whose status you need to change.**

2. **In the Tax Withholding section of the Employee Details page that appears, click the Edit icon to edit the employee's tax withholding information, as shown in Figure 8-12.**

3. **On the What Are [Employee's] Withholding page, scroll down, and expand Tax Exemptions, as shown in Figure 8-13.**

As shown in Figure 8-14, the Employee screen has been revamped to include a Profile tab, which I walk you through in Chapter 4. The Paycheck List tab, as you might surmise, includes a list of paychecks. The Documents tab, as of this writing, only allows you to view and download or print Form W-4, which is predicated on the inputs you made on the Profile tab. A fourth tab enables you to enter notes.

4. **Click Done when you finish editing.**

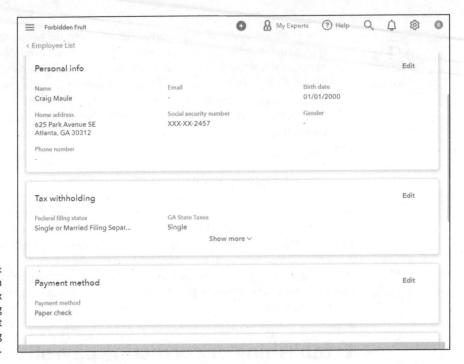

FIGURE 8-12:
Click the Edit icon in the Tax Withholding section to edit withholding information.

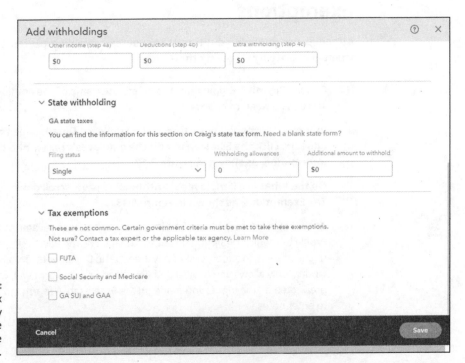

FIGURE 8-13:
Click Tax Exemptions only when you are certain they are applicable.

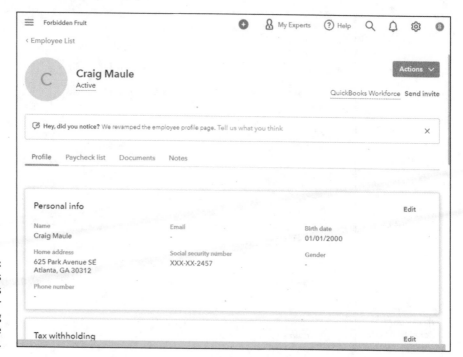

FIGURE 8-14:
QuickBooks
Payroll includes
four tabs for
managing
employee
information.

TIP

To void or delete a paycheck, click Paycheck List in the top-right corner of the Employee page, select a paycheck, and then click the Void or Delete button above the list. A series of questions helps you get the job done.

Printing payroll reports

When you complete payroll, you may want to print payroll-related reports. Choose Reports ⇨ Reports (Business Overview ⇨ Reports) on the left menu bar to display the Reports page. Scroll down to the payroll reports, shown in Figure 8-15. Along the way, you may see an Employees section that has reports related to time tracking.

You can click any payroll report to print it to the screen and, subsequently, to your printer. See Chapter 14 for more details.

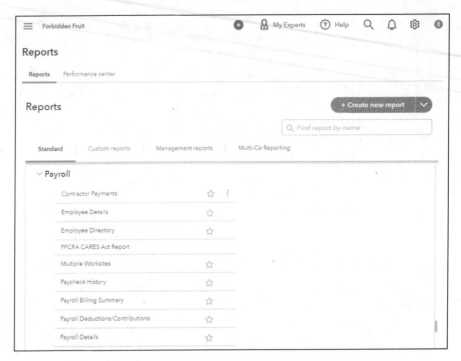

FIGURE 8-15:
Scroll down the Reports page to locate payroll reports.

Managing Payroll Taxes

As I mention at the beginning of this chapter, the payroll process doesn't end with preparing and producing paychecks. On a schedule determined by the IRS, you need to remit payroll taxes and file payroll tax returns, not to mention state and in some cases local payroll tax returns.

Paying payroll taxes

Using rules established by the IRS, most employers pay payroll taxes semiweekly, monthly, or quarterly, depending on the amount you owe (called your *payroll tax liability*). All versions of QuickBooks Payroll now include the option of automated tax deposits and forms, so your payroll tax compliance can be automated, or you can file your returns on your own. Payroll Premium and Elite handle local taxes where applicable.

To manage how payroll taxes are paid:

1. **Choose Settings ⇨ Payroll Settings ⇨ Taxes and Forms, and then click the Edit button.**

2. **Clear the Automate Taxes and Forms option if you *don't* want QuickBooks to handle your taxes and forms for you.**

3. **Optional: If you're handling taxes on your own, choose between I'll Initiate Payments and Filings using QuickBooks or I'll Pay and File the Right Agencies Through Their Website or by Mail, as shown in Figure 8-16.**

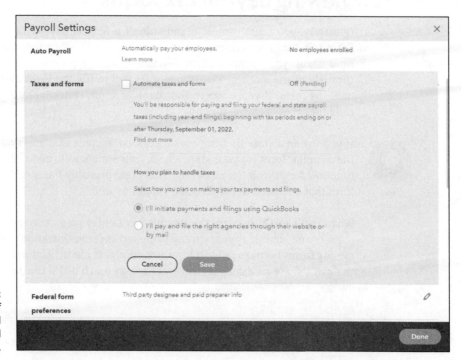

FIGURE 8-16:
How to opt out of
automatic payroll
tax payments and
form filings.

WARNING

Don't wait until the 11th hour to file payroll tax returns, because you may end up with late filings due to buffers needed for both electronic filing and electronic payments.

You must make federal tax deposits by electronic funds transfer by connecting your bank account to QuickBooks Online. If you opt out of this service, you need to make federal tax deposits using the Electronic Federal Tax Payment System (EFTPS; www.eftps.gov), a free service provided by the U.S. Department of the Treasury. QuickBooks Payroll doesn't use EFTPS, but pays directly on your behalf. For this reason, you need to complete and sign IRS Form 8655 (Reporting Agent Authorization) before your tax deposits and form can be filed on your behalf.

To see your payroll taxes that will be paid, choose Taxes ⟹ Payroll Tax to display the Payroll Tax Center. Normally, I'd show you what this page looks like, but I don't here because I'm not using a real company. I can tell you that once you've paid employees, the Payroll Tax Center displays taxes that are due, along with their due dates and e-payment cutoff dates. You can preview how much you owe by printing the Payroll Tax Liability report; click the View Your Tax Liability Report link on the Payroll Tax Center page.

Viewing payroll tax forms

Quarterly, you must complete and submit a federal payroll tax return by using Form 941, which identifies the total wages you paid, when you paid them, and the total taxes you withheld and deposited with appropriate taxing authorities throughout the quarter. The IRS permits you to file the form electronically or to mail the form. If you connect your bank account, QuickBooks Payroll automatically files these returns for you.

TIP

If you live in a state that imposes a personal income tax, you typically also must file a similar form for your state; check your state's website for the rules you need to follow for payroll tax reporting. Your state probably has a state unemployment form that you need to prepare and submit as well.

When you click Filings on the Payroll Tax Center page, the reports you need to prepare and submit appear. In my sample company, QuickBooks refused to show me any forms because I didn't have real employer identification numbers to enter, so I can't share an example with you here, as much as I'd like to.

Paying Contractors

Paying contractors is pretty much a straightforward experience. You can wait until you receive a bill from a contractor, enter it, and then pay it, as described in Chapter 7. But to ensure that you can accurately report payments you made to contractors, you need to ensure that they're set up as vendors who will receive Form 1099-NEC. I'll call these folks *1099-eligible contractors* going forward.

TIP

The IRS has reactivated Form 1099-NEC as a reporting vehicle for compensation paid to contractors. Previously, nonemployee compensation was reported in Box 7 of Form 1099-MISC. Now you report these amounts on Form 1099-NEC.

REMEMBER

I use the term *1099-eligible* because if you hire someone as a contractor but don't pay that person at least $600 — the threshold established by the IRS — technically, you don't have to produce a 1099 for that contractor. Further, if you don't pay a contractor more than $600, QuickBooks doesn't show payments to that contractor on certain reports.

1099-eligible contractors are people who work for you but who aren't your employees. Specifically, the IRS distinguishes between 1099-eligible contractors and employees based on whether you, the employer, have the means and methods of accomplishing the work or simply have the right to control and direct the result of the work. If you have the means and methods to accomplish the work, the person who works for you is an employee, not an independent 1099-eligible contractor. If you're at all uncertain, ask your accountant.

In this section, I focus on setting up 1099-eligible contractors, paying them (without using direct deposit), reporting on 1099 payments you've made, and preparing 1099s for those of your contractors who need them.

TIP

If you use QuickBooks Payroll, you can pay contractors (as well as employees) via direct deposit for a fee is $5 per contractor per month. First, you must complete direct-deposit setup for your company's payroll subscription, which involves supplying the routing and bank-account information for paying contractors and employees. To set up a contractor as a direct-deposit recipient, choose Workers⇨Contractors. On the page that appears, click the Check It Out button, and follow the onscreen directions to add a contractor's banking information and initiate payment the same way you would for employees if you're willing to pay a monthly fee on a per-contractor basis. Keep in mind that it may be far less expensive to add ACH capabilities to your bank account and pay contractors directly unless you only have one or two contractors that you'd like to pay this way. If you're not using QuickBooks Payroll you can subscribe to Contractor Payments for $15/month to pay up to 20 contractors, plus another $2/month for each additional contractor that you add. All plans include 1099 e-filing.

Setting up 1099-eligible contractors

You can set up 1099-eligible contractors in two ways, with the same result:

>> You can use the information in Chapter 4 to set up a new vendor. Make sure that you select the Track Payments for 1099 checkbox.

>> You can use the Contractors page to set up a contractor. Any contractor you add from this page becomes a 1099-eligible contractor.

Because you also saw how to set up new employees in Chapter 4, I'll focus here on using the Contractors page to create a new contractor. Follow these steps:

1. Choose Payroll ⇨ Contractors.

The Contractors page appears.

2. Click the Add Your First Contractor button.

3. **Provide the contractor's name, and if you want the contractor to complete their profile, enter their email address.**

TIP

If you provide the contractor's email address, Intuit contacts the contractor and gets their 1099 information for you, including the contractor's signature on the W-9 form that the IRS requires you to keep on file. Intuit uses the form information to populate the contractor's record and leaves a PDF of the W-9 form for you on the Contractors page (Documents section).

4. **Click Add Contractor.**

The contractor's details page appears.

5. **Click Add (or Waiting for Info if you opted to send the contractor an email) to provide details about the Contractor Type, as shown in Figure 8-17.**

This information is used when you prepare 1099s for the year.

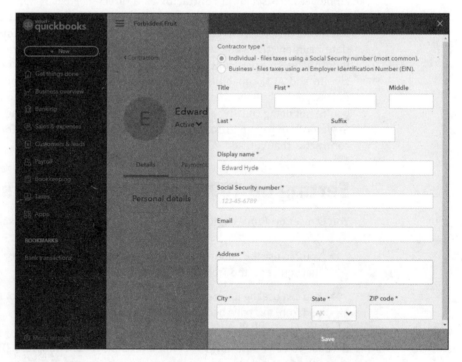

FIGURE 8-17:
Provide the Contractor Type information needed for Form 1099 preparation.

6. **Click Save.**

The contractor's details page appears again, showing the details you just provided.

Paying contractors

You pay contractors the same way you pay any other vendors; see Chapter 5 for details on entering bills, expense transactions, and checks. If a contractor sends you a bill, you can enter it and pay it when appropriate.

Reporting on 1099 vendor payments

Here comes the tricky part. QuickBooks offers 1099 Contractor Summary and 1099 Contractor Detail reports, but both reports show information only on outstanding bills — *not* on bills you've paid. You can think of these reports as being accounts-payable reports for contractors.

To view payments you've made to 1099-eligible contractors, you need to do the following:

>> Make sure that you've set up your company to prepare 1099s.

>> Prepare the 1099 Transaction Detail report, which shows contractors whom you've paid more than $600, the IRS-specified threshold.

REMEMBER

The report excludes payments you make to contractors by using a credit card, because you aren't responsible for providing a 1099-NEC for credit card payments. Instead, the contractor's payment processor will provide the contractor a Form 1099-K.

QuickBooks e-files 1099s with the IRS on your behalf, e-delivers 1099s to your contractors, and prints and mails hard copies of 1099s to your contractors. I regret to inform you that you pay a fee for these services, one way or another. There's no additional fee if you subscribe to QuickBooks Payroll or Contractor Payments, otherwise here's what you'll be on the hook for:

>> **1099s filed by January 15:** $12.99 for your first 3 forms, $2.99 for each additional form up to 20, and no charge for 1099s beyond the first 20. If you had 25 forms to file, your cost would be $63.82 ($12.99 + $2.99 x 17 + $0 x 5).

>> **1099s filed on or after January 16:** $14.99 for your first 3 forms, $3.99 for each additional form up to 20, and no charge for 1099s beyond the first 20. If you had 25 forms to file, your cost would be $82.82 ($14.99 + $3.99 x 17 + $0 x 5).

You can also order a 1099 kit that allows you to print your 1099s on paper. As of this writing, pricing starts at $58.99 for ten forms, so opting in to the e-filing method is cheaper and requires much less involvement on your part.

Because of the new e-filing automation in QuickBooks, you can't access the 1099 process whenever you like; you have to wait for certain time frames during the year to carry out these steps:

1. **Choose Payroll ⇨ Contractors.**

   The Contractors page appears, listing the 1099-eligible contractors you have set up.

2. **Click the Prepare 1099s button in the middle of the page.**

   The resulting screen explains what happens as you go through the process.

3. **Click Let's Get Started.**

   Due to changes in QuickBooks, you may be able to process 1099s only during certain time frames. If you're outside one of those time frames, you'll see the dates when you can start preparing to file your 1099 forms. When you can click Let's Get Started, you're prompted to review and (if necessary) edit your company's name, address, and tax ID number.

   If you've partially completed the 1099 process, you see a Continue Your 1099s button instead of Let's Get Started.

4. **Click Next.**

   You're prompted to categorize payments you made to your contractors.

   In most cases, you check Box 7, Nonemployee Compensation, and then select an account from your Chart of Accounts list where you assigned your 1099-eligible contractor payments.

5. **Click Next.**

   On the next page, you can review information about the contractors you've set up. Only contractors who meet the $600 threshold appear on this page. You review the contractor's address, tax ID, and email address, and you can click Edit in the Action column if you need to make changes.

6. **When you finish reviewing contractor information, click Next.**

   The total payment you've made to each contractor appears for you to review; you can print the information shown on the page or view a report of the information.

You've now set up your company sufficiently to view reports on 1099 information.

7. **If you're not ready to prepare 1099 forms, click Save and Finish Later.**

You can print the 1099 Transaction Detail report at any time during the year. This report gives you detailed information about the amounts you've paid to 1099-eligible vendors who met the IRS's $600 threshold. Click Reports on the navigation bar, and enter **1099** in the search box to locate the report.

REMEMBER

If you paid any of your 1099-eligible vendors by credit card, those payments won't appear in the 1099 Transaction Detail report because payments made by credit card are reported to the IRS by the credit card company.

Preparing 1099s

There's really not much to say here; you follow the steps in the preceding section except Step 7; click Finish Preparing 1099s and follow the onscreen instructions to print Form 1099s for you and for your contractors who qualify to receive them.

Chapter **9**

Working in Registers

I n Chapters 6 and 7, I show you how to enter transactions such as checks, sales receipts, invoices, customer payments, and more, while Chapter 8 shows you how to process payroll. I also show how you to search and filter existing transactions. In this chapter, I'll show you how to use registers to carry out these actions. As I explain, registers give you a bird's-eye view of transactions that affect certain accounts in your books. In accounting parlance, these are known as balance sheet accounts.

Understanding Registers

Registers are chronological lists of transactions for a particular account, and used to be maintained on paper before the advent of computers. Those of us of a certain age may recall dutifully maintaining paper checkbook registers for our personal checking accounts.

You can only view a register for the following account types:

» Bank

» Accounts Receivable

» Other Current Assets

» Fixed Assets

» Other Assets

» Accounts Payable

» Credit Card

» Other Current Liabilities

» Long-Term Liabilities

» Equity

Retained earnings, income, and expense accounts don't have registers. But you can run reports that show the transactions within these accounts, which is fairly close to having a register. To view the register for a particular account, follow these steps:

1. **Choose Settings ⇨ Accounting ⇨ Chart of Accounts in the Your Company column.**

   If necessary, click the See Your Chart of Accounts button to display your chart of accounts.

   TIP

2. **Click the View Register link in the Action column shown in Figure 9-1 to display the register of your choice.**

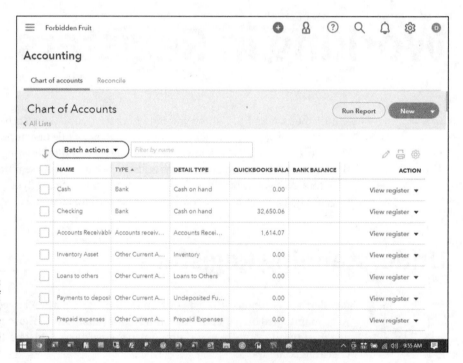

FIGURE 9-1:
Use the Chart of Accounts page to open a particular account's register.

3. **The register appears, as shown in Figure 9-2.**

   Click Back to Chart of Accounts at the top left-hand corner to close the register.

   If you've connected your bank account to QuickBooks, the bank balance appears alongside the bank account name, while the book balance always appears in the top-right corner of the register. Differences between the two balances represent transactions that you've recorded but that haven't cleared the bank yet.

   REMEMBER

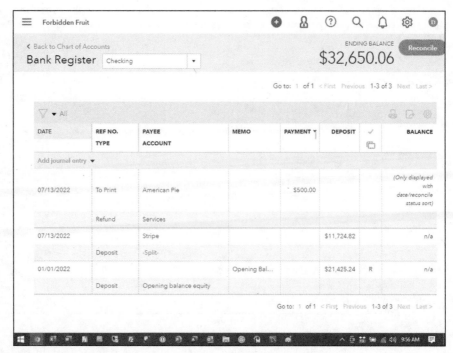

FIGURE 9-2: A typical bank account register.

Within the register, column headings identify the information contained in each column for every transaction, and at the right edge of a register page, you see a running balance for the account. All the transactions in a bank account register affect that bank account and at least one other account on your Chart of Accounts (which QuickBooks often euphemistically refers to as a *category* on most transaction screens), as dictated by the rules of accounting. (*Double-entry bookkeeping*, a founding principle of accounting, means that every transaction affects at least two accounts.) At the right edge of a register page is the Balance column, which has the running balance for the account as long as the register is sorted by date.

Customizing the Register View

You can also show or hide columns in most registers. Click the Table Settings button above the Balance column on the right edge of the register. As shown in Figure 9-3, you can toggle certain columns on or off.

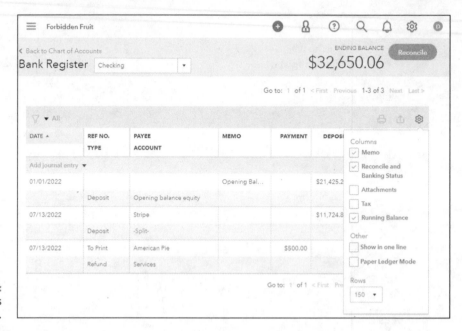

FIGURE 9-3:
Table Settings
menu.

Typically, a QuickBooks register displays transactions in two-line format, but the Show in One Line option on the Table Settings menu enables you to collapse the register to a single line for each transaction when you click the Table Settings button and select the Show in One Line checkbox. This action may hide the Memo, Reconcile, and Banking Status columns in certain registers. You can turn these fields back on by clearing the Show in One Line checkbox on the Table Settings menu.

The next command on the Table Settings menu enables you to kick your ledger old school by presenting it in Paper Ledger Mode:

1. **Click the Settings icon above the Balance column.**

2. **In the Settings menu, click the checkbox for Paper Ledger Mode.**

   As shown in Figure 9-4, the transactions appear in date order from oldest to newest.

That's right baby, we're gonna do our accounting like it's 1979. Of course, you can turn off Paper Ledger Mode by clearing the checkbox in Step 2. You can also enable or disable Show in One Line in conjunction with Paper Ledger Mode. The world is your oyster.

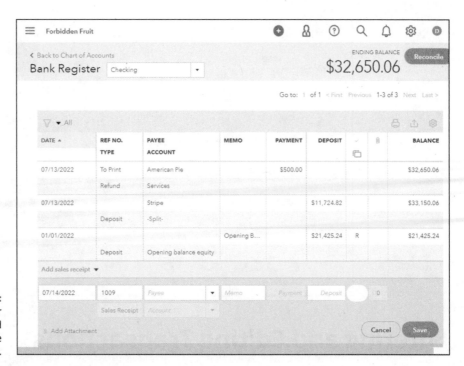

REMEMBER

Any customizations that you make in one register, such as changing the display to Paper Ledger Mode, are get applied to all your registers automatically.

The final command on the Table Settings menu allows you to control how many rows appear on a single page of your register. Click the Table Settings button and choose 50, 75, 100, 150, or 300.

TIP

First, Previous, Next, and Last links always appear above and below the right-hand side of your register to enable you to navigate forward and back through a multi-page register.

Finally, you can change the size of any column by positioning your mouse over the right-hand side of a column heading, such as in Figure 9-5, where I'm resizing the Memo column. Drag the double-headed arrow mouse pointer to the left to make the column narrower or to the right to make the column wider, just like in a spreadsheet. As you drag, a solid vertical line helps you determine the size of the column. Release the mouse button when the column reaches the size you want.

FIGURE 9-4:
Paper Ledger Mode enabled and Show in One Line disabled.

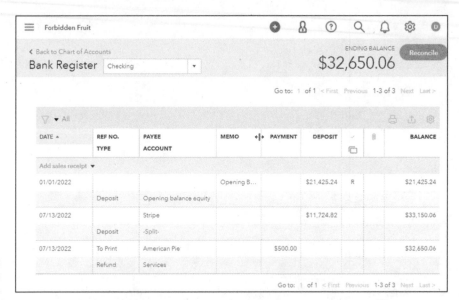

FIGURE 9-5:
Resizing a
column.

Entering and Editing Transactions

The Paper Ledger Mode, shown in Figure 9-5, shows a transaction entry area that appears at the bottom of most QuickBooks registers that offers a quick, easy way to enter simple transactions. This area limits you to a single transaction row, however, and you can't reference inventory items here. But if you need to enter a handwritten check or Venmo transaction quickly, then this is the place. Notice that the register in Figure 9-2 does not display a transaction input screen, but you can use the Add drop-down menu that appears just below the Date heading to open a transaction entry screen. The Add button remembers the last transaction type that you created.

Bank account registers enable you to add the following transaction types: check, deposit, sales receipt, receive payment, bill payment, refund, expense, transfer, or journal entry. Most other registers only allow you to directly record transfers and journal entries. The Transfer window shown in Figure 9-6 enables you to move funds between bank and/or equity accounts.

WARNING

Journal entries make direct adjustments to your books and are easy to book backwards, meaning that you enter what should be a debit into the credit column and vice versa. It's always best to defer to an accounting professional if you have any uncertainty about recording a journal entry.

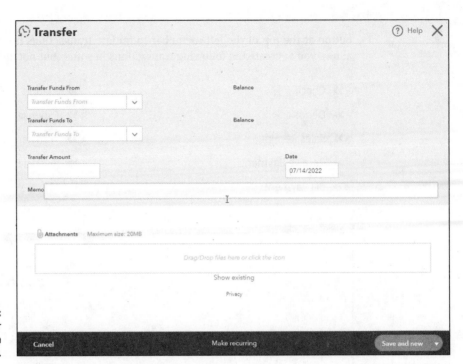

FIGURE 9-6:
A transfer transaction window.

REMEMBER

You can't enter transactions in the Accounts Receivable or Accounts Payable registers. Use the Invoice or Bill transaction windows, respectively, which you can access by clicking the New button at the top of the navigation bar.

Registers in most accounting programs reflect columns for debits and credits, but in Figure 9-7 you see columns for Payments and Deposits, and only a single row. Fortunately, a more traditional journal entry screen, shown in Figure 9-8, is available when you choose New ⇨ Journal Entries. *Always use this window when you want to record a journal entry.* The simplified journal entry transaction shown in Figure 9-7 defies accounting logic and raises the odds that you'll enter the journal entry incorrectly due to the confusing interface.

Entering transactions

If you consider yourself to have a strong accounting background, you can enter a variety of transactions in a register. Keep in mind that you're limited to a single row, which means you cannot divide a transaction among multiple accounts, nor can you reference inventory items. You can avoid all of these caveats by using the New button at the top of the left menu bar to initiate transactions instead. QuickBooks allows you to create the following transactions in some (but not all) registers:

- » Check
- » Deposit
- » Sales Receipt
- » Receive Payment
- » Bill Payment

- » Refund
- » Expense
- » Transfer
- » Journal Entry

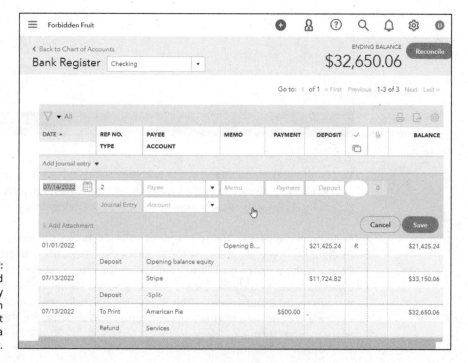

FIGURE 9-7:
The abbreviated journal entry transaction window that appears within a register.

QuickBooks suggests a default transaction type for a given register or remembers the last type of transaction that you entered in that register. If you want to change the transaction type, click the Add button to choose any of the transaction types in the preceding list. The Add button for transactions appears at the top of the register unless you activate Paper Ledger Mode, in which case the Add button moves to the bottom.

You'll be working blindly if you add certain transaction types, such as Receive Payment or Bill Payment, as you won't be able to see open invoices or bills. This means that amounts you entered are applied arbitrarily by QuickBooks.

WARNING

FIGURE 9-8:
A traditional journal entry transaction window.

To add a transaction to a register, follow these steps:

1. **Click the down arrow next to the Add button and choose a transaction type.**

   Today's date is filled in, and fields related to the transaction appear. Remember that you're limited to a single row when working within the register, and you cannot split amounts between more than two accounts, one of which is the account for the register that you're working in.

2. **Choose a transaction type.**

3. **Change the transaction date, if necessary.**

4. **Optional: Enter a reference number.**

   The Ref No. Type column shown in Figure 9-9 is disabled for certain types of transactions, such as deposits, transfers, and refunds.

5. **Optional: Enter a payee name, if permitted.**

   You can choose existing names from the list or add a new name on the fly.

6. **Choose an account if permitted.**

   You can't choose an account for certain transactions, such as sales receipts, bill payments, and refunds.

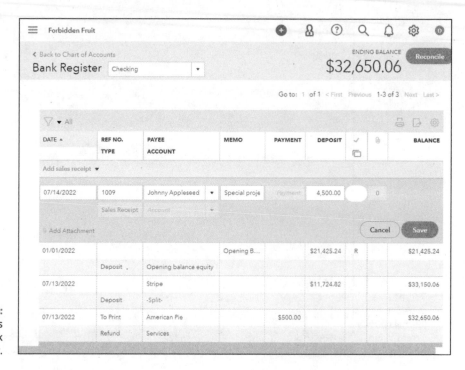

FIGURE 9-9:
Entering a sales receipt in a bank account register.

7. **Optional: Fill in the Memo field, if it's available for the transaction type you chose.**

   If the Memo column isn't shown in your register, click the Settings button above the Balance column, and toggle the checkbox. You can enable the Class and Location fields in the same fashion, depending on your preferences and subscription level.

8. **Enter an amount in the Payment or Deposit field.**

   QuickBooks sometimes disables one field or the other. Payment is disabled for Sales Receipts and Receive Payment transactions, for example, whereas Deposit is disabled for Bill Payment and Refund transactions.

9. **Modify Reconcile Status at your own peril.**

   The Reconcile and Banking Status column may, and perhaps should, be hidden in your register, but you can enable it as discussed earlier in this chapter. This field is blank, contains C for Cleared, or contains R for Reconciled. When the column is blank, the transaction is neither cleared nor reconciled. Although you can set the reconciliation status of a transaction here, doing so is one of those "not that you should, but you could" situations. You should modify the reconciliation status of a transaction only through the Reconcile screen in QuickBooks, as I discuss in Chapter 10.

WARNING

I'm so nice that I'll say it twice: Do not be tempted to adjust the reconciliation status of a transaction from this screen. Doing so adjusts the account's reconciled balance in a way that won't show up in reconciliation reports. You can quickly have a mess on your hands if you modify the reconciliation status outside the reconciliation process. Ask me how I know.

If the account is connected electronically to your financial institution, the Reconcile and Banking Status column indicates whether transactions were added or matched when transactions were downloaded via the account's bank feed. I discuss how to connect your bank account in Chapter 11.

10. **Optional: Click in the Attachments field if you want to link one or more electronic documents, and then click Add Attachment.**

If you've displayed it by way of the Table Settings menu, the Attachments column displays the number of attachments linked to a given document.

11. **Click the Save button.**

The transaction is saved and replaced by a blank transaction screen of the same type.

WARNING

You can't change the sales account for a sales receipt when entering a transaction directly in the checking register. You can edit transactions through the respective transaction form, however, which does enable you to change the account if necessary.

Editing a transaction

It's often remarkable what you see when you look at something in a new light. As you peruse a register, you may discover errors or missing data related to a particular transaction. To make revisions, follow these steps:

1. **Click on the transaction within the register.**

2. **Click the Edit button that appears to display the original transaction screen.**

It can be tempting to just make the adjustment directly in the register, and if you're a bookkeeper or accountant, then feel free. Otherwise, always click the Edit button and make your changes on the transaction screen instead of within the register to avoid solving one problem and inadvertently creating a new one.

Performing Other Register Activities

It's pretty useful to be able to add and edit transactions in a register, but wait, there's more! You can also sort and filter your transactions, create a printout of the register, or export the printout to a spreadsheet that you can access in Microsoft Excel or Google Sheets.

Sorting transactions

Looking for a transaction by skimming the register — eyeballing it — can be a nonproductive way of finding it. Instead, sorting the register based on any column can help you zero in on a particular transaction.

Click any column heading to sort the register in that order. Figure 9-2 shows transactions in the default order of newest to oldest, while the Paper Ledger Mode in Figure 9-5 lists transactions from oldest to newest. Regardless, you can click the Date column heading to toggle the order of the transactions or click the Payee column heading to sort transactions in alphabetical order by payee. Click the Payee column heading a second time to sort in reverse alphabetical order.

WARNING

You can sort by any column heading except Account, Foreign Currency Exchange Rate, Balance, Memo, and Attachment. Sorting on any column other than Date causes the Balance column to display "n/a" because the balances can't be computed in that order.

Filtering transactions

Filtering is a more effective means of sifting through a sea of transactions than sorting. To do so, click the Filter button that appears above the Date column to display the menu shown in Figure 9-10.

TIP

The current filter criteria appear to the right of the Filter button. The word All appears when no filter criteria have been set.

Here are some examples of filter criteria:

» Enter **1234** in the Find field to display all transactions with 1234 in the memo or reference field.

» Enter **$5000** or **5000** in the Find field to display all transactions that have a total of $5,000; don't enter commas for the thousands position.

» Enter **<$25** or **<25** in the Find field to display all transactions with amounts less than $25.

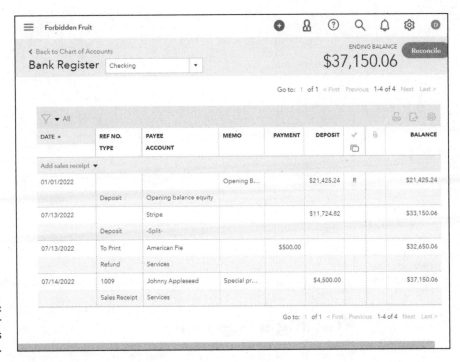

FIGURE 9-10:
You can filter transactions within a register.

You can fill any or all of the fields shown in Figure 9-10, which means that you could search for the Not Reconciled checks written to a particular vendor in a specific period.

REMEMBER

Unfortunately, you can't search for transactions between $500 and $1,000. Quick-Books accepts only a single criterion in the Find field and doesn't support <= or >=. Use <500.01 if you want to search for transactions that are less than or equal to 500. Invalid search criteria turn red within the filter field, almost as though they're radioactive.

Any transactions that meet the criteria you specify in the Filter window appear in the register after you click Apply. As shown in Figure 9-11, the filter criteria appear beside the Filter button. Click the Clear Filter/View All link to clear the filter and redisplay all transactions in the register.

REMEMBER

A bank account register may not be the best place to search for Receive Payment transactions if you use the Payments to Deposit Account (Undeposited Funds). The register reflects Deposit transactions that are comprised of one or more Receive Payment transactions. This means QuickBooks may display the message, "There are no transactions matching the selected criteria," for transactions that you know are in QuickBooks somewhere.

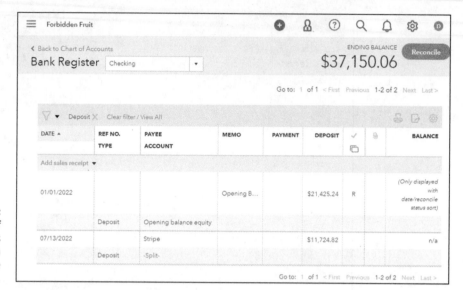

FIGURE 9-11:
A list of
transactions
based on criteria
specified in the
Filter window.

Printing a register

You can always generate an old-school paper copy of your register when necessary. To do so, click the Print button beside the register's Table Settings button above the Balance column. As shown in Figure 9-12, a Print tab appears, offering a preview of your report.

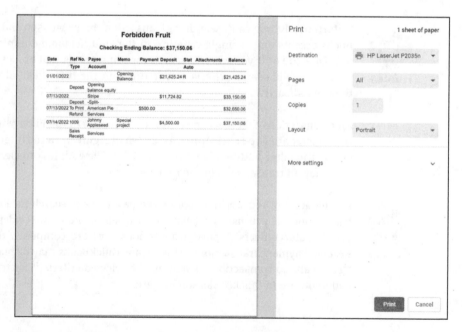

FIGURE 9-12:
Printing a
register.

On the right side of the tab, select the printer you want to use, and make any other necessary selections, such as pages to print, number of copies, and orientation. When you finish selecting settings, click Print. When the report finishes printing, you can close the Print tab to return to your electronic register.

TIP

You aren't restricted to printing to paper. You can choose Save As PDF or Microsoft Print to PDF on the Print tab to send your register to a PDF document. You can even choose Save to Google Docs if you sign in to Google Cloud Print.

Exporting a register

The Export to Excel button next to the Table Settings button shown in Figure 9-12 allows you to export the register to an Excel spreadsheet. You can open the resulting file in Microsoft Excel or Google Docs and then use the more robust filtering tools available in those platforms to perform more-granular searches than are possible in QuickBooks Online. In Chapter 15, I discuss ways to analyze QuickBooks data in Excel, and in Chapter 19, I show you how to automate Excel analysis with Power Query.

Chapter **10**

Administering Bank and Credit Card Accounts

I n this chapter, I show you not only how to set up bank and credit card accounts in QuickBooks, but also how to reconcile bank and credit card accounts. If you're wondering how to record credit card transactions in QuickBooks, see Chapter 7, as you record credit card transactions in the same fashion as you record transactions that post to your bank account.

Setting Up a Bank or Credit Card Account

In Chapter 2, I discuss adding new accounts to your chart of accounts, which QuickBooks sometimes confusingly refers to as categories. The steps for adding a bank or credit card account to QuickBooks are a little different than simply adding a revenue or expense account, so let's walk through the process.

1. Choose Settings ➪ Switch to Accountant View, unless you see Switch to Business View, in which case you can skip this step.

TIP

Trust me, you really want to switch to Accountant View for this task; otherwise, you are likely to get wildly confused, frustrated, or both.

2. **If necessary, choose Settings ⇨ Chart of Accounts from the Your Company column to display your chart of accounts.**

3. **Click the New button on the Chart of Accounts page to open the Account task pane, shown in Figure 10-1.**

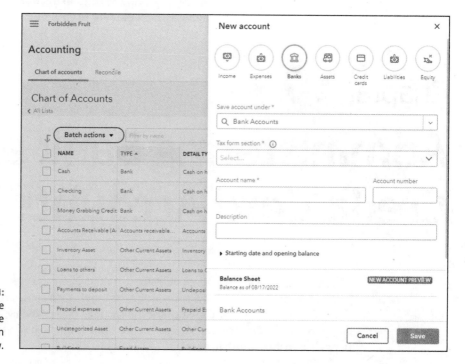

FIGURE 10-1: The task pane you use to create an account in Accountant View.

4. **Click either the Banks or Credit Cards icon at the top of the task pane, as appropriate.**

5. **Choose either Bank Account or Credit Card, as appropriate, from the Save Account Under list.**

6. **In the Tax Form Section, choose the account type that is most appropriate, which will probably be checking, money market, or savings; otherwise, choose Credit Card if you're adding a credit card.**

WARNING

If you create a credit card account in Business View, the Tax Form Section list is named Account Type and only shows you bank account types, with no option to choose credit card. If you forge ahead and choose a bank account type from the list, your credit card account then appears in the banking section of your chart of accounts instead of in the liabilities section near Accounts Payable.

7. **Fill in the Account Name field.**

WARNING

In Business View, the Account Name field is called Category Name, which might leave you scratching your head when you try to relate a Category Name to the name of a bank or credit card account. This is another reason to switch to Accountant View, at least temporarily, when creating bank or credit card accounts.

8. **Optional: If the Account Number field is shown, enter a general ledger account number for the new account.**

WARNING

Don't enter your credit card number in this field. The words *Account Number* refer to the general ledger account number, not the number on the face of your credit card.

9. **Optional: Enter a description for the account.**

I don't recommend entering the full account number here either, but it is safe to use the last four digits if you want to have a way to identify the account number. It's never good to leave your bank or credit card account numbers lying around in plain text when you can avoid it.

10. **Optional: Specify a currency if you enabled the multicurrency feature in your QuickBooks company.**

11. **Optional: Specify a start date to start tracking the account in QuickBooks.**

You can choose Beginning of This Year, Beginning of This Month, Today, or Custom Date. You need to enter any transactions that have posted to your bank or credit card account since this date.

12. **Optional: If you chose a start date then enter a starting balance in the Account Balance field.**

WARNING

If you enter a balance, QuickBooks updates both the account balance and the Opening Balance Equity account. Make sure to notify your accountant if you fill in the starting balance so that they can make any adjustments necessary to keep your books in sync with last year's tax return.

13. **Click Save.**

The Chart of Accounts page displays your new account in the list.

14. **Optional: If you switched from Business View to Accountant View and want to return to the left menu that you've become accustomed to, choose Settings ⇨ Switch to Business View.**

You can also stick with Accountant View if you find that the expanded menu hierarchy is easier to navigate. Don't worry, your secret is safe with me.

REMEMBER

You won't be able to reconcile your bank or credit card account until you enter any transactions that have occurred since the start date that you specified. In Chapter 4, I discuss how to record customer payments that post to your bank account, while Chapter 5 covers recording bills and expenses that you may have paid with your credit card.

Making a Bank Deposit

In Chapter 6, I discuss using the Payments to Deposit (or Undeposited Funds) account to record payments from customers. I strongly recommend that you use that when you record Receive Payment transactions as well. As you may surmise from the name, Payments to Deposit is simply a stopover along the way to your bank account. To create a bank deposit transaction, follow these steps:

1. **Click the New button and select Bank Deposit in the Other column.**

   The Bank Deposit transaction window appears, as shown in Figure 10-2. Existing payment transactions appear in the Select the Payments Included in This Deposit section. You can use the lines in the Add Funds to This Deposit section shown in Figure 10-3 to add new payment transactions that aren't associated with an outstanding invoice, such as refund checks, reimbursement payments, that check for $1.63 that you received from a class-action lawsuit settlement, and so on.

WARNING

   Don't try to record a payment from a customer for an outstanding invoice in the Add Funds to This Deposit section. Doing so doesn't mark an outstanding invoice as paid, so you may end up trying to collect it again. Instead, create a Receive Payment transaction (which I discuss in Chapter 6), which then appears in the Select the Payments Included in This Deposit section of the Bank Deposit transaction window.

2. **Choose the bank account into which you plan to deposit the payments, using the From Account drop-down list at the top of the window.**

3. **Select each transaction you want to include in the deposit in the Select the Payments Included in This Deposit section.**

4. **Optional: Specify a payment method for each transaction you intend to deposit.**

TIP

   Intuit Payments automatically posts deposits in a QB Payments section, which is collapsed by default for the benefit of users who don't rely on that service. If you have your own merchant account, credit card transaction receipts may get deposited in your bank account as often as daily. Make sure to record a separate deposit for each day so that the amounts mirror what's hitting your physical bank account. Then create a separate deposit to group any checks and cash payments into a bank deposit.

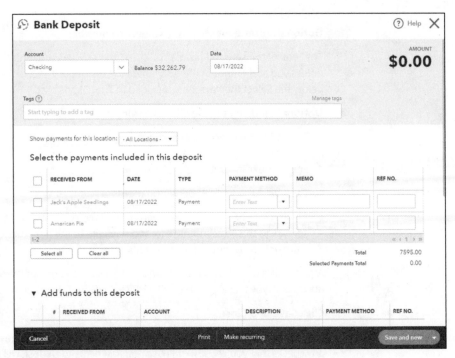

FIGURE 10-2:
Use the Bank Deposit transaction window to select payment transactions to deposit.

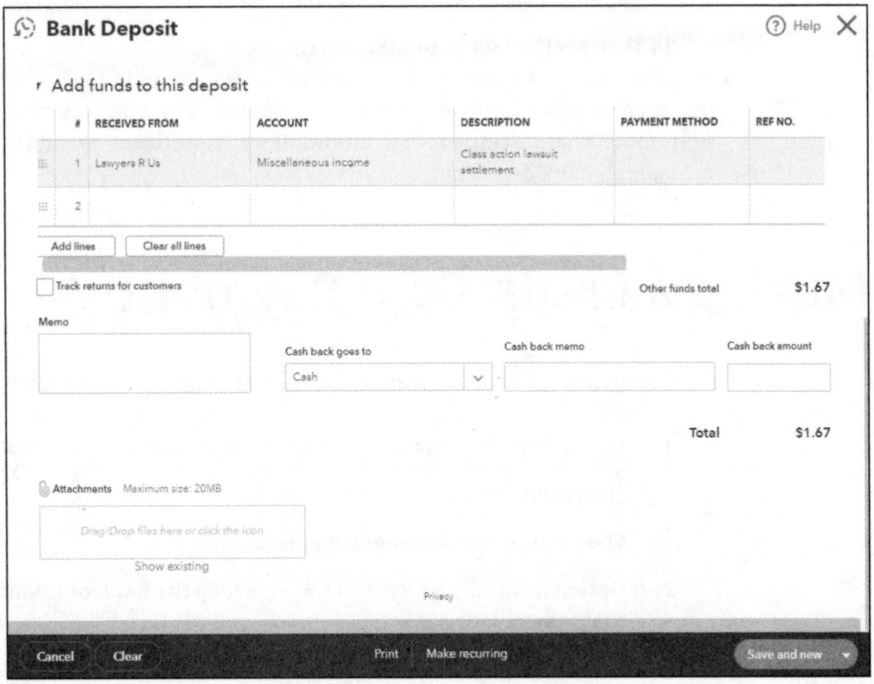

FIGURE 10-3:
Record payment amounts that are unrelated to customer invoices in the Add Funds to This Deposit section.

5. **Optional: Enter a memo and a reference number.**

   The total of the selected payments — and the amount you intend to deposit unless you add entries in the Add Funds to This Deposit section — appears below the Select the Payments Included in This Deposit list.

6. **Optional: Add any or all of the following:**

   - Memo for the deposit transaction itself, which is an additional level of documentation you can add apart from the memo field available on each line of the transaction.

   - Cash-back amount, account, and memo.

   - An attachment, such as a scanned copy of the paper deposit ticket. To do so, click in the Attachments box and navigate to the document, or drag the electronic copy into the Attachments box.

   Attachments must be no more than 20MB in size, and one of the following document types: CSV, DOC, GIF, JPEG, PDF, PNG, TIFF, XLSX, or XML.

   TIP

7. **Click Save and Close.**

   The Payments to Deposit (or Undeposited Funds) account balance is reduced by any checks that you chose in this deposit. Payments to Deposit will have a zero balance whenever you have deposited all of the checks that you have in hand.

All that's left to do is to take a trip to the bank. Or, if you're mobile-savvy, ask your banker whether you can deposit checks remotely via your mobile device. If you receive a significant number of paper checks, you may be able to sign up for a remote check scanner that eliminates a significant amount of drudgery from making bank deposits.

Making a Credit Card Payment

QuickBooks offers a dedicated screen for making credit card payments:

1. **Choose + New ⇨ Pay Down Credit Card from the Other column.**

   The Reconcile window appears, as shown in Figure 10-4.

2. **Choose or enter the name of your credit card.**

3. **Optional: Specify a payee name, typically the bank or financial institution that issued your card.**

4. **Enter your payment amount in the "How Much Did You Pay?" field.**

5. **Confirm the payment date.**

6. **Select your bank account from the "What Did You Use to Make This Payment?" field.**

7. **Optional: Expand the Memo and Attachments section to write a note about the transaction, and/or to include an attachment, such as a PDF copy of your credit card statement or an Excel spreadsheet (`.xlsx`) version of your statement that you downloaded from your provider.**

8. **Click Save and close, or Save and new if you have an additional credit card payment to make.**

TIP

I discuss entering credit card charges in Chapter 7.

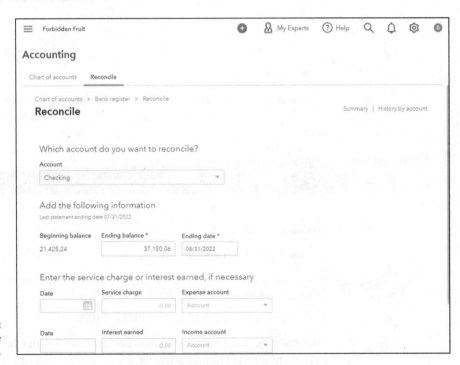

FIGURE 10-4:
The Reconcile window.

Recording a Credit Card Credit

Let's say that a refund gets posted to your credit card, such as for goods that you've returned. Nope, you're not going to enter a Credit Memo; that type of transaction relates to giving *your* customers a refund. Instead, you're looking to enter a Credit Card Credit. After you try saying that three times fast, carry out these steps to record the transaction.

1. **Choose + New ⇨ Credit Card Credit from the Vendor column.**

   The Credit Card Credit window appears, as shown in Figure 10-5.

FIGURE 10-5:
The Credit Card
Credit window.

2. **Choose a payee.**

3. **Choose your credit card account.**

   TIP

   You can use this window to enter debit card refunds as well, by simply choosing your bank account instead.

4. **Enter the refund date in the Payment Date field.**

5. **Optionally: Fill out any other fields onscreen and fill in the Category Details and/or Item Details sections.**

   Entering credit card charges and credits works the same as entering bills and expenses; see Chapter 7 if you're unclear how to use these sections.

   REMEMBER

   Even though you're entering a credit, you're going to record it as a positive amount. So, record that $50 refund as $50, and not –$50. Otherwise, QuickBooks responds with "Tut, tut, you can't do that!"

6. **Click Save and close, or Save and new if you have an additional credit card credit to record.**

Reconciling a Bank or Credit Card Account

Some people's least-favorite task is reconciling their bank statement, but I like knowing that my books are aligned with my bank; it's a great way to avoid surprises. I am not a fan of reconciling credit card statements, but we must all face the music. Fortunately, if you're diligent about entering transactions in QuickBooks and recording bank deposits and credit card payments as described in the preceding section, then reconciling your bank or credit card statement should be a fairly easy process. Grab your most recent statement, and follow these steps:

1. **Choose Settings ⇨ Reconcile from the Tools section.**

   Make sure that you click the Settings button, and not the + New button.

2. **Select the account you want to reconcile, as shown in Figure 10-6.**

   The fields related to recording service charges and interest do not appear for accounts that you have connected to your bank because this information downloads automatically.

REMEMBER

   You may see a Get Started button that you can click to see a summary, road map–style, of the reconciliation process. At the end of the wizard, click Let's Get Reconciled to continue and display the page, as shown in Figure 10-6.

TIP

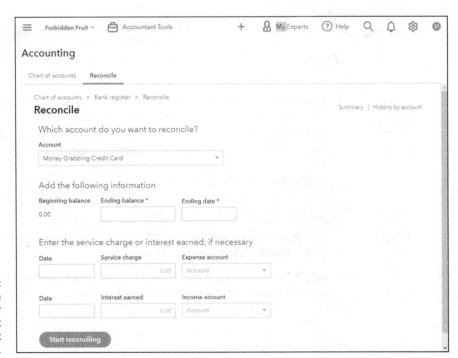

FIGURE 10-6: Enter information from your bank or credit card statement on this page.

3. **Enter the ending date and balance from your statement and the click Start Reconciling button.**

   The Reconcile page appears, as shown in Figure 10-7.

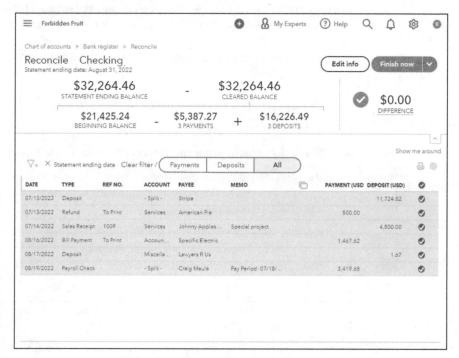

REMEMBER

Enter bank and credit card balances so they are the same as the balance on your credit card statement. For example, if the bank says you owe $750 on your credit card, then you enter $750 in the Ending Balance field. However, if you overpaid and your credit card statement reports a balance of –$125, then you enter –125 as the ending balance. Typically, you always enter a positive number for your bank account balance — that is, unless you're reconciling an overdrawn account.

TIP

Click the Edit Info button if you need to return to the initial screen to correct your ending bank balance or to record a service charge or interest. Click Save to return to the reconciliation window.

4. **Select each transaction that appears in your statement and on the Reconcile page by clicking the rightmost column.**

TIP

Paychecks divided between two bank accounts show up as two distinct transactions in QuickBooks, so they should be easy to match up during reconciliation.

By selecting a transaction, you're marking it as having cleared the bank. Your goal is to have the Difference amount at the top right-hand corner of the Reconcile page equal $0. If your account is connected to your bank, many transactions might already display a checkmark in the rightmost column because the transactions have been downloaded from the bank and matched with your accounting records. See Chapter 11 for details on connecting your bank and credit card accounts to QuickBooks.

By default, the Reconciliation page displays all uncleared transactions dated before the statement ending date, but you can click Payments or Deposits to filter by either of those options, like the way most bank statements are organized. Any transactions with dates later than the statement ending date are hidden by default. If, after you select all the transactions you see, the Difference amount isn't $0, click the X next to Statement Ending Date to look for additional transactions to mark as cleared. You can also take advantage of the Filter icon (which looks like a funnel) to limit the transactions in a way that works best for you. Be sure to compare the total payments and deposits with the corresponding numbers on the bank statement. This comparison can help you determine whether deposits and/or payments are missing.

TIP

You can click the Bank Register or Credit Card Register link in the top-left corner of the page to view the register for the account you're reconciling. When you finish viewing the register, click the Reconcile button in the top-right corner of the register page (not shown). If you'd like to see more transactions on the reconciliation page, click the upward-pointing arrow to collapse the header.

5. **When the Difference amount equals $0, click the Finish Now button.**

The Success message, shown in Figure 10-8, gives you the opportunity to view the Reconciliation report by clicking the View Reconciliation Report link. The Reconciliation report looks like the one shown in Figure 10-9. The report is broken into a summary section that you can see in Figure 10-9 and a detail section (not entirely visible) that lists all transactions you cleared.

REMEMBER

You don't have to finish your reconciliation in a single sitting. Click the drop-down arrow on the Finish Now button and then choose Save for Later if you get interrupted or you simply can't get the reconciliation to zero out. Returning with a fresh eye can often make discrepancies jump off the screen. You can also choose Close Without Saving if you want to abandon the entire process.

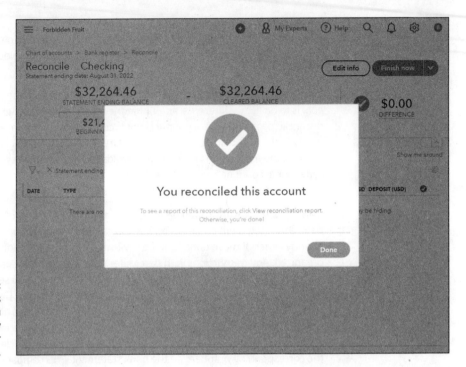

FIGURE 10-8:
QuickBooks
confirms that you
successfully
reconciled your
account.

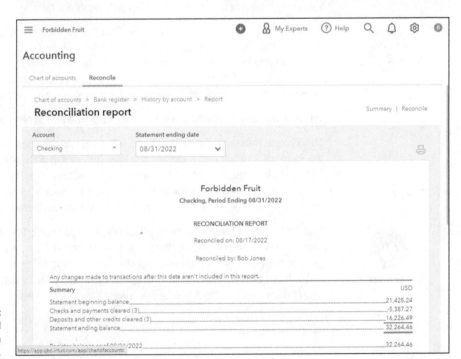

FIGURE 10-9:
A typical
Reconciliation
report.

TIP

There's an age-old bookkeeping trick that calls for dividing the unreconciled difference by 9. If it divides cleanly, the chances are exceedingly high that your difference is caused by a transposition. For instance, if your unreconciled difference is $90, you may have entered $450 when you should have entered $540 for a transaction.

You can click any transaction in the report to view it in the window where you created it. To produce a paper copy of the report, click the Print button in the top-right corner of the report window.

You can view the Reconciliation report at any time. Just redisplay the Reconcile page shown in Figure 10-6 (by choosing Settings ⇨ Reconcile). After you reconcile an account, a History by Account link appears in the top-right corner of the page. When you click the link, the History by Account page appears, listing earlier reconciliations for an individual account, as shown in Figure 10-10. Click the View Report link beside any reconciliation on this page to see its Reconciliation report.

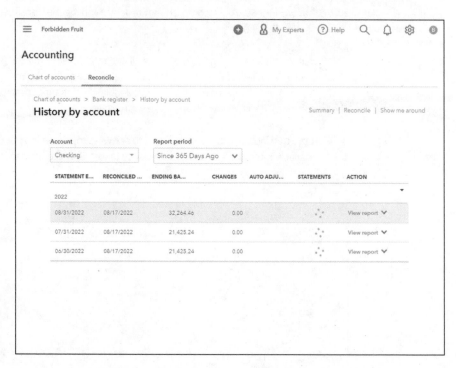

FIGURE 10-10:
Previous Reconciliation reports that you can view.

To view reconciliations for other accounts, choose a different account from the Account drop-down list.

WHEN THE OPENING BALANCE DOESN'T MATCH THE STATEMENT

It happens sometimes. You go to reconcile an account, and its opening balance doesn't match the ending balance of the previous reconciliation period. You need to fix the beginning balance before you can reconcile the account.

Good news: QuickBooks provides a tool that helps you fix the problem. This tool is in the form of a Reconciliation Discrepancy report, which lists transactions associated with the erroneous beginning balance. When you select an account to reconcile that has a beginning-balance problem, a prompt identifies the amount by which the account beginning balance is off and offers a Let's Resolve This Discrepancy link. Click the link to display a Reconciliation Discrepancy report that lists the transactions affecting the erroneous beginning balance. Typically, the report contains transactions that were changed after they were reconciled or that weren't reconciled when they should have been. The Reconciliation Discrepancy report also contains a Difference amount, and your goal is to make that amount $0. You accomplish that task by handling the transactions in the Reconciliation Discrepancy report.

If you want to explore what happened to the listed transactions that caused the discrepancy, click the View link of the transaction (it appears in the right column of the report) to display an Audit report for the transaction, detailing the changes that were made in the transaction.

To correct a transaction, click it in the report to see ways to correct it. When you correct the transaction in the Reconciliation Discrepancy report, the account is ready to reconcile.

» Joining your accounts to your financial institutions directly

» Finding indirect methods to connect accounts

» Making use of app transactions

» Uncovering how to convert paper receipts to electronic transactions

Chapter **11**

Synchronizing with Financial Institutions

Earlier chapters focus on manually entering transactions into QuickBooks, which is a necessary part of mastering any accounting software. In this chapter, I turn your attention to automating portions of your accounting by synchronizing your bank and credit card accounts with your financial institutions. Doing so can streamline the reconciliation process, and eliminate pesky reconciliation issues that can arise when you type $450 and meant to type $540. I also discuss how to convert email or paper receipts to electronic transactions.

Connecting QuickBooks Accounts to Financial Institutions

What does it mean to connect your QuickBooks accounts to a financial institution? It means that the activity that posts to a bank or credit card can get synchronized with your books, which can simplify your reconciliation process. QuickBooks offers a "choose your adventure" approach:

>> Connecting directly

>> Connecting indirectly, through QuickBooks Web Connect or by importing transactions stored in a Microsoft Excel or Google Docs file

>> Not connecting at all

If the third option appeals to you, skip to the end of the chapter and at least consider posting receipts electronically to QuickBooks as a starting point. If you are contemplating one of the first two options, allow me to first share a cautionary tale.

Connecting . . . or not connecting

As you can see from the cautionary tale in the sidebar, a paraphrased version of Hamlet's famous quote applies here: "To connect or not to connect, that is the question." Connecting requires a commitment on your part to act on the transactions rather than let them pile up unattended. Of course, even if you want to connect, your financial institution may not have the proper infrastructure in place. A direct connection streamlines the process for you, but there are two semi-manual alternatives that you can pursue.

DON'T LET THIS HAPPEN TO YOU

My friend Stephanie Miller learned a tough lesson about connecting bank accounts to QuickBooks. A couple of years ago, she connected her bank account to QuickBooks and downloaded a significant number of transactions. Life got in the way, and she didn't review the transactions. Such unreviewed transactions hang out in limbo in the For Review list, which I discuss in the section, "Managing uploaded or downloaded activity," later in this chapter. Stephanie disconnected her bank account, and all was good until a well-meaning temporary bookkeeper reconnected the account and downloaded the original transactions again, plus all subsequent transactions. None of this was a problem yet — until the bookkeeper selected all the transactions and clicked Accept. The result was that Stephanie had to decide whether to find and delete hundreds of duplicate transactions one at a time, or start a new set of books.

Connecting your books to your financial institution isn't something you can kinda, sorta do. Either fully embrace the concept and follow through by reviewing and accepting the transactions each time you connect or import, or you run the risk of compromising your accounting records at some point in the future. The download and import processes that I'm about to share with you bring in new sets of transactions each time; they don't overwrite existing transactions in the For Review list. If you can't act on downloaded transactions immediately, it's best to select all transactions and choose Exclude. You can always undo the exclusion later without setting up a potential accounting nightmare for yourself.

REMEMBER

Before I dive into connecting, it's important to explain that *you don't have to connect.* You can work quite happily in QuickBooks without ever connecting to an account in a financial institution. You just manually enter the transactions that affect the appropriate account and periodically reconcile your accounts. Many folks choose to reconcile monthly, but there's nothing stopping you from performing interim reconciliations in the middle of a month if that gives you assurance with regard to your financial position.

You can disconnect your accounts at any time if you find it doesn't work as expected. With that said, you'll probably really like being able to electronically compare the transactions recorded in QuickBooks with the transactions your financial institution has on file.

TIP

See Chapters 6, 7, and 8 for details on entering transactions that affect a bank or credit card account. You typically use an Expense transaction to record credit card purchases and a Credit Card Credit transaction to record refunds to a credit card. You can also use the Pay Down Credit Card transaction to record payments you make to reduce your credit card balances.

REMEMBER

You must set up your bank and credit card accounts in QuickBooks *before* you can connect to your financial institution.

Accessing bank and credit card–related pages in QuickBooks

Writing this next section took me back to the "hall of mirrors" at the fairground, where nothing seemed to physically be where I thought it was. I'm about to show you a set of banking-related commands, which may or may not show up in QuickBooks for you where you think they should. As I discuss throughout this book, the left menu bar has at least two modes: Accountant View and Business View.

I say at least two views because QuickBooks has been dallying with a third Partner/Owner view, but you can't switch to that — it's basically a customized version of Business View based upon you telling QuickBooks at some point that you have an ownership stake.

Let's first assume that you want to connect a bank or credit card account, and are either already in Accountant View, or want to use Accountant View:

1. Skip this step if the first command on your left menu bar is Overview; otherwise, choose Settings ⇨ Switch to Accountant View.

2. **Choose Banking from the left menu bar to display the page shown in Figure 11-1.**

    A Connect Account button appears if you haven't connected any accounts yet.

Now, let's say that you're in Business View or want to use Business View:

1. **Skip this step if the first command on your left menu bar is Get Things Done; otherwise, choose Settings ⇨ Switch to Business View.**

2. **Choose Bookkeeping ⇨ Transactions to display the page shown in Figure 11-2.**

REMEMBER

As shown in Figure 11-3, the Banking command on the left menu bar in Business View tries to entice you into signing up for a new bank account. If you're looking to connect your accounts, you must start with the Bookkeeping command instead.

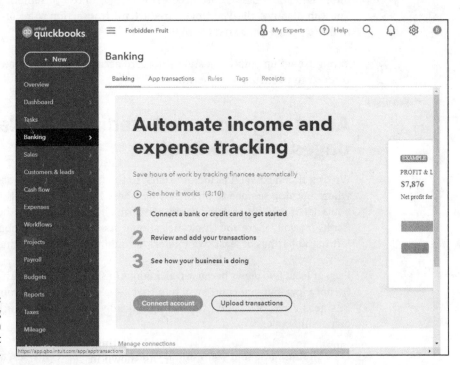

FIGURE 11-1: The Banking page in Accountant View.

TIP

Click Add a Bookmark (or click the three-dot menu adjacent to most commands in the left menu bar, and then choose Customize this Menu), choose Bank Transactions from the list, and then click Save to create one-click access to your Bank Transactions page. If you change your mind later, click the three-dot menu next to Bank Transactions and choose Remove this Bookmark.

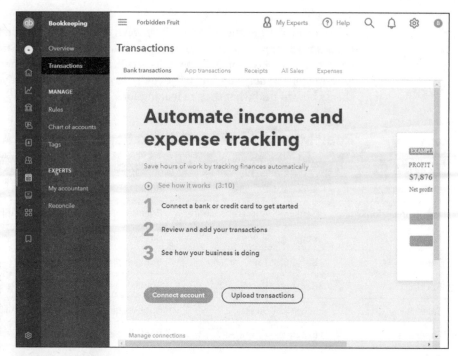

FIGURE 11-2:
The Bank
Transactions
tab of the
Transactions
page in
Business View.

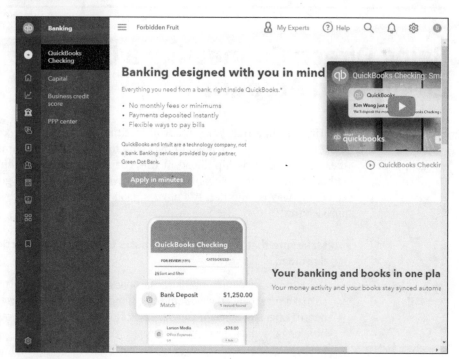

FIGURE 11-3:
The Banking page
in Business View.

Now let's play "spot the difference" between the Banking page in Figure 11-1 and the Transaction page in Figure 11-2. Both have five tabs, but one tab is in a different position, and two of the other tabs are different. I put together Table 11-1 as a Rosetta Stone to help you find what you're looking for, or so that you can tell your clients how to find what they're looking for.

TABLE 11-1   ## Road Map to Banking-Related Pages

Page	Accountant View	Business View
Connected Accounts	Banking ➪ Banking	Bookkeeping ➪ Transactions
App Transactions	Banking ➪ App Transactions	Bookkeeping ➪ Transactions ➪ App Transactions
Rules	Banking ➪ Rules	Bookkeeping ➪ Rules
Tags	Banking ➪ Tags	Bookkeeping ➪ Tags
Receipts	Banking ➪ Receipts	Bookkeeping ➪ Transactions ➪ Receipts
Sales	Sales ➪ All Sales	Bookkeeping ➪ Transactions ➪ All Sales
Expenses	Expenses ➪ Expenses	Bookkeeping ➪ Transactions ➪ Expenses
QuickBooks Checking	Not available	Banking ➪ QuickBooks Checking

Being Direct: Connecting a Bank or Credit Card Account

Let's first assume that your financial institution offers direct connections with QuickBooks. Don't worry, it won't take long to make this determination. If you hit a dead end, you can skip ahead in this chapter to the two indirect connection methods that I share in upcoming sections, which means you're going to get connected one way or another. It's always good to be direct in life, so let's try that approach first:

1. **Make sure that you have a few minutes to allow the transactions time to download.**

   QuickBooks downloads recent transactions as part of the connection process, so make sure that you have some quiet time to allow QuickBooks to do this. It doesn't offer a meaningful progress indicator, so it's hard to forecast exactly how long the initial download will take.

2. **Retrieve your online banking credentials in your password manager so that you have the information handy.**

   What? You're *not* using a password manager? Get thee a password manager subscription *today*. Two reputable managers include www.lastpass.com and www.1password.com.

TIP

I resisted using password management software for far too long. One day, I was struggling to remember a password when the guy I was meeting with said, "My password manager software saves me so much time." I heard that advice in the right moment, and writing this reminds me that I need to get my two teenagers set up on a password manager as well. You do have a choice: reusing passwords on more than one site, which is a huge identity-theft risk, or using a password manager to have unique and complex passwords for each site that you need to log into, which includes QuickBooks. You install the password manager app on each of your devices, and then create a passphrase to serve as a master key. You'll be shocked at the number of sites you're logging into once you have them all in one list.

REMEMBER

It's easy to solve one problem and inadvertently create new ones. Password managers suggest credentials to use based up on the web page that you're on. This means that a password manager may try to suggest your Intuit account credentials instead of, say, your financial institution's. If this happens, you can open the password manager directly and copy and paste your banking credentials into the correct fields.

3. **Choose Banking ⇨ Banking in Accountant View (Bookkeeping ⇨ Transactions in Business View).**

4. **Click Connect Account or Add Account to display the Connect an Account page shown in Figure 11-4.**

5. **Choose a logo from the list if your financial institution is one of the eight choices; otherwise, type a name in the Search box, and then select a match from the list.**

TIP

When I searched on one of my banks, QuickBooks returned 9,869 choices, until I removed the word "Bank" from my search — then, 141 choices appeared. The list shows the website address for each bank to help you ensure that you're making the correct choice.

REMEMBER

Don't worry if you can't find your bank on the list, or if you have any trepidation about connecting QuickBooks to your financial institution. First, it's a one-way feed, meaning *their* transactions come into *your* books, not the other way around. See the section, "Downloading Web Connect and text files," later in this chapter if you want or need an alternative to a direct connection.

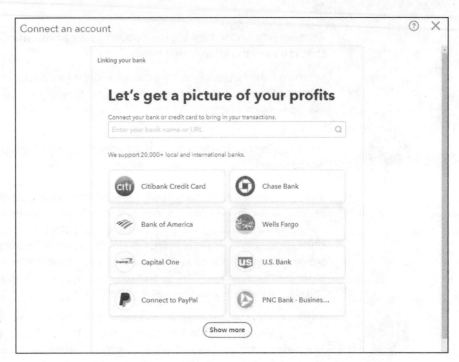

FIGURE 11-4: Identify your financial institution.

6. **Follow the onscreen instructions, which will vary.**

   You may be directed to go to your bank's website and sign in, after which you're returned to the connection process. Or if you're connecting to PayPal, you're walked through a three-step process.

TIP

   You may have to prove your "nonrobotness" by way of a reCAPTCHA. Who doesn't like looking for stoplights in grainy photos? Fortunately, this method is falling out of favor, so you may be prompted instead to authorize an OAuth connection. Just follow the onscreen prompts.

   If all goes as expected, a new page displays the accounts you have at the financial institution and lets you choose which ones you want to connect to QuickBooks, as shown in Figure 11-5.

7. **Choose the accounts you want to connect.**

   For each account you choose, QuickBooks asks you to choose an existing Bank or Credit Card account, or allows you to create a new account. QuickBooks also asks you how far in the past you want to pull transactions for the account. Depending on your bank, options may include Today, This Month, This Year, or Last Year, or you may be able to specify a custom range.

8. **Click Connect, and then wait while your accounts download.**

FIGURE 11-5:
Select the
accounts you
want to connect,
their type, and a
transaction
range.

The Connect button is disabled until you select an account, specify a type, and choose a date range for downloading transactions.

9. **Follow any additional onscreen prompts you see to finish setting up the account.**

The automatic download of transactions is only the first phase of the process; you must still review and accept the transactions. I first show you how to do this manually, and then how to automate the process with the Rules feature.

Managing uploaded or downloaded activity

Any accounts to which you have uploaded or downloaded activity will appear as connected accounts on the Banking Transactions page, as shown in Figure 11-6. You determine the schedule for files that you upload, while QuickBooks typically downloads activity from your financial institution nightly, but the pace of any updates is controlled by your financial institution. In the case of Figure 11-6, the Checking account is a direct connection to one of my banks, while the two credit card accounts represent fictional transactions that I uploaded.

TIP

See the section, "Uploading Web Connect and text files," later in this chapter if you are unable to establish a direct connection with your financial institution.

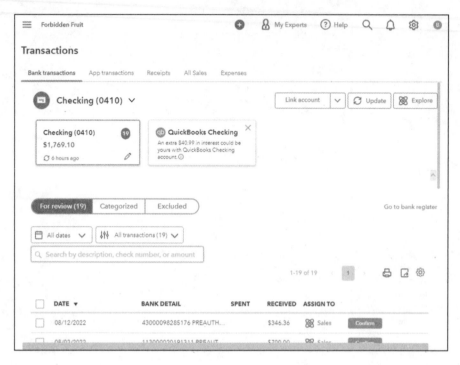

FIGURE 11-6: The Banking Transactions page shows accounts that you have uploaded or downloaded activity to.

You can make the following changes in the information that appears in the table shown in Figure 11-7 on the Banking page:

>> Display check numbers.

>> Display payee names.

>> Display class names.

>> Display location names.

>> Turn on grouping to group transactions by month.

>> Show amounts in one column, or in separate Spent and Received columns.

>> Show the Tags field.

>> Make the date field editable so that you can change it if necessary.

>> Copy bank detail information into the Memo field.

>> Show suggested rules (which allow QuickBooks to classify accounting transactions automatically).

>> Show bank details, which I chose in Figure 11-6 to maintain a modicum of privacy about the transactions that run through this account.

» Enable suggested categorization (QuickBooks makes guesses as to which category, meaning an account from your chart of accounts, the transaction should post to).

» Display 50, 75, 100, or 300 transactions per page.

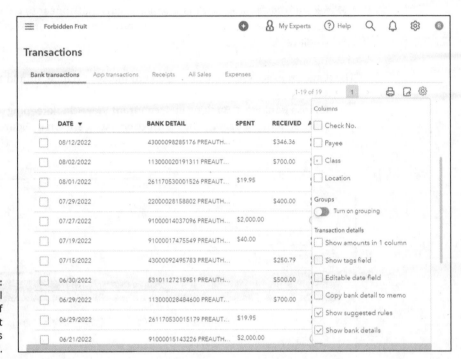

 To make a change in the page's table, click Settings just above the Action column, and add or remove checkmarks to display or hide columns. You can also adjust the column widths; QuickBooks remembers any column-width adjustments you make, even after you sign out and then sign back in. If you need to display the Memo field in an individual bank register, see Chapter 10 for directions.

Reviewing transactions

Getting transactions from a financial institution into QuickBooks is only the first part of the process. You need to review each transaction and, as appropriate, accept or confirm that you want to post it to your books. QuickBooks tags transactions for review in one of four ways:

» *Confirm* or *Add* indicates that the Category or Match field reflects QuickBooks' best guess.

» *Match* signifies transactions for which QuickBooks found an exact counterpart in your books.

» *View* means that two or more transactions in your books potentially match the banking transaction. The number of matches is shown in the Category or Match column.

» *Record Transfer* or *Review* marks transactions that appear to be a transfer between bank accounts or a payment on a liability account such as a credit card.

The Bank Transactions page allows you to match, exclude, or add transactions:

1. **Choose Banking ➪ Banking in Accountant View (Bookkeeping ➪ Transactions) to display the transaction listing shown in Figure 11-8.**

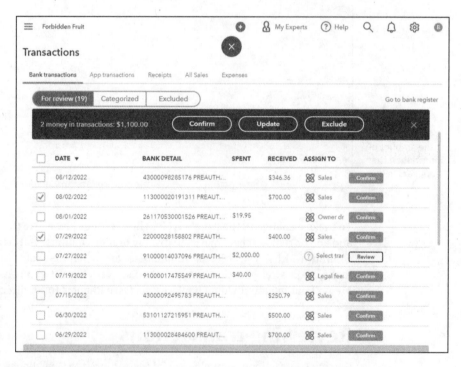

FIGURE 11-8: Uploaded or downloaded transactions awaiting review.

2. **Choose a bank or credit card account to display any related transactions you need to review.**

    Three tabs appear just below your account(s).

    ● **For Review:** Unreviewed transactions that await your attention.

- **Categorized:** Transactions that you've reviewed and accepted or confirmed, either manually or by way of a rule.

- **Excluded:** Transactions that you've opted not to post to your books at the present time. You can select one or more transactions and choose Undo to return the transactions to the For Review list, or you can choose Delete to remove the transactions from QuickBooks.

TIP

Note that the Delete command does not ask you if you're sure, so think twice before clicking Delete. See the section, "Using Indirect Connections to Financial Institutions," later in this chapter if you inadvertently delete transactions directly downloaded into QuickBooks, as you may be able to recover what you deleted by manually downloading the transactions from your financial institution again and then uploading into QuickBooks.

3. **QuickBooks automatically classifies as many transactions as it can, based on built-in rules that you can override with your own specifications.**

   a) **When you select one transaction at a time, you can use the following commands:**

   - **Accept (or Confirm).** Accepts the category/account that QuickBooks assigned the transaction to and posts the transaction to your books.

   - **View (Review, or click on the transaction).** Displays the screen shown in Figure 11-9, from which you can do the following:

   - Choose the Categorize radio button to change the vendor/customer, category, location, class, tags, or memo.

   - Choose the Find Match radio button to view potential matches or search for other matches.

   - Choose the Record As Transfer radio button to select an offsetting account for the transfer.

   - Add an attachment, such as a PDF copy of a receipt.

   - Create a rule (which I discuss in the sneakily named section, "Creating rules").

   - Exclude a transaction so that it doesn't post to your books.

   - View the categorization history for similar transactions when you choose the Categorize option.

   - Split a transaction that you're categorizing among two or more categories.

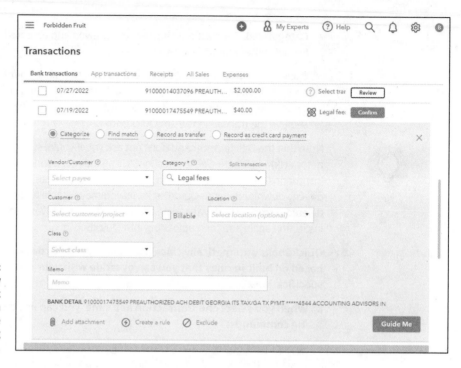

FIGURE 11-9:
Choose View
(Review) or click
any transaction
to see the
underlying
details.

b) **When you select two or more transactions on the list (using the checkboxes along the left), you can then Confirm, Update, or Exclude them, as shown in Figure 11-8.**

- **Confirm.** Accepts the transactions, which means that they post to your books and appear on the Categorized tab.

- **Update.** Displays the Update Selected dialog box shown in Figure 11-10.

TIP

QuickBooks may ask if you want to create a rule to automatically apply the transactions in the future. I discuss Rules in more detail later in this section. Click Don't Show Me This Again if you don't want QuickBooks to suggest creating rules.

- **Exclude.** Moves the transactions to the Excluded tab. As noted previously, you can later select one or more transactions and choose Undo to move transactions back to the For Review tab, or you can delete the transactions.

4. **Keep working the list until you have reviewed all transactions.**

You may be able to speed up the process by making one of the following choices from the All Transactions filter.

- **Recognized:** View transactions that have been recognized (you updated the category manually).

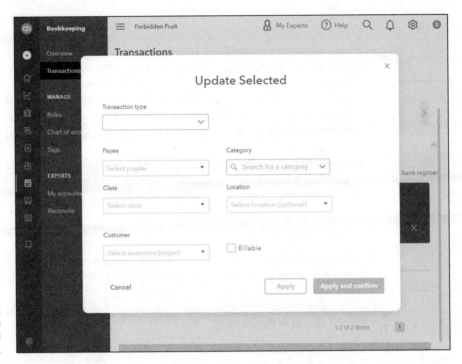

FIGURE 11-10:
The Update
Selected
dialog box.

- **Matched:** See transactions in which a match was made between the transaction downloaded from your financial institution and your accounting records.

- **Transferred:** See transactions that are deemed to be a transfer between accounts, such as a credit card payment, or a transfer of funds between two bank accounts.

- **Rule Applied:** View transactions that are automatically updated by a rule, which I discuss later in the section, "Creating rules."

- **Missing Payee/Customer:** See a list of transactions for which the payee or customer couldn't be identified.

- **Unassigned:** View a list of transactions that have a status other than Add and haven't been processed yet.

Now that you see how to manually review and process transactions, let's eliminate some repetitive work by creating rules.

Automating downloaded activity with rules

Rules instruct QuickBooks how to automatically update and optionally post uploaded or downloaded transactions. Let's say that you often buy gas for your business vehicles at Shell stations. You can either manually categorize such transactions as Fuel Expense, or you can set up a rule to automate the process going forward. Rules are applied based upon the accounts, transaction types (money in or money out), and criteria that you specify. Rules can assign categories (meaning income/expense accounts) and modify other fields as well. This means that you can create a rule that updates one or more fields, and then leaves the transaction in the For Review list. Or, you can create a rule that updates one or more fields, and accepts the transaction, which means it will post to your books and then appear in the Categorized list. Either way, you can always amend a transaction by choosing it from the Categorized list, using the Search feature to locate the transaction, or by clicking on the transaction within a report.

Creating rules

As noted previously, as you manually review transactions, QuickBooks may prompt you to create a rule. Or, you can always create a rule directly:

1. **Choose Banking ⇨ Rules (Bookkeeping ⇨ Rules) to display the Rules page shown in Figure 11-11.**

FIGURE 11-11:
The Rules page.

2. Click the New Rule button to display the Create Rule task pane shown in Figure 11-12.

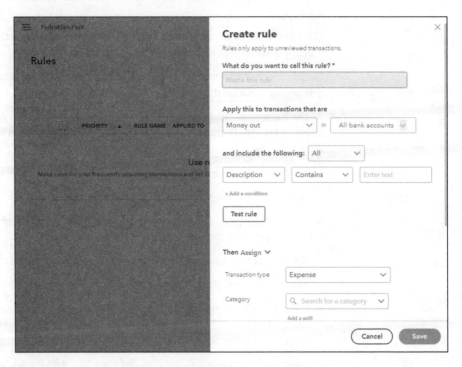

FIGURE 11-12:
The Create Rule
task pane.

3. Assign a meaningful name to the rule.

You can't use special characters like the apostrophe (') in a rule name.

4. Indicate whether the rule applies to money coming in or money going out, and select the account(s) to which you want the rule to apply.

5. Set the transaction criteria for the rule by using the drop-down lists in the Include the Following section.

Use the Add a Condition link to set additional criteria, and to specify if a transaction should meet all or any of the criteria. Specifying All is more stringent and makes QuickBooks more selective about applying the rule.

TIP

The first list box in the section enables you to specify whether QuickBooks should compare the transaction description, the bank text, or the transaction amount with a condition you set. For those inquiring minds out there, *Description* (the transaction description) refers to the text that appears in the Description column of the Bank and Credit Cards page. The *Bank Text* option refers to the Bank Detail description the bank downloads; you can view the

Bank Detail description if you click any downloaded transaction. The Bank Detail description appears in the bottom-left corner of the transactions being edited. *Transaction Amount* is of course the dollar amount of an individual transaction.

6. **Click Test Rule to determine how many unreviewed transactions the rule will apply to, as shown in Figure 11-13.**

   QuickBooks won't show you the actual transactions, but you'll at least know that you've specified the criteria correctly to match one or more transactions.

7. **At the bottom of the Create Rule panel, set the information you want to apply to transactions that meet the rule's criteria, as shown in Figure 11-13.**

   You can do one or more of the following:

   - *Select a transaction type to assign to the transaction.*

   - *Select a category and (optional) split to use for classifying the transaction.* Splits can be based on percentages or dollar amounts.

   - *Select a payee to apply the transactions that meet the rule's conditions.*

   - *Specify one or more tags for grouping related transactions.*

   - *Optional: Click Assign More to add a memo to each transaction that meets the rule's conditions.* For more on ways to use the Memo field, see the nearby sidebar, "The Memo field and transaction rules."

   - *Toggle off Automatically Confirm Transactions This Rule Applies To if you do not want to automatically add transactions that meet the rule's conditions to your company.*

REMEMBER

   This setting instructs QuickBooks to bypass the For Review list and post transactions directly to your books. Such transactions will appear on the Categorized tab, along with any transactions that you manually post, and you can make changes later if you experience an unexpected outcome with a rule.

8. **Click Save in the bottom-right corner of the Create Rule panel.**

   Your rule appears on the Rules page, and the rule is applied to any matching transactions in the For Review lists for your accounts.

REMEMBER

You cannot manually run a rule in QuickBooks Online. You can create a rule that makes changes and keeps the transaction in your For Review list, or you can allow QuickBooks to automatically update and post transactions, but you cannot select specific transactions that you want to apply a rule against.

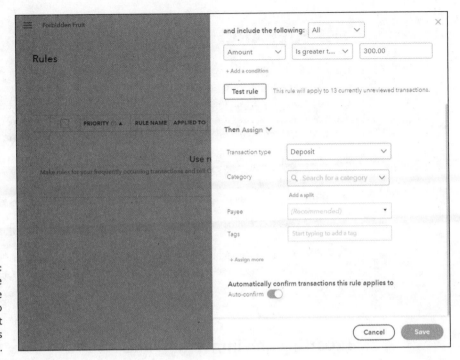

FIGURE 11-13:
Specify the changes to be made to transactions that meet the rule's criteria.

TIP

Choose Copy in the Action column of the Rules page to replicate a rule to use as a starting point (instead of starting from scratch). You can also edit, disable, or delete rules.

TIP

See the section, "Exporting and importing rules," later in this chapter to see how to transfer rules between QuickBooks companies.

THE MEMO FIELD AND TRANSACTION RULES

QuickBooks uses special icons in the register to identify transactions posted automatically with rules, but you can't filter a register to see only transactions that were added via a rule. You can, however, add a search term, such as "Added by Rule" to the Memo field, which you can then use to filter an account register.

Exporting and importing rules

Rules can be exported from one QuickBooks company and then imported into another. This is helpful when you have multiple entities that use the same conventions. You can also create a set of generic rules to use as a starting point for crafting rules in other companies. Here's how to transfer rules from one company to another:

1. **Choose Banking ⇨ Rules (Bookkeeping ⇨ Rules) in the company that has the rules that you want to transfer to display the Rules page, as shown in Figure 11-11.**

2. **Choose Export Rules from the New Rule drop-down menu.**

   QuickBooks creates an Excel file containing the rules, and stores it in your Downloads folder. The name of the file includes the QuickBooks company name whose rules you exported and the words Bank_Feed_Rules.

   The Export Rules command is disabled if a given company doesn't have any rules established.

REMEMBER

3. **Click Close.**

4. **Switch to the company into which you want to import these rules.**

5. **Choose Banking ⇨ Rules (Bookkeeping ⇨ Rules) in the company that has the rules that you want to transfer.**

6. Choose Import Rules from the New Rule drop-down menu.

The first screen of the Import Rules wizard appears.

7. Select the file you created in Step 2 and then click Next.

8. On the second wizard screen, select the rules you want to import and then click Next.

9. Optional: On the third wizard screen, select categories for the rules that match the chart of accounts of the client to which you are importing the rules, and make any changes you want.

10. Click Import.

A message tells you how many rules imported successfully.

11. Click Finish.

The Rules page for the company you opened in Step 4 appears.

12. Verify that the rules you wanted to import appear.

You can edit or delete the rules in the same way as if you had created them by hand.

The combination of a direct connection to your financial institution and a series of well-crafted rules creates an automated process that will keep your books up to date on a set-and-forget basis. There are always exceptions to the rule, so let's see how to correct transactions that you reviewed by hand or where a rule caused an unexpected outcome.

Fixing mistakes in uploaded or downloaded transactions

Whether you're accepting transactions manually or on autopilot with rules, sometimes mistakes or mispostings can happen. There's no need to worry; you can use the same steps in either case.

REMEMBER

QuickBooks treats downloaded transactions as having cleared your bank; be careful to edit as opposed to delete transactions that have been accepted or confirmed.

Follow these steps to undo an accepted transaction:

1. Choose Banking ⇨ Banking in Accountant View (Bookkeeping ⇨ Transactions).

2. Select the bank or credit card that the transaction posted to.

QuickBooks maintains separate transaction lists for each account.

3. **Click the Categorized tab on the Bank Transactions page, as shown in Figure 11-14.**

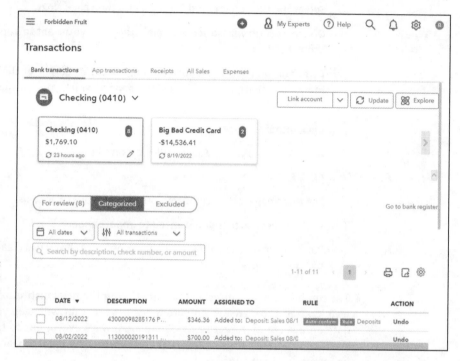

FIGURE 11-14:
Use the Categorized tab to find transactions accepted into QuickBooks.

4. **Locate the transaction and click Undo in the Action column to send the transaction back to the For Review list.**

Alternatively, click on the category name in the Added or Matched column to display the corresponding transaction screen and make your edits there.

5. **Switch to the For Review tab, edit the transaction as needed, and then accept (confirm) or exclude the transaction.**

If necessary, you can delete transactions from the Excluded tab. To do so, click one or more transactions and then click the Delete button. Remember, QuickBooks does not ask you if you're sure that you want to delete, so move deliberately through the process.

The steps to review and/or automatically post transactions are the same, no matter how transactions arrive in QuickBooks. Up to this point, I assumed a direct connection to QuickBooks, but now let's see how to handle situations where you need or want to upload transactions manually.

Using Indirect Connections to Financial Institutions

In some cases, you can't connect your financial institution to an account in Quick-Books, or you can connect, but transactions don't download. All is not lost. You can still update a Bank or Credit Card account with financial institution information by first downloading a QuickBooks Web Connect file or a text file from your financial institution. You can then immediately upload Web Connect files without modification, but you may need to make some minor modifications to text files.

TIP

QuickBooks Online Advanced subscribers can also use the Spreadsheet Sync feature to post transactions from within an Excel spreadsheet directly to QuickBooks. I discuss this at the end of Chapters 6 and 7.

Downloading Web Connect and text files

Most financial institutions at least allow you to download your transactions in some form from their website. The process isn't as automated as a direct connection, but the result is the same. Once you upload the transactions to QuickBooks, you can edit and accept them in the same fashion as a direct connection.

WARNING

You should not use a public computer to download Web Connect or files, as the files are not encrypted and contain sensitive information about your bank or credit card account.

Follow these steps to download transactions from your financial institution:

1. **Log in to your financial institution's website and look for a link that enables you to download to QuickBooks or to a text file.**

Some websites have a Download button associated with each account, whereas others offer a Download to QuickBooks or CSV/TXT link. Others may offer a QuickBooks Web Connect link. If you can't find a link, odds are that your financial institution doesn't offer this functionality. But don't just assume; ask for help. Sometimes, what you're looking for is hiding in plain sight in the form of an icon with an arrow pointing down.

2. **Select any of the following file formats that your financial institution offers:**

- .qbo (QuickBooks)
- .qfx (Quicken)
- .ofx (Microsoft Money)

- Any file format that references QuickBooks or QuickBooks Online

- .csv (comma-separated value file)

- .txt (tab-delimited text file)

TIP

I've listed these files in priority order, meaning always choose one of the first four types if available, as you won't have to edit the file. The last two types are last-resort options that may require some editing before you can import them into QuickBooks.

3. **Specify a date range for the transactions you want to download.**

WARNING

The account's opening balance will change if you download transactions with dates that precede the opening balance, so double-check the dates you choose here and don't go too far back in time.

4. **Save the file to a location on your computer where you'll be able to find it later.**

Many people use the Downloads folder or their computer's desktop.

Easy enough, right? If you chose a Web Connect file, meaning a QuickBooks (.qbo), Quicken (.qfx), or Microsoft Money (.ofx) file, then you can skip the next three sections and resume again with the section, "Uploading Web Connect and CSV files." Otherwise, read on to see the hopefully minor changes you may have to make to the text file that you download.

TIP

Even if you can't download the transactions, you may be able to copy and paste them or enter them into a Microsoft Excel workbook or Google Sheets spreadsheet. The next section describes the prescribed format and how to save your work to a comma-separated value file that you can then upload. You truly can get there from here.

Opening text files in Microsoft Excel or Google Sheets

If you downloaded a .csv or .txt file from your financial institution, you may be able to import the transactions into QuickBooks without modification, or you may have to make some edits. Both of these are considered text files, so I often refer to .csv and .txt files collectively as text files until you get to saving the file. The first time around, you want to open and review the text file to make sure that it conforms to the minimum requirements that I lay out in the next section. But first, here's how to open a text file in Microsoft Excel:

1. **Choose File ➪ Open.**

2. **Change the File Type field to Text Files.**

3. **Browse to the folder where your .csv or .txt file resides, select the file, and then click Open.**

Meanwhile, in Google Sheets, you do this instead:

1. **Create a blank spreadsheet.**

2. **Choose File ⇨ Import ⇨ Upload.**

3. **Click Select a File from Your Device, browse for the file, and then click Open.**

4. **Make a choice from the Import Location list, and then click Import Data.**

5. **Change the File Type field to Text Files.**

6. **Browse to the folder where your `.csv` or `.txt` file resides, select the file, and then click Open.**

Now let's see how to edit your text file to conform to what QuickBooks expects.

Editing text files

QuickBooks accepts text files formatted in three or four columns, as shown in Tables 11-2 and 11-3. Keep in mind that these columns are the minimum required. A text file that you download may include additional columns that QuickBooks will ignore, so don't obsess about making the file just so. What you do need is a single row of titles and the columns shown here. The order doesn't matter.

TABLE 11-2   An Acceptable Three-Column Format

Date	Description	Amount
1/1/2022	Example check, fee, or credit card charge	–100.00
1/1/2022	Example deposit or credit card payment	200.00

TABLE 11-3   An Acceptable Four-Column Format

Date	Description	Debit	Credit
1/1/2022	Example check, fee, or credit card charge	200.00	
1/1/2022	Example deposit or credit card payment		100.00

In either case, edit the spreadsheet to conform with the formats in Tables 11-2 or 11-3 by adding or removing columns. Remember, QuickBooks ignores any additional columns beyond the minimum requirements.

There are three special situations that you must resolve before saving your text file.

» **Amounts:** Make sure that your transaction amounts are positive or negative, or appear in the proper columns, meaning Debit or Credit as shown the tables. An easy way to flip the sign in a column of numbers is to type **–1** in a blank worksheet cell, select the numbers you want to change the sign on, and then choose Home ⇨ Paste ⇨ Paste Special ⇨ Multiply and then click OK. In Google Sheets, let's say that cell C2 contains positive amount that you want to be negative. Type **–C2** in any blank cell, such as D2, and then copy the formula down as many rows as needed. Copy the formulas from Column D and choose Edit ⇨ Paste Special ⇨ Values Only, and then delete Column D to avoid confusion.

» **Date formats:** Make sure that the date column only contains dates as opposed to dates and times. Let's say that cell A2 contains 01/01/2024 08:00 AM. In Microsoft Excel, you can enter **=ROUND(A2,0)** in a blank cell, such as E2, and then copy the formula down. You then copy the formulas in Column D, choose Home ⇨ Paste drop-down ⇨ Paste Special ⇨ Values, and then click OK. You can use this same formula in Google Sheets, and use the Paste Special method described for amounts.

TIP

In Google Sheets, you can also use the formula =DATEVALUE(A2) to remove the time portion. This doesn't work in Excel, though, as =DATEVALUE(A2) returns #VALUE!

WARNING

Dates within spreadsheets are serial numbers that represent the number of days that have elapsed since December 31, 1899. That means that 1/1/2024 may appear as 45,292 instead. If so, in Excel, select the date serial numbers and then choose Home ⇨ Format ⇨ Format Cells, make a selection from the Date section of the Number tab, and then click OK. In Google Sheets, choose Format ⇨ Number ⇨ Date. QuickBooks does not accept dates that are saved to a text file in serial number format.

» **Splitting columns:** You may encounter situations where, say, the description or memo column in your text file contains extraneous text that you don't want to import into QuickBooks. You may be able to split the data into two or more columns and then discard what you don't want. Copy the data in question to an unused area of your spreadsheet, so that you don't accidentally overwrite any data. Next, in Microsoft Excel, select the data in question, choose Data ⇨ Text to Columns, and then work through the wizard. In Google Sheets, select the data, choose Data ⇨ Split Text into Columns, and then select or enter a separator from the list that appears.

The next step is to save your text file as a comma-separated value (`.csv`) file.

Saving CSV files

You may have noticed that the two previous sections refer to *text files*. When downloading from your financial institution, any sort of text file will do, but when you're ready to upload to QuickBooks, you want to make sure to use the comma-separated value format.

Here's how to do so in Microsoft Excel:

1. **Choose File ⇨ Save As.**

2. **Change the File Type field to CSV (Comma Delimited).**

3. **Browse to the location where you want to save the file and then click Save.**

   Make sure that you choose a location you can remember, because you'll be choosing this file in QuickBooks.

4. **Choose File ⇨ Close.**

   This step is crucial to a successful upload. First, it ensures that your changes get saved, and second, your operating system may lock open files and prevent you from uploading.

You can also create CSV files with Google Sheets:

1. **Choose File ⇨ Download ⇨ Comma Separated Values (.csv).**

2. **Browse to the location where you want to save the file and then click Save.**

   As with Excel, make sure that you choose a location you can remember, because you'll be choosing this file in QuickBooks.

3. **Choose File ⇨ Close.**

   It's not as crucial to close a Google Sheets spreadsheet as it is in Excel, but doing so will ensure that you don't make any changes onscreen that won't be in the copy that you downloaded.

REMEMBER

QuickBooks says that it accepts .txt files as an upload format, but this is somewhat misleading. Most .txt files are either tab-delimited or fixed-width files, which QuickBooks does not recognize.

You're now ready to upload your transactions to QuickBooks.

Uploading Web Connect and CSV files

Remember, it's not necessary to edit Web Connect (.qbo, .qfx, .ofx) files, and in fact, it may be destructive to do so, in that you may inadvertently alter the file structure. If you downloaded a text file from your financial institution, make sure that you run through the open/edit/save process in the preceding sections to ensure that your format conforms to QuickBooks requirements. No matter the source, you're now ready to upload your transactions into QuickBooks.

1. **Choose Banking ➪ Banking (Bookkeeping ➪ Transactions) to display the Banking Transactions page.**

2. **Click the Link Account drop-down menu and choose Upload from File, as shown in Figure 11-15.**

   The Import Bank Transactions page appears, as shown in Figure 11-16.

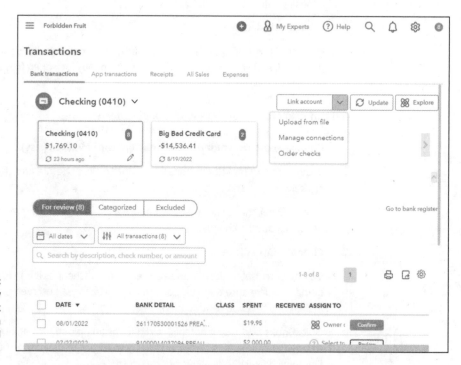

FIGURE 11-15:
Click the arrow beside the Link Account button and select Upload from File.

3. **Click the Select Files link, navigate to and then select your transaction file.**

4. **Click Continue in the bottom-right corner.**

5. **On the next page, select the bank or credit card account where the transactions should appear and then click Continue, as shown in Figure 11-17.**

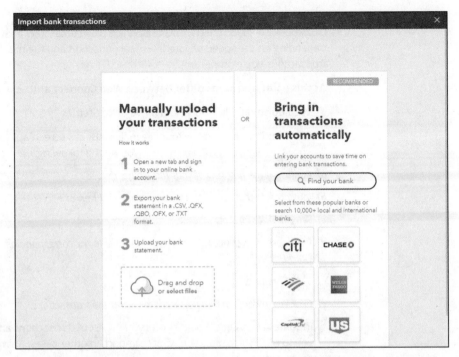

FIGURE 11-16:
The Import Bank
Transactions
page for
uploading
Web Connect or
.csv files.

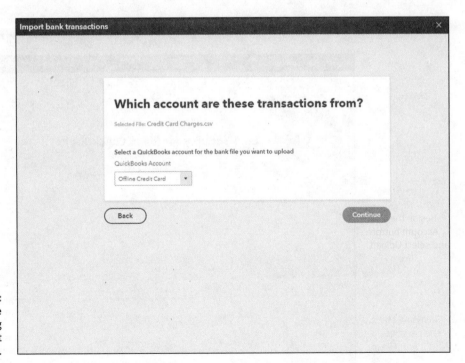

FIGURE 11-17:
Select the
corresponding
bank or credit
card account.

QuickBooks uploads the transactions, which could take a few minutes, depending on the speed of your Internet connection and the number of transactions you're importing.

6. **At this point, the steps differ between Web Connect and .csv files.**

- **Web Connect:** Click Done and move on to Step 7.

- **CSV file:** The Let's Set Up Your File in QuickBooks screen appears, as shown in Figure 11-18. From here, you do the following:

a) *Confirm if the first row of your file is a header.*

b) *Indicate whether your file has one amount column or two.*

c) *Select a date format.*

d) *If needed, map the columns in your .csv file to the corresponding QuickBooks fields.*

e) *Click Continue.*

f) *Click Yes to confirm that you want to import the transactions.*

In some cases, QuickBooks shows you the list of transactions and allows you to pick which ones you want to import. In other cases, a simple confirmation prompt appears.

g) *Click Done.*

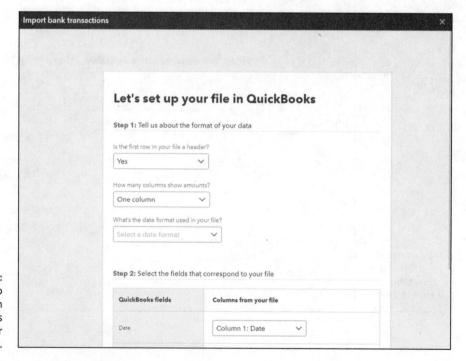

FIGURE 11-18:
The Let's Set Up Your File in QuickBooks window for .csv files.

7. **You're now ready to review and accept the transactions by following the instructions in the section, "Managing uploaded or downloaded activity," earlier in this chapter.**

Always delete Web Connect files after importing them, because they contain sensitive information about your financial accounts that can be viewed by anyone who gains access to the file.

When you import transactions from a CSV file, the bank balance in QuickBooks may be reported as zero. Don't panic! This simply means that the balance amount isn't available in the CSV file. See Chapter 10 for the steps to take to reconcile your QuickBooks account with your bank.

Connecting to Online Providers through App Transactions

The App Transactions tab enables you to connect QuickBooks to certain online providers as another means of automatically importing data. Built-in providers include Amazon Business, Square, and eBay Payments. To get started, choose Banking⇨App Transactions (Bookkeeping⇨Transactions⇨App Transactions). Choose the app you want to connect, or use the search box to find other apps that you can connect. In some cases, you may need to subscribe to a third-party app, such as for importing Stripe or Clover transactions.

As shown in Figure 11-4, PayPal appears among the available banks rather than as an app.

Converting Paper Receipts to Electronic Transactions

QuickBooks enables you to convert paper or electronic receipts or bills to transactions without having to key in all the details. To get started, choose Banking⇨Receipts (Bookkeeping⇨Banking⇨Receipts). You can capture receipts in four ways, three of which are shown in Figure 11-19:

>> Upload files from your computer.

>> Upload files from Google Drive.

» Forward from email, which means establishing a special @qbodocs.com email address. The benefit of forwarding is that you can establish a filter in your email to automatically forward receipts that you receive by email for automatic posting to QuickBooks.

» Take pictures of receipts onscreen or on paper with the QuickBooks Online mobile app (not shown in Figure 11-19).

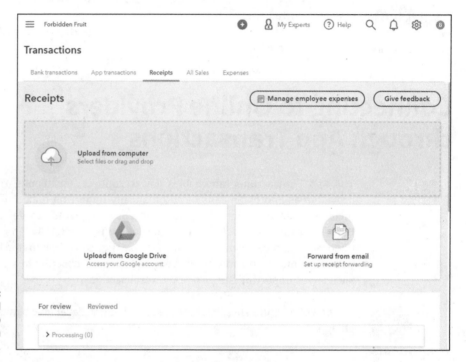

FIGURE 11-19: You can send receipts or bills to QuickBooks in several ways.

TIP

To create an email address, click Manage Forwarding Email on the Receipts page. You are prompted to create a special @qbodocs.com email address, as shown in Figure 11-20, that has a maximum of 25 letters to the left of the @ symbol. Click Next, Looks Good, and then click Done to create the email address. Now you can email receipts to that address to have the activity appear in QuickBooks. Keep in mind that you can send receipts only from registered accounts. Click the Manage Forwarding Email button and add new users in the Manage Receipt Senders section. You can choose only users who have credentials for your QuickBooks company.

No matter which route you take, receipts appear in the For Review section, as shown at the bottom of Figure 11-21.

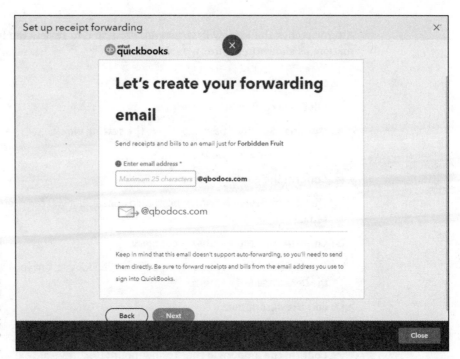

FIGURE 11-20:
You can establish an @qbodocs.com email address that you forward receipts and bills to for automatic posting into QuickBooks.

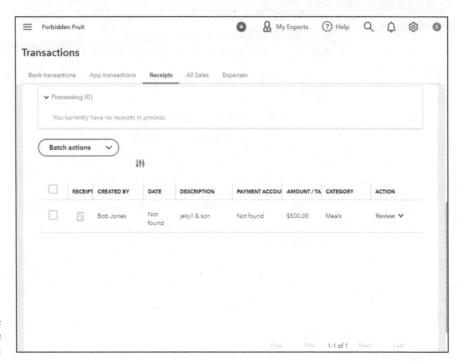

FIGURE 11-21:
A receipt to be reviewed.

After you click the Review link, you are prompted to review the following information, as shown in Figure 11-22. Here's how:

1. Specify a document type.

Choose Receipt or Bill.

2. Optional: Specify a payee, or leave the setting blank.

3. Choose a Bank or Credit Card account.

4. Confirm the payment date.

The date from your receipt or bill should appear, but you can override this setting if necessary.

5. Confirm the account and/or category.

QuickBooks attempts to classify the transaction for you, but you can change the default value if necessary.

6. Edit the description.

You can override the default description, if necessary.

7. Confirm the amount in the "Total Amount (Inclusive of Tax)" field.

QuickBooks attempts to capture this amount for you, but you can correct the amount if necessary.

8. Optional: Enter a memo (not shown in Figure 11-22).

This field allows you to write a paragraph or more about the transaction if you'd like.

9. Optional: Set the following options.

- Click Make Expense and Items Billable if you plan to be reimbursed by a customer.
- Choose a customer from a drop-down list.
- Add a reference number, such as a receipt or invoice number.

10. Click Save and Next to post the transaction and review the next transaction in the queue.

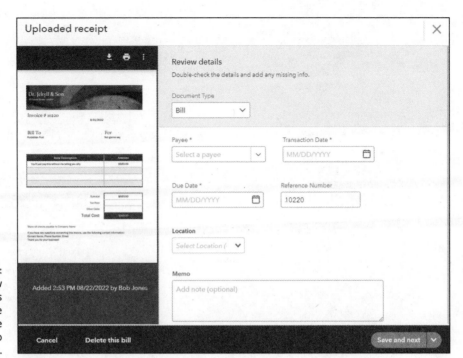

FIGURE 11-22:
You can review uploaded receipts or bills before you commit the transaction to your books.

Chapter **12**

Working with Purchase Orders, Estimates, Projects, and Tags

I n Chapter 6, I discuss most, but not all, of the sales-related transaction forms in QuickBooks, including invoices, sales receipts, credit memos, bank deposits, and refund receipts. Chapter 7 covers most, but not all, expense-related transaction forms, including expenses, checks, bills, and vendor credits. In this chapter, I round out the sales and expense cycle with a discussion of purchase orders and estimates, as well as projects and tags.

Purchase orders, often called POs, can be thought of as pre-bills, as they track amounts that you will ultimately pay to vendors once goods are delivered or services are rendered. This chapter shows how purchase orders and estimates can be closely related if you want. If a purchase order is a pre-bill, then estimates are pre-invoices, in that they track amounts that your customers will eventually pay.

Finally, projects and tags allow you to aggregate together all the revenues and expenses for, you guessed it, a project, so that you can keep tabs on its profitability or group related revenues and costs together. The difference between projects and tags is that projects are related to a single customer, whereas tags can be used in transactions for as many customers as you want.

NONPOSTING TRANSACTIONS

Purchase orders and estimates are two examples of nonposting transactions. Nonposting transactions don't affect your accounting records in any way, but they're helpful because they enable you to track potential transaction information you don't want to forget. Other nonposting transactions include Delayed Charges and Delayed Credits.

Delayed Charges record potential future revenue, much like estimates. In fact, you can convert a Delayed Charge to an invoice in the same way that you convert an estimate to an invoice. For details, see the section, "Converting an estimate to an invoice," later in this chapter.

Conversely, if you want to stage a credit memo to be posted against an invoice later, you can create a Delayed Credit. Unlike Credit Memo transactions that affect your books upon entry, Delayed Credit transactions affect your books only when they're applied to an invoice. This is helpful for situations where you want to post a credit to a customer's account on a contingent basis, such as when the credit will only apply if they place another order in the future.

Creating either transaction is much like creating an invoice, which I discuss in detail in Chapter 6.

Working with Purchase Orders

Businesses that order lots of stuff from vendors often use purchase orders to keep track of the items on order. The purchase-order feature is available only to Plus and Advanced subscribers, so you cannot create purchase orders if you have a Simple Start or Essentials subscription.

Purchase orders don't affect any of your accounts; they simply help you keep track of what you have ordered. When the order arrives, you can compare the goods that come in the door with the ones listed on the purchase order to make sure that they match, and then convert the purchase order to a bill to be paid, which also records the new inventory that you received.

Businesses that use purchase orders typically have a workflow such as the following:

>> You place an order with a vendor and then enter a purchase order in QuickBooks that matches the order you placed.

>> Once you receive the items you ordered, you apply the purchase order against an expense, check, or bill. If the purchase order includes inventory items, applying the purchase order against a payment transaction also updates your on-hand inventory quantities.

>> An Expense or Check transaction indicates that you've already paid the bill, while a Bill transaction indicates that you'll pay the vendor at a later date.

If you use estimates, then your workflow may be a little different:

>> You record the order for goods and/or services from your customer as an estimate.

>> You convert the estimate to a purchase order (this keeps the estimate open but saves you from retyping what you need into a purchase order form).

>> Upon receipt of the goods or services, you apply the purchase order against an expense, check, or bill.

>> An Expense or Check transaction indicates that you've already paid the bill, while a Bill transaction indicates that you'll pay the vendor at a later date.

I discuss estimates in more detail in the section, "Working with Estimates," later in this chapter.

Enabling the purchase order feature

 There are a few settings that you need to turn on or at least consider before you can start using purchase orders in QuickBooks:

1. **Choose Settings ⇨ Account and Settings ⇨ Expenses.**

2. **Toggle on Show Items Table on Expense and Purchase Forms in the Bills and Expenses section.**

3. **Click Save to record your change to the Bills and Expenses section.**

4. **Click on the Purchase Orders section and then toggle on Use Purchase Orders in the Purchase Orders section, as shown in Figure 12-1.**

5. **Optional: Toggle on Custom Transaction Numbers in the Purchase Orders section.**

   Turn this setting on if you want to assign your own transaction numbers to purchase orders. If you leave the setting turned off, QuickBooks will automatically assign purchase order numbers to your transactions.

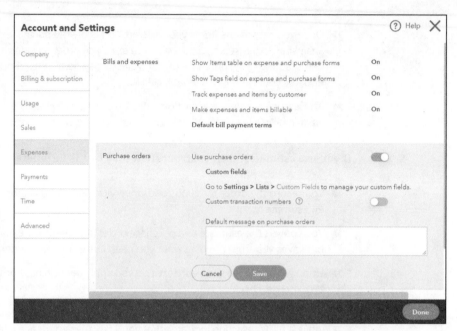

FIGURE 12-1:
Turn on the
purchase-orders
feature and set
up a customized
message to
include purchase
orders to your
vendors.

6. **Optional: Fill in the Default Message on Purchase Orders.**

   This allows you to add boilerplate language that you would like to appear on every purchase order.

7. **Click Save to record your change to the Purchase Orders section.**

8. **Optional: Click in the Messages section to customize the default email message.**

   You can customize the subject line and email body, and then choose to send yourself a copy, as well as copy and/or blind copy one or more email addresses.

9. **Click Save to record your change to the Messages section.**

10. **Click Done to close the Account and Settings window.**

Now you're good to go and ready to start creating purchase orders.

Creating purchase orders

I show you how you can convert an estimate to a purchase order in the upcoming section, "Working with Estimates," but you can also create a purchase order from scratch on your own:

1. **Choose New ⇨ Purchase Order from the left menu bar.**

   A new purchase order window appears, and the purchase order status is set to Open, as shown in Figure 12-2. Purchase orders only have two statuses: Open or Closed.

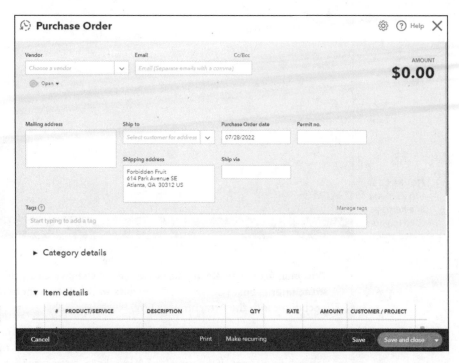

FIGURE 12-2:
A pristine
purchase order
window.

2. **Choose a vendor.**

   The vendor's mailing address appears.

3. **Optional: Choose a customer from the Ship To field.**

   This enables you to instruct the vendor to deliver the goods and/or services directly to your customer.

4. **Add at least one line item either to the Category Details or Item Details sections, as shown in Figure 12-3.**

   Category Details gives you the flexibility to order anything under the sun without having to create an inventory, non-inventory, or service item. As you may surmise, the Item Detail section enables you to choose existing items or add new items on the fly.

5. **Optional: Fill in the Your Message to Vendor field with any special instructions, and/or enter a Memo, which is an internal note that your vendor cannot see.**

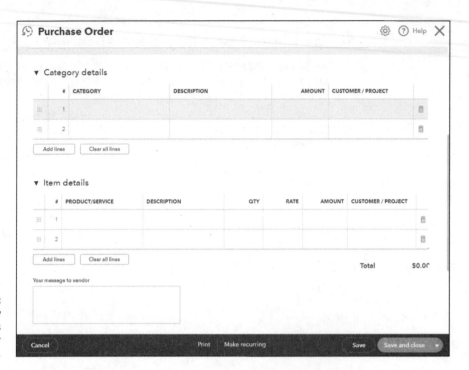

FIGURE 12-3:
Add as many line items as needed to your purchase order.

6. **Optional: Attach an electronic document to the invoice by clicking the Attachments box. You can then navigate to the document or drag the document into the Attachments box.**

   Supporting documents must be no more than 20MB in size, and one of these file types: PDF, JPEG, PNG, DOC, XLSX, CSV, TIFF, GIF, or XML. This means you can include pictures of the product, schematics, or blueprints for an item to be manufactured, and so on. If your vendor sends you a sales order or estimate confirming the transaction, you can add a copy of that document here as well.

7. **At the bottom of the window, you can choose any of the following options:**

   - *Cancel* if you want to discard the purchase order and close the window.

   - *Print* displays a print preview of the purchase order, from which you can download a PDF copy of the PO or print a paper copy.

   - *Make Recurring* to schedule the transaction as a recurring invoice.

   - *More* to Copy, Delete, or view the Audit History of a PO.

TIP

   Don't be alarmed, the More button only appears at the bottom of the screen after you have saved the purchase order or clicked Print to display the print preview.

- *Save* to assign a PO number and save the transaction.

- *Save and Close* to save the PO and close the Purchase Order window.

- *Save and New* to create a new PO.

- *Save and Send* to assign a purchase order number, save the PO, edit the default email message, preview the PO, and then send a copy to the vendor.

Choose between Save and New, Save and Send, and Save and Share Link by clicking the arrow on the button. The option you choose becomes the default behavior for invoices until you make a different selection in the future.

You can also convert an estimate to a purchase order, instead of creating the document from scratch like I just did. I give you the lowdown on this in the section, "Working with Estimates," later in this chapter.

Copying an existing purchase order

Copying a purchase order enables you to make an exact duplicate, which is helpful when you need to reorder the same set of items that you've ordered in the past, or you have converted an estimate to a purchase order and then need to order items from more than one vendor. Simply click the Copy command at the bottom of the Purchase Order screen. After you edit the new PO, you can click the clock icon in the top left-hand corner to view recent purchase orders if you need to remove unwanted items from the first PO. Other ways to open an existing PO include selecting from a vendor's Transaction List or using the Search command on the dashboard to search for the PO.

Receiving items against purchase orders

Once you receive the goods or services that you ordered, you can add all or part of a purchase order to a Bill, Check, or Expense transaction. You record what you've received, and later add the remaining items to another transaction as needed until the entire purchase order is fulfilled. QuickBooks can link multiple transactions to the purchase order and automatically closes the purchase order when you've received everything, or you have clicked the Closed checkbox for any line items that you will not receive in full.

Let's say that you have a purchase order with three items, as shown in Figure 12-4, and you receive one of the three items. Here's how to receive the items against the purchase order:

1. **Open the New menu, and choose Bill, Check, or Expense.**

For this example, I'm using a check.

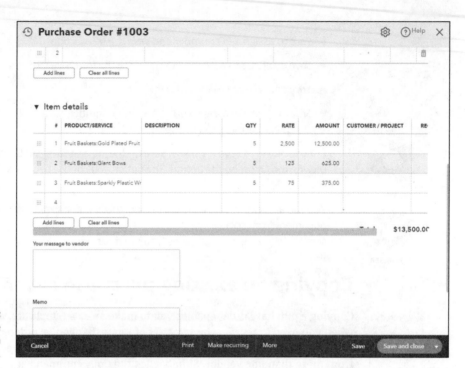

Purchase Order #1003

#	PRODUCT/SERVICE	DESCRIPTION	QTY	RATE	AMOUNT	CUSTOMER / PROJECT	RE
1	Fruit Baskets:Gold Plated Fruit		5	2,500	12,500.00		
2	Fruit Baskets:Giant Bows		5	125	625.00		
3	Fruit Baskets:Sparkly Plastic Wr		5	75	375.00		
4							

Total $13,500.00

Your message to vendor

Memo

Cancel   Print   Make recurring   More   Save   Save and close

FIGURE 12-4:
A purchase
order with
multiple lines.

2. **Select the vendor.**

   Open purchase orders for the vendor appear in the panel on the right side of the screen, where you can see some of the lines on the purchase order as well as its original amount and current balance, as shown in Figure 12-5.

3. **Click Add on the purchase order in the panel.**

   This action adds all the lines on the purchase order to the Item Details or Category Details section, starting at the first available line in the appropriate section.

4. **Edit the quantity or amount for each line to reflect the portion you want to record as partially received or paid.**

   In Figure 12-6, I set the quantities on the first and last lines to zero to indicate that I haven't received those items yet and am not paying for them. I also set the second line to fully receive the ordered item.

REMEMBER

   Note that you can partially pay a line on the purchase order by changing the quantities on that line from the original number on the purchase order to the number you receive.

5. **Save the transaction.**

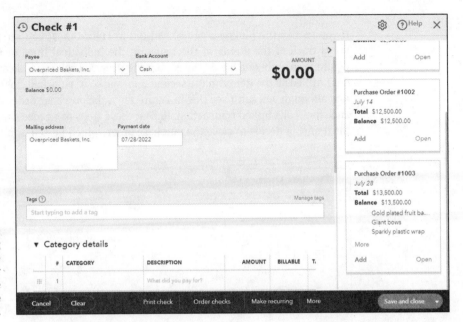

FIGURE 12-5:
A check showing an available purchase order with multiple lines for the selected vendor.

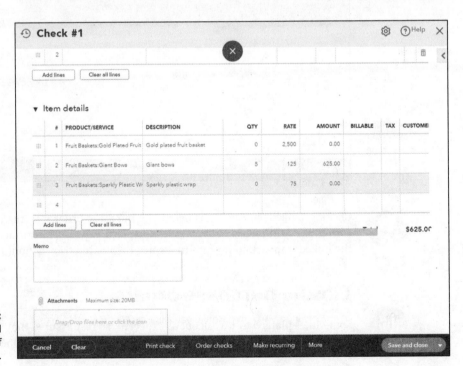

FIGURE 12-6:
Receiving and paying for part of a purchase order.

If you reopen the purchase order, as I did in Figure 12-7, you see that QuickBooks keeps track of the status of the items on the individual lines of the purchase. In Figure 12-6, only one line is closed, but the Received column indicates that the vendor fulfilled all the items on the second line, and so it's marked closed in Figure 12-7. And although you can't see this in Figure 12-7, the purchase order itself is still open and shows one linked transaction. Repeat these steps as needed until you receive all the items, or decide to close the purchase order, which I discuss in the next section.

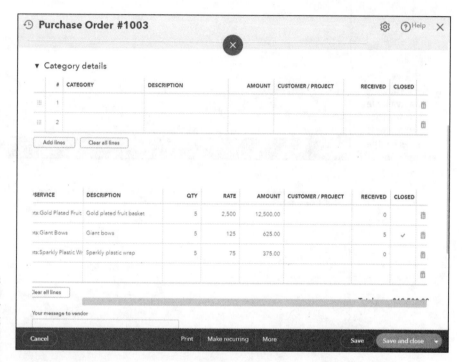

FIGURE 12-7:
Reviewing a purchase order after receiving some of the items on it.

TIP

Clicking Linked Transactions below the purchase order's status in the top-right corner of the Purchase Order window displays any linked transaction types. Click the linked transaction prompt to display the related transaction(s).

Closing purchase orders

Sometimes plans don't work out as expected, so rest assured that you can close an entire purchase order at any time by changing its status from Open to Closed:

1. **Choose Expenses from the left menu bar, and then activate the Vendor tab.**

2. **Click on the vendor that you issued the purchase order to.**

   The vendor's transaction page appears.

3. **Click Filter, choose Purchase Orders from the Type list, optionally set a Date filter, and then click Apply.**

4. **Click on the purchase order in the list or choose View/Edit from the drop-down menu in the Action column.**

   The purchase order appears onscreen.

5. **Click the Open button beneath the Vendor field, change the Purchase Order Status to Closed, and then click anywhere on the PO screen to dismiss the status window.**

6. **Click Save and Close.**

TIP

Rest assured that you can always open a closed purchase order and change its status back to Open, so there's no need to fret about closing out the wrong PO.

Tracking open purchase orders

The Open Purchase Orders Detail report, shown in Figure 12-8, enables you to keep tabs on the status of your pending purchase orders. Choose Reports (Business Overview ⇨ Reports) and start entering **Open Purchase Orders** in the search field. Click the report name from the resulting list. You can also use the Open Purchase Order List report. For more on reports, see Chapter 14.

FIGURE 12-8:
The Open Purchase Orders Detail report.

Working with Estimates

You can use estimates — also known as quotes or bids — to prepare documents that forecast what you'll charge a client to complete a project. Estimates don't affect your general ledger or financial statements but do enable you to keep track of proposals you make to customers. If necessary, you can convert an estimate to a purchase order to facilitate ordering the items needed to complete the job. You can also convert an estimate to an invoice when it's time to bill your customer, which eliminates redundant typing.

WARNING

You can only convert estimates with a Pending or Accepted status to purchase orders or invoices. Converting an estimate to an invoice sets its status to Closed, so convert estimates to purchase orders first if you need both.

Preparing an estimate

Creating an estimate is identical to creating an invoice, and similar to creating a purchase order. Choose New⇨Estimate to display the Estimate page, shown in Figure 12-9. Alternatively, choose Sales⇨All Sales on the navigation bar, click the New Transaction button, and click Estimate. From there, all the steps are the same as those for creating an invoice, so refer to Chapter 6 if you're unclear about the process.

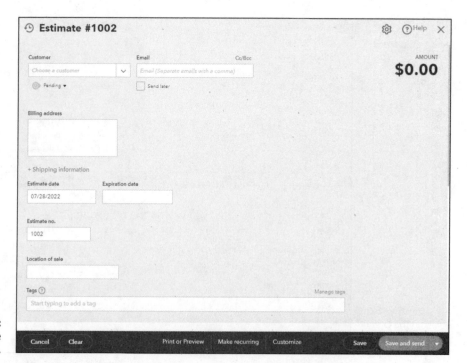

FIGURE 12-9: The Estimate page.

Estimates don't affect your financial reports. If you enter an estimate for $10,000, you won't see that $10,000 in your Profit & Loss report until you convert the estimate to an invoice, as I explain in the sidebar, "Nonposting transactions," near the start of this chapter.

If you are working on a project, you can choose Business Overview ➪ Projects, select the project, and click Add to Project. Doing so gives you the ability to see all transactions related to a project in one place. I discuss projects in more detail later in this chapter.

Invoices have a status of Unpaid or Paid, whereas estimates have a status of Pending, Accepted, Closed, or Rejected. An estimate's status remains Pending if the estimate is open and has not expired, been marked as Accepted or Rejected, or converted to an invoice. The status drop-down menu appears just below the customer's name. You can change the status of an estimate from Pending to any of the following:

>> Accepted, meaning that the estimate is approved

>> Closed, indicating that the job is complete

>> Rejected, recording the fact that your customer declined your offer

Opening an existing estimate works in a similar fashion to opening an existing purchase order. You can click the clock icon at the top left-hand corner of the Estimate screen to view recent transactions, choose the estimate from a customer's Sales Transactions list, or use the Search command on the QuickBooks dashboard.

If you scroll down the Estimate page, you see the additional fields shown in Figure 12-10. If you have enabled sales tax or discounts on your invoice form, those fields appear on your estimates as well. You must customize your invoice screen as described in Chapter 6 if you want to have those fields appear on your estimates. As with purchase orders, you can enter a message to your customer, write an internal memo about the estimate, and/or attach supporting documentation, such as the spreadsheet you used to build the estimate, pictures of the job site, or anything else that you want to be able to reference easily later.

At the bottom of the page, you can do the following:

>> Click Cancel to discard the estimate before you've saved it or to cancel any changes after you've saved it and close the Estimate window.

>> Click Clear to erase an estimate and keep the Estimate window open. A Revert button appears in this position instead of when you edit an existing estimate that will undo any changes you've made.

>> Click Print or Preview to print the document now or mark it to print later.

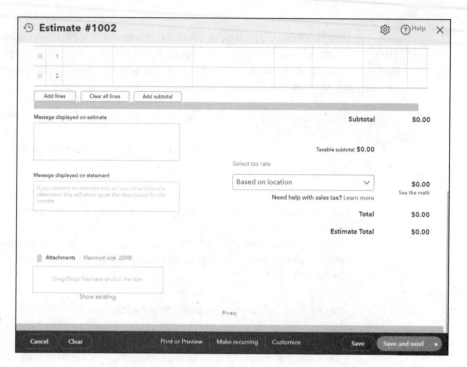

FIGURE 12-10:
The bottom of
the Estimate
page.

>> Click Make Recurring to schedule the transaction as a recurring estimate.

>> Click Customize to choose or create a customized estimate form, as described in Chapter 2.

>> Click More to copy or delete the estimate, as well as view its audit trail. This button appears only after you've saved the estimate.

>> Click Save to assign a number to the estimate and save the transaction.

>> Click Save and Send to assign a number to the estimate, save it, and email a copy to the customer. After you send your estimate, the email time- and date-stamp information appears in the header.

QuickBooks offers an Estimates by Customer report that you can filter by status to generate a list of estimates.

Copying an estimate to a purchase order

Good news! Your customer wants to purchase based on the quote you provided. In this case, you may want to use the estimate information to prepare a purchase order for a vendor. Plus and Advanced subscribers can convert an estimate with a status of Pending or Accepted to a purchase order; these versions turn on this feature by default.

WARNING

Converting an estimate to an invoice automatically changes the estimate's status to Closed. You can convert Pending or Accepted estimates only to purchase orders, so make sure that you create purchase orders before invoices if you're using both types of documents.

In Chapter 5, I discuss creating inventory items, and how to set the I Purchase This Product/Service from a Vendor option for products and services that you set up. Purchase orders are created only for such items. Conversely, all items in an estimate appear in invoices. If you discover that an item isn't appearing on a purchase order as expected, edit the inventory item to turn on the purchase option.

You can convert any estimate with Pending or Accepted status to a purchase order by following these steps:

1. **Create and save a new estimate or open an existing pending estimate.**

   To open an existing estimate, choose New ⇨ Estimates, and click the clock icon to the left of the estimate number in the top-left corner of the screen to see a list of recent estimates.

2. **Click the arrow next to the Create Invoice button and choose Copy to Purchase Order from the drop-down menu, as shown in Figure 12-11.**

   You may see a message that some items on the estimate won't carry over to the purchase order. This situation occurs when one or more items in the estimate don't have the I Purchase This Product/Service from a Vendor option enabled within your item list.

REMEMBER

   The Create Invoice button appears on the Estimate window after you click Save. So, no, you aren't going crazy if you were just scouring a blank estimate window looking for the button.

3. **Click OK if a prompt indicates that some items may not carry over to a purchase order.**

   As shown in Figure 12-12, a purchase order appears.

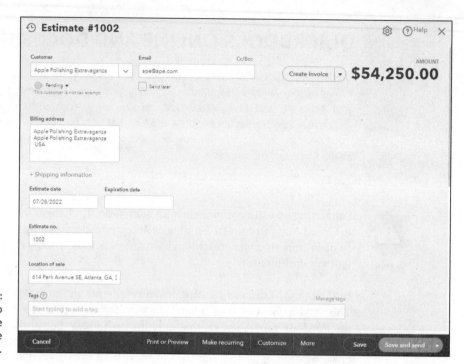

FIGURE 12-11:
Getting ready to
copy an estimate
to a purchase
order.

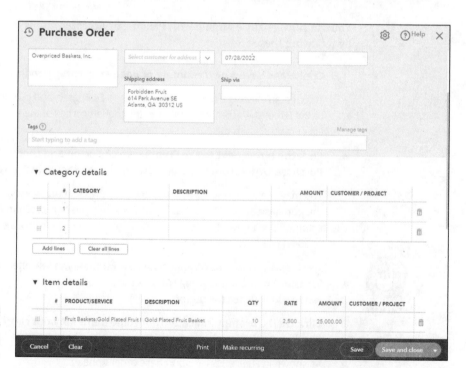

FIGURE 12-12:
A purchase order
created from an
estimate.

4. **Edit the purchase order as necessary, selecting a vendor and adding any more items you want to the purchase order.**

   In this case, the estimate was for ten gold-plated fruit baskets. Five were in stock in inventory, so the purchase order represents the additional five items that must be ordered to fulfill the estimate.

5. **Choose Save and Send, Save and New, or Save and Closed, as appropriate.**

Converting an estimate to an invoice

You've finished the project and/or delivered the goods, so it's time to send your customer an invoice. You're most of the way there; you simply need to convert the estimate to an invoice. You can adjust the invoice by adding or removing lines as needed. You have several ways to create an invoice from an estimate.

REMEMBER

Converting an estimate to an invoice changes the status to Closed, which means that you can no longer convert the estimate to a purchase order. If you need to generate a purchase order from an estimate, make sure to do that first before you create the invoice.

Use one of these options to create an invoice from an estimate:

» Open the Invoice window and select a customer with the open estimate. As shown in Figure 12-13, you see a list of available documents you can link to the invoice, including any estimates. Click the Add button below an estimate to add the line items to your invoice.

» Filter a customer's Sales Transactions page to display only open estimates and click the Create Invoice link in the Action column next to the estimate you want to convert, as shown in Figure 12-14. This action creates a new invoice based on the estimate.

» On a customer's Sales Transactions page, open the estimate, and click the Create Invoice button. This button is available when the estimate status is Pending or Accepted. You can't create invoices from Closed or Rejected estimates.

TIP

No matter which routes you take, creating an invoice from an estimate changes the status of the estimate to Closed, even if you don't invoice the customer for all lines on the estimate. You can change an estimate's status from Closed to Pending or Accepted (or even Rejected), but doing so makes *all* lines on the estimate available for invoicing, which means that you could accidentally invoice your customer twice for the same items. If you need to create a partial invoice, it's best to first make a copy of the invoice that has only the pending items in it and then close the original estimate.

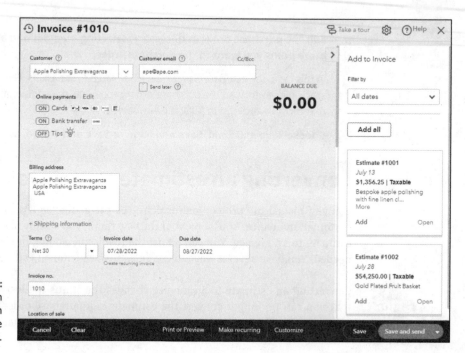

FIGURE 12-13:
Copying an
estimate to an
invoice from the
Invoice window.

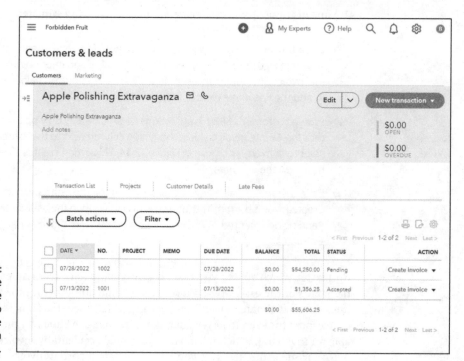

FIGURE 12-14:
Click the Create
Invoice link in the
Action column to
use estimate
information in an
invoice.

If you frequently need to send an invoice for only a portion of an estimate, progress billing may be a better fit for you. Read more in the section, "Creating a progress invoice for an estimate," later in this chapter.

Copying an existing estimate

Copying an estimate enables you to make an exact duplicate, which is helpful if you want to send a partial invoice, or another customer wants the same set of items. Open an existing estimate from a customer's Sales Transactions list or choose New ⇨ Estimates and click the clock icon to the left of the estimate number. Figure 12-15 shows an estimate with a status of Closed.

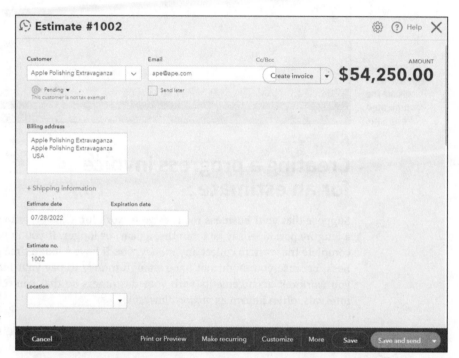

FIGURE 12-15: Choose Copy from the More menu to duplicate an estimate, even if it's closed or rejected.

Click the More button at the bottom of the screen and choose Copy from the pop-up menu. A copy of the estimate appears, along with a message explaining that you're viewing a copy of an estimate, as shown in Figure 12-16. You might change the customer, for example, or add, delete, or modify the pricing. Click Save or Save and Send in the bottom-right corner of the window, as appropriate.

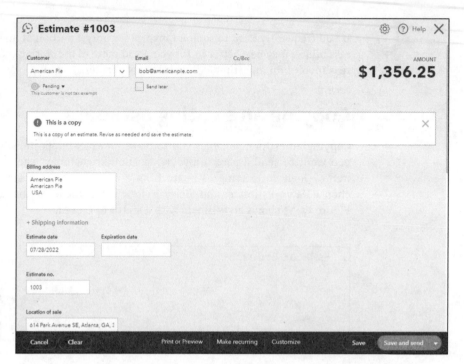

Estimate #1003

Customer
American Pie

Email
bob@americanpie.com

Cc/Bcc

AMOUNT
$1,356.25

Pending ▾
This customer is not tax exempt

Send later

ℹ **This is a copy**
This is a copy of an estimate. Revise as needed and save the estimate.

Billing address
American Pie
American Pie
USA

+ Shipping information

Estimate date
07/28/2022

Expiration date

Estimate no.
1003

Location of sale
614 Park Avenue SE, Atlanta, GA, 3

Cancel   Clear   Print or Preview   Make recurring   Customize   Save   Save and send ▾

FIGURE 12-16:
Edit and then save the duplicated estimate.

Creating a progress invoice for an estimate

Suppose that your business requires your work for a customer to stretch out over a lengthy period — say, six months, a year, or longer. If you must wait until you complete the work to collect any money, you'll have a tough time staying in business, because you might not have enough money to pay your bills. Accordingly, you work out arrangements with your customers so that you're paid at various intervals, often known as *progress invoicing*.

TIP

Progress invoicing often goes hand in hand with project work, which I discuss later in this chapter. You don't have to use the Projects feature to generate progress invoices, but if you plan to use projects, make sure to set the project up before you create even an estimate.

Progress invoicing lets you send invoices to your customers at periodic milestones that you and your customer agree on. In short, you can create as many invoices as you need for a given estimate until the work is completed in full, or all goods have been provided.

REMEMBER

To enable the progress invoicing feature, choose Settings ⇨ Account and Settings ⇨ Sales. As shown in Figure 12-17, click the switch in the Progress Invoicing section, click Update to confirm that you're cool with updating your invoice template to accommodate progress invoicing, click Save, and then click Done.

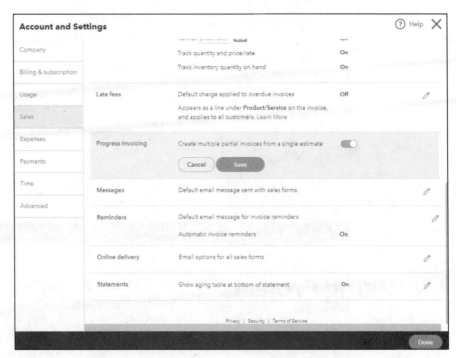

FIGURE 12-17:
Turn on the option to create partial invoices.

Next, create an estimate in the usual fashion, as described earlier in this chapter. When you're ready to invoice a portion of the estimate, create an invoice, which displays the window shown in Figure 12-18.

Based on the choice you make in this window; an invoice is created with the appropriate values filled. If you opt to create an invoice with custom amounts for each line, an invoice is created with no amounts filled in so that you can supply them. You create additional progress invoices for the estimate as appropriate until the estimate is closed out.

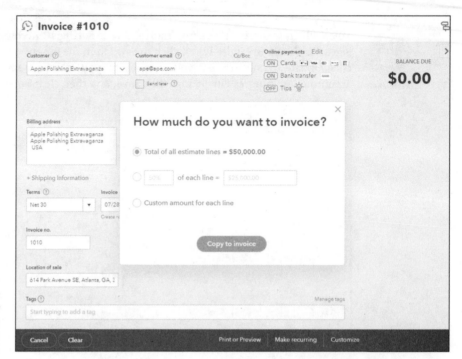

FIGURE 12-18:
Use this window to establish the amount of a progress invoice.

Managing Projects

If your business completes projects for your customers, the Projects feature helps you organize, in one central location, all the pieces — that is, associated transactions, time spent, and necessary reports — that make up, well, a project. Also, the reports included in the Projects feature help you determine each project's profitability and keep on top of unbilled time and expenses as well as nonbillable time. You'll still complete all the various sales transaction forms described in this chapter in the same way that I describe them, with one change: Instead of starting from the Sales Transaction list or the New menu, you'll be able (but not required) to start from the Project tab. If you enable the Projects feature before you enter transactions, your picture of a project's profitability will be clearer.

TIP

The Tags feature allows you to track revenues and expenses across multiple customers if needed. In fact, you can go wild and use both projects and tags together if you need that level of tracking. I discuss this in the section, "Tagging Transactions," later in this chapter.

Turning on the Project feature

You must have a Plus or Advanced subscription to use the Projects feature, which means this feature is not available to Simple Start or Essentials subscribers.

REMEMBER

The Projects feature is enabled by default in the Plus and Advanced editions of QuickBooks. You must manually enable it in QB Accountant.

Follow these steps to enable the Projects feature:

1. **Choose Settings ⇨ Account and Settings ⇨ Advanced ⇨ Projects.**

2. **Toggle on the Organize All Job-Related Activity in One Place option, as shown in Figure 12-19.**

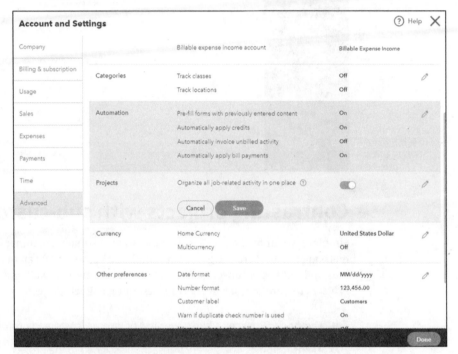

FIGURE 12-19:
Enabling projects
in QuickBooks.

3. **Click Save to record your change.**

4. **Click Done to close the task pane.**

   A Projects command now appears on the left menu bar in Accountant View, as shown in Figure 12-20; otherwise, you find it under Business View ⇨ Projects. Either way, you are prompted to start your first project when you choose the Projects command.

TIP

The primary admin user in a QuickBooks company can turn the projects feature off. In Step 2 you would toggle Organize All Job-Related Activity in One Place option off, instead of on.

Before you jump in and start creating projects, read on.

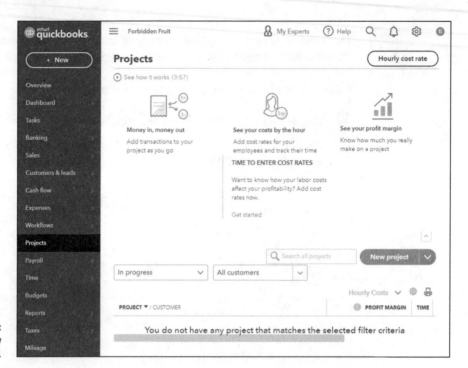

FIGURE 12-20:
Starting a new
project.

Contrasting projects with sub-customers

Simple Start and Essentials subscribers can use sub-customers as a simplistic method of project tracking — I say simplistic because you can only track invoices. Plus and Advanced subscribers create sub-customers as well, but can also use the Projects feature to track every transaction type. Each project's page has five tabs:

>> **Overview:** Provides a bird's-eye view of income, costs, and profit margin.

>> **Transactions:** Shows every transaction assigned to the project.

>> **Time Activity:** Displays view activity by time period and then by employee or service.

>> **Project Reports:** Three project-specific reports are available.

>> **Attachments:** Shows files that you have chosen to upload to QuickBooks Online.

TIP

See the section, "Creating a New Record," near the start of this chapter, for details on the types of files that you can attach.

The Projects feature keeps all the information for each project in one place. Sub-customers don't offer this centralization — unless you convert them to projects.

>> Any sub-customers that you wish to convert to projects must be marked as billed to the parent customer. To confirm this setting, edit the sub-customer record and then ensure that Bill Parent Customer is enabled just below the Parent Customer field.

>> You can choose which sub-customers you want to convert to projects, and which ones you don't.

>> You can't undo the conversion of a sub-customer to a project.

First, I show you how to create a project, and then I show you how to convert sub-customers to projects.

Creating a new project

You can create projects by following steps that are similar to adding records to the other lists I've discussed in this chapter, or you can convert a sub-customer to a project. Let's first create a project by following the steps that are similar to creating customers or vendors:

1. **Choose Projects (Business Overview ⇨ Projects) on the left menu.**

2. **Click Start a Project if you haven't created a project yet, or click New Project.**

3. **At a minimum, fill in the Project Name and Customer fields on the New Project task pane, shown in Figure 12-21.**

   You can optionally specify start and end dates as well as project status, and add notes. You cannot add attachments to a project, but you can add attachments to customer records as well as customer-related transactions.

4. **Click Save to display the page for your project, as shown in Figure 12-22.**

   Although you specified customer, no transactions appear on the Projects page. Newly created projects have no transactions, so there is nothing to see just yet.

To convert a sub-customer to a project, choose Sales ⇨ Customers (Sales & Expenses ⇨ Customers). A message asks whether you want to convert the first level of sub-customers to projects. Click Convert Now in the message window, and select eligible sub-customers to convert, as shown in Figure 12-23.

TIP

If the Convert Sub-customers to Projects prompt doesn't appear on your Customers screen, choose Projects on the left menu, and then choose Convert from Sub-customer from the New Project drop-down menu.

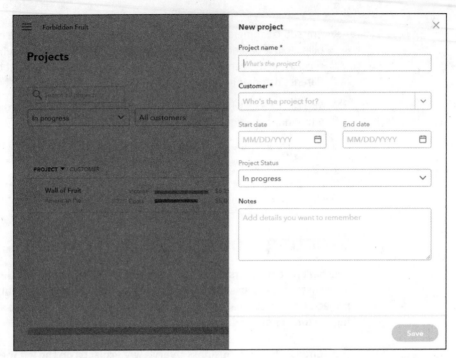

FIGURE 12-21:
Creating a
project.

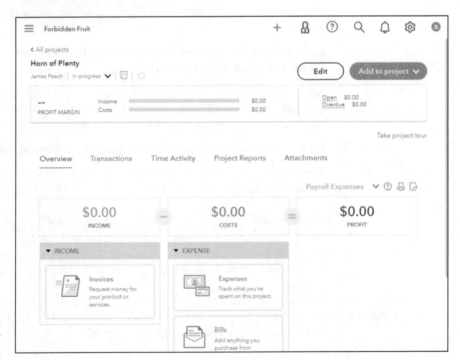

FIGURE 12-22:
Projects page for
a new project.

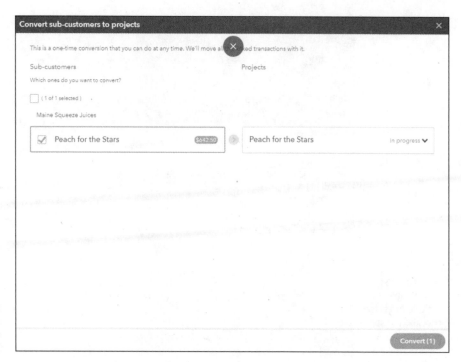

FIGURE 12-23:
Converting a
sub-customer to
a project.

After you click Convert (see Chapter 4; this is not shown in Figure 4-13), a message explains that you're about to convert a sub-customer to a project — and that there's no going back. If you're sure you want to do this, click Continue to convert the sub-customer(s), set the status of the project(s) to "in progress," and then decide whether you want to go to the Projects Center or redisplay the Customer list. Any previous activity for the sub-customer now appears on the corresponding Projects page.

WARNING

Be careful if you're thinking about changing the customer name in existing transactions to pull those transactions into the project. Changing the customer can have repercussions throughout QuickBooks. If you try to change the customer assigned to a payment transaction that you've deposited, for example, you're warned that you must remove the transaction from the deposit before you can change the customer name, which will mess up your deposit unless you remember to add the payment to the deposit again. So you see, things can get complicated very quickly. Even though there's a connection between a customer and sub-customer or project, entries in the Customers list are unique list elements.

TIP

You can choose whether to show projects in your customer list alongside any sub-customers. To do so, choose Sales ➪ Customers (Sales & Expenses ➪ Customers) to display the Customers page. Click the Table Settings icon just above the Action column, and then click Include Projects, as shown in Figure 12-24. You can see projects on the Customers page and in list boxes on transactions, as well as on the Projects Center page.

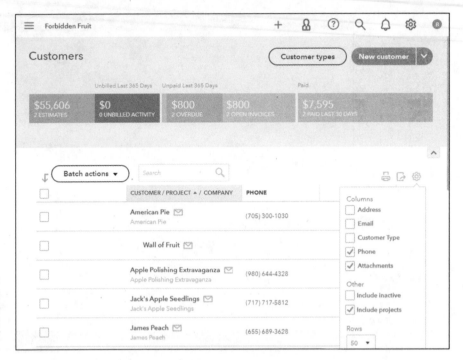

FIGURE 12-24:
Enable the
Include Projects
checkbox to see
projects in your
customer list.

Adding transactions to a project

There's no special, secret way to add transactions to a project. Nope, I'm not talking double secret probation from *Animal House*. In fact, you have two choices. First, you can create transactions in the manner I discuss in Chapter 6, but you choose the project name from the Customer drop-down list rather than choosing the customer name itself, as shown in Figure 12-25.

Second, you can start most, but not all, transactions by clicking Add in the Projects Center, which prefills the project name on the transaction. Inexplicably, the Projects Center resolutely does not allow you to create a Sales Receipt transaction, so simply choose New ⇨ Sales Receipt instead.

Reporting on projects

The power of projects becomes apparent once a project accumulates some activity, such as invoices, time charges, expenses, and so on. The Project Center allows you to list your transactions on the Transactions and Time Activity tabs, while the Project Reports tab offers three reports:

>> Project Profitability is a Profit & Loss report for the project, as shown in Figure 12-26.

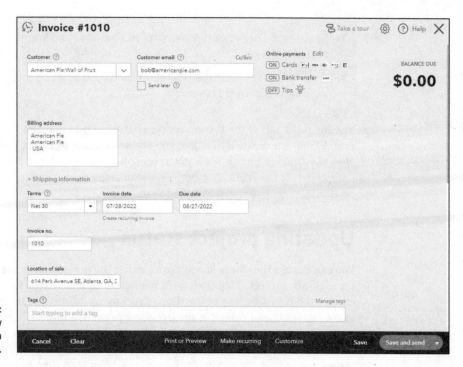

FIGURE 12-25:
Creating a new
transaction for a
project.

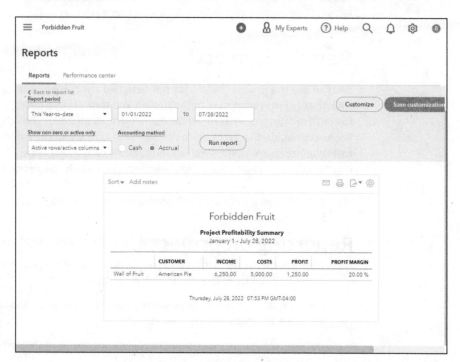

FIGURE 12-26:
A sample Project
Profitability
report.

>> Time Cost by Employee or Vendor reflects the labor and external service fees posted to the job.

>> An Unbilled Time and Expenses report shows you time and costs assigned to the project but not yet billed.

The Overview tab of the Project center enables you to manage the status of projects. When you create a new job, the status defaults to In Progress, but you can click the Options button for a given project to change the status to Not Started, Completed, or Canceled. The Options menu also enables you to delete a project if no transactions have been assigned to it.

Updating project status

You can change the status of a job from either the project list or the Overview page for a specific project. Click Options in the Action column on the Project list page, or change the status by way of the drop-down menu adjacent to the customer name at the top left-hand corner of the Overview page for a project. You can change the status of any project to Not Started, In Progress, Completed, or Cancelled. The first drop-down field above your list of projects enables you to filter the project list by status, the second allows you to filter by customer, and then to the right of that, a Search field enables you to search based upon a portion of the project name.

Deleting projects

You can delete a project if you have not assigned any transactions to it yet. To do so, click the Options menu next to the project and then choose Delete Project. Click Yes to confirm that you wish to delete the project. Remember, though, that in Quick-Books Online, no list items are truly deleted. Contrary to the convention of inactivating unnecessary customers, vendors, and so on, Projects use the term *Delete* as if you could truly delete them. Rest assured, you can always revive deleted projects:

1. Click the settings button just above your list of projects, and then choose Show Deleted Projects.

2. Choose All Statuses from the Status field above your list of projects.

3. Click Options in the Action column for any deleted project, and then make a choice from the list, as shown in Figure 12-27.

4. Click the settings button just above your list of projects, and then clear the Show Deleted Projects checkbox.

WARNING

You can't see your active projects until you clear the Show Deleted Projects checkbox from the Project Settings menu.

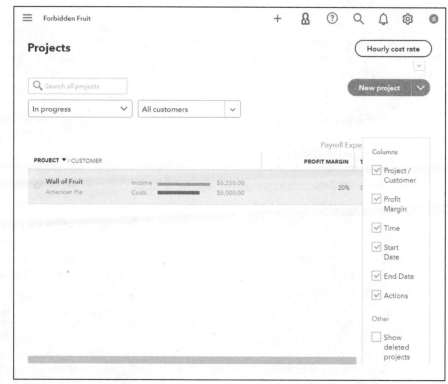

Tagging Transactions

Tags offer an additional dimension for categorizing and reporting on related transactions. As you saw in the previous section, Projects allow you to group related revenues and expenses together for work that you do for a specific customer. Tags are far less structured, meaning that you can tag just about every type of transaction except for transfers and journal entries.

TAGS, CATEGORIES, PROJECTS, CLASSES, LOCATIONS, AND CUSTOM FIELDS

Yikes, that is quite a title for this callout section! Modern society tends to offer overwhelming levels of choices, and QuickBooks is riding that wave for sure when it comes to ways that you can group related transactions together. First off, QuickBooks confusingly uses the words Categories and Accounts interchangeably when referring to

(continued)

(continued)

accounts on your chart of accounts, which is the most basic level of grouping related transactions together. Keep in mind that any changes you make to categories or accounts affect your books and financial statements. You might think of the other options as shadow-reporting capabilities that do not affect your books.

As I discuss in this chapter, the Projects feature offers a way to group transactions together for specific projects. There are also *four* other ways to group related transactions.

- **Tags:** This feature is automatically enabled in QuickBooks, and as you'll see, you can create tags as well as sub-tags.

- **Classes:** Plus and Advanced subscribers can assign a class at the top level of a transaction, meaning all line items are associated with a single class, or assign one or more classes to specific rows within a transaction. When enabling classes, you can instruct QuickBooks to remind you when a transaction isn't assigned to a class.

- **Locations:** Location tracking isn't as granular as class tracking, which means it works more like tags. When enabling Locations, QuickBooks allows you to pick a single label for the Location field, which can be Business, Department, Division, Location, Property, Store, or Territory.

- **Custom Fields:** Essentials and Plus subscribers can add up to three custom fields to sales forms, while Plus subscribers can also add up to three custom fields to purchase orders. Advanced subscribers can add up to 12 custom fields to each type of form, which includes sales forms, expense forms, purchase orders, customer profiles, and vendor profiles. Custom fields can also be included in reports.

To enable classes and locations, choose the Gear icon ➪ Account and Settings ➪ Advanced ➪ Categories and then toggle on Track Classes and/or Track Locations; adjust the options if desired, and then click Done. Enabling the Class feature unlocks five new reports: Class List, Profit and Loss by Class, Purchase by Class Detail, Sales by Class Detail, and Sales by Class Summary. Enabling the Location feature unlocks the same five reports, but based upon location instead of class. As you'll see, the Tag feature only offers two reports: Profit and Loss by Tag Group and Transaction List by Tag Group.

You can create or manage custom fields by choosing the Gear icon ➪ Custom Fields. Depending upon your subscription level, you're able to choose which forms a custom field appears on and whether the custom field prints.

Keep in mind that none of these tracking features are exclusive to each other. You always have to assign transaction rows to an account or category, but you can then go farther by assigning transactions to customers, sub-customers, or projects, in addition to class, location, custom field, and/or tag.

Creating Tag Groups and Tags

You can quickly add tags on the fly when creating new transactions by typing a tag name in the Tags field and then clicking Add. However, you need to create any tags in advance that you want to assign to existing transactions. Here's how to create such tags:

1. **Choose the Gear icon ⇨ Tags to display the Tag list.**

You can also choose Banking ⇨ Tags (Bookkeeping ⇨ Tags).

REMEMBER

The left menu bar has two different modes: Accountant View and Business View. As noted throughout this book, the command names in the left menu bar differ between the two views. Similarly, when using Accountant View, the Tags window appears as a tab in the Banking window, whereas in Business View, the Tags window appears on its own. Apart from that, everything looks the same, but this doesn't explain why the Tags window might appear on the Banking page in some companies and as its own page in others. Click the Gear icon and choose either Accountant View or Business View at the bottom right-hand corner to switch between the views.

2. **Click New, and then choose Tag Group or Tag.**

In QuickBooks vernacular, tag groups are parent tags, while tags are treated as children tags, or sub-tags. Each tag group can optionally have one or more sub-tags associated with it.

3. **Create a tag group or tag.**

You can choose one of the following:

- **Tag Groups:** As shown in Figure 12-28, you assign a tag group name, optionally assign one of 16 colors to the tag group, and then click Save. You can then fill in the Tag Name field and click Add as needed to add sub-tags to the group. Click Done to close the Tag Group task pane.

TIP

The number of tag groups you can create depends on your subscription level. Simple Start, Essentials, and Plus users can create 40 tag groups, whereas Advanced users have unlimited tag groups. In any version of QuickBooks, you can assign up to 300 tags across all your tag groups. You can create unlimited ungrouped tags, which QuickBooks refers to as "flat" tags. Tags that are not within a group cannot be viewed in reports, but you can use them for searches to return lists of transactions that have that tag.

- **Tags (sub-tags):** As shown in Figure 12-27, the Create New Tag task pane only has two fields, Tag Name and Group. You are returned to the Tag list when you click Save. Accordingly, it's more efficient to use the Tag Groups command when you need to create multiple tags.

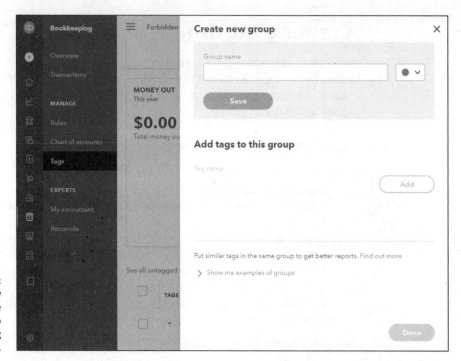

FIGURE 12-28:
The Create New Group task pane enables you to establish new tag groups and tags.

REMEMBER

Each tag can only be associated with a single group. For instance, if you sell fruit baskets internationally and domestically, you might create tag groups for Domestic Sales and International Sales. In this case, a Fruit Basket tag (sub-tag) can only be associated with Domestic Sales or International Sales, but not both. One solution could be to have Fruit Baskets be the tag group and to set up Domestic Sales and International Sales as tags (sub-tags). Fortunately, you can delete tags and tag groups (as opposed to marking them inactive, which is what QuickBooks requires for most list items).

- **Tags (flat tags):** A flat tag is not associated with a group. Although it's not readily apparent, you can fill out the Tag field on the Create New Tag task pane, leave the Group field blank, and then Click Save. You can't choose flat tags in your reports, but you can use the various transaction filter options in QuickBooks to unearth transactions that have flat tags assigned.

Tagging existing transactions

When you have at least one tag or group created, you can start tagging existing transactions:

1. **Choose Banking ➪ Tags (Bookkeeping ➪ Tags).**

2. **Click Start Tagging Transactions in the Money In or Money Out sections or choose See All Untagged Transactions.**

A list of your transactions appears.

3. **As shown in Figure 12-29, select one or more transactions that you want to tag.**

You can use the Filter button to select groups of transactions if you like.

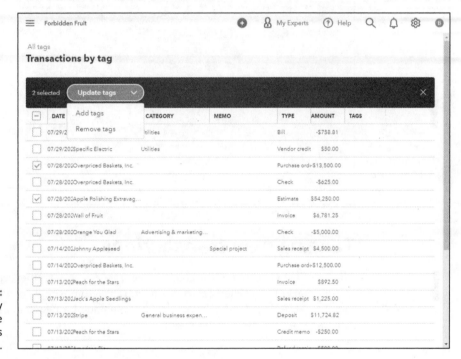

FIGURE 12-29: You can apply tags to multiple transactions at once.

4. **Choose Update Tags ⇨ Add Tags.**

You can also choose Remove Tags from the Update Tags drop-down menu if you want to reassign tag transactions.

5. **Choose or type the name of the tag and click Apply.**

Tags appear in the new Tags column.

REMEMBER

You can assign as many tags as you want to a transaction, but you can only choose one tag (sub-tag) per tag group (parent tag). The nuance goes further, as you cannot assign a tag group (parent tag) to a transaction — you must choose a tag (sub-tag) that is associated with a tag group (parent tag).

Figure 12-30 shows the Bananas and Grapes tags added to the Peeling Services group, along with Apples and Pears in the Polishing Services group.

CHAPTER 12 **Working with Purchase Orders, Estimates, Projects, and Tags** **309**

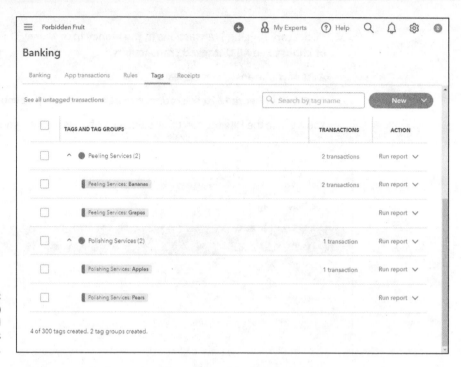

FIGURE 12-30:
Tags (sub-tags) have been added to two tag groups (parent tags).

Tagging new transactions

The Tag field appears on just about every transaction screen except for transfers and journal entries. When creating a new transaction, simply choose one or more tags from the Tags field or start typing the name of a new tag, and then choose Add Tag from the drop-down menu.

Disabling the Tags feature

Although the Tags feature is automatically enabled, you can always choose to turn it off if you don't plan on using it. You need to turn the feature off in two places by following these steps:

1. **Choose the Gear icon ⇨ Account and Settings ⇨ Sales ⇨ Sales Form Content.**

2. **Toggle off the Tags feature and then click Save.**

3. **Choose Expenses ⇨ Bills and Expenses in the Accounts and Settings window.**

4. **Toggle off the Tags feature and then click Save.**

5. **Click Done to close the Account and Settings window.**

3

Budgeting, Reporting, and Analysis

Create and track budgets at the company and class level.

Run and customize reports in QuickBooks.

Analyze QuickBooks data in Excel.

Chapter **13**

Creating Budgets in QuickBooks

Many businesses create annual budgets that enable them to project revenues and expenses for the coming year. As the year rolls on, actual results are compared to the budget to determine if things are going as planned. As you'll see in this chapter, Plus and Advanced subscribers can create budgets based upon current or prior fiscal year actual results or import a budget from a CSV file that you edit in a spreadsheet program such as Microsoft Excel or Google Sheets. Once you have created a budget, you can then run Budget Overview or Budgets vs. Actual reports in QuickBooks.

Creating a Budget

You're free to create budgets at any time in QuickBooks, but most businesses tend to create budgets toward the end of one fiscal year for the following year. Let's walk through the steps:

1. **Choose Settings ⇨ Account and Settings ⇨ Advanced ⇨ Accounting and confirm that the first month of your fiscal year is set correctly.**

   Click on the section or choose the pencil icon to edit the fiscal year if needed.

2. **Choose Budgets (Business Overview ⇨ Budgets).**

   The Budgets page appears.

3. **If you haven't created a budget before, click Add Budget to display the New Budget page shown in Figure 13-1.**

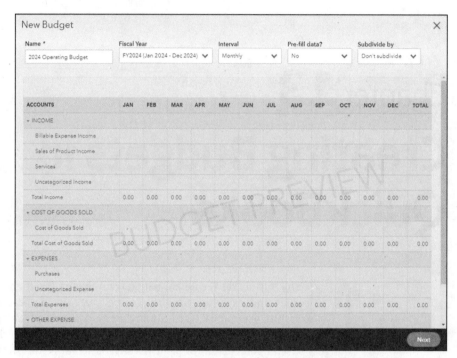

FIGURE 13-1:
The New
Budget page.

4. **Assign a name to your budget, such as 2024 Operating Budget.**

5. **Choose a fiscal year from the list.**

   QuickBooks allows you to create a budget for the current year and any of the six subsequent years.

6. **Choose Monthly, Quarterly, or Yearly from the Interval list.**

7. **Choose No or pick Actual Data for the previous or current fiscal years from the "Pre-Fill Data?" list.**

8. **Choose Don't Subdivide, Customer, Class, or Location from the "Subdivide By" list.**

9. **Click Next to create your budget.**

   The budget appears, as shown in Figure 13-2.

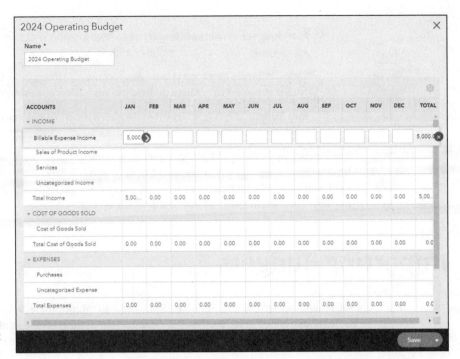

ACCOUNTS	JAN	FEB	MAR	APR	MAY	JUN	JUL	AUG	SEP	OCT	NOV	DEC	TOTAL
▾ INCOME													
Billable Expense Income	5,000												5,000.0
Sales of Product Income													
Services													
Uncategorized Income													
Total Income	5,00...	0.00	0.00	0.00	0.00	0.00	0.00	0.00	0.00	0.00	0.00	0.00	5,00.
▾ COST OF GOODS SOLD													
Cost of Goods Sold													
Total Cost of Goods Sold	0.00	0.00	0.00	0.00	0.00	0.00	0.00	0.00	0.00	0.00	0.00	0.00	0.0
▾ EXPENSES													
Purchases													
Uncategorized Expense													
Total Expenses	0.00	0.00	0.00	0.00	0.00	0.00	0.00	0.00	0.00	0.00	0.00	0.00	0.0

FIGURE 13-2:
The Budget
input page.

10. **Complete the budget and remember to click Save periodically so that you don't lose your work.**

    You can safely type over any numbers that are prepopulated if you brought in the actuals from the prior or current year.

    TIP

    As shown in Figure 13-2, a blue arrow appears whenever you select a cell that is in the first through eleventh month of your budget; you can click this arrow to copy the amount for that month through the end of the fiscal year.

11. **Choose Save and Close from the Save drop-down menu when you're ready to leave the budget.**

12. **Your budget now appears on the Budget page.**

    The Action menu offers the following choices:

    - **Edit** returns you to the budget page shown in Figure 13-2 so that you can continue working on the budget or make other changes.

    - **Copy** enables you to duplicate the budget.

    - **Delete** removes a budget from the list.

- **Run Budgets vs. Actuals Report** generates a report that compares your actual results against your monthly budget.

TIP

Click Customize and then choose Accounts vs. Quarters or Accounts vs. Total if you want to create a quarterly or annual comparison report.

- **Run Budget Overview Report** generates a report that details your budget.

TIP

The Budget vs. Actuals and Budget Overview reports are also available in the Business Overview section of the Reports page, or you can type the word **Budget** in the Find Report by Name field. In this case, you need to choose the budget you want to use from the Budgets list at the top of the report.

Importing Budgets

As I mention in the previous section, you can prepopulate your budget within QuickBooks based upon previous or current year actuals. You can also import budgets that you create Microsoft Excel or Google Sheets into QuickBooks instead.

WARNING

Make sure that you add any new accounts to your chart of accounts before you create the budget template. You cannot add new accounts to the chart of accounts by importing a budget template.

REMEMBER

There's a bit of chicken versus egg involved here, as the Import Budgets button you need to click isn't available until you have created at least one budget. Follow the steps in the previous section, if needed, to create a budget; you don't have to change or type any values. You can delete the temporary budget after you've imported your true budget.

Here's how to create a budget in Microsoft Excel or Google Sheets:

1. **Choose Budgets (Business Overview ⇨ Budgets) and then click Import Budget.**

2. **Click Sample.csv as shown in Figure 13-3 to generate a template that you can populate in a spreadsheet platform.**

3. **Change the name and location of the template file if you want, and then click Save.**

4. **Open the budget template.**

   - **Microsoft Excel:** Choose File ⇨ Open and then change the File Type list to Text Files. Select the .csv file and then click Open.

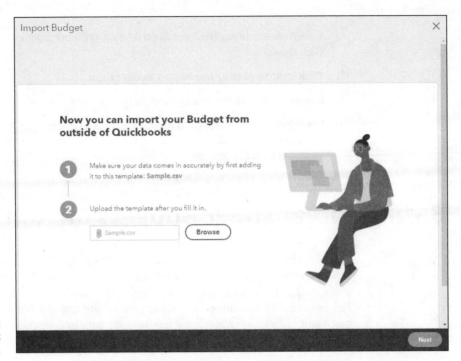

FIGURE 13-3:
The Budget
Import page.

- **Google Sheets:** Choose File ⇨ Import ⇨ Upload. Make another choice from the Replace Spreadsheet list if needed, and then click Import.

The columns in the budget template are based upon your fiscal year, while the rows are based upon your chart of accounts. Make sure that you do not add any additional rows or columns to the template format.

TIP

5. **Once you've completed your budget, the next step is to save the .csv file.**

- **Microsoft Excel:** Choose File ⇨ Save and then File ⇨ Close.

It's important to close the budget file to ensure that it uploads cleanly to QuickBooks. Leaving files open in a software program sometimes creates operating system locks that can prevent files from opening or cause them to be corrupted upon upload.

TIP

- **Google Sheets:** Choose File ⇨ Download ⇨ Comma Separated Value (.csv), specify a name and location for the file, and then click Save. Click the Sheets Home button to the left of the File command to close the spreadsheet so that you aren't tempted to make changes that won't be in the .csv file that you created.

6. **In QuickBooks, choose Budgets (Business Overview ⇨ Budgets) ⇨ Import Budget.**

7. **Click Browse, select the `.csv` file that contains your budget, and then click Open.**

8. **Click Next to display the Import Budget page.**

9. **Assign a name to the budget and then click Save.**

   The Import Budget page is simply another version of the page that you use to edit a budget in QuickBooks, and you can feel free to override any of the values imported from the `.csv` file.

Basing Spreadsheet Budgets on Actuals

The budget template that you can download from QuickBooks may appear to be rather spartan. Since you're expected to not insert any rows or columns may make you wonder, "What's the point?" For one, in Microsoft Excel or Google Sheets, you can copy and paste values from other worksheets into the budget template. You may want to do so by copying the numbers for your budget and then pasting them as values.

>> **Microsoft Excel:** Choose Home ⇨ Paste ⇨ Paste Special ⇨ Values and then click OK. You can also choose a Paste Values option from the Paste drop-down menu.

>> **Google Sheets:** Choose Edit ⇨ Paste Special ⇨ Values Only.

Another approach is to export the Profit and Loss by Month report to Microsoft Excel or Google Sheets, and then use the SUMIF function to pull the budgeted amounts into your budget template:

1. **In QuickBooks, choose Reports (Business Overview ⇨ Reports) and then select the Profit and Loss by Month report.**

2. **Choose a period to base your budget on, such as Last Year.**

   Choose Last Year or This Year, but not Last Year-to-Date or This Year-to-Date so that you have 12 consecutive periods in the report.

REMEMBER

3. **Choose Cash or Accrual from the Accounting Method section.**

4. **Click Run Report to update the report.**

5. **Choose Export ⇨ Export to Excel.**

6. **Open the spreadsheet.**

- **Microsoft Excel:** Click the file on your browser's Downloads bar, or choose File ⇨ Open ⇨ Browse and then select the resulting spreadsheet and choose Open.

- **Google Sheets:** Advanced subscribers can choose Export ⇨ Export to Google Sheets. All other subscribers can choose Export ⇨ Export to Excel, and then in Google Sheets, choose File ⇨ Import ⇨ Upload and then select the resulting Excel workbook.

7. **Move the worksheet into the same spreadsheet as your budget template.**

   - **Microsoft Excel:** Make sure that the budget template is open in Excel. Activate the Profit and Loss by Month worksheet and then choose Home ⇨ Format ⇨ Move or Copy Sheet. Choose the budget template from the To Book list and then click OK.

   - **Google Sheets:** Click the arrow on the sheet tab of the Profit and Loss by Month worksheet, and then choose Copy To ⇨ Existing Spreadsheet. Click Recent to locate your budget template and then click Select. Click Open Spreadsheet to open the combined workbook.

8. **Double-click the worksheet tab that your Profit and Loss by Month report appears on and change the name to something easy to remember, like** Data.

9. **Select cell B2 of the budget template worksheet and then enter this formula:** =SUMIF(Data!$A:$A,"*"&$A2,Data!B:B). **Copy the formula across to December and then down to the last account row.**

   The SUMIF function has three arguments.

   - **Range:** A range of cells where Excel or Sheets should look for a criterion. In this case, referencing $A:$A accomplishes two things. First, the $ instructs Excel or Sheets not to change the column letter when you copy to the right. Second, leaving out the row numbers instructs the spreadsheet to reference the entire column, which is a way of future-proofing the formula.

   - **Criteria:** What to look for — in this case, an account name. Note the $ here, which causes the formula to always reference Column A.

   The SUMIF function requires an exact match, but in some cases, QuickBooks adds extra spaces before certain account names. The asterisk (*) in the formula is known as a wild card, while the ampersand (&) enables you to combine two pieces of text together. The result is a formula that searches for any row that ends with the account name, rather than looking for cells that are comprised of just an account name and no additional spaces. Combining text with an ampersand is an alternative to the CONCAT and CONCATENATE functions.

- **Sum range:** What to add up when a match is found in the cells specified by the range argument. There is no $ in this case because you want the formula to change the column references as you copy the formula across to the right.

You can now make revisions as you want on the Data worksheet, which contains formulas for the subtotal rows and total column.

WARNING

Comma-separated value (.csv) files can only contain a single worksheet, and no formulas. If you're working in Excel, make sure to choose File ⇨ Save As and save your workbook as an Excel workbook so that you can preserve your formulas.

When you're ready to import your completed budget template into QuickBooks, activate the budget template worksheet and start with Step 5 in the section, "Importing Budgets," earlier in this chapter, to create the .csv file. You can disregard any warnings Excel gives you about losing your formulas if you've saved your work as an Excel workbook beforehand.

Deleting Budgets

Deleting usually means marking items as inactive, but there are exceptions to the rule, including budgets. Deleted budgets cannot be recovered from within QuickBooks, but you can import the .csv file again. Here are the steps for deleting a budget:

1. Choose Budgets (Business Overview ⇨ Budgets) from the left menu bar.

2. Choose Delete from the menu in the Action column adjacent to the budget you want to remove.

3. Click Yes to confirm the deletion.

IN THIS CHAPTER

» Navigating the Reports page

» Knowing how to locate a report you want

» Printing and customizing reports

» Sending reports to Excel, PDF, or Google Sheets

» Using Spreadsheet Sync to customize reporting

Chapter **14**

Utilizing QuickBooks Reports

QuickBooks Online reports help you keep tabs on the pulse of your business, as well as do a deep dive into the details whenever warranted. This chapter provides an overview of the reporting capabilities QuickBooks offers and shows how you can export reports to Microsoft Excel, PDF files, or Google Sheets. Advanced subscribers can also use the Spreadsheet Sync feature to create custom reports and graphs in Microsoft Excel that are directly tied to your books, meaning that you can refresh the reports at any time to pull in the latest details from QuickBooks.

Looking at the Reports Page

When you click Reports (Business Overview ⇨ Reports) on the left menu bar, you see a page like the one shown in Figure 14-1.

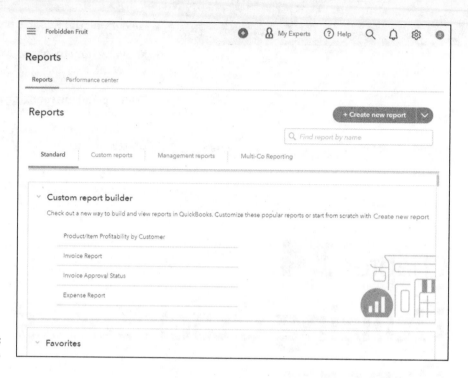

FIGURE 14-1:
The Reports page.

Reports are typically organized into three tabs — Standard, Custom Reports, and Management Reports — and Advanced subscriptions have an additional Multi-Co Reporting tab. As you scroll down the Reports page, you find the Standard reports organized in the following categories:

>> Custom Report Builder (requires an Advanced subscription)

>> Favorites

>> Business Overview

>> Who Owes You

>> Sales and Customers

>> What You Owe

>> Expenses and Vendors

>> Sales Tax

>> Employees

>> For My Accountant

>> Payroll

REMEMBER

The list of available payroll reports depends on whether you have a payroll subscription. If you don't have a payroll subscription, you see only an Employee Contact list and two reports related to time tracking. Also, you see Sales Tax listed only if you have the Sales Tax option enabled.

All QuickBooks users have the ability to customize the standard reports, which I talk about in the section, "Customizing Reports," later in this chapter. Advanced subscribers have access to Spreadsheet Sync (which I discuss in the section, "Custom Reporting with Spreadsheet Sync"), along with a Custom Report Builder option that enables you to build reports from scratch. Advanced subscribers access the Custom Report Builder by clicking the + Create New Report button, shown in Figure 14-1.

TIP

If the Reports menu feels overwhelming, click the down-pointing arrow next to a section heading, such as Favorites, to collapse that section of the page temporarily, or enter part of a report name in the Find Report by Name field.

Finding the Report You Want

Reports in QuickBooks are organized in three or four categories, depending upon your subscription level:

>> Standard

>> Custom Reports

>> Management Reports

>> Multi-Co Reporting (requires an Advanced subscription)

Click the corresponding tab, shown in Figure 14-1, to access a particular set of reports.

Examining standard reports

The reports available to you on the Standard tab of the Reports page are based on your subscription level, the features you use, the preferences you've set, and the add-ons you've installed.

TIP

In Figure 14-2, I've scrolled down the Standard tab to show you many of the reports in the Business Overview section of that tab in QuickBooks Advanced. Your list of reports may differ if you have a different subscription level.

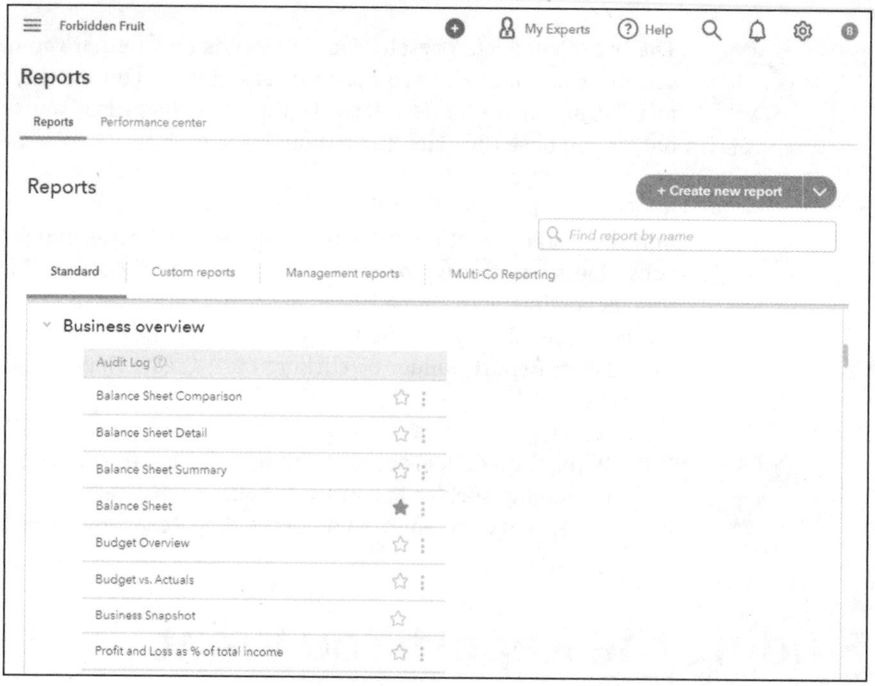

Forbidden Fruit   My Experts   ? Help

Reports

Reports   Performance center

Reports

+ Create new report ∨

Q Find report by name

Standard | Custom reports | Management reports | Multi-Co Reporting

∨ **Business overview**

Audit Log ⓘ

Balance Sheet Comparison ☆ ⋮

Balance Sheet Detail ☆ ⋮

Balance Sheet Summary ☆ ⋮

Balance Sheet ★ ⋮

Budget Overview ☆ ⋮

Budget vs. Actuals ☆ ⋮

Business Snapshot ☆

Profit and Loss as % of total income ☆ ⋮

FIGURE 14-2:
Business
Overview reports.

If you're following along onscreen, note the star next to the Balance Sheet report; the star is green, but in this black-and-white book, it looks dark gray at best. Green stars indicate *favorite* reports. The Balance Sheet report appears in the Favorites section of the Standard tab, also shown in Figure 14-1.

Click the star next to any report to place it in your Favorites section. If a report falls out of favor with you, simply click the star to free up space on your list of besties. Any reports on your Favorites list always appear in their normal sections as well, so the Favorites section simply serves as a quick access feature.

Finding customized reports

When you first click the Custom Reports tab, you may think, "Welp, nothing to see here!" Hang tight; I show you how to add reports to this tab in the upcoming section, "Saving a customized report." For now, know that the Custom Reports tab is a repository for reports that you've customized and saved to run again later. You can store report groups here as well. As you may have guessed, report groups are a batch of related reports that you want to run in one fell swoop.

Saving a customized report in QuickBooks Online is the equivalent of memorizing a report in QuickBooks Desktop.

TIP

Reviewing management reports

The Management Reports tab, shown in Figure 14-3, lists three predefined management report packages that you can prepare and print by clicking the View link in the Action column.

These report packages are quite elegant. Each package contains a professional-looking cover page, a table of contents, and several reports that correspond to the report package's name:

>> The Company Overview management report contains the Profit and Loss report and the Balance Sheet report.

>> The Sales Performance management report contains the Profit and Loss report, the A/R Aging Detail report, and the Sales by Customer Summary report.

>> The Expenses Performance management report contains the Profit and Loss report, the A/P Aging Detail report, and the Expenses by Vendor Summary report.

When you click View in the Action column of a management report, a Print Preview window appears, as shown in Figure 14-4. You can click Print, or if you move your mouse to the preview area, you can click the Download button on the toolbar to save the report in PDF format. Alternatively, if you click the View arrow in the Action column, you have some additional choices:

» *Edit* allows you to add your logo to the cover page, add more reports to the package, include an executive summary, and add end notes to the package. Click the icons along the left side of the screen to modify each section of the report.

» *Send* allows you to email the report package as a PDF file.

» *Export as PDF* allows you to save your report package as a PDF file.

» *Export as DOCX* saves your report package in a format compatible with Microsoft Word, Google Docs, and other word processing platforms.

» *Copy* creates a new version of the report package while keeping the original intact. QuickBooks adds a number to the report name, such as Company Overview–1, but you can change the name if you want.

» *Delete* appears only next to management reports that you've copied. You can't delete the three default report packages.

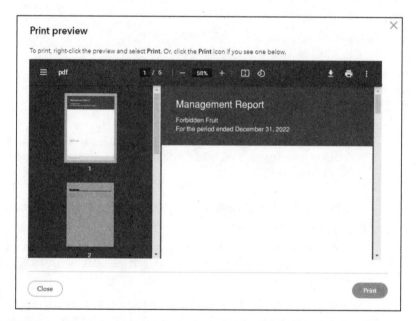

FIGURE 14-4:
Print Preview of a management report.

Contemplating Multi-Co reporting

The new Multi-Co Reporting option in QuickBooks Advanced allows you to group two or more QuickBooks companies into a single consolidated financial report. You can also create custom key performance indicators (KPIs), which are metrics you can use to measure certain aspects of your businesses. This feature also allows you to set up performance targets and alerts for your group.

Searching for a report

You can enter part of a report name in the Find Report by Name search box in the top-right corner of the Reports page. As shown in Figure 14-5, any report names that include the letters you type appear in a drop-down list. Click the report that you want to view, or enter a different combination of letters if the desired report doesn't appear.

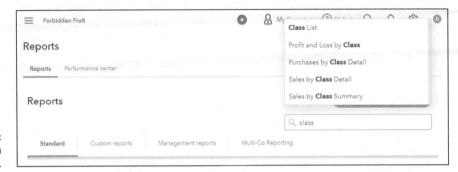

You also can use the Search tool, adjacent to the Settings menu in the top-right corner of the screen, to search for a report from anywhere in QuickBooks.

TIP

Printing a Report

Click a report's title to display the report using its standard settings. On most reports, you can drill down to view the details behind the report's numbers. Click any Income or Expense account value in the Profit and Loss report, for example, to display the transactions that make up the number, as shown in Figure 14-6. QuickBooks Advanced subscribers may then see a Try Modern View button, which displays the reimagined reporting screen shown in Figure 14-7. You can click Switch to Classic View if you're just not feeling the modern vibe, man.

Figure 14-7 includes a Pivot Table button that wasn't functional for me as of this writing. Once the feature is built out, you'll be able to choose fields to display in rows, columns, and values sections, just like creating PivotTables in Microsoft Excel, which I discuss in Chapter 15.

TIP

To redisplay the original report — in this case, the Profit & Loss report — scroll up to display the top of the report, as shown in Figure 14-6, and click the Back to Report Summary link. Alternatively, click Reports (Business Overview⇨ Reports) on the left menu bar to return to the Reports listing.

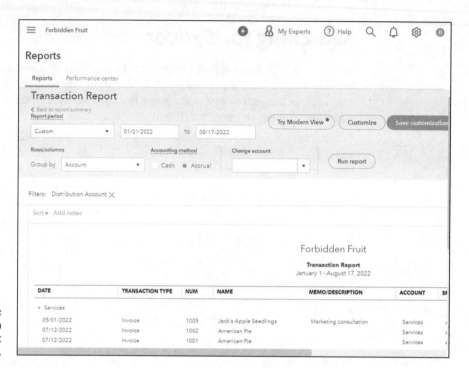

FIGURE 14-6:
Transaction
report in Classic
View.

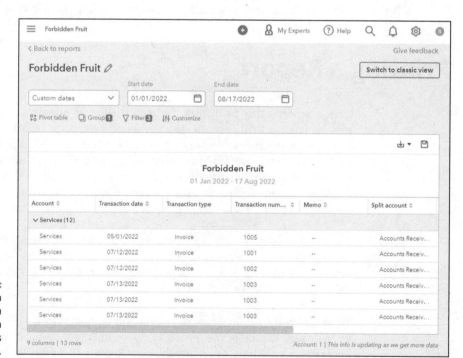

FIGURE 14-7:
Transaction
report in Modern
View in
QuickBooks
Online Advanced.

The Back to Report Summary link is only available when you're viewing a report that has been generated by clicking an amount to drill down into the details.

If you want to keep the original summary version of the report open and also view the details from drilling down, duplicate the browser tab that contains the summary version of the report before you drill down to view details. When you finish working with the details, you can close the second tab. To duplicate a tab in Google Chrome, right-click the tab and choose Duplicate from the shortcut menu. For all other browsers, consult the browser's Help menu for instructions on duplicating a tab.

Customizing Reports

You can customize most reports, such as choosing between cash-basis and accrual-basis on accounting reports. Some reports allow you to change the date range; most reports allow you to control which columns appear. Click the Run Report button to refresh the report each time you make any changes in the report settings.

Suppose that you want to customize the Profit and Loss report, which appears by default in the Favorites section of your Reports page. Click the Customize button at the top of the report to open the Customize panel; the choices available may vary from report to report.

As shown in Figure 14-8, the Customize Report panel typically contains several sections. The General section, for example, may allow you to choose between cash and accrual accounting methods for a given report.

Click the right-pointing arrow next to a section name, such as Rows/Columns, to see the available options. For example, if you click the Change Columns link shown in Figure 14-8, you see the panel shown in Figure 14-9, where you can control the columns and rows that appear in the report and add a variety of comparison and percentage columns.

When you choose columns to add to your report, the field names move above the list of available columns below Select and Reorder Columns. This separate section lets you easily see the columns you've added. As shown in Figure 14-10, certain reports allow you to change the order of the fields by using the waffle buttons adjacent to each column name.

You can use the Filter section, shown in Figure 14-11, to control the data that appears on some reports. For instance, you may be able to specify distribution accounts, either by type or by account name/number, or apply filters such as vendor, employee, product/service, and much more. The filters that are available can vary from one report to the next. Click the checkbox to apply a given filter, and then use the adjacent drop-down menu to specify your filter criteria.

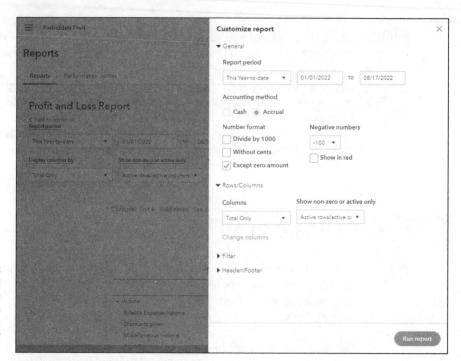

FIGURE 14-8:
The General section of the panel you use to customize a report in greater detail.

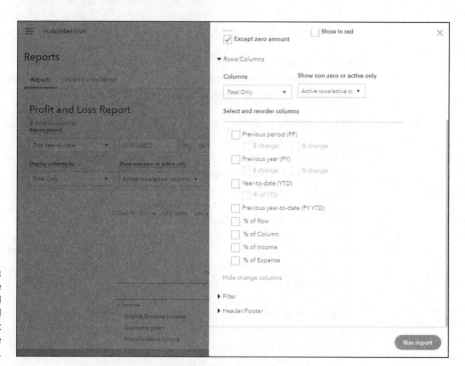

FIGURE 14-9:
Use these settings to control the rows and columns that appear in the report.

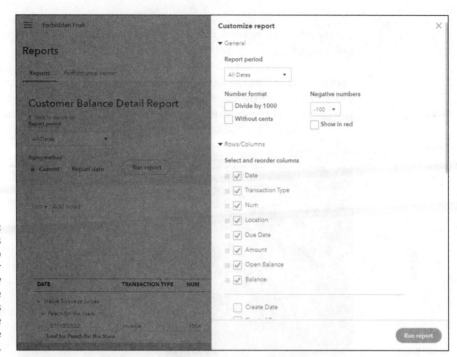

FIGURE 14-10:
Some reports allow you to change the order of the fields by dragging the waffle buttons located to the right of the columns.

FIGURE 14-11:
The filtering options you can control in the Profit & Loss report.

REMEMBER

Filters limit the amount of information included on the report. Use the Rows/Columns section when available to control which fields appear on the actual report.

Figure 14-12 shows the settings you can control in the header and footer sections of the report. Use the checkboxes to select the information you want to display in the header and footer of the reports. The Alignment section enables you control the alignment of the header and footer on the page, meaning left, right, or center.

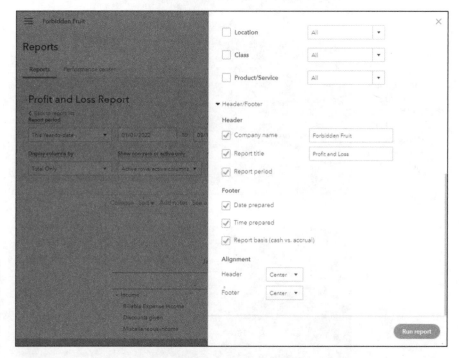

FIGURE 14-12:
The header and footer settings you can customize in the Profit & Loss report.

When you're finished customizing the report, click Run Report in the bottom-right corner of the Customize Report panel to display the report onscreen, using your customized settings shown in Figure 14-13. Then you can click the Print button to print the report on paper or to a PDF file. Alternatively, you can click the Email button to email the report; you can also click the Export button to export the report to Excel, a PDF file, or (if you're an Advanced subscriber) Google Sheets.

Saving a customized report

Now that you've tailored the report to your liking, click the Save Customization button at the top of the report page to display a panel like the one shown in Figure 14-14. Accept the default name for the report, or provide a more meaningful name that reminds you of the customizations you made.

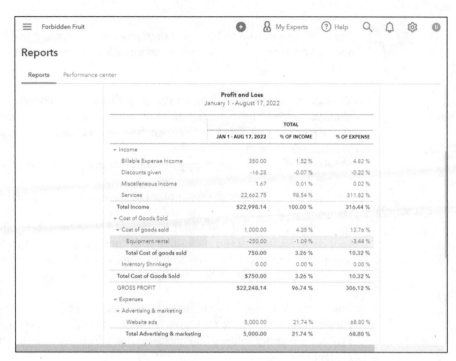

FIGURE 14-13:
The report after customization, which includes % of Income and % of Expense columns.

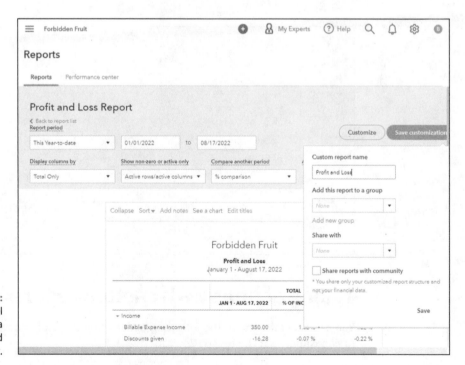

FIGURE 14-14:
Use this panel to save a customized report.

TIP

Click the Save button in the panel that appears, as opposed to clicking Save Customization again; otherwise, you'll end up discarding any changes you've made, such as to the report name.

You can add any report to a report group by clicking the Add New Group link, which displays the New Group Name box. Enter a name in the New Group Name box, and click the Add button. Going forward, when you want to add other reports to the group, you can select the group name from the Add This Report to a Group list box in the panel. Report groups make it easy to attach two or more reports to one email as well.

TIP

You can choose to share the customized report with other QuickBooks users in your company, and accountants can share reports with users in their firm. Click the Share With list box and then select All, or select None to prevent others from seeing your customization. If you click Share with Community, other QuickBooks users are able to use your customizations in their companies. Rest assured that Intuit shares only the report settings — never your data. Click Save to confirm your choices.

The saved report appears on the Custom Reports tab of the Reports page or within a report group. In Figure 14-15, my customized version of the Profit & Loss report appears in a group called (uninspiringly) Bob's Group. Click the title to display the custom report.

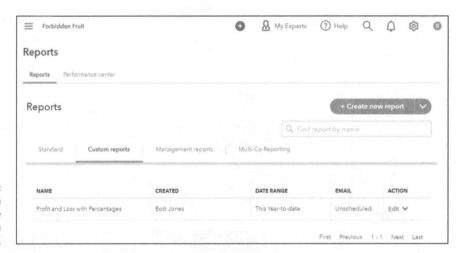

FIGURE 14-15:
The My Custom Reports page after you create a custom report.

Taking actions with custom reports

You can also take any of the following actions if you click the down arrow in the Action column for the report. You can

>> Create a PDF version of the report by clicking Export as PDF.

» Export the report to Excel by clicking Export as Excel.

» Delete the customized report by clicking Delete.

TIP

The Action list for Advanced subscribers doesn't offer an Export to Google Sheets option, but if you display the report onscreen, you can choose to export to Google Sheets from the preview window, as I discuss in more detail in the section, "Exporting to Google Sheets," later in the chapter.

To change a custom report's name or group, click the Edit link in the Action column for the report. You can also use this link to set an email schedule for the report group, as shown in Figure 14-16. The email interval defaults to Daily, but you can change it to Weekly, Monthly, or Twice a Month. Note that every interval allows you to specify the frequency for emailing the reports, as well as ending options. Fill in the Email Information, making sure to separate email addresses with a comma (,). You can customize the subject of the report email. There wasn't space to show it in the figure, but if you scroll down, you can click the Attach the Report as an Excel File checkbox at the bottom of the screen if you prefer that format to a PDF file.

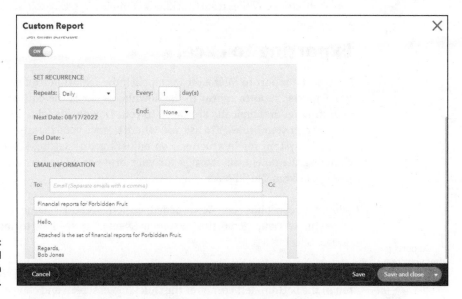

FIGURE 14-16:
Set an email schedule for a report group.

For report groups, click the down arrow in the Action column of a report group to do the following:

» Export the group in PDF format.

» Delete the group.

WARNING

Be aware that deleting a group has more consequences than just removing a named group from the Custom Reports page. If you choose Delete from the Action drop-down menu for a report group, you delete the report group and all custom reports that the group contains.

Exporting Reports from QuickBooks

All subscribers can export reports directly to Microsoft Excel and to PDF documents, and at least indirectly into Google Sheets. Advanced subscribers can export reports directly to Google Sheets and, as I discuss later in this chapter, create customized reports in Excel by way of the Spreadsheet Sync feature. A downside of exporting is that reports can become out of date as soon as you enter or edit a transaction in QuickBooks. As I show later in this chapter, Spreadsheet Sync eliminates the repetition of exporting, but on the other hand, for most QuickBooks subscribers, exporting is the only available avenue within QuickBooks.

TIP

QXL (www.qxl1.com) offers one-click exporting from QuickBooks Online to Excel spreadsheets or CSV files from QuickBooks Simple Start, Essentials, Plus, or Advanced.

Exporting to Excel

To export a report to Microsoft Excel, click the Export button shown in the margin. Exported reports appear in the downloads bar at the bottom of the screen in your browser and typically are saved to your Downloads folder. Alternatively, you can instruct your browser to ask you where to save your reports. (See your browser's help system for instructions on adjusting this setting.) Keep in mind that changing the download settings for your browser will affect all downloads, not just those from QuickBooks.

When the report has been downloaded, click the report's name to open it in Excel, or see the section, "Exporting to Google Sheets," to see how to open Excel files in Google Sheets.

TIP

In most browsers, you can click the up arrow on the right side of the report's button in the bottom-left corner of the QuickBooks screen and choose Show in Folder if you want to navigate to the location where the report is stored.

When you open the downloaded report in Excel, the file is in Protected View, and you have to click Enable Editing to work with it. If you don't, you can't make any changes in the report, such as deleting rows or performing calculations on the side. As shown in Figure 14-17, Protected View may also mask the actual amounts in your report with zeros.

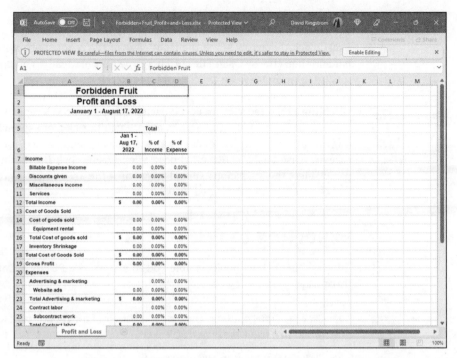

FIGURE 14-17:
Protected View in
Excel requires
you to click
Enable Editing
before you can
modify or view
numbers on
reports exported
from QuickBooks.

The Protected View feature in Excel perceives reports downloaded from the Internet as being potential security threats. You should certainly be careful when opening unfamiliar email attachments or website downloads, but if clicking Enable Editing over and over again feels onerous, you can disable this feature, as follows:

1. **Choose File ➪ Options in Excel.**

   The Options task pane opens.

2. **Choose Trust Center in the left column and click the Trust Center Settings button on the right.**

   The Trust Center task pane opens.

3. **Click Protected View in the left column, and clear the checkbox titled Enable Protected View for Files Originating from the Internet.**

   Optionally, you can clear the checkbox titled Enable Protected View for Outlook Attachments as well, but be sure to leave the checkbox titled Enable Protected View for Files Located in Potentially Unsafe Locations turned on.

4. **Click OK twice to close the Trust Center and Options task panes.**

Now you no longer have to click Enable Editing whenever you open a QuickBooks report in Excel. You streamline the export process by having files open automatically in Excel from QuickBooks. The next time you export a report to Excel, click the arrow along the right edge of the report button in the downloads bar and then choose Open Files of This Type Automatically. You now have a seamless integration between QuickBooks and Excel.

WARNING

Disabling Protected View makes it easier for you to access reports that you export from QuickBooks, but doing so can expose you to risk from spreadsheets that you download outside QuickBooks. Fortunately, you can enable Protected View on a case-by-case basis. In Excel, choose File ⇨ Open, click Browse in the Open task pane, select the suspicious spreadsheet, click the arrow next to the Open button, and choose Open in Protected View.

Exporting to PDF

All versions of QuickBooks enable you to export to a PDF file. You can do this in three ways:

>> Click the Email button in the top-right corner of the report to attach your report to a blank email as a PDF file.

>> Click the Print button and then click Save as PDF.

>> Click the Export button and then choose PDF.

TIP

You can open and edit many PDF files in Microsoft Word 2013 and later. Choose File ⇨ Open, click Browse in the Open task pane, and then select your PDF file the same way you would a Word document. Some reports don't convert cleanly, so your mileage may vary. Google Docs extracts text from PDF files, so you may lose some of the look and feel of the report. You can explore add-ins for Google Drive that offer a better experience.

Exporting to Google Sheets

Advanced subscribers can export reports directly to Google Sheets by way of the Export button (which looks like an up arrow in the top-right corner of the screen) and then choose Export to Google Sheets. In any other version of QuickBooks, follow these steps to export to Excel and then open the file in Google Sheets:

1. **Click the Export button and then choose Export to Excel.**

    This step places the report in your Downloads folder unless you customized your browser to specify alternative download locations.

2. **In Google Sheets, choose File ⇨ Import and then click Upload.**

You must upload any files stored locally on your computer so that they can be accessible in Google Sheets.

3. **Drag a file into the window or click Select a File from Your Device.**

   If you have a Windows Explorer or Apple Finder window open, you can drag a file from there into the upload window. Otherwise, use the Select a File from Your Device button to select the file.

4. **Confirm the Import Location and then click Import Data.**

   Among other things, the Import Location list allows you to replace or insert sheets into an existing spreadsheet or create a new spreadsheet entirely.

Once your spreadsheet appears in Google Sheets, you can edit, save, or delete it as you would spreadsheets that you've created from scratch. For more details, see *Google Apps For Dummies*, by Ryan Teeter and Karl Barksdale.

Custom Reporting with Spreadsheet Sync

The Spreadsheet Sync feature enables Microsoft Excel spreadsheets to become a direct extension of QuickBooks. At the end of Chapter 4, I describe how Advanced subscribers can install the Spreadsheet Sync Add-In in Microsoft Excel. In Chapters 5 and 6, I describe how you can use Spreadsheet Sync to review, edit, and create transactions in Excel that you can optionally post directly to QuickBooks, but that's only half of what Spreadsheet Sync offers. Let's look at how to create custom reports in Excel that remain connected to QuickBooks and can be updated on demand:

1. **Open an existing spreadsheet that you want to connect to QuickBooks or create a blank workbook.**

2. **Choose Home ⇨ Spreadsheet Sync in Excel unless the Spreadsheet Sync task pane is already displayed.**

   You must carry out the installation steps in Chapter 4 on each computer on which you want to use Spreadsheet Sync.

REMEMBER

3. **Sign into your QuickBooks Online company if prompted.**

4. **Choose Get Started.**

5. **Click Build a Report.**

6. **At this point, you have three options, as shown in Figure 14-18; I chose My QuickBooks Data because that is the most complex option.**

- **My QuickBooks Data:** This enables you to choose the company or companies that you want to retrieve data from, along with an existing QuickBooks report that you want to use as the basis.

- **Advanced Template:** This enables you to choose between prebuilt Smart Profit and Loss or Simple Management Report templates that enable you to retrieve data from one or more QuickBooks companies.

- **Existing File:** Once you have created and saved one or more workbooks using Spreadsheet Sync, this command enables you to save an existing workbook with a new name to use as a template for new reports.

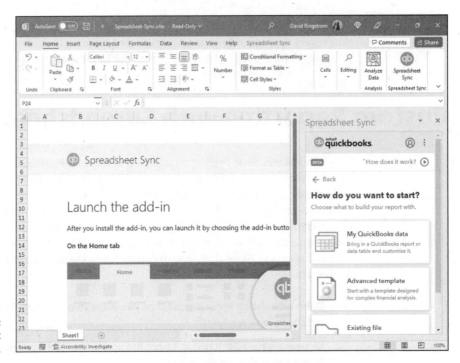

FIGURE 14-18:
Spreadsheet Sync reporting options.

7. **Optional: If you have two or more QuickBooks Advanced subscriptions, you can choose a company or create a reporting group.**

   Reporting groups allow you to create consolidated reports that aggregate the results from all companies in the group.

8. **Click Select Data Source.**

   The Spreadsheet Sync task pane displays a searchable list of reports and data tables, as shown in Figure 14-19.

TIP

Many of the reports, such as Sales by Customer Summary, only summarized results. If you want the nitty-gritty details of your sales, choose Data Tables ⇨ Transactions Core ⇨ Invoices instead.

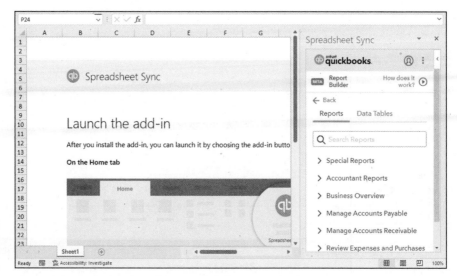

FIGURE 14-19:
Spreadsheet Sync
Reports and
Tables lists.

9. **Choose a report or data table.**

   QuickBooks returns you to the workflow list. Click the Change button if you decide that you want to pull data other than what you chose.

10. **Click Select Data to Get to display the Filter dialog box shown in Figure 14-20.**

    Make selections from the drop-down lists to refine the data set that you wish to present in a Microsoft Excel worksheet.

11. **Click Add to Current Sheet to create a report in the active worksheet or click Add to New Sheet to add a new worksheet to your workbook.**

    As shown in Figure 14-21, a Spreadsheet Sync tab appears in the Excel ribbon. This tab only appears when you are working in a workbook that utilizes Spreadsheet Sync.

REMEMBER

The Spreadsheet Sync command is a permanent part of the Home tab in the Excel ribbon unless you remove the add-in, which I describe in Chapter 4.

The Spreadsheet Sync tab, located in the Excel menu interface known as the Ribbon, contains the following commands.

>> **Company Settings:** Redisplays the Spreadsheet Sync task pane if you have closed it and enables you to add companies and create reporting groups.

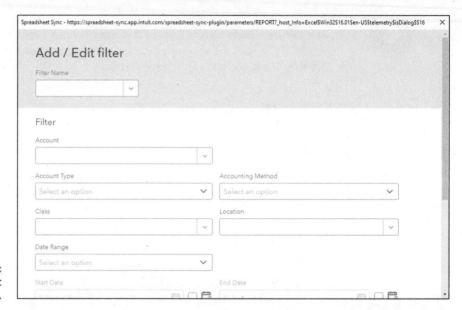

FIGURE 14-20:
Spreadsheet Sync
Filter options.

FIGURE 14-21:
The Spreadsheet
Sync tab.

>> **Get Started:** Displays the three reporting options I discuss earlier, My QuickBooks Data, Advanced Templates, and Existing File.

>> **Build Reports:** Enables you to choose which data to pull, and also to specify filters.

>> **Refresh:** Contains options to refresh the current worksheet. *Current worksheet (Quick)* uses your existing filters, *Current Worksheet* displays the Filter dialog box shown in Figure 14-20, *All Sheets* refreshes all worksheets in the workbook that are tied to Spreadsheet Sync, and *Automatic Refresh* enables you to have Excel refresh your workbook when you open it, which enables you to have self-updating reporting.

>> **Manage Records:** Enables you to choose which report or table to retrieve data from.

Other commands appear on the Ribbon tabs as well and are related to posting transactions, accessing help documentation, signing out of your QuickBooks company, and giving feedback on the feature to Intuit.

Chapter **15**

Analyzing QuickBooks Data in Excel

A longtime complaint that I've had about QuickBooks and other accounting programs is that it often feels that accounting records are literally trapped under glass. You may find, for example, that you can't quite get to the report format you want to see inside QuickBooks. In this chapter, I share some of my favorite tricks and techniques for unlocking your accounting data and viewing it the way you want to see it. If you don't have much experience in Excel, the book *Microsoft Excel For Dummies*, by Greg Harvey, can help you get up to speed.

For much of this chapter, I'm using the sample company available for QuickBooks Online, which you can access at https://qbo.intuit.com/redir/testdrive. I chose this example so that you have an easy way to generate reports that contain actual data, in case you haven't started using QuickBooks Online. You can and should follow along with your own data, of course, but it's always good to have options. The Spreadsheet Sync feature can only be enabled by way of a QuickBooks Online Advanced company.

I used the Microsoft 365 version of Excel when writing this chapter. Everything I discuss in this chapter can be carried out in older versions of Excel, but in some cases, menus or commands may differ slightly from what you see in this chapter.

Automatically Opening Excel Reports Exported from QuickBooks

When teaching Excel webinars, I often use the phrase, "death by a thousand cuts," as a metaphor for how many people carry out tasks in a slightly inefficient way. In isolation, it's not a big deal. However, the more times you carry out a task, the greater the propensity it has to eat into your day. Suppose that you decided to export a Profit & Loss report to Excel from QuickBooks. You would probably follow these steps:

1. **Choose Reports (Business Overview ⇨ Reports) on the left menu bar.**

   The Reports page appears.

2. **Choose Profit & Loss in the Favorites, Business Overview, or For My Accountant section.**

   Reports can appear in multiple sections, so choose whichever section is easiest for you to access, or click the star next to a report to add it to the Favorites section.

3. **Click the Export button and then choose Export to Excel.**

   See Chapter 14 for more information about running reports in QuickBooks.

4. **Click the report name on your browser's downloads bar or in your Downloads folder.**

   Depending upon your browser of choice, files that you download may appear in the downloads bar across the bottom of your screen. If you close this bar or your browser doesn't offer this feature, you can generally choose Downloads from your browser's main menu to redisplay the bar, or you can navigate to the Downloads folder on your computer.

5. **Click Enable Editing on the message bar shown in Figure 15-1 to access your report.**

   Protected View is a sandbox environment in which you can open an Excel report to determine whether it's hazardous — something to consider if you're downloading an Excel template from an unknown website. Conversely, it can be a major speed bump if you're exporting reports to Excel multiple times a day.

I can't do anything about Steps 1 to 3, but I can help you eliminate the last two steps if your downloads appear in a downloads bar within your browser. First, set your browser to open Excel files automatically by following these steps:

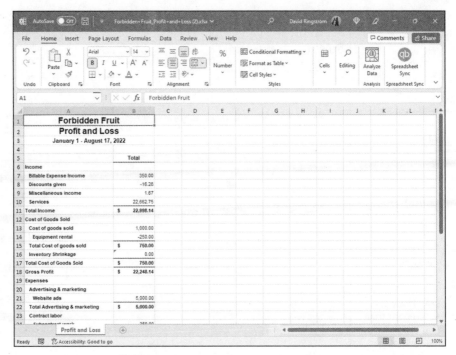

FIGURE 15-1:
QuickBooks
reports that you
export to Excel
generally open in
Protected View,
which sometimes
hides the
amounts
temporarily.

1. **Carry out Steps 1–3 of the preceding list.**

   Make sure that you don't click the report name on the downloads bar this time.

2. **Click the arrow to the right of the filename and choose Always Open Files of This Type from the pop-up menu, as shown in Figure 15-2.**

   This command instructs your browser to automatically open files that you download in the associated program, eliminating the need to open the file manually. I discuss this function in detail in Chapter 20, including how to turn it off.

   TIP

   Alternatively, you can set your browser to prompt you for a location where you want to save each report, instead of every report being dumped into your Downloads folder. It is an either/or choice, so you'll have to decide if the greater benefit is to have files open immediately in Excel, or if you'd rather open them from the Downloads bar after choosing a location and file name. Chapter 20 covers both options.

3. **Click the report name on the downloads bar one last time.**

   Going forward, your reports will open automatically in Excel, but you'll need to click on the report name one last time.

4. **If necessary, click Enable Editing to clear Protected View.**

   In Chapter 14, I show you how to eliminate repetitive work by turning off Protected View.

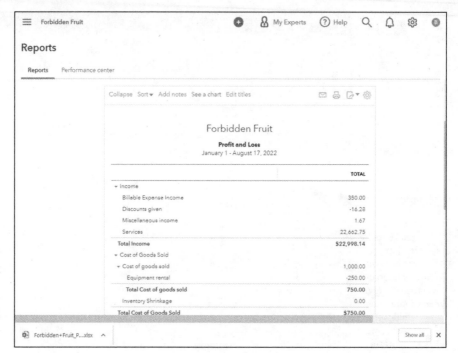

FIGURE 15-2:
Choose Always
Open Files of
This Type to
seamlessly open
Excel reports that
you export from
QuickBooks.

Sifting through Excel Reports

Now that I've helped you pave the way for faster exports from Excel, I'll show you how to transform QuickBooks data into meaningful reports. In this section, I use the Transaction List by Date report, shown in Figure 15-3. I like this report more than the Transaction Detail by Account Report shown in Figure 15-4; you can probably tell why. Notice that the Transaction List by Date report is a simple transaction listing, which gets very close to the optimal analytical report format in Excel because it has the following features:

» Columns are contiguous, so there are no blank columns.

» Rows are contiguous, so there are no blank rows.

» The report doesn't have subtotal or total rows; you can use Excel to add them if necessary.

» The report doesn't have headings within the data, such as the account headings shown in Figure 15-4.

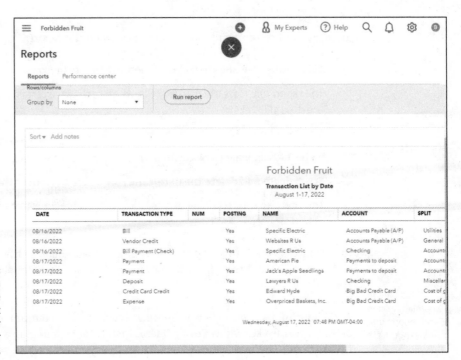

FIGURE 15-3:
The Transaction List by Date report is best suited for analyzing your data in Excel.

FIGURE 15-4:
Most transaction list reports have headings or subtotals that make Excel analysis more difficult.

Here's what I recommend that you do to clean up the report:

1. **Select Rows 1–4 and then choose Home ⇨ Delete in Excel.**

   The report title rows use merged cells, which can stymie certain analytical activities in Excel.

2. **Delete Column A.**

   It's best to eliminate blank columns in spreadsheets whenever possible.

3. **Scroll down and delete the date/time row at the bottom of the report.**

   This row also consists of merged cells. You'll thank me for eliminating this potential snag.

TIP

At this point, I encourage you to save your Excel workbook so that you don't have to redo the cleanup as you try the various techniques that I'm about to walk you through.

TIP

In Chapter 19, I show you how to automate cleanup of accounting reports by using an Excel feature known as Power Query. Instead of cleaning up a monthly report by hand over and over, you can use Power Query to prescribe a set of automated steps to be performed on the report. After you export the report from QuickBooks the first time, you can pull the data from the report into Power Query, and your cleaned-up results appear in a second workbook. Going forward, you can save over the monthly report workbook as needed with new exports from QuickBooks, and then update the results workbook by clicking the Refresh button on the Data menu in Excel. This makes for a set-and-forget approach to reporting.

Filtering data

The Filter feature is one of my favorites in Excel because it enables me to get a bird's-eye view of data within a report. I can also collapse a report to see just the information that interests me. Follow these steps to use the Filter feature:

1. **Click any cell in your report and then choose Data ⇨ Filter or Home ⇨ Sort & Filter ⇨ Filter.**

   I used the Transaction List by Date report in Figure 15-5. You could also press Ctrl+Shift+L (Cmd+Shift+L for Mac users).

2. **Click any Filter button at the top of the columns shown in Figure 15-5.**

   As shown in Figure 15-5, the resulting filter menu shows you one of each item in the column, ordered in alphanumeric sequence, which makes for a nice overview of your data.

If you click the Filter button in the Amount column, you see the smallest number in that column at the top of the list. Scroll down to the bottom of the list to see the largest number in the column. Most users resort to sorting reports to see information in this format. Filtering allows you to keep transactions in their original order.

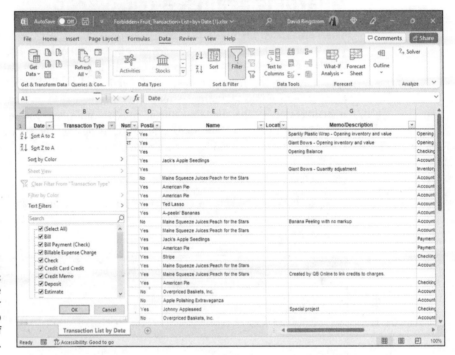

FIGURE 15-5:
The Filter feature adds a Filter button to the top of each column of your data.

3. **Optional: Clear the Select All checkbox, choose the specific data that you want to see, and then click OK.**

   You can filter in this fashion on as many columns as you want.

4. **Optional: Choose Data ➪ Clear or Home ➪ Sort & Filter ➪ Clear to remove all the filters from a list.**

   You can also clear filters for individual columns by clicking the Filter button and then choosing the Clear command from the drop-down menu.

When you filter data in Excel, information in any hidden rows is protected. If you color-code, delete, or otherwise alter anything in any of the visible rows, nothing in the hidden rows is affected. Conversely, if you delete an entire column, the hidden rows are *not* protected because the entire column is removed.

TIP

I don't have enough room to talk about this function in any detail, but if you're using Microsoft 365 or Excel 2021, you can use the FILTER worksheet function to filter data with a worksheet function instead of manual commands. This technique enables you to filter a list by changing the criteria in an input cell.

Guarding against a tricky trap

The Transaction List by Date report has one tricky aspect that I want to bring to your attention because it can surface in other QuickBooks reports. Look closely at Column A in Figure 15-6, which you can see is comprised of dates. To your eye, they may look like normal dates, but if you dig below the surface, you'll find that these dates are masquerading as text. This means that Excel treats them as words instead of dates. Click the Filter button for Column A, and you see each date listed individually instead of automatically grouped by month. Follow these steps to transform the text-based dates into numeric dates that Excel treats as such:

1. Select Column A, as shown in Figure 15-6.

You do this by clicking the column letter on the worksheet frame to highlight the entire column.

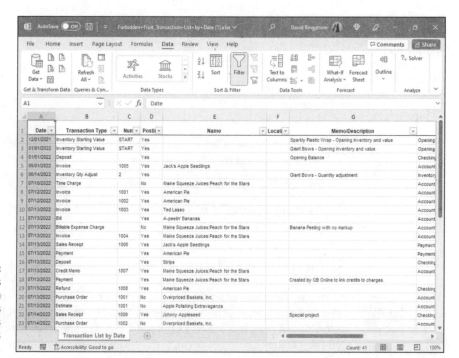

FIGURE 15-6:
Text-based dates exported from QuickBooks sometimes masquerade as numeric dates.

2. **Choose Data ⇨ Text to Columns.**

The Text to Columns wizard appears. Ostensibly, this feature allows you to take text in one column and split it into two or more columns. In this case, I'm using the feature to transform text-based dates to numeric values that Excel recognizes as dates instead of a group of characters that happen to look like a date.

3. **Click Finish.**

The Text to Columns wizard has three steps, but you don't need to carry any of them out in this case. Simply click Finish, and your dates are transformed into dates that Excel recognizes as such.

WARNING

At this point, you may encounter a prompt that says, in effect, "We can't do that to a merged cell." Exactly who is this *we*, Excel? Regardless, I warned you about this situation earlier in the chapter. If you skipped the step of removing the title rows at the start of the section, "Sifting through Excel Reports," you have one or more merged cells impeding your progress. You have two choices: Delete the title rows and then repeat the preceding steps, or select the cells that contain dates and then repeat the steps.

4. **Click the Filter button in Column A again, and then optionally pick one or more time periods.**

You should see the dates grouped by month; if your report spans more than one year, they're grouped by year as well. You can expand any grouping to make a granular selection. Your spreadsheet should now only show you the rows that match the time period(s) that you selected.

5. **Filter on as many columns as needed.**

This means that you can display sales from one or more customers for a specific time period or perhaps determine which customers bought one or more products.

TIP

Click the Filter button in a number column, such as quantity or total sales, and choose Filter and then Number Filter to reveal options such as greater than, less than, and Top 10. Top 10 would be better named Top *x*, where *x* can be whatever number you want it to be for filtering the largest or smallest amounts within a list.

Slicing your data

I'd like to bring the Slicer feature to your attention. I often describe slicers as being a remote control for the Filter feature. A *slicer* is a floating object that you can add to your worksheet that displays one of each item within a column of data. If you click an item within the slicer, Excel filters the list for that item. You can hold down the Ctrl key (Cmd key for Mac users) and make multiple choices from a slicer if you want to filter for multiple items. This saves you from having to click the Filter button in a column and make choices from the list. One of my favorite aspects of slicers is that you can also easily determine which items are presently hidden within the list. Items that you've "sliced" (or more correctly filtered on) have shading behind them within the slicer, whereas hidden items are disabled or have no shading, as shown in Figure 15-7.

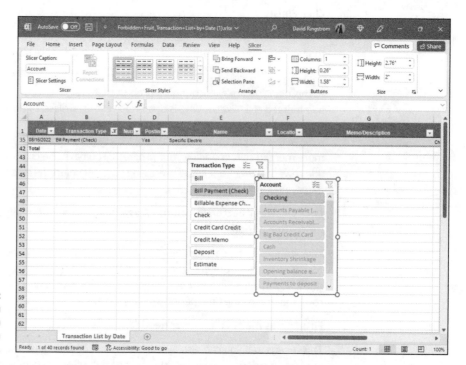

FIGURE 15-7: Slicers allow you to filter data in a table with a single click.

You can apply the Filter feature to any range of cells that you want in Excel, but you can only use the Slicer feature with lists that are formatted as a table:

1. **Choose any cell in your data.**

   Sometimes, users think that they have to select all the cells in a report before carrying out an action in Excel. Selecting everything is necessary for applying formatting (such as colors, fonts, and number formats), but it's not necessary for performing data actions.

2. **Choose Insert ➪ Table, and then click OK in the Table dialog box that appears.**

   The My Table Has Headers checkbox should be selected automatically, confirming that the first row of your list contains column titles.

3. **Optional: Choose Table Design ⇨ Total Row.**

This command adds a total row to the bottom of your list. The last column is automatically summed or counted, depending on whether that column contains numbers or other content (such as dates or text). Click any other cell in the total row to display a button that looks similar to a Filter button, but in this case is a menu from which you can choose a mathematical function such as sum, average, count, and so on. When you make a choice from the list, Excel adds the corresponding formula to the total row for that column. If you then filter or slice the table, the total row only tallies the visible rows.

4. **Click any cell in your table, and then choose Table Design ⇨ Insert Slicer to display the Insert Slicers task pane.**

You can use slicers only with data that is formatted as a table or a pivot table. I show you how to create a pivot table in the section, "Creating Custom Reporting with Pivot Tables," later in this chapter.

WARNING

Make sure to select a cell near the top of your table when inserting slicers. If you select a cell near the bottom of the table, your slicers may vanish off of the screen when you make a selection. If this happens, click the Clear command on the Data menu to reset the table.

5. **Choose one or more fields and then click OK.**

A slicer appears for each field that you choose. You can add as many slicers as you want, but keep in mind that it usually doesn't make sense to slice on columns that contain dates or numbers. Slicing works best for text-based cell contents in situations where items you want to slice on appear multiple times.

6. **Click any item in a slicer.**

Your list gets filtered with one click, as shown in Figure 15-7.

TIP

Hold down the Ctrl key in Windows or the Cmd key in Excel for Mac to select two or more items. The total row reflects the sum of only the visible rows.

TIP

If you use two or more slicers, the second and later slicers reflect any matches based on choices made in the first slicer. In Figure 15-7, Bill Payment (Check) is selected, which means that the only account that has activity is the Checking account. All other accounts are disabled, with no activity in them.

To reset a slicer, click the Clear command, which looks like a funnel with an x.

You can make choices from as many slicers as you want. As shown in Figure 15-7, any items on the slicer that are being displayed in the list have shading behind them. Items that do not have shading or that are disabled are either hidden or not available, respectively. Conversely, when you use the Filter feature, you don't have any visual cues as to what data has been hidden based upon your choices.

I could tell you much more about the Table feature because it's a fantastic automation opportunity in Excel. However, this book is about QuickBooks, so I'll close this discussion with a few tips:

TIP

>> Expand the Quick Styles section of the Table Design menu and then click the first icon at top left to remove the shading from the table or choose other colors.

>> Right-click a slicer and choose Remove from the shortcut menu if you change your mind about using the feature.

>> Choose Table Design ⇨ Convert to Range if you no longer want the data to be in a table. This command removes any slicers you have in place.

Sorting data

Sorting enables you to rearrange data sequentially, such as from A to Z or highest to lowest. Sort commands appear when you click a Filter button. Sort commands also appear on the Home and Data menus. In Excel, you can sort on up to 64 columns. To sort data in Excel, follow these steps:

1. **Choose any cell that you want to sort on.**

   Excel is always tracking what's referred to as the *current region,* the contiguous block of cells surrounding your cursor. For this reason, you don't need to select all your data in advance.

2. **Choose Data ⇨ Sort A-Z, Data ⇨ Sort Z-A, or Home ⇨ Sort & Filter.**

   The names of these commands are Sort A to Z or Sort Z to A if your cursor is in a column of text, and Sort Smallest to Largest or Sort Largest to Smallest if your cursor is in a column of numbers.

3. **Optional: Click the Sort button to display the Sort task pane if you want to sort based on two or more columns.**

   You can also use the Sort task pane to sort based on color or conditional formatting. If you dig deep enough, you'll find that you can sort on custom lists or even sort lists sideways, meaning sorting columns from left to right or right to left versus sorting rows up and down the spreadsheet.

TIP

Here I go again: If you're using Microsoft 365 or Excel 2021, you can use the SORT or SORTBY worksheet functions to sort data with a worksheet function instead of using manual commands. Any changes you made in the original data are reflected by the worksheet functions.

Creating Custom Reporting with Pivot Tables

Many users are intimidated by pivot tables. The name itself can be intimidating. Rest assured, however, that pivot tables are among the easiest features to use in Excel. Pivot tables allow you to transform a list of data in Excel into meaningful reports simply by clicking checkboxes or dragging field names. Even better, nothing you do in a pivot table affects the original data, and you'll unlock a drill-down capability that's similar to drilling down into reports within QuickBooks.

Understanding pivot table requirements

Although Excel is forgiving when it comes to how your data is laid out, when it comes to pivot tables, you must conform to the rules I describe earlier in the section, "Sifting through Excel Reports," for creating analysis-ready formats in Excel. Every column must have a unique heading, for example.

Although doing so isn't required, for best results you should make your data into a table, as shown in the section, "Slicing your data." When you do, a Summarize with PivotTable command appears on the Table Design menu. This command is important if you have reports to which you want to add data, such as a year-to-date report to which you add a new month of data after each accounting period. The Table feature enables a pivot table to "see" any data that you add. If you don't use the Table feature, there's a good chance that the new data you add to your list will be left off your pivot table report. In the section, "Removing fields," I show you how to manually resize your pivot table source data if you choose not to use the Table feature.

Follow these steps to create a pivot table:

1. **Select any cell in your list.**

   Make sure that you've cleaned up your data, as described in the section "Sifting through Excel Reports."

2. **Choose Insert ⇨ PivotTable.**

   The Create PivotTable task pane appears.

3. **Accept the default settings by clicking OK.**

   A blank pivot table canvas appears on a new worksheet in your workbook, along with a PivotTable Fields task pane. You also see two new tabs in the Excel ribbon: PivotTable Analyze and Design.

The PivotTable Analyze and Design tabs, as well as the PivotTable Fields task pane, are context sensitive. If you move your cursor to any cell outside the pivot table canvas, the menus and task pane disappear; they reappear when you click inside the pivot table canvas again. This behavior can be a bit disconcerting if you're new to the feature.

Adding fields

At this point, you're ready to add fields to your pivot table. You have one or two choices, depending upon your version of Excel:

» In Windows, you can select the checkbox for any field. Text or date fields appear in the Rows quadrant of the PivotTable Fields task pane; these fields are displayed as rows in the report. Number-based fields appear in the Values section as new columns in the report.

» In Windows or Mac, drag fields from the field list into any of the quadrants.

In Figure 15-8, I added Account to the Rows quadrant, Date to the Columns quadrant, and Amount to the Amount quadrant. In Excel 2019 and later, dates should group by month and/or year automatically. I didn't apply any number formatting to the numbers in Figure 15-8, so that you can see the raw format that first appears. You can change the formatting in a pivot table in the same fashion as any other cells in Excel.

If you're using a current version of Excel and instead find all the individual dates listed, refer to the section, "Guarding against a tricky trap," earlier in the chapter, because your dates are most likely being stored as text. To make your pivot table reflect your changes, right-click the pivot table and choose Refresh from the shortcut menu. At this point, however, you need to group your columns manually (which is also the case in older versions of Excel). Right-click a date and choose Group from the shortcut menu. Choose Months and Years in the Grouping task pane and click OK to group your dates by month and year. If your data spans more than one year, and you don't see a total by year, right-click any date and choose Subtotal from the shortcut menu.

Removing fields

Excel can feel overwhelming because you often have three or four ways to carry out almost every task, such as removing fields from a pivot table. Rest assured that you don't need to commit all the options to memory. Instead, use the approach that makes the most sense to you:

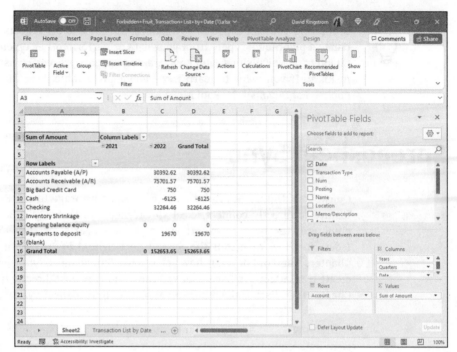

FIGURE 15-8:
Pivot tables allow you to create instant summaries of your data by dragging and dropping fields.

>> Clear the checkbox for a field in the main area of the PivotTable Fields task pane to remove a field from your report.

>> Drag any field out of a quadrant and off the PivotTable Fields task pane. When you release your mouse button, the field is removed from the pivot table.

>> Click the arrow on the right side of any field in a quadrant and choose Remove Field from the drop-down menu.

>> Right-click the field within the pivot table and choose Remove from the shortcut menu.

WARNING

The data displayed by a pivot table doesn't recalculate automatically, the way formulas do in Excel. If you make any changes in the underlying data, you need to right-click the pivot table and choose Refresh from the shortcut menu, or choose PivotTable Analyze ⇨ Refresh. If you append data to your existing list, the pivot table reflects the new data when you refresh if that data is within a table, as discussed earlier in the section, "Understanding pivot table requirements." If your data resides in a regular range of cells, you need to choose PivotTable Analyze ⇨ Change Data Source and reselect your list to include any new rows of data in your report.

TIP

If you find yourself repetitively cleaning up QuickBooks reports so that you can create a pivot table report from your data or perform other types of analysis, see Chapter 19, which shows you how to automate this process by using Power Query in Excel. If you want to learn more about pivot tables, see *Microsoft Excel Data Analysis For Dummies*, by Paul McFedries.

Spreadsheet Sync

QuickBooks Online Advanced users can take advantage of the Spreadsheet Sync feature to directly connect Excel spreadsheets to their QuickBooks data, which eliminates the need to export and clean up reports. At the end of Chapter 4, I describe how to install the Spreadsheet Sync Add-In in Microsoft Excel. In Chapters 5 and 6, I describe how you can use Spreadsheet Sync to review, edit, and create transactions in Excel that you can optionally post directly to QuickBooks. In Chapter 14, I discuss the reporting aspects of Spreadsheet Sync.

4

Features for Accountants

Get started in QuickBooks Online Accountant (QB Accountant).

Manage your client's books.

Leverage accountant-only tools.

Use Power Query to automate QuickBooks data analysis.

Chapter **16**

Introducing QB Accountant

P arts 1 and 2 of this book cover the details of QuickBooks Online, which allows your clients to maintain detailed accounting records for their businesses. Supporting multiple QuickBooks Online clients can quickly feel like herding cats, particularly when you are juggling multiple sets of credentials. Layer in tasks that your clients don't want to touch, such as making journal entries or writing off bad debts, and things really can feel like a circus; this is where QuickBooks Online for Accountants (QB Accountant) can save the day. This free practice management platform enables you to to easily switch to designated clients' QuickBooks companies on the fly with a single sign-on. Authorized team members then have access to every area of your client's books (limited to the features offered by their subscription level, of course). Accounting practice owners receive a free QuickBooks Online Advanced subscription and a free Payroll Elite subscription for use in managing the accounting records for their firm. Further, you can receive an ongoing discount by allowing Intuit to bill you directly for the subscription fees that one or more of your clients pay, or you can have your clients pay Intuit directly and then receive a share of certain fees they pay for up to one year.

Getting Started with QuickBooks Online Accountant

Unlike QuickBooks Online, which provides an optional 30-day free trial, Quick-Books Online Accountant (QB Accountant) is free in perpetuity. To create your account, visit `https://quickbooks.intuit.com/accountant` and then click the Sign Up for Free button on the left side of the page.

WARNING

Abbreviating the URL to qbo.intuit.com/accountant results in a "page not found" error, so make sure to spell out QuickBooks when accessing that page.

Once you create your account, you can sign in and start a short tour of the QB Accountant interface. When you complete the tour, your home page looks like Figure 16-1. Going forward, you can use the same page to log in to QuickBooks Online Accountant that your client uses to log in to QuickBooks Online: `https://qbo.intuit.com`.

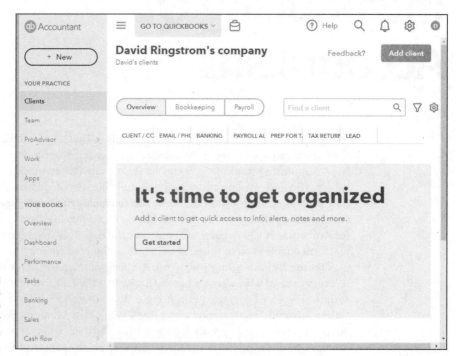

FIGURE 16-1:
A typical QB Accountant home page after creating an account.

REMEMBER

Just as you'd expect, by clicking the Finish button, you're agreeing to Intuit's terms of service, the end-user license agreement, and the privacy policy for QuickBooks Online Accountant.

TIP

In addition to the video tour, QuickBooks displays cards you can click to get more information about certain subjects, such as how to save time while you work in QB Accountant. You can click the X in the top-right corner of any card that you don't want to see.

Setting Up Your Team

Whoever creates the QB Accountant account for your firm becomes the master administrator and can set up as many other team members as necessary. Each team member has their own login credentials, and can selectively be assigned rights to clients' books, as well as the firm's books. All team members can utilize the Accountant tools described in Chapter 18.

REMEMBER

Creating individual users, as opposed to sharing a single account, bolsters security in QB Accountant by limiting access to product subscriptions and billing information.

QB Accountant users can be assigned one of three access levels.

>> **Basic:** Users can access QuickBooks companies for designated clients.

>> **Full:** Users can access QuickBooks companies for designated clients as well as the firm's books.

>> **Custom:** This provides a middle ground between Basic and Full, meaning users have at least one permission that has been customized.

Either the master administrator or any full-access users can set up and control user privileges in this fashion:

1. **Log in to QB Accountant as a primary admin or full-access user.**

2. **Choose Team from the left menu bar to display the Team page shown in Figure 16-2.**

3. **Click the Add User button.**

   The three-step Add User wizard begins.

4. **On the first page of the Add User wizard, fill in the name, email address, and (optional) title of the team member you want to add.**

5. **Click Next.**

FIGURE 16-2:
View, edit, and add QB Accountant team members.

The second page of the Add User wizard appears in Figure 16-3. On this page, you identify the privileges related to your firm that you want to provide to the team member. In this example, I set up a team member with custom access. This team member has access to the books of certain clients but doesn't have access to the firm's books or to firm-administration functions.

6. **Select the type of access you want to give to the team member.**

   Assign Basic access to give access to client companies only, Full Access to give access to client companies and the firm's books, or Custom access to create a hybrid set of privileges.

7. **Click Next in the bottom-right corner of the page.**

   The last page of the Add User wizard appears, as shown in Figure 16-4. On this page, you identify the clients for whom the team member should be able to perform work.

8. **Deselect clients if necessary and then click Save.**

   The new user is added to your team and assigned the status of Invited. In addition, the Status column of the Team page indicates that an email invitation was sent to the user. After the user accepts the invitation, their status changes to Active.

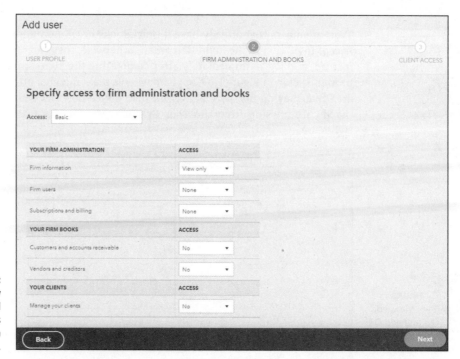

FIGURE 16-3:
Specify the new user's access level to your firm's administration and books.

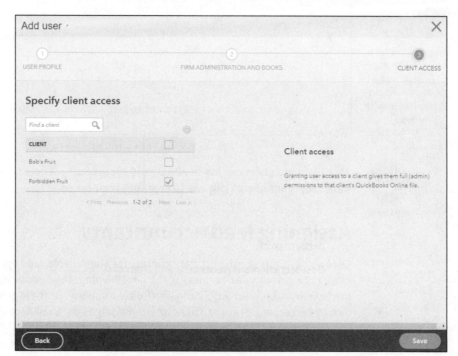

FIGURE 16-4:
You can give a team member access to your firm's clients on a selective basis.

Team members that already have a QuickBooks or QB Accountant login can click Accept Invitation in the invitation email; otherwise, they can click Create Account instead, and log in immediately after completing the sign-up process. The error prompt shown in Figure 16-5 appears when a team member attempts to access an area that they do not have access to. Also notice how the Team and Apps commands are missing from the Your Practice area for this user who has limited rights.

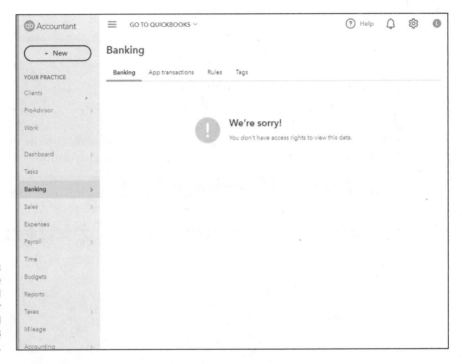

FIGURE 16-5:
The home page of an invited team member who has limited privileges in QB Accountant.

REMEMBER

Your team members can log in at https://quickbooks.intuit.com, which is the same page your clients can use to sign into their books.

Assigning lead accountants

Lead accountants are the primary contact for your clients, and typically have primary responsibility for overseeing the bookkeeping. Lead accountants can also be the primary admin for a QuickBooks Online company, or these roles may be handled by two separate people. QB Accountant assigns the Lead Accountant role when

>> **A client invites an accountant.** After the accountant accepts the invitation, the accounting firm has access to the client, and the invited accountant — who is a member of the firm — is assigned the Lead Accountant role.

>> **A firm member creates a client company.** The team member within the firm that creates a client company in QB Accountant becomes the lead accountant.

Once assigned, the lead accountant can only be changed by a firm admin, meaning the primary admin for a QB Accountant account. Here are the steps to reassign a lead accountant:

1. Log in to QB Accountant as a primary admin or full-access user.

2. Choose Clients, click the Filter icon, and choose Edit Leads.

3. Choose a client for which you want to reassign the lead accountant.

4. Select a new lead accountant in the Lead column.

5. Choose Save.

TIP

You can also assign a lead accountant by selecting the checkboxes for two or more clients, choosing a name from the Assign To drop-down list, and then clicking Save.

Examining the QB Accountant Interface

The QB Accountant interface focuses on giving accountants access to tools they need to manage multiple clients. As you'll see, there are three ways that you may find yourself using QB Accountant:

>> As a practice management tool

>> As an accounting software platform to maintain the books for your practice

>> As a single sign-on platform that enables you access to the books for any of your clients

Although the view in the interface depends on where you're working in a client's books or not, two elements remain constant:

>> The left menu bar appears in light gray when you're in your practice and dark gray when you access a client's books.

>> A QB Accountant toolbar runs across the top of the page.

As with QuickBooks Online, a New button appears at the top of the left menu bar. When you're working in QB Accountant, this button enables you to create transactions in *your* books. When you activate a client's set of books, the New button that appears creates new transactions in *their* books. Now let's look at the rest of the left menu bar.

Using Your Practice commands

The Your Practice section of the left menu bar contains a set of practice management commands.

- >> **Clients:** This command displays, well, a list of your clients. Choose this command any time you want to return to your client list. The Clients command enables you to search for a client, see overview information about each client, and open a client's QuickBooks company. You can also control some aspects of the Clients page, which I discuss in the section, "Working with the Client List," later in this chapter.

- >> **Team:** This command enables you to set up the users in your firm who will have access to various client companies. For more information, see the section, "Setting Up Your Team," later in this chapter.

- >> **ProAdvisor:** This command enables you to access information related to the benefits and training offered through the Intuit ProAdvisor program. A free Silver membership is created for you automatically if you aren't already enrolled in the ProAdvisor program. More details are available at https://quickbooks.intuit.com/accountants/tools-proadvisor.

- >> **Work:** This command displays practice-management tools that I discuss in more detail in Chapter 18.

- >> **Apps:** Choose this command to launch the App Center, where you can search for apps that extend the capabilities of both QuickBooks and QB Accountant. You can also view the apps you've already installed.

The Your Books section appears immediately beneath the Your Practice commands and includes the same commands that can be seen by your clients who have Advanced subscriptions.

REMEMBER

The left menu bar transforms into the same left menu bar that your clients see when you switch to their set of books. The Your Practice and Your Books sections reappear once you exit their set of books.

Toolbar commands

Across the top of the interface, you find a toolbar with the following elements, from left to right.

» **QB Accountant:** This button, which features the QuickBooks logo, offers you another way to display the page shown in Figure 16-2, which contains a list of your clients.

» **Expand/Collapse:** This button, which has three horizontal lines, hides and displays the left menu bar in the same fashion as within QuickBooks.

» **Go to QuickBooks:** You can use this feature to display a drop-down list of your clients; clicking a client name in the list opens the client's company.

» **Accountant Tools:** Think of this button as being an accountant-specific version of the New button, offering quick links and tools that accountants frequently use when they're working on a client's books, as shown in Figure 16-6. See Chapter 18 for details on these tools and on practice-management tools.

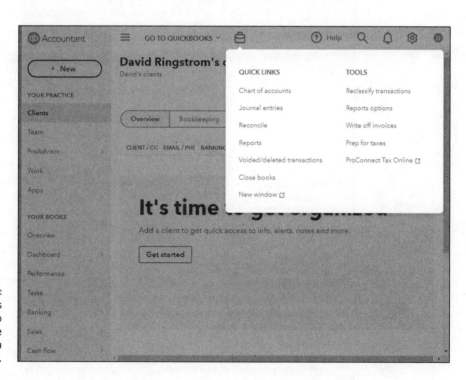

FIGURE 16-6:
The tools available to accountants while working in a client company.

>> **Help:** This command displays help documentation for QuickBooks and QB Accountant.

>> **Search:** This feature enables you to find a list of recent transactions or reports, just as in QuickBooks.

>> **Notifications:** This feature displays messages from Intuit about new features in QuickBooks, webinars for accountants, and other information.

 >> **Settings:** This command displays the Settings menu, from which you can manage settings for your own company, your client's company, and your QB Accountant account, as shown in Figure 16-7.

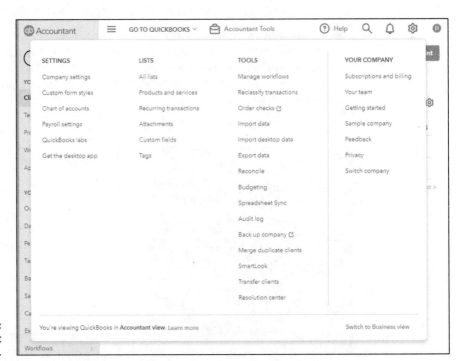

FIGURE 16-7:
QB Accountant
Settings menu.

>> **Sign Out:** Your first initial appears on this button, which enables you to sign out of the software, as well as access your ProAdvisor profile and manage your Intuit account.

TIP

Intuit's free ProAdvisor program entitles you to Online, Advanced Online, and Payroll Certified ProAdvisor designations at no cost. QuickBooks Desktop certification is available to those who purchase the desktop bundle add-on through the ProAdvisor program. As an added bonus, the certification programs provide free continuing education credit (CPE) for certified public accountants (CPAs). QuickBooks Accountant University offers free CPE as well by way of webinars, virtual conferences, and in-person events.

Adding Companies to the Client List

You can add a client company to the Client List in two ways:

» By letting your client create a company and then invite you to access it

» By creating a client's company for the client

If you participate in the ProAdvisor Preferred Program that I discuss later in this chapter, you can opt to manage clients' subscriptions for them. In this case, Intuit bills you for clients' subscriptions, and then you bill your clients. Alternatively, your clients can opt to manage their own QuickBooks subscriptions but still give you access to their books.

TIP

You're not bound by one choice or the other — that is, managing a client's subscription or not managing a client's subscription. You can change who manages the subscription at any time if you participate in the ProAdvisor Preferred Program.

Chapter 17 discusses working with a client's set of books within QB Accountant.

REMEMBER

Inviting you to be the accountant user

When a client creates their own company, they accept the responsibility to pay for their company's QuickBooks subscription. Even so, your client can invite you to access the company by using the Invite Accountant process. You can manage any type of QuickBooks subscription in QB Accountant, including Schedule C and ProConnect Tax Online clients.

Your client should follow these steps:

1. **Choose Setting ⇨ Manage Users in the Your Company column.**

   The Manage Users page identifies the company's primary admin and enables your clients to add users to their QuickBooks subscription by way of the Users and Accounting Firms tabs. The Roles tab enables Advanced subscribers to more tightly control access levels for users.

2. **Click the Accounting Firms tab shown in Figure 16-8.**

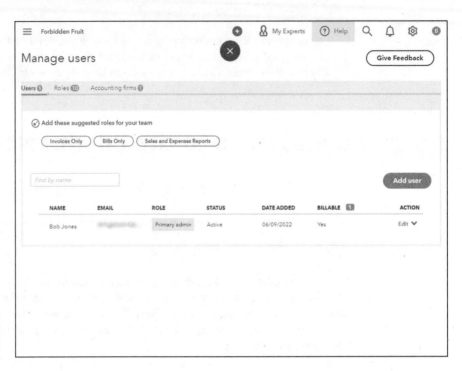

FIGURE 16-8:
The Manage Users page.

3. **Provide your email address (meaning their accountant's email address if that's not you) and then click Invite.**

   The Accounting Firms tab of the Manage Users page reappears, showing your email address with a status of Invited. Your clients can click Resend Invite from this screen if needed.

In turn, you click the Accept Invitation button in the invitation email to open the QB Accountant login page. A Welcome Back screen appears once you log in, from which you choose the accounting firm you want to use to accept the invitation, and then click Continue. The new client appears in your client list, as shown in Figure 16-9. By default, QB Accountant gives access to the team member invited by your client and to your primary admin. If you click the Edit Client link to the right of any client's name, you can use the Edit Client page to identify additional people in your firm who should have access to the client's QuickBooks Online books by way of the Team Access section.

You also receive an email telling you that the client has been added to your QB Accountant account.

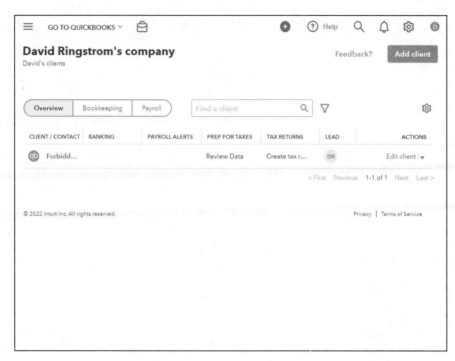

FIGURE 16-9:
A Client List page
after you accept
an invitation from
a client to be the
accountant.

Adding a client to your practice

You can initiate a QuickBooks subscription for any client that wants Simple Start or above, or add a client without creating a subscription. QuickBooks Self-Employed subscribers must create their own company and then invite you to be the accountant for their QuickBooks company, as described in the section, "Inviting you to be the accountant user," earlier in this chapter.

Follow these steps to start a QuickBooks subscription for your client:

1. **Choose Clients on the left navigation bar.**

2. **Click Add Client in the top right-hand corner.**

   The Client Contact Information page appears, as shown in Figure 16-10.

3. **Select Business or Person, depending on whether you're adding a business or a self-employed individual.**

4. **Provide a name and an email address for the company.**

   QB Accountant adds any existing company that uses the name and email address you provide to your account; otherwise, it creates a new QuickBooks Online company.

FIGURE 16-10:
The Client
Contact
Information
page of the Add
Client wizard.

5. **Optional: Click Add More Info to provide billing and shipping addresses, as well as the company phone number and website address.**

6. **Choose Subscription or No Subscription.**

Choose No Subscription and then click Save if you simply want to add the client to your client list — you can always add a subscription later. Otherwise, choose Subscription and continue on to Step 7.

7. **Choose a billing option.**

You can choose to be billed directly for your client's subscription at a discounted rate, extend a temporary 12-month direct discount to your client, or receive a revenue share for up to 12 months. I cover all of the ins and outs in the section, "ProAdvisor Preferred Pricing versus ProAdvisor Revenue Share," later in this chapter.

8. **Select a QuickBooks subscription level (Advanced, Plus, Essentials, or Simple Start) or Payroll Standalone Subscription (Payroll Elite, Payroll Premium, or Payroll Core).**

REMEMBER

QuickBooks Online subscriptions offer a choice between direct or wholesale billing. Your clients can receive your discount on payroll standalone subscriptions but will be billed directly by Intuit.

9. Specify whether you should become the client company's primary admin.

If the client is the primary admin, they receive a link to QuickBooks so that they can sign in. If you're the primary admin, you can log in and then add your client as a user.

The Make Me the Primary Admin checkbox doesn't appear on the screen until you select a subscription level.

TIP

10. Click Save.

The company is created and appears in the list of companies on your Clients page. If by chance the new company doesn't appear, refresh your browser page or log out of QB Accountant and then log back in again.

Your client only has 60 days to import their data from QuickBooks Desktop if they created their company directly. Conversely, you have 180 days to import data from QuickBooks Desktop if you create the company for your client in QB Accountant. You can replace existing data in QuickBooks Online by importing more than once during either of these windows, but you cannot import once the respective window closes.

REMEMBER

Accepting primary admin rights from your client

QuickBooks Online companies have a single primary admin user who is a super-user with full access from top to bottom within a QuickBooks company. This is not to be confused with admin users, who have more rights than the average user, but less than the primary admin. Clients that you might generously describe as, say, control freaks, will probably want to retain the primary admin rights for themselves. Other clients might think, "Whoa, that's too much power for me," and decide that they'll be better served asking you to be their primary admin instead. Here's what those clients need to do:

1. Choose Setting ⇨ Manage Users in the Your Company column.

2. Click the Accounting Firms tab.

3. Choose Make Primary Admin from the drop-down menu in the Action column adjacent to the accountant that they wish to foist, or, shall we say, convey this power upon.

4. The equivalent of an "Are you sure?" prompt appears, from which your client clicks Make Primary Admin.

As you'll see in the next section, you can always transfer the primary admin rights back to your client, so nothing is getting etched in stone here.

5. **A message briefly appears on the screen, informing your client that you have been invited to be the primary admin.**

QuickBooks doesn't offer any indication that you've been invited, so if your client is frazzled, they might forget whether they invited you or not.

At this point, you can expect an email with a subject line that has your client's company name and the phrase, "Account Privileges Granted." Within the email, you see links to Accept or Decline this responsibility. If you accept, you're asked to log into and verify your Intuit account; once you've done so, a screen informs you that primary account administrator privileges have been successfully transferred to you, and that the previous primary account administrator has been notified by email.

Transferring primary admin rights to your client

As you can see, your client can designate you as the primary admin for their QuickBooks company. Or, you might purposefully or unwittingly make yourself as the primary admin when creating a company on a client's behalf. No matter how it landed on your plate, rest assured that you can always transfer the primary admin role back to your client:

1. **Choose your client's company from the Go To QuickBooks list at the top of the QB Accountant screen.**

2. **Choose Settings ⇨ Manage Users in the Your Company column.**

The Manage Users page appears, initially showing only the accountant user who created the company.

3. **Choose Make Primary Admin from the drop-down menu in the Action column next to your client's name, as shown in Figure 16-11.**

4. **Choose Make Primary Admin from the Action column.**

A message explains that only one user can serve as primary admin and transferring that role downgrades your access to admin.

5. **Click Make Primary Admin to confirm the transfer; otherwise, click Cancel.**

An automatic email invites your client to become the primary admin. When they accept the invitation, they're prompted to log in to QuickBooks. A message explains that the primary admin role has been transferred successfully and that you, the former primary admin, have been notified.

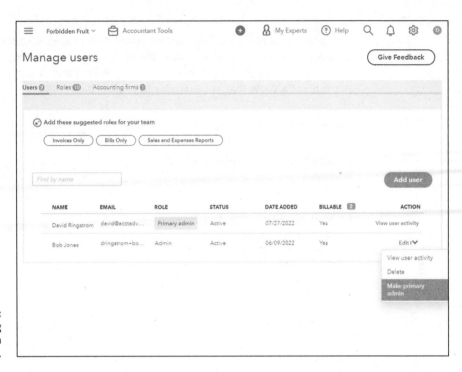

FIGURE 16-11:
Transferring
primary admin
rights.

Once your client accepts the invitation, the next time you log in to the client's QuickBooks company, you no longer appear in the Manage Users section of the Manage Users page. Your client is now the primary admin for the company, and you have become an admin user.

REMEMBER

A distinction between admin and primary admin is that the primary admin is a superuser with rights that can't be changed by other admins. The primary admin can relinquish their role, but primary admin rights can't be changed or altered by other users.

Working with the Client List

You can open any client's set of books by clicking the QuickBooks logo in the Status column of the Client List page unless their subscription has expired. As shown in Figure 16-12, when you hover over the QB logo, a tip informs you of the client's subscription level. If the word *Cancelled* appears, then you can no longer access the books. Alternatively, you can also open a company by way of the Go to QuickBooks drop-down list on the QB Accountant toolbar, but this avenue doesn't tell you in advance if a subscription has been cancelled. You're alerted to this fact by way of a screen that invites you to restart the billing for the company. I talk all about working with your client's books in Chapter 17, and I dig into the suite of Accountant's Tools that are available to you in Chapter 18.

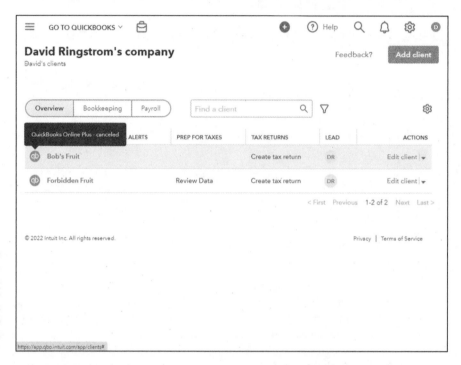

FIGURE 16-12: Click a QuickBooks logo or use the Go to QuickBooks drop-down list to open a client's company.

Clicking a client's name instead of the QuickBooks logo displays overview details such as tasks to complete in the client's books, the account watch list, and payroll alerts, instead of opening the company.

REMEMBER

Customizing the Client List

You can also customize the Client List page by using the list box above the table to filter the list to show all clients, for example, or only the QuickBooks Payroll clients in your list. You can also control the columns of information that appear on the page, and you can hide or display inactive clients. (I show you how to make a client inactive in the next section.) Click Settings just above the list of clients and make choices from the Settings menu shown in Figure 16-13.

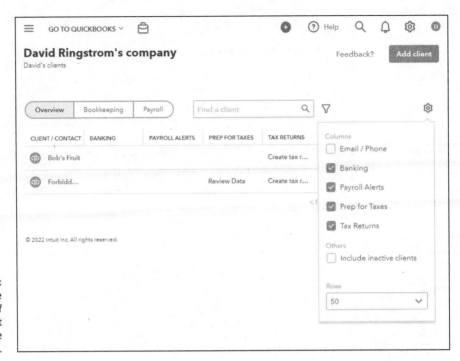

FIGURE 16-13:
Control the appearance of the Client List page with the Settings menu.

REMEMBER

QB Accountant contains multiple Settings menus. One of them appears on the QB Accountant toolbar and is visible on most QB Accountant pages, even while you work in a client's company; you use that Settings menu to provide information about your QB Accountant account, establish settings, view lists, and access tools. On the Clients page, the Settings menu appears above the list of clients; you use that menu to control the information that appears on the page.

Removing Clients from Your Client List

You'll be hard-pressed to find anywhere QuickBooks allows you to delete a list item, and clients are no exception to this rule; you must mark a client as inactive instead. Here's how:

1. **Choose Clients from the left menu bar.**

2. **Choose Make Inactive from the Action column drop-down list next your former client's name.**

   A prompt asks whether you're sure you want to make the client inactive.

3. **Click Yes.**

   The page shown in Figure 16-14 appears, and the client no longer appears in the Client List.

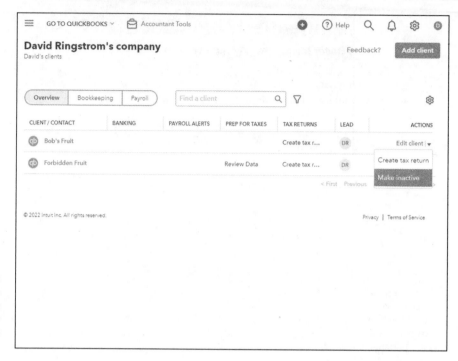

FIGURE 16-14:
Choose Make
Inactive
command to
hide a client on
your list.

TIP

Don't worry; you can always change the client's status back to Active again. Click Settings above the Action column on the Clients page and enable the Include Inactive option shown in Figure 16-9. Click Make Active in the Action column next to the client's name. You can then turn the Include Inactive option off again in the Settings menu for your Clients page.

ProAdvisor Preferred Pricing versus ProAdvisor Revenue Share

The free ProAdvisor Preferred Pricing program offers an ongoing 30 percent discount on most QuickBooks products; it is available to accounting professionals that allow Intuit to charge their bank account or credit card automatically for their clients' subscriptions. Alternatively, the ProAdvisor Revenue Share program rewards accountants that create new subscriptions on behalf of their clients with 30 percent of the fees paid for QuickBooks subscriptions, along with 15 percent of payroll subscription fees for 12 months.

TIP

ProAdvisor Preferred Pricing has gone by other names in the past, such as Wholesale Pricing and Wholesale Billing.

Signing Up for ProAdvisor Preferred Pricing

You have immediate access to the free ProAdvisor Preferred Pricing program once you log into QB Accountant for the first time, but the program isn't activated until you complete your Billing Profile in QB Accountant:

1. **Choose Settings ➪ Subscriptions and Billing in the Your Company column.**

   The Subscriptions and Billing page appears, displaying four tabs:

   - **Accountant-Billed Subscriptions.** This tab lists exactly what you'd expect: clients whose subscriptions you're managing, the QuickBooks product (Essentials, Plus, and so on), the subscription price, and the status.

   - **Client-Billed Subscriptions.** This tab lists all your clients that are paying Intuit directly for their QuickBooks subscriptions.

   - **Billing Details.** This tab enables you to add billing information for accountant-billed subscriptions, and then details any monthly charges that you incur as time goes by.

TIP

   The Action column of the Billing Details tab enables you to export the charges for any month to a PDF or CSV file so that you can determine which clients you need to invoice for their subscription fees.

   - **Revenue Share.** This tab allows you to opt into a revenue sharing arrangement with Intuit. This program entitles you to 30 percent of certain subscription fees that your clients pay for up to one year. See the section, "Signing Up for ProAdvisor Revenue Share," later in this chapter.

2. **Click the Billing Details tab.**

3. **Fill in all Payment Information fields.**

4. **Click Subscribe.**

   The Your Account page reappears, and ProAdvisor Preferred Pricing is activated.

You receive a consolidated bill each month for all the QuickBooks subscriptions you manage. You can, in turn, either use the invoice templates that QB Accountant offers to bill your clients the normal subscription price, or share all or part of the discount with them. Alternatively, you can offer your clients a 30 percent discount that lasts for 12 months when Intuit bills them directly. See https://quickbooks. intuit.com/accountants/products-solutions/pricing-promotions/papp/ for all the latest details.

Adding existing clients to your consolidated billing

You can move clients onto your consolidated bill if they meet certain criteria:

» Their next payment date must be within 33 days of the day you attempt to add the company to the ProAdvisor Preferred Pricing subscription. You can find this date in the client company by choosing Settings ⇨ Account and Settings ⇨ Subscriptions and Billing.

» Clients must have an active monthly billing subscription and must be listed on your Clients page.

REMEMBER

You can add only monthly QuickBooks subscriptions to the ProAdvisor Preferred Pricing program — annual subscriptions aren't eligible. Annual billing subscriptions receive roughly a 10 percent discount and can be changed to monthly billing subscriptions 30 days before the next annual billing date.

» Clients must be in the region of QuickBooks that corresponds with your region of QB Accountant (United States, United Kingdom, Australia, France, or Canada).

>> QB Accountant users in the United States can add QuickBooks Self-Employed companies to ProAdvisor Preferred Pricing subscriptions if the client is subscribed to the standalone plan.

REMEMBER

Note that ProAdvisor Preferred Pricing isn't available to QuickBooks Self-Employed/Turbo Tax bundle users, because QB Accountant has its own default tax software. Turnaround time for the client to be moved to ProAdvisor Preferred Pricing is 24 hours. The discount is also not available to clients that were transferred from another accountant and were paying full price on a direct bill basis for any period of time.

TIP

Clients that transfer their books to you from another accountant will retain any existing preferred pricing.

Phew! Now that that rigmarole is out of the way, here's how to add a client to your consolidated bill:

1. **Choose Settings ⇨ Subscriptions and Billing from the Your Company column.**

   The Subscriptions and Billing page appears.

2. **Click Client Actions in the Action column, and then choose Transfer Billing to Me.**

   Note: This button is available only if you've completed the Billing Profile.

3. **Review the charges in the Subscription Summary section, confirm or adjust your payment method, and then click Transfer Billing to Me.**

   The client now appears on the Accountant-Billed Subscriptions tab of your Subscriptions and Billing page.

Removing clients from your consolidated billing

Rest assured, you can remove a client from your consolidated bill at any point:

1. **Choose Settings ⇨ Subscriptions and Billing in the Your Company column.**

   The Subscriptions and Billing page appears.

2. **Choose Transfer Billing to Client in the Action column for the company you want to remove from your consolidated billing subscription.**

   The Transfer Billing to Client confirmation page appears.

3. **Review the information shown, and then click Confirm Transfer.**

   The client no longer appears on your Accountant-Billed Subscriptions listing.

If you're no longer working with a client that you've removed from your consolidated bill, you need to mark them as inactive on your client list, as I discuss in the section, "Removing Clients from Your Client List," earlier in this chapter.

REMEMBER

When you remove a QuickBooks company from your consolidated billing subscription, that company is no longer eligible for the ProAdvisor Preferred Pricing discount, and all previous discounts are removed as well. The client is billed the standard rate for their subscription as of the date the subscription is removed, unless they establish a relationship with another QB Accountant user. In that case, the client regains the discounts starting from the ProAdvisor Preferred Pricing activation date.

Stopping consolidated billing

At some point, you may decide that you don't want to participate in the consolidated billing subscription or manage QuickBooks subscriptions for your clients at all. You can't cancel the ProAdvisor Preferred Pricing subscription, but you can remove all your clients from the plan, as discussed in the previous section. Once you do, Intuit no longer bills you because you don't have any clients in your consolidated billing subscription.

Signing up for ProAdvisor Revenue Share

Based upon customer feedback, Intuit has discovered that the consolidated billing option solves one problem, giving accountants a discount on Intuit services, while creating new problems, namely, accountants being on the hook for their clients' subscription fees. The Revenue Share is basically a twist on the ProAdvisor Preferred Pricing program where clients that are billed directly can get a 30 percent discount on their QuickBooks fees. Under this program, the direct discount is paid to accountants instead of being passed along to the client. When creating a new company in QuickBooks Online Accountant, you see three billing options, as shown in Figure 16-15:

>> **ProAdvisor Discount:** Your firm is billed for the subscription at 30 percent off the normal price, and you then charge your client each month for their subscription fee. There is no time limit on this 30 percent discount, which you can choose to keep or pass along, in part or fully, to your clients.

» **Direct Discount:** Your client receives a 30 percent discount for the first 12 months of their subscription and they are billed directly.

» **Revenue Share:** The first month of your client's subscription is free, followed by a 50 percent discount for three months. Your client pays Intuit directly, and Intuit pays you 30 percent of what the client gets billed for their subscription plus 15 percent of any employee fees for 12 months. Your client is not made aware of this commission arrangement.

FIGURE 16-15:
Billing options available for new companies that you create within QB Accountant.

Follow these steps if you want to opt into the ProAdvisor Revenue Share program:

1. **Choose Settings ➪ Subscriptions and Billing ➪ Revenue Share Payouts and then click Get Started.**

The Revenue Share application page appears.

2. **Fill out the four-page application and then click Submit.**

Among other details, you are asked to provide your entity type, tax identification number, address, and phone number.

Using Your Free QuickBooks Online Advanced Subscription

As I mention at the beginning of this chapter, QB Accountant users get one free QuickBooks Advanced subscription to use for their firm's books, which is an upgrade from the Plus subscription offered in the past. QB Accountant users also get a free Payroll Elite subscription as well.

REMEMBER

The Your Books subscription integrates with QB Accountant, and is intended to house your accounting firm's data, not a client's data or a subsidiary of your accounting firm. Every client in your QB Accountant Client List is automatically set up as a customer in the Your Books company, but team members are not set up as employees.

As I discuss in Chapter 3 and Appendix B, you can import your current accounting records from QuickBooks Desktop. Alternatively, Chapters 4 and 5 discuss importing list information.

REMEMBER

QB Accountant users have up to 1,060 days to import from QuickBooks Desktop into QuickBooks Online. This is different from the 60-day window that your clients get when they create their company on their own, or the 180-day window that you get when you create a client's company within QB Accountant.

Refer to Parts 1 and 2 of this book when you want to enter transactions and create list items. The links in the Your Books portion of the left menu bar match the links your client sees when they view their QuickBooks company. For instance, you can choose Overview from the left menu bar to open the Dashboard page of your own QuickBooks company. The Dashboard typically displays outstanding invoice and expense information, a list of your bank account balances, profit and loss information, and sales in interactive filters. Click part of any graphic on this page to display the details that make up that part of the graphic.

Chapter **17**

Managing Your Clients' Books

A client's QuickBooks company looks and feels the same in QuickBooks Online Accountant (QB Accountant), with the addition of some accountant tools that you can use but that your clients cannot access. In this chapter, I give you a tour of the accountant tools so you'll know what to expect when you're working in a client's books.

Opening a Client's Company

Unless they have multiple QuickBooks subscriptions, your clients are typically managing a single set of books. You, on the other hand, are potentially overseeing numerous sets of books. Accordingly, you have two options for opening a QuickBooks company via QB Accountant (as shown in Figure 17-1):

» Click the QB logo to the left of any client's name in the Client/Contact column of the Client's page.

TIP

The current status of a client's subscription appears in a caption when you hover over the QB logo in the Client/Contact column. This enables you to see the subscription level and status, as well as if a client has a payroll subscription.

» Click Go to QuickBooks at the top of any QB Accountant page and choose the name of the company you want to open.

TIP

The company name that you choose replaces the Go to QuickBooks button. Click the company name to choose Back to Practice to return to your Clients page or choose another QuickBooks company from the list. You can also click the QB Accountant logo to return to your Clients page.

As shown in Figure 17-2, the client's company appears within QB Accountant.

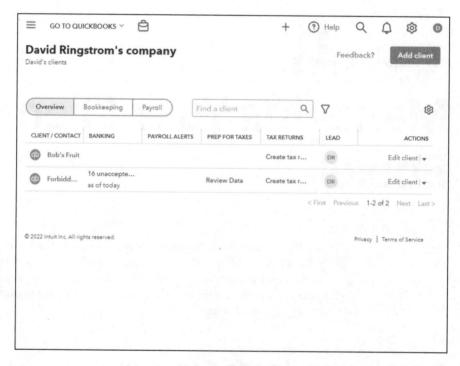

FIGURE 17-1: Click the QB logo to the left of the client's name or use Go to QuickBooks to open a client's company.

You'll immediately notice that accessing your clients' books through QB Accountant is tremendously easier than logging into their books directly. QB Accountant provides a single sign-on, which means once you log into QB Accountant, you can switch to any client's books without signing in again. You can sign out of QB Accountant by clicking the button with your first initial on it at the top right, and then choose Sign Out, as shown in Figure 17-3.

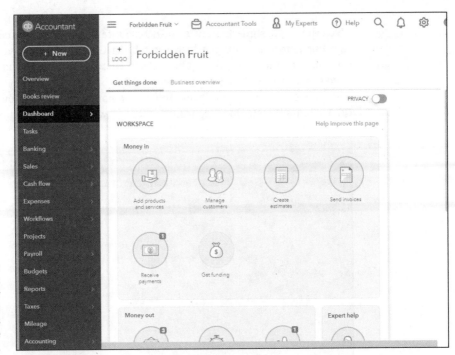

FIGURE 17-2:
A client's company displayed within QuickBooks Online Accountant.

WORKING IN MULTIPLE WINDOWS

Hands down, the easiest way to have multiple windows is to use the QuickBooks Online Advanced Desktop app for Windows. This free app allows you to access multiple QuickBooks companies at once, and you can access your client's books no matter what subscription level they have.

If you're using a web browser, you can open two or more pages at the same time within a single QuickBooks Online company. To do so, click the Accountant Tools button, shown in Figure 17-2, and then choose New Window to duplicate the page you are viewing in another browser tab. Now you can use either tab to navigate to a different page within the company.

All the major browsers let you duplicate tabs, so the New Window command is simply a convenience. In most browsers, if you right-click any tab, the shortcut menu should include a command that contains the word *Duplicate*.

Note that if you want to access two or more QuickBooks companies at the same time, you can't simply open another browser tab. Instead, you need to use separate browsers, such as Google Chrome, Mozilla Firefox, or Microsoft Edge. In Chapter 20, I show how you can use profiles in Chrome to access multiple QuickBooks companies simultaneously.

Given the single sign-on nature of QB Accountant, you want to make sure that you sign out before closing the browser tab. In Google Chrome, you can click the three-dot menu at the top right, choose History, and then choose QuickBooks from the Recently Closed page to access QB Accountant again if you closed the tab without signing out. I didn't test this to see how long the window of getting into QB Accountant lasts, but I do want you to be aware of this exposure.

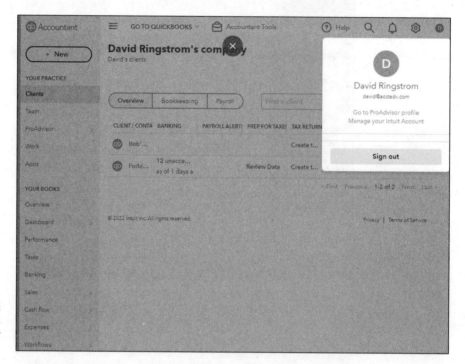

FIGURE 17-3:
Exit QB Accountant by signing out.

Utilizing the Client Overview page

The Client Overview page is designed to give you a quick read on the status of a client's company from several perspectives. Within a client's company, choose Overview at the top of the left menu bar to display a page that you can see but that your clients cannot. The Client Overview page has four sections:

» **Company.** This section allows you to see a client's subscription level and any connected apps, as well as the status of their payroll subscription, if any, and if sales tax has been enabled or not, as shown in Figure 17-4.

» **Banking.** This section, also shown in Figure 17-4, lists bank and credit card accounts along with the bank balance for connected accounts. You can see the book balance for all accounts, and whether any transactions need to be accepted, along with the date that the accounts were last reconciled. The transaction counts in the Unaccepted and Unreconciled columns are clickable links to the For Review tab of the Banking Transactions page and the corresponding account register, respectively.

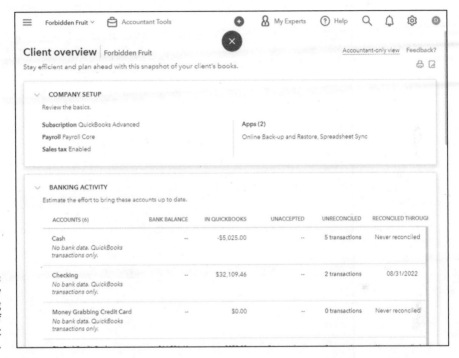

FIGURE 17-4:
The Company and Banking sections of the Client Overview page.

>> **Common Issues.** This section calls out any undeposited funds and uncategorized transactions, as well as significantly overdue A/R and A/P transactions. The opening balance equity amount is shown, as well as the number of negative asset and liability accounts, as shown in Figure 17-5. There's also a link to view the chart of accounts and a View Reports button that allows you to run a Balance Sheet or Profit & Loss report. Each section contains a clickable link to an account register or Quick Report.

>> **Transaction Volume.** As shown in Figure 17-6, this section provides counts by transaction type so that you can see how active a client's company is, and how much review work may be ahead of you. Most sections contain a clickable link to a corresponding Transaction List by Date report.

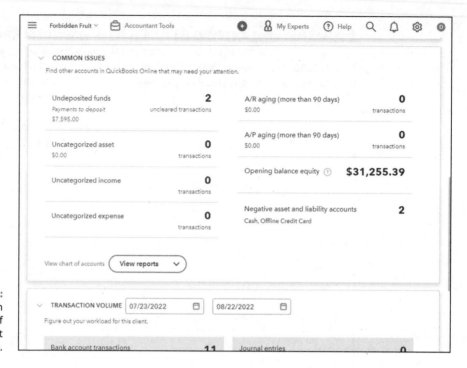

FIGURE 17-5:
The Common Issues section of the Client Overview page.

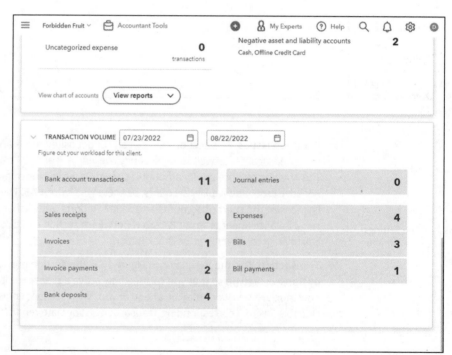

FIGURE 17-6:
The Transaction section of the Client Overview page.

Examining company setup information

You can review company setup information to make sure that the client's company uses the correct accounting method, employer identification number (EIN), and legal business organization, as well as enable account numbers in the chart of accounts:

1. **Choose Settings ➪ Account and Settings within a QuickBooks company, as shown in Figure 17-7.**

   The Account and Settings task pane appears, with the Company tab selected, as shown in Figure 17-8.

   TIP

   Company Settings appears in place of Account and Settings when you click the Settings button in QB Accountant.

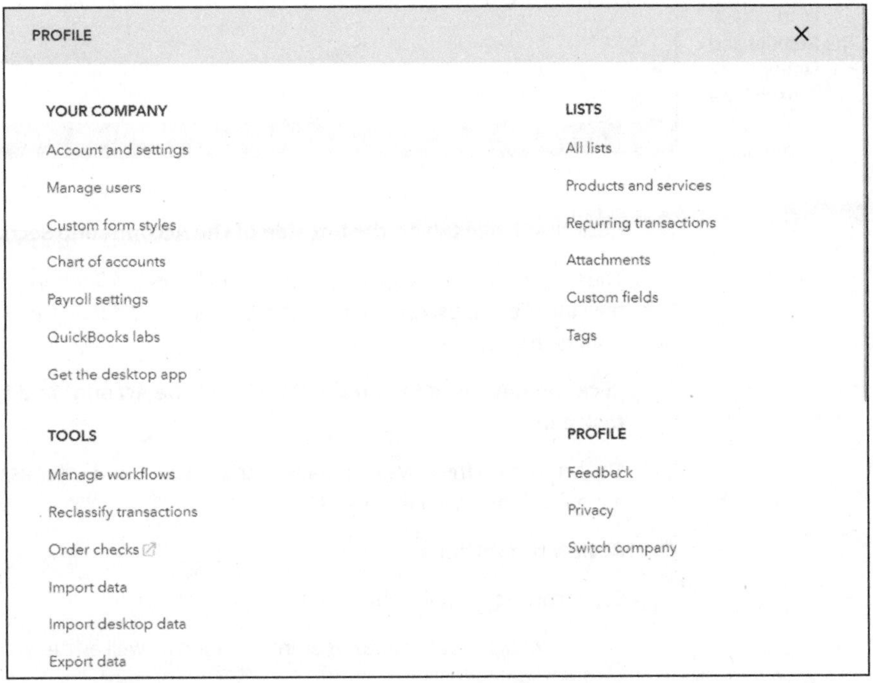

PROFILE	✕

YOUR COMPANY	LISTS
Account and settings	All lists
Manage users	Products and services
Custom form styles	Recurring transactions
Chart of accounts	Attachments
Payroll settings	Custom fields
QuickBooks labs	Tags
Get the desktop app	
TOOLS	**PROFILE**
Manage workflows	Feedback
Reclassify transactions	Privacy
Order checks ⬈	Switch company
Import data	
Import desktop data	
Export data	

FIGURE 17-7:
The Settings menu.

2. **Review the settings.**

   In particular, set or correct Company Name, Legal Name, and EIN. If you need to make changes, click any setting or click the pencil icon that appears in the upper-right corner of the section of settings. Make your changes and click Save.

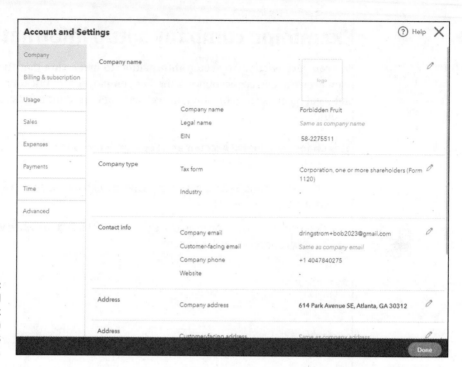

Account and Settings

Company	Company name		logo
Billing & subscription			
Usage		Company name	Forbidden Fruit
Sales		Legal name	*Same as company name*
Expenses		EIN	58-2275511
Payments	Company type	Tax form	Corporation, one or more shareholders (Form 1120)
Time		Industry	.
Advanced			
	Contact info	Company email	dringstrom+bob2023@gmail.com
		Customer-facing email	*Same as company email*
		Company phone	+1 4047840275
		Website	.
	Address	Company address	614 Park Avenue SE, Atlanta, GA 30312
	Address	Customer-facing address	*Same as company address*

(?) Help ✕

Done

FIGURE 17-8:
The Account and Settings task pane for a QuickBooks company.

3. **Click the Usage tab on the left side of the Account and Settings task pane.**

   The Usage Limits tab appears, as shown in Figure 17-9, where you can review how the client subscription fits within the use limits for a given subscription. I discuss these limits in Chapter 1.

4. **Click the Advanced tab on the left side of the Account and Settings task pane.**

   The settings on the Advanced page of the Account and Settings task pane appear, as shown in Figure 17-10.

5. **Review the settings.**

   Set or correct the following options.

   - *Accounting:* Fiscal and tax year information as well as the accounting method.

   - *Company Type:* The tax form setting.

   - *Chart of Accounts:* Whether to use numbers in the chart of accounts.

   - *Automation:* Whether QuickBooks should prefill forms, automatically apply credits, invoice unbilled activity, and apply bill payments.

   - *Other Preferences:* Information such as warnings when duplicate check numbers and bill numbers are used. (This section isn't shown in Figure 17-10.)

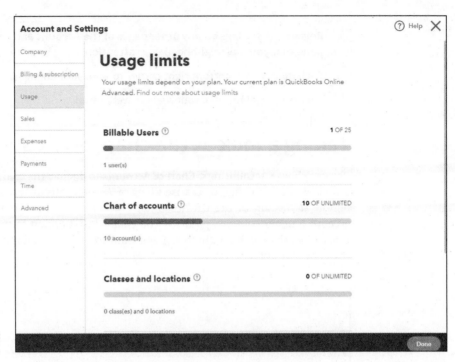

FIGURE 17-9:
Usage limits.

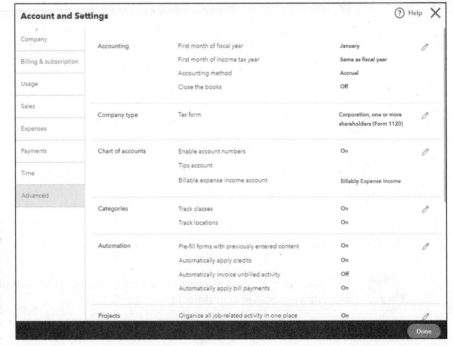

FIGURE 17-10:
Review and, if
necessary,
change settings
on the Advanced
tab of the
Account
and Settings
task pane.

6. Review the settings on any other pages of the Account and Settings task pane that you feel might need your attention.

7. Click Done in the bottom-right corner to save your changes.

A message confirms that your changes were saved.

Taking a look at the chart of accounts

You can choose Accounting ⇨ Chart of Accounts to display the chart of accounts for a QuickBooks company, or choose Chart of Accounts from the Accountant tools button at the top of the QB Accountant screen. As shown in Figure 17-11, an account number column appears if you enabled that option in the company settings. Click the Batch Edit button if you want to assign account numbers to more than one account at a time.

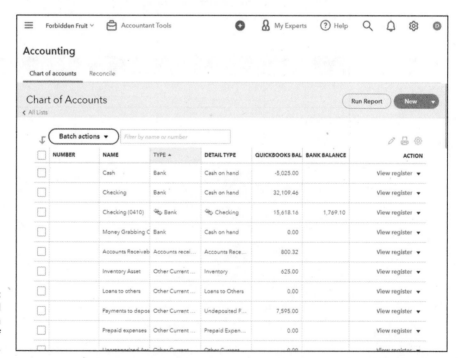

FIGURE 17-11:
You can add and edit accounts on the Chart of Accounts page.

I discuss maintaining the chart of accounts in Chapter 2, including importing a chart of accounts into QuickBooks.

Reviewing list information

There's no secret way to view customers, vendors, employees, inventory, and other lists in QuickBooks. You do this in the same fashion that your clients do:

>> Sales ⇨ Customers let's you curate the Customers page, shown in Figure 17-12.

>> Expenses ⇨ Vendors is a way to view the Vendors page.

>> Payroll ⇨ Employees unveils the Employees page.

>> Payroll ⇨ Contractors causes the Contractors page to appear so that you can review 1099 vendors.

To see most other lists in QuickBooks, you can choose Settings ⇨ All Lists. I think that menu command is disingenuous, because to me, a true All Lists page, shown in Figure 17-13, would include customers, vendors, employees, and contractors as well.

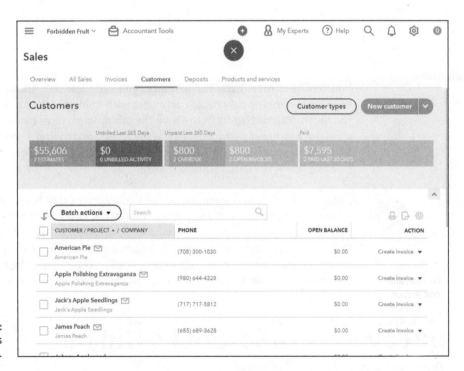

FIGURE 17-12:
The Customers
page.

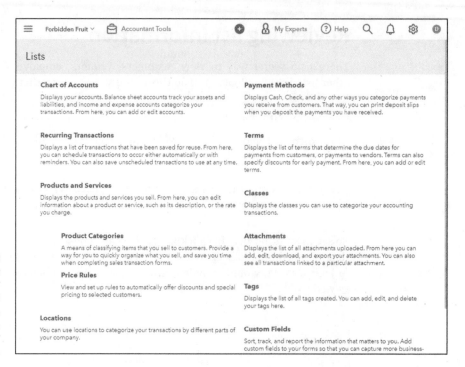

FIGURE 17-13:
The All Lists page doesn't offer access to customers, vendors, employees, or contractors.

You can filter most lists. For instance, you can view only those customers with overdue invoices or only those customers with unbilled activity. And you can click the Batch Actions button (just above the table) to perform batch actions, such as emailing a group of customers, or use the Search box to find a particular list entry. You can also sort lists by name or by open balance by clicking the appropriate heading below the Batch Actions button.

I discuss creating and maintaining lists in Part 2 of this book. Chapter 4 covers customers, vendors, and employees. Chapter 5 covers sales tax, services, and inventory. In both chapters, I discuss the Spreadsheet Sync feature available to QuickBooks Advanced subscribers that allows you to review lists in Excel and then make changes that you post back to QuickBooks. You're going to wish every one of your clients had an Advanced subscription once you experience it.

Discovering QuickBooks Online Accountant Tools

Accountants often need to reclassify transactions, examine voided and deleted transactions, write off invoices, and perform other activities. QB Accountant contains tools that make performing these activities easy. Click the Accountant Tools button at the top of any QuickBooks company that you have accessed through QB Accountant to display the list of quick links and tools shown in Figure 17-14.

TECHNICAL STUFF

Allow me to get pedantic for a moment. The term *write off* is a phrasal verb representing an action, whereas the term *write-off* is a noun representing the result of said action. (In some quarters, the term *writeoff* is vying for attention, but for now, *write off* remains the commonly accepted term.) In case you're wondering, QuickBooks Online Accountant uses the term *write off*.

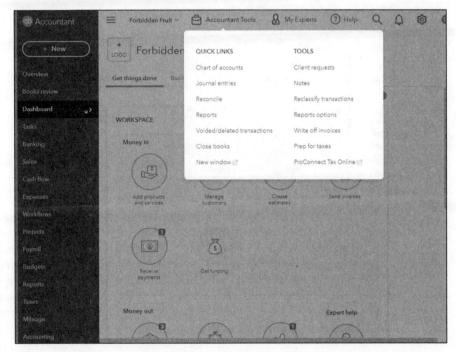

FIGURE 17-14: The Accountant Tools menu contains commands specifically designed to aid the accountant.

Reviewing reports

I'm afraid I don't have a sneaky way for you to run reports in QB Accountant; you have to do that the same way that most people do in QuickBooks Online by choosing Reports from the left menu bar or from the Accountant Tools menu. QuickBooks does try to curry your favor, though, by grouping the reports that you'll probably find of greatest interest into the For My Accountant section of the Reports page, as shown in Figure 17-15.

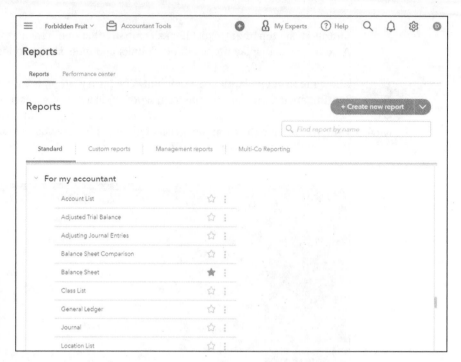

FIGURE 17-15:
Accountant-
oriented reports
available in
QuickBooks
Online.

What *is* sneaky, though, is the Reports Options command on the Accountant Tools menu. This displays the Reports Options page shown in Figure 17-16. Any changes that you make in the Report and Tool Defaults section override the default settings for reports that you run in QuickBooks Online. This page also informs you if the books are closed and provides a convenient Close Books button to facilitate this activity. The Reconciliation Status section shows you the reconciled and current balance of bank and credit card accounts and provides one-click access to the corresponding reconciliation pages.

TIP

Click the star next to any report to mark it as a favorite; this places a copy of the report in the Favorites section at the top of the Reports page. Don't worry, these are *your* favorites; your clients won't know about your proclivity to run Profit and Loss by Month reports.

I discuss the Reports page in detail in Chapter 14, so I won't repeat that information here. I do want to call your attention to Chapters 15 and 19, though. In Chapter 15, I discuss several ways that you can analyze data from QuickBooks in Excel, including using the Spreadsheet Sync feature in QuickBooks Online Advanced to create custom reports in Excel that are refreshable. That means no exporting; just click a menu button to update the report. In Chapter 19, I discuss using Power Query in Excel to automate report cleanup, which also creates refreshable reports. The Spreadsheet Sync feature obviates some of what I discuss in these chapters, but remember, that feature is only available to Advanced subscribers.

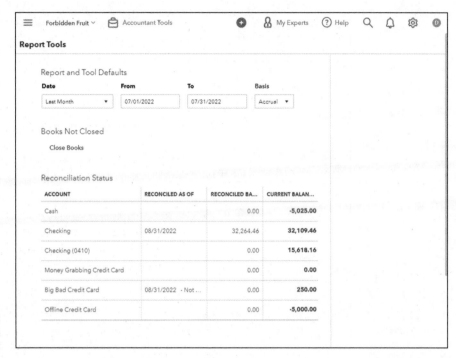

ACCOUNT	RECONCILED AS OF	RECONCILED BA...	CURRENT BALAN...
Cash		0.00	-5,025.00
Checking	08/31/2022	32,264.46	32,109.46
Checking (0410)		0.00	15,618.16
Money Grabbing Credit Card		0.00	0.00
Big Bad Credit Card	08/31/2022 - Not ...	0.00	250.00
Offline Credit Card		0.00	-5,000.00

FIGURE 17-16:
The Reports
Options page.

Examining voided and deleted transactions

The Accounting Tools ⇨ Voided/Deleted Transactions command displays the QuickBooks Audit Log and filters it to show voided and/or deleted transactions. Alternatively, here are the steps your clients can use to view deleted or voided transactions in a QuickBooks company, and that you can potentially use to expand the scope of your periodic review by making additional choices from the Events list:

1. **Choose Accountant Tools ⇨ View Deleted/Voided Transactions.**

The Audit Log page appears, as shown in Figure 17-17.

TIP

Your clients can choose Reports from the left menu bar and then click Audit Log in the Business Overview section. They can then choose Deleted/Voided Transactions from the Events list. While we're here, I should mention that the Events list enables you to monitor a wide array of activity. Make sure that you scroll down past Permissions because that is far from the last choice on the list. Also, you can make multiple selections from the Events list.

2. **Optionally, use the Date Changed field to set a date range.**

3. **Optionally, choose an individual from the Users list.**

You can only filter the Audit Log for one user at a time.

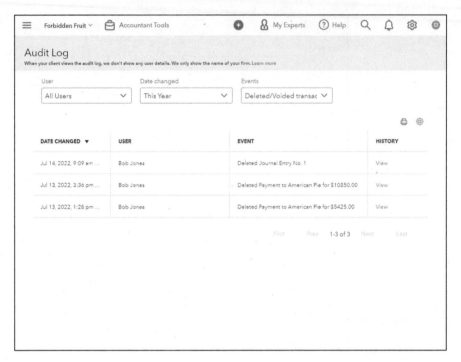

FIGURE 17-17:
Use the Audit Log page to view all kinds of activity in the QuickBooks company.

Now let's say that you want to work with this report in Excel or Google Sheets. Notice that the Audit Log doesn't offer the Export button that is available on all other QuickBooks reports. Fortunately, you *can* get there from here:

1. **Click the Print button on the Audit Log report and then click Cancel.**

   A browser tab that contains your Audit Log results appears, as shown in Figure 17-18.

2. **Press Ctrl+A (Cmd+A for Mac) to select the entire page.**

   All the text on the page should now be selected.

3. **Press Ctrl+C (Cmd+C for Mac) to copy all of the text to the clipboard.**

4. **Select cell A1 of a blank Excel workbook or Google Sheets spreadsheet, and then paste the data.**

   - Microsoft Excel: Choose Home ⇨ Paste.

   - Google Sheets: Choose Edit ⇨ Paste.

   TIP

   You can also press Ctrl+V (Cmd+V for Mac) on either platform if you prefer to use a keyboard shortcut to paste.

Forbidden Fruit

Date changed	User	Event	History
Aug 22, 2022, 2:24 pm Eastern Daylight Time	Online Banking Administration	Completed Deposit of $400.00	View
Aug 22, 2022, 2:24 pm Eastern Daylight Time	Online Banking Administration	Completed Deposit of $400.00	View
Aug 22, 2022, 2:24 pm Eastern Daylight Time	Online Banking Administration	Added Credit Card Credit for $2000.00	View
Aug 22, 2022, 2:24 pm Eastern Daylight Time	Online Banking Administration	Completed Deposit of $750.00	View
Aug 22, 2022, 2:24 pm Eastern Daylight Time	Online Banking Administration	Completed Deposit of $787.50	View
Aug 22, 2022, 2:24 pm Eastern Daylight Time	Online Banking Administration	Added Credit Card Credit for $2000.00	View
Aug 22, 2022, 2:24 pm Eastern Daylight Time	Online Banking Administration	Completed Deposit of $346.36	View
Aug 22, 2022, 2:24 pm Eastern Daylight Time	Online Banking Administration	Added Credit Card Credit for $500.00	View
Aug 22, 2022, 2:24 pm Eastern Daylight Time	Online Banking Administration	Added Credit Card Credit for $500.00	View
Aug 22, 2022, 2:24 pm Eastern Daylight Time	Online Banking Administration	Completed Deposit of $500.00	View
Aug 22, 2022, 2:24 pm Eastern Daylight Time	Online Banking Administration	Completed Deposit of $400.00	View
Aug 22, 2022, 2:24 pm Eastern Daylight Time	Online Banking Administration	Completed Deposit of $304.15	View
Aug 22, 2022, 2:24 pm Eastern Daylight Time	Online Banking Administration	Completed Deposit of $500.00	View
Aug 21, 2022, 4:32 pm Eastern Daylight Time	David Ringstrom	Added Journal Entry No. 3	View
Aug 21, 2022, 4:24 pm Eastern Daylight Time	David Ringstrom	Added Journal Entry No. 2	View
Aug 21, 2022, 2:53 pm Eastern Daylight Time	David Ringstrom	Added Bill to A-peelin' Bananas for $350.00	View
Aug 21, 2022, 2:50 pm Eastern Daylight Time	David Ringstrom	Recorded expense for American Express for $55.00	View

FIGURE 17-18: The browser tab Chrome creates to print the report offers a gateway to Excel or Sheets.

5. **You can now filter the list:**

- Microsoft Excel: Here's one way to filter the results.

  a) Click on cell A3.

  b) Choose Data ➪ Filter to display the Filter arrows.

  c) Make selections from the filter buttons in cells A3:D3 to collapse the log down to the results you want to see.

- Google Sheets: The steps are a little different.

  a) Click on cell A2.

  b) Choose Insert ➪ Rows ➪ Insert 1 Row Above.

  c) Choose Data ➪ Filter Views ➪ Create a Filter View.

  d) Make selections from the filter buttons in cells A3:D3 to collapse the log down to the results you want to see.

TIP

If you're not able to copy and paste the report in the fashion I describe, you can try printing the Audit Log to a PDF file. Microsoft Word 2013 and later, as well as Google Docs, allows you to open and edit PDF files. If you can get the data cleanly into Word or Docs, you can then use Steps 2 to 5 to get the data into Excel or Sheets.

Looking at Books Review

TIP

The Books Review command on the left-hand menu bar displays a page with four tabs that give you a bird's-eye view of potentially problematic transactions in QuickBooks, allow you to monitor the status of account reconciliations, perform a final review, and then do a wrap-up. A fifth tab, labeled Settings, appears if you choose Cleanup from the Monthly drop-down menu, adjacent to the words *Books Review* at the top of the page.

Click the pencil icon next to the month and year shown at the top-left in Figure 17-19 to perform a Books Review for a different period.

Let's review the tabs:

» **Settings.** This tab only appears when you choose the Cleanup option. It gives you an overview of the company's subscriptions, provides links to financial statements, and gives you the ability to make opening balance adjustments, as shown in Figure 17-19. Other sections reflect disconnected bank feeds, accounts without activity for more than 90 days, and an additional items list that you can edit or add to.

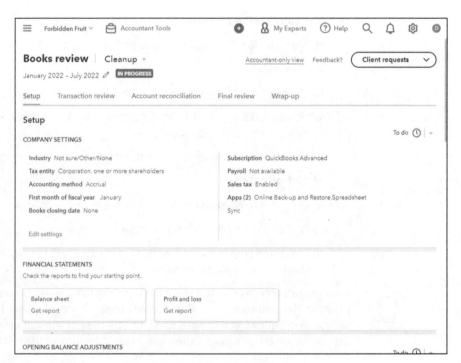

FIGURE 17-19:
The Books Review setup.

TIP

Every tab in Books Review has an Additional Items or Reports section at the bottom of the page that allows you to edit existing items or add new items. You can change the name and/or link name of the item and add details. The QuickBooks Page Link field allows you to store the URL of a given page, which you can copy from the address bar of your browser. Choose Accountant Tools ⇨ New Window to open an additional browser window that you can navigate to within the same QuickBooks company.

» **Transaction Review.** As shown in Figure 17-20, the Transaction Review tab displays lists of any uncategorized transactions, transactions without payees, and additional items you may want to monitor each month. If you scroll further down on your screen, you also see a To Do Checklist that includes reminders to Check for Personal Transactions, Review Loan Payments, and Record Cash Transactions.

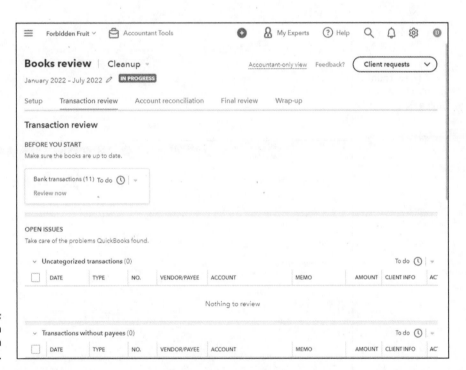

FIGURE 17-20:
The Transaction Review tab in Books Review.

» **Account Reconciliation.** This tab displays the status of bank and credit card reconciliations, as shown in Figure 17-21.

» **Final Review.** This tab, shown in Figure 17-22, allows you to track unusual or unexpected balances, along with A/R and A/P transactions over 90 days old. You can also maintain a running list of reports that you want to review each month. You can toggle the status for each report between To Do, Waiting, and Done.

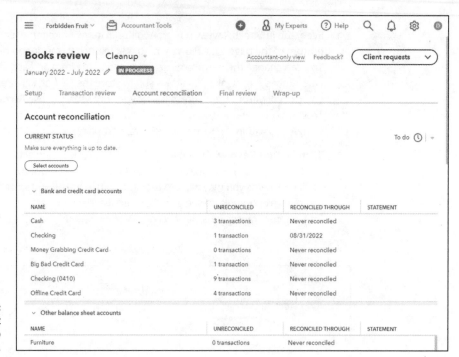

FIGURE 17-21:
The Account
Reconciliation tab
in Books Review.

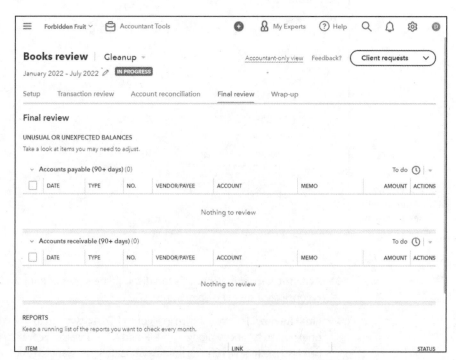

FIGURE 17-22:
The Final Review
tab in Books
Review.

>> **Wrap-Up.** This tab, shown in Figure 17-23, allows you to put a bow on your month-end process by allowing you to choose reports to send to your client. There are three major sections on this page:

- **Prepare Reports.** Click Select to customize the Basic or Expanded Company Financial Reports. The Basic reporting package includes a cover letter, table of contents, optional preliminary pages, the Profit and Loss, Balance Sheet Summary, and Statement of Cash Flows reports, along with an optional End Notes page. The Expanded package includes the Profit and Loss, Balance Sheet, Statement of Cash Flows, A/R Aging Detail, and A/P Aging Detail reports. You can add or take away reports as desired.

- **Send Report Package.** Click Send to open a browser tab that displays the Management Reports tab of the Reports page. Choose an option from the Action column to edit, send, or save the reports in PDF or DOCX format.

- **Close the Books.** Click Close Now to start the process of setting a closing date, which I discuss in more detail later in this chapter.

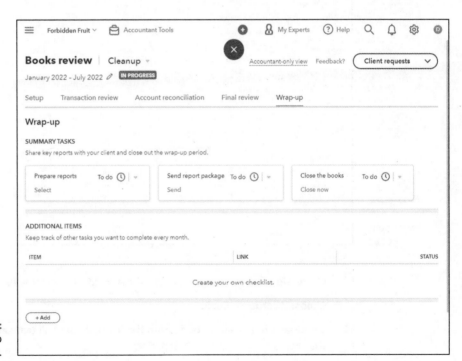

FIGURE 17-23:
The Wrap-Up tab in Books Review.

Reclassifying transactions

The Reclassify Transactions page shown in Figure 17-24 allows you to reclassify transactions for any period, regardless of the closing date, which means be careful! Reclassifying means changing the account, class, and/or location, depending upon your subscription level. You can reclassify multiple transactions if you choose. Follow these steps to reclassify transactions:

1. **Choose Accountant Tools ⇨ Reclassify Transactions.**

   The Reclassify Transactions page appears, as shown in Figure 17-24.

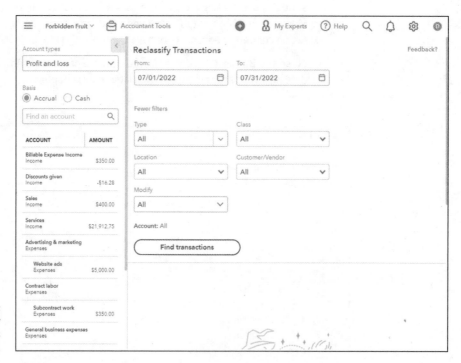

FIGURE 17-24:
The Reclassify
Transactions
page.

2. **Choose Profit and Loss or Balance Sheet from the Account Types list.**

3. **Choose Accrual or Cash.**

4. **Optional: Choose an account from the list to display all transactions for that account for the specified period.**

5. **Optional: Adjust the date range.**

6. **Optional: Make selections from the filter lists to isolate the transactions that you want to reclassify.**

7. **Click Find Transactions if you changed the date range or filters.**

8. **Choose one or more transactions from the resulting list, and then choose Reclassify.**

9. **As shown in Figure 17-25, optionally change the Account, Class, and/or Location for the transactions, and then click Apply.**

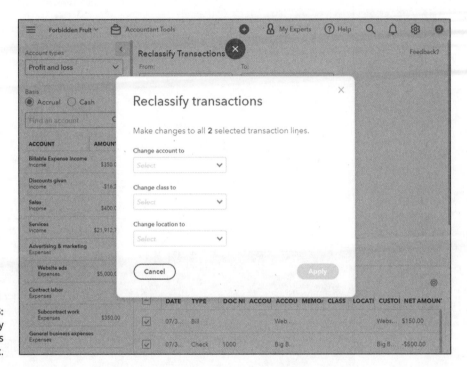

FIGURE 17-25: The Reclassify Transactions dialog box.

Writing off invoices

Choose Accountant Tools ⇨ Write Off to display the Write Off Invoices page shown in Figure 17-26, which enables you to view invoices and then write them off to an account of your choice. At the top of the page, you set filters to display the invoices you want to review. You can view invoices more than 180 days old, more than 120 days old, in the current accounting period, or in a custom date range that you set. You can also set a balance limit. Select any invoices that you want to write off, and then click the Write Off button. A confirmation task pane opens, as shown in Figure 17-27. Select an account if needed, and then click Apply to write off the invoices; otherwise, click Cancel.

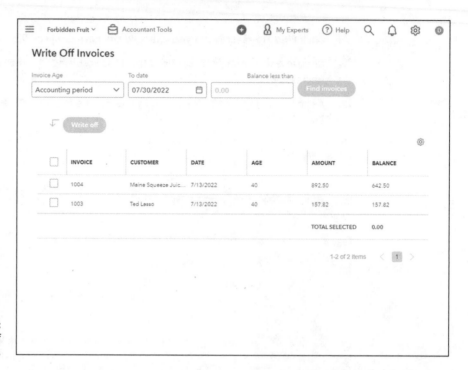

FIGURE 17-26:
The Write Off
Invoices page.

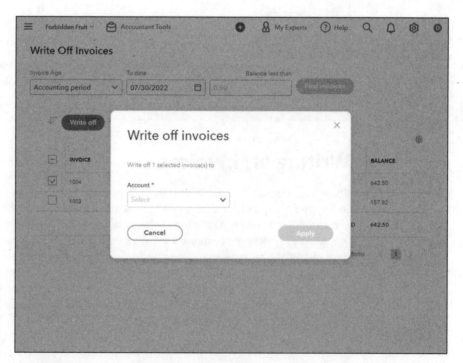

FIGURE 17-27:
Confirm that you
want to write off
the selected
invoices.

WARNING

The Write Off feature doesn't make adjusting entries in the current period; instead, it adjusts the period in which the transaction was originally created, which can affect closed periods negatively. See the last section in Chapter 6 to see how to write off an invoice without affecting a prior period.

Closing the books

Unlike with other accounting programs you may have used, closing the books is purely optional in QuickBooks because there are no accounting periods — it's all one continuous stream of transactions. With that said, closing the books can lock prior transactions, which means they can no longer be edited. Fortunately, you can provide an override option. Here's how to close the books:

1. **Choose Accountant Tools ⇨ Close Books.**

   TIP

   Other ways to do so include choosing Settings ⇨ Account and Settings ⇨ Advanced or choosing Accountant Tools ⇨ Reports Options and then clicking Close Books.

2. **Click on the Accounting section and then toggle on Close Books if needed.**

   A closing Date field appears, as shown in Figure 17-28.

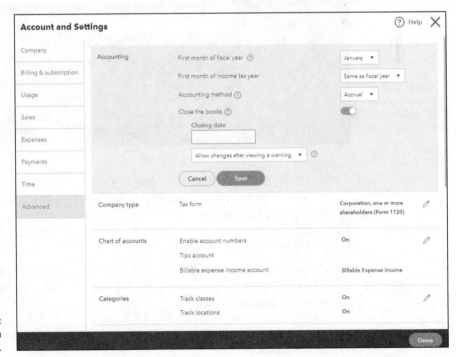

FIGURE 17-28: Setting a closing date.

3. **Enter the closing date of your choice.**

Rest assured that you can always "unclose" the books by editing the closing date or toggling off Close Books.

4. **Decide how restrictive you want the closing to be:**

- *Allow changes after viewing a warning.* This option alerts users that they are trying to enter or edit a transaction in a closed period. They can click Yes on the prompt shown in Figure 17-29 and post the change or new transaction.

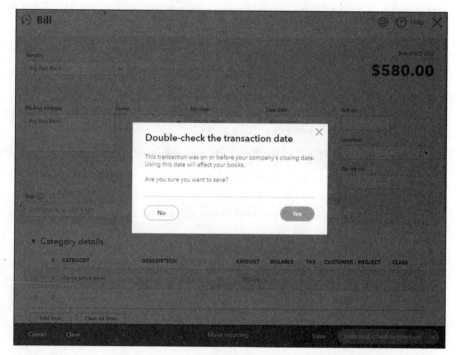

FIGURE 17-29: Warning prompt for new transactions or edits to existing transactions dated prior to the closing date.

- *Allow changes after viewing a warning and entering a password.* This option reveals Password and Confirm Password fields to specify a password that you want users to enter before they can edit or create transactions dated prior to the closing date. In that case, users encounter the prompt shown in Figure 17-30.

TIP

There's no need for password anxiety here. If you forget the closing date password, simply toggle off the Close Books setting. You can then toggle it back on again and assign a new password.

REMEMBER

Only users with administrative rights to a QuickBooks company can close or unclose the books.

FIGURE 17-30:
Password-
protected
warning prompt
for transactions
dated prior to the
closing date.

Understanding the Prep for Taxes page

You can use the Prep for Taxes tool to adjust and review accounts before preparing your client's taxes. Choose Accountant Tools ⇨ Prep for Taxes to view a page that includes the following tabs:

REMEMBER

>> **Year-End tasks.** A to-do list of items to be completed as part of the tax return filing process, shown in Figure 17-31. You can add or remove items from the list.

Tasks that you add here do not appear in the Work page in QuickBooks Online Accountant, which I discuss in Chapter 18.

REMEMBER

>> **Documents.** Enables you to upload and organize supporting documents for your client's income tax return, as shown in Figure 17-32.

Documents that you upload here do not appear in the My Accountant ⇨ Shared Documents tab that I discuss in Chapter 18.

FIGURE 17-31:
The Year-End
Task tab of the
Prep for Taxes
page.

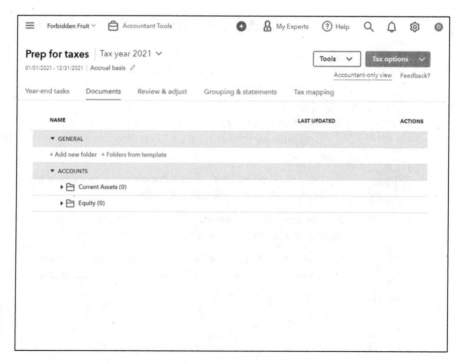

FIGURE 17-32:
The Documents
tab of the Prep
for Taxes page.

»» Review & Adjust. This tab, shown in Figure 17-33, allows you to compare the current tax year with the previous tax year and adjust the Opening Balance Equity and Retained Earnings accounts. There are a few things to note about this tab:

- You can't actually adjust anything directly on this page, but you do see Make Adjustment links that open the Journal Entry page and preselect the Adjusting Entry checkbox. As shown in Figure 17-34, the Prep for Taxes page then asks you to accept the changes.

- You can delete adjusting entries that you have accepted. Click the amount of the adjusting entry to display a report that lets you drill down to the underlying journal entry. At the bottom of the Journal Entry screen, click More ⇨ Delete, and then confirm that you want to delete the transaction. The Prep for Taxes page prompts you to accept these changes as well.

- You can click any dollar value that appears as a link to display a transaction report that details the balance. As with journal entries, you can make corrections and then accept the changes when prompted.

- The Actions menu includes commands that allow you to add notes and attach documents so that you can support the changes that you make.

- You can track your progress by clicking the checkmark to the left of a category or account as you complete your work.

- Click the + button to the right of any account to add a note.

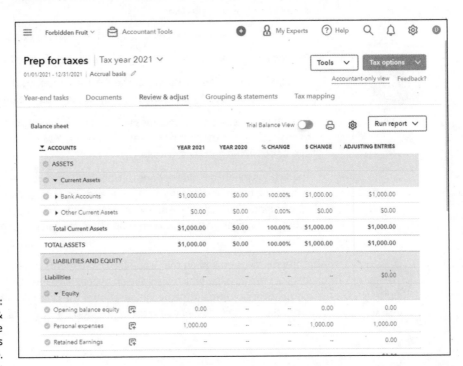

FIGURE 17-33:
The Review & Adjust tab of the Prep for Taxes page.

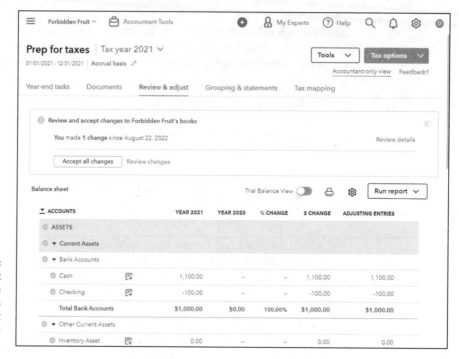

FIGURE 17-34: You must accept changes to a QuickBooks company that would affect the tax return.

» **Grouping & Statements.** This tab, shown in Figure 17-35, allows you to group accounts in any fashion you like:

- Click the Create New Group link to display the Create Group task pane.

- Provide a group name and optionally a reference code, and then click Save.

I couldn't close the task pane by way of the X in the corner, so I had to create a group and then delete it by choosing Ungroup in the Action column.

- Drag the six-dot button, sometimes referred to as a waffle button, adjacent to an account into the group to create a grouping. You can drag accounts into or out of the group as needed.

- The Actions menu includes options to Update the group, which means change the name and/or reference code, and add notes as well as attachments. The Actions menu includes Add Note and Add Attachment options, as well as an Ungroup command that you can use to delete the group.

Attachments that you add on the Grouping & Statements page do not appear on the Documents page, which feels like an oversight to me. Further, any attachments or notes are discarded if you choose the Ungroup command. You are asked to confirm that you want to ungroup the accounts.

TIP

Choose Run Report ⇨ Export as Excel to create a reporting package in Excel that includes the following worksheet tabs: Cover Page, Notice to Reader (NTR), Balance Sheet (BS), Income Statement (IS), and Leadsheets Schedule.

I included the actual worksheet names in parentheses where they differ from the full names.

» **Tax Mapping.** This page allows you to map your client's books to their tax return. Most accounts are mapped automatically for you, but as shown in Figure 17-36, you're prompted to assign any accounts that QuickBooks couldn't match. Click Assign Tax Line to display a task pane from which you choose a line from the tax form, and then click Save.

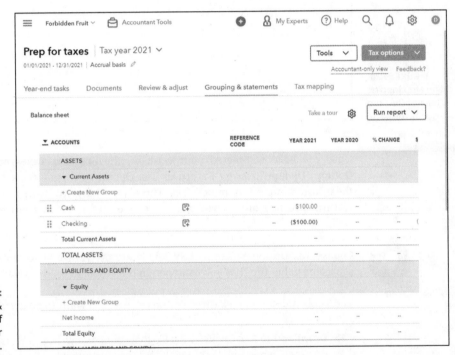

FIGURE 17-35:
The Grouping & Statements tab of the Prep for Taxes page.

TIP

The Tax Mapping tab prompts you to choose a tax form for the QuickBooks company if you haven't yet selected one. Click the Edit button, which looks like a pencil, if you need to make changes.

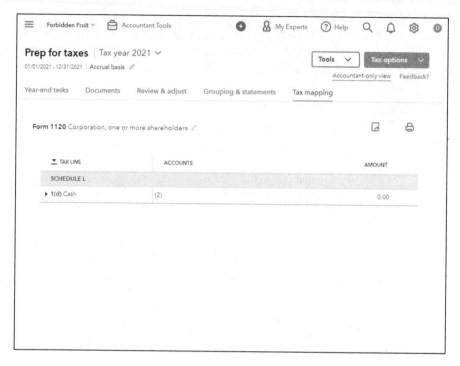

FIGURE 17-36:
The Tax Mapping
tab of the Prep
for Taxes page.

Once you have completed your work on the Prep for Taxes pages, click Tax Option ⇨ Update Existing Return or Tax Option ⇨ Create New Return to transfer the information to ProConnect Tax. There's no charge for using the Prep for Taxes feature; you pay only when you print or e-file a return from ProConnect Tax Online.

TIP

Choose Tax Options ⇨ Export CSV File to export your adjustments to a comma-separated value file that you can open in Microsoft Excel or Google Sheets.

The Tools menu includes three options that you'll want to be aware of:

>> **Download to Zip.** Creates a Zip file that contains any attachments you've uploaded, along with Excel workbooks that document the financial statements, your adjustments, and the tax mapping.

>> **Carry Forward Previous Year.** Use this command if you want to start over and replace the entirety of the Tax Mapping page with files, folders, groupings, reference codes, and tax mappings from the prior year. You are asked to confirm because any activity on the page will be overwritten.

>> **Lock.** Use this command to enable a lock icon on the Prep for Taxes page and establish a closing date for the QuickBooks company. See the section, "Closing the books," for more about what this entails.

Taking a brief look at other accountant tools

The Accountant Tools menu contains a few other tools that make an accountant's life easier:

- » *Chart of Accounts* displays the Chart of Accounts window. I describe working in this window in Chapter 2.

- » *Journal Entries* displays the Journal Entry window.

- » *Reconcile* displays the Reconcile page, where you can choose an account or review existing Reconciliation reports. For more details on reconciling accounts, see Chapter 10.

- » *New Window* allows you to open a new window quickly in QB Accountant, as I discuss in Chapter 16.

- » *Client Requests* enables you to send a message to your client that they must respond to within QuickBooks. I discuss Client Requests in Chapter 18.

- » *Notes* allow you to see the same notes that you can add from the Notes page that appears when you click a name on your client list.

- » *ProConnect Tax Online* launches a new browser window that takes you to Tax Hub in ProConnect Tax Online, another Intuit product. Tax Hub allows you to track the status of your clients' tax returns. ProConnect Tax Online connects to your QB Accountant account but is a separate product.

Chapter **18**

Practice Management

QuickBooks Online Accountant makes it easy for you to monitor your clients' individual QuickBooks companies. The single sign-on feature alone means QB Accountant saves you a lot of time and hassle. You can take things further by utilizing its practice management features. For instance, QB Accountant can generate an automated to-do list that alerts you when work needs to be completed within a particular QuickBooks company, such as reviewing downloaded transactions or processing payroll. You can supplement this to-do list by creating projects comprised of tasks that you can assign to yourself or to team members. You can also initiate and track client requests, rather than running the risk of correspondence getting buried in your email inbox. Let's begin with a look at the Work page.

Introducing the Work Page

The Work page in QB Accountant is a centralized to-do list that all your team members — but not your clients — can access. You can further determine which elements of the Work page each team member can see. As shown in Figure 18-1, the Work page enables you to track work to be completed for both your clients and your own firm. This is a mix of automated notifications from your clients' QuickBooks companies, projects that you create and populate with tasks, and requests that you send to your clients. The Work page in Figure 18-1 is mostly blank because I haven't set up any projects yet.

I discuss adding team members to QB Accountant in Chapter 16.

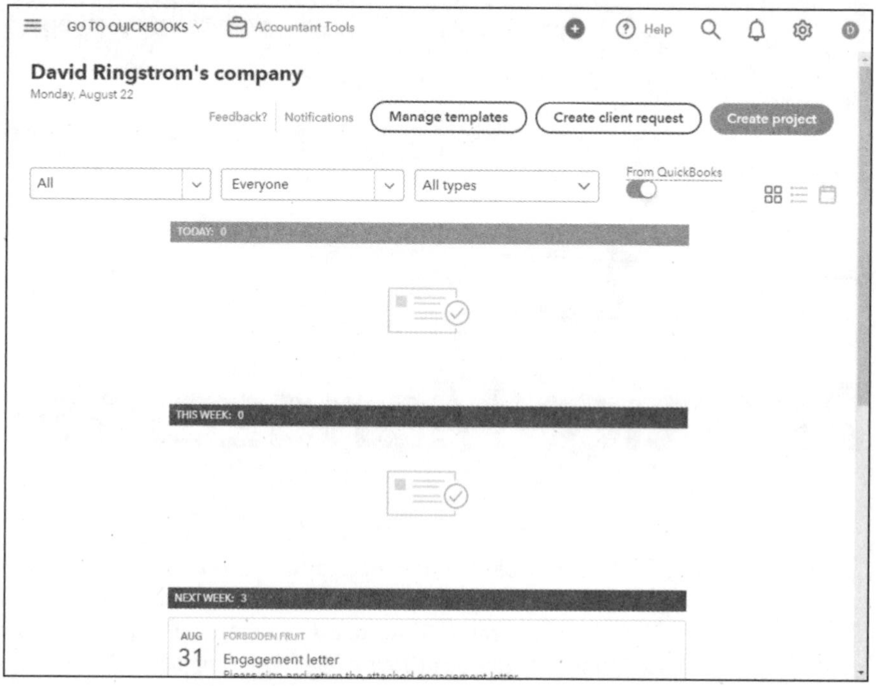

TIP

FIGURE 18-1:
A mostly
unpopulated
Work page within
QB Accountant.

REMEMBER

The word *Projects* has two different connotations in QuickBooks. Plus and Essentials users can use the Projects feature within a QuickBooks company to track related transactions to monitor the profitability of a particular endeavor. In QB Accountant, Projects are containers for one or more tasks to be completed.

The Work page offers three different views — Grid, List, and Calendar — that you can filter by using three buttons and a toggle:

>> **All.** The first filter defaults to giving you a birds'-eye view of your practice. From this list, you can choose Clients Only to only see tasks related to your clients, or Firm Only to only view internal tasks. You can also choose a specific client as well.

>> **Everyone.** The second filter shows you tasks assigned to everyone in the firm, but you can choose Me to see your personal to-do list or choose a specific team member.

>> **All types.** The third filter controls which types of items appear onscreen. You can choose Projects, Tasks, or Requests from this list.

>> **From QuickBooks.** This toggle controls whether automated notifications generated by each client's QuickBooks company appear on your Work page.

You can use all three filters in conjunction with each other, so that you see as much or as little detail as you need in each moment.

The Work page also has three buttons in the top right-hand corner:

>> **Manage Templates.** This button displays the Templates page that allows you to create project templates, which are basically pre-configured to-do lists for work to be done on an ongoing basis. As shown in Figure 18-2, the Templates page includes four Quick Start templates that are prepopulated with related tasks. You cannot modify the built-in templates, but you can duplicate them as starting points for your own templates.

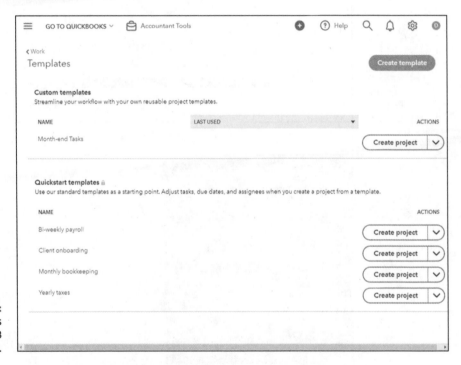

FIGURE 18-2:
The Templates page within QB Accountant.

>> **Create Client Requests.** This button displays the Create a Request task pane, shown in Figure 18-3, that you can use to document a request that you're making of a client. You can optionally notify your client of the request, which saves you from having to log the request and then separately email the request as well.

>> **Create Project.** This button displays the Create Project task pane, shown in Figure 18-4, for situations where there is work to be completed that doesn't fit within a template that you've created.

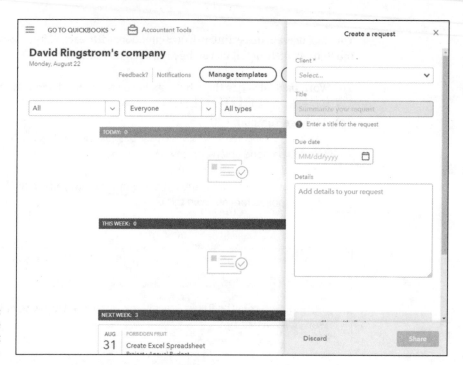

FIGURE 18-3:
The Create a Request task pane.

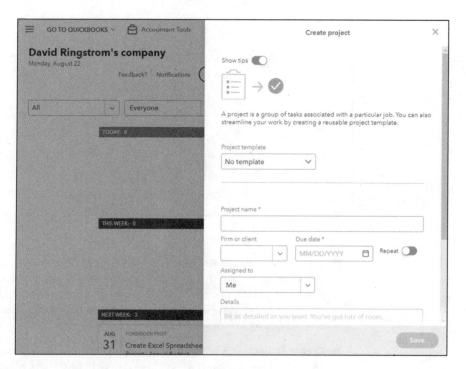

FIGURE 18-4:
The Create Project task pane.

The tasks and requests that you create can be viewed in three different ways on the Work page, but first let's see how to create templates.

Creating templates

The repetitive nature of accounting-related tasks means it's easy for items to fall off of your radar or blur into the woodwork. You can counter this by creating project templates that are comprised of tasks or steps to be completed. Here's how to create a template:

1. **Choose Work on the left menu and then click Manage Templates.**

   The Templates page shown in Figure 18-2 appears.

2. **Click Create Template to display the task pane shown in Figure 18-4.**

3. **Assign a name to the template, such as Month-End Tasks.**

4. **Optional: Enable the Repeat toggle to display the Due Date options shown in Figure 18-5.**

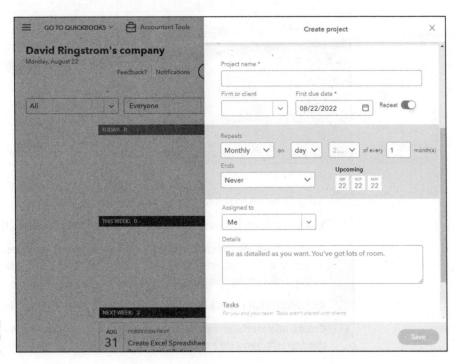

FIGURE 18-5: Establishing a recurring project.

Projects can be set to recur on a weekly, bi-weekly, monthly, quarterly, or yearly basis on specific days of your choice. The scheduling options presented vary, based upon the frequency that you select.

5. Optional: Use the Details field to add any narrative information about the project.

6. Click Add a Task to display the fields shown in Figure 18-6.

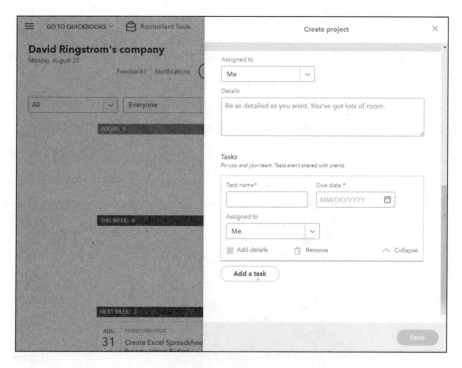

FIGURE 18-6:
Adding a task.

7. Assign a name to the task, such as Bank Reconciliation.

8. You can choose between Set Later or Offset in the Due Date field.

Offset enables you to schedule the task a specified number of days prior to the project due date. *Set Later* means that you'll need to set the due date when you create a new project based upon this template.

9. Add additional tasks as needed, and then click Save Template.

10. Create additional templates as needed, and then click the Work link at the top left-hand side of the page or choose Work from the left menu bar.

TIP

The Save Template button is disabled if you haven't filled in a required field in the task pane.

Creating client requests

A client request can be anything related to a client's QuickBooks company or your business relationship with them. Here's how to create a client request:

1. **Choose Work on the left menu and then click Create Request.**

The task pane shown in Figure 18-3 appears.

You can also choose Accountant Tools ⇨ Client Requests within a QuickBooks company to display a task pane that shows pending requests and allows you to add requests.

TIP

2. **Choose a client name from the list.**

3. **Enter a title for the request, such as Engagement Letter.**

This is similar to crafting a subject line for an email.

4. **Specify a due date for the request.**

The due date is a required field that you must complete.

5. **Enter the details of the request, much like the body of an email.**

6. **Optional: Click Documents to upload one or more documents related to the request.**

This is similar to adding an attachment to a QuickBooks transaction.

7. **The Notify Client option defaults to enabled, but you can turn it off if you don't want to notify your client of the request.**

8. **Click Share to save the request.**

The Share button retains its label even if you toggle off the Notify Client option.

9. **The request appears on your Work page, as shown in Figure 18-6.**

A Sent indicator appears if you notified your client of the request.

If you choose to notify your client, they will receive an email message notifying them of the request, plus the request will appear within their QuickBooks company. Here's how your clients can view requests that you make of them:

1. **Choose My Accountant (Bookkeeping ⇨ My Accountant) from the left menu bar.**

The My Accountant page shown in Figure 18-7 appears and can be sorted by Due Date or Recently Updated.

You can view the My Accountant page when you access your clients' companies through QB Accountant by choosing My Accountant from the left menu bar.

TIP

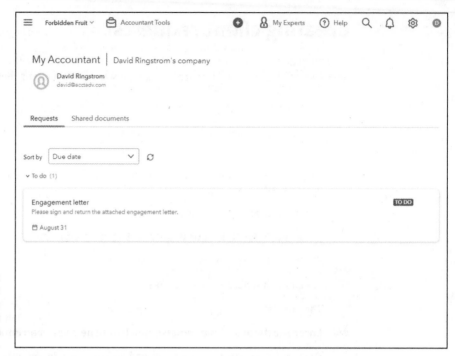

FIGURE 18-7:
The My
Accountant page
within a client's
QuickBooks
company.

2. **Click on any task to display the task pane shown in Figure 18-8.**

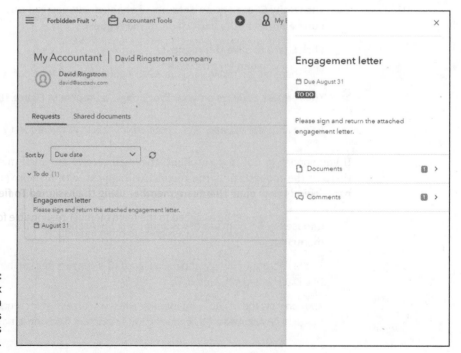

FIGURE 18-8:
The To Do task
pane within
a client's
QuickBooks
company.

3. **Optional: Your client can expand the Documents section to view documents you've shared or upload new documents.**

4. **Optional: Your client can expand the Comments section to respond to the request and then click Post Comment.**

   You will receive an email notification that your client responded.

WARNING

Comments added to a request are not editable and cannot be deleted.

Your clients cannot delete requests, but you can. Click on any request on the Work page to display a task pane that shows the request and any responses. Click the trash can icon at the top right to delete the request. You can also change the status of a request to In Progress or Completed. Your clients cannot change the status.

Managing projects and tasks

Projects typically are a collection of tasks to be completed by a specified date. Each project will be assigned to a client or to your firm, and each task within a project will have a due date and will be assigned to a team member. Here's how to create a task-tracking project:

1. **Choose Work on the left menu and then click Create Project.**

   The panel shown in Figure 18-4 appears.

2. **Optional: Choose a template from the Project Template drop-down list.**

3. **Enter a name for the project, such as Annual Budget.**

4. **Choose between My Firm or a client name from the Firm or Client drop-down list.**

   Use My Firm to track internal projects that aren't related to a specific client.

5. **Set a project due date.**

   The due dates for any tasks associated with this project must be scheduled on or before the project due date.

6. **Assign the project to a team member using the Assigned To field.**

   The project should be assigned to the team member responsible for the overall project. Tasks can be assigned to other individuals.

TIP

   Click the Repeat slider to set up the time frame to use for recurring projects, such as monthly bank statement reconciliation or quarterly payroll tax filings.

7. **Enter narrative information about the project in the Details field.**

8. **Optional: Click Add a Task to add one or more tasks to the project.**

9. **Click Save to save the project.**

TIP

Projects scheduled for more than 30 days in the future don't appear on the Grid View of the Work page, but do appear in List View, as I discuss later in this chapter.

You can edit any project or task that you add, but you cannot edit the automatic tasks that are posted by a QuickBooks company. Click on any project or task on the Work page to display a task pane like what you used to create the project. You can edit the project details, as well as add, remove, or update tasks. Buttons along the bottom of the task pane enable you to delete the project, convert it to a template, or duplicate the project.

TIP

You can't convert a project into a task or a task into a project.

As you make progress on a task, you can update its status directly from Grid View on the Work page. Click the arrow on a task card to change its status, as shown in Figure 18-9.

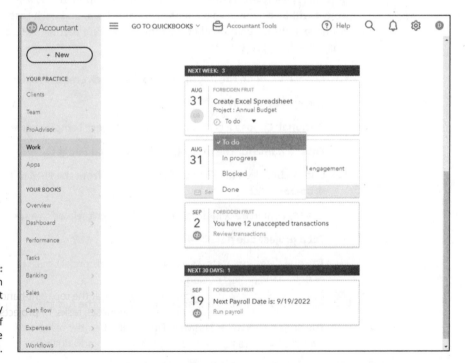

FIGURE 18-9:
Use the arrow on a task or project card to display the list of available statuses.

Tasks can have a status of To Do, In Progress, Blocked, or Done. You use Blocked status when something is stopping you from completing a task.

Looking at Work page views

As I discussed previously, the Work page allows you to filter your to-do list as granularly as you want. The Work page also offers three different views:

>> **Grid.** This default view uses cards that allow you to monitor requests, projects, and tasks due within the next 30 days, as shown in Figure 18-10.

NEXT WEEK: 3

| AUG 31 | FORBIDDEN FRUIT |
| Create Excel Spreadsheet |
| Project : Annual Budget |
| ⊘ To do ▾ |

| AUG 31 | FORBIDDEN FRUIT |
| Engagement letter |
| Please sign and return the attached engagement letter. |
| ✉ Sent |

| SEP 2 | FORBIDDEN FRUIT |
| You have 12 unaccepted transactions |
| Review transactions |

NEXT 30 DAYS: 1

| SEP 19 | FORBIDDEN FRUIT |
| Next Payroll Date is: 9/19/2022 |
| Run payroll |

FIGURE 18-10: The Grid View.

>> **List.** The List button appears at the top right-hand corner of the Grid and displays all requests, projects, and tasks in list form, as shown in Figure 18-11.

>> **Calendar.** The Calendar button also appears at the top right-hand corner of the grid, and shows you the number of requests, tasks, or projects that are due on a given day, as shown in Figure 18-12.

REMEMBER

Filters that you apply affect all three views.

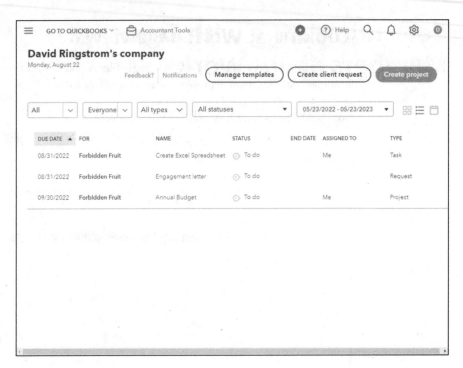

FIGURE 18-11:
The List View.

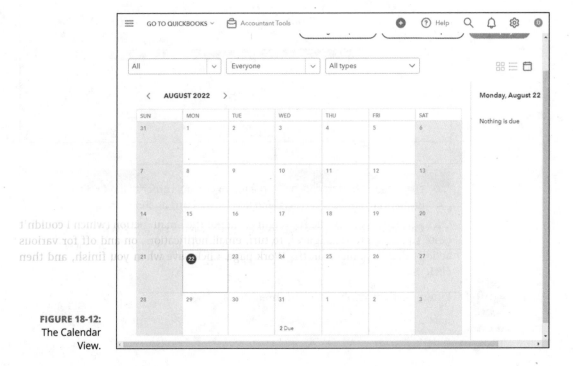

FIGURE 18-12:
The Calendar
View.

Communicating with Team Members about Work

At the risk of stating the obvious, communication is paramount when you're working in a team environment. You can provide notifications by email for a variety of actions associated with the projects and tasks that appear on the Work page. Click the Notifications link at the top of the Work page shown in Figure 18-10 or Figure 18-11 if you want to turn notifications on or off. Doing so displays the Notifications tab of the Company Settings task pane shown in Figure 18-13.

FIGURE 18-13: Set up email notifications for team members regarding work.

Click the pencil icon in the top-right corner of the Email section (which I couldn't quite squeeze into the figure), to turn email notifications on and off for various actions that take place on the Work page. Click Save when you finish, and then click Done.

TIP

By default, each team member gets notifications of new assignments and due dates, but team members can log into their QB Accountant accounts and enable any additional notifications they'd like to receive.

Chapter **19**

Automating QuickBooks Analysis with Power Query

n Chapter 15, I explain how you can analyze QuickBooks reports in Microsoft Excel. The steps require some manual effort, which can become tedious if you need to perform them frequently or for multiple clients. In this chapter, I show you how you can automate the steps by using the Power Query feature of Excel.

I also show you how to create self-updating reports in Excel, and I give an explanation of how to unpivot data in a QuickBooks report. *Unpivoting* means transposing data from columns going across the worksheet into rows that travel down. You can then more easily filter the data and create pivot tables from it, as I discuss in Chapter 15.

Introducing Power Query

Power Query is an Excel feature that allows you to automate report analysis in a similar fashion to what you'd do in Excel. The difference is that Power Query keeps track of the steps that can be applied automatically to future versions of

QuickBooks reports and other data. Even better, Power Query is often referred to as a code-free solution, which means that you can automate repetitive tasks without writing any programming code.

REMEMBER

Power Query has been around since Excel 2010 and is built into Excel 2016 and later versions. Excel 2010 or 2013 users need to perform an online search for "Power Query download" and follow the instructions. This chapter is best suited to readers who are using Excel 2016 or later (especially as part of Microsoft 365) on a Windows computer, but as of this writing, Power Query is being beta-tested in Excel for Mac.

For this chapter, I used the sample company for QuickBooks Online, which you can access at https://qbo.intuit.com/redir/testdrive. I chose this company so that you have an easy way to generate reports that have actual data in them. You can also follow along with your own data.

Connecting to QuickBooks Reports

This section explains how to automate the manual steps you may have performed in Chapter 15 when cleaning up the Transaction List by Date report. The end result is a set-and-forget approach. In other words, going forward, when you export the report from QuickBooks, you save the new Excel workbook over the previous Excel workbook that contained the QuickBooks report. Your cleaned-up data appears in a second workbook that is linked to your report. You can choose to have the second workbook update itself automatically, or you can manually click Data ⇨ Refresh All to refresh the workbook with the latest information that you exported from QuickBooks.

Begin by exporting the Transaction List by Date report from QuickBooks. Follow these steps:

1. **Choose Reports or Business Overview ⇨ Reports.**

   The Reports page appears.

2. **Start typing** Transaction List by Date **in the search field, and then choose that report title in the search results.**

   The search field makes it easy to locate reports without scrolling through the entire list.

3. **Select a date range, such as This Year, and then click Run Report.**

   Many QuickBooks reports default to the current month, but you can designate any time period.

4. **Click the Export button and then choose Export to Excel on the resulting menu that appears.**

   See Chapter 14 for more information about running reports in QuickBooks.

5. **Open and save the report in a location that you'll be able to remember.**

   By default, reports that you export from QuickBooks land in your Downloads folder. In this case, you want a more permanent location for this report because you'll be saving over this file again in the future.

6. **Close the Excel report.**

   You don't always have to close a file before you can analyze data in Excel. You can put your cursor within a list of data in a spreadsheet and then choose Data ⇨ From Table/Range, or Data ⇨ From Sheet, to load the data into the Power Query Editor. In this exercise, though, you want to access a workbook that has been closed.

7. **Press Ctrl+N or choose File ⇨ New ⇨ Blank Workbook in Excel to create a blank workbook.**

8. **Choose Data ⇨ Get Data ⇨ From File ⇨ From Workbook.**

   If you're using Excel 2016, choose Data ⇨ New Query. If you're using Excel 2010 or 2013, a similar New Query type of command appears on the Query menu.

9. **Browse for and select the QuickBooks report that you saved in Step 5, and then click the Import button.**

   A Navigator dialog box appears.

10. **Click the worksheet that contains the data you want to access, and then click Transform Data to open the Power Query Editor, as shown in Figure 19-1.**

    If you were to click Load, Power Query would return the data to a new worksheet without making any modifications. If you want to automate the manual cleanup process described in Chapter 15, click Transform Data instead.

At this point, you're ready to start the cleanup process. The work that you've done so far has connected your report to Power Query. Now let's eliminate two extraneous steps that could pose issues down the line.

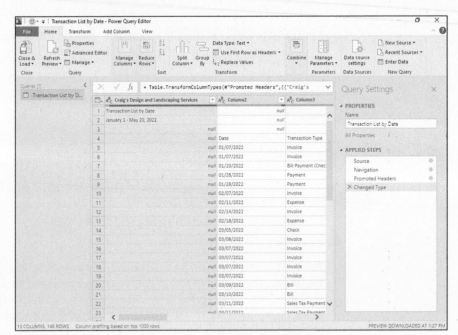

FIGURE 19-1:
The Power Query Editor shows the QuickBooks report that you just imported.

Removing header rows

As you see in Figure 19-1, several blank rows appear at the top of the report, and the column headings appear in Row 4. For a cleaner report, it's a good idea to remove those rows and then promote the contents of Row 4 to be the true column headings. First, remove two unneeded default steps that Power Query tends to add by following these steps:

1. Right-click on the third step in the Applied Steps pane on the right side of the screen, and choose Delete Until End from the shortcut menu.

Every Power Query transformation has a Source step, and typically has a Navigation step as well. The Navigation step allows you to see the data in the worksheet. I can tell you from hard-fought experience that it's best to remove any other steps that Power Query "helpfully" adds to your transformation. In this case, you're removing the Promoted Headers and Changed Type steps, which you'll add back in a different fashion.

2. When the Delete Step prompt appears, click Delete.

You can also hover your mouse over a step in the Applied Steps pane and then click the X to the left of its name to remove it from the list.

3. **Choose Home ⇨ Remove Rows ⇨ Remove Top Rows.**

   The Remove Top Rows dialog box appears, as shown in Figure 19-2.

   The Remove Rows command allows you to remove rows from the top or bottom of a report. You can also remove duplicates, alternate rows, and rows that contain errors.

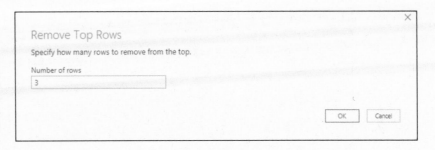

FIGURE 19-2:
The Remove Top
Rows dialog box
allows you to
remove rows
from the top of a
report.

Remove Top Rows

Specify how many rows to remove from the top.

Number of rows

3

OK   Cancel

4. **Enter 3 in the Number of Rows field and then click OK.**

   The goal is to make the headings in Row 4 move up to the first row of the listing.

5. **Click the first column of the report and then press Delete on your keyboard.**

   Unlike in Excel, you can remove columns in Power Query by clicking a column and pressing Delete. You can also choose Home ⇨ Remove Columns or right-click a column and choose Remove from the shortcut menu.

At this point, the report format is starting to shape up, but you can still make some additional improvements.

Promoting headers

If you scroll down on your report in its current state, you'll find that the headings in Row 1 scroll off the screen. In an Excel worksheet, you can choose View ⇨ Freeze Panes to freeze one or more rows at the top of the screen. In Power Query, you can freeze a single row at the top of the screen by choosing Home ⇨ Use First Row As Headers. This command moves the column headings from Row 1 up to the frame of the Power Query grid. If you change your mind about this action, hover your mouse over Promoted Headers in the Applied Steps pane and then click the X that appears to the left of the step.

Notice that Power Query added a Changed Type step to the Applied Steps pane in Figure 19-3. Changed Type means that Power Query changed the data type for one or more columns. On this report, the dates in the first column were stored as text. I show in Chapter 15 how to use the Text to Columns feature in Excel to convert text-based dates to numeric format. Conversely, Power Query noticed the dates stored as text and converted them automatically.

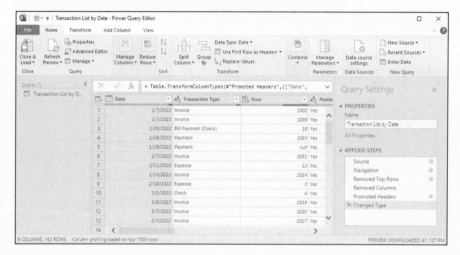

FIGURE 19-3:
The Applied Steps pane shows the transformation steps being carried out on a report.

TIP

Power Query isn't always this prescient when it comes to recognizing data types, which are represented by an icon on the left-hand side of each column's header. For instance, one or more columns of numbers may get changed to the Text data type, which means you won't be able to sum the numbers or do other types of math in Excel. If you see an ABC in the header of a column of numbers, make sure to click the icon and choose a value-based data type, such as Decimal Number, Currency, or Whole Number unless you're trying to preserve leading zeros, such as in ZIP codes or Social Security numbers.

At this point, the report is clean enough that you could send it back to Excel. First, though, I want to show you some additional actions that you can take in Power Query.

Removing unwanted columns

In this section, I show you how to use the Choose Columns command to indicate which columns you want to keep and which you want to remove. For instance, you may not want to include the Num, Posting, and Split columns in the final data set that you're building. Follow these steps to remove any extraneous columns:

1. **Choose Home ⇨ Choose Columns.**

   Many command buttons in Power Query are bifurcated. For instance, if you click the top half of the Choose Columns command, the Choose Columns dialog box opens, as shown in Figure 19-4. If you click the bottom half, a menu appears from which you have to click Choose Columns a second time. On the other hand, this action also reveals the Go to Column command. The Go to Column command allows you to navigate to a specific column in your report by selecting the column name in a list.

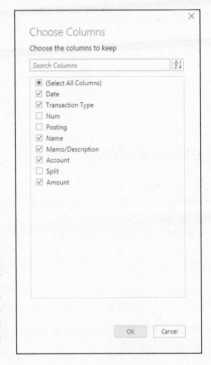

2. **Clear the Num, Posting, and Split checkboxes and then click OK.**

   The fields in the Choose Columns dialog box are initially presented in the order in which they appear in the report. If you click the AZ button to the right of the Search Columns field, you can choose Name from the drop-down list to sort the list alphabetically, if that makes it easier for you to find the fields you want to remove.

3. **Click Settings next to the Removed Other Columns step in the Applied Steps pane, as shown in Figure 19-5.**

   You can revise a step that you've added to a Power Query transformation if a Settings icon appears.

4. **You can now remove any other columns you missed the first time, so you might clear the Memo/Description checkbox and then click OK.**

   At this point, the report should have five columns, as shown in Figure 19-5.

FIGURE 19-5:
The report is in a much easier-to-analyze format than it was in Figure 19-1.

Filtering unnecessary rows

In an Excel worksheet, you can select one or more rows, right-click the worksheet frame, and then choose Delete from the shortcut menu to remove the rows. You can't remove rows from a Power Query grid in that fashion, but you can filter out rows that you don't want to see by following these steps:

1. **Click the filter arrow at the top of any column, such as Transaction Type.**

   In the case of the Transaction Type column, a menu containing an alphabetical listing with one of each Transaction Type appears. Blank rows appear as *(null)*.

2. **Clear the Select All checkbox, select the items you want to keep (such as Invoice and Sales Receipt), and click OK.**

   If you're creating a list of sales-related transactions, the Power Query grid now displays only invoice and sales receipt transactions, as shown in Figure 19-6.

   You can apply filters to as many columns as you want. Also, you're not limited to choosing options from the list. Depending on the column's contents, context-specific options on the filter menu such as Text Filters, Date Filters, or Number Filters appear. Depending upon context, additional options such as Contains, Does Not Contain, Begins With, Greater Than, Less Than, and Between may become available as well.

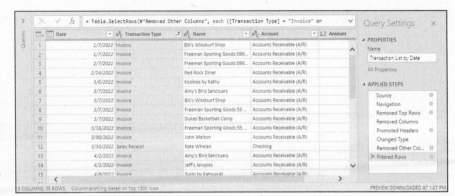

FIGURE 19-6:
You can't delete specific rows from the middle of the Power Query grid, but you can use filters to show specific data.

Returning the data to Excel

Choose Home ⇨ Close & Load to return the data from Power Query to Excel. Doing so closes the Power Query Editor and enables you to continue working in Excel. The data appears in a new worksheet in your workbook as a table in Excel. I discuss the Table feature in Chapter 15.

Instead of returning the data to Excel as a table, you can opt to create a pivot table, pivot chart, or simply a data connection by following these steps:

1. **Choose Home ⇨ Close & Load in Power Query (click the words "Close & Load" as opposed to the icon), and then click Close & Load To on the resulting menu.**

The Import Data dialog box opens, as shown in Figure 19-7.

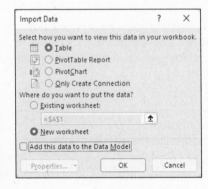

FIGURE 19-7:
The Import Data dialog box allows you to choose how and where your data is returned to Excel.

2. **Choose an option in the top section of the dialog box.**

   The default options include the following:

   - *Table,* which creates a list of data in an Excel worksheet
   - *PivotTable Report,* which creates a blank pivot table canvas in a worksheet
   - *PivotChart,* which creates a blank pivot chart canvas in a worksheet
   - *Only Create Connection,* which stages data in Power Query that you want to append to or merge with another data set

   If you choose the Table option, your data appears in a new Excel worksheet.

   If you choose PivotTable or PivotChart, then a blank pivot table and/or pivot chart appears in your workbook. Unlike with the Table option, you don't see the underlying raw data in your Excel worksheet unless you double-click a number within the pivot table. For this reason, most users prefer to send data to Excel as a table, and then create a pivot table based on the table so that they can have the detail and a summary.

3. **In the second section of the dialog box, choose an option.**

   You can choose Existing Worksheet and make a choice from the drop-down list to place the data in an existing worksheet instead. Keep in mind that depending on where you place the Power Query data, you could end up erasing some existing information, so it's better to accept the default of New Worksheet.

4. **Click OK.**

   If you click the Cancel button instead, Power Query returns the data to your Excel workbook, and you can delete the worksheet from the workbook to remove any unwanted data.

TIP

Mission accomplished! You've successfully transformed a QuickBooks report into an analysis-ready Excel format. You can close the Queries & Connections task pane shown in Figure 19-8, which appears automatically whenever you send data to Excel from Power Query.

FIGURE 19-8:
The Queries & Connections task pane appears automatically every time you import data via Power Query.

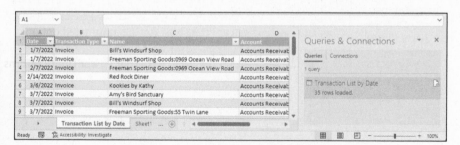

TIP

The Queries & Connections task pane allows you to monitor the data connections that you've established within a workbook. You can right-click any connection and choose commands from the shortcut menu to rename, edit, or delete the connection. Choosing Edit returns you to the Power Query Editor. Deleting the connection doesn't remove the data from the worksheet, but prevents it from being refreshed, which you may want to do if you want to preserve a permanent archive of the data. (I discuss refreshing Power Query data later in the chapter.) If you close this task pane, choose Data ➪ Queries & Connections to display it again.

Creating Self-Updating Reports

The gold standard for many accountants is establishing set-and-forget reports. In this case, the process is partly manual because you still have to export the Quick-Books report each time you want to update your Excel spreadsheet.

TIP

In Chapter 15, I discuss the Spreadsheet Sync feature for Advanced subscribers that enables you to connect QuickBooks Online directly to Excel workbooks. Simple Start, Essentials, and Plus subscribers can procure a third-party ODBC driver for QuickBooks Online that allows you to connect spreadsheets directly to Quick-Books, thereby eliminating the export process. After you install the ODBC driver, you can use Power Query to pull data directly into Excel. Two such drivers are available at www.cdata.com and www.qodbc.com.

Setting Power Query to refresh automatically

Although Power Query allows you to establish a connection to other workbooks and data sources, it's not a live feed to your spreadsheet. Rather, Power Query returns a snapshot of your data. If the data changes, because you either edited the data you connected to or saved a new version over a QuickBooks export, the new data doesn't appear in your spreadsheet until you refresh. In the section, "Refreshing reports," at the end of this chapter, I discuss three ways to refresh data from Power Query, but here are the steps for the automated option:

1. **Click any cell within the list of data that Power Query returns.**

    Certain Excel features are context-sensitive, so supporting menu commands aren't available unless you click a cell containing data related to a command. For instance, you only see pivot table–related commands when you click inside a pivot table. With regard to Power Query, the Query menu only appears in the Excel ribbon when you click any cell within data that has been brought into Excel from Power Query.

2. Choose Query ➪ Properties.

The Query Properties dialog box appears, as shown in Figure 19-9.

REMEMBER

You don't see the Query menu unless you've clicked the Power Query data.

An alternative way to access the Query Properties dialog box is to choose Data ➪ Properties to open the External Data Range Properties dialog box and then click the Query Properties button to the right of the Name field.

TIP

3. Clear the Enable Background Refresh checkbox, select the Refresh Data When Opening the File checkbox, and (if available) select the Enable Fast Data Load checkbox.

The Enable Background Refresh option has good intentions; it's designed to enable you to keep working in your spreadsheet while data from an external source is being refreshed. In my experience, though, this option can lead to confusion because you can initiate a refresh and not be sure whether anything is happening. If you deselect this option, you can't carry out any actions while the refresh occurs, but the refresh is much faster.

The Refresh Data When Opening the File option is where the automation happens. This option causes your spreadsheet to reach out to the external workbook automatically and grab the latest version of the data, so you see the newest information in your workbook.

Fast Data Load purportedly speeds the refresh process. I'm not convinced, but enabling it doesn't hurt.

REMEMBER

You can change these options at any time. For example, you might turn off Refresh Data When Opening the File if you want to archive a snapshot of a data set for a particular point in time.

4. **Click OK to close the Query Properties dialog box.**

REMEMBER

Query properties that you set are unique to each Power Query connection, so you need to carry out the preceding steps every time you establish a new data connection via Power Query.

Now that you've set the query properties for your Power Query connection, you need to eliminate one other speed bump to streamline the update process. Follow these steps to disable the Enable Content security prompt that otherwise appears every time you open your workbook:

1. **Save and close your workbook that contains a Power Query connection.**

2. **Reopen your workbook.**

   A security prompt appears.

   Don't click Enable Content in the prompt. If you do, you won't be able to prevent the prompt from appearing again. If you did click Enable Content, close your workbook, reopen it, and proceed to Step 3.

3. **Choose File ➪ Info ➪ Enable Content ➪ Enable All Content to suppress the security prompt.**

   As shown in Figure 19-10, the Enable All Content option makes the document a trusted document. When you mark a document as such, Excel no longer requires you to choose Enable Content before you refresh the workbook.

FIGURE 19-10:
Setting a workbook to be a trusted document eliminates the need to click Enable Content every time you open the file.

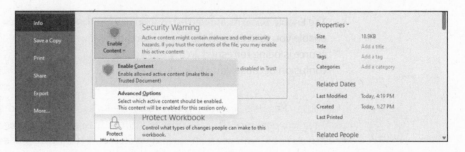

If you're presenting the data in the form of a table, you're all set. But if you're using the pivot table feature, which I discuss in Chapter 15, you need to change one more setting to ensure that your report is completely self-updating. Follow these steps:

1. **Select any cell within a pivot table, and choose the PivotTable Analyze menu.**

The pivot table menus are context-sensitive, so the PivotTable Analyze and Design menus vanish when your cursor isn't within a pivot table.

2. **Choose PivotTable Analyze ⇨ Options.**

The PivotTable Options dialog box appears, as shown in Figure 19-11.

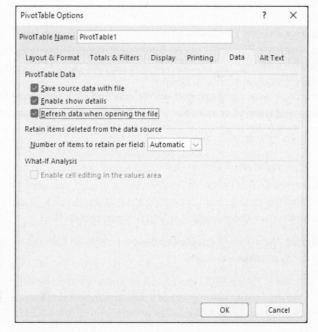

3. **Click the Data tab, select the Refresh Data When Opening the File checkbox, and then click OK.**

This option instructs Excel to refresh your pivot table when you open the workbook.

WARNING

Make sure that you set both your Power Query connection and any pivot tables based on Power Query data to refresh automatically when you open the file; otherwise, you could find yourself reviewing stale information. Choose Data ⇨ Refresh All in Excel to be absolutely certain that everything in your workbook is updated.

Adding a total row

Data that you return to Excel from Power Query always appears within a table. I discuss the table feature in more detail in Chapter 15. Also, you can easily add a total row to any table in Excel by following these steps:

1. **Click anywhere inside a table.**

This step displays the Table Design menu, which appears only when your cursor is inside a table.

2. **Choose Design ⇨ Total Row.**

A total row that automatically sums or counts the last column is added to your table. If the last column is composed of numeric values, Excel sums the column. If the column is composed of words or dates, Excel counts the number of records instead.

REMEMBER

The total row in a table tallies only the visible rows, which means that it automatically recalculates any time you filter or slice the contents of a table.

3. **Optional: Select any cell in the total row and click the arrow to display a drop-down menu that allows you to add or remove a mathematical calculation for that column, as shown in Figure 19-12.**

You can choose from 11 mathematical functions, but most likely, you'll opt to sum, average, or count the records.

FIGURE 19-12:
You can sum, average, count, or perform other mathematical calculations in any column of a table's total row.

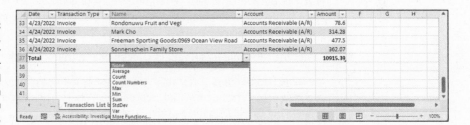

Date	Transaction Type	Name	Account	Amount	F	G	H
33	4/23/2022 Invoice	Rondonuwu Fruit and Vegi	Accounts Receivable (A/R)	78.6			
34	4/24/2022 Invoice	Mark Cho	Accounts Receivable (A/R)	314.28			
35	4/24/2022 Invoice	Freeman Sporting Goods:0969 Ocean View Road	Accounts Receivable (A/R)	477.5			
36	4/24/2022 Invoice	Sonnenschein Family Store	Accounts Receivable (A/R)	362.07			
37	Total			10915.39			

None
Average
Count
Count Numbers
Max
Min
Sum
StdDev
Var
More Functions...

Transforming QuickBooks data

Automating report cleanup is a huge benefit of Power Query. But Power Query can do much more. One of my favorite features is unpivoting reports.

The Transaction List by Date report makes it easy to filter because all the data appears in rows. Other reports, such as Profit and Loss by Customer, are oriented differently, with a row for each account and a column for each customer. If you want to see the total activity for a certain account for two customers at the same time, you don't have a good way to get that information quickly. Also, you can't easily create a pivot table from that type of report layout. In that case, unpivoting the data can be helpful. All the data appears in rows, and then you can filter or slice it.

Here's how to run the Profit and Loss by Customer report:

1. **Choose Reports or Business Overview ⇨ Reports.**

   The Reports page appears.

2. **Start typing** Profit and Loss by Customer **in the search field and then choose the report title.**

3. **Click the Export button and then choose Export to Excel from the resulting menu.**

   This report may be rather wide, so you may have to scroll the report to the right to access the Export button.

4. **Open the report, and click the first customer name.**

   This positions your cursor so that Excel will recognize the list that you want to import into Power Query.

5. **Choose Data ⇨ From Sheet or Data ⇨ From Table/Range.**

   The Create Table dialog box appears, as shown in Figure 19-13.

   Microsoft is going through what it's calling a "visual refresh" for Microsoft 365, which includes renaming certain commands. Your version of Excel may have a From Table/Range command or a From Sheet command. Both commands get you to the same place.

6. **Select the My Table Has Headers checkbox and then click OK.**

   My Table Has Headers confirms that your list of data has unique column headings across the first row. This report doesn't have a heading in the first column, but Excel fills in the gap with a generic heading.

FIGURE 19-13:
The My Table Has
Headers setting
allows you to
confirm that your
list has titles at
the top of most
or all columns.

At this point, your data appears in the Power Query Editor. The next step is unpivoting the columns.

Unpivoting columns

The sample report that I ran has 30 columns, which makes analysis tricky or even impossible unless you unpivot the data. The Unpivot command allows you to unpivot specific columns in a report. Unpivot Other Columns is helpful when you want to unpivot a contiguous group of columns. If unpivoting the data jumbles your data, click the X next to the Unpivoted Other Columns command in the Applied Steps pane to remove the transformation.

Follow these steps to unpivot columns:

1. **Right-click on the first column in your report, and choose Unpivot Other Columns from the shortcut menu.**

    Your report has three columns: Column1, Attribute, and Value, as shown in Figure 19-14.

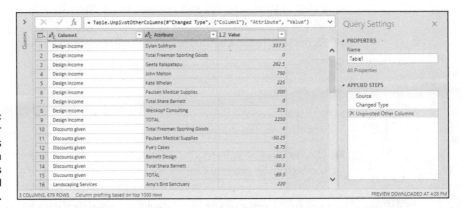

FIGURE 19-14:
The customer data that was presented in columns has been transposed into rows instead.

2. **Double-click the Column1 heading, replace Column1 with** Account, **and press Enter.**

    You can double-click any column heading in Power Query and type a new name.

3. **Change the name of the Attribute and Value columns to** Customer **and** Amount, **respectively.**

    Renaming columns is a great way to prevent confusion so that no one misconstrues data in a column that has a cryptic name.

4. **Click the Filter arrow in the Amount (or Value) column, and clear the checkbox for 0 (zero).**

    It's doubtful that every customer will have activity in every account, so filtering out zeros eliminates noise from your report.

5. **Optional: Click the step immediately above Unpivoted Other Columns in the Applied Steps pane, in this case Changed Type.**

   This step allows you to see what the report looked like before you unpivoted the data. Click the Unpivoted Other Column step again to see the unpivoted data. In effect, Power Query lets you walk around within the transformations so that you can see what the data looks like at various points. Click the last step in the Applied Steps pane to see the final output.

6. **Click Home ⇨ Close & Load.**

   Power Query returns the cleaned-up, unpivoted data to a new worksheet in your workbook. The original report remains in place in the form of a table.

Refreshing reports

Remember, Power Query isn't a live feed from any data source but instead returns a snapshot of your data. You can refresh Power Query data manually in five ways:

» Right-click the list, and choose Refresh from the shortcut menu.

» Click any cell in the list, and choose Table Design ⇨ Refresh in Excel.

» Choose Data ⇨ Refresh All in Excel.

» Right-click a connection in the Queries & Connections pane, and choose Refresh from the shortcut menu.

» Choose Query ⇨ Refresh. This menu is available only when Power Query connects to an external data source.

REMEMBER

You need to refresh a report only when the underlying data has changed.

If you'd like to learn more about Power Query, please see *Excel Power Pivot & Power Query For Dummies* by Michael Alexander.

5

The Part of Tens

Chapter **20**

Ten Cool Chrome Shortcuts Plus Ten Bonus Excel Shortcuts

O ver the years, I've observed that some folks like to use their mouse to carry out most, or all, commands on the computer. There's nothing wrong with this approach, but it can take more time to carry tasks out, because the mouse cursor must always be moved from one part of the screen to another. I've also seen people that pretty much act as if they don't know what a mouse is and carry out every command with their keyboard. Accordingly, sometimes one must use several keystrokes in conjunction to carry out a task. I'm a bit of a purist. To me, if it involves pressing more than three keys at once, such as Ctrl-Alt-Delete to display the Task Manager in Windows, then it's not truly a shortcut. Therefore, I tend to use my mouse a fair amount, but I also use keyboard shortcuts as well. Given the repetitive and transactional nature of accounting work, having at least a handful of keyboard shortcuts at your fingertips can definitely help you streamline certain tasks. In this chapter, I get you started with ten keyboard shortcuts that you may find helpful in Google Chrome. Chances are pretty good that these shortcuts will work in other browsers as well. I then follow this up with ten bonus shortcuts for Microsoft Excel and show you how to unearth even more shortcuts for both Chrome and Excel.

TIP

If you're looking for QuickBooks Online keyboard shortcuts, I have you covered at www.dummies.com. Search for *QuickBooks Online For Dummies* to find this book's Cheat Sheet.

Chrome Keyboard Shortcuts

Let's look at ten shortcuts that you may find helpful in conjunction with Quick-Books Online. Along the way you'll see that I mention supplemental shortcuts that complement the ten primary shortcuts that I've chosen. You can access a complete list of keyboard shortcuts for Chrome at https://support.google.com/chrome/answer/157179.

Opening and activating a new tab

Press Ctrl + T in Windows or Cmd+T on a Mac to create and activate a new browser tab. Your cursor will appear in the address bar, ready for you to type a web address, often referred as a URL (uniform resource locator).

REMEMBER

Ctrl + N in Windows or Cmd + N on a Mac creates a new tab as well, but in a separate window. Chrome allows you to press Ctrl + Shift + Tab or Cmd + Option + Left Arrow to jump to a previous tab within a window, but creating a new window means you have to use Ctrl + Tab or Cmd + `(grave symbol, which resides on the same key as ~) to move between windows.

Closing the current tab

Press Ctrl + W or Cmd + W to close the current tab. If you only have a single tab open, this will close your Chrome window as well, otherwise other tabs in the window will remain open. Use Ctrl + Shift + W or Cmd + Shift + W to close the current window.

TIP

Press Alt-F4 to close a Chrome window, which includes all open tabs, in Windows, or hold down Cmd + Q on a Mac.

Navigating to web sites faster

Type a site name, such as **intuit** in the address bar and then press Ctrl + Enter to automatically add www. and .com to the beginning and end, respectively, and then navigate to that site.

REMEMBER

This technique only works for primary domains, like www.intuit.com. You can't navigate to https://qbo.intuit.com in this manner because the site's address is qbo.intuit.com, versus www.qbo.intuit.com.

Saving open tabs as a bookmark group

Press Ctrl + Shift + D or Cmd + Shift + D to create a new folder with bookmarks to your current set of open tabs. This is a great way to remember your place when carrying out a research project that involves multiple web pages. You can also press Ctrl + D (Cmd + D) to create a bookmark for the currently open tab.

Toggling full-screen mode

Chrome's full-screen mode means two different things depending upon which operating system you're using. On a Windows computer, you can press F11 to toggle the tabs, address bar, and bookmarks bar on or off. On a Mac, Ctrl + Cmd + F expands or contracts the size of a Chrome window, but doesn't affect the tabs, address bar, or bookmarks.

Opening your home page in the current tab

Press Alt + Home or Cmd + Shift + H to open your home page in the current tab. With that said, you may need to enable the Home Page feature. To do so:

1. **Click the 3-dot button in Google Chrome and then choose Settings.**

2. **Enter the word Home in the Search Settings field.**

3. **Toggle Show Home Button on and then specify a home page, such as https://qbo.intuit.com to display the login page for QuickBooks Online.**

Activating a specific tab

Press Ctrl + 1 or Cmd + 1 to activate the first tab in your Chrome Window. You can use 1 through 8 to access the first eight tabs. Ctrl + 9 (Cmd + 9) activates the last open tab, so if you have ten open tabs you cannot jump directly to the ninth tab.

REMEMBER

You can press Alt + Left Arrow or Cmd + Option + Left Arrow to navigate one tab to the left or use Alt + Right Arrow (Cmd + Option + Right Arrow) to move one tab to the right.

Displaying the Downloads page

Press Ctrl + J or Cmd + Shift + J to display the Downloads page in a new tab. This provides easy access to reports that you have recently exported to Microsoft Excel from QuickBooks Online.

TIP

Press the Tab key twice to navigate to the first download. You can then use the Down Arrow key to navigate through the Downloads list. In Chrome for Windows, you can press Enter to open a download or use your mouse to click Show in Folder. In Chrome for Mac, pressing Enter will download the file again, or you can click Show in Finder with your mouse.

Displaying the History page

Press Ctrl + H or Cmd + Y to display the History page. As with the Downloads page you can press the Tab key to navigate to a specific link. Press Enter to open the link in the current tab, which will replace the History page.

Creating a tab in a new profile

Press Ctrl + Shift + M or Cmd + Shift + M to choose a different profile and create a new Chrome window, which in turn enables you to log into an additional Quick-Books Online company at the same time.

TIP

Press Alt + Tab to switch between windows in Chrome for Windows, or Ctrl + Left Arrow or Ctrl + Right Arrow to switch between windows on a Mac. Ctrl + Tab allows you switch between applications on a Mac.

Microsoft Excel Keyboard Shortcuts

There are over 200 keyboard shortcuts within Microsoft Excel, which makes choosing just ten to focus on feel like being asked to choose a favorite child if you have more than one kid. In Chrome and QuickBooks Online we all tend to follow similar paths, but in Excel keyboard shortcuts that resonate wildly with me may fall flat for you. A comprehensive list of keyboard shortcuts is available at http://support.microsoft.com when you use the search term **Excel keyboard shortcuts**. Alternatively, you can access a free template that shows 50 common shortcuts in:

>> **Excel for Windows:** Choose File, New, and then enter the word **Shortcuts** and press Enter. Click on the first option presented and then click Create.

>> **Excel for Mac:** Choose File, New from Template, and then type **Shortcuts** in the Search field at the top of the dialog box and then press Enter. Double-click 50 Time Saving Keyboard Shortcuts for Excel for Mac.

Switching between open documents

Press Ctrl-Tab in Excel for Windows to switch between open workbooks. Maddeningly, for me at least, there's not a keyboard equivalent on the Mac, which means I have to choose Window and then Switch Windows to activate another open workbook.

Switching between worksheet tabs

Press Ctrl + Page Down or Option + Right Arrow to activate the next worksheet tab to the right, or Ctrl + Page Up (Option Left + Arrow) to activate the next worksheet to the left.

These keyboard shortcuts stop working when you reach the first or last worksheet in a workbook, so rest assured that you won't find yourself suddenly in a different workbook.

REMEMBER

Closing an open workbook

Press Ctrl + W or Cmd + W to close an open workbook. This is particularly helpful in Excel for Windows, as clicking the Close button in the top right-hand corner of the screen closes Excel as well if you only have one workbook open, which means you must then launch Excel again if you wish to work on another workbook.

Moving to cell A1 of a worksheet

Press Ctrl + Home in Excel for Windows or fn + Ctrl + Left Arrow in Excel for Mac to move your cursor to cell A1.

Press Home in Excel for Windows or fn + Left Arrow in Excel for Mac to move your cursor to column A of the current row.

TIP

Saving your work

Press Ctrl + S or Cmd + S to save your work. An exception to this rule arises when you save your workbooks to Microsoft's OneDrive service and enable the AutoSave option at the top left-hand corner of the Excel screen. Otherwise, I can tell you from decades of hard-fought experience that you want to develop the muscle memory of periodically pressing Ctrl + S or Cmd + S to save your work because it's frightfully easy to have hours of spreadsheet work vanish off the screen.

TIP

In Excel for Windows, you can choose File, Open, and then Recover Unsaved Files to see if you can access a back-up copy of a workbook that you closed accidentally. Disappointingly Excel for Mac doesn't offer equivalent functionality.

Undoing your work

Press Ctrl + Z or Cmd + Z to undo your last action. In fact, you can use this keyboard shortcut repeatedly to undo up to the last 100 actions that you've carried out. Alternatively, you can display the Undo dropdown menu to select one or more consecutive steps that you wish to undo.

WARNING

Certain actions in Excel will clear the Undo stack, which is that list of up to 100 actions that can be undone. Three that particularly come to mind include deleting a worksheet, running a macro, and removing subtotals from a list by day of the Subtotals command on the Data tab of Excel's Ribbon.

Toggling absolute or mixed references

This shortcut relates to worksheet formulas. Let's say that you want to create a formula that always refers to cell A1 on a particular worksheet. To do so, you can enter =A1 into any other cell, such as B1. Now let's say that you click on cell B1 and then drag the Fill Handle in the bottom right-hand corner either down the column or across the row. Copying down will cause the row numbers to increment on each row, so that the formula in cell B5 will refer to A5, instead of A1. Similarly, dragging across will increment the column letters, such that the formula in cell E1 will refer to cell D1, instead of A1. You can freeze column and/or row references by manually inserting a $ before the column and/or row, or use the F4 key in Excel for Windows, or Cmd + T in Excel for Mac. Each time you press the shortcut Excel will toggle the positions of the dollar signs, including removing the dollar signs completely before cycling through the positions again.

Toggling Enter versus Edit mode

Many dialog boxes in Excel enable you to specify or enter a cell reference. Such fields are known as RefEdit fields, and depending upon the context, you may sometimes type text in such fields instead of a cell reference. Frustration can ensue though when you go to use the arrow keys in such a field, because rather than navigating within the field you'll find that Excel inserts cell references instead. The answer lies at the bottom left-hand corner of Excel's screen. When you click in a RefEdit field, the word Enter appears at the bottom left-hand corner of the Excel screen, on Excel's Status Bar. When you use the Left Arrow or Right Arrow keys in a RefEdit field in Enter mode, Excel assumes you want to append a new cell reference to the field. Conversely, press the F2 key to toggle to Edit mode, which will enable you to use the arrow keys to navigate back and forth within the RefEdit field.

Calculating a portion of a formula

Troubleshooting Excel formulas can be an exercise in frustration if you're not aware of the Evaluate Formula command on the Formulas menu in Excel for Windows. Unfortunately, Mac users are out in the cold with regard to this helpful feature, but any Excel users can select a portion of a formula and then press F9 to calculate a portion of the formula. This includes converting a cell reference to its equivalent value, or a portion of the formula, such as an argument within a worksheet function.

WARNING

Tread carefully with this shortcut. If you use F9 to convert a portion of a formula to its equivalent value and then press Enter, you'll permanently remove any underlying cell references for the part of the formula that you converted. When editing formulas, Excel only allows you to undo a single change within a cell or the formula bar. Your options include pressing Ctrl-Z or Cmd-Z to restore the formula back to its previous state if you pressed Enter accidentally, or if you're still amidst editing a formula, you can press Escape to discard any changes that you've made.

Summing a range of cells

Press Alt + = in Excel for Windows or Cmd + Shift + T in Excel for Mac to enter the SUM function into any worksheet cell. Excel will automatically sum the values of any contiguous cells.

TIP

You can add the SUM function to two or more cells at once by selecting the cells before using the keyboard shortcut. To do so, hold down the Shift key and use the arrow keys to select two or more cells that you wish to sum.

Index

P

packing slips, printing, 136–137

paid invoices, 144–146

Paper Ledger Mode, 212–213

paper receipts, converting to electronic transactions, 269–273

parent tags, 309–310

partial invoices, creating, 294–296

password managers, 245

Pay Bills window, 167

pay bill transactions
 about, 158
 adjusting payment amounts, 169
 check numbers for, 168
 paying two or more bills at once, 166–168
 payment date, 168
 scheduling payments, 169
 writing checks for, 169–170

paychecks
 deleting, 199
 reviewing and generating, 194–197
 voiding, 199

Payments preferences, 44–45

Payments tab, 43

Payments to Deposit (Undeposited Funds) account, 138, 142

payroll
 desktop data conversion and, 53
 enabling employee time tracking, 193–194
 establishing or correcting exemptions, 197–199
 preparing, 191–200
 printing reports, 199–200
 recording information, 192–193
 reviewing and generating checks for, 194–197
 voiding or deleting paychecks, 199

Payroll Settings page, 187–188

Payroll Tax Center, 201–202

payroll taxes
 managing, 200–202
 paying, 200–202
 setting up, 189–191
 viewing forms, 202

payroll tax liability, 200–202

PDF, exporting reports to, 338

pencil icon, 36

pending estimates, 291

PivotChart option, 444

PivotTable Analyze and Design tabs, 356

Pivot Table button, 327

PivotTable Report option, 444

pivot tables
 adding fields, 355
 creating, 355
 custom reporting with, 355–357
 removing fields, 356–357
 requirements, 356

plus (+) icon, 26

Plus version
 vs. Essentials version, 15–16
 Projects feature, 296–297
 purchase-order feature, 276
 subscription pricing, 10
 usage limits, 16

portable file (*.QBM), 54

Power Query (Excel), 348–349
 about, 435–436
 connecting to QuickBooks reports, 436–438
 filtering unnecessary rows, 440–442
 promoting headers, 439–440
 refreshing reports, 452
 removing header rows, 438–439
 removing unwanted columns, 440–442
 returning data to Excel, 443–445
 setting to refresh automatically, 445–448
 transforming QuickBooks data, 449–450
 unpivoting columns, 451–452

Premium tier, 11–12

Prep for Taxes page
 documents, 413–414
 review & adjust, 415–417
 tax mapping, 417–418
 year-end tasks, 413–414

previewing, estimates, 287

pricing
 add-on pricing, 13
 payroll, 11–13
 ProAdvisor Preferred, 11
 subscription, 10
 time track, 11–13

pricing rules, 110–112

About the Author

David Ringstrom, CPA, is president of Accounting Advisors, Inc., an Atlanta-based spreadsheet and database consulting firm. David's consulting work focuses on streamlining repetitive accounting tasks. He helps clients use software such as QuickBooks more effectively and creates automated tools in Microsoft Excel.

David spends much of his time teaching webinars on Microsoft Excel and occasionally QuickBooks. He also owns StudentsExcel, an online service that helps accounting professors teach Excel more effectively to their students. Since 1995, David has written freelance articles about spreadsheets and accounting software, some of which have been published internationally. He has served as the technical editor for over three dozen books, including *QuickBooks Desktop For Dummies*, *Quicken For Dummies*, and *Peachtree For Dummies*, and is the author or co-author of five books, including *Idiot's Guide to Introductory Accounting* and *Exploring Microsoft Excel's Hidden Treasures*.

He resides in a historic neighborhood in Atlanta, Georgia, with his wife Erin, his children Rachel and Lucas, dogs Ginger and Eddie, and cat Arlene Frances (Francie).

Author's Acknowledgments

I took over as the lead author for *QuickBooks Online For Dummies* during the first year of the COVID-19 pandemic and have since been the sole author for this edition and the prior edition. Dan Delong is a technical editor extraordinaire whose suggestions have made all three books better. I appreciate how my editors Linda Brandon and Marylouise Wiack improved the readability of this book. Also, I want to give a shout out to everyone else on the Wiley team that helped bring this book to life. This is the fifth book that I have authored or co-authored, so my wife Erin and my children Rachel and Lucas have become accustomed to the writing process, but I'm always grateful for their love and support. Working on a book is no small undertaking, but it is always rewarding. This year life came at me fast and I wrote two books at the same time, while recovering from breaking my arm in a mountain biking accident. I won't ever look at working on just one book the same!

Each time I write a book, I like to look back and thank people who have helped my career along. Thank you to Vicki Darrah — my first consulting client way back in the early 1990s — Jana Broder and her father Jerry — who were my second clients, and the countless others who I have had the pleasure of helping over the subsequent decades.

Publisher's Acknowledgments

Acquisitions Editor: Kelsey Baird
Project Editor: Linda Brandon
Copy Editor: Marylouise Wiack
Technical Editor: Dan DeLong

Production Editor: Tamilmani Varadharaj
Cover Image: © andresr/Getty Images